FISCAL STRESS AND PUBLIC POLICY

SAGE YEARBOOKS IN POLITICS AND PUBLIC POLICY

Sponsored by the **Policy Studies Organization**

Series Editor: **Stuart S. Nagel**, *University of Illinois, Urbana*

Books in this series:

Volume 9. Sage Yearbooks in Politics and Public Policy

FISCAL STRESS
AND
PUBLIC POLICY

CHARLES H. LEVINE
and
IRENE RUBIN
Editors

SAGE PUBLICATIONS   Beverly Hills   London

For information address:

SAGE Publications, Inc.
275 South Beverly Drive
Beverly Hills, California 90212

SAGE Publications Ltd
28 Banner Street
London EC1Y 8QE, England

Printed in the United States of America

Library of Congress Cataloging in Publication Data

Main entry under title:

Fiscal stress and public policy.

  (Sage yearbooks in politics and public policy ; v. 9)
  Originally presented as lectures at a colloquium sponsored by the University of Maryland's Institute for Urban Studies and held during the spring semester, 1980.
  Bibliography: p.
  Includes index.
  1. Finance, Public--United States--Congresses. 2. Government spending policy--United States--Con-gresses. I. Levine, Charles H. II. Rubin, Irene. III. Maryland. University. Institute for Urban Studies.
HJ257.2.F56   336.73   80-24515
ISBN 0-8039-1553-5
ISBN 0-8039-1554-3 (pbk.)

FIRST PRINTING

CONTENTS

SERIES EDITOR'S INTRODUCTION

This is the ninth volume in the series of Yearbooks in Politics and Public Policy published by Sage Publications in cooperation with the Policy Studies Organization. This volume on *Fiscal Stress and Public Policy,* edited by Charles H. Levine and Irene Rubin, is especially important for two almost opposed reasons. One reason is that (more so than the previous volumes, which emphasize policy problems that are not so specific in time) this volume emphasizes a contemporary crisis. It focuses on the governmental financial crisis that began in the late 1970s and resulted in considerable pressure to cut back on many governmental programs. A second reason is that (more so than the previous volumes) this volume deals with a problem that has always been with us and always will be. That is the problem of how governments do, can, and should deal with scarce resources.

The immediate crisis of fiscal stress in government results from a pincer movement of (1) increased expenses and (2) decreased taxes or taxes that are not increasing proportionately. The increased expenses are partly due to unusually severe inflation, which in its severity may be a short-run phenomenon. Substantial inflation may, however, be chronic in the American economy, partly due to prices and wages that can be readily raised by business firms and unions. The increased expenses are also due to long-run pressures for a more positive role on the part of government in dealing with such increasing problems as urbanism, defense, the economy, education, and crime, and more recent governmental concerns, such as energy-environment, discrimination, and health. Taxes have not increased proportionately, partly due to unemployment and lowered productivity, which in its severity may be a short-run phenomenon. Substantial unemployment or underemployment may, however, be chronic in the American economy, partly due to technological developments which may make full employment unlikely or in need of redefinition, and partly due to more effective foreign competition. Taxes have also not increased proportionately, due to the increasing difficulty, both political and economic, of taxing people at constantly higher levels. That is especially so within an economic system where the government cannot in effect levy taxes by controlling wages, as governments do where they are virtually the only employer.

There have been at least three major effects of the fiscal stress in government. One has been cutbacks in budgets of government agencies, as measured in real dollars adjusting for inflation. A second effect has been cutbacks in the outputs that government agencies are capable of producing, given their reduced budgets. A third effect that is particularly relevant to policy analysis has been the stimulus to try for more output per dollar from the reduced budgets. That effect has manifested itself in an increased concern for government efficiency and program evaluation. Government agencies, like people, have always tried to some extent to be efficient, but that concern becomes greater in a time when budgets are going down and one's goals or external pressures to produce may be going up. A side effect has been the stimulus to the policy studies or policy evaluation field within political and social science.

Reactions to these effects by government agencies depend to a considerable extent on whether the agency is acting in its role as an allocator or an allocatee. All agencies are both. Even the highest-level agencies, such as the White House or Congress, operate within some budgetary constraints as an allocatee. Even the most grass-roots agencies also allocate resources, as, for example, when police departments make decisions on the allocation of police to neighborhoods or activities. In good and bad times, allocators and allocatees are concerned with manipulating resources, goals, and processes. In times of retrenchment, allocators tend to respond by (1) allocating less to various places and activities, (2) lowering their output expectations, and (3) trying to get those to whom they allocate to operate more efficiently. In times of retrenchment, allocatees tend to respond by: (1) seeking to be allocated at least as much as they have been; (2) arguing they cannot or should not lower their output expectations, but eventually doing so in order to avoid the frustrations of too wide a gap between goals and achievement; and (3) arguing they are operating as efficiently as they can, but simultaneously seeking to be more efficient so as to minimize the output effects of the input reductions.

Reactions to these effects by policy analysis people has partly been to emphasize how, through more efficient policy analysis and program evaluation, one can get more output from a given budget, and maybe even more output from a reduced budget. For example, suppose a police force has been allocating its resources between two activities or places on a 60 percent, 40 percent basis, and having a crime detriment of 200 crimes. By reallocating a reduced budget on a 30 percent, 70 percent basis to the same activities or places, the police force might be able to have a crime detriment of even fewer than 200 crimes. Making that kind of improved allocation decision, though, requires a careful analysis of the relations between crime occurrence and alternative allocations over time or across police forces. Likewise, if an environmental agency has been seeking to keep pollution at a level of 75 on a 0 to 100 scale, that agency may be missing on improving the difference between pollution damages avoided (as a benefit) and clean-up expenditures incurred (as a cost) by not seeking to operate at a 65 or 85 on such a scale. In other words, a careful analysis might show that benefits minus costs at a 75 level are $100,000,000, but they would be $200,000,000 at an 85 level. Allowing more pollution up to a point may not cause the pollution damages to go up as rapidly as the increased savings in clean-up costs. In addition to optimum allocation analysis and optimum level analysis, the policy analysis field has developed methods for arriving at more profitable decisions in such situations as being faced with a set of choices where contingent probabilities are involved, or being faced with how to optimally sequence a series of events so as to minimize expensive time consumption. If fiscal crisis stimulates more use of optimizing analysis and related methods in government, and it thereby causes more benefits for given costs, then that would be one desirable effect of the contemporary crisis in governmental financing.

The organization of this excellent treatment of *Fiscal Stress and Public Policy* is in three parts. The first part emphasizes the causes of fiscal stress, including the slowdown in economic development and taxpayer resistance, as key factors adversely affecting the resources available for government programs. The second part emphasizes budgeting or input reactions to fiscal stress, including budgetary adaptations to resource scarcity, budgetary reform, budgetary flexibility, and borrowing as a taxing supplement. The third part emphasizes the efficiency and output reactions to fiscal stress, including the ultimate output reaction of terminating government programs. Each part consists of four chapters by experts on the subjects discussed. The analysis deals with government at all levels, including national, state, and local. The analysis is also broad in time and place, frequently referring to historical and cross-national perspectives.

This volume fits well with the previous volumes in the Sage Yearbooks in Politics and Public Policy. Some of the volumes emphasize the important and increasing roles that government and public policy play in society. That emphasis on growth is consistent with the present volume's emphasis on retrenchment. There is a long-term trend in the growth of American government since 1789 (along with short-term growth spurts), while at the same time there are long-term trends toward chronic inflation, underemployment, taxpayer resistance, and foreign competition (along with short-term fiscal crises). Some of the volumes also emphasize the important and increasing role of systematic policy analysis in improving government policy. That policy analysis movement is partly an effect of fiscal stress, and it can be a partial influence on the reduction of fiscal stress. Each volume in this series tends to be integrated with the other volumes and tends to be integrated within itself. *Fiscal Stress and Public Policy* fits well within the good track record which this series has established.

Stuart S. Nagel
Urbana, Illinois

VOLUME EDITORS' INTRODUCTION

ECONOMIC GROWTH, DECLINE, AND POLICY CHANGE

Living amidst great wealth in the United States, it has become easy to forget that resources are scarce, limited, and exhaustible. When it comes to government revenues, the explosive growth of the post-World War II economy and the massive expansion of public programs almost buried the classic debate between advocates of limited government and free-market capitalism and proponents of an active interventionist state (Bell, 1960). During the 1950s and 1960s, the ability of government to solve public problems seemed unlimited and the resources needed to fund public programs appeared boundless. This optimism has not always dominated public attitudes about government. During the 150 years prior to the great explosion of economic growth brought forth by the opening up of rich western territories and by the industrial revolution, policy making in the United States was dominated by a conservative ideology: mankind's problems were largely preordained and government intervention was an unlikely source of relief (Fox, 1967).

The economic growth of the nineteenth and twentieth centuries created an abundance of taxable resources that became channeled into the public

AUTHORS' NOTE: *The twelve essays in this volume were originally presented as lectures at the University of Maryland's Institute for Urban Studies during the Spring semester of 1980. They were part of a colloquium sponsored by the Institute intended to bring the latest thinking on problems of fiscal stress and public policy to an audience of students, faculty, and practitioners associated with the Institute. To our knowledge, this is the first colloquium on this subject in the United States. If the predictions for slow economic growth throughout the 1980s prove out, it will hardly be the last.*

In aggregate, these essays are an exploratory attempt to derive a conceptual handle on a developing policy problem. We hope that they will prove useful to other scholars and policy makers as a base from which to develop more theoretically elegant conceptualizations and more finely grained policy responses to the difficult issues involved in coping with fiscal stress.

We are grateful to Sage Publications and the Policy Studies Organization for making it possible to share these essays with a wider audience.

sector by war and defense taxation. These new public revenues combined with the development of Keynesian economics and the success of the New Deal programs of the Roosevelt Administration to change public attitudes about "big government." The prevailing liberal ideology was premised on the assumption of a limitless economy: if only the abundance of resources attained through continuous economic growth could be properly directed, eventually all our public and private problems would melt away.

The post-World War II era was an especially heady time in the United States. In 1945, the United States produced 50 percent of the Gross National Product of the capitalist world; Keynesian economics promised that the turbulent peaks and valleys of the prewar economy could be smoothed out and stabilized so that inflation and unemployment could be made forever tolerable, and the social insurance reforms of the New Deal promised a secure and stable economic life for everyone.

So strong was the belief of Americans in the power of abundance that the issues of revenue raising and taxation that dominated the first century-and-a-half of the nation's life became transformed into issues of resource allocation and distribution. Politicians debated not the existence of the social security system, for example, but its coverage and distribution. During the 1950s, it became fashionable in social science circles to argue about the "end of ideology" and the development of a policy science, a new form of social engineering combining the power of economic growth and an activist state with the knowledge generated by the social sciences (Lerner and Lasswell, 1951).

The policy sciences needed another decade-and-a-half to attract much scholarly support. During most of the late 1950s and 1960s, the study of politics and policy making tended to conceive of resources as givens or as one among several inputs to the policy-making process. The division of labor in policy studies relegated concern for resources to economists; political scientists concerned themselves more with developing theory about policy formulation and processes of resource allocation. Topics such as taxation, bonding, and fund accounting were studied by public finance economists, while appropriations, law making, and budgeting were the province of political scientists. With the exception of the literature on comparative state policy (Dye, 1966), few social scientists explicitly examined the link between resources and politics. Not one major study in the United States addressed the problems that austerity might pose for democratic regimes.

Since the mid-1970s, the boundaries between economics and political science have been breaking down and blending together into a unified field of public policy studies. There are several reasons for the blurring of boundaries between the social sciences; one of them is the obvious artificiality of hard disciplinary borders in studying the effects of the slowdown in economic growth on the political stability of advanced industrial nations (Klein, 1976). During the 1970s, the average annual growth rate of the economies of developed countries declined from about 4.9 percent to 3.4 percent. For the early 1980s, this rate is projected to decline to 1 or 2 percent. This slowdown has already produced inflation, unemployment, and budget deficits, causing austerity programs to be promulgated and rapid turnover in leadership and in parliamentary coalitions. If the glum forecasts about the 1980s become reality, we can expect even greater distress and political turmoil in these nations.

From 1945 until the mid-1970s, political leaders in the United States and other nations used abundance to extend their economic and regulatory roles and to strengthen their hold on the electorate (Brittan, 1975). Economic growth lived up to its promise of making everyone better off while enhancing political stability. Growth slowdown, on the other hand, has threatened to put an end to this happy condition. Skyrocketing energy costs have hastened inflation and unemployment, antagonists that heretofore had operated independently. Far from dying, the ideological debate over the scope of government—over the size and reach of the welfare state—has been joined anew. All over the capitalist world, conservative political parties who promise to cut back the size of welfare and other government programs have flourished, while the liberal social programs that characterize welfare states, such as national health insurance, welfare, and employment programs, have been deferred, reduced, or terminated (Rose and Peters, 1978). These changes have obvious political causes and consequences that are affected by and affect the distribution of power and influence in society.

Economic slowdown has highlighted the reciprocal influence of politics and economics. Austerity programs exacerbate all the conflicts and cleavages of pluralist politics, pitting haves against have nots, debtors against creditors, organized workers against unorganized employees, wage earners against pensioners, and growing states, regions, and cities against economically stagnant areas (Thurow, 1980). For most of the past fifty years, these national cleavages were modulated and submerged by growth as organized interests drew greater and greater shares of national wealth. Now that this share is beginning to shrink, policy making has become more contested as tradeoffs between programs and beneficiaries become more obvious. In short, policy making has become both more constrained and more contested, making the study of public policy more challenging and more relevant.

STRESS AND CHANGE

No government can incur deficits indefinitely. Eventually, runaway inflation, the devaluation of currency, and defaulted bonds and loans will be the consequences of a continuous gap between revenues and expenditures. This gap creates stress, and stress, in turn, creates change in the policies and processes of government. Whether it means a rise in taxation to pay for increased activity and benefits or, as is more likely in developed countries, a trimming down of public programs, closing this gap poses major political questions that strike at the heart of pluralist political theory and interest-group liberalism (Bell, 1974). For example:

(1) How can tradeoffs be arranged between programs when the policy-making system is by design fragmented and disjointed?

(2) How can new interest groups and policy demands be accommodated when expenditures cannot be expanded and established programs are being retrenched or terminated?

(3) How can programs be reduced without asking for extraordinary sacrifices from those with the least power: the poor, the aged, and the unemployed?

(4) And how can viable federalism be maintained when state and local governments cannot raise sufficient funds to finance services through self-generated revenues?

These questions are not easily answered. In fact, they may be insoluble within the present framework of pluralist policy-making and implementation structures (Barnet, 1980). But their resolution is a necessary condition for resolving the fiscal problems that surely will confront the United States in the 1980s.

The brunt of the burden of adjusting governments to the pressures of fiscal stress falls on their budgetary and management systems. These systems will be expected to respond with new procedures which will smooth out the potential negative repercussions of reduced resources while targeting resources to maintain and enhance high-priority public programs. In the budgeting arena, politics and economics merge, as managers, legislators, clients, and public employees strive to protect their favorite programs. The strategies of budgetary politics weaken central control and planning, calling forth another set of perplexing policy issues:

(1) How can agencies be retrenched or terminated without intense and debilitating political conflict?

(2) How can budgets be balanced if resources decline and programs are not cut back?

(3) How can budgetary authority be centralized and public officials held accountable for deficits when scarce resources fragment authority?

(4) How can agencies maintain management flexibility when political officials demand budgetary centralization to control expenditures?

Closely related to these budgetary issues is a series of managerial problems. Reduced revenue calls forth three kinds of managerial responses: (1) finding new sources of revenues; (2) improving productivity; and (3) reducing programs (Levine, 1980). Ideally, program reductions should follow priorities, with low-priority programs taking large cuts or being terminated. But these responses are not easily accomplished and raise several additional policy issues:

(1) How can new revenues be raised when taxation is already straining public tolerance?

(2) How can productivity be improved when declining resources have a demoralizing effect on work forces?

(3) How can programs be prioritized when the intensity of supporters for small, limited service programs often outweighs the wide but diffuse support of the general public for other programs with collective benefits?

(4) How can public managers be induced to retrench agencies when the measure of successful public management has been budgetary expansion?

These three sets of four questions of political economy and public management are addressed directly and indirectly by several of the essays in this book. These essays are intended to raise and analyze issues of major political and managerial significance that arise under conditions of economic stress. Taken together, the essays explore many of the links between policy, politics, economics, and management, and provide a wide-angle examination of the effects of austerity on the public sector.

ABOUT THIS BOOK

The twelve essays in this book are grouped in three sets: the first set of essays deals with broad issues of definition, examining the sources and extent of fiscal stress at the societal level; the second set deals with the immediate impacts of fiscal stress on budgeting and financial management; and the third set discusses some of the less immediate impacts—emerging policy choices, and limits on the range of governmental responses to fiscal stress.

PART I: SLOW GROWTH, TAXPAYER RESISTANCE, AND FISCAL STRESS

Primary among the causes of fiscal stress is the slowdown of economies that had been growing rapidly for several decades. This theme is documented and analyzed by B. Guy Peters in his essay, "Fiscal Strains on the Welfare State: Causes and Consequences." Peters argues that the growth in public policy expenditures during the post-World War II period in Western nations was achieved without doing serious damage to the take-home pay of workers. With a slowing of economic growth, the tradeoff between collective goods and personal disposable income has become much more obvious to the taxpaying public. Peters outlines a number of political consequences of this problem, including the possibilities for tax evasion, corruption, and political alienation as citizens withdraw their support for the welfare state.

It can be argued that the withdrawing of public support for increased governmental spending will result in a smaller public sector, but David R. Beam and Cynthia C. Colella question this prediction in their essay, "The Federal Role in the Eighties: Bigger, Broader, and Deeper or Smaller, Trimmer, and Cheaper?" They argue that government growth is not so much a result of increased citizen demands for services and benefits as it is of bureaucratic demands for more resources and the need of politicians to spend money to build and maintain voter coalitions. Beam and Colella conclude that these basic facts of political life will prevent deep cuts in federal spending when citizen demand declines and will make whatever cuts do occur as politically innocuous as possible.

John J. Kirlin approaches the question of decline in demand for public services from the perspective of the state rather than the federal government. In his essay, "Accommodating Discontinuity: Adjusting the Political System of California to Proposition 13," he explores the political responses to Proposition 13 and the significant issues raised by the taxation limits imposed by popular referendum in California. Kirlin discusses the reasons behind propositional politics and the implications of revenue limitations for (1) the realignment of state and local authority and (2) the agenda of issues confronting state political leaders.

While the Beam and Colella essay and the Kirlin essay discuss the possible impacts of declining support for public expenditures on the relationships between state, local, and federal governments, John P. Ross and James Greenfield broaden the argument in their essay, "Measuring the Health of Cities," by considering different definitions and causes of fiscal stress (other than declining demand). The possible role of the federal government in alleviating local stress is a central consideration of this essay.

To determine an appropriate federal fiscal response to local fiscal stress, Ross and Greenfield propose several criteria for assigning responsibility for service delivery to different levels of government in the federal system.

PART II: FISCAL STRESS, BUDGETING, AND FINANCIAL MANAGEMENT

Financial stress impacts most directly on the processes of budgeting and financial management. It is to these processes that one should look first for signs of change. Some of these changes are explained in Allen Schick's essay, "Budgetary Adaptations to Resource Scarcity." Schick argues that scarcity is a fact of budgetary life but its severity can change, causing modifications in the behavior of participants in the budgetary process. His essay develops a typology of budgetary scarcity that clearly links problems of fiscal stress with both budgetary procedures and political dynamics. The first stage, chronic scarcity, conforms to incremental budgeting and pluralist politics. This is followed by relaxed scarcity, a brief period of relative affluence in which new programs are launched and new capital expenditures incurred. The final two stages, acute and total scarcity, describe the downward path of governments undergoing fiscal crises. Under conditions of acute scarcity, money is not available to either initiate new programs or maintain equipment and physical facilities. Under conditions of total scarcity, resource deficiencies lead to an undermining of the integrity of fund accounts and behavior that borders on illegality as officials struggle to balance resources against ongoing demands.

Naomi Caiden's essay argues, in agreement with Schick, that one should not expect improved financial management as scarcity increases. She illustrates the argument with reference to prerevolutionary French monarchy in her essay, "Negative Financial Management: A backward Look at Fiscal Stress." The response to growing expenditures and limited capacity to tax was fragmentation of revenues, deconcentration of accounts, cash-flow manipulation, and diversion of budgetary purposes. These four consequences combined to undermine budgetary control and the legitimacy of the tax system. Caiden concludes that the lessons learned from prerevolutionary France may be transferable to today's governments in spite of their more modern budgetary practices.

Evidence to support Caiden's argument is contained in Irene Rubin's essay, "Retrenchment and Flexibility in Public Organizations," which describes the budgetary responses of contemporary universities and cities. Rubin discusses the degree of flexibility in the budget, treating it as a variable that changes with resource levels. She argues that organizations tend to have the least flexibility when they need it most, and strive to re-create budgetary flexibility with a limited resource base. In re-creating flexibility, they take a variety of actions which have unintended consequences that change the organization. Rubin also observes that the particular actions taken to recreate flexibility depend on the degree of autonomy over resources: organizations with more autonomy tend to borrow and manipulate cash flow; organizations with less autonomy tend to buffer and create pools of uncommitted resources.

The fourth piece in this section deals not with budgetary processes, but with an area of financial management equally responsive to fiscal stress—long-term borrowing in credit and bond markets. John E. Petersen's essay, "Changing Fiscal Structure and Credit Quality: Large U.S. Cities," discusses the impact of urban fiscal stress on the quality of cities' bond ratings since the New York City fiscal crisis. The New York City crisis, he argues, exaggerated the differences in interest rates associated with different bond ratings. It tended to give high-rated cities a fiscal bonus and low-rated cities a fiscal penalty. He also notes geographic effects, in which midwestern and northeastern cities are doing worse financially than other areas of the country. His analysis discerns an overall improvement in cities' bond ratings in recent years, despite an increasing dependence on intergovernmental revenues, which introduces some uncertainty about future revenues. Finally, Petersen includes a discussion of how closely changing conditions in the city, such as population growth or decline, or tax effort, relate to bond ratings. In general, he finds socioeconomic indicators fairly good predictors of bond rating.

PART III: MANAGING RETRENCHMENT

The third section of the book deals with the less immediate impacts of fiscal stress, the long-term policy issues of what should be done and how policies should be carried out. The major issues include whether to increase revenues (if possible) or cut back expenditures. If expenditures are to be cut back, can they be cut back without reducing service levels (increasing productivity)? Are cuts best made across the board or selectively; all at once or gradually; by attrition or by layoffs? Are there minimal levels of operation beyond which it makes more sense to cut an entire facility or program or department?

While organization theory suggests that it might be best to terminate some programs to keep others functioning effectively, and that drops in resource levels are liable to trigger increases in productivity, such theories are normally intended to apply to organizations with a strong central authority capable of carrying out unpopular decisions. Public organizations are typically not of this type; they are appropriately concerned about responses to their actions and about opposition they might stir up. The political aspects of public organizations may affect the responses taken by public officials; they may be unwilling to take any action at all, or, if they take action, choose the path that rouses least resistance, regardless of the consequences for efficiency and effectiveness.

The pieces in this section deal with managerial responses to fiscal stress in the public sector. Richard Rose introduces some definitions and strategies for making cutbacks. In his essay, "Misperceiving Public Expenditure: Feelings About 'Cuts,' " Rose introduces some cross-national comparisons, and uses the austerity policies of Great Britain during the past several years to illustrate the difficult political choices confronting policy makers intent on balancing budgets and rekindling economic growth.

Harold Wolman's essay on cities' responses to fiscal stress, "Local Government Strategies to Cope with Fiscal Pressure," reflects the constraints of politics on fiscal policy making. In his sample of cities, Wolman found that cities preferred to maintain the level of their budgets as much as possible, even when this meant raising additional revenue, or changing traditional program mixes in order to obtain federal funds. They were reluctant to reduce budgets or personnel, let alone make deep targeted cuts. When cuts had to be made, these cities were most reluctant to cut programs for which there were federal matching funds, because such cuts would have disproportionate effects on total budget levels. As a result, federally sponsored programs for the poor seemed to survive cuts quite well even though much of the impetus behind tax protests has an antiwelfare bias.

Robert D. Behn's essay, "Can Public Policy Termination be Increased by Making Government More Businesslike?" discusses the desirability of comparing rates of policy termination of business and government organizations. Behn discusses the basic differences between business organizations and public agencies that affect their termination rates, and concludes that they are so fundamentally different that it makes no sense to expect government to terminate at the same rate as business.

In a similar vein, R. Scott Fosler's essay, "Local Government Productivity: Political and Administrative Potential," discusses the possibility of increasing public-sector productivity as a means to alleviate fiscal stress. Fosler incorporates politics into traditional notions of productivity derived from business by outlining political actors and their motivations to increase or decrease productivity. He also lays out short-term and long-term actions to improve productivity in fiscally stressed localities, given the special political constraints operating in the public sector.

In summary, the essays in this book cover a range of topics from disillusionment with the public sector to the limits of administrative response to fiscal stress. Nearly all the essays document the relationships between economics, politics, and public policy. The pieces were chosen not just for breadth of coverage and individual sparkle, but also to generate discussion and further research. The authors sometimes support and extend the arguments of other authors in the book, but as often disagree or suggest other lines of inquiry. Both the disagreements and the agreements should prove stimulating to the concerned scholar or public policy analyst.

REFERENCES

BARNET, R. (1980) The Lean Years: Politics in the Age of Scarcity. New York: Simon & Schuster.

BELL, D. (1960) The End of Ideology: On the Exhaustion of Political Ideas in the Fifties. Glencoe, IL: Free Press.

––– (1974) "The public household–On fiscal sociology and the liberal society." The Public Interest 37 (Fall): 29-68.

BRITTAN, S. (1975) "The economic contradictions of democracy." British Journal of Political Science 5 (April): 129-159.

DYE, T. R. (1966) Politics, Economics and the Public. Chicago: Rand-McNally.

FOX, D. M. (1967) The Discovery of Abundance. Ithaca, NY: Cornell University Press.

KLEIN, R. (1976) "The politics of public expenditure: American theory and British practice." British Journal of Political Science 6 (October): 401-432.

LERNER, D. and H. D. LASSWELL. [eds.] (1951) The Policy Sciences. Stanford, CA: Stanford University Press.

LEVINE, C. H. [ed.] (1980) Managing Fiscal Stress, Chatham, NJ: Chatham House.

ROSE, R. and G. PETERS (1978) Can Government Go Bankrupt? New York: Basic Books.

THUROW, L. (1980) The Zero-Sum Society, New York: Basic Books.

PART I

SLOW GROWTH, TAXPAYER RESISTANCE, AND FISCAL STRESS

FISCAL STRAINS ON THE WELFARE STATE:
CAUSES AND CONSEQUENCES

B. GUY PETERS

Center for Public Policy Studies
Tulane University

The majority of articles in this Yearbook are concerned with the management of fiscal problems of specific institutions faced with decline and retrenchment. The decline of these institutions does not occur in a vacuum, however, but is related to broader political and economic changes which have been occurring in the United States and other Western industrialized societies. Arguably, some of these institutions might be in decline anyway, regardless of the condition of the larger economy and polity. Local governments are burdened by high costs and restrictions on their revenue-raising potential, while universities face declining enrollments and low prestige with many potential funding agencies. The problems of these institutions are, however, exacerbated by the socioeconomic and public policy predicaments in which we now find ourselves. This essay will concentrate on these broad problems, with some examination of their possible explanation and some prescriptions for change. And an attempt will be made to link these conditions to the particular situations of local governments and other institutions threatened with the most severe financial problems.

THE CURRENT CONDITION

The period from the end of World War II until the 1970s was an era of truly remarkable political, economic, and social progress. In these days of uncertainty and cynicism, we to some degree look back fondly on the "Roaring Sixties"; at least there was a belief that anything could be done if only we, the citizens of the United States, or the world, just decided to do it. The mood at the beginning of the 1980s is very different. A pervasive pessimism, apparently justified by the facts, tells us that little is possible. The economy is no longer the great engine of growth that it once was, and citizens increasingly have lost faith in the ability of the political system to manage the political economy effectively.

The postwar period was also one of remarkable growth in the benefits produced by government, as well as those produced by the economy (Rose and Peters, 1978). The welfare state became a reality in some form in all industrialized countries. Even the United States, which is commonly cited as a welfare state "laggard," developed programs such as Medicare and Medicaid which provide health insurance for one-fifth of the population, Supplemental Security Income as a step toward a guaranteed annual income, and a (largely unsuccessful) "war on poverty" (Aaron, 1978). And what is perhaps more important is that the expectation was institutionalized in these societies that government could provide for the good life in the future.

It is instructive at this point to compare the record of the 1970s with that of the 1960s along a number of economic and political-economic dimensions. We will compare the state of certain economic indicators for 1978 with those of 1963. As with any comparison of arbitrarily selected points in time, there are obvious difficulties in the selection of these years, but at a minimum they will be illustrative of the changes which have taken place. We will look at conditions in seven major Western nations which again are arbitrarily selected but are representative of the range of experiences of the Western industrialized world: the United States, the United Kingdom, France, West Germany, Sweden, Italy, and Canada.

In almost all cases, given the usual value systems of Western societies, economic conditions in the late 1970s are not as good as in the early 1960s (see Table 1). Economic growth has slowed significantly, with the most rapid growth rate from 1977 to 1978 (3.3 percent in Canada) being slower than the slowest from 1962 to 1963 (3.5 percent in the United Kingdom). Not surprisingly, unemployment was also higher in 1978 than it had been in 1963. In each country other than the United States, unemployment was at least 50 percent higher than in 1963, and in one country—West Germany—it was five times higher as a percentage of the labor force. More surprisingly, with "stagflation," inflation has also increased. In every country except West Germany, the average annual rate of inflation was at least double in 1968-1973 what it had been from 1958 to 1963; in West Germany it was "only" 48 percent higher.

Table 1   Changing Conditions in the Political Economy

	Average Annual GDP Growth Rate (1973-1978)	Average Annual Inflation Rate (1973-1978)[a]	Unemployment Rate	Public Expenditure as a Percentage of GDP	Average Annual Growth of Public Expenditure (1973-1978)	Government Deficit as a Percentage of GDP[b]
			1978			
America	1.8	7.5	6.0	32.6	5.2	2.1
Britain	0.9	15.6	5.8	40.8	4.8	5.2
Canada	3.3	10.4	8.4	37.0	6.6	4.4
France	2.6	10.4	na[c]	40.9	4.8	4.0
W. Germany	2.2	4.6	4.3	41.3	5.2	2.0
Italy	2.1	16.8	7.2	42.5	17.9	15.4
Sweden	1.3	11.2	2.2	55.6	7.4	5.3
	(1958-1963)	*(1958-1963)*	**1963**		*(1958-1963)*	
America	4.2	1.4	5.7	26.1	4.7	1.1
Britain	3.5	2.3	2.4	31.2	5.2	2.8
Canada	4.0	1.4	5.5	25.5	6.2	1.4
France	5.6	4.7	na[c]	32.7	8.4	+0.8
W. Germany	5.7	3.1	0.8	30.3	8.6	+1.1
Italy	6.6	3.7	2.5	27.3	7.6	5.2
Sweden	4.8	3.4	1.4	30.6	6.8	2.9

SOURCES: International Monetary Fund, *International Financial Statistics, 33*, 5 (May 1980); OECD, *National Accounts of OECD Countries, 1962-1977,* Vol. I (Paris: OECD 1979); OECD, *National Accounts of OECD Countries, 1950-1968,* (Paris: OECD 1969); OECD, *Main Economic Indicators,* 80, 2 (February 1980).

[a]Change in Consumers Price Index or equivalent.

[b](+) indicates a government surplus.

[c]The French government does not report an unemployment rate.

The values attached to the condition of the public sector are less homogeneous, but the changes are nonetheless evident. The government share of Gross Domestic Product has increased greatly, almost doubling in Sweden. For some countries, such as the United States, which had a very small public sector, this may indicate the development of much-needed welfare state services, although in all cases it meant an increase in taxation. Likewise, expenditure growth in most countries increased in the 1973-1978 period more than in the earlier period, although not perhaps as much as might have been anticipated. The rate of increase was especially pronounced in Italy. Finally, the public-sector deficit as a percentage of Gross Domestic Product has also increased dramatically, rising to more than 15 percent in Italy. Apparently, faced with growing expenditure demands as well as demands for tax reductions or controls, many public-sector officials have chosen to borrow rather than seek the necessary tax increases to cover the expenditures. According to the traditional Keynesian position, these deficits should stimulate economic growth and reduce unemployment, although, being faced with inflation simultaneously, the medicine may not be exactly what was ordered (Buchanan and Wagner, 1977).

THE SOURCE OF THE STRAINS:
SUPPLY, DEMAND, AND THEIR MIX

In short, citizens and politicians both have genuine cause for concern. The long boom is over, and, even in optimistic moments, organizations such as the OECD do not see a return to the historic growth rates of the 1950s and 1960s (OECD, 1977a, 1977b). The absence of growth and the continuing pressures to spend do indeed place a significant strain on the welfare state to continue in the way it has.

At a broad level, we can understand the source of the fiscal strains on the welfare state as coming from failures in the supply of resources, e.g., the slowing of economic growth, or as emanating from the demand side of the equation with rapidly increasing levels of public expenditure, leaving aside whether those expenditure demands are generated by the public or within the political system itself. Finally, there is a problem of the mixture of supply and demand. Levels of economic growth in public expenditure growth which would not produce difficulties under more "normal" economic circumstances have become quite troublesome under conditions of slower economic growth, and further there is the "juggernaut" of growth in the public sector which becomes more difficult to control as the public sector itself becomes expanded (Rose and Peters, 1980).

ECONOMIC GROWTH AND THE SUPPLY OF REVENUE

Daniel Bell has referred to economic growth as the "political solvent" which has helped to hold together the postwar world (1974). Economic growth has generated expectations that the conditions of society will improve, but, more importantly, provides the wherewithal to make those improvements. Certainly, massive economic growth enabled Western countries to fund significant increases in the quantity and quality of public programs during the 1950s and 1960s at the same time that private consumption was being increased (Rose and Peters, 1978: Chap. 2).

The expectations generated by previous economic growth may persist, but, as we have shown, the reality of that growth does not. The economies of Western countries are now growing slowly, and in some years not at all. There is no longer the fiscal dividend from which increases in public expenditure can be painlessly financed, and consequently any increase in public expenditures must come from other programs, or from private consumption. With the political solvent absent, there will be an increased probability of political conflicts.

A number of diagnoses and remedies have been offered for the problems of the contemporary economic system. We will discuss three of the most commonly espoused: the market, neo-Marxism, and organizational change. In many ways, these three correspond quite closely to categories put forward by Alford to describe proposed reforms in health care policy: market reformers, radical reformers, and bureaucratic reformers (1976).

Market reformers and the dismantling of the welfare state. The conventional wisdom for conservative political and economic analysts is that the source of fiscal strain on the welfare state is the welfare state itself. This analysis ranges from unsubstantiated political claims that government "handouts" discourage people from seeking employment, and that bureaucratic "red tape" stifles the competitive market system, to more sophisticated analyses of the interaction of markets and the public sector (Lindblom, 1978; Benjamin, 1980). As Lindbeck has pointed out, it is often a mistake to discuss the economy as if political considerations were exogenous, and indeed there are very complex and important interactions between politics and markets (1976).

In this discussion, we will concentrate on one of the more interesting attempts to relate the growth of the public sector to the decline of industrial productivity. This is Bacon and Eltis's examination of the British economy, *Britain's Economic Problem: Too Few Producers* (1978).

The argument presented by Bacon and Eltis is similar in many ways to others presented before and since, but differs from most in clearly linking political choices to economic outcomes and in documenting analyses and conclusions. The fundamental argument is that the principal reason for slow productivity growth in Britain, and consequently for slow economic growth, is that too few people are working in manufacturing industries ("traded goods"), which tend to have higher rates of productivity growth than do service industries such as the public services. In the British case, there is a definite political background to this argument, since Government had made a commitment to full employment in 1946, and was therefore placed in the position of being an employer of last resort whenever economic slowdowns occurred and unemployment threatened to increase. In particular, employment was created in the social services and education (Bacon and Eltis, 1978: 12-13). Few would argue that these services are bad or harmful per se; in fact, they are quite pleasant things for the community. The difficulty is that they make a very slight direct contribution to economic growth as compared to an alternative use of manpower.

The previously cited changes in employment through deindustrialization may create a downward spiral in the economy (Blackaby, 1979). As more employees are taken into relatively less productive social service jobs, there is a tendency for the economy to slow, which in turn may result in more people being taken into government jobs in order to maintain full employment. This in turn is argued to create a further slowing of the economy. While this downward spiral is certainly not deemed to be inevitable, it is difficult to break once it is begun, barring significant policy changes by government.

Eltis points out elsewhere that poorly or self-taught Keynesianism pervaded this period of public decision making (1979). The logic was that if only the public sector would spend, then the economic problems which seemed so prominent at the time would disappear. Further, hiring people who might otherwise be unemployed for public-sector jobs was not seen as wasting resources but rather as putting them to use. The period of affluence in the 1950s and 1960s, then, was a time in which spending was quite possible politically and economically, but which built up very large ongoing expenditure commitments which began to come due in the 1970s and will continue to do so, perhaps forever.

The underlying analysis here is that the slower growth of service industries as compared to manufacturing industries would hold true whether those services were produced by government or by private industry. So the shift of production into the tertiary sector of the economy in most Western societies—it accounts for 59 percent of employment in Sweden and 60 percent in the United States—should on average produce slower rates of growth. The argument of Bacon and Eltis is, however, that at least privately provided services have some discipline in the marketplace, while those provided by government are not priced and lack any such discipline. Also, since government employees are more difficult to remove than private-sector employees, they develop vested "property rights" in their jobs, and become extremely difficult to relocate into possibly more productive uses of their energy.

In short, the market reformers are arguing that what is needed to improve the position of Western economies is to return to a greater dose of marketplace discipline rather than depend upon the services of the public sector. Some, as do the advocates of the Laffer curve, argue that this would in fact over time increase the revenue available to government and then enable a return to the condition of treble affluence with both public and private growth.

The neo-Marxist analysis. A quite different analysis of the problems of contemporary welfare states is provided by the Marxist or neo-Marxist school of analysis, the most widely cited work being James O'Connor's *The Fiscal Crisis of the State* (1973). Whereas the problems identified by the market reformers are in many ways the function of the success of the welfare state in extending its programs and policies, the neo-Marxists (or radical reformers, in Alford's terminology) see structural problems in "late capitalism" which can be solved only through the end of that system (Gough, 1975; Offe, 1974).

The structural problems, as they relate to the fiscal problems of the state, arise from the capitalist classes' use of the state as a means of furthering the process of capitalist accumulation. In fact, in this analysis, the state is central to the process of accumulation. The state must spend public funds of two types in order to further the accumulation of capital.

The first broad category is social capital expenditures, which expand surplus value for the capitalist classes. That is, they make private accumulation more profitable. There are two subcategories of social capital expenditures. The first is social investment, which increases the productivity of a single unit of labor. The best example would be expenditures on education, which make each worker more productive. The second subcategory is social consumption expenditures, which lower the reproduction costs of labor, i.e., make individuals more willing to join the labor force. An example would be social insurance expenditures which guarantee workers a reasonable existence in retirement in return for work during the more productive years.

The second major category of expenditures is "social expenses," intended to maintain social harmony and fulfill the legitimation function for the state. The category of expenditures includes a number of welfare state expenditures directed at the bottom of the income distribution ladder, such as AFDC, food stamps, and Medicaid in the United States. In O'Connor's analysis, these expenditures are necessary to paper over the deep socioeconomic divisions in these societies and thereby to legitimate the existence of the capitalist system.

The fiscal crisis of the state in capitalist societies is argued to result from a number of structural features in these societies. Most fundamental is the nature of late capitalism itself, with the confluence of monopoly powers of big business, big labor, and big government. The ability of these large forces in the society to appropriate the fruits of the economy for themselves will necessarily lead to a slowing of economic growth.

Additionally, the contributions of social capital expenditures to productivity will always lag behind their costs, so that there is an inherent structural gap. The costs of maintaining the capitalist state will therefore outrun the ability of the state to pay.[1] And there is the continuing need to legitimate the capitalist state through social expenses, with those legitimation expenditures increasing until the "legitimacy crisis of late capitalism" is reached.

Another aspect of the fiscal crisis is that the capitalist state cannot raise sufficient revenue to fund its expenditure needs. Late capitalism is controlled not only by the capitalist classes, but by the conjunction of the capitalists, labor organizations, and big government, and both labor and capital oppose the imposition of the necessary taxes to fund expenditure requirements. Likewise, because of the appropriation of many of the benefits of social investment expenditures for private gain, the state can never reap the benefits of its own activities, and will be in a perpetual and growing state of penury.

What is perhaps most remarkable about these discussions of the fiscal crisis of the state is the degree of similarity between the market and radical reformers. They both see a direct connection between the political and economic factors in determining the current condition of the welfare state. The downward spiral which both sets of analysts conceive of as almost inherent in these systems is the result of the need of the systems to legitimate themselves. For the "radicals," this need is inherent in the capitalist system and its structural deficiencies, while for the market reformers the need is based more upon specific political considerations and commitments such as the pledge to full employment, or the fear of the political consequences of high unemployment. Likewise, while the market reformers regard the shift of employment into education and social services as slowing economic growth, the radical reformers see it as creating a range of benefits which are appropriated by individuals or corporations rather than being shared with society. The solutions offered by these two sets of reformers are, of course, quite different, but they both see the problems arising from the same features, albeit assigning different meanings to those features.

The bureaucratic reformers: tinkerers and structuralists. Bacon and Eltis divide economic analysts into two broad categories: tinkerers and structuralists (1978: 1). Structuralists regard the problems in the contemporary economy as inherent in the economic structure and consequently believe these problems can only be addressed by changing those structures. Tinkerers, on the other hand, regard the structures as fundamentally sound and seek to improve economic performance by more indirect means, e.g., through manipulating the size of the government deficit or the money supply. As we carry through with Alford's categorization of reformers, we find "bureaucratic reformers" who are both tinkerers and structuralists.

The tinkerers are those who seek to manage to economy through traditional instruments such as monetary and fiscal policy. This is the Keynesian legacy, which now suffers from the demise of the famous Phillips Curve describing the tradeoff between inflation and unemployment (Phillips, 1958; Robinson, 1972). The contemporary problem of "stagflation," with both high unemployment and high inflation, makes simple attempts to move from one position to another along this curve rather inefficient as a means of producing acceptable policy outcomes. While stagflation may not yet have created a legitimacy crisis for the state as a whole, it certainly has for the economic managers, whose favorite tools and prescriptions are now in grave doubt. A semi-official OECD report, which is perhaps the most profound statement of the views of contemporary tinkerers, attributes the current slow growth of Western economies to "an unusual bunching of unfortunate disturbances unlikely to be repeated on the same scale, the impact of which was compounded by some avoidable errors in economic policy." (OECD, 1977a). Later reports from the same organizations were, however, less sanguine concerning the long-term prospects of these economies, but emphasized their underlying strength and durability (1977b).

The structuralist among the bureaucratic reformers, instead of attempting to cure economic problems through bureaucratic means, seeks to do so through debureaucratizing the economy. In particular, Mancur Olson argues that the primary cause of stagflation is the development of large, bureaucratic complexes in both the corporations and labor which make wages impervious to downward pressures, but displace those downward pressures into lowered production (Silk, 1980). Olson explains the relative economic success of Japan and West Germany not in terms of the destruction of their factories during World War II and the consequent rebuilding of a newer capital stock as compared to Britain or the United States, but rather the destruction of older organizations. The organizational networks in the Anglo-Saxon countries remained in place and have created an organizational and economic "rheumatism" in these countries. And in the United States, the relative success of the Sunbelt states in economic growth is explained by their lower level of institutionalization of organizations for both business and labor. A similar analysis is provided by Weintraub (1978), who argues for a Tax-Based Incomes Policy, with the major instrument tax penalties on corporations who allow wage increases greater than productivity. This is seen as a means of lessening some of the organizational power which has produced what he considers to be inflationary wage settlements. While both of these authors are interested in returning the determination of economic outcomes to the marketplace, we have discussed them here because of their emphasis on the effects of organizations and bureaucracies on the economy.

The tax system. A rapidly growing economy provides relatively little for the political system other than pride of producing or guiding such an economy if the tax system is not capable of extracting needed revenue from that economy. While the tax systems of Western governments have been quite efficient in including almost every category of economic activity—income, sales, value-added, wealth, or payrolls—in the tax base, several factors currently create difficulties for public-sector managers attempting to raise revenue.

The most obvious problem is the growing resistance to taxation. This has been manifested most obviously in the United States in the form of Proposition 13 and the numerous tax-limitation proposals which have followed (Oakland, 1979). At the federal level, ideas such as the Roth-Kemp tax-cut plan indicate some interest at all levels of government in reducing or controlling the size of tax obligations for citizens. Resistance to taxation has not been confined to the United States, however, as Mogens Glistrup and the Progress Party in Denmark, Mrs. Thatcher and Sir Geoffrey Howe in the United Kingdom, and the Anders Lange Party in Norway all indicate. Even the Italian Communist Party has stated publicly that it does not wish to see the size of the public sector in Italy increase.

Wilensky has argued that taxpayers' resistance can be explained by the visibility of the taxes citizens have to pay (1976). Highly visible taxes such as the income tax tend to provoke more resistance than less visible taxes such as the value-added tax. Unfortunately for those who must raise the revenue, however, it is the visible taxes which are most buoyant in an inflationary period. With inflation, income earners with no more real income will be paying higher rates of income tax because they are moved into higher tax brackets. Thus, rather painlessly for politicians who do not consciously have to pass tax increases which might be prominently featured in the media, government receives more money in "real" terms and as a percentage of Gross National Product.

The second problem which arises relative to the tax system is that the revenues generated, and particularly new revenues, are not evenly distributed. It is common for central governments or, in the United States, state governments to restrict the types of taxation, or even rates of taxation, of local governments. The Scandinavian countries have significant local income taxes, but most other local governments must depend upon property, sales, and excise taxes, etc., which do not grow nearly as rapidly as a progressive income tax (Wolman, 1979).

Local or regional governments are also constrained to some degree in raising tax levels by the existence of a "quasi-market" in taxation. That is, even when local governments can set their own tax rates, they may compete among themselves to attract residents or industry in part on the basis of giving the most favorable tax treatment (Tiebout, 1956). While there are a number of fixed costs which deter industries or individuals from picking up and leaving their current locations, when that move is to be made anyway, local tax systems and other aspects of the local political situation, such as laws on unionization, can have a significant impact on that decision. The success of the Sunbelt states in attracting industries from the Northeast is indicative of the attractiveness of tax breaks in promoting relocation. Likewise, the existence of high tax rates may deter relocation in an area, so that local governments may not be able to raise revenue to the extent that they might otherwise wish.

Summary. Public-sector managers are faced with the difficult task of trying to generate the revenues their expenditure programs require. Economies are growing slowly and promise to do so for some time in the future. Revenues do not painlessly roll into treasuries as they did in the 1950s and 1960s. Thus, decisions to spend in the public sector will frequently involve making decisions not to spend for other programs, or to consciously diminish private consumption. These managers will not receive a great deal of help from citizens in expanding the public sector, and in fact there are strong political pressures to limit or diminish the size of public revenues and expenditures. There are, however, strong pressures on the demand side to increase expenditures in the public sector. These forces are not inexorable but are still important for understanding how the dynamics of the political economy function.

THE PRESSURES TO SPEND: DEMAND FOR PUBLIC EXPENDITURE

The inevitability of public expenditure increases has been very much overemphasized by critics of the public sector and its policies. The round of budget cutting by the Carter administration in the Spring of 1980 is one indication of the ability of political leaders to "bite the bullet" and to reduce expenditures. And if President Carter bit the bullet, Mrs. Thatcher and her Chancellor of the Exchequer swallowed it whole through several rounds of rather deep cuts in expenditure.

In regard to the Carter cuts, however, it can be argued that they were ones which were easy to make. They were made in programs with relatively little powerful political support or which did not create great financial hardships. Thus, the cuts concentrated on urban programs such as UDAG and CETA, and on revenue sharing for the states—most of which were already running surpluses. Cuts have yet to be made in major entitlement programs. The available evidence is that when and if such cuts are attempted, they will provoke serious political reactions. For example, when a newly reelected Schmidt government in West Germany attempted to delay the indexing of public pensions by six months to reduce expenditures, the outcry forced a return to the original plans. And, as Rose points out in this volume, cuts are not always cuts, but frequently involve only cuts in projections or cuts in expectations for future growth (1980a).

Expenditures can be cut, but they are not always cut, and there are strong pressures to increase them. We can look at these pressures on the demand side of the fiscal crisis as being in three broad categories: demographic, economic, and political.

Demography. Ben Wattenberg has a television program entitled "Demography is Destiny," and much the same could be said of public expenditures. The population structures of most Western countries have a dynamic in them which apparently will call for increasing expenditures in the foreseeable future.

The primary demographic force for future expenditure is the aging of the population. Already in the United States, 25 percent of the federal budget in 1981 was directed toward the elderly through Social Security, Medicare, and a variety of other programs (Washington Post, 1980). The populations of most Western countries are aging rather rapidly. The average age of the U.S. population is already over 30 and is increasing each year. Over 12 percent of the United States population is already over 65 years of age, and this segment of the population is increasing by 2.5 percent per annum, while the population as a whole is tending to increase by less than 1 percent per year. However, compared to many Western European countries, the United States remains a very young country. For example, almost 16 percent of the population in Sweden is over 65, and if this percentage were similar to the percentages of other Western countries, public expenditures for health care alone would have been almost 15 percent less (OECD, 1978: 28).

Given that social security systems are financed by payroll taxes, one of the impacts of aging populations is likely to be more tax resistance. For example, in the United States, each social security recipient is supported by payroll taxes from six workers. In 2025, this figure will be decreased to four, and by 2050, to three, given current population projections (Parsons and Munro, 1977). Social security taxes are not so visible perhaps as some other forms of taxation, but these demands may require the introduction of the value-added tax in the United States as a means of funding this program less visibly.

Unfortunately for public budget managers, the demographic impetus to spend more does not work so easily in reverse. The declining segments of the population are the young, so the obvious place for savings is in education. However, savings in educational costs tend not to be proportional to declines in enrollment. A school teacher must still be employed and is paid the same amount whether a classroom has 25 or 30 pupils. Certainly, some savings can be effected by consolidation and closings, but even those come much harder than the upward adjustments of pensions and Medicare expenditures.

Migration is another demographic factor which tends to push public expenditure upward. The American population, as is true for all nations, is shuffling itself around in space. For most of the postwar period, there has been a flight from central cities to suburban or exurban communities. This trend has been reversed, at least partially, in response to increased energy costs. However, this has produced two additional pressures on expenditures. First, the new suburban communities must spend to provide the type of services which their citizens expect. In general, they must perform especially well in education and in providing recreation and other amenities, given the middle-class constituency which they serve. However, the inner cities can save very little from this exodus. They have exactly the same capital infrastructure to maintain, and, as with the earlier education example, they save very little when providing direct services to the remaining population. And, of course, the population remaining tends to be the disproportionately poor and elderly, the two groups of people who tend to consume very high levels of public services.

Much the same thing has happened with the shift of population from the Frostbelt to the Sunbelt states. Declining areas of the industrial Northeast are left to maintain or replenish their capital infrastructures despite declining industrial and population bases. On the other end, the boom areas of the West and South must build up the same sort of capital stock in the public services. And again, it is frequently the poor, although not necessarily the elderly, who remain in the declining areas, placing additional expenditure requirements onto a declining tax base.

Economic factors. There are also factors associated with the economics of providing public services which tend to drive the costs of the public sector upward. Some of these involve particular features of the public sector, while others are features of the economic environment which indirectly affect the public sector through the need to subsidize certain types of firms in the private sector. Also, although these factors are labeled economic, in many instances they would not be a problem without a political system to make them a problem. The potential bankruptcy of Chrysler is an economic problem, but it is exacerbated because of the fear of massive unemployment concentrated in a number of areas during an election year.

General economic factors affecting public-sector expenditures are rather well known. As energy prices pass through the economy, they will certainly affect public-sector costs as much as private-sector costs. In the public sector, however, these costs will be potentially offset by a windfall profits tax at the federal level, and the deregulation of oil and gas will produce a huge windfall in severance taxes for the energy-rich states.

Likewise, the possibility or probability of a general recession in the early 1980s will also significantly affect public expenditures. It is commonly estimated that each additional 1 percent in the unemployment rate requires some $4 billion in additional expenditures from the federal government for unemployment insurance benefits, social security payments, welfare, food stamps, etc. To this would have to be added the costs incurred by state and (especially) local governments to cover the same type of expenses. And, of course, a recession also means a slowdown of economic activity with a subsequent slowdown in tax revenues.

Inflation also affects public-sector expenditures. In the first place, many public programs are now "indexed," or have their benefits linked to the Consumer Price Index (CPI). Many governments also have their employees' salaries linked to the price index. Thus, any increases in price will soon show up directly in the costs of public programs.

And even if public sector salaries and wages are not directly tied to the CPI, there will still, in all probability, be an effect of inflation on the need for public expenditure. This is because of the "Relative Price Effect" (Baumol, 1971; Klein, 1976; Beck, 1979). The public sector is heavily labor intensive, with wages and salaries a larger component of the total costs than is true for most other industries. In an inflationary period, the costs of producing public-sector programs will therefore tend to increase more rapidly than for private-sector goods and services. Thus, to produce the same package of goods and services from one year to the next, the government share of the economy will have to increase, and proposals made in the United States to impose a limitation on the share of economic production of a state, or the country as a whole, which can be devoted to public expenditure imply a slow diminution of the volume of public services, despite the constant share of the economic pie. For example, in the United Kingdom, the Treasury has estimated that to provide the same services in a given year, the share of Gross National Product taken for public expenditure would have to increase by 0.7 percent (H.M. Treasury, 1972). This is not a rapid increase by any means, but it does indicate that there is pressure, due to the very nature of the provision of public services, to increase public-service costs, and that to stay constant actually implies a cut in real services.

A final economic problem besetting those in the public sector and in the general public seeking to limit the increasing share of production taken for government expenditure is the lumpiness of the economy. A general recession may produce general unemployment, with the effects scattered throughout the country. When a major corporation such as Chrysler or Lockheed threatens to go bankrupt, the effects would be concentrated geographically and might be sufficiently large to have an effect on the economy as a whole. These problems are exacerbated when the firm in question produces a product which is highly valued by the public sector itself, as Lockheed does with its aircraft and Chrysler does with its tanks. Thus, the structure of modern economies, with huge corporations rather than many small producers, makes it difficult for market forces to work without political interference, with pressure to keep the large corporations running through public subsidies or loan guarantees.

Political factors. Perhaps the ultimate constraint on the ability of public-sector managers to control expenditures is politics. All the problems of a demographic or economic nature would be relatively easily manageable were it not for the political forces which underlie the inability or unwillingness of the public sector itself to restrict the supply of goods produced through public expenditure.

The most important problem in controlling the expenditure growth of the welfare state involves the entitlement programs which have been institutionalized in these systems. The use of social insurance as a means of attaining the ends of the welfare state has been an excellent means of legitimating these programs, but has become less efficacious as pressures for restricting expenditure growth have grown. Most of the programs of the welfare state are not perceived as "giveaways," but rather as rights earned through contributions. This quasi-contractual nature of the programs is a major barrier to the adjustment of program costs. As Franklin Roosevelt said when his social security program was being passed (Leuchtenberg, 1963):

> We put those payroll contributions there so as to give the contributors a legal, moral and political right to collect their pensions and employment benefits, with those taxes in there, no damn politician can ever scrap my social security program.

And he was right.

One measure of the impact of entitlement programs on public expenditures is the controllability of the budget, that is, the proportion of the budget which can be cut in any one year without a major political conflict. This percentage has been increasing, so that in the 1981 budget proposed by President Carter, the uncontrollable expenditures accounted for 75 percent of total expenditure (Executive Office of the President, 1980). And the remaining controllable portions of the budget were very heavily concentrated in defense spending. The political climate of the early 1980s indicates that these expenditures are unlikely to be cut, so that in practice almost all of the budget may be uncontrollable.

There are also features of the political marketplace which have a significant influence on the growth of public expenditures. As the economic marketplace has externalities, the political system attempts to internalize those costs, but, in so doing, tends to produce rather peculiar patterns of decision making. One important feature is the lack of a budget constraint on the part of the individual citizens seeking benefits from the public sector, so that the politics which develop are dedicated to concentrating benefits and spreading costs (Brittan, 1976). Individuals who want a certain type of benefit are able to mobilize groups who as consumers may be directly benefited by the expenditure, while taxpayers have traditionally had difficulty mobilizing to block expenditures. Their interests tend to be more diffuse, so the organizational efforts necessary to create an effective political lobby might not be worth the personal savings in taxes from blocking any additional programs.

Likewise, over the period of affluence in the "long boom," Western countries developed a pattern of making decisions by log rolling. In a period of affluence, it is easy to paper over divisions and conflicts within a society by using the fiscal dividend of growth to pay for benefits for everyone (Heisler and Peters, 1978). This has been very useful for the resolution of ethnic and regional conflicts in a number of countries, but presents intense political problems once it must be terminated by the absence of resources.

The structure of decision making in government, and especially in the United States, also presents problems for the management of public expenditures. Tax and expenditure decisions are frequently divorced, and while almost everyone likes expenditures and few like taxation, the two are never made to balance. Frequently, spending committees and organizations will approve of expenditures without any knowledge of how the costs incurred will be covered. And, even within the expenditure process itself, the committee and subcommittee system in the United States produces a very narrow consideration of many expenditure decisions. Within the context of macroeconomic management, the division of taxation and expenditure decisions among a number of levels of government presents additional difficulties. The federal government may decide that for economic growth a tax cut is required, but the effects of that tax cut may be negated by the activities of state and local governments trying to increase their own revenues. This is precisely what happened in the case of the Kennedy tax cut in 1963, when the effects of federal tax cuts were almost exactly offset by increased taxation by subnational governments. Likewise, the federal government has a number of instruments for stimulating local governments to spend money if it believes the economy is slowing and needs a boost, but lacks the delicate instruments required to slow spending while still guaranteeing needed services will be provided, especially in inner-city areas.

Governments also make decisions based upon their experiences and expectations, just as individuals do. Arguably, governments have a built-in "permanent income hypothesis" about the future of their revenues and economic growth. That is, the period of growth during the 1950s and 1960s produced a generation of decision makers who assume that any spending decisions they make will be funded very easily by the fiscal dividend of growth (Alt and Chrystal, 1978). Such socialization or conditioning by a period of growth may be difficult to overcome in a short period of time, so that a certain psychological inertia, as well as the more physical inertia of entitlement programs, is built into continuing patterns of expenditure growth (Rose and Peters, 1978: Chap. 9).

Finally, there are important pressures for continuing public expenditure growth coming from within the public sector itself. As the public sector

has become increasingly professionalized, these individuals with professional qualifications and status are capable of lobbying for improvements
in quality to bring service standards up to acceptable professional norms,
and they are also very good at protecting their own interests and positions.
At lower levels in the bureaucracy, the unionization of many public
servants also creates pressures for job retention and for improvements in
salaries and benefits (Peters, 1980; Rose, 1980b) which are backed by real
threats of strikes. In general, public employees have more clout as we enter
the 1980s and consequently can have a major impact on keeping the
public sector large and growing.

One recent analysis, however, places the credit or blame for the expansion of the public sector in the United States more on congressmen than
on the bureaucracy (ACIR, 1980). Whether acting from genuine interests
of their own, the expressed wishes of constituents, or the desire to make
political hay, congressmen are argued to be a major force in developing
new public programs and in pushing the boundaries of the public sector
into areas which had previously been private. It has long been argued that
the congressional need for "porkbarrel" has been related to continuing
public works expenditures (Fiorina, 1978), but this analysis argues that
congressmen use new programs and the associated spending as a way of
enhancing their own careers and building certain types of monuments to
themselves.

The summation of the above catalogue of pressures is that there are
powerful pressures pressing to expand the size of the public sector. For
economic, demographic, and political reasons, we should expect the public
sector to expand, despite all the best efforts of politicians and public-
sector managers to reduce or to control that expansion. A limitation of
growth is by no means impossible, but it will require more than a few
clever political tricks or one-time efforts to accomplish.

PUTTING SUPPLY AND DEMAND TOGETHER

As we move into the 1980s, the interface of supply and demand
problems in the public sector is becoming more acute. On the one hand,
the supply of public revenues, both from the fiscal dividend of growth and
from the willingness of the public to pay taxes, is decreasing, or at least
not growing as rapidly as it once did. On the other hand, the growth in the
pressures on governments to spend money has perhaps slowed but is still
significant. And, as the public sector is now a larger proportion of the total
economy, the relative rates of growth of the public sector and the
economy are crucial for maintaining the mixture of the mixed economy.

As government grows as a share of total economic production, its growth commands a larger share of the total growth of the economy. For example, if the public sector accounts for 25 percent of Gross National Product, and the public sector grows at a rate of 8 percent, then 2 percent GNP growth is required to fund the growth in the public sector, with any economic growth above that available for private consumption or investment. The figures outlined above are not unreasonable for the 1950s, and during that period most Western economies far exceeded a 2 percent annual growth rate. However, when the public sector increases to 50 percent of total GNP and continues to grow at 8 percent annually, then a 4 percent growth rate is required simply to cover the rate of public-sector growth, before anything can be added to the private consumption of citizens. The bad news is that the 50 percent figure is not unreasonable for many Western governments, and the average annual growth rate is now well beneath 4 percent per annum.

Table 2 points to the differences between the experiences of the 1950s and the 1970s (Rose and Peters, 1980). In the 1950s, the "front-end load" of government expenditures, or the growth rate required simply to fund public expenditure growth, averaged less than 50 percent of GNP growth for the period for the seven countries discussed previously. By the 1970s, however, the front-end load accounted for an average of 131 percent of economic growth rates. In other words, the rate of economic growth was not keeping pace with the demands for increases in private consumption. On average, citizens were getting less in their take-home pay at the end of the month or week than they were in previous years.

Just as do citizens, governments face difficulties when they begin to do their sums. They have increased revenues, if for no other reason than that the general inflation has provided them the revenue. However, their expenditure requirements will, on average, have increased more than their revenues, leaving them the options of increasing revenues—in the face of growing taxpayer resistance and increasing indebtedness—or reducing their expenditures, or both. This problem is evident at the local level, which has a number of programs for which continued spending is required, but which also lacks the buoyant tax system of the federal government. State governments have been faring best, lacking many entitlement programs and having more buoyant tax structures than local governments.

The underlying disequilibrium in the political economy is a fundamental problem for the public sector and the welfare state. While there may be many crises and problems in the welfare state (Janowitz, 1976), the existence of this underlying imbalance is certainly a major force in bringing citizens to question the efficacy of the system. For the middle-

Table 2   The Disequilibrium of the Mixed Economy

	A) The Experience of the 1950s		
	(1)	(2)	(3)
	Costs of Public Policy as % of National Product	Front End Load: Growth of Public Policy as % of National Product	Front End Load as % of Annual Growth of National Product
America	27	1.3	54
Britain	34	1.2	52
Canada	29	1.3	33
France	33	2.6	80
Germany	31	2.5	37
Italy	23	1.7	32
Sweden	27	1.8	55
	B) The Experience of the 1970s		
America	36	1.8	62
Britain	50	2.2	122
Canada	39	2.8	68
France	41	3.6	100
Germany	46	3.7	142
Italy	47	5.2	200
Sweden	54	3.8	224

SOURCES: OECD *National Accounts of OECD Countries, 1950-1968* (Paris: OECD 1969), Tables 1, 2, and 7 for each country; OECD, *National Accounts of OECD Countries, 1977,* Vol. 2 (Paris: OECD 1979), Tables 1, 2, and 9 for each country; Vol. 1 pp. 31, 63, 67, 83, 107, and 119; OECD, *Main Economic Indicators,* February, 1980, p. 168.

class taxpayer, the apparent inefficiencies and the very level of taxation may force a skeptical or hostile attitude (Citrin, 1979). For the client who depends upon public programs for some or all of his or her livelihood, the threats to the continuation of those programs raise questions as to whether the public sector is the solution to problems it was once portrayed to be.

IMPLICATIONS

What does the imbalance which has been described mean for the average citizen and for the average government? The first thing to consider is that there is no average citizen or government. One of the major implications of the "crisis" of the welfare state is the redistribution of goods, services, and power within both the public and private sectors. We have already pointed out that the crisis is generally felt most strongly at the local levels of government, which frequently lack the ability—either economic or legal—to increase their revenues, and whose expenditure commitments continue to increase.

Likewise, there are important differences among the several countries for which we presented data. Some, such as Canada and West Germany, if not smiling through the apocalypse, are at least holding their own. Others, such as the United Kingdom and Italy, are doing anything but smiling. The two do differ, however, in how they reached their unhappy junctures. Italy was pushed to the precipice by an apparently uncontrollable rate of public expenditure growth, albeit with quite high rates of economic growth. The United Kingdom, on the other hand, has been extremely frugal in public expenditure when compared to others, but has had such low rates of economic growth that even those slowly growing expenditures could not be funded without cutting private consumption and investment.

This "crisis" also will have redistributional effects on individuals. Obviously, there will be some redistribution between those who receive their income through the "social wage" and those who receive their wages as wages. There are, however, two possible scenarios for this redistribution. In one scenario, the public could learn to accept and perhaps even enjoy a decline in personal take-home pay. In such a scenario, people would value the benefits created by the public sector more than those created by private consumption, and would agree to the social desirability of redistribution from wage earners to those receiving public benefits. In the other scenario, the principal reaction to the imbalance in the public sector would be to cut the size of the public sector, with those depending upon public benefits suffering. The interesting thing is that to some degree both of these scenarios are occurring simultaneously. Many public programs are being cut back or terminated, while others continue to grow and to match inflation in the economy. The obvious difference between the fates of CETA and Social Security in the United States is representative of the varying response to the "crisis." While there is a differentiation of public programs in many industrialized countries, there is an overall decline in the take-home pay of citizens, so that the net beneficiaries are those who work for government or who receive a large share of their income through public programs.

As well as class implications, there are also redistributional consequences for ethnic or sexual groups. One of the findings concerning the effects of Proposition 13 in California was that as well as affecting services for the less affluent, it also affected the employment of minority group members in public programs. Blacks and Chicanos were the last hired and were among the first laid off. This was particularly unfortunate because of the special training programs to prepare those individuals for white-collar jobs in the public sector (Pascal et al., 1979). Likewise, the effects of many of Mrs. Thatcher's cuts in British public expenditure have apparently fallen very heavily on women (Turner, 1979). Programs such as day care for working mothers and attendance allowances have been among the programs most severely cut, so that the attempts of British women to move into the work force have apparently been seriously affected.

The reaction of citizens to the crisis in the public sector can also be seen through several scenarios, neither of which is very happy. One scenario postulates that the major form of reaction will be attempts by citizens to flee the power of the state, especially its powers of taxation, through a variety of illegal and quasi-legal activities (Rose and Peters, 1978). One possible reaction to increasing taxation and decreasing services would be to try to opt out of the system entirely, take Hirschman's exit option (1971), and engage in barter, demonetization of one's labor, and tax evasion. There is some evidence to support the proposition that this type of behavior has in fact been increasing over the past several years (Gutmann, 1977).

The alternative scenario is one of increasing political conflict over the distribution of the benefits and burdens of society as the nexus between public and private gains becomes more evident and the tradeoff between different public programs also becomes evident. In this scenario, rather than acting as individuals and seeking to escape from the burdens of taxation, citizens will continue to act as members of groups and use the political process to influence the allocation of benefits (Heisler and Peters, 1978). This will be especially true in European countries which have adopted a more corporatist conception of politics and for which the existence of organized political groups is more central to the allocative process (Heisler, 1974). These two scenarios are not necessarily mutually exclusive, and both already may be occurring simultaneously, but they do constitute an interesting means of examining the political implications of the crisis of the welfare state.

One of the common responses to the perceived crisis is to devise mechanisms that presumably prevent governments from spending more than a percentage of Gross National Product, or require a balanced budget. Some have already been imposed. Local governments and many state governments function with laws placing limits on their capital bonding. Many have restrictive provisions for their operating budgets, as well as recently passed state referenda pegging state expenditures and/or revenues to levels of economic activity within the state. Similar restrictions have been proposed for the federal government.

These provisions present at least two significant difficulties. The first is the difficulty of budgeting to stay within the parameters. The planning for a federal budget begins approximately sixteen months prior to its implementation, and making the budget requires building in a number of assumptions about economic conditions that will exist during the budget period. This means that, unwittingly, budget makers may be put into a position of breaking a law, or conversely, of forcing existing programs to slow down their spending and perhaps seriously affect the implementation of programs. In the long run, these possible outcomes may do more damage to public confidence in the ability of the public sector to manage its own affairs than increasing expenditures.

Second, the need to evade any such restrictions may produce more of the mutation of the state which has begun to be observed in most Western countries (Sharkansky, 1979). When there are restrictions on how much local government can tax and spend, there has been a tendency to produce new organizations which are not covered by these restrictions, such as quasi-governmental corporations and special district governments. This presents even greater difficulties in controlling the public sector than now exist, both in financial terms and in terms of policy. And again, this may produce as great a disaffection for the state as have the tax and expenditure problems we have outlined.

The problems of the welfare state are not only those of taxation and expenditure control. There are problems of program effectiveness and of providing human relationships in a more mechanical society. But merely covering the costs of the welfare state is presenting sufficient problems in the early 1980s to question the long-term viability of the arrangements developed so painfully over such a long period of time. The crisis is real and does not appear to be amenable to solution by simple mechanical means. What appears to be needed is more political will and political judgment rather than attempts to find quick and easy remedies.

REFERENCES

AARON, H. (1978) Politics and the Professors. Washington, DC: Brookings.
Advisory Commission on Intergovernmental Relations [ACIR] (1980) The Growth of Government in the United States. Preliminary Report to the Commission. Washington, DC: Government Printing Office.

ALFORD, R. R. (1976) Health Care Politics. Chicago: University of Chicago Press.

ALT, J. and A. CHRYSTAL (1978) "Endogenous government behaviour." Presented at Conference on Politics of Inflation, Unemployment, and Growth, Stanford, California.

BACON, R. and W. ELTIS (1978) Britain's Economic Problem: Too Few Producers, 2nd ed. London: Macmillan.

BAUMOL, W. J. (1971) "Macroeconomics of unbalanced growth: the anatomy of urban crisis," in R. L. Heilbroner and A. M. Ford (eds.) Is Economics Relevant? Pacific Palisades, CA: Palisades.

BECK, M. (1979) "Public sector growth: a real perspective." Public Finance 34 (Winter): 313-356.

BELL, D. (1974) "The public household." The Public Interest 37 (Fall): 29-68.

BENJAMIN, R. (1980) The Limits of Politics: Collective Goods and Political Change in Postindustrial Society. Chicago: University of Chicago Press.

BLACKABY, F. (1979) De-Industrialization. London: Heinemann.

BRITTAN, S. (1976) "The economic contradictions of democracy." British Journal of Political Science 6 (April): 129-160.

BUCHANAN, J. M. and R. E. WAGNER (1977) Democracy in Deficit: The Political Legacy of Lord Keynes. New York: Academic.

CITRIN, J. (1979) "Do people want something for nothing: public opinion on taxes and government spending." National Tax Journal (Supplement) 32 (June): 113-130.

DENISON, E. F. (1979) "Where has productivity gone?" pp. 71-78 in W. Fellner (ed.) Contemporary Economic Problems 1979. Washington, DC: American Enterprise Institute.

ELTIS, W. (1979) "How rapid public sector growth can undermine the growth of the national product," in W. Beckerman (ed.) Slow Growth in Britain. Oxford: Oxford University Press.

Executive Office of the President, Office of Management and Budget (1980) U.S. Budget in Brief, 1981. Washington, DC: Government Printing Office.

FIORINA, M. (1978). Congress: Keystone of the Washington Establishment. New Haven, CT: Yale University Press.

GOUGH, I. (1975) "State expenditures in advanced capitalism." New Left Review 92 (April): 53-92.

GUTMANN, P. M. (1977) "The subterranean economy." Financial Analysts' Journal (November/December): 26, 27, 34.

HEISLER, M. O. (1974) "The European Polity Model," in Heisler (ed.) Politics in Europe. New York: McKay.

––– (1979) "Authority and strains in the political economy of the welfare state–or, if, as Rose and Peters suggest, we are heading for political bankruptcy, how will our creditors collect?" Presented at the annual meeting of the International Studies Association, Toronto.

HEISLER, M. O. and B. G. PETERS (1978) The Implications of Scarcity for the Management of Conflict in Multicultural Societies. Studies in Public Policy, No. 20. Glasgow, Scotland: Centre for the Study of Public Policy, University of Strathclyde.

H. M. Treasury (1972) Public Expenditure White Papers: Handbook on Methodology. London: HMSO.

HIRSCHMAN, A. O. (1971) Exit, Voice and Loyalty. Cambridge, MA: Harvard University Press.

JANOWITZ, M. (1976) Social Control of the Welfare State. Chicago: University of Chicago Press.

KLEIN, R. (1976) "The politics of the budgetary process: American theory and British practice." British Journal of Political Science 6 (April): 401-432.

LEUCHTENBERG, W. E. (1963) Franklin D. Roosevelt and the New Deal, 1932-1940. New York: Harper & Row.

LINDBECK, A. (1976) "Stabilization policy in open economics with endogenous politicians." American Economic Review 66 (May): 1-19.

LINDBLOM, C. (1978) Politics and Markets. New York: Basic Books.

OAKLAND, W. H. (1979) "Proposition 13–Genesis and Consequences." National Tax Journal (Supplement) 32 (June): 387-409.

O'CONNOR, J. (1973) The Fiscal Crisis of the State. New York: St. Martin's.

OECD (1977a) Towards Full Employment and Price Stability. McCracken Report. Paris: OECD.

——— (1977b) Economic Outlook 22 (December).

——— (1978) Studies in Resource Allocation, No. 5. Public Expenditure Trends. Paris: OECD.

OFFE, C. (1974) "Structural Problems of the Capitalist State," pp. 31-58 in K. von Beyme (ed.) German Political Studies. Beverly Hills, CA: Sage.

PARSONS, D. and D. MUNRO (1977) "Intergenerational transfers in social security," in M. Boskin (ed.) The Crisis in Social Security. San Francisco: Institute for Contemporary Studies.

PASCAL, A. H. et al. (1979) Fiscal Containment of State and Local Government. Santa Monica, CA: Rand.

PETERS, B. G. (1980) Public Employment in the United States: Growth and Change. Studies in Public Policy, No. 63. Glasgow, Scotland: Centre for the Study of Public Policy, University of Strathclyde.

PHILLIPS, A. W. (1958) "The relation between unemployment and the rate of change of money wage rates in the United Kingdom, 1861-1957." Economica 25 (November): 283-299.

ROBINSON, J. (1972) "The second crisis of economic theory." American Economic Review 62 (May): 1-9.

ROSE, R. (1980a) "Misperceiving public expenditures," in C. Levine and I. Rubin (eds.) Fiscal Stress and Public Policy. Beverly Hills, CA: Sage.

——— (1980b) Changes in Public Employment: A Multi-Dimensional Comparative Analysis. Studies in Public Policy, No. 61. Glasgow, Scotland: Centre for the Study of Public Policy, University of Strathclyde.

ROSE, R. and B. G. PETERS (1978) Can Government Go Bankrupt? New York: Basic Books.

——— (1980) "The juggernaut of incrementalism," in P. Aronson and P. Ordeshook, Causes and Consequences of the Growth of Government. Lexington, MA: Lexington.

SHARKANSKY, I. (1979) Wither the State? Chatham, NJ: Chatham House.

SILK, L. (1980) "Interest groups and stagflation." New York Times (May 2).

TIEBOUT, C. M. (1956) "A pure theory of local expenditures." Journal of Political Economy 65 (October): 416-424.

TURNER, J. (1979) "Women and the cuts." New Society (December): 645-646.

Washington Post (1980) "Aiding elderly." January 29.

WEINTRAUB, S. (1978) Capitalism's Inflation and Unemployment Crisis: Beyond Monetarism and Keynesianism. Reading, MA: Addison-Wesley.

WILENSKY, H. L. (1976) The "New Corporatism." Centralization and the Welfare State. Beverly Hills, CA: Sage.

WOLMAN, H. (1979) Local fiscal problems in OECD countries, Working Paper 1368-02. Washington, DC: The Urban Institute.

2

THE FEDERAL ROLE IN THE EIGHTIES: BIGGER, BROADER, AND DEEPER OR SMALLER, TRIMMER, AND CHEAPER?

DAVID R. BEAM
CYNTHIA C. COLELLA

Advisory Commission on Intergovernmental Relations

THE CLOUDY CRYSTAL BALL

Forecasting public policy is a notoriously tricky business. And, while prognostication of any sort is quite difficult, policy foresight seems to pose special problems. Many of the best minds in the business have made serious errors, and instances of accuracy are few. In short, the task should be approached with extreme trepidation and more than a little humility.

It is worth recalling, for example, the state of expert opinion circa 1960. There was little recognition that the nation was then nearing a period of rapid expansion of government in general and of federal domestic responsibilities in particular. Quite the contrary. Indeed, such an insightful commentator as John Kenneth Galbraith was explaining the

AUTHORS' NOTE: *This article is a revision of a paper prepared for presentation at the Forty-First National Conference of the American Society for Public Administration, San Francisco, California, April 13-16, 1980. The views expressed are solely those of the authors, and should not be attributed to the members of the Advisory Commission on Intergovernmental Relations or its staff. The authors would like to acknowledge the helpful criticisms of many of their colleagues, especially Michael Mitchell, David B. Walker, and John F. Shannon, and their debt to Timothy Conlan, presently at Harvard University, who shared fully in the research on federal policy making described here.*

"inherent tendency" for the production of public services to lag behind private-sector growth (1958: 205), while Anthony Downs was propounding the theoretical reasons for government budgets being inevitably "too small" in a democracy (1960). And, as late as 1963, James MacGregor Burns was warning of the political "deadlock and drift" expected to carry on into the indefinite future (1963: 2).

None of these analysts should be condemned: the evidence in favor of their opinions was quite ample. Government was a "five-and-dime" operation in 1960, more appropriately compared to the limited state propounded by the Founders than to the sprawling Leviathan it was to become in less than twenty years. Despite the programmatic and constitutional revolutions of the New Deal era, important remnants of "dual federalism" remained in practice, and seemed very firmly entrenched.

Think back to the halcyon days surrounding the Kennedy inauguration. The welfare explosion had not yet begun. Although the number of AFDC recipients had increased somewhat in the 1950s and 1960s, the percentage of children receiving benefits was stable, and payments were low (Levitan and Taggart, 1976: 49). Little of the legislative outpouring of the coming years was then visible, and with good reason. While the "war on poverty" was the dominant theme of the decade, poverty simply was not a major public concern in 1960. Indeed, the problems of poverty, economic inequality, and discrimination were considered to be largely outside the realm of the "political" branches of government (Aaron, 1978: 16). A majority of economists, including those within the Kennedy Administration, believed that economic growth would sop up most of the unemployed, and that special manpower measures targeted to the disadvantaged were unnecessary. Those few experts who were concerned fixed their attention chiefly upon the potential plight of the older, mostly white, mostly male workers apt to be displaced by automation, rather than upon the youths, blacks, and women who became the principal targets of new federal employment policies.

In other related social fields as well, major policy breakthroughs seemed unlikely. Efforts to establish a major federal role in education and health had been frustrated for decades. Having surveyed the dismal record of efforts to enact a major program of aid to schools through 1961, Munger and Fenno declared that there was no "end ... in sight" (1962: 170), although passage of the landmark Elementary and Secondary Education Act (and thereafter a number of related bills) was then just four years away. Only a daring few would have predicted the creation of a very substantial federal role in health care, as provided with the enactment of Medicare and Medicaid in 1965 and a host of other services and regulatory legislation thereafter. Prior to the 1960 Presidential campaign, at least, the adoption of a major health benefit program appeared to be a legislative impossibility (see Marmor, 1973; Sundquist, 1968: 287-321). Despite continuing popular interest, both major political parties had repudiated national health insurance in the 1950s, while the American Medical Association provided a textbook example of the powerful "veto group."

Although government had changed dramatically by the late 1960s, the policy trends which were to dominate the coming decade again were not perceived widely in advance. The three Es—energy, environment, and the economy—were back-burner issues, and seemed likely to remain so. No one could have anticipated the string of events that would lead to the creation of a national Department of Energy or efforts to establish a national energy policy. Two careful students of the environment, Richard Cooley and Geoffrey Wandesford-Smith, could plausibly assert in 1969 that the national concern about the environment had passed, although the nation then stood poised on the very eve of the "environmental decade" (1970: 93). Moreover, it was widely believed that the business cycle had been whipped, that both excessive unemployment and inflation were things of the past (Okun, 1970). No one expected the coming stagflation, or the imposition of wage-price guidelines and controls, or the vast expansion of public employment make-work programs.

The probable course of social policy in other fields also was unclear. The election of Richard Nixon could easily have been taken as marking a shift toward decentralization, devolution, and deregulation in federal policy, and, in fact, was so regarded. In 1971, Richard P. Nathan predicted the adoption of major programs of flexible "overhead aid" for state and city governments in the 1970s, together with a movement toward the wholesale consolidation of grants-in-aid programs in other functional areas and a drastic reduction in the role of categorical assistance programs (1972: 362-369). Yet, while more modest programs of overhead aid are now in place, categorical programs continue to dominate the scene, and federal intergovernmental regulation, far from declining, has grown sharply. Nathan also foresaw a shift toward centralization of welfare programs by the adoption in 1972 of a uniform-support category, with nationwide benefit levels and eligibility standards, thus guaranteeing a minimum income level for all (1972: 367). This still has not come to pass.

In short, then, policy analysts seem to have an even poorer predictive record than that for which meteorologists are so mercilessly chided. They are weak in prognostication—though often rather clever about explaining the course of events after the fact. Indeed, what seems inevitable in retrospect (Sundquist, 1968: 507) often looked improbable in advance.

Unlike classical physics, long the model discipline for all rigorous inquiry, policy analysis simply is not a predictive science. Perhaps, like evolutionary biology, it never will be.[1]

THE "FISCAL CONSTRAINT" SCENARIO:
A DECLINING FEDERAL ROLE

Despite this disheartening record, the air at present is rife with prophecy. Policy trends for the next decade are being foretold as frequently, and with only slightly less confidence, than they were ten or twenty years ago. The dominant view is that the nation has now turned a corner where domestic policy is concerned, that the next decade will be one of a dwindling federal role and a substantial decentralization of governmental authority. In capsule form, the projection is for "fewer federal dollars, fewer programs, and fewer regulations."

One of the best examples of this assessment is provided by Rochelle L. Stanfield, a leading journalistic commentator on intergovernmental trends. Stanfield (1980: 105) foresees a reversal of the trend toward centralization, with the "decisive factor" being

> the economic condition of the federal government. Washington simply cannot afford to treat the states and cities as its children. The trend may have begun in 1978, when the ratio of federal aid to state and local expenditures reached a peak and started to fall. It may become much more evident in the 1980s, and with it will come less federal control of state and local affairs.

The standard fiscal constraint scenario holds that the period from 1978 to 1980 marked a major shift in intergovernmental fiscal relations. The era of dramatic increases in federal domestic outlays in general, and especially of federal aid to the states and localities, is thought to be over, with relatively slow growth on both counts predicted for the 1980s. Supportive evidence is provided by the actual and projected declines in federal grants in constant dollars in recent years, as well as reductions in grants as a percentage of state-local receipts, total federal outlays, and gross national product, as indicated in Table 1.

National economic conditions and the post-Proposition 13 "tax revolt" are taken as the principal causal factors. An effort to control inflation is expected to result in reductions in federal spending, deficits, taxes, and regulations, all of which add to the cost of living and the costs of doing

Table 1 Federal Grants-In-Aid in Relation to State-Local Receipts from Own Sources, Total Federal Outlays, and Gross National Product, 1955-1981 Est.

	Dollar Amounts in Billions						
	Federal Grants-In-Aid (Current Dollars)					Exhibit:	
			As a Percentage of			Federal Grants in Constant Dollars (1972 Dollars)	
Fiscal Year[1]	Amount	% Increase	State-Local Receipts from own Source[2]	Total Federal Outlays	Gross National Product	Amount	% Increase/ Decrease
1955	$ 3.2	4.9	11.8	4.7	0.8	$ 5.8	5.5
1960	7.0	7.7	16.8	7.6	1.4	11.4	7.5
1965	10.9	7.9	17.7	9.2	1.7	15.7	5.4
1970	24.0	18.2	22.9	12.2	2.5	27.0	11.1
1971	28.1	17.1	24.1	13.3	2.8	29.5	9.3
1972	34.4	22.4	26.1	14.8	3.1	34.4	16.6
1973	41.8	21.5	28.5	16.9	3.4	39.6	15.1
1974	43.4	3.8	27.3	16.1	3.2	37.8	−4.5
1975	49.8	14.7	29.1	15.3	3.4	39.1	3.4
1976	59.1	18.7	31.1	16.1	3.6	43.2	10.2
1977	68.4	15.7	31.0	17.0	3.7	45.9	6.5
1978	77.9	13.9	31.7	17.3	3.8	48.5	5.7
1979	82.9	6.4	30.9	16.8	3.6	47.2	−2.7
1980 Est.	89.8	8.3	30.5	15.8	3.5	45.8	−2.9
1981 Est.	91.1	1.4	28.3	14.9	3.2	42.0	−8.3

SOURCES: ACIR staff computations based on U.S. Office of Management and Budget, *Budget of the United States Government*, annual; *Fiscal Year 1981 Budget Revisions*; and unpublished data; U.S. Department of Commerce, Bureau of Economic Analysis, *The National Income and Product Accounts of the United States, 1929-74*; *Survey of Current Business*, various issues; and ACIR staff estimates.

[1] For 1955-1976, years ending June 30; for 1977-1981, years ending September 30.

[2] As defined in the national income accounts.

business. Widespread popular disillusionment with big government and the ineffectiveness of federal programs will add fuel to the fire.

According to this scenario, the new fiscal crunch means that the federal government will have to get "back to basics," chief among them national defense and the maintenance of the Social Security system. Both will place increasing claims on scarce federal tax dollars. Spending for most domestic programs—even including some of the big welfare entitlement programs like AFDC and Medicaid—is likely to be reduced, and new program proposals will be subjected to far tougher scrutiny than in the past.[2]

Selected evidence from the public opinion polls is frequently cited in support for these newly emerging national priorities. Such polls do in fact indicate that inflation and its control are the paramount national concern, that both federal deficits and taxes are regarded as too high, that increases in defense spending are thought to be necessary to rebuild our strategic posture, and that there is growing opposition to the high levels of federal "welfare" spending.

Of course, state and local governments are not immune to these belt-tightening pressures, as many recent events show. Still, many states now seem to be in better financial shape than in past years, and—with federal revenue hemmed in—may well be forced to meet a greater share of domestic needs. Local governments will look more to the states, and less to Washington, to meet their own financial requirements, and a strengthening of local revenue systems (with local income or sales taxes) or an expansion of state revenue-sharing programs for localities may be expected. The net result could be the reemergence of a stronger subnational role within the federal system. This, at least, is the standard view.

AN ALTERNATIVE SCENARIO: MORE PROGRAMS, MORE REGULATIONS, FEWER BUCKS

"Futurologists"—either because they have more experience or less confidence in forecasting than most policy analysts do—usually prepare two or more alternative and often equally plausible scenarios, rather than a single projection of "how things will be" (World Future Society, 1977: 6). They recognize, as novelists must, that there is always more than one way to write the final chapter.

The lesson is a good one, especially in the light of past experience. Alternative forecasts should be prepared. And, indeed, there is a second, perhaps even more defensible, policy scenario for the new era of fiscal constraint. In summary form, it is this: "More programs, more regulations, fewer bucks."

PREMISES: HOW POLITICS WORKS

The difference between the two projections rests chiefly in different interpretations of the political process—of how politics works. The standard scenario emphasizes the role of public opinion as a determinative force. The political system is described as a process for converting citizen desires into public goods, just as the market economy is often described as a mechanism which converts consumer desires into private goods. The underlying analytical model, it might be said, is a variant of the classic democratic credo—government *of, by,* and *for* the people—with elections and the political parties playing crucial transmission roles. The model assumes a high degree of rationality on the part of politicians and voters alike, and implies that political actors will scurry around cutting budgets, eliminating programs, and snipping regulatory strings to satisfy the demands of an inflation-aroused electorate. Indeed, this is the traditional view, shared by many political scientists and economists, and nicely presented in the previously noted article by Anthony Downs. "In a democratic society," he said, "the division of resources between the public and private sectors is roughly determined by the desires of the electorate" (1960: 76).

Yet this perspective is open to serious criticism, both empirical and theoretical. First, it is by no means clear that public opinion is as strongly opposed to federal expenditures as the standard cutback scenario suggests. On the contrary, many reports indicate that popular opposition to big spending is very "soft." Throughout the tax revolt, as in years past, the public has supported current or expanded expenditure levels for most major federal (as well as state and local) functions (see Ladd and Lipset). That is, the public's tastes incline it toward a smaller overall fiscal pie but one serving somewhat larger pieces—quite a difficult culinary feat. Furthermore, opinion on tax questions has failed to show the high and rising levels of opposition one would expect. A series of Louis Harris polls indicated that the proportions of the public declaring their federal, state, and local taxes to be "too high" held roughly constant during the period 1969 to 1978 (Public Opinion, 1978). Although the Roper Organization found that those feeling that the federal income tax is "excessively high" rose sharply in the wake of the Proposition 13 referendum (from 26 to 41 percent in just two months), this concern fell to its previous level a year later. By that time, the tax revolt seemed to be "faltering" (Washington Post, 1979).

Second, from a theoretical point of view—and consistent with these findings—it is quite inappropriate to regard public opinion (or any other single factor) as the principal driving force behind public policy. Other considerations are frequently (indeed, usually) more decisive in Washington than the preferences recorded by polling firms. Policy trends frequently lead or lag "public opinion," and can diverge sharply from it. This is recognized by most specialists in the field. Two leading experts, Everett Carll Ladd, Jr., and Seymour Martin Lipset, have declared that

> public opinion is clearly not the sole or even the main determinant of public policy at the national level. Many of the specific reactions that are voiced to pollsters reflect weakly held views. Opinion surveys have reported sharp reversals in popular sentiment following decisive actions by the President and Congress [1980: 82].

Furthermore, as they add, the "contradictory values" normally existent

> leave abundant room for leaders and political forces of diverse orientations to attain majority support among the electorate. Lead-

ership . . . can still be a major force in determining policy outcomes
[1980: 82].

Politics as an "insider's game." Whether or not "leadership" is the
appropriate term in many instances, an alternative perspective locates the
most important policy actors within or in close proximity to government
itself. Policies are thought to be more consistent with the immediate goals
or needs of these actors than with those of a public far removed from the
site of decision making. In this view, members of the Congress, bureaucrats, and interest groups play the leading roles in both the design and
enactment of legislation, as well as in budgetary actions.

The summary model might be described (with only modest levity) as
government *of* the Congress, *by* the bureaucrats, and *for* special interest
lobbies. Indeed, the growth of federal programmatic responsibilities, especially over the past twenty years, is far more accurately described as a
product of the interplay of these proximate actors under conditions of
relative freedom from constitutional, political, and fiscal constraints than
as a response to the "demands" or preferences of the general public.

For over two years, the staff of the Advisory Commission on Intergovernmental Relations has been studying the continual addition to, and
expansion of, the federal government's now myriad functional roles (see
Colella, 1979: 6-11). The bulk of this work has focused on a series of
historical/political case studies examining public assistance, elementary
and secondary education, higher education, environment, unemployment,
libraries, and fire protection. While these functional areas constitute only a
fraction of the federal government's current business, they nonetheless
provide insight into a wide and representative range of governmental
endeavors from the massive to the relatively minute. Each of the case
studies was designed to illustrate the overall dynamics of the policy
process and thus to determine the forces responsible for governmental
growth.

If any broad generalization might be made from these findings, it is that
the expansion of federal activities has been determined primarily by the
activities of *internal* policy actors—the Congress, interest groups, bureaucracy, the President, and courts—and only secondarily by external actors:
public opinion, elections, political parties, and the media, as well as various
socioeconomic environmental influences. Summary findings for each of
the seven fields studied are presented in Table 2.

The ACIR study also stressed the very different patterns found in two
distinct stages of policy development. First, it noted the widespread
existence of policy entrepreneurs within government at the time of pro-

Table 2 Major Actors and Forces in Policy Development and Growth

	Functional Fields – ACIR Case Studies						
	Public Assistance	Elementary and Secondary Education	Higher Education	Environment	Unemployment	Libraries	Fire Protection
Internal Policy Actors							
Congress	X	X	X	X	X	X	X
President		X			X		
Interest groups		X		X	X	X	X²
Bureaucracy				X	X		X
Courts		X		X			
External Policy Actors							
Public Opinion	X¹			X			
Elections							
Political Parties					X		
Press	X¹			X			
Environmental Influences							
Demographic & Social Trends	X	X	X				
Dislocations (wars, depression)	X	X	X		X		

SOURCE: Advisory Commission on Intergovernmental Relations.
¹Food stamps only.
²Interest groups were crucial in the creation of the U. S. Fire Administration only.

gram initiation or "first generation" policy making. A policy entrepreneur is so named because he or she acts in the public sector much like a business entrepreneur in the private sector. That is, the policy entrepreneur perceives something as a problem or potential national public issue, devises a strategy (usually either a grant or regulatory program) for addressing the problem, and then sees, or attempts to see, the strategy through to programmatic or policy fruition by securing the cooperation of other political actors. While policy entrepreneurship is by no means a new phenomenon, the study found that, in the 1960s and 1970s, program initiation of this sort became a relatively unrestrained activity. Without the constitutional, political, and institutional leadership, and, until quite recently, fiscal constraints which limited the activities of their relatively few counterparts throughout most of American history, modern policy entrepreneurs have tended to seek issues and devise programs with untempered abandon. There now seem to be no mechanisms left for separating large-scale injustices from small grievances, important issues from trivial questions, or problems of national significance from those of state or local interest. In short, the old complaint about government not being responsive has been turned upside down. Through the process of unconstrained policy entrepreneurship, the federal government has become almost indiscriminately hyperresponsive.

In the postinitiation or "second-generation" policy phase, an entirely different political dynamic was disclosed, one which tends to change hyperresponsiveness into policy intransigence. In sharp contrast to the conventional wisdom that new programs are made by and for special interests, the case studies demonstrated the opposite causal pattern: new special interests are formed, more often than not, by and for new programs. So, for example, a common scenario sees the creation of a program by a policy entrepreneur. And, upon creation of the program, groups—often entirely new groups—who perceive themselves to be potential beneficiaries will rush to fill the newly created policy space. Having built themselves rapidly around the program, and into the policy space, these "resultant interests"—together with allies in the Congress and bureaucracy—thereafter strive to keep the program alive, enlarge the policy arena, and/or add on to it with additional, related programs. For all practical purposes, the policy-interest nexus becomes institutionalized; major reform, or termination, becomes very difficult.

At no point in this two-stage process, it might be added, are policy makers usually held closely accountable to the wishes of the public through the partisan election process. Though electoral outcomes may change the cast of players, they do not write the script. Indeed, the steady institutionalization of policy making goes far to explain the tattered condition of the national two-party system and perhaps the rising levels of citizen alienation as well.

Although this interpretation does run counter to the traditional paradigm, it has in fact been confirmed (in whole or part) by many other close observers of American politics.[3] One crucial conditioning factor seems to be the "overloading" of government itself. Once public activities reach a certain size, scope, and complexity, policy making usually becomes an "insider's game." Samuel H. Beer, among others, has contended that explanations of public-sector growth which stress changes in the electorate or socioeconomic developments, or the activities of interest groups or the major political parties (1977: 8)

> become less adequate as in the course of political development the public sector of the polity grows in scale, specialization, and complexity. In economic and social development, increasing specialization and increasing scale provide much of the dynamic for growth. Similar changes within the public sector of the polity give it an increasing degree of autonomy in generating and shaping changes in government output.

This possibility was in fact recognized by some of the sharpest proponents of the traditional model, including Anthony Downs, who noted that great potential sensitivity of political outcomes to changes in information costs. As government becomes bigger, broader, and deeper, information costs rise sharply and communication patterns change. Political actors specialize out of intellectual necessity. Since knowledge is power, power too becomes specialized. The "atomization" of the political process is not a surprising consequence (King, 1978).

Actors and goals. If the "Washington insider's" model of politics is correct, it then is necessary to consider the objectives of the proximate political actors in order to gauge their probable responses to an increasingly stringent fiscal and political environment. *Their* goals and needs, rather than those of the public at large, become the primary tool of political analysis and provide the basis for policy forecasting.

Individual politicians differ, of course, and so do individual political strategies and goals. Still, the commission's case studies (and other recent literature) do suggest a number of broad generalizations. One objective is overarching—shared by almost every type of actor in the system. This is a tendency toward personal activism. The policy-making impulse is now all-pervasive. Nearly all politicians have come to share in what Edward

Banfield has described as the "service motto" of the American upper classes: "DON'T JUST SIT THERE. DO SOMETHING." And second, "DO GOOD!"

At bottom, this reflects the replacement of the earlier ideal of the "negative" liberal state by the "positive" liberal state. The ultimate achievement of the New Deal was institutionalization of the principle of governmental responsibility for the condition of American society. As a matter of course, politicians now receive blame and get credit for matters which once were attributed to Divine Providence or the "natural" laws of the market. Thus, even conservatives must devise some "plan" for dealing with unemployment, inflation, poverty, crime, health care, old age, education, environmental quality, energy resources, and the nation's other dilemmas. From this there is no escape.

Other goals are associated with particular governmental roles, for, as Miles's Law specifies: "Where you stand depends on where you sit." Every political actor looks at government through the prism of his or her own particular responsibilities and opportunities. More specifically, it might be said that:

- Members of Congress seek to advance their political careers through individual policy entrepreneurship;
- Interest groups seek to identify beneficial programs, maintain them, and, if possible, expand their scope or increase their benefits;
- Bureaucrats seek to protect and, if possible, to enhance their security and status—personal, professional, and institutional.

As suggested previously, each of these actors also tends to specialize in the pursuit of these personal objectives. This is necessarily true of bureaucrats and group leaders, but it applies with equal force to legislators, since one's status and influence in the Congress depends upon expertise, upon subcommittee and committee memberships and chairmanships, and upon access to staff. In a complex world, useful knowledge exists only in a highly specialized form; power thus becomes specialized (and diffused) as well.

The resulting collectivities of interrelated specialists have been termed "policy communities" (Milward, 1980: 260-264) or "issue networks" (Heclo, 1978: 87-124). As described by Milward, their members typically include the chairmen of relevant legislative committees and their staffs, a variety of affected interest groups (including professional associations, subnational policy implementors, the suppliers of goods and services, and various policy intellectuals), and bureau chiefs and line agency administrators (Milward, 1980: 260-264). Though tripartite in composition, these policy communities must be distinguished from "subgovernments" or "iron triangles" as traditionally described in that they are somewhat larger, more loosely coupled, more diverse, and more fluid.

The presidential domestic policy role is the most difficult to describe, for presidents, by virtue of their nationwide constituency and immense visibility, are forced to be issue universalists. Furthermore, presidents seem as often to advance the objectives of other actors (members of Congress, interest groups, bureaucrats) as any distinctly their own. Yet what is most unique to the office is the almost cosmic span of responsibilities of the modern presidency. No one else need regularly address "the state of the union" in its entirety. The President is also at least titular head of the budgetary and administrative processes and, unsuccessful vetoes notwithstanding, he is the tail of the legislative process in every functional field. For this reason, presidents seek to enhance their reputations for effective national leadership by proposing comprehensive policy innovations. Aspirants to the presidency must do likewise. Though everyone else is forced by the press of business to narrow his or her attention, the President must attempt to take a more general view. What is obvious from the record of the past decade, however, is that many of these presidential efforts bear little (or bitter) fruit. In most fields, the policy communities of legislators, interest groups, and bureaucrats hold the real reins of "power." And, in a world of dispersed power and specialized knowledge, comprehensive policies are disdained; the generalist, more often than not, is doomed to failure.

WHAT HAPPENS NEXT?

Money is a key political resource and, in the recent past, all the proximate political actors have advanced their own objectives by spending more of it. Funds were readily available, for a rising economic tide and a supportive, sometimes enthusiastic, public were the backdrop against which policy entrepreneurs played out their roles over the last two decades. The relevant question, then, becomes: "Will political actors be able to advance their traditional goals with fewer dollars to spend?"

The probable answer, perhaps unfortunately, is "yes." This perception lies at the heart of the alternative fiscal constraints scenario. Reducing the stakes does not change the rules of the game: penny-ante poker is played the same way as that at the $500 table. There are a number of "low-budget" strategies for the realization of traditional political goals. These include:

(1) the adoption of new, small program proposals, to provide at least the appearance of action;

(2) introduction of new programs with low "front-end" costs but which require higher outlay levels in later years;

(3) increasing use of regulatory programs, which involve very low federal budget outlays, to accomplish national objectives;

(4) increasing use of federal policy mandates, which transfer program costs to state and local governments;

(5) expansion of loan and loan guarantee programs, which fall outside of the traditional budget control process.

Proximate political actors might also be expected to attempt to keep the game going by increasing available revenues in comparatively invisible or unobjectionable ways. Again, there are several possibilities. These include:

(6) automatic income tax increases as inflation moves individuals into higher tax brackets;

(7) improved tax administration to maximize actual receipts;

(8) increased reliance on revenues from the least politically visible sources;

(9) a tightening of program regulations to maximize efficiency and eliminate "waste, fraud, and abuse."

Finally, when actual funding reductions must be made, the following possibilities suggest themselves:

(10) marginal "across-the-board" reductions which spread burdens without disadvantaging particular organized group, bureaucratic, or congressional interests;

(11) substantial cuts in those few large programs providing highly generalized benefits or having weakly organized beneficiaries;

(12) Delays in the enactment of costly new programs, regardless of their national priority.

A review of this listing suggests the reason for the more programs, more regulations, fewer dollars forecast. There is a strong tendency to maintain or expand the present complex programmatic structure (items 1, 2, 3, 4, 5, 10, 11, and 12), while regulation in several forms becomes a more attractive policy tool as revenues decline (items 3, 4, and 9). Each of these points also suggests why the imposition of fiscal constraints may be unlikely to produce a measured decentralization of governmental authority and may actually result in far greater national intervention into state and local affairs, rather than the reverse. (The pattern already found in the field of higher education—declining federal financial assistance but rising federal control—may well become universal.)[4] Furthermore, the fiscal and political straitjacket already forming around state and local governments, coupled with already high levels of fiscal dependency on federal funds, makes it unlikely that state and local governments will be able to resist Washington's own policy inclinations. More likely, they will seek to maximize externally generated revenues, and be willing to accept them under whatever terms they are offered (for a discussion, see Levine and Posner, 1979).

CONCLUSION:
THE RECORD SO FAR

The two fiscal constraint scenarios point in quite different directions. Each reflects a different interpretation of how politics works, and each suggests a different policy path which the nation may follow. The standard view, emphasizing "demand" side explanations for policy development, foresees a new era of fiscal cutbacks and governmental decentralization. The alternative view, which stresses "supply" side characteristics, looks toward a continuation and even expansion of federal programmatic and regulatory activities, but on a low-budget basis. Both scenarios are plausible and, indeed, both are possible outcomes.

So far, however, the record is more consistent with the alternative cutback scenario than with the standard model. Indeed, most of the specific policy forecasts read like items from yesterday's newspapers. Despite growing budgetary pressure, there is yet little evidence of a sharp reduction in federal programs or of a measured decentralization of governmental authority. The number of categorical aid programs, and the red tape associated with them, has continued to mount—as have tax incentives, loan guarantees, and other expressions of the activist spirit. With the proliferation of policy mandates and across-the-board regulatory requirements, federal assistance has become decidedly more coercive than ever before.[5]

In 1979, the tax revolt had little impact on the development of federal policy, according to a year-end summary prepared by *Congressional Quarterly*. Indeed, in CQ's assessment, the first session of the 96th Congress is apt to "pass into history as a contradiction" (Arieff, 1979: 2877):

> Members came to Washington this year spurred by a nationwide anti-government mood. Legislators, even some of the more liberal ones, talked bravely of the need to limit federal spending. They agreed that the influence of Uncle Sam had become too pervasive and needed to be curbed.

> But this session of Congress probably will not be remembered as a conservative one that restrained the powers of government.

It more likely will be recalled as just the opposite: a session where members voted for massive new spending efforts and laid the groundwork for significant new federal involvement in the lives of American businesses and citizens.

Although the session did begin under the influence of the Proposition 13 mentality, initial plans to focus attention on the oversight of existing programs, rather than the enactment of new ones, were quickly abandoned (Arieff, 1979: 2880).

The budget-making process for fiscal 1981, still under way, has taken a similar guise. The President's initial budget proposals showed little evidence of the comprehensive zero-based program reviews that he pledged in 1976, and earlier commitments to bring the budget into balance and reduce federal spending to 21 percent of GNP also were abandoned. While the budget did propose a reduction in the size of the federal deficit, it also called for the continuation of most domestic programs, sharp boosts in defense spending, and substantial federal tax increases. If adopted, federal taxes would have risen to some 21.7 percent of GNP—the highest level since 1944—while individual income-tax payments would have averaged 11.8 percent of personal income, the highest level in any year since World War II (Berry, 1980).

Despite the President's own characterization of the budget as "prudent and responsible," it seemed to much of the press to offer "business as usual" and appeared to Rudolph Penner (1980) to embody the principle of "don't make anyone too angry." Others agreed. In the view of Robert J. Samuelson (1980), the budget's theme was

> no theme. For all the rhetoric—deploring inflation, promoting energy savings and urging restrained spending—the latest proposals do little to stem dependence on oil imports and promise significantly higher levels of taxing and spending.

> The White House is mostly drifting, accommodating the constituencies—mainly for sustained spending—that seem nearest, most visible and most politically important. . . . Carter has willingly allowed himself to become the prisoner of short-term political pressures.

Carter's revised budget and anti-inflation plan, announced March 14, offered little more in the way of decentralization or deregulation than its predecessor. The President declared his intention to bring the budget into balance by trimming an additional $13 billion from his previous budget—a surprisingly small amount, considering that the Congressional Budget Office had estimated the actual deficit for 1981 as close to $25 billion. He also proposed increasing federal receipts by some $11 billion a year through the imposition of an additional ten-cent-a-gallon gasoline tax, an "anti-inflation" measure calculated to boost the Consumer Price Index half a point, and thus raise indexed expenditures as well (New York Times, 1980).

Although funding cutbacks were clearly anticipated, the President was either unable or unwilling to specify most of the areas in which they would be made until the end of the month. The largest decreases announced involved federal revenue sharing to states ($1.7 billion) and high-unemployment urban areas ($1 billion). State and local officials were naturally shocked, for, of the 500-odd grant programs, revenue sharing offers its recipients the most financial flexibility and the smallest degree of national regulation. Indeed, to Governor Richard A. Snelling of Vermont, general revenue sharing is "the last visible evidence that the federal government recognizes decentralization as an important part of our national heritage" (Peirce and Hagstrom, 1980).

The absence of clear presidential direction encouraged Congress to set new spending targets and develop "cutback proposals" of its own. However, even this activity has taken on all the characteristics of policy entrepreneurship, with individual members of the budget committees, in both Houses, banking committees, demographically based caucuses, and others each vying to devise the "best" hit list. So far, none have much willingness to terminate categorical programs, eliminate agencies, or cut back on the scope of federal activities. Instead, the budget-balancing process on Capitol Hill, as in the White House, appeared to Joseph Kraft (1980) to be aimed

> at finding a multitude of tiny cuts that nobody can feel or even perceive—the budgetary equivalent of hairline fractures. Far from being an impressive move that gets out in front of the problem, the budget-balancing act already shapes up as a mere Band-Aid certain to foster, after a brief lapse, another crisis of confidence.

If this spirit persists, what might be called the "upside-down cake" model of federalism also will remain. Reversing the traditional "layer-cake" conception of separated national and state-local functional allocations, the upside-down cake model recognizes the federal propensity to intervene in essentially every local activity, and its concomitant unwillingness to assume its own paramount responsibility for meeting basic human needs through income redistribution. Indeed, two years into the tax revolt, welfare reform appears much less likely than it did a decade ago, and hopes for a national system of health-care financing have faded. But maintenance of the patchwork system of nearly 500 aid programs—many of them comparatively petty in funding levels and even objectives—still seems assured.

Of course, substantial changes in the direction of national policy remain possible, in either the weeks and months ahead or at some future date. It may be too soon to count the standard fiscal cutback scenario "down and out." However, its realization will require a far greater degree of national commitment and national leadership than has yet been in evidence. Unless these are forthcoming, the possibility for a substantial reduction in the functional scope and regulatory depth of the national government's domestic role appears slight. Instead, the operative political slogan for the coming decade may be, "I can get it for you wholesale."

NOTES

1. For a discussion of the analogies between biological and policy evolution, see Beam and Colella (1979).

2. For discussions, see Clark (1979), Bowen (1979), Congressional Quarterly Weekly Report (1979).

3. For a discussion and partial review of recent literature, see Milward (1980).

4. See Cheit (1977).

5. For a discussions of these regulatory issues, see Lovell and Tobin (1980) and Advisory Commission on Intergovernmental Relations (1978).

REFERENCES

AARON, H. J. (1978) Politics and the Professors: The Great Society in Perspective. Washington, DC: Brookings.

Advisory Commission on Intergovernmental Relations (1978) Categorical Grants: Their Role and Design. Washington, DC: Government Printing Office.

ARIEFF, I. B. (1979) "First session of the 96th: a contradiction." Congressional Quarterly Weekly Report (December): 2877-2880.

BEAM, D. R. and C. C. COLELLA (1979) "One thing leads to another: an evolutionary perspective on governmental growth." Presented at the Fortieth National Conference on Public Administration, Baltimore, Maryland, April 1-4.

BEER, S. H. (1977) "Political overload and federalism." Polity 10 (Fall): 5-17.

BERRY, J. M. (1980) "Raising taxes." Washington Post (January 29): A1.

BOWEN, W. (1979) "The decade ahead: not so bad if we do things right." Fortune (October 8): 82-104.

BURNS, J. M. (1963) The Deadlock of Democracy. Englewood Cliffs, NJ: Prentice-Hall.

CHEIT, E. F. (1977) "The benefits and burdens of federal financial assistance to higher education." American Economic Review 67 (February): 90-95.

CLARK, L. H. (1979) "Long look ahead." Wall Street Journal (September 13): 1.

COLELLA, C. C. (1979) "The creation, care and feeding of Leviathan: who and what makes government grow." Intergovernmental Perspective 5 (Fall): 6-11.

COOLEY, R. A. and G. WANDESFORD-SMITH [eds.] (1970) Congress and the Environment. Seattle: University of Washington Press.

Congressional Quarterly Weekly Report (1979) "Tax revolt consequences: possible strain in federal, state relations." August 25: 1748-1750, 1819.

DOWNS, A. (1960) "Why the government budget is too small in a democracy." World Politics 7 (July): 541-563.

GALBRAITH, J. K. (1958) The Affluent Society. New York: New American Library.

HECLO, H. 1978) "Issue networks and the executive establishment," pp. 87-124 in A. King (ed.) The New American Political System. Washington, DC: American Enterprise Institute.

KING, A. [ed.] (1978) The New American Political System. Washington, DC: American Enterprise Institute.

KRAFT, J. (1980) "Big issues—but only tiny steps." Washington Post (March 9): 67.

LADD, E. C., Jr., and S. M. LIPSET (1980) "Public opinion and public policy," pp. 49-84 in P. Duignan and A. Rabushka (eds.) The United States in the 1980s. Stanford, CA: Hoover Institution of Stanford University.

LEVINE, C. H. and P. L. POSNER (1979) "The centralizing effects of austerity on the intergovernmental system." Presented at the annual meeting of the American Political Science Association, Washington, DC, August 31-September 3.

LEVITAN, S. A. and R. TAGGART (1976) The Promise of Greatness. Cambridge, MA: Harvard University Press.

LOVELL, C. H. and C. TOBIN (1980) "Mandating—a key issue for cities," pp. 73-79 in The Municipal Yearbook 1980. Washington, DC: International City Management Association.

MARMOR, T. J. (1973) The Politics of Medicare. Chicago: AVC.

MILWARD, H. B. (1980) "Policy entrepreneurship and bureaucratic demand creation," pp. 255-277 in H. M. Ingram and D. E. Mann (eds.) Why Policies Succeed or Fail. Beverly Hills, CA: Sage.

MUNGER F. and R. FENNO (1962) National Politics and Federal Aid to Education. Syracuse, NY: Syracuse University Press.

NATHAN, R. P. (1972) "Intergovernmental relations in the year 2000," pp. 362-369 in H. S. Perloff (ed.) The Future of the U.S. Government. Englewood Cliffs, NJ: Prentice-Hall.

New York Times (1980) "Once more up inflation hill." March 16: 18E.

OKUN, A. M. (1970) The Political Economy of Prosperity. Washington, DC: Brookings.

PEIRCE, N. R. and J. HAGSTROM (1980) "The cities, not the states, may bear the brunt of revenue sharing cutbacks." National Journal (April 19): 639.

PENNER, R. G. (1980) "The president's 1981 budget." The AEI Economist (February): 10-11.

Public Opinion (1978) "The tax revolt." July-August: 29.

SAMUELSON, R. J. (1980) "Part of the problem." National Journal (February 2): 204.

STANFIELD, R. L. (1980) "If you want federal dollars, you have to accept federal controls." National Journal (January): 105.

SUNDQUIST, J. L. (1968) Politics and Policy: The Eisenhower, Kennedy, and Johnson Years. Washington, DC: Brookings.

Washington Post (1979) "The faltering tax revolt." August 15: A24.

World Future Society (1977) An Introduction to the Study of the Future. Washington, DC: World Future Society.

3

ACCOMMODATING DISCONTINUITY: ADJUSTING THE POLITICAL SYSTEM OF CALIFORNIA TO PROPOSITION 13

J O H N   J.   K I R L I N

Sacramento Public Affairs Center
University of Southern California

Proposition 13, passed by a two-thirds plurality of the Californians voting on June 6, 1978, dramatically reduced property tax levies in that state. While the direct revenues of the state government were not affected, as it receives no property tax revenues, the state-level political system was immediately and dramatically impacted. Indeed, the consequences of passage of the Jarvis-Gann Initiative are at least as great for that political system as they are for California's local governments. This chapter analyzes these "secondary" effects of the initiative, arguing that among the consequences are new fiscal and political demands upon the state. The processes of state policy making have, in the ensuing two years, begun to accommodate these new demands and even to institutionalize adaptive responses.

The causes of this immediate and substantial impact are three. First, California, as is the case in most states, is a major "banker" to local governments (Hamilton, 1978), collecting revenues statewide, then appropriating, subvening, and otherwise transferring approximately three-quarters of those monies to local governments. Second, the state had accumu-

AUTHOR'S NOTE: *The research upon which this chapter is based has been supported by the John Randolph and Dora Haynes Foundation.*

lated a substantial surplus (totaling $3.7 billion in June 1978, up nearly $2 billion that fiscal year), due largely to its income-elastic tax policies (Kirlin, 1979; Oakland, 1979; Rodda, 1980). Despite preelection pronouncements that no local government fiscal relief would be made available, substantial relief (described below) was quickly provided. Third, the political shock waves of such an overwhelming rejection of policy directions the legislature and governor had been pursuing (culminating in their defeated alternative to Proposition 13) arrived immediately and remain strong.

A useful organizing framework for an analysis of how the State of California is accommodating the discontinuity of its tax revolt is to distinguish between a first and a second period of adjustment since passage of Jarvis-Gann, and then to turn to a broader analysis of impacts upon the political system of the state. The two periods correspond to legislative and electoral cycles rather than calendar or fiscal years, with the first encompassing the period from passage of the initiative through the elections of November 1978, and the second the period from those general elections to the elections of June 1980. At this writing, the second period has not yet ended, but victory or defeat of the second Jarvis Initiative (Proposition 9, halving California's income tax rates and indexing income tax brackets) at that election will mark the beginning of a third period.

A. THE FIRST PERIOD: QUICK FISCAL RESPONSE AND SENSING THE POLITICAL ENVIRONMENT

Within the three weeks between passage of the initiative and the new fiscal year (July 1, 1978) for the state and most California local governments, the legislature developed its first-year, stop-gap fiscal response (SB 154). David Doerr, Chief Consultant to the Assembly Revenue and Taxation Committee and key staff participant, provides a firsthand account of the period (1979: 1-3):

> The pressures on legislators during those June days were fierce. Schools, cities, counties, and special districts were all vying for a larger share of limited resources—recognizing that what was allocated would be insufficient. Advocates of programs were seeking to have their programs fully protected by legislation, while local governments pleaded for maximum flexibility.

> Local employee groups in each district made sure each member heard from home. From the other side, the self-proclaimed leaders of the revolution let it be known that they would not tolerate any

tax increases, that they wanted "essential services maintained" but they wanted the "fat in government" cut.

The organization of the "bail-out" effort was critical. An unprecedented joint conference committee, comprised of the Legislative leadership of both houses, was created. Senior Legislative staff were assigned to the Committee. Public input was received. Staff gathered data and prepared alternative strategies. Continual meetings were held by the party caucuses of each house for feedback. And a plan took shape.

It was decided to (1) define the key elements of the new property assessment procedure put into place by Proposition 13, (2) allocate the remaining property tax resources among local governments based on their historic share of the tax and (3) to provide enough additional resources to each government so that they would be "held harmful" to approximately 10 percent less revenue (from all sources) than projected for 1978-79 absent Prop. 13. This third objective, the so-called "bail-out," was accomplished by the state takeover of the funding of the SSI-SSP program, the Medi-Cal program and AFDC program and by the appropriation of block grant amounts to counties ($436 million), to cities ($250 million), to special districts (originally $125 million, but a total through subsequent bills of $192 million). From these amounts, there was subtracted one-third of any local reserves in excess of 5 percent of the local agency's 1977-78 revenues. In order to qualify for these funds, the Legislature required all jurisdictions to freeze employee salaries, a provision subsequently declared unconstitutional by the State Supreme Court.

To free up state revenues for the "bail-out" effort, the Legislature substantially reduced the then pending 1978-79 State budget. State general fund expenditures were held to $12.2 billion, a 4.3 percent increase over the $11.7 billion in 1977-78, the smallest percentage increase in the memory of most capital observers.

The extraordinary conference committee described by Doerr worked under even more difficulty than he recounts. A major source of uncertainty was lack of information concerning the revenue and expenditure patterns of the state's 5000-plus local governments. Even after the magnitude of state assistance to be allotted had been decided, apportionment among local jurisdictions remained a thorny problem. The availability of information concerning expenditures on various functions and perceptions of state responsibility ultimately shaped this decision process. Elsewhere, I have described the dynamics as follows (1979: 13-14):

Schools were seen as an area of high state responsibility (prior to Proposition 13, state funds totaled approximately 40 percent of statewide K-12 school expenditures), much was known about school finances and they had minimal alternative revenue sources. Health and welfare expenditures were largely mandated on the counties by the state, and good information was available concerning these functions, particularly in large counties. The finances of cities varied more, information was poor, and they were perceived as having more alternative revenue sources. Finally, special districts were multitudinous (over 4,000), of a mind-boggling variety, little data was available concerning their financing, and many legislators believed they should be put under the control of general purpose governments. The distribution of state assistance under SB 154 clearly reflected the consequences of these orientations: schools and counties received 83 percent of the funds, cities 6 percent, and special districts 3 percent.

As analysts of political processes suggest often occurs (Schattschneider, 1960), other issues were introduced into this debate. Opponents of state financial assistance for abortions succeeded in making reduction of that funding a condition of passage of the bailout. Some Republican legislators sought, unsuccessfully, to place a revenue or expenditure limit upon the state. Even so, the relatively narrow focus of debate on this issue contrasts with a common legislative strategy of seeking to advance policy proposals by amending them into "major," but unrelated, bills. Time pressures and the uncertainties of a volatile political situation served to focus attention on the major task at hand.

One explanation for this devoted attention to coping with the consequences of Proposition 13 by a legislature that had foundered for a decade on the issue of tax reform (Kirlin and Chapman, 1978) can be found in the then upcoming November election, in which Governor Brown, all Assembly, and half of the Senate seats would be on the ballot. Those elections were also a major factor in spurring passage of a one-time $1 billion income tax rebate later in the summer of 1978. A tax rebate had always been a possible use of the state surplus, but it had not received serious consideration before passage of Jarvis-Gann. As a condition for support of the June bailout bill, Republican legislators had been promised that revenue or expenditure limits would be considered during the session. When no agreement on lids could be reached, the one-time tax rebate emerged as politically desirable. The bill which was ultimately passed and signed rebated $675 million of 1978 income taxes (by reducing tax liability for that year) and created temporary, partial indexing of state income-tax brackets (inflation greater than 5 percent was offset during

1979). In addition, the bill provided for a once-in-a-lifetime exclusion of up to $100,000 in capital gains received upon sale of a residence and provided permanent income-tax relief for senior citizens, welfare recipients, and disabled persons.

This preelection positioning was largely effective. Jerry Brown won reelection as governor by a larger plurality than that gained in his initial term, helped not only by a lackluster campaign by Republican candidate Evelle Younger, the State Attorney General, but also by his strong commitment to implementation of Proposition 13. Indeed, he earned the epithet of "Jerry Jarvis" in the eyes of some who opposed his proposed policies. Most vocal in this regard were state employees for whom Brown proposed no salary increases in his revised FY 1978-79 budget. Being loudly booed at summer gatherings of the California State Employees' Association added considerable credence to Brown's campaign to be perceived as a tax cutter.

Not all candidates for reelection were so fortunate. Aided partly by direct mailings bearing (computerized) "personal" messages from Howard Jarvis, several challenges to incumbents were successful. Of the Assembly incumbents seeking reelection, six Democrats were defeated; in the Senate, two incumbent Democrats were defeated. This rate of defeats is high, suggesting an episodic wave of voter dissatisfaction with incumbents.

B. THE SECOND PERIOD: INSTITUTIONALIZING RESPONSES TO JARVIS-GANN EVEN AS NEW FISCAL CONSTRAINTS LOOM

In the second period after passage of Proposition 13, the state enacted a plan for "long-term fiscal relief" for local governments, passed legislation "cleaning up" various ambiguities in Proposition 13 (most notably concerning assessment practices), institutionalized procedures for closer monitoring of revenues and expenditures, and adopted full, though still temporary, indexing of the state personal-income tax. A "Spirit of 13" expenditure-limit initiative was adopted by the electorate (Proposition 4, developed by Paul Gann) in the November 1979 election, and Jarvis II ("Jaws II" to its opponents) qualified for the June 1980 ballot. Broadly perceived, public institutions sought long-term accommodation with Proposition 13 during this period while the organizers of tax-revolt-oriented initiatives sought further victories.

Developing successor legislation to SB 154 was the major issue confronting the California Legislature in its 1979 session (this discussion adapted from Kirlin, 1979: 16-21). A long-term bill was ultimately passed, but its passage was often in doubt. Governor Brown vacillated on the choice between a long-term plan and a second one-year bailout, at first being sympathetic to a long-term bill, then arguing that another one-year bill was all that was possible, and ultimately signing AB 8, the long-term bill passed by the legislature. Speaker of the Assembly Leo McCarthy strongly and consistently advocated a long-term approach. Governor Brown's initial long-term proposal, which gave all of the remaining property-tax revenues to the schools, was not seriously considered by the legislature. Similarly, Speaker McCarthy's first proposal, which took sales-tax revenues away from cities and counties, received scant attention. Following the procedure used in developing SB 154, the first bailout, a Joint Conference Committee composed of three members of the Assembly and three of the Senate was created to provide an arena for resolution of this issue.

Assemblyman Leroy F. Greene served as Committee Chairman, and his AB 8, originally a school finance bill, became the vehicle for development of a long-term local government financial system. In addition to being a long-term as opposed to a one-year bill, AB 8 differs from SB 154 in other critical respects. It is a much more complex bill, 108 pages in length (compared to 50 pages for SB 154), including not only matters relating directly to the fiscal relations of local governments and the state, but also "extraneous" issues, such as increased state contributions to the state-run teachers' retirement fund. Where SB 154 had constrained local governments' allocation of funds among activities through such devices as giving priority to police and fire expenditures, AB 8 eschews such mandates but does empower the Auditor General to audit local-government financial transactions. Finally, because the capability of the state budget to accommodate the projected expenditures into the indefinite future was uncertain, a "deflator" clause was added which reduces state assistance to local governments should its revenues fall below estimates. The deflator reduces local-government fiscal assistance by the amount that state revenues fall below a 1979-80 base level, adjusted annually for increases in the Consumer Price Index and in population of the state.

Some continuities exist between SB 154 and AB 8. Abortion funding was again an issue, delaying passage of AB 8 until satisfactory resolution could be found in the state budget, which was being enacted contemporaneously. The same priority of claimants for state assistance was carried forward, with schools and counties receiving more generous allocations than did cities and special districts.

Tables 1 and 2 provide information on the fiscal features of AB 8. Table 1 compares the cost to the state general fund of SB 154 (FY 1978-79) to appropriations for the first year under AB 8 (1979-80) and projections for the second year (1980-81). Appropriations for assistance to

Table 1 General Fund Cost Summary (in millions)

	1978-79	*1979-80*	*1980-81*
School Finance			
K-12:			
Revenue limit	$ 6,370	$ 6,800	$ 7,252
STRS	144	144	168
Categoricals and other	959	1,159	1,234
Total, K-12	$ 7,473	$ 8,103	$ 8,654
County superintendents	276	319	361
Community colleges	1,141	1,226	1,321
Total cost	$ 8,890	$ 9,648	$10,336
Less local share	− 2,507	− 1,913	− 2,085
State share	$ 6,383	$ 7,735	$ 8,251
Less amount in budget	− 3,927	− 4,147	− 4,271
Fiscal relief, education	$ 2,456	$ 3,588	$ 3,880
Replacement of property tax shifted to other local governments	−	757	823
Net fiscal relief, education	$ 2,456	$ 2,831	$ 3,057
Health and Welfare			
AFDC − Family payments	$ 244	$ 204	$ 231
BHI pyaments	79	100	115
Administration	85	−0−	−0−
SSI/SSP	182	200	218
Food stamp administration	22	−0−	−0−
Medi-Cal	459	505	550
County health services	−0−	267	286
Waiver of state hospital match	−0−	6	−0−
Other	−0−	17	18
Fiscal relief, health and welfare	$ 1,071	$ 1,299	$ 1,418
Block Grants			
Counties	$ 436	$ −0−	−0−
Cities	250	−0−	−0−
Special districts	190	−0−	−0−
Total block grants	$ 876	$ −0−	$ −0−
Reduction in BIE reimbursement			
Counties	$ −0−	$ 17	$ −0−
Cities	−0−	21	−0−
Total fiscal relief[a]	$ 4,401	$ 4,849	$ 5,298

SOURCE: Conference Committee Report.

[a]Does not include $14 million in funds previously appropriated by SB 154 to be released to cities under redefinition of reserves (AB 227).

Table 2   Property Tax Redistribution, 1979-80 (in millions)

	Schools	Counties	Cities	Special Districts
1978-79 Property tax revenues[a]	$ 2,409	$ 1,349	$ 448	$ 362
Estimated 1979-80 property tax revenues before redistribution	$ 2,670	$ 1,475	493	398
Revenue redistribution: Amount transferred to replace block grants	$– 908	$ 480	$+228	$ +200
Reduction in state reimbursement for inventory exemption (1979-80 only)		17	– 21	
Amount transferred to replace reduction in AFDC buyouts	– 116	+ 116		
Amount transferred to offset new state support for county health programs[a]	+ 267	– 267		
Net transfer	$– 757	$+ 312	$+207	$ 200
Estimated 1979-80 revenues[b] after redistribution	$ 1,913	$ 1,787	$ 700	$ 598

SOURCE: Conference Committee Report.

[a]Includes state subventions for tax relief but excludes debt services levies.

[b]These figures constitute the new property tax *base* under AB 8; local governments receive in property taxes each year an amount equal to the prior year's "base," plus revenues from assessed value growth on "situs" (i.e., location of new construction or changes in ownership).

schools increased 15 percent between FY 1978-79 and FY 1979-80; health and welfare assistance is up 21 percent. Block grants to counties, cities, and special districts are terminated and a one-year reduction in business inventory exemption reimbursement of $17 million for counties and $12 million for cities is imposed.

In place of the lost block grants, counties, cities, and special districts are to receive increased property taxes shifted to them from the schools. Table 2 reports these reallocations. A major flaw of SB 154 was not returning increased property-tax revenues to jurisdictions in which new construction occurred. Faced with the high probability of increased expenditures to provide services to the new development without compensating new revenues, jurisdictions hesitated to allow development. AB 8 remedies this weakness of the earlier legislation by assigning increased property-tax revenues (created by new construction, transfer of ownership, or the 2 percent annual increase allowed by Proposition 13) on a situs basis to the jurisdictions in which it occurs.

Proposition 13 required sweeping changes in property-assessment practices. A "market-value" based system was replaced with a "base-value plus adjustments" system. Among the legal and technical questions requiring resolution before full transition to the post-Proposition 13 system were definition of the 1975 base, change of ownership, and new construction. Millions of dollars of tax liabilities/revenues rode on these decisions, and the language of the Jarvis-Gann Initiative and related constitutional and statutory provisions left much ambiguity. Some issues were decided in the courts (e.g., that the unsecured property roll was controlled by Proposition 13). But most of the questions were resolved legislatively through two "clean-up" bills, AB 1488 and AB 1019. In general, the definitions and interpretations adopted favor taxpayers as opposed to tax collection. For example, transfer by a partner of an interest in a property is treated as equivalent to sale of stock in a corporation; change of ownership (and reassessment to full market value) occurs only when the partnership itself ceases to have immediate beneficial use of the property. As another example, when alteration of an existing structure is substantial, it qualifies as new construction to be assessed at full market value but does not trigger reassessment of the preexisting structure or the underlying land. Undoubtedly, hesitation to "tamper" with the popular initiative should be given some of the credit for this posture, but the decisions also are reasonable in terms of their technical attributes (e.g., ease of application) and balancing of secondary economic effects (e.g., not discouraging property improvement).

Beyond specific adjustments to Proposition 13, broader institutional modifications were also adopted during this second phase. The most important and formalized of these was creation of a new "Commission on State Finance." Carried by State Senate President Pro Tem James Mills and supported by State Treasurer Jesse Unruh, the commission, composed of four legislators and three members of the executive branch, provides quarterly estimates of general-fund revenues, expenditures, and surplus levels. The commission will have an executive officer and an annual budget of under $100,000. It is intended to rely in part on existing legislative and executive branch support, and is subject to a 1984 sunset provision. While the major impetus behind the creation of the commission is desire to avoid the surprises and political embarassment of fluctuating (but usually too low) surplus estimates characteristic since 1974, the commission's June estimates provide the trigger for the deflator clause of AB 8. A less formal but still important response can be seen in the types and quality of fiscal analyses being undertaken by some legislative committees. As would be expected, the "money" committees in the Assembly and the Senate (e.g., Senate Finance, Assembly Revenue, and Taxation) are the locus of this effort. Passage of Propositions 13 and 4 and the prospect of Proposition 9 encouraged more extensive and careful analyses of the California public sector. Particularly noteworthy is the clear recognition of interdependence of state and local government finances.

A final institutional accommodation to the spirit, if not the requirements, of Proposition 13 is the full indexing of the California personal-income tax and abolition of the business-inventory tax. The partial indexing bill passed before the November 1978 elections was described earlier. A year later, in the summer of 1979, full indexing was achieved by extending tax brackets the final 3 percent excluded in the earlier bill. However, the measure is subject to a 1982 sunset provision. Reduction of property taxation on business inventories had been a legislative objective since 1968, with increasing exemptions passed episodically since that time (e.g., 15 percent in 1968, 30 percent in 1971, 50 percent in 1974-75). The state replaced the revenues lost to local property-taxing jurisdictions. Contemporaneously with the indexing of the personal income tax, the business-income tax was repealed. As a part of AB 8, described previously, the state reimbursement to cities and counties for lost revenues was reduced a total of $39 million for FY 1979-80.

While the legislature was still seeking accommodation with dislocations caused by Proposition 13, more fiscal limits were in the future. Proposition 4, the "Spirit of 13" expenditure limits sponsored by Paul Gann, was overwhelmingly approved in the November 1979 elections, substantially surpassing the plurality achieved by Proposition 13 (76 to 65 percent yes votes). A proposed initiative to abolish the state sales tax failed to qualify. But Howard Jarvis's second initiative, Proposition 9, the principal effects of which are to fully index personal income-tax brackets and halve personal income-tax rates, qualified for the June 1980 ballot.

While Proposition 13 cut the property-tax rate and changed assessment practices to a base period plus limited adjustments method, Proposition 4 takes the approach of imposing a limit on overall expenditures, an approach favored by some commentators as preserving more flexibility in governmental decision making. Proposition 4 has six major provisions (Cal-Tax News, August 1-14, 1979):

(1) Appropriations of state and local government from tax sources are limited to a formula based on changes in population and the cost of living (Consumer Price Index). Growth of per capita personal income is used to adjust the limit if this figure is less than CPI.

(2) The limitation may be adjusted temporarily by a majority vote of the electors.

(3) Tax revenues in excess of the limit must be returned to the taxpayers within two years.

(4) The State is required to reimburse local governments for new programs or higher levels of service which it mandates.

(5) Fees and charges in excess of the cost of providing the service are within and controlled by the limit.

(6) Provisions are made for emergencies, for government debt service, for new entities of government, and for transfers of functions from one entity to another or from a tax source to a fee.

As with Proposition 13, ambiguity exists concerning certain key definitions in Proposition 4, although this initiative appears to have fewer such issues than does the earlier property-tax limit. A useful exploration of these issues is provided by the California Legislative Analyst (1979). That publication also provides a schematic detailing the operation of the limit for the state (1979: 4).

Operation of Proposition 4 for local governments follows similar calculations. The initiative provides important incentives for use of nontax revenues (e.g., user fees up to the cost of service provision) and generally encourages much more careful attention to cost accounting. A particularly important case of this general incentive concerns state-mandated local-government expenditures, which must be reimbursed by the state and included within its limit, while being excluded from the local-government limit.

Projection of the operation of the limit (which does not become operational until FY 1980-81) is made difficult by the distinction between limited and nonlimited appropriations. For example, $8.3 billion of the state's FY 1978-79 appropriations of $14.2 billion are subject to limit. Moreover, the limit may be adjusted, for a maximum of four years, by a vote of the people, and a one-year "emergency" surpassing of the limit is possible, provided that appropriation limits for the following three years are reduced to prevent an aggregate increase in expenditures. The Governor's budget for FY 1980-1981 projects appropriations of $16.0 billion, well below the limit of $16.8 billion. Some analysts believe that the limit would rarely be operational; others forecast reaching the limit within the near future.

Passage of Proposition 9 in the June 1980 elections would have made the limit moot for several years. That measure would have reduced state revenues between $1.8 and 3.8 billion for FY 1980-81 and $3.6 to 4.0 billions for FY 1981-82, depending upon how the state (and the courts)

Total Income of the State

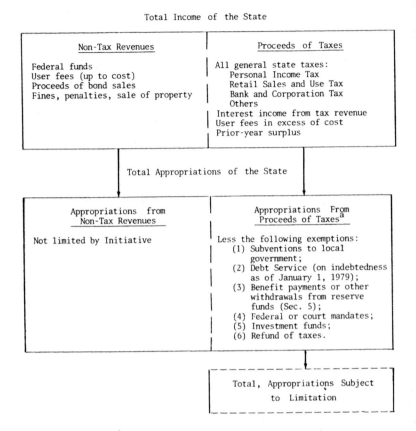

SOURCE: Legislative Analyst, State of California.

a. Any "proceeds of taxes" *not* appropriated (that is, surplus funds) would be subject to Section 2 of the initiative, which requires that surplus funds be returned to the people.

Figure 1   Determining "Appropriations Subject to Limitation" for State Government

implemented Proposition 9 (Rodda, 1980b: 1-13). A revenue reduction of this size is beyond what anyone believes could be handled through the AB 8 deflator. Senator Rodda, Chairman of the Senate Finance Committee, anticipated that an extraordinary process would again be invoked by the legislature (Rodda, 1980b). The model immediately at hand, of course, is the kind of joint committee which developed SB 154 and AB 8. The substantive proposal which Rodda viewed as most feasible would entail reducing AB 8 appropriations by 50 percent and all other state budget appropriations by "appropriate" percentages, averaging 15 percent across the board (Rodda, 1980b: 30-31). Proposition 9 was defeated, however, obviating the need for extensive budget reductions.

C. BROADER IMPACTS UPON THE POLITICAL SYSTEM OF THE STATE OF CALIFORNIA

While the specific features of California's public fiscal system are still being redefined, the major impacts of two years of tax revolt are reasonably clear. Unless a substantial revenue-reduction measure passes (i.e., of the magnitude of the rejected Proposition 9), public-sector expenditures will be somewhat lower than they would have in the absence of Proposition 13, and Proposition 4 will provide a (weak) lid on future increases. But these reductions must be understood in the context of the state's historically high public expenditures. In 1976-77, California was the third-ranked state (behind Alaska and New York) in total state and local tax collections measured either per capita or per $1000 of personal income, 23 percent above the national average (Jamison, 1979: Sect. III D). Expenditures, in contrast, were only 6 percent above the national average per $1000 of per capita income, with the state surplus and sizable local government reserves explaining the discrepancy. Adjusting to Proposition 13 has, to date, involved depletion of these reserves. For example, the state ran a deficit of current revenues to current expenditures of $1 billion in FY 1978-79, anticipates a deficit of $900 million in FY 1979-80, and the Governor's budget projects a deficit of $1.4 billion on this measure for FY 1980-81, effectively depleting the accumulated general-fund reserve (commonly referred to as "the surplus"). If these projections should occur, and they are dependent upon estimates of levels of economic activity in the state, small errors in which create large swings in revenues, an annual deficit of current revenues to expenditures of something more than $1 billion would be faced from FY 1981-82 forward.

This eventuality *could* result in greater service cuts than have been experienced to date (and selected services have already been reduced by some jurisdictions). Still, the revenue-generation capacity of the California public sector remains impressive, and what is most likely to occur is moving California state and local expenditures to a range approximating the national norm. This is not the same as saying that all will agree this is a desirable overall outcome, that the resulting distribution of expenditures will be optimal. On the latter point, available evidence suggests that capital and maintenance expenditures have been cut disproportionately to date, not a desirable long-range strategy. Recent state employment estimates show that city employment, off 5.2 percent from 1978 to 1979, is the unusual case, with the average decline for all state-local employment being 1.3 percent (calculated from Cal-Tax News 21, 9, May 1-14, 1980: 6).

Even a modest constraint on the growth of California's public sector would, of course, upset a wonderful money machine that had been created. Before Proposition 13, the state's general-fund taxes had an elasticity of 1.6 (California State Governor's Budget for 1979-80, 1979: A-99). As a professional assessment system kept property assessments close to rapidly escalating property prices, most local governments were also experiencing sizable revenue increases at constant, or even slightly declining, tax rates. In retrospect, earlier tax reform would have blunted the appeal of Proposition 13 and subsequent initiatives, but available evidence suggests that the rapid increase in revenues was an unplanned surprise (the income-tax rates, the greatest contributor to increased state revenues, had been set in the Reagan administration during the 1971-72 mini-recession, and the explosion of housing prices following the 1974 recession was unexpected). Without doubt, however, the California Legislature (and Governor Brown) found it hard to grapple with tax reform (Kirlin and Chapman, 1978). But so do their equivalents in Washington, D.C. and most capitals. Current legislative proposals to index income-tax brackets permanently and fully and to reduce the inheritance and gift tax will reduce the elasticity of the state tax system and, if enacted, would make future budget choices more constrained.

Among the nonfiscal and nonservice impacts of California's experience with fiscal limits, four are most interesting. First, much greater interdependence exists among California state and local governments. Second, "proper" state-local interelationships are now an exlicit question. Third, some latent policy issues were given much greater exposure, and sometimes urgency, as a result of changes in the fiscal system. Finally, an era of "propositional politics" was launched. Each of these consequences is briefly analyzed.

Interdependence. The increased fiscal interdependence resulting from Proposition 13 and Proposition 4 is seen most obviously in the bailout bills and interaction of state and local expenditure limits. A less obvious, but not subtle, increased competition for revenue sources also creates increased interdependence. Beyond these fiscal causes/manifestations of increased interdependence, others also exist. Policy and pragmatic interdependence is already evident in three areas. In "buying out" county shares of health and welfare expenditures, the state was essentially assuming fiscal responsibility for services it and the federal government already largely directed, but now the state stake in policy making in these areas is heightened, and state officials should be more conscious of the cost consequences of their policies and of any local policy initiatives. Proposition 4 requires state reimbursement of costs mandated upon local governments, creating a need for much more accurate cost accounting that can only be achieved through vastly more precise determinations of existing local activities and of state-mandated increments. Finally, the impacts of revenue availability upon land development were made obvious by the disincentives to new development created by SB 154.

Yet another area of increased interdependence concerns personnel policies. SB 154 prohibited local governments receiving state bailout funds from granting pay increases to their employees, and Governor Brown insisted that state employees would receive no raises either. When court decisions struck down the prohibition against local government pay increases, and most granted them, pressure for state employee increases mounted, with the legislature enacting a retroactive (lump-sum) raise, the Governor vetoing the measure, the legislature overriding the veto, and an appeals court ruling it was unconstitutional. More generally, the question of equivalence in personnel practices between state and local governments in functions where the state now plays an increased fiscal role is bound to arise.

State-local balance. The fiscal and policy interdependencies just discussed are an important example of the questions concerning the appropriate roles of state and local governments after Jarvis-Gann. For many, the question has ideological overtones and can be addressed through adherence to "home rule" or to "equity." While most public dialogue focuses upon fiscal issues, with secondary concern given to programs, the ultimate questions are political. For example, what is the relative weight to be given to decisions made by a "representative" city council compared to those made by a "representative" state legislature? Unless some legitimacy can be preserved for local governments as political units appropriately making value judgments for their citizens, their long-term future is as administrative arms of central authorities. Recognition of both the desirability of maintaining local governments as effective political units and desire to reduce the onslaught of functionally oriented special interests apparently contributed to the legislature imposing fewer strictures upon expenditures of the bailout funds in AB 8 than in SB 154.

New policy issues. The fiscal-limits movement also "advantaged" some policy issues by focusing greater attention upon them and "disadvantaged" other issues by detracting attention from them. An example of the former is housing; of the latter, school finance equalization. Housing was already a sizable issue in California, with a well-publicized leap in prices from 1975 onward providing clear evidence of a shortage of owner-occupied units given strong demand. Proposition 13 is credited/blamed by some for sparking a wave of local rent-control initiatives or ordinances in California (e.g., San Francisco, Los Angeles City, Santa Monica, Davis, Berkeley). The organizing cry for the rent-control movement became: "Homeowners got relief from Proposition 13, renters can get it from rent control." Proposition 13 also upset established practices for real-estate development, reducing the property-tax revenues jurisdictions received from any new development to the point where many questioned whether new development provided sufficient revenues to cover increased expenditures (California State Office of Planning and Research, 1979). Jurisdictions coped by increasing fees and user charges (Chapman and Kirlin, 1980), and by entering into innovative agreements with developers (Kirlin and Chapman, 1980).

Two other issues given increased visibility by the tax revolt are public pensions and alternative methods of delivering public services (e.g., contracting): the pensions issue is the familar problem of unfunded liability while the alternative serviced delivery issue focuses upon cost reduction. In neither case has much progress been made, but both are receiving somewhat more attention than they did when the public purse looked plumper.

Propositional politics. California is the only large state in which the initiative (adopted in 1911) can be used to adopt both statutes and constitutional provisions. From 1912 to 1979, 434 initiatives were circulated in the state. One hundred sixty-five of these qualified to be placed on the ballot (receiving 5 percent of the total number of votes for governor in the last election in the case of statutory initiatives and 8 percent in the case of constitutional initiatives), and 45 were adopted by the voters. Prior to passage of Proposition 13, only one of nearly 100 proposed initiatives dealing with taxation had been adopted (abolition of the poll tax in 1914).

Initiative activity has quadrupled since 1970. Prior to 1970, attempts to qualify initiatives were made 4.7 times per year on the average. Annually since 1970, 15.3 initiatives have been circulated on the average. Fewer initiatives have qualified for the ballot in recent years (15 percent since 1970 versus 55 percent in the prior years), but the percentage then approved by the electorate had been in the 27-30 percent range over the seven decades.

Many initiatives are circulated by "mainstream" political actors. Tax reform initiatives were qualified in the decade-and-a-half prior to Jarvis Gann by then Governor Reagan and (twice) by then-Los Angeles County Assessor Watson. All three measures were rejected by the electorate. In general, whether proposed by political officeholders, interest groups, or "citizens," the initiative process is a device to avoid, shortcut, or surmount inaction in the legislative arena. Proposition 13 is a classic example of an initiative surmounting a paralyzed state legislative process (Kirlin and Chapman, 1978).

In addition to the increased frequency of initiatives in the last decade, three other features of the current situation are distinctive and important enough to warrant the expectation that propositional politics will set the tone of California politics in the immediately foreseeable future. The first feature is the continued paralysis of the established political processes. California's state political system is institutionally weak, being characterized by feeble political parties, strong interest groups, and a "professionalized" state legislature. Marginal adjustments to existing programs, statutes, and regulations are made, but major issues are mired in deadlock. In addition, Governor Brown's flirtation with the presidency further weakened his already low capacity to exercise policy leadership on major issues. And a continuing battle for control of the position of Speaker of the Assembly, usually considered the second most important office in the state, has reduced the capacity of that institution.

The second feature is the increasing attraction of the initiative to interest groups willing to spend large sums to qualify and support initiatives, which in turn often elicit large expenditures in opposition. Opponents of an initiative to ban smoking in most public areas spent over $6 million in 1978. Proponents of state standards for local rent control will spend approximately $5 million before the June 1980 election. An initiative is now being circulated to mandate that local expenditures on "safety" services (police and fire) do not fall below pre-Proposition 13 base levels, regardless of what other services must be cut to achieve this result. Supporters of K-12 education are preparing a similar initiative. Of course, not all of these initiatives will qualify, nor will all be adopted. And money does not ensure success: in only about half of twenty high-spending initiative campaigns of this decade has the side spending the most won.

An important innovation in the initiative qualification process is the third distinctive feature encouraging propositional politics. Initiatives have traditionally been qualified through face-to-face solicitation of signatures on the qualifying petition by either volunteers or paid signature gatherers. In contrast, Proposition 9 was qualified "without human hands," by direct mail. Butcher-Forde, the campaign/public relations firm working with Jarvis, has developed an impressive technology for qualifying initiatives. Working from lists of signatures of the qualifying petition for Proposition 13 and of contributors to that campaign, plus sophisticated stratifications of voter-registration lists by census tract characteristics, Butcher-Forde mailed out 6 million pieces of mail on Proposition 9. Each envelope contained a qualifying petition, a solicitation of contributions to the campaign, and a letter from Jarvis extolling the importance of the initiative and referring (as the mail campaign progressed) to a specific individual on the addressee's block or nearby who had both signed the qualifying petition and contributed to the campaign. The 400,000 responses received contained 820,000 signatures on qualifying petitions, and 200,000 also contained contributions, totaling $1.8 million. The initiative qualification had not only succeeded, but returned more than twice its cost in contributions, a good start toward campaign financing. However, opponents of Proposition 9, largely public-employee groups, ultimately raised a larger campaign war chest than did its supporters. This same computerized technology is now being used in the attempt to qualify the initiative concerning expenditures on safety functions and is being considered for other campaigns.

D. BEYOND INTEREST GROUP POLITICS

Born in frustration with the incapacity of the legislative processes of the State of California to provide relief from rapidly increasing tax burdens, Proposition 13 may well mark a significant modification of the state's political system. By the mid-1970s, the progressives' dreams of the early twentieth century (at which time not only the initiative, but many other major features of California's political institutions were shaped) had been realized. Parties were weak, the legislature among the most professionalized and well-staffed in the nation, the administrative agencies were organized consonant with civil-service concepts, and one of the nation's most stringent political contributions reporting systems (itself adopted by initiative in 1974) kept the "mother's milk" of politics visible.

But the legislative process deadlocked on some issues of critical importance to the electorate, of which tax reform is the preeminent example. It is an instructive example, because principal among the causes of the deadlock was the fact that tax relief became important to such a large proportion of the state's residents as to be a "general" issue. But the legislature could not deal with it in these terms, seeking consistently over nearly a decade to treat taxation policy as if it had only specialized interest components. For example, all tax-related legislative proposals receiving leadership or gubernatorial support sought to "balance" any tax cuts with tax increases and to make any tax-relief redistributive (e.g., through devices such as property tax circuit breakers, or renters' credits in personal income taxes). Paralysis resulted when no sufficient coalition of potential tax winners was ever constructed to overcome the opposition of potential losers.

The legislature and interest groups did much to perfect their symbiotic relationship over the past decade and a half: legislators learned how to derive campaign contributions from the introduction of bills (most of which died without serious consideration); extensive staff had been developed, the functions of which were as much negotiation with interest groups as analysis; ever-increasing numbers of interest groups established legislative liaison/lobbying units, and higher percentages maintained offices in Sacramento.

Increased recourse to the initiative process, development of new techniques for initiative qualification, and increased spending on initiative campaigns portend movement of a major part of the struggle over public policy in California away from the legislative arena. Direct plebiscitary democracy is at least supplementing, and probably "guiding," political processes based upon representation. If this present trend continues, the political system of the State of California will be quite different from that which existed before Proposition 13.

REFERENCES

California Legislative Analyst (1979) "Analysis of proposition 4, the Gann 'spirit of 13' initiative." Sacramento, CA: Legislative Analyst.

California State Governor's Budget for 1979-80 (1979) Sacramento, CA: Governor's Office.

California State Office of Planning and Research (1979) "Does housing pay its way?" Sacramento, CA: Office of Planning and Research.

CHAPMAN, J. I. and J. J. KIRLIN (1980) "Land use consequences of proposition 13." USC Law Review 53, 1.

DOERR, D. R. (1979) "The California legislature's response to proposition 13." Delivered at a conference, "Proposition 13: A First Anniversary Assessment," sponsored by the Lincoln Institute of Land Policy, Cambridge, Massachusetts, June 19-20.

HAMILTON, E. K. (1978) "On non-constitutional management of a constitutional problem. Daedalus 107 (Winter): 111-128.

JAMISON, C. D. (1979) California Tax Study: An Analysis of Taxes and Expenditures of State and Local Government in California. Los Angeles, CA: Security Pacific Bank.

KIRLIN, J. J. (1979) "The impacts of proposition 13 upon California governments." Los Angeles, CA. (mimeo)

KIRLIN, J. J. and J. I. CHAPMAN (forthcoming) "Active approaches to local government revenue generation." The Urban Interest.

——— (1978) "The causes and impacts of proposition 13." Presented at the Conference on Tax Limitation sponsored by the U.S. Department of Housing and Urban Development, Santa Barbara, California, December.

OAKLAND, W. H. (1979) "Proposition 13—genesis and consequences." National Tax Journal (Supplement) 32 (June): 387-409.

RODDA, A. S. (1980a) Fiscal Implications of Jarvis II for the State of California Local Government, Including the Schools, as Viewed from the Perspective of a Practical Politician. Sacramento, CA: California Senate Finance Committee.

——— (1980b) Supplement to January 15 Paper on Fiscal Implications of Proposition 9. Sacramento, CA: California Senate Finance Committee.

SCHATTSCHNEIDER, E. E. (1960) The Semi-Sovereign People: A Realist's View of Democracy in America. Hinsdale, IL: Dryden.

MEASURING THE HEALTH OF CITIES

JOHN P. ROSS
JAMES GREENFIELD

U.S. Department of Housing and Urban Development

INTRODUCTION

Often, the most straightforward policy questions prove to be the most difficult to answer. For example, one of the questions frequently asked by urban policy makers today is which cities have the most severe urban problems and, as a corollary, how well are our federal aid programs targeted to solve those problems? It is not that the urban experts have not tried to answer these questions. Many authors have discussed ways to describe "urban distress" in which the relative "need" of various cities might be compared. Yet, despite the rhetoric surrounding the problems of "distressed" cities and the urgency felt by some policy makers to target increasingly scarce governmental resources to particularly "needy" urban areas, no consensus exists within the government and academic communities as to what the concept of "urban distress" really means. There is even less agreement on how to measure this "urban distress." The real policy problem is not that this question remains unanswered—there are many such questions without answers—but rather that policy is made as if we could not only answer the question, but as if we already had.

Two points should be made clear from the very beginning of this essay. First, the question itself is subjective, inherently political, and not well

AUTHORS' NOTE: *The views expressed in this chapter are those of the authors and do not necessarily reflect the views of the U.S. Department of Housing and Urban Development.*

suited to economic tools. As such, the definition of "need" itself has become a political issue and must necessarily be tied to an existing ideology of the state. As a subjective concept, there is no reason to expect complete agreement on the most appropriate method for measuring urban "needs." It is possible, however, to come much closer to agreement than presently exists.

Second, the concept of urban distress is relative and only has meaning in comparison with other places. This suggests that there will always be some places experiencing urban stress. Unlike present definitions of poverty which are based on absolute levels of income, relative definitions of urban stress imply that the problem will never be completely resolved—there will always be some places better off than others.

The purpose of this essay is to review various efforts to measure the health of cities and to suggest the policy implications of the present state of the art. The question of where to go from here will also be discussed. The remainder of the essay is divided into four sections. The first examines the purpose of place-related "needs" measures, looking in some detail at the issue of people versus place indicators. The second reviews some of the major problems generally associated with attempts to measure urban needs. The next section examines some of the more important studies which have rated the degree of urban distress for various cities, and the final section reviews the policy implications of these studies, suggesting directions that might be pursued in the future.

EXPLORING THE CONCEPT OF "URBAN NEEDS"

Government actions have a number of intended and unintended impacts on both people and places. These actions may be intended to equalize opportunities between groups of people or between groups of places, to better develop specific groups or specific areas, or to efficiently determine resource use in either a human or a spatial context (Edel, 1980). It does not follow, however, that if aid is targeted to a particular spatial unit it will necessarily benefit specific groups within that unit. Nor does it follow that aid targeted to specific groups will necessarily benefit particular geographic areas. The justifications for targeting aid to people differ from those for targeting to places; the impacts, both intended and unintended, are different, and it has even been suggested that the levels of government providing aid to people should be different from those providing aid to places, with the federal government helping people while the states aid places, specifically, cities.

EQUITY WITH RESPECT TO PERSONS

In his classic work, *The Theory of Public Finance* (1959), Richard Musgrave suggested that in addition to its role ensuring the proper functioning of a free market, the public sector has three principal responsibilities. The first is to provide for the production of public goods—the allocation function. The second is to achieve certain macroeconomic goals such as full employment, stable prices, and an acceptable rate of economic growth—the stabilization function. The third is to provide for the redistribution of wealth among individuals in a manner which society has determined to be equitable—the distribution function.

The first two of these functions concern the efficient use of resources. Market imperfections are to be overcome, and factors of production are to be combined so as to maximize output and achieve a theoretically definable optimal welfare position for society.

Musgrave recognizes the uniqueness of the third function by pointing out that a theory of efficient factor use is not a theory of distributive justice. In other words, in the interest of what a society determines politically to be "just," that society may choose to transfer resources to bring particularly impoverished individuals up to a minimal standard of living. Individual "need" in this equity sense represents the difference between one's income and society's minimum standard, a standard which for Musgrave is determined outside the economic realm in the domain of politics.

Note the tidiness of this approach to individual equity. The unit of measure, income, is given and the degree of inequality is presented as both absolute and measurable. Once the political process provides the absolute minimum standard, the difference between that standard and the individual's income level can be determined and measured. The government, through its grants system, can redistribute income to eliminate individual "need."

PEOPLE VERSUS PLACE

While individual "need" may be thought of in terms of individual income, the "need" of places presents a much more complex problem. Neat, abstract discussions of efficiency and social justice often ignore the fact that economic activity occurs in a geographic context and over time, leaving in its wake a spatial array of fixed capital, economic and political institutions, and constraints on the mobility of production factors. Because public goods, such as roads, are generally consumed in a fixed location, government must examine the needs of places to fulfill its allocation function. More important, government policies must consider spatial need to perform the stabilization function. Just as an unconstrained market may swing violently through boom and bust cycles over time, its impacts may also fluctuate widely over space, leaving numerous costs behind. A government policy seeking to provide stable economic growth may want to impose a countercyclical policy sensitive to spatial differences as a supplement to its normal macroeconomic stabilization concerns.

There has been a great deal of discussion about the distinction between people and place needs and, as Robert A. Levine has suggested, a "tendency exists to confuse poor people with poor areas" (Levine, 1970: 41). This confusion stems from the contention that a place is needy simply because the people in it are needy. In other words, the characteristics of the place are the simple summarization of the characteristics of the people in the place. Therefore, if the federal government provides aid to a poor place, it will automatically be providing aid to the poor people in that place. An economic development program and an antipoverty program become almost interchangeable under this kind of reasoning.

In "'People' versus 'Places' in Urban Impact Analysis" (1980), Matt Edel suggests two problems with the preceding argument. First, because not all needy people live in needy places and because not all people who live in needy places have need, redistribution of wealth by location misses some needy people while unduly benefiting others. Second, and more important, much of the assistance intended for needy people in poor areas may accrue to people who own property in the area but live outside the "needs" area and are not in poverty themselves. For example, the benefits of weatherization rehabilitation in a poor neighborhood intended to reduce the energy costs of poor tenants may pass on to landlords in the form of both capital improvements to their property and potentially higher rents. Thus, it does not automatically follow that aiding a place that is in poor health means aiding poor people in that place.

PLACE NEED

There are, however, a number of strong arguments favoring the use of spatial criteria in both program design and evaluation for some types of programs. These criteria make important the ability to measure urban differences. Edel has suggested that one of these factors is the fiscal crisis facing many local governments, particularly urban local governments. The imbalance between tax revenues and demands for public services precipitating the local fiscal crisis requires programs designed with spatial dimensions as a major component. Governments facing a fiscal crisis are not made up solely of poor residents; neither does the majority of poor people reside within the boundaries of governments with severe budget constraints. Thus, if places with a public-sector fiscal crisis are to be made financially sound, they must be aided by programs designed with spatial considerations in mind.

A related argument concerns those programs designed to aid in the provision of necessary public-sector capital infrastructure. A healthy business climate within a community requires the provision of good roads, streets, water, and sewage systems. Programs designed to aid in the provision of that infrastructure must be designed with spatial criteria in mind.

Government also may choose to direct policy by geographic need in order to address an area's structural economic problems which lie behind the poverty of individuals living there. Government policy based solely on individual need can do little to remove the structural barriers which maintain the poverty of individuals. A program such as CETA, which hopes to lift individuals out of poverty by augmenting their job skills, can make few lasting improvements if the individuals coming out of the program find no private-sector jobs in which to use their improved skills. Thus, government may choose to implement policy which improves the profitability of capital investment in the area, hoping that the spinoff benefits of this investment will trickle down in the form of jobs and wages to the disadvantaged.

Because of the great degree of residential segregation among individuals and families by income level within and among cities, government policy may choose to avoid the high administrative cost of certifying the eligibility of every family for income transfer programs by allocating aid strictly by the location of individuals or families. For example, in New York City, the city government distributes funds from the Federal Energy Crisis Assistance Program—a program set up to help low-income individuals pay for rising fuel oil costs—on the basis of residence in a census tract which in aggregrate falls below a certain income standard.

The federal government may direct aid on the basis of geographic need simply because of politics. The division of residents by geographic boundaries (municipalities, counties, states) ignores the tremendous diversity of "need" among individuals within these boundaries. As a result, providing aid based on spatial criteria may actually reduce conflict. It might be impossible to pass a bill which would provide financial support to a particular group of people, whereas it may be much less difficult to pass a bill that aids the kinds of jurisdictions within which those people reside.

In the congressional world of log rolling, where the important question for members evaluating an aid proposal is "how much money will my district receive?" need becomes not a phenomenon of individuals or classes of people but rather a phenomenon of political places. To gather sufficient support to pass through Congress, federal aid programs must be seen to be benefiting places with need as much as people with need.

Finally, the federal government may provide aid to a lower level of government rather than directly to individuals because that lower level of government is in a better position to equitably distribute that assistance than is the federal government. Being much closer to the electorate than is the federal government, lower-level government may be able to better define uses for those funds than can the federal government.

For all of these reasons, it is important to be able to measure the differences between places, particularly cities, and to be able to determine those suffering the greatest urban distress.

MEASUREMENT PROBLEMS

Before turning to studies of urban stress, some of the general measurement problems common to all of these efforts will be discussed. In some cases, these problems are quite severe and limit the conclusions which can be drawn concerning differences between cities. In other instances, the problems can be overcome by better understanding the goals of the measurement effort (Cuciti, 1978).

DATA

One of the most serious problems facing any attempt to measure differences in urban need is the lack of high-quality, timely data. In some cases, there is simply no data available to directly measure factors which are known in principle to be important. For example, how does one measure differences in business climate or in the quality of the educational system between various places? These factors are important in determining differences in urban needs, but there is no directly available data to measure them.

There are also many indicators for which data is inaccurate, available infrequently, and/or available for a relatively limited number of places. For example, information on race and poverty characteristics, two important indicators of urban needs, are only available once every ten years. Other kinds of information are available on a regular basis only for large jurisdictions, effectively eliminating the variable from consideration when large numbers of cities are to be compared.

A practical result of these problems is that for some programs, formula and evaluation criteria are based on what is available rather than what would be ideal. For example, when the formula for the antirecession fiscal assistance program was being developed, a variable was needed which was both cyclically sensitive and available for all jurisdictions. The only one that could be found which met those criteria was the unemployment rate. While the unemployment rate is certainly not the ideal measure of cyclical impacts on local jurisdictions, it was used in the formula because it was the only variable which was readily available.

It is interesting to note that it was later determined that local unemployment rates as then collected were subject to large errors—large enough for some to argue that they were no better than random numbers. As a result of this experience, the accuracy of local unemployment rates has been greatly improved.

LEVELS VERSUS TRENDS

Most measures of urban health can be expressed as either a level for a given point in time or a rate over time. The former measures where we are, the latter measures the direction in which we are going. A place which is in bad shape but getting better is clearly in a better condition than a place which is in bad shape and getting worse. It is not clear, however, whether a place that is in bad shape and getting better is in better or worse condition than a place which is in good shape but getting worse.

As a practical matter, measures of urban distress are most often expressed as levels (for an example of an exception, see ACIR, 1977). The reason for this is twofold: (1) levels are often easier to interpret than trends; and (2) the data needed for the indicators is more often available at a point in time rather than over time. This practice does not imply that the level measure is always preferred. For example, in the antirecession case cited earlier, the change in unemployment may have been a better measure of cyclical sensitivity than the unemployment level which was actually used in the formula. That decision generated an entire debate over whether or not a place that had an unemployment rate of 3 percent which went up to 6 percent was better or worse off than a place that went from 12 to 13 percent unemployment as a result of the recession. Thus, while point-in-time measures are most often used as indicators of urban distress, it is not always clear that they are the preferred measures.

GEOGRAPHIC AREA

The next major problem concerns the appropriate geographic area for analysis. Two separate issues are involved: the area and the comparison. Some experts suggest that city differences can only be understood within a neighborhood area context. They argue that the analysis should begin with the characteristics of the various neighborhoods in the city. These characteristics should be aggregated up to the city as a whole.

Others suggest that cities' differences can only be understood within the context of their states or regions. A poor city in a rich state cannot possibly be in as difficult a position as a poor city in a poor state. Thus, the appropriate method according to this argument is to begin with the larger geographic area and disaggregate down to the city.

Again, as a practical matter, most of the studies completed use the political unit, the city, as the geographic unit for analysis. Data is often more easily available by political unit, and within the U.S. system, policy implications of the analysis can often only be implemented on the basis of political boundaries.

Since measures of urban stress are relative, the second part of this question concerns the geographic unit of comparison. In other words, a city is better or worse off relative to what? The two standard techniques most often used are to either compare the city to other cities of similar size or to compare the city to its surrounding suburban area. As may be expected, the results differ depending upon the comparison chosen. The city-suburb comparison usually finds that large cities in the Northeast and Midwest are suffering the greatest urban problems, whereas city-to-city comparisons find that many large cities in the Northeast are no worse off than cities in the South or Midwest.

There is no clearly superior choice for the appropriate unit of comparison. The point that has to be recognized, however, is that the choice of that comparison will make a substantial difference in the findings.

COMBINING MEASURES AND MEASURING "WORSE"

Two additional problems must be faced when attempting to measure differences between cities. The first concerns the way in which the various measures of city problems are to be aggregated. Many of the dimensions of urban stress cannot be collapsed into a single unit such as income or price and some other method must be used. There is any number of ways to aggregate the data to form an index. The index may be additive, multiplicative, or some combination of the two. The problem is that the method chosen to index the variables affects the rankings of city problems. In addition, the more complicated the indexing procedure, the less clear the final rankings.

Because of the various yardsticks which must be used, it is not at all clear how much "worse off" is. A place with a 12 percent rate of unemployment is certainly not twice as badly off as a place with a 6 percent rate of unemployment.

These are some of the major measurement problems which must be faced by each of the studies of city distress. Each study solves these problems in one way or another. The way in which they are solved, however, may be more important in determining the outcome of the results than the actual differences between the cities.

STUDIES OF URBAN DISTRESS

There are two general approaches to measuring the level of city distress. One approach, the disaggregate method, identifies the various dimensions of place need and chooses indicators for each dimension. The indicators may be aggregated into an index for each of the various dimensions, but no attempt is made to aggregate the various dimensions into one index of urban distress.

The second approach, the aggregate approach, concentrates on one dimension of distress and aggregates the indicators of that dimension into a single index of urban distress. This method results in a single number which purports to rank cities according to the severity of their urban problems.

THE DISAGGREGATE APPROACH

Probably the most sophisticated of the disaggregate studies was done by Peggy Cuciti of the Congressional Budget Office for the House Subcommittee on the City (1978). In this study of 45 large cities, Cuciti divides city problems into three basic dimensions: social need—the condition of people; economic need—the condition of business; and fiscal need—the condition of governments.

The composite index of social problems developed for this study includes those measures of urban hardship developed by Nathan and Adams (1976) and combines them with current measures of unemployment and per capita income. The economic-needs dimension is made up of percentage of change in manufacturing jobs, percentage of change in population, percentage of change in per capita income, percentage of change in total employment, density, and proportion of housing stock built before 1940. Finally, the measure of fiscal problems includes tax effort, property-tax base, and two comprehensive measures developed by Harold Bunce that include service needs (1976).

The results of the Cuciti study are reported in Table 1. She suggests the following conclusion from this study (1978: 39):

> The determination of which cities have greatest need is largely dependent on which dimension of need is emphasized:
>
> - Social problems are most severe in southern cities of all sizes and in large cities in the Northeast and Midwest. Recent income data suggest that smaller Northeastern cities should also be counted among the neediest. On the income measures, Western cities appear to be relatively well off. Large cities in that region, however, have unemployment and crime rates that are well above the national average.
>
> - Problems stemming from a declining economy are concentrated in the Northeast. Larger cities have had the greatest difficulties but smaller cities in the region are also losing population and business. Large Midwestern cities also have serious economic problems.
>
> - Fiscal problems are greatest in medium and large sized Northeastern and Southern cities, and in large Midwestern cities.

It is interesting to note that Cuciti made no attempt to combine these three dimensions of place needs into a single index. The closest the study comes to combining the various dimensions is contained in Figure 1, where the top ten cities in each of the needs categories are shown. Only Newark and St. Louis appear within the top ten cities on all three of the composite needs indexes.

SINGLE-DIMENSIONAL MEASURES OF NEED

Most of the other studies of the needs of a place have concentrated on one of the three dimensions suggested by Cuciti. In order to provide the flavor of this work, some of the studies will be briefly reviewed below.

Studies of fiscal needs. Perhaps as a result of the urban fiscal crisis, the dimension of fiscal needs or the needs of government has received the greatest attention. Beginning with the work of Philip Dearborn and Susan Calkins for the Advisory Commission on Intergovernmental Relations (1973), these studies have attempted to assess the financial well-being of

Table 1

City	Social Need		Economic Need		Fiscal Need	
	Score	Rank	Score	Rank	Score	Rank
Northeast						
Albany	NA	–	59	21	28	28
Boston	45	15	74	8	72	2
Buffalo	61	6	77	5	44	13
Jersey City	48	13	78	3	47	8
Newark	100	1	84	1	65	4
New York	41	21	80	2	67	3
Paterson	NA	–	72	9	45	12
Philadelphia	49	12	70	12	53	6
Pittsburgh	43	20	71	10	37	18
Rochester	44	19	70	11	36	19
Midwest						
Akron	37	25	64	17	27	29
Chicago	46	16	76	6	NA	–
Cincinnati	45	17	65	16	44	14
Cleveland	67	2	78	4	42	16
Columbus	34	26	51	28	28	26
Detroit	62	4	66	15	46	9
Gary	58	8	58	22	31	24
Indianapolis	21	35	37	37	22	32
Kansas City	29	30	56	24	NA	–
Milwaukee	37	23	64	18	NA	–
Minneapolis	20	37	62	20	23	31
Oklahoma City	30	29	34	39	NA	–
St. Louis	64	3	74	7	61	5
South						
Atlanta	47	14	45	30	NA	–
Baltimore	55	9	63	19	52	7
Birmingham	51	11	45	31	46	10
Dallas	11	39	35	38	NA	–
El Paso	NA	–	30	41	34	21
Houston	21	34	26	43	NA	–
Louisville	45	18	51	27	35	20
Miami	60	7	42	34	31	23
New Orleans	61	5	53	26	45	11
Norfolk	30	28	40	36	44	15
Tampa	51	10	29	42	29	25
Washington, D.C.	NA	–	54	25	84	1

continued

Table 1   (continued)

	Social Need		Economic Need		Fiscal Need	
City	Score	Rank	Score	Rank	Score	Rank
West						
Anaheim	NA	–	31	40	10	38
Denver	20	36	41	35	33	22
Los Angeles	27	31	57	23	18	34
Phoenix	24	32	16	45	18	33
Sacramento	40	22	43	33	24	30
San Bernardino	NA	–	49	29	28	27
San Diego	30	27	43	32	17	35
San Jose	37	24	24	44	12	37
San Francisco	22	33	68	13	39	17
Seattle	16	38	66	14	13	36

SOURCE: Peggy Cuciti, "City Need and the Responsiveness of Federal Grants Programs," Report for U.S. House of Representatives, Committee on Banking, Finance, and Urban Affairs, Subcommittee on the City, 95th Congress, 2nd Session, August 1978, p. 53.
NOTE: N.A. = not available. Composite measure of need could not be created because one or more data items were not available.

various local governments. The variables that are generally used include data such as budget deficits, debt burdens, and tax-effort ratios.

Studies of fiscal needs have taken three general directions. Some of the studies concentrate on the differences between the fiscal capacity of various local governments and the costs to those governments of providing one standard unit of public service—e.g., the work of Steve Barro et al. for the National Science Foundation's study of the general revenue-sharing formula (1975). Fiscal need is defined as the difference between the tax capacity of the local government relative to other local governments and its cost for delivering a unit of service, again relative to the cost of other local governments for delivering that same unit of service. The purpose of federal aid under this approach is to equalize potential service delivery across jurisdiction. In other words, the aid should be targeted so as to equalize the difference between tax capacity and service costs among jurisdictions.

While this approach to fiscal need has the strongest theoretical basis, it is also the most difficult of the three approaches to implement. Since units of public service often have neither a direct price nor quantity dimension, it becomes very difficult to standardize the units of output and associate cost with each unit.

The second type of fiscal need study examines both the demand for public services and the ability of the local jurisdiction to meet that

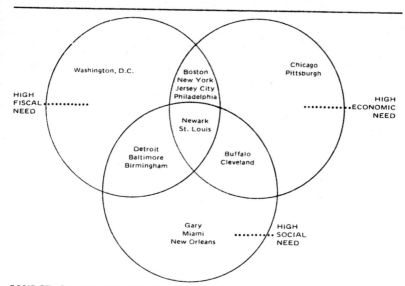

SOURCE: Peggy Cuciti, "City Need and the Responsiveness of Federal Grants Programs." Report for U.S. House of Representatives, Committee on Banking, Finance, and Urban Affairs, Subcommittee on the City, 95th Congress, 2nd Session, August 1978, p. 52.

Figure 1   Overlap between Cities with High Social, Economic and Fiscal Need

demand (Schmid et al., 1975; Bunce, 1976). Cities are ranked according to the jurisdiction's ability to meet service demands.

Again, in a study of the general revenue-sharing formula, Schmid et al. developed an index of service requirements, an index of the jurisdiction's ability to finance those requirements, and an index of the jurisdiction's tax effort. The index of fiscal need was equal to service requirements times effort divided by the jurisdiction's ability to pay.

Harold Bunce (1976) uses the same type of approach in his attempt to evaluate the Community Development Block Grant Formula. Using factor analysis, Bunce combined twenty measures of community development into a single index of need. Weights for each factor were provided by the factor analysis. The factors were poverty with a weight of .40, age and decline with a weight of .35, and crime and density with a weight of .25. Based on this analysis, Newark, New Orleans, St. Louis, and Cleveland were the four cities with the greatest urban needs. Bunce then combined this index with measures of tax effort and fiscal capacity to generate a composite fiscal-need index. The CDBG formula was evaluated using the combined fiscal-needs index.

The major problem with this approach is the definition of service "needs." A city's fiscal distress depends to a large degree upon its public-service requirements, and no agreed-upon objective methods for measuring service requirements have as yet been developed.

The third approach to measuring fiscal stress concentrates almost exclusively on budget parameters (Aronson and King, 1978; Howell and Stamm, 1979). Generally, the purpose of this approach is to determine whether or not a city is headed for financial problems. For example, using measures such as long-term debt retired, total interest payments, short-term debt, etc., Aronson and King conclude that trends in short-term debt are the best single indicator warning of coming fiscal problems.

The problem with this type of study is that the finances of a city are treated as if they were those of an individual applying for an automobile loan. Just as with an individual, if a city does not spend too much and if it is not too far in debt, then it is judged to be financially healthy enough to qualify for a loan. A city's ability to repay debt is not an appropriate indicator of its overall fiscal health. By itself, a city's balance sheet neither measures the economic well-being of the jurisdiction nor does it necessarily indicate the future financial circumstances of the jurisdiction. Unlike the individual or private business, the goal of the city is not to accumulate financial assets nor to maximize its income or profits. Rather it is to provide services to people—a goal which cannot be measured by a city's accounting records alone.

Studies of social needs. There have also been a number of studies which concentrated on measuring the social needs of various places (Clark et al., 1976; Ross et al., 1975; Nathan and Adams, 1976). Perhaps the best known of these studies was done by Richard Nathan and Charles Adams. They combined six variables—unemployment, per capita income, poverty, dependency, education, and crowded housing—to estimate two separate indexes of urban hardship.

The results of these two indexes are reported in Table 2. The first, the intercity hardship index, is based on a comparison of the standardized scores of an individual central city with the scores of the other central cities in the sample. The second index, the intrametropolitan disparity index, ranks cities in the sample based on the disparities between the central city and its surrounding suburbs with respect to the six variables listed above. Under this index, cities in the Northeast and Midwest registered the greatest hardship. Using the intercity index, little difference in hardship was found between northeastern, midwestern, and southern cities. Only Newark, St. Louis, Baltimore, and Cleveland were in distress on both indexes.

Table 2   Indexes of Urban Hardship Conditions

	Intercity Hardship Index	*Intrametropolitan Disparity Index*
U. S., All Cities	46.7	160
Northeast	51.1	193
Newark	85.5	422
Buffalo	57.2	169
Jersey City	56.6	129
Hartford	56.2	317
Providence	52.7	121
Springfield, Mass.	52.0	152
Philadelphia	50.0	205
Pittsburgh	47.1	146
Rochester	46.3	215
Boston	45.8	198
New York	45.3	211
Syracuse	40.8	103
Allentown	29.1	100
Midwest	48.8	178
St. Louis	75.5	231
Gary	70.0	213
Youngstown	60.3	180
Cleveland	59.6	331
Detroit	58.6	210
Cincinnati	53.5	148
Grand Rapids	50.3	119
Chicago	49.3	245
Dayton	46.9	211
Akron	43.4	152
Milwaukee	42.2	195
Toledo	41.4	116
Indianapolis	40.3	124
Kansas City, Mo.	38.9	152
Omaha	35.3	98
Columbus, Ohio	34.9	173
Minneapolis	28.9	131
South	47.0	139
New Orleans	72.6	168
Miami	62.5	172
Birmingham	61.8	131
Baltimore	60.0	256
Louisville	55.9	185
Tampa	50.9	107
Atlanta	50.1	226
Richmond	46.2	209
Norfolk	43.4	82
Ft. Worth	42.8	149
Houston	38.2	93
Oklahoma City	35.5	128

continued

Table 2   (continued)

	Intercity Hardship Index	Intrametropolitan Disparity Index
Dallas	32.6	97
Greensboro, N.C.	28.2	43
Ft. Lauderdale	24.0	64
West	36.2	110
Sacramento	50.4	135
San Jose	41.9	181
Los Angeles	37.9	105
Portland, Oregon	37.7	100
Salt Lake City	37.6	80
San Diego	33.2	77
Denver	30.0	143
San Francisco	28.8	105
Seattle	28.5	67

SOURCE: Richard P. Nathan and Charles Adams, "Understanding Central City Hardship," *Political Science Quarterly,* Vol. 91, No. 1 (Spring 1976), pp. 47-62, as listed in Cuciti. "City Need and the Responsiveness of Federal Grants Programs," Report for U.S. House of Representatives, Committee on Banking, Finance, and Urban Affairs, Subcommittee on the City, 95th Congress, 2nd Session, August 1978, pp. 22-23.

The major problem with these studies of social needs is interpreting the results. The meaning of the final index, whether derived by factor analysis or some other technique, is not at all clear. Looking again at the intra-metropolitan disparity index reported in Table 2, both Allentown and Portland, Oregon have scores of 100. Does this score mean that their social problems are similar and that the cities deserve the same amount of federal attention? Since Richmond has a score of 209, are its problems twice as severe as either Allentown or Portland? Setting the actual scores aside for a moment, why not use other variables in the index? Is social need completely captured by these six variables? Finally, why should these variables be given the same weight in an index? Is not the percentage of families in poverty more important than the percentage of people with less than a twelfth-grade education as far as measuring social problem is concerned?

These are some of the questions that make it very difficult to interpret the indexes of social need. The fact underlying these problems is that there is no well-developed theory explaining the social needs of a place. Until that theory is developed, it will be impossible to provide anything more than the most general interpretation of these indexes.

Studies of economic need. Measures of the economic strength of a city may be the most important single indicator of its overall health. The economic condition of a place helps to determine both fiscal and social well-being. Yet the economic dimension has received the least attention of the three needs areas. Aside from the work of Cuciti, the only other study that has attempted to examine and directly compare the economic needs of places was done by Seymour Sacks for the ACIR (ACIR, 1977a). That work examines disparities between central cities and their surrounding suburbs for the 85 largest SMSAs. Sacks's work does not attempt to index the cities studies. Instead, it simply compares the various central cities with their suburbs both over time and at a given point in time using a large number of different variables.

Other studies of need. There is one additional study of city need that deserves attention but cannot be included in the preceding categories. That study, entitled *Report on the Fiscal Impact of the Economic Stimulus Package on 48 Large Urban Governments,* by the U.S. Department of the Treasury, attempts to develop an index of urban strain for 48 large cities (U.S. Department of the Treasury, 1978). The results are reported in Table 3. The first column shows cities ranked according to the Treasury's strain measures. These included change in population, change in per capita income as compared to change in national per capita income, change in per capita own-source revenues as compared to change in per capita income, change in per capita debt outstanding as compared to change in per capita income, and change in full market value. The variables were weighted and standardized to form an index. The remaining columns in Table 3 report the results of other studies of urban strain.

The next step, the development of a composite index, is most interesting. The Department of the Treasury (1978: 62) explains the process as follows:

> To maximize the significance of the categories of fiscal strain, city rankings from the six urban strain studies were combined. A composite ranking was developed by (a) using the raw rankings of the six indices, (b) applying a "median polishings" technique to insert missing rankings, and (c) determining the composite rank based on resulting median ranks. For purposes of this study the 48 large city governments were classified according to relative fiscal strain among these 48 cities. The cities are grouped according to high, moderate, and low degrees of fiscal strain although it might be argued that any one city, independently, may not be under any fiscal strain relative to all cities in America.

As might be expected, the result of this procedure was to change the rankings of the cities. Los Angeles, Long Beach, and Oakland dropped out

Table 3   Comparative Rankings (Studies on Urban Strain)

City	Treasury Ranking	Urban Conditions Index (Brookings)[a]	Hardship Index (Brookings)[b]	Clark Study[c]	NPA Study[d]	Derived Urban Institute Index[e]
New York	1	16	17	1	1	6
Newark	2	2	1	3	11	8
Los Angeles	3		27	9	12	16
Buffalo	4	3	9	5	9	14
Cleveland	5	4	7		6	7
Long Beach	6			18	28	26
Oakland	7	17			26	19
Chicago	8	13	14	13	2	
Detroit	9	12	8		4	1
Boston	10	7	16	2	17	4
Toledo	11	28	22		24	2
Minneapolis	12	18	35	15	23	10
Seattle	13	29	37	7	19	12
St. Louis	14	1	2	12	7	
Kansas City	15	22	25		22	
San Francisco	16	15	36	4	16	
Fort Worth	17		19	20	37	
St. Paul	18	24		14		
Atlanta	19	23	12	6	36	21
Dallas	20		33		30	
Louisville	21	14	10		27	17
Cincinnati	22	8	11		10	22
Philadelphia	23	11	13		3	3
Indianapolis	24		23		14	
Washington, D.C.	25	19			13	
Pittsburgh	26	6	15	16	8	13
Birmingham	27	10	5	11		25
New Orleans	28	5	3		18	5
Tulsa	29					29
Oklahoma City	30		29		39	
Milwaukee	31	21	20	17	15	9
Baltimore	32	9	6		5	18
Portland	33	20	28		25	15
Norfolk	34	27	18			24
Denver	35	26	34		21	
Columbus	36		31		35	11
Nashville-Davidson	37				40	
Omaha	38		30			
San Diego	39		32		31	
Houston	40		26		29	
Honolulu	41					28
El Paso	42					
Jacksonville	43			8	20	

Table 3   (continued)

City	Treasury Ranking	Urban Conditions Index (Brookings)[a]	Hardship Index (Brookings)[b]	Clark Study[c]	NPA Study[d]	Derived Urban Institute Index[e]
Memphis	44			10	33	27
Miami	45	25	4			20
San Antonio	46				32	23
Phoenix	47		24	22	34	
San Jose	48		21	21	38	

SOURCE: U.S. Department of The Treasury, Office of State and Local Finance, *Report on the Fiscal Impact of the Economic Stimulus Package on 48 Large Urban Governments,* Washington, D.C., January 1978, p. 61.

[a]Richard Nathan, "Decentralizing Community Development," Report to the Department of Housing and Urban Development, January 1978, Brookings Institution, Washington, D.C.

[b]Richard Nathan, and Charles Adams, "Understanding Central City Hardship," *Political Science Quarterly,* Vol. 91, No. 1, Spring 1976, pp. 47-62, Washington, D.C.

[c]Terry Clark et al., "How Many New Yorks—New York Fiscal Crisis in Comparative Perspective," University of Chicago, July 5, 1976, Chicago.

[d]John Craig and Michael Kolleda, "Outlook for the Municipal Hospital in Major American Cities," National Planning Association, April 1976, Washington, D.C.

[e]Harvey A. Garn, Thomas Muller, et al., "A Framework for National Urban Policy," The Urban Institute, December 15, 1977, Washington, D.C.

of the high-strain category while New Orleans, Philadelphia, and St. Louis were added to the high-strain category. The composite index was used as an evaluation tool to measure the targeting of various federal programs.

This study is included as an example of the extremes to which some studies go to measure the needs of places. The Treasury study does develop a composite index of urban strain and it does use that index to rank cities. Because of the way the index was developed, however, it is impossible to understand or interpret what the index measures or means.

CONCLUSIONS AND POLICY IMPLICATIONS

The purpose of this essay was to review some of the efforts to measure the health of cities and to suggest the policy implications of the present state of our knowledge. After suggesting the subjective nature of this entire exercise, the essay went on to argue that people "needs" and place "needs" are not necessarily the same thing. Providing aid to needy places does not always imply that the aid will go to help "needy" people. There are, however, a number of reasons for targeting aid based on place criteria, and therefore it is important to be able to measure the relative problems that various places face.

The essay went on to discuss three distinct dimensions of place need and to suggest some of the problems inherent in measuring each of these dimensions. Lacking a theory of the "needs" of a place and an understanding of the impacts the various dimensions make on each other, it is almost impossible to understand or give meaning to the rankings which emerge from the various studies. The result is often only a vague, intuitive idea of which cities face the worst problems.

If measuring the health of cities were simply an academic exercise, the lack of knowledge in this area would not be considered a severe problem. It would simply mean that there was much more research to be done. Many policy makers however, made decisions as if the health of cities could already be measured with reasonable accuracy. Billions of federal dollars are distributed each year based on various different formulas which are supposed to measure the relatively severity of the problems faced by different cities. Thus, the state of the art has a number of important policy implications. Some of the most important are as follows:

DATA

The lack of timely data covering large numbers of cities is one of the most difficult problems facing any attempt to compare the health of cities. Indexes are often constructed using data which are known to be second best, but which are available. Data can be collected on many of the variables known to be important in determining urban "needs." Rather than simply taking what is available and trying to make it fit, we should specify what is needed and go collect it. If adequate indexes of place need are to be developed, the first step is to agree upon and collect the appropriate data.

SIMPLICITY

The second point that should be recognized is that given our present state of knowledge on this subject, there is a great deal to be said for "keeping it simple." While the motives may be exemplary, the more complicated the indexes become, the harder they are to understand and the less useful they become. Thus, there is much to be said for keeping the indexes as simple and understandable as possible at this time.

TARGETING

Since much of the importance of this work is derived from the fact that it is used to both target federal aid and evaluate the results, it is imperative to understand the limits of the research to date. Given the present state of the art, these studies should not be used as the sole evaluation criteria, nor should more be expected from them than they can provide. Placing too much reliance on any one particular index presents a real danger in that the result may be a misallocation of funds, particularly for programs with specific purposes and not intended as general assistance to places.

RESEARCH

The final question concerns where we go from here. The missing link is a theory of needs of places. Without such a theory, there is no reasonable way to evaluate one index as compared to another and there is no way to understand the relationships between the various dimensions of city need. Continuing to simply correlate variables and derive new indexes is not a particularly useful exercise. What is needed at this point is more research on the causes of urban distress and the ways in which those causes interact with each other.

REFERENCES

Advisory Commission on Intergovernmental Relations [ACIR] (1973) City Financial Emergencies: The Intergovernmental Dimension, A-42. Washington, DC: Government Printing Office.

––– (1977a) Trends in Metropolitan America, M-108. Washington, DC: Government Printing Office.

––– (1977b) Measuring the Fiscal "Blood Pressure" of the States–1964-75, M-111. Washington, DC: Government Printing Office.

ARONSON, J. R. and A. E. KING (1978) "Is there a fiscal crisis outside of New York?" National Tax Journal 31, 2: 135-155.

BAHL, R. (1978) The Fiscal Outlook for Cities. Syracuse, NY: Syracuse University Press.

BARRO, S. M. et al. (1975) Equalization and Equity in General Revenue Sharing: An Analysis of Alternative Distribution Formulas. Santa Monica, CA: Rand Corporation.

BRADBURY, K. L. (1979) "Concepts and measures of city fiscal distress." Prepared for presentation at the Eastern Economic Association annual meetings, Boston, Massachusetts, May 10-12.

BUNCE, H. (1976) An Evaluation of the Community Development Block Grant Formula. Washington, DC: Department of Housing and Urban Development.

CLARK, T., I. RUBIN, L. C. PETTLER, and E. ZIMMERMAN (1976) "How many New Yorks–New York fiscal crisis in comparative perspective." University of Chicago. (unpublished)

CRAIG, J. and M. KOLLEDA (1976) "Outlooks for the municipal hospital in major American cities." Washington, DC: National Planning Association.

CUCITI, P. (1978) City Need and the Responsiveness of Federal Grants Programs. Report for U.S. House of Representatives, Committee on Banking, Finance and Urban Affairs, Subcommittee on the City, 95th Congress, 2nd Session, August.

DEARBORN, P. M. (1977) Elements of Municipal Financial Analysis. Special Report, New York: First Boston Corporation.

EDEL, M. (1980) " 'People' versus 'places' in urban analysis," pp. 175-191 in N. J. Glickman (ed.) The Urban Impacts of Federal Policies. Baltimore, MD: Johns Hopkins University Press.

GARN, H. A. et al. (1977) "A framework for national urban policy." Washington, DC: The Urban Institute.

HOWELL, J. M. and C. F. STAMAN (1979) Urban Fiscal Stress. Lexington, MA: Lexington.

LEVINE, R. A. (1970) The Poor Ye Need Not Have with You: Lessons from the War on Poverty. Cambridge, MA: MIT Press.

MUSGRAVE, R. A. (1959) The Theory of Public Finance. New York: McGraw-Hill.

NATHAN, R. (1978) Decentralizing Community Development. Report to the Department of Housing and Urban Development. Washington, DC: Brookings.

NATHAN, R. and C. ADAMS (1976) "Understanding central city hardship." Political Science Quarterly 91 (Spring): 47-62.

PETERSEN, J. E. (1974) The Rating Game. New York: Twentieth Century Fund.

ROSS, J. P. et al. (1975) Alternative Formulae for General Revenue Sharing: Population Based Measures of Need, NSF Report 74-27. Blacksburg, VA: Virginia Polytechnic Institute and State University, Center for Urban and Regional Study.

SCHMID, G., H. LIPINSKY, and M. PALMER (1975) An Alternative Approach to General Revenue Sharing: A Needs Based Allocation Formula, SR-43. Washington, DC: Institute for the Future.

U.S. Department of the Treasury, Office of State and Local Finance (1978) Report on the Fiscal Impact of the Economic Stimulus Package on 48 Large Urban Governments. Washington, DC: Government Printing Office.

PART II

FISCAL STRESS BUDGETING AND FINANCIAL MANAGEMENT

5

BUDGETARY ADAPTATIONS TO RESOURCE SCARCITY

ALLEN SCHICK

Library of Congress

Budgeting is a creature of scarcity. If public resources were available in unlimited quantity (or sufficient to satisfy all public wants), governments would not have to ration their funds. But this euphoric condition is rarely experienced by modern governments. Even in the oil-rich countries, new wants have outstripped the growth in revenues with the result that budget controls have been applied to the public sector.

Scarcity is ubiquitous. Not a single government possesses enough wealth to fulfill all the public interests of its citizens. That is why all governments must have some form of budgeting. But not all scarcities are alike. In the mid-1960s, the U.S. Government was beginning to explore possible uses for the projected surpluses that would be harvested from its productive tax system; in the 1980s, it is struggling to make ends meet and to cope with burgeoning demands for "guns and butter." Yet the federal government's predicament has not been as severe as the recurring fiscal crises which have forced many states and cities to raise taxes every year or two in a struggle to bring revenues into line with rising costs. The fiscal problem generally is most difficult in the old inner cities where a declining economic base has been combined with rising demands for public services. Resource scarcity tends to be extreme in poor countries, which lack the wherewithal to meet the rising expectations of their citizens. Among the poorest countries of the world, governments and people alike live a hand-to-mouth subsistence in which scarcity is the number one fact of life.

Not only does the intensity of scarcity vary among governments; so too does the duration. Few of the impoverished countries existing on the edge

113

of subsistence can expect any significant easing of their economic plight in the foreseeable future. But the U.S. Government has some prospect of an easier future if a growing economy (and inflation) deliver higher tax revenues to the Treasury. Among American governments, there is a big difference between those which need only to ride out a shortage of funds until the next fiscal year (or a fresh source of money) arrives and those which expect the next year to be as bleak as the current one.

There also is a difference between scarcity which is self-imposed and that which occurs beyond the control of the affected government. During the 1920s, the U.S. Government practiced budgetary frugality in a successful effort to drive down taxes, expenditures, and the national debt. Scarcity was contrived as a means of bolstering financial control by the new Bureau of the Budget. For most governments, however, scarcity is a matter of circumstance. Local governments, in particular, have comparatively little control over their fiscal fate.

Scarcity is a two-sided condition: how much governments have in relation to how much interests and agencies want. Both conditions are essentially subjective: they are defined as much by the aspirations and perspectives of budget makers as by the objective condition of the budget. The federal budget is more constrained in 1980 than it was in 1970, even though federal revenues have climbed during the decade from less than $200 billion to more than $500 billion. In this context, the size of the budget surplus or deficit is not an appropriate indicator of budgetary scarcity. A surplus might either indicate self-restraint—as it did in the 1920s—or the availability of an ample budget margin. On the other hand, a deficit can mean either a willingness to expand available resources by borrowing or a desperate shortage of funds to meet established commitments.

Scarcity, then, is a matter of both attitude and circumstance. The poor who dwell in the midst of plenty have different aspirations than those who know only total squalor. The agency which has come to expect regular budget increases may be pinched more tightly by a sudden cutoff of new funds than an agency which has lived with stable budget expectations. Scarcity is determined by the perceived relation of supply to demand, not according to some objective standard (see Stanley, 1968: 855-870).

Because it is perceived rather than "real" scarcity that determines the budget condition, it is difficult to design precise empirical measures of the different kinds of scarcity. If the excess of requested funds over actual budget allocations were taken as an indicator of scarcity, it would be easy to measure the gap between available and demanded resources. But this indicator would overstate scarcity by including false demands (for ex ample, requests inflated in anticipation of expected budget cuts) or might understate scarcity by excluding repressed expectations (for example, an agency's judgment that it would be unwise to ask for all that it really wants). As noted, the actual budget surplus or deficit can be a misleading measure, for a government willing to borrow might be in an easier situation than one determined to live within its current income. An accurate and complete measure, therefore, would have to encompass: (1) ability and willingness to tax, borrow, and use other resources; and (2) expressed and latent demands for public funds.

Just as the types of scarcity differ, so too do the uses of budgeting by contemporary governments. Some governments use their budget powers primarily to guard the legality of expenditures or to achieve a balance between income and expenses. In these circumstances, the budget serves as a central control over administrative discretion. Other governments use the budget more flexibly to improve administrative performance or to accomplish the organizational objectives set by the executive and the legislature. A few governments have tried to use the budget for setting public goals and program priorities (on the purposes of budgeting, see Schick, 1966: 243-258). There also are governments which use their budgets to veil the true condition of their finances; the figures in their budgets do not correspond to actual receipts and expenditures.

What is the relationship between the various types of scarcity and the different uses to which budgeting is put? The budget literature does not tackle this question. During the 1960s, when planning-programming-budgeting (PPB) innovations were in vogue, it was generally assumed that budgeting was not (or ought not to be) significantly affected by a particular government's financial condition. Whether money is easy or tight, and the government affluent or mendicant, it was argued that major resource decisions should be made on the basis of thorough analyses of program alternatives and their multiyear consequences. Yet in the 1970s, when zero-based budgeting (ZBB) became popular, it was evident that the receptivity of many governments to this reform had something to do with their financial plight. The marketability of budgetary innovations, as well as the use of more entrenched budget practices, depends more on scarcity than on the promotion of budget ideas. Indeed, no reform can succeed, no matter how much support it garners from high government officials, if it is not relevant to the government's fiscal circumstance.

This article attempts to make a start toward an understanding of the connections between budgets and scarcity. Four types of scarcity are identified and described: relaxed scarcity, chronic scarcity, acute scarcity, and total scarcity. These range from the least to the most constraining situation. For each type, the defining characteristic is the availability (or lack) of incremental budget resources. The typology thus derives from the now familiar incremental scheme described and defended by Aaron Wildavsky in *The Politics of the Budgetary Process* (1979). Wildavsky wrote of a budget process which has different decisional rules for the "base" and the "increment." The base consists of the continuing costs of ongoing programs; the increment is the source of funds for new and expanded programs.

My core proposition is that a government blessed with incremental resources will behave differently than one which must struggle to make ends meet, and that the differences will be reflected in the budget and planning processes of government.

In the following sections, the various types of scarcity are linked to particular time periods and levels of government. My intent is to amplify and illustrate each of the types of scarcity, not to precisely label any particular time or government in terms of the scarcity it has experienced.

RELAXED SCARCITY

Relaxed scarcity is a situation in which governments have sufficient resources to continue existing programs and to undertake substantial new budget commitments. In terms of the budget increment, there are enough resources to fund all ongoing activities plus normal cost and workload increases, plus major program initiatives. This favorable condition can occur as a consequence of special circumstances: a tax structure that yields higher incremental revenues than are required for ongoing programs; enactment of a major increase in taxes above immediate needs; a willingness to borrow in order to finance program expansions; windfall revenues from outside sources or from changes in governmental policy.

It is important to distinguish between relaxed scarcity and a budget surplus. While a surplus might mean a greater ability or willingness to spend, it also might represent a decision to limit the use of resources for public purposes. The federal government had a surplus through most of the 1920s, but the budget process was utilized in ways that might have suggested an acute fiscal crisis. During World War II, many states accumulated large surpluses as a consequence of their high taxes and low expenditures, but despite the surpluses, budgeting was used to dampen spending and to discourage program expansion.

Under conditions of relaxed scarcity, there is virtually no incentive to review or evaluate old programs. The incremental rise in the cost of existing programs can be paid out of available resources with enough left over for significant program additions. The primary focus of the budget process, therefore, will be on program development. Faced with the opportunity for substantial program growth, but lacking resources to do everything that might be wanted, policy officials might try to develop a strategy for planning new programs such as was envisioned by the PPB model. That is, rather than add new programs in an ad hoc manner appropriate for incremental choice, they might be willing to use a planning procedure for canvassing new program options and for comparing the prospective costs and utilities of alternative programs. They also might try to extend the budget horizon beyond the ensuing fiscal year to some multiyear period (conventionally, five years) appropriate for planning and analysis. Because there is little compulsion to economize in established programs, the budget process can be liberated from its pressure-point concentration on immediate needs and can focus instead on future opportunities. Policy makers are not bound by the routines of incrementalism, and they can consider programs outside the "shopping lists" presented in agency budget requests. Moreover, a relaxed fiscal atmosphere breeds confidence about future financial conditions: not only are resources abundantly available now, they will continue to be available in the future. Hence the feeling that the future can be volitionally planned by current policies and actions.

Relaxed scarcity, then, induces these tendencies in budgeting: (1) a reorientation of budgeting from control (and/or management) functions to planning; (2) little review or evaluation of existing programs which are permitted to continue and grow in incremental fashion; (3) a drawing together of planning and budgeting processes under the aegis of the chief executive or other top policy officials; and (4) increased attention to program analysis and multiyear budgeting.

Relaxed scarcity is not a common condition. The most prolonged and significant recent period of relaxed scarcity of the federal government occurred during the early to mid-1960s. A combination of favorable circumstances and policies produced a relaxation of federal budget constraints. The Kennedy Administration abandoned traditional balanced budget norms in favor of economic growth. Economic growth stimulated substantially higher tax collections. The buoyant economic and fiscal situation whetted the program initiatives of the New Frontier and Great Society.

By the mid-1960s, federal economists were able to foresee a new type of budget situation—a "fiscal dividend" of billions of dollars of unencumbered resources which could not be spent through incremental budgeting. It was not happenstance that the governmentwide planning-programming-budgeting system was introduced during a period of relaxed scarcity. When PPB was announced in August 1965, the fiscal outlook still was favorable, and it appeared feasible to look ahead to years of program growth. PPB was an appropriate response to the perceived fiscal condition of the federal government, for it broadened budgeting to a multiyear, analytic perspective.

Few states or cities have experienced extended periods of relaxed scarcity. Sometimes the imposition of a new tax allows an easing of constraints, but before this improved condition can impact on budgeting and planning, the incremental growth of existing programs consumes the new funds and the government must pull in its belt and cope with recurring budget crises.

Many states and localities have established public corporations and authorities to liberate preferred programs from financial (and other) constraints. These corporations generally are vested with authority to charge for their services and to borrow funds to finance the expansion of their operations and facilities. Such corporations often display the characteristics of relaxed scarcity and tend to be more oriented to multiyear budgeting and planning than regular governmental agencies. Quite commonly, while regular agencies are functioning under severely constrained budgets, the public corporations have bountiful resources with which to chart new opportunities. This double standard is born out of the recognition that it is easier to release preferred programs from conventional budget constraints than to ease the budget condition of all public agencies. A similar double standard is at work in poor countries which give special treatment to their development budgets.

If it is short-lived, the relaxation of scarcity might have no impact on budget practices, for it often takes much more than a temporary alleviation of resource constraints to induce a reorientation of established traditions and perspectives. Thus, the periodic easing of the fiscal problems of some governments has not brought corresponding changes in their budget operations. A case in point has been the reaction of many states and localities to the general revenue-sharing windfalls of the early 1970s. Because they had experienced boom and bust cycles of budget surpluses and deficits, these governments apparently avoided treating revenue sharing as a relaxation of their basic budget condition. Studies of revenue sharing showed that many states and localities applied their new resources to non-recurring expenditures (such as capital projects) or to tax reductions rather than to program expansion (see Nathan et al., 1975). They correctly perceived that the revenue-sharing bounty would be spent within a few years and they might be left with higher budgets to finance with their own funds.

The absence of protracted budget relaxation in state and local governments explains why efforts to extend PPB to these levels in the 1960s were misapplied and doomed to failure. In the face of recurring financial difficulties, there was little inclination to plan or budget ahead. No matter how many policy alternatives it considers, a city must deliver its standard package of municipal services. After they dutifully went through the PPB motions, many conscientious states and cities found that their budget routines had not been affected by the new process (see Schick, 1971, for a discussion of PPB efforts in the states).

Ordinarily, relaxed scarcity cannot persist for an extended period of time. When resources are plentiful, governments will be tempted and pressured to turn a portion back to the private sector (via tax reductions and subsidies) and to undertake major program expansions. Inevitably, the new programs start small, but they generate much higher spending in future years, thereby leading to a tightening of resources. (Note Parkinson's Second Law: "Expenditure rises to meet income.") Relaxed scarcity can persist only when the tax structure possesses sufficient elasticity to produce steadily higher yields above the incremental growth of expenditures.

By the time federal PPB was launched in August 1965, the fiscal situation had begun to change, but the transformation was not recognized at once. The costs of Vietnam escalation were not yet apparent, nor were those spawned by the Great Society initiatives. In effect, PPB was a process whose time had passed before it had a chance to be applied. The "guns and butter" rhetoric was a vain effort by a beleaguered President to deny the fiscal realities which confronted the nation. In his first budget message (for fiscal 1967) after PPB was launched, President Johnson declared:

> We are a rich nation and can afford to make progress at home while meeting obligations abroad. . . . For this reason, I have not halted progress in the new and vital Great Society programs in order to finance the costs of our efforts in Southeast Asia.

Despite this optimistic note, signs of budgetary stringency already were abundantly evident. The President campaigned for—and ultimately got—a 10 percent tax surcharge; Congress enacted a ceiling on total federal outlays; and there emerged a growing gap between authorized and appropriated levels of expenditure.[1] The 1969 budget message (delivered in January 1968) marked the official recognition of changed fiscal conditions (Congressional Quarterly Service, 1968: 750):

Faced with a costly war abroad and urgent requirements at home, we have had to set priorities. And "priority" is but another word for "choice." We cannot do everything we would wish to do, and so we must choose carefully among the many competing demands on our resources.

The era of relaxed scarcity was ended for the federal government, and so too was any realistic prospect of applying the planning and analytic perspectives of PPB of federal budgeting.

CHRONIC SCARCITY

Chronic scarcity is the normal budget predicament for most American governments. There are enough funds to continue what is already being done because public resources are growing as fast as the cost of established services. But they are not growing as new claims on the budget and, consequently, there is not enough money to cover all demands on public resources. In terms of the budget increment, there is some slack for limited program growth, but not enough for substantial program expansion.

This kind of scarcity encourages use of the budget to constrain new demands for resources. There is only a weak incentive, however, to review existing commitments, for the government does not have to retrench in order to balance its budget or to fund modest program growth. Wild-avsky's classic study of incremental budgeting applies perfectly to this situation. First published in 1964, before the federal government experienced its brief period of relaxed scarcity, *The Politics of the Budgetary Process* depicts the strategies appropriate for budget participants who can look forward to the incremental growth of federal programs.

Chronic scarcity thus induces foot-in-the-door strategies for new programs. First year start-up costs are held low and the bulk of the additional costs is shifted to future years. All parties to budgeting can benefit (at least in the short run) from this incremental ploy. The chief executive is able to build an attractive program record without having to raise the resources to pay for its accomplishment. Legislators can squeeze in some of their own program initiatives without unbalancing the executive budget. Agencies can use the foot-in-the-door technique to build a higher base for future budgets.

Governmental responses to chronic scarcity depend upon whether it is regarded as a welcome constraint against spending pressures or as an interference with program aspirations, and on whether it is seen as a harbinger of future bad times or as a temporary reversal of normally favorable budget fortunes. If the government wishes to promote further program expansion, it will be disinclined to do much multiyear budgeting or planning. A multiyear perspective would disclose the future costs of incremental growth and would therefore inhibit the ability of budget participants to fund new programs. However, if government leaders want to combat incremental expansion and alert the public to prospective financial difficulties, they might favor multiyear budgeting. At least until recently, this type of political leader was not very common on the American scene. The more likely strategy has been to engineer some margin for program expansion in the budget.

One of the reasons for the shift to zero-based budgeting has been the widening belief that chronic scarcity—or worse—is here to stay. Depressed economic conditions and spiraling governmental costs have rooted out the optimism of an earlier decade. On the federal level there is no fiscal dividend. For states and cities, revenue sharing brought only momentary relief, while inflation and collective bargaining have combined to load these governments with costs that grow faster than revenues.

Regardless of the attitude to chronic scarcity, program planning and analysis are likely to be downgraded because they would invite agencies to intensify their pressures for more programs. In practice, analysis and planning are almost always biased in favor of program expansion. The planner identifies the good that could be accomplished if only the necessary funds were forthcoming; the analyst identifies cost-effective alternatives that should be considered. But when budget resources are chronically scarce, it would be futile to set into motion a wide search for new spending ideas. Inevitably, most of those turned on by the search would come away from the budget process disappointed. Not only would they be chagrined at their failure to win new program commitments; they also would be irked by the fact that they were duped to invest in problem initiatives.

Under the influence of chronic scarcity, then, the following pattern is likely to prevail. (1) The budget will not be used primarily for close control of spending, but emphasis will be placed on management improvements. Management efficiency is desired because it exerts some downward pressure on expenditures, increases funds available for new programs, and conveys a sense of doing something about the budget situation. (2) Program analysis and evaluation are neglected. Evaluation (of established programs) has low priority because sufficient funds are available for continuation; analysis (of new programs) is unwelcome because funds are not available for substantial expansion. (3) Program development is sporadic and unsystematic. The preferred strategy is to approve a few programs that have low initial costs. (4) The multiyear implications of current policies are not emphasized, except when political leaders want to dampen budget demands. (5) Planning is isolated from budgeting and policy making.

Chronic scarcity is the stable and prevalent condition for many American governments. It is difficult to move from chronic to relaxed scarcity, though it is easy to slip from relaxed to chronic conditions, as was explained earlier. As government agencies escalate their expectations in accord with increased resource availability, demands remain somewhat higher than supplies. If a government had 1980 resources to pay 1975 demands, it would be in a most favorable situation. But this never is the case because demands find some equilibrium with supply: demands exert pressure for more resources; availability of resources begets increased demands.

It is somewhat easier to drop from chronic to acute scarcity. A severe setback in resources can produce this slippage, as can the spiraling of demands beyond the incremental increase in budget resources. Only when resources increase according to incremental expectations and demands are stable can chronic scarcity be maintained. Given its elastic tax resources, the federal government should be expected to fare no worse than chronic scarcity. However, recent budget battles between Congress and the President, the establishment of the new congressional budget process in 1974, and renewal of the "guns versus butter" conflict provide some indication that the federal budget situation now may be regarded as more acute than usual.[2]

After World War II, chronic scarcity was the perceived condition of many state and local governments. At first, states dipped into their wartime surpluses to finance growing public demands, but when these were depleted, many looked for comparatively easy tax sources to help balance their budgets (for example, conversion to income-tax withholding, penny increases in the sales tax, and additional nuisance taxes). When governments adopt resource-producing strategies, they do not ordinarily consider long-range needs. Rather, they are content to put together a revenue package that covers today's needs, leaving tomorrow's problems to tomorrow's leaders. Even when they adopted new income taxes, few states secured a sufficiently elastic supply of revenues to avoid budget stringencies for more than a few years.[3] As a consequence, most states rarely have been able to do better than chronic scarcity.

Since the 1950s, many older cities have been beset by the flight of industry and population to the suburbs, but the full extent of their predicament was not recognized for many years. The demand on public resources was held down by the failure of the new urban minorities to articulate their interests and by the failure of municipal employees to organize effectively for higher compensation. These restraints have been weakened by the advent of collective bargaining for public employees and the mobilization of minorities into active and sometimes militant political forces.

In retrospect, one might argue that the plight of these cities was much more acute than it was perceived to be, but through most of the postwar era there still was pervasive confidence about the ability to cope with the urban crisis. Muddling through until full relief arrived was considered an appropriate and statesmanlike accommodation to the conditions of the times.

ACUTE SCARCITY

Acute scarcity prevails when available resources do not cover the incremental rise in program costs. New programs cannot be encouraged, though the chief executive or the legislature might find funds for a few of their pet ideas or for demands that cannot be deferred. The main business of budgeting must be to force the demand for funds into alignment with available resources. This often is engineered on both the demand and supply sides of the budget. Demands are suppressed by various budget-cutting strategies applied to the aggregate and details of expenditure. The aggregate is controlled by across-the-board slashes, ceilings on spending totals, allotment controls, disallowance of any program increases, and similar tactics. The details are controlled by line-item surveillance of items of expense, freezes on new hirings, travel and purchasing restrictions, and the like. Established programs are subjected to line-item scrutiny in an effort to capture savings, not to ascertain their effectiveness.

The hunt for revenues concentrates on immediate needs to bridge the budget gap, not on means to secure the future solvency of the government. Sometimes opportunistic, sometimes desperate, the search covers numerous potential sources of additional revenues. Nuisance taxes often are favored, but there also is a tendency to adjust tax rates and fee schedules to bring in more money. Increasingly in the 1970s, the search focused on outside sources of assistance. Local governments pressured their states for more aid and/or for more taxing authority. Both state and local governments intensified the quest for federal grants as a substitute for their own funds.

The fate of planning and evaluation depends in substantial measure on the political temper of the government. Acute scarcity can evoke fiscal conservatism, a belief that government is in trouble because it has over-extended itself with too many program commitments and that it must retrench in order to avoid a bigger debt or higher taxes. The call is for economy and efficiency, not for a grand reappraisal of government's role and its future course of action. In this climate, program planning tends to be shunted aside in favor of short-term savings. This kind of response was dominant in earlier periods of American history, when fiscal conservatism was popular and pervasive. What looking ahead there is, is fixed to the cost side of the budget to spotlight the precarious finances of the government or to sound an alarm, not to chart an expansive course for the future.

A substantially different kind of reaction might occur if political leaders still prefer an expansionist policy in the face of financial diffi-culties. While they might be compelled to engage in a holding action—no major program starts—to buy another year's balance, and would exercise tight control over current spending, policy officials might take advantage of the crisis for a new burst of planning in which the purposes and capabilities of the government were reexamined and its priorities recast. Planning for the future might serve as a substitute for current action, or it might be used for finding a way out of the current predicament.

The fate of evaluation also depends on the political inclination of the times. One might expect acute scarcity to provoke a reassesment by a troubled government of its program and spending commitments, but this course is likely to be avoided when demands for more services are intense and difficult to turn away. This is particularly likely for local governments, where the demands are much more direct and immediate than at the other levels, and where the standard municipal services must be continued regardless of the fiscal condition. Rather than face budget realities and scale down their activities, local governments might prefer to intensify their muddling-through improvisations.

Acute scarcity, like the other forms, can be brief or prolonged. Even governments with abundant resources sometimes find themselves in a temporary bind during the closing months of a fiscal year as a result of higher than anticipated expenditures or a shortfall in revenues. A typical response is to impose temporary controls which are lifted once the next year begins and the fiscal picture brightens. States ban out-of-state travel, cities defer the filling of vacancies, equipment purchases are postponed, all for the purpose of saving enough money to avert a cash deficit. Many states and localities react in this manner when mandatory expenses such as welfare payments (which probably were underestimated in the first place) soar above projections and threaten to unbalance the budget.

One would expect the federal government to have a sufficiently elastic source of revenues to overcome any acute budget difficulties. After all, the elasticity of personal income taxes is significantly above 1.0, which means that the yield of these taxes grows faster than GNP. Even without any increase in tax rates, it should be possible to secure additional revenues. Moreover, because of the steep progressivity of the tax structure, inflation actually generates (at least in the short run) a bigger increase in revenue than in expenditures. In fact, federal revenues more than doubled between 1970 and 1980, with the annual increases averaging more than $30 billion.

Although stagflation has held federal revenues below their full employment potential, the main explanation for the fiscal stress is that increments no longer are routinely available in sufficient amounts to cover both the built-in increases in the budget and claims for new programs. Nowadays, much of the annual budget battle revolves around future increments. Inasmuch as the current budget increment already has been consumed by past decisions, various claimants maneuver to gain an advance commitment of resources that will become available in future years. This means that when the next year arrives, its normal increment already will have been encumbered by past decisions and it is necessary to buy budget peace by claiming some later year's share. The acute predicament thus becomes self-perpetuating.

The primary mechanism for committing future increments has been the establishment of mandatory entitlement programs which, in recent years, have accounted for most of the growth in federal expenditures. Many entitlement programs are indexed to designated economic changes. For example, social security benefits are linked to the consumer price index. Similarly, civilian and military pay, retirement benefits, food stamps, and other programs are tied to one or another index. Largely as a consequence of the entitlement programs, the percentage of the federal budget which is uncontrollable has climbed from 59.2 percent in 1967 to an estimated 76.6 percent in the 1981 budget.

Of course, the acuteness of the federal predicament must be measured in terms of the magnitude and the elasticity of its resources, as well as its unmatched access to capital markets. Countless cities and states probably would be willing to exchange their crises for the crunch which now besets federal budget makers.

Acute scarcity was widespread in state government during the Depression years. Many states reacted to rising expenditures and declining revenues by establishing potent fiscal controls centered in gubernatorial budget staffs. Because many of the states had biennial budgets (and part-time legislatures), they had to concentrate on controls during budget execution to prevent unanticipated deficits and to preserve the balanced budgets required by their constitutions (see Schick, 1964). Accordingly, the acute scarcity led to short-term budget improvisations rather than to long-term planning.

In recent years, signs of acute fiscal crisis have reappeared in some states, especially those which have experienced above-average growth in the budgets or whose revenues have been constrained by statutory or constitutional limitations. The high-budget states are constrained on both the supply and demand sides. Their taxes already are high by comparison with those of other states; hence, they no longer possess the revenue options they once had. When a state already levies a sales tax, an income tax, dozens of nuisance taxes, and is pressed from above by federal income taxes and from below by mushrooming local adoption of sales and income taxes, it no longer has much freedom to expand its tax base.

On the demand side, past spending fuels current demand and expectations, especially when it is built into ongoing programs which force steep annual increases in mandatory spending. When acute scarcity afflicts a government which regards program cutbacks as unacceptable, its only available option might be to intensify the search for outside sources of assistance. In the case of state governments, this means turning to Washington for additional financial support, a strategy which partly accounts for the huge jump in federal grants to states and localities from $10 billion in fiscal 1965 to almost $90 billion in fiscal 1980.[4] State (and local) budgeters shift from controllers of their own spending agencies to claimants for federal aid. Inasmuch as the outside assistance brings fiscal relief only if it can be used as a substitute for the state's own funds, budget makers invest a great deal of effort in identifying programs for which federal assistance can be claimed.

An extraordinary pursuit of this strategy occurred in the early 1970s in the State of Illinois, which was faced with a $100 million overrun in its welfare programs. The Governor rejected cutbacks in welfare assistance, and he and his budget aides turned instead to the federal government in an effort to gain federal funding of various social programs. After months of intensive political and administrative pressure, Illinois won the additional federal assistance it sought, thereby opening up a multibillion dollar loophole in federal assistance for social services grants. As other states lined up for the new federal aid, Congress was forced to put a $2.5 billion cap on social services grants in order to prevent the program from getting completely out of control.[5]

It is now recognized that many of the older cities are mired in a severe fiscal crisis. The forces which held the crisis at bay in earlier years now are rampant: pent-up demands of municipal workers for a larger share of the pie, and the poor demanding more public benefits and taking increased advantage of those available. The characteristic fiscal crisis of poor cities is one of fixed expenses rising much faster than revenues from current sources. If revenues grow at 5 percent but expenses at 10 percent, the city faces a 5 percent budget gap each year. Virtually all of its budget energies must be devoted to closing this gap, and this induces a one-year-at-a-time rather than a long-range perspective. Since not very much can be done to mandated spending, the budget process is oriented to: (1) eliminating the new spending demands of municipal agencies, (2) deferring postponable expenditures such as maintenance and equipment purchases, and (3) searching for new revenue sources. The effects of this predicament on the city's budget process are sensitively reported in Arnold Meltsner's *The Politics of City Revenue,* which deals with the situation in Oakland, California. Meltsner notes that much of the revenue search "is devoted to obtaining only enough resources for maintaining the city system but not for coping with its severe problems" (Meltsner, 1971: 6).

In sum, the effects of acute scarcity are: (1) use of the budget to limit spending by means of both aggregate and itemized controls; (2) retrenchment directed against the most vulnerable portions of the budget—discretionary programs (such as libraries and museums), administrative and overhead costs, and maintenance activities: (3) not much budget-related planning, both because of the fixation on short-term gapsmanship and the sense that the government cannot determine its own fate; (4) a modest increase in evaluative activities, more so in governments able to face up to their hardships than in those in which the demand for public service cannot be resisted; and (5) renewed emphasis on management efficiencies.

TOTAL SCARCITY

Total scarcity exists when available resources are not adequate for ongoing government programs. Unlike acute scarcity, where the government is unable to finance the incremental costs of its programs, total scarcity is a condition in which the government cannot pay for the programs it already has. Under total scarcity, the government either is not delivering many of the programs it wants to provide (it is committed to universal education but cannot furnish the schools and the teachers; it wants to combat disease but lacks doctors and hospitals) or it yields to pressures for services by spending above its means.

Total scarcity, then, exists either when a government is very poor or when the demands for services are exceedingly high. Often these two conditions go hand in hand, if only because poverty in an age of rising expectations begets demands for more public assistance.

It is futile for a government afflicted by total scarcity to try to balance supply and demand via the budget process. Resources cannot (or will not) be enlarged to meet the demands, and the demands cannot be trimmed to suit the resources. The problem is much more desperate than merely that of a budget gap; in fact, the gap cannot be closed except by papering it over. Rather, there is a preoccupation with cash flow, with having enough money on hand to pay the bills, or at least those bills which cannot be deferred any longer.

When the budget situation is so precarious that it cannot be resolved by realistic means, the government tries to do dishonestly that which it cannot achieve honestly. Total scarcity, therefore, invites escapist budgeting, a tendency to fabricate unreal plans and inaccurate budgets. Governments confronted by total scarcity might be tempted to conceal the gap between reality and aspirations rather than publicize it in official budget documents. The budget becomes a pretense, a paper balance that is ignored in practice and not taken seriously by insiders. It serves to present an appearance of government accomplishment and fiscal responsibility, two incompatible strivings when the budget is wracked by total penury. Few knowledgeable public officials have confidence in the figures or act strictly according to the dictates of the budget. The budget tells outsiders (who often include "important" government officials) that the government is doing something about their expectations; it tells the media and good-government groups that the government is operating in a fiscally responsible manner. If more resources are needed than are shown in the budget, the printing presses can manufacture additional currency, for a high rate of inflation is more tolerable than a high rate of political instability. When the balance in one account is exhausted, officials covertly turn to others to pay the bills. When all balances are exhausted, the government borrows against future or imagined income.

Escapist budgeting breeds pervasive public corruption. One might expect the poorest governments to be the most honest, but this is a luxury which only the rich seem to afford. To understand why corruption widely practiced, let us consider a situation in which a fairly well-to-do agency faces a temporary shortage of funds as the fiscal year draws to a close. Suppose that the agency is financed out of two accounts: for one, a year-end surplus is projected; for the other, a deficit is feared. What would happen if the agency decided to cover the shortfall in one account by coding its expenses (only till the next fiscal year starts) to the other account? Rather than being regarded as mischievous, this fabrication is apt to be greeted as a responsible solution of the agency's problem. Surplus funds would be put to good use, the agency and its programs can continue without disruption, everybody wins. Surely, this kind of improvisation would not be regarded by its practicioners as a seedbed of corruption.

But what happens when privation is not limited to one agency or to one account? What happens when scarcity is not a temporary thing, but a year-in, year-out fact of existence? Miscoding of accounts grows into more pernicious forms of corruption until the whole budget becomes a massive escape from truth. Corruption becomes a way of life, a functional adaptation to the intractable limitations on government. Corruption becomes the way things get done, a way out for those who know its rules and are able to bear its costs.

Corruption is a very costly enterprise, which is one of the reasons why poor governments find it difficult to alleviate their distress. There are brokers of corruption who exact their tribute, kickbacks are sought and tendered, vendors pad their bills, employers their payrolls. Funds are siphoned off to hidden accounts, scarce resources are diverted to illicit uses. The poorest governments pay more, and become ever more anchored to escapism and corruption.

Escapist budgeting is paralleled by escapist planning. Just as the budget announces today's fancied accomplishments, the plan promises tomorrow's fantasized objectives. The plan might look good to AID and World Bank visitors as well as to locals, but it does not correspond to the real intentions of the government. There is a simple test to determine whether a plan is escapist or not. Are any concrete steps being taken to move toward realization of the plan? If the answer is no, escapism is rampant. An escapist plan is a salient part of a government's political strategy and therefore, paradoxically, cannot be entrusted to a fringe bureau. In countries affected by total scarcity, the planning agency often is one of the most important ministries. The government is actively involved in planning; it invests the plan with status and in return benefits from the plan's political appeal. In effect, the plan promises that which the budget cannot afford to buy.

The control and management functions which loom so large in American budgeting have little meaning in total scarcity. Fiscal efficiency cannot save enough money to make much difference. Strict adherence to budget controls is vitiated by the falsification of accounts. Evaluation also has no place in total scarcity, for it would be futile to evaluate that which wasn't done. Evaluation must be grounded on the bedrock of reality, but poor governments engage in running away from reality.

Total scarcity is the fate of some undeveloped countries which have been thrust headlong into the twentieth century. The rising expectations and frustrations of their citizens, combined with their meager resources, have made realistic planning and budgeting impossible. When total scarcity is accompanied by great uncertainty about future resources, poor countries muddle through in the manner described by Caiden and Wildavsky in *Planning and Budgeting in Poor Countries*. Such countries have a "disappearing budget"; they practice "repetitive" and "cash-flow" budgeting, hoping to make it through their impossible predicament (Caiden and Wildavsky, 1974: 67).

> Characteristic of this turbulent financial environment are the many changes that take place after the budget has been approved. . . . Rich countries normally get by with only a few changes, however, while poor ones face the necessity of constant alteration.

Under repetitive budgeting, "the budget is not made once and for all when estimates are submitted and approved; rather, as the process of budgeting is repeated, it is made and remade over the course of the year" (Caiden and Wildavsky, 1974: 72). Behavior which would be regarded as unwise in other circumstances comes to be a rational response to total scarcity for the poorest countries of the world.

In general, the United States has not had total scarcity because it possesses abundant resources. Yet patches of this condition have cropped up in some older cities. Given the disposition of the poorest to escape, it is not suprising that some of the worst cities have some of our best plans. The blueprint for tomorrow's model city clashes with the realities of today's blight and despair. Faced with seemingly insoluble problems, some decaying inner cities have engaged in a good deal of escapist planning: the planners are divorced from the centers of power and the plan clearly is unrealistic in terms of the capability or intent of the government to mobilize resources in pursuit of the alluring objectives planned for the future. This divorcement occurs because—unlike developing countries—the planning ethic is not implanted in the United States.

Escapist budgeting probably is much more widespread in the United States than is openly recognized. Because the budget (even for a small government) can be difficult to interpret and because there is very little looking for corruption (the public administration profession, for example, is more concerned about efficiency than about honesty), the amount of escapism practiced in public budgets probably is much more than is reported. Some "token" escapism probably is widely practiced in the form of illicit transfers among funds, borrowing for current operations, postponing the payment of bills, and detailing personnel from an authorized to a nonbudgeted activity. These practices by themselves do not indicate the onset of total scarcity, for they often are limited in duration or application.

To get a glimpse at total scarcity requires that the curtain of escapism be drawn aside and that the fabrications used by the afflicted government be exposed to public scrutiny. But inasmuch as the escapists are not wont to confess their sins and the government watchers are not apt to look for them, widespread escapism can go undetected for long periods of time. This is precisely what happened in New York City for approximately a decade, from the time its fiscal situation began to worsen in the mid-1960s until the bankers and news media blew the whistle on its extraordinary budgetary escapism in the mid 1970s. For many years, New York City practiced a routine form of escapism involving the line items in the budget. Thousand of employees worked "out of line," while thousands more were "loaned and borrowed" among city agencies, carried on one budget account but working for another. The lines in the budget always added up to much more than the amounts appropriated for city agencies. The difference between the two amounts was made up by "required accruals," actions barring agencies from filling authorized positions. Millions more in dollars were exacted from agencies in the form of "excess accruals" imposed by the Mayor's Budget Bureau. Each budget contained thousands of "dead" lines whose real status was normally known only by insiders. The capital budget also was prey to escapism; year after year, funds were authorized for schools that never would be built, for parks that never would be rehabilitated, for community projects that never would be carried to realization. It was less painful politically to promise these projects than to present a honest statement of city intent and capability.[6]

As New York City's fiscal plight worsened in the mid 1960s, its repertoire of escapist tactics was significantly broadened. Whereas the improvisations previously were concentrated on the line items, now they focused on the budget aggregates. According to a leading expert on New York City budgeting, "the tradition in New York is that the budget is a fake piece of paper from the start of the fiscal year. There's confusion, lack of knowledge, obscurity, and stealth" (Dick Netzer, quoted in Weisman, 1975: 71). With this tradition in place, the ground was set for more venturesome escapism. During the course of a decade, the expense budget exploded from about $3 billion to more than $11 billion. In an average year, expenses climbed 15 percent, while existing revenue sources provided only 5 percent more. Some experts warned of a looming crisis and urged that the city adopt a more modest role in providing services and benefits for its residents (Netzer, 1970: 651-711). But this course of action was unpalatable for top city officials, and they pressed instead for more outside assistance and taxing authority. The pressure tactics worked, but rarely enough to close the real budget gap. Budgetary escapism, therefore graduated to gimmicks which would forge the appearance of a balanced budget. Some of the tactics were legal, though probably unwise and rarely comprehended by outsiders: collective bargaining agreements were back loaded to thrust the full costs onto future rather than current budgets, contract negotiations were stretched out until the start of the next fiscal year, permitting the payment of retroactive wage increases out of the capital budget. Some were done under the cover of state law: periodically the Local Finance Law was amended by the New York State Legislature to authorize the shift of certain recurring costs to the capital budget. Sometimes the gimmicks violated standard accounting practices: raiding special funds and deferring the payment of bills. Sometimes they violated state requirements that the budget be balanced: overestimating revenues and then floating budget notes to make up the shortfall. Sometimes the gimmick was a product of utter fabrication: posting uncollectable amount as receivables and borrowing in anticipation of them.

Between 1965 and 1975, New York City debt quadrupled from $2 billion to $9 billion, for each avenue of escape was paved with borrowed funds. As long as banks and other investors were willing to finance the gimmicks (often with short-term debt rolled over one or more times a year), the city could persist with escapist budgeting. Like other escapists it had no incentive to own up to its true predicament. For many years, the incredible obscurantism of the city budget coupled with indolence by city watchers enabled New York to go its extraordinary ways. But in 1974 and 1975, the maze of budgetary lies was penetrated, the city suffered a series of cash-flow crises, and was brought to the precipice of fiscal bankruptcy.

New York City behaved like others more fortunate might if they were steeped in total scarcity. The lessons of New York relate not to the caprices of public leaders but to the way governments respond to their budget conditions. No less than those blessed with relaxed scarcity, those confronted with total poverty are swayed by the fiscal situation within which budgets and plans are shaped.

NOTES

1. In June 1970, the Advisory Commission on Intergovernmental Relations estimated that the gap between authorizations and appropriations for 169 federal grant programs rose from $7.7 billion to $8.5 billion.

2. The events leading to the Congressional Budget Act of 1974 are examined in Schick (1974a).

3. For example, between 1959 and 1968, the states as a whole levied 309 rate increases and imposed 26 new taxes (Federation of Tax Administrators, 1969).

4. The trend in federal assistance to state and local governments is analyzed in U.S. Office of Management and Budget (1976).

5. The story of the social services grant debacle is told with insight and clarity in Derthick (1975).

6. For an assessment of the budgetary practices of New York City, see Schick (1974b).

REFERENCES

Advisory Committee on Intergovernmental Relations (1970) The Gap Between Federal Aid Authorizations and Appropriations. Washington, DC: Government Printing Office.

CAIDEN, N. and A. WILDAVSKY (1974) Planning and Budgeting in Poor Countries. New York: John Wiley and Sons.

Congressional Quarterly Service (1968) Congressional Quarterly Almanac 1968. Washington, DC: Congressional Quarterly, Inc.

DERTHICK, M. (1975) Uncontrollable Spending for Social Services Grants. Washington, DC: Brookings.

Federation of Tax Administrators (1969) Tax Administration News (February).

MELTSNER, A. J. (1971) The Politics of City Revenue. Berkeley: University of California Press.

NATHAN, R. P. et al. (1975) Monitoring Revenue Sharing. Washington, DC: Brookings.

NETZER, R. (1970) "The budget: trends and prospects," pp. 651-711 in L. C. Fitch and A. Walsh (eds.) Agenda for a City: Issues Confronting New York: Beverly Hills, CA: Sage.

SCHICK, A. (1964) "Control patterns in state budget execution." Public Administration Review 24: 97-106.

——— (1966) "The road to PPB: the stages of budget reform." Public Administration Review 34: 243-258.

——— (1971) Budget Innovation in the States. Washington, DC: Brookings.

——— (1974a) "Budget reform legislation: reorganizing centers for fiscal power." Harvard Journal on Legislation 11 (February): 303-350.

——— (1974b) Central Budget Issues Under the New York City Charter. New York: State Charter Revision Commission for New York City.

STANLEY, M. (1968) "Nature, culture, and scarcity: forward to a theoretical synthesis." American Sociological Review (December): 855-870.

U.S. Office of Management and Budget (1976) Special Analyses Budget of the United States Government Fiscal Year 1976. Washington, DC: Government Printing Office.

WEISMAN, S. R. (1975) "How New York became a fiscal junkie." New York Times Magazine (August 17).

WILDAVSKY, A. (1979) The Politics of the Budgetary Process. Boston: Little, Brown.

6

NEGATIVE FINANCIAL MANAGEMENT:
A BACKWARD LOOK AT FISCAL STRESS

N A O M I   C A I D E N

Graduate School of Administration
University of California, Irvine

> *History, by itself, if we knew it ten times*
> *better than we do, could ... prove little*
> *or nothing: but the study of it is a correc-*
> *tive to the narrow and exclusive views*
> *which are apt to be engendered by obser-*
> *vation on a more limited scale.*
>
> —John Stuart Mill

In the rhetoric of the tax revolt, slim is beautiful. Proponents of tax limitations assert that fiscal stress would provide a healthy impetus to efficiency in the administration of public finance, and might even achieve by indirect means reforms which appear to have eluded direct efforts. Common sense suggests that if officials and politicians have fewer resources at their disposal, they will have to accomplish objectives more efficiently. Analogies abound. Economic theory relies on competition for scarce resources in the marketplace to force optimal choices: similar restriction of public resources might replicate this condition in the public arena with equally happy results. An inherited ethic extols thrift and condemns prodigality. The application of stress to a system determines its limits and ensures it is working to capacity. Through adaptation to stress it may be held that the body becomes stronger, extending its limits, and the image of the lean and purposeful organization is compelling.

As increasing pressure is placed on public resources, the question of the effects of fiscal stress on public management processes takes on a new urgency. It seems apparent that the good years for public finance are over and lean years loom ahead. Can we expect fiscal stress to bring about greater efficiency in the use of public resources? Will pressure on available resources force priorities and optimal choice, cut waste, increase accountability, and improve planning of expenditures? Will stringency encourage innovation and produce a climate for successful reforms? If so, we might look forward to a period of positive financial management and better public budgeting.

The probable increase in financial stringency over the next few years will undoubtedly give rise to many opportunities to detect various impacts of fiscal stress on financial management and policy. Fiscal stress has come as a shock and a novelty: we do not know what its effects will be. So far, experience has been limited and few case studies exist. But we do not need to wait for their results in total ignorance. We have become so accustomed to the availability of fiscal resources for public purposes that we often forget that until relatively recently, fiscal stress in government budgeting was the rule.

The capacity of public authorities to raise resources on a large scale is a characteristic of modern industrialized societies. It is an achievement virtually unparalleled in other periods and places, and is quite untypical of most of human history. Even today, poor countries have trouble raising revenues and sustaining government functions (Radian, 1980). Historically, fiscal stress has been ubiquitous, arising out of predominantly agricultural subsistence economies and the exemption of the wealthy and powerful from taxation.

It might be thought that rulers who had such difficulty in raising resources would be careful in spending them, and that strong budget systems would have developed simultaneously with the growth of successful state power. However, the concepts and practices of public budgeting are a relatively recent development. Although certain elements of budgeting processes, such as audit, had been incorporated into many financial systems, these were generally ineffective up to at least the nineteenth century. Even when the formal principles and procedures of public budgeting and accounting had become known, there were considerable difficulties in putting them into practice. It was only when industrialization and democratization assured a regular and flexible flow of resources that the budget practices with which we are familiar today were instituted and developed. Until then, governments coped with fiscal stress without the aid of budgets.

This article explores the effects of fiscal stress on financial management practices in a prebudgetary era. It deals with governments which survived and accomplished their goals despite fiscal stress. Their success in doing so rested not on their conformity to modern budget principles but on their skill in employing a variety of financial management practices quite contrary to those principles. Such negative financial management was highly effective in ensuring a flow of resources to rulers, but its use entailed heavy costs and made lasting reforms an impossibility.

It is not, of course, possible to cover the entire world history of government finance in the span of a short essay. Nor would any purpose be fulfilled in doing so. The intention is not to prove that fiscal stress necessarily causes negative financial management, erosion of budget practices, or recalcitrance to reform. It is rather to indicate that fiscal stress may result in practices detrimental to public budgeting, and has frequently done so in the past.

At the outset, then, it is important to recognize the limitations of an historical approach. Treated without care, history is like a mirror: it is always possible to see in it a reflection of what we want to find. The historical record upon which we rely is always partial—both in the sense that it is necessarily incomplete, and that it is biased toward our own preconceptions. The data that are available or that we select tend to reflect our preoccupations rather than those we study. Moreover, facts do not stand for themselves but require careful interpretation. Where we are dealing with relatively hazy and argumentative categories, such as budgetary effectiveness and fiscal stress, difficulties of selection and interpretation are overwhelming. Definitive stipulation of cause and effect in such conditions is extremely hazardous, while exact replication of historical circumstances is, of course, out of the question. We should not look to history, then, to solve our problems or to predict the future on the basis of what has happened in the past. Rather, we should use historical data to help us generate hypotheses, seek out likely outcomes, and analyze the patterns of events which appear to spring from particular identifiable circumstances.

For these purposes, a single example is sufficient. Most European states suffered from acute fiscal stress up to the early years of the nineteenth century and employed well-accepted methods to cope with it. Rulers were constantly short of money, and financial affairs were conducted in an atmosphere of routine crisis. Since the bulk of expenditures went for wars, payoffs, and extravagant living, it might also be said that the most successful states were those that suffered the most fiscal stress, and by the same token, employed the most successful strategies to overcome it. Preeminent among these was the prerevolutionary French monarchy, whose financial system elicited widespread admiration throughout Europe. Over the long period which stretched from medieval times to the Revolution, its structures underwent remarkably little change. They became larger, handled greater sums of money and refined their basic features, but their essentials remained the same. Their strength lay in their ability to do what rulers demanded of them—to produce a steady flow of resources as and when they were required and to overcome financial constraints which would otherwise have doomed royal ambitions to wishful thinking. So famous was French financial management that in 1766 the Prussian monarch imported French experts to improve his own financial administration (Harsin, 1950: 5). Because the French monarchy was so successful in its financial strategies, and because its methods were so widely imitated in other contemporary European states, it provides a useful example for the analysis of how governments managed fiscal stress in a prebudgetary era.

THE NATURE OF FISCAL STRESS IN A PREBUDGETARY ERA

The concept of fiscal stress is a vague one. It is difficult to identify the exact point at which a shortfall between tax revenues and public expenditures becomes fiscal stress. The measurement of different degrees of fiscal stress is also a problem. Where accurate and comprehensive accounts are not available, the existence of fiscal stress may be arguable and uncertain. Moreover, it may take a number of forms. Its effects at a high level of revenues and expenditures may be substantially different from those at a low level. Lack of tax revenues may be less significant where nontax revenues are available. Involuntary fiscal stress, where economic conditions preclude raising revenues, may be quite different from induced fiscal stress, where the choice has deliberately been made not to collect available revenues. Finally, whereas it seems obvious that an authority which incurs persistent deficits through failing to hold down expenditures to the level of plausible revenues is suffering from fiscal stress, it is not clear whether a different authority which has cut down its commitments to achieve budget balance should be regarded as similarly afflicted.

The broad scope of history provides ample opportunities for argument over ambiguities in definitions of concepts and interpretation of evidence. But in the case of prerevolutionary France, there is little problem in identifying the endemic fiscal stress which plagued the monarchy throughout the centuries from its inception till its fall. Though financial authorities (for reasons which will become apparent) rarely knew their exact financial position, and rulers did not care, the prevailing impression was one of lasting and continuous financial crisis.

A. ACCELERATING STATE EXPENDITURES

On the expenditure side, fiscal stress derived primarily from the need of monarchs to fight long wars to maintain, consolidate, and expand their realms in the face of external enemies and internal revolts. Traditionally, kings relied on feudal obligation to furnish armies and fight wars as the need arose: the king's vassals would come to his aid personally and at their own expense. By the end of the thirteenth century, this system was breaking down. Such extended enterprises as the Crusades, followed by wars in Flanders and the Hundred Years War, demanded paid soldiers and more expensive military technology. Even after the end of the war, military expenditures continued unabated as successive rulers consolidated their positions by the creation of a permanent professional army and standing militia (Wolfe, 1972: 38). A variety of smaller internal conflicts had to be dealt with, while policies of gifts, pensions, offices, and privileges to the influential were also expensive.

By the beginning of the sixteenth century, the crown was already in financial trouble. Military expenditures had created persistent deficits, but pressures for increased spending did not cease (Knecht, 1969: 10-11). This was the period of the emergence of the absolute state, an age marked by "the carefree magnificence of kings and courtiers who do not need to count because they do not have to earn" (Trevor-Roper, 1968: 59). Assertions of power against foreign powers at home and abroad involved the heavy upkeep of armies and expensive military campaigns and diplomacy. Advances in military hardware (artillery, field fortifications, and firearms for infantry) contributed to a rising spiral of expenditure which entailed heavy deficits. Even the periodic cessation of hostilities brought little relief. The Peace of Cambrai in 1529, for example, involved huge ransoms (Wolfe, 1972: 86). Price rises diminished the purchasing power of royal revenues, while nobles, deprived of the employment and opportunities of war, clamored for gifts of money, land, and official positions.

At the end of the 1550s, the state was effectively bankrupt, unable to service its debt to the bankers of Lyons. The second half of the sixteenth century was no less costly. Religious wars tore the country apart and further pushed up demands for money to finance military activities and to satisfy its supporters' demands. Once again, expenditures consistently outran revenues, though because of the general breakdown in the financial system, assessments of the financial position were impossible to make.

The end of the religious civil wars brought only a brief interlude of stability. The first half of the seventeenth century was characterized by "tension, frequent rebellion and deepening crisis" (Moote, 1971: 36). During this period, the monarchy was occupied in consolidating its hold over the kingdom, overcoming independent sources of power, and establishing military and administrative machinery to enable it to maintain its grip. Such activities were expensive. The participation of France in the Thirty Years War and open civil war in the 1640s were responsible for spiraling expenditures which grew from about 32 million livres in 1610 to nearly 150 million in 1642. When, in 1660, the Sun King, Louis XIV, assumed personal control of the kingdom, annual expenditures were running at about 115 million livres (see Lublinskaya, 1968; Buisseret, 1968; Bonney, 1978: 825-836).

Apart from brief intervals, Louis XIV's war policies maintained expenditures at high levels. War with the Dutch, which began in 1672, tripled the annual deficit (Goubert, 1970: 137). The war of the League of Augsburg demanded double the normal revenues. The War of Spanish Succession required between 91 million livres to 130 million livres a year for nearly fifteen years (Scoville, 1960: 200-202). By the death of Louis XIV and the end of the war in 1715, there was an estimated gross debt of between 2 and 3 billion livres of which 400 million livres was due for payment, while the revenues for the next three years had already been spent. Between 1684 and 1714, it has been estimated that the government spent over 5 billion livres (Scoville, 1960: 377).

Again, a brief period of relative peace reduced the strain on government finances for a while but was broken by the Seven Years War in the mid-eighteenth century. Between 1756 and 1759, the annual deficit grew from 67 million livres to 118 million livres and partial bankruptcy was declared. During the rest of the war, the annual average debt was running at around 2 billion livres, with approximately the same amount falling due each year. The end of the war in 1763 brought little relief because of the continued need to service the debts accumulated during it. Finally, support of the American War of Independence imposed a burden of expenditure which could not be met, but the extent of the deficit was disputed (Harris, 1970).

B. LIMITED CAPACITY TO TAX

The pressure by rulers to maintain high levels of expenditure was not matched by their capacity to tax. In the first place, they faced difficulties in raising revenues from a primarily subsistence economy. Exchange of goods was limited so that few opportunities for taxation were available. It was necessary to make estimates of several kinds of crop yields which fluctuated from year to year according to the weather. Concealment was relatively easy. The surplus remaining from subsistence was small, and as the taxes which ate into it were repressive, they were often resisted. Over and above these difficulties were recurrent plagues and epidemics, as well as intermittent warfare which destroyed crops, left fields unsown, and produced bands of marauding troops to prey on the peasantry.

Yet the economy was not poor. As time passed its wealth and diversity increased. Manufacturing and commerce grew, urban centers prospered, and the acquisition of colonies furthered overseas trade. The problem for the crown was how to tap this growing stream of wealth.

There were a number of difficulties in doing so. The major stumbling block was the disputed power of the king over his subjects. Originally, the king had been a feudal lord, exercising feudal rights over his own estates, but with no general right to take the property of any other persons. The king was expected to "live on his own," though in times of emergency he could call on other lords to come to his aid militarily. Gradually, as warfare became more sophisticated, this military support was commuted into cash payments, but as a regular source of revenue, these lacked reliability: they could only be called on in time of war and they were dependent on the consent of powerful lords whose cooperation was uncertain. Moreover, as feudalism broke down and social structure and distribution of wealth became more complex, more was needed than consultation with a few powerful barons. The old noble families had been overshadowed by a new nobility and a bourgeoisie based on new towns and communities. The lines between classes had blurred as expanded avenues of mobility and wealth had opened up in trade, the church, and public office.

The king might assert absolute sovereignty which gave him "power to legislate, power to judge, power to control" (Lewis, 1968: 84), but as far as taxing power was concerned, things were not so simple. Royal military power and administrative capacity were inadequate to extract resources from an unwilling populace (Major, 1967: 8). It was necessary to seek intelligence about possible resources and to avoid conflict that might result in refusals to accede or delays in collection (Strayer and Taylor, 1939: 21). Therefore, when kings wanted to impose taxes they would call assemblies, which represented not individuals, but the mosaic of over-lapping groups with which the king had to deal—areas, towns, commu-nities, feudal estates, corporations, clergy, nobility, bourgeoisie. Few of these assemblies were national, owing to problems of distance and communication, and even when promises of support were forthcoming from them, they required ratification at regional and local levels. Their powers were vague. Created almost entirely by royal initiative, they would seize the opportunity to present grievances, seek trade privileges, and demand exemptions in return for the taxes they voted (Lewis, 1968: 98-99). Whenever the king was desperately short of money and the regime was weak, assemblies pressed demands for open accounts and administrative reforms. But as soon as the king felt strong enough, he was able to ignore or repress such demands and would continue to collect taxes on his own authority.

As far as possible the king tried to do without assemblies, and they were never convened on a regular basis or as a right. National assemblies, or Estates General, died out at the beginning of the seventeenth century, and provincial ones during the reign of Louis XIV. But the king still did not have an untrammeled right of taxation. The role of the assemblies was taken over by sovereign courts or *parlements,* in particular the Paris Parlement, which became the focus of opposition to the financial ambitions of the crown. The Parlement was essentially a court whose interest in financial affairs originally only concerned the alienation of the royal domain and its revenues (forbidden by fundamental law). It did possess the right to register royal legislation, together with the concomitant rights to amend, refuse to register, and remonstrate against specific pieces of legislation. These rights were by no means clear-cut. They could be overridden by the king, and royal legislation could also be registered in a different court, but the Parlement saw itself as the bulwark against illegal use of royal authority. It took the attitude that financial exactions by the crown should depend upon the support of the subject, and that the king was obliged to respect the rights and privileges of all classes and communities in the state. Since it had no power to refuse revenue proposals, its main tactic was obstruction. As time went on, it acted more and more as a block against efforts to impose new taxes, and also against attempts to reform taxation along more equitable lines (Shennan, 1968).

The crown thus suffered formidable constraints in raising taxes. As in most primary economies, the main tax was on the agricultural produce of land, but for traditional reasons, noble and church lands were exempt. The wealthy obstructed any attempt to impose effective direct taxes on them, which meant that the brunt was borne almost entirely by the peasantry. Not only was this inequitable, but it meant that the crown was left with an inferior revenue base whose yield was limited. The growth of commerce allowed for further revenue expansion by means of indirect taxes, but these were also limited by resistance. They were not uniform but were imposed at differing rates, commodity by commodity, varying according to region. In order to increase taxation, it was necessary to devise an entirely new tax each time, which would meet with obstruction from the Parlement, and might provoke serious tax riots.

Fiscal stress, then, was the natural consequence of profligate spending policies and hated fiscal policies. Financial authorities were pinched between inexorable demands for expenditures and a limited base for satisfying them. Their recurring predicament was well summarized by one seventeenth-century financial official, who wrote: "Expenditure in cash is up to at least 40 millions, the *traitants* [financiers] are abandoning us, and the masses will not pay either the new or the old taxes. We are now at the bottom of the pot (Ranum, 1963: 145). The elements of the situation are no doubt familiar to many present-day financial officials—uncontrollable expenditures, low credit ratings affecting ability to borrow, failing revenues, resistance to increased taxation, and inability to meet immediate commitments. In the prebudgetary state, these were the normal conditions of financial management. Yet, in spite of fiscal stress, the wars were fought, the soldiers were paid, and the court maintained its luxurious way of life. How was all this achieved?

THE STRATEGIES OF FISCAL STRESS MANAGEMENT

Today, the usual remedies proposed for dealing with fiscal stress are reductions in expenditures, economies in staffing, more accurate accounting, tighter estimates, and an effort to demonstrate efficiency and effectiveness in the use of public money. In short, financial authorities are urged to strengthen the basic features of public budgeting as a means to control expenditures, restore public confidence, and set public finances on a firmer footing.

Their historical counterparts dealt with fiscal stress quite differently. They had no budgets. They converted the constraints of their situation into opportunities and exploited them to the hilt. Patchwork revenues, poor communications, problems in meshing receipts and payments, and difficulties in maintaining control of financial officials were transformed by a series of ingenious strategies into an administrative system whose flexibility and apparently infinite capacity for expansion enabled it repeatedly to surmount fiscal stress. The major features of this system were the fragmentation of revenues, deconcentration of accounts, cash-flow manipulation, and profitable diversion of financial purposes.

1. Fragmentation of revenues. Modern budgeting systems have relied to a large extent on the ease and certainty with which resources may be raised. Current expenditures have been met largely from tax revenues which are concentrated in relatively few high yielding sources such as income tax. Based on acknowledged principles of equity and efficiency, they provoke little resistance. Such revenues have been administratively cheap and simple to collect, and dependable within relatively narrow margins. Budget makers assured of reliable forthcoming large blocks of revenue have been able to forecast receipts with reasonable certainty and have generally expected tax yields to increase with economic growth. Budgeting has therefore been largely incremental in nature, with the main base of both revenues and expenditures taken for granted.

Financial authorities in prebudgetary systems could not rely on a solid revenue base which would cover the major part of expenditures. Every revenue source was problematical, demanding separate calculation, and subject to unpredictable fluctuations. Tax increases faced formidable obstacles:

> The government had to take into account myriads of rights, exemptions and traditions. For new taxes, new cadres had to be formed and trained. Public opinion was a potent impediment to bizarre fiscality. The peasant masses and the lower class urban groups lived near the level of subsistence. And the nation's stock of specie was only slightly responsive to the will of even an absolute monarch [Wolfe, 1972: 98-99].

It is thus not surprising that financial authorities taxed indiscriminately everything from belfries to playing cards without concern for efficiency or equity. They exercised considerable ingenuity discovering new taxes, such as the creation of a category of "illegal" housing in the capital, which was then subjected to a fine. But mostly, taxes fell heavily on necessities, such as salt and foodstuffs, because these were hard to avoid, and taxes were collected on goods passing from one part of the country to another and on entering towns. Though these strategies might raise money, they aggravated inequities and hampered trade. The tax system remained regressive, fragmented, inelastic, complex, and uncertain. Most important, it did no tap the real economic potential of the country.

Financial authorities therefore turned to nontax revenues, which might be roughly divided into two kinds: selling things and borrowing. Monarch strapped for ready cash traditionally sold produce from their estates mortgaged their land, or gave up domain revenues for a lump sum. Later they found they could exploit a much more lucrative source through sale of offices in a growing bureaucracy. Venality, of course, was nothing new offices had traditionally been bought and sold not because of the value of their salaries (which might or might not be available or worthwhile) but because of the fees officials could charge for their services. Office was seen as property and an instrument of plunder. At the beginning of the sixteenth century the king himself began to create and sell offices for profit, and virtually all offices became venal. The potentialities were enormous. For example, with one master stroke, revenues were doubled by creating "alternates" for each office, whose occupants performed their duties every other year (Wolfe, 1972: 131). Useless and redundant offices were invented to raise money, and office bore less and less relation to function. From the beginning of the seventeenth century, the king demanded an annual payment from officials in return for which the occupant of the office might sell or bequeath it at any time. Office thus became hereditary, but every nine years the right had to be renewed, which was of course an occasion for further payment. The proportion of revenues raised through venality varied, but at times represented as much as 40 percent of total revenues.

Borrowing was somewhat more problematical and had to be approached more carefully because of the monarchy's poor credit record. State bankruptcy in the mid-sixteenth century seemed to have put a stop to borrowing from merchant bankers who were the main source of credit in those days. But once again ingenuity triumphed. A little while before, an enterprising monarch had realized that if his own credit was bad, he could use that of others, notably the municipalities of the newly burgeoning towns, particularly that of Paris. A fruitful new relationship was instituted, and borrowing through intermediaries was established as an important way of doing state business. The king also expected to borrow from his officials, and an essential qualification for the chief finance officer was to be rich enough to guarantee his master's debts and so ensure a ready flow of credit.

The crown gained flexibility and increased revenues by diversifying tax and credit resources. These were multiplied by a dazzling array of expedients, such as sale of noble titles, forced ennoblement, debasing of the coinage, taxes on non-Catholics, exemptions from specific taxes, clerical levies, and many others. An accomplished finance minister could play on expedients, producing new ones as the older ones became exhausted. But the diversity of revenue sources served a broader purpose than directly providing funds for expenditure: each source acted as collateral for borrowing. Specific taxes, blocks of offices, or discounted credit notes could be bought up by financiers, in return for cash or further credit. As time passed, state finance became more and more dependent on the continuing servicing of these debts, while borrowing was greatly aided by the nature of financial administration.

2. *Deconcentration of accounts.* One of the cardinal principles of modern financial management is budget unity: ideally, all revenues should be received in a single consolidated fund so that their spending can be centrally controlled. The scattering of money in earmarked funds robs the center of decision-making power. It leads to inefficiencies in which some parts of the system have idle funds while others are forced to borrow for short-term needs. Except where there are special reasons, efforts are made to integrate all receipts and expenditures in a single budget document.

In prebudgetary systems, however, since communications were poor, it was more logical to make local payments out of local revenues rather than attempt to transport large sums to the center and out again. Local officials were therefore appointed to take charge of the collection of a particular revenue and its safekeeping in an account or fund. Each of these accounts would be earmarked for the specific local payments to be made out of it. There were sometimes separate officials for receiving and paying. Since these were all venal officials who had paid for their offices, the accounts were operated as private businesses.

Where revenues and payments were known in advance, the system worked well, as in the case of the land taxes. It was much more difficult to administer where receipts and payments were irregular and unpredictable in amount. This problem was solved by means of tax farming, which has been defined as

> a method by means of which a holder or proprietor of a legal right to an income or source of revenue assigned that right for a limited time to an individual, known as the revenue farmer in return for a lump-sum payment or the guarantee of a steady income in installments. The difference between the amount paid to the proprietor and the amount of revenue actually collected (less the costs of that collection) constituted the profit of the revenue farmer [Matthews, 1958: 9].

The practice had been developed by the proprietors of landed estates, among them the king, when they began to accept money instead of services in kind as feudal dues. The king merely extended the principle from the dues he received from his personal domain to public taxation and by the mid-fourteenth century the practice was firmly entrenched. Indirect taxes were particularly amenable to a tax-farming arrangement and it seemed administratively sensible for the crown to exchange the prospect of uncertain and fluctuating revenues, which were difficult to ascertain, for a fixed and certain sum. Private businessmen bid for lease which allowed them to collect a specific tax or taxes. The tax farmers paid lump sums at regular intervals to the government, and pocketed the profits from their collections over and above these amounts.

This contracting out of receipts and payments offered great potential for credit. Governments could make payments in advance of receiving actual revenues, as officials and tax farmers were willing to advance funds, at a price. Gradually, the system came to be perfected, and the business of farming the indirect taxes was handled by a single company taking up regular leases and offering a major line of credit to the state. Long after the original reasons of uncertainty and poor communications had disappeared, tax farming and deconcentrated earmarked funds continued to thrive because of their credit potential. By the eighteenth century, the government's debt to the tax farmers was often in excess of a whole year's revenue.

3. Cash-flow manipulation. In rich jurisdictions, at least, the handling of cash flow today has ceased to be a major problem. Where revenues and expenditures are fairly predictable in their amount and timing, financial authorities are able to schedule expenditures accordingly, and to limit short-term borrowing by means of revenue-anticipation notes which are quickly paid off. The disbursement process is dominated by legal authorization, accurate information as to balances, and planned timing of expenditures. The regularity of cash-flow management is an indispensable condition for budget implementation which converts annual budget estimates and authorizations into expenditures for the purposes for which they were allotted.

In contrast, in a prebudgetary system, the scattering of government revenues in hundreds of earmarked and local accounts posed an enormous headache in keeping track of receipts and payments. No one really knew how much was in each account. There were attempts at annual statements but these were often little more than enlightened guesses. The central accounting system was based on local estimates and accounts sent in annually by responsible fiscal officials. These statements did not relate income and expenditure, but rather affirmed how much the king was owed and also showed from which accounts authorized expenditures would be met. The documents were far from comprehensive, leaving out increasingly frequent secret payments, "special" authorizations for military needs, mortgaged or donated revenues, and the costs of collection. As time passed, they tended to become less effective as financial administration became more complicated and conditions more difficult. There was no way of knowing precisely what was happening to the royal finances at any given point (Dent, 1973: 31).

But the opportunities such a system offered for manipulation of cash flow were immense. In order to pay bills, financial authorities did not need to wait for revenues to come in. They could assign debts to a particular fund. In time of straitened finances, all assignations were not equal; some persons could collect easily, others not for some time, if at all. As war and financial crisis deepened, assignations were given on revenues not due to be paid until the following year. Through such anticipations, it was possible to postpone payments, or to borrow from officials in charge of funds on the security of revenues not yet received.

This system enormously complicated accounting. Robert Harris explains how it worked (1979: 76):

> Each officer who handled the king's money, a *comptable,* was required to keep records of his transactions and make a detailed account for each fiscal year (*exercice*). When completed it was sent to the Council of Finance. Because of arrears in the collecting of revenue, and also delays in the spending of it, several years were required before all these "true accounts" (*états au vrai*) could be completed and the council of finance could draw up a general account for the fiscal year. This was then sent to the Paris Chamber of Accounts for detailed verification. By that time the "true account" had become highly fictitious in describing the total amount of money received and spent by the royal government for a fiscal year. . . . It was the practice to assign a certain amount of anticipations received in a given fiscal year retroactively to previous fiscal years, and some portion was assigned to future years. Each fiscal year, then, spent funds drawn from previous and future fiscal years by way of anticipations.

Orderly budgeting in the sense of prioritizing expenditures in advance and adjusting them to revenues was out of the question. But the crown profited by postponing debts and choosing the time when it would have to meet them. The system met the needs of cash flow in a period in which taxes might take years to collect. As long as the tax farmers and officials played their part, governments were freed from the pressures of immediate fiscal stress.

4. Diversion of budgetary purposes. The purposes of public budgeting are by now well established. Though there may be some debate regarding the desirability or feasibility of incorporating planning and efficiency elements into the budget process, there is widespread agreement that the basic function of the budget is to maintain accountability for the use of public monies in the public interest. The budget is a public document. It is debated and ratified by representative elected bodies. It is implemented strictly in accordance with prior legal authorization. It is finally audited to ensure that its provisions have been carried out with accuracy, probity, and good faith.

In a prebudgetary system, the functions of mobilizing revenues and allocating expenditures were carried out without a formal budget. Fiscal stress was managed by a combination of revenue fragmentation, deconcentration of accounts; and cash-flow manipulation. These strategies ensured financial solvency, and in this sense they substituted for a budget. But in every other way, the financial system was totally at odds with accepted budget purposes. Far from existing to uphold accountability, its primary aim was to sustain the autonomy of the crown against any constraint at all. Institutions which asserted even a tentative opposition to the financial policies of the king were crushed, weakened, or evaded. Administrative regularity and control were subordinated to the demands of credit and maintaining cash flow. Through its financial strategies, the crown accomplished its short-term aims and overcame fiscal stress. But the means it chose to do so damaged its financial capacity, opened up its processes to systemic corruption, and made it prisoner to the very system it had itself created.

Initially, the crown's strategy was one of evasion of the claims of any body which might seek to limit its financial freedom of action. Expedients, venality, indiscriminate taxation on helpless groups, and the use of private credit avoided the need to apply to representative assemblies for consent to taxation. Secret payments, tax farming, and scattered funds stultified audit processes. Regularity and integration counted for less than access to ready credit and evasion of controls. Revenue fragmentation, deconcentration of accounts, and cash-flow manipulation became a viable way of managing fiscal stress.

But this was not the end of the story. In exempting itself from control, the crown had simultaneously opened itself up to private exploitation. The muddle of accounts, arrears in payments and receipts, anticipations and assignments, and lengthy audit processes precluded knowledge of what was going on. Administrative control had been a constant headache even in feudal times. Much effort had gone into superimposing one layer of officials over another and sending out special inspectors to check on transactions. These efforts at control had not been very effective, and things had been made much worse by the strategies used for coping with fiscal stress. Venality, the maintenance of tax receipts in private hands, and reliance on officials to make advances mingled private and public capacity, aggravated officials' independence, and laid open wide areas for abuse. Officially accepted private dealings, such as deduction of fees for services and use of tax receipts for private investment, easily shaded into outright extortion, fraud, and embezzlement.

The expedients employed by the crown not only increased the permeability of financial administration to private interests, but eventually realigned it so that its primary purpose was to serve those interests. This displacement of purpose occurred because of the crown's constant need for credit and the nature of the expedients themselves. The difficulty was that the expedients were not uniformly successful. The market for offices became sated. Guarantees by intermediaries lost their effectiveness because of recurring abuse by the crown. Officials were unable to keep their links with potential credit sources. In order to maintain solvency, the crown turned to financiers who would make immediate advances in exchange for rights to specific future tax revenues, or would buy bonds or blocks of offices at a heavy discount. Moreover, the same career financiers bought offices in the central administration of finance for themselves, to conduct these profitable transactions on their own behalf from the inside. There were numerous examples of fortunes made by unscrupulous financiers, such as one Hervart, who as controller general

> spent much of his time concocting the fraudulent documents by which illegal interest payments were made, altering the figures on Ordonnances after they had been ratified by the *Conseil des Finances,* tearing off corners which specified legal payees and inserting the names of his fellow-financiers, and, deplorably, even those of his own employees [Dent, 1967: 252].

Dishonesty added to incompetence, confusion, and official independence created a kind of looking-glass world in which nothing worked as it was supposed to on paper. Attempts at control, through audit or special tribunals, were ineffective as long as the crown was dependent on the good will of its creditors to service one loan with another. The crown had surmounted fiscal stress, but only at the cost of its own subversion.

It would be easy to dismiss these practices of an alien form of government in a distant land and remote period as stemming from preindustrial conditions and ignorance of authorities unenlightened in modern budgetary wisdom. Royal domains, tax farming, and systematized sale of office appear bizarre and of no relevance to our own budgetary predicaments. Yet it would be wrong to believe that statesmen who were so skilled in manipulating royal finances were either foolish or had no conception of any alternative means of conducting their business. They were well aware of the dysfunctions of the financial systems with which they grappled. The idea of a budget was well in advance of its accomplishment in practice. Why then did negative financial practices persist for so long? Why did fiscal stress not result in reforms establishing regular budgets?

FISCAL STRESS AND BUDGETARY REFORM

The elaboration of negative financial management practices was accompanied by persistent efforts to reform them. Some of these changes made little difference to the structure as a whole, and simply concentrated on making the existing system work better. For example, tax farmers were grouped in larger companies, or attempts were made to keep detailed control of every transaction. New sources of revenue were added and new institutions created to deal with them. Monarchs tried to shortcut the intricacies of financial administration by taking personal control, bypassing official procedures or taking them over.

While the short-term results of such initiatives were often excellent, their long-term effects were to entrench negative management more firmly. Administrative additions furthered fragmentation, undermined existing controls, and offered new opportunities for patronage and venality. Consolidation increased the power and wealth of tax farmers. Attempts to keep track of the complexity of scattered accounts was doomed to failure as the system increased in size without concomitant efforts to reform the accounting system or deprivatize the accounts in which funds were held. Efforts to substitute personal control for official procedures further undermined those procedures and added to formalism. But some real attempts were made to institute structural reforms. Why did they fail, so that ultimately it took a revolution to destroy the system along with the monarchy it had supported for so long? There appear to be three main explanations—the pressure for increased expenditures, the strength of vested interests, and the lack of outside support for reform.

1. Pressure for increased expenditures. The fiscal stress which had given rise to negative financial management practices was in large measure also responsible for preventing their reform. Governments were constantly pushing expenditures beyond the limits taxation could reasonably be held to supply. Briefly, the path of reform would lead in the direction of consolidating revenues and expenditures, redeeming existing debts and limiting further borrowing, instituting economies and curbing corruption, and insisting upon regularity and accuracy in day-to-day accounting. The happy result of this strategy would soon be increasing revenues from existing tax sources and reduced expenditures—in short, at least a balance and even a surplus. But invariably war would intervene, and demands for immediate and heavy payments to service it would force the authorities back into the older modes.

An example of this process may be taken from the work of one of the most renowned finance ministers of the seventeenth century, Colbert, controller of finance for Louis XIV. Colbert was appointed to clean up the royal finances once and for all in 1660. He instituted a tribunal which diligently spent some years uncovering and prosecuting maladministration and corruption. He established a royal council of finance which met three times a week. He drew up a detailed inventory of the state of financial affairs. He created a special body for the revision of all debts. He received every day from the central administration a resume of all transactions. He also codified the muddle of indirect taxes, consolidated tax farming in a single company, and placed the authority of the state behind local and private revenue collecting and disbursement mechanisms.

For about ten years Colbert was successful. Tax receipts increased, costs and duplication were reduced, and the system worked with greater regularity and certainty. But with the outbreak of war in 1670, Colbert was forced to reverse his policies to cope with mounting deficits. Old taxes were increased and new ones invented. Offices, titles, and tax exemptions were sold. Royal estates were mortgaged. Revenues were anticipated. Bit by bit, financiers reinfiltrated the financial administration and consolidated their links to the court. Colbert's work was largely undone by monarchical ambitions involving large-scale warfare in Europe, and the integrity of financial administration was subordinated to the channeling of resources for a powerful war machine (see Neymarck, 1970). Similar experiences had befallen several of his predecessors, and in each case the reason was similar—the determination of political authorities to achieve their ends despite fiscal stress and the capacity of negative financial management practices to do what regular budget practices could not.

2. Vested interests. A crucial element in negative financial management was the cooperation of those possessing resources with the state—venal officials, tax farmers, financiers. These were obviously unwilling to acquiesce in changes in profitable arrangements without resistance. For this reason, early reforms were often by way of addition, as new layers of officialdom were superimposed upon older ones deemed to have become too corrupt or unresponsive. Later, state finances were too dependent on tax farmers to collect revenues and advance credit to do without them. Only when profits were too low and the tax farmers refused to bid for leases were state commissions substituted to carry out their functions. But as soon as times improved, tax farming would be reinstituted, for the commissions could not carry out the credit function of the tax farmers and lacked their expertise.

Sometimes the tax farmers would themselves run the commissions, and would thus have an interest in their failure. For example, on the death of Louis XIV in 1715, following several years of disastrous warfare in which it had been impossible to farm the taxes, the Company of General Farmers once more took up its lease. However, the whole of the first year's revenue was consumed in outstanding debt. An attempt to prosecute tax farmers and financiers failed because their cooperation was essential to maintaining revenues and credit. Into this situation stepped a Scotsman, John Law, with a scheme for taking over tax collection and credit through a state bank and joint stock company. Unfortunately, largely owing to speculation and maneuvering by the tax farmers, the scheme failed. A state commission took over tax collecting and repaired the damage, but it was directed by a syndicate of the tax farmers. These ensured the low profitability of the commission until they were ready to take over the lease again at a low price (Matthews, 1958).

3. Lack of support for reform. The primary aim of the financial management system was to uphold the autonomy of the crown. In this it succeeded all too well. By the time the regime was drawing to its close, there were no institutions left to challenge its aims or methods of business. No representative assemblies existed. The sovereign courts, such as the Parlement, had been attenuated by intimidation and even temporary exile. Audit institutions existed but were totally ineffective. Even the tribunals which had earlier been held periodically to prosecute financiers had disappeared.

The effect was to leave the crown isolated. By weakening the institutions which might check its policies, it had also deprived itself of their support. When finally, after the American War of Independence, the crown made a serious attempt at reform of its financial administration and tax structure, it lacked the backing to carry it out. Proposals to make taxation more equitable, abolish venal office, make economies, and restructure the accounting system met with virulent opposition. The crown could summon few resources against the pressures of a parasitic court, venal officials, tax farmers, and financiers. The institutions which still existed, such as the audit chambers and the Parlement, were profoundly conservative, obstructive, and concerned only with protecting their own interests. By the time the need for reform had become indisputable, it was too late, and events were overtaken by revolution (Harris, 1979; Bosher, 1970).

The French Revolution entailed destruction of the prebudgetary financial system. Tax farmers were executed, taxation overhauled, and the system of independent earmarked accounts ended in favor of a central treasury. It might therefore be argued that in the long run, fiscal stress brought about reform. But it should be noted that revolution by no means resulted in the immediate institution of an effective budgeting system. In the early revolutionary years, the state was financed through inflation, while Napoleon relied on resources from occupied territories and a system of semi-secret interlocking accounts to evade budgetary accountability. It was only at the end of the Napoleonic Wars, when pressure for expenditures slackened, and determined statesmen deliberately eschewed negative financial management practices in favor of regularity, strict accounting, and control over expenditures, that a system of budgetary accountability was instituted (Bruguiere, 1969).

CONCLUSIONS

It would be misleading to regard this excursion into the past simply as an amusing diversion, much less as a demonstration of ancestral ignorance or underdevelopment as against modern enlightenment and superiority. The historical inability of governments to budget was not the result of ignorance of techniques or principles but was related to an environment in which fiscal stress was an important element. Budget capacity should not be taken for granted. The formal processes set out in law and regulation depend on a complex set of behavioral interactions, mutual expectations, habits, and understanding of the rules of the game. Recent experiences in implementing budget reforms emphasize how difficult it is to change these, and how easily formal regulations may be undermined to the detriment of budgetary purposes. Just as budget systems may develop, they may also deteriorate and decay.

Those who relate fiscal stress and positive financial management assume that the same public purposes may be achieved with the use of fewer resources, and that expenditures will be scaled down automatically commensurate with reduced revenues. These assumptions are not necessarily true. Politicians and officials may not accommodate to fiscal stress by restricting expenditures, scaling down objectives to fit fiscal realities, or seeking to attain the same objectives with fewer resources. Although they may concede a general need for economy, where their own sphere of action is concerned they will fiercely resist cuts, seek to protect their own position, and employ strategies remarkably similar to those of their historical counterparts. These may be briefly summarized as follows:

1. *Revenue fragmentation.* Efforts are made to find new sources of taxation, preferably in areas where they are little noticed, irrespective of efficiency or equity. Pressure on tax revenues may also result in an enhanced interest in nontax revenues. These may derive from the sale of assets, or their use as security for borrowing. Both long- and short-term borrowing become prevalent as a means of financing operating expend-

tures, and capital accounts may be used for current purposes. Expedients abound.

2. Deconcentration of accounts. As tax revenues become harder to acquire, attempts are made to earmark them in special funds for particular purposes. Agencies attempt to maintain separate accounts outside the regular budget so they may be protected from others' depredations. Autonomous and semi-autonomous entities spring up, with their own sources of funding, and often freed of the financial constraints on their parent agencies.

3. Cash-flow manipulation. The fewer resources available, the harder it is to pass a budget which satisfies everyone who has any power over it. Budgets may not be passed in time for the financial year to which they apply. But even when they have been passed, budgets may disintegrate during the financial year as competition for scarce funds continues, transfers and supplementaries nullify original appropriations, and financial authorities preaudit expenditures to ensure funds do not run out. The eventual pattern of expenditures may bear little resemblance to the original budget, which has become a fiction.

4. Diversion of budget purposes. The classic budget purposes of accountability, management, and planning are subordinated to cash-flow manipulation. Strategies initially undertaken to maintain and protect essential public functions from the indiscriminate effects of fiscal stress came to serve the purpose of bureaucratic self-maintenance. In the process, controls evaded for legitimate reasons are weakened, so that budget procedures become increasingly permeable to those who wish to use public organizations for private purposes. Even as budget institutions cope with fiscal stress in the short run, their long-run capacity to maintain acknowledged budget purposes erodes.

Such strategies for coping with fiscal stress are by no means hypothetical. "Creative budgeting" in New York City and the strategies of the Chicago school board in recent years bear a striking resemblance to the methods of the prebudgetary systems. George Hale and Scott Douglass have documented budget disintegration in state governments (1978), and Allen Schick has drawn attention to breakdowns in control in federal budgeting (1978). In California, observers have noted a growth in revenue fragmentation since the passage of Proposition 13, and the proliferation of statutory corporations and special districts based on revenue bond financing has become a marked feature of public business (Walsh, 1978). The impact of poverty and uncertainty upon the budgetary processes in poor countries has been similar in many respects to that of fiscal stress in prebudgetary systems (Caiden and Wildavsky, 1980).

In the historical case, the short-term advantages of the strategies to rulers were outweighed by their long-term costs. First, while they preserved cash flow, this was at the cost of knowledge of the real financial position. Second, it is worth noting that stress may be defined as "a force exerted on a body that tends to strain or deform its shape" or "the resistance or cohesiveness of a body resisting such force" (Webster's New Twentieth Century Dictionary, 1977: 1801). The effects of fiscal stress were to distort the financial system and displace its purposes. Third, while strategies for managing fiscal stress undoubtedly aided the interests of rulers and their circles, they were against the interests of those who ultimately paid the costs. In fact, they provided a mechanism for excluding accountability to the majority of the population and, by preventing for so long the translation of legitimate grievances into public policy, contributed to ultimate revolution.

It has not been the intention of this essay to prove that fiscal stress will invariably give rise to negative financial management practices, or that such an outcome is inevitable or predetermined. It is merely to indicate that such a relationship is possible given certain circumstances, and that historically such practices were prevalent. Stripped of the obvious archaisms and any overtones of historical determinism, the experience of managing fiscal stress in other times and places may provide a valuable field of study for those grappling with it today. At the very least, historical study may prevent the temptation of taking for granted the institutional foundations upon which public finances are conducted. These foundations may be more fragile than they appear. If we wish them to sustain further vicissitudes, we should do well to look to their maintenance.

REFERENCES

BONNEY, R. (1976) "The secret expenses of Richelieu and Mazarin 1624-1641." English Historical Review 91 (October): 825-836.
BOSHER, J. F. (1970) French Finances 1770-1795: From Business to Bureaucracy. Cambridge: Cambridge University Press.
BRUGUIERE, M. (1969) La Première Restauration et son Budget. Geneva: Droz.
BUISSERET, D. J. (1968) Sully and the Growth of Centralized Government in France. London: Eyre & Spottiswoode.

CAIDEN, N. and A. WILDAVSKY (1980) Planning and Budgeting in Poor Countries. New Brunswick, NJ: Transaction.

DEANE, P. (1978) The Evolution of Economic Ideas. Cambridge: Cambridge University Press.

DENT, J. (1967) "An aspect of the crisis of the seventeenth century: the collapse of the financial administration of the French monarchy 1653-1661." Economic History Review 20 (August): 252.

——— (1973) Crisis in Finance: Crown, Financiers and Society in Seventeenth Century France. Newton Abbot: David & Charles.

GOUBERT, P. (1970) Louis XIV and Twenty Million Frenchmen. London: Allen Lane.

HALE, G. and S. DOUGLASS (1978) "The politics of budget execution: financial manipulation in state and local government," pp. 488-493 in A. C. Hyde and J. M. Schafritz (eds.) Government Budgeting: Theory, Process, Politics. Oak Park, IL: Moore.

HARRIS, R. (1979) Necker: Reform Statesman of the Ancien Regime. Berkeley: University of California Press.

HARRIS, R. D. (1970) "Necker's 'compte rendu' of 1781: a reconsideration." Journal of Modern History 42 (June): 161-183.

HARSIN, P. (1950) "Les finances belges sous l'ancien régime," in Finances Publiques en Belgique. Brussels: Emile Bruylant.

KNECHT, R. J. (1969) Francis I and Absolute Monarchy. London: Historical Association.

LEWIS, P. (1968) Later Medieval France: The Polity. London: Macmillan.

LUBLINSKAYA, A. D. (1968) French Absolutism: The Crucial Phase 1620-1629. Cambridge: Cambridge University Press.

MAJOR, J. R. (1967) Representative Institutions in Renaissance France 1421-1559. Madison: University of Wisconsin Press.

MATTHEWS, G. T. (1958) The Royal General Farms in Eighteenth Century France. New York: Columbia University Press.

MOOTE, A. L. (1971) The Revolt of the Judges: the Parlement of Paris and the Fronde 1643-1652. Princeton, NJ: Princeton University Press.

NEYMARCK, A. (1970) Colbert et son Temps. Geneva: Slarkine.

RADIAN, A. (1980) Resource Mobilization in Poor Countries. New Brunswick, NJ: Transaction.

RANUM, O. A. (1963) Richelieu and the Councillors of Louis XIII. Oxford: Clarendon Press.

SCHICK, A. (1978) "Contemporary problems in financial control." Public Administration Review 38 (November-December): 513-519.

SCOVILLE, W. C. (1960) The Persecution of Huguenots and French Economic Development 1680-1720. Berkeley: University of California Press.

SHENNAN, J. H. (1968) The Parlement of Paris. Ithaca, NY: Cornell University Press.

STRAYER, R. and C. H. TAYLOR (1939) Studies in Early French Taxation. Cambridge, MA: Harvard University Press.

TREVOR-ROPER, H. R. (1968) The Crisis of the Seventeenth Century. New York: Harper & Row.

WALSH, A. H. (1978) The Public's Business: The Politics and Practices of Government Corporations. Cambridge, MA: MIT Press.
WOLFE, M. (1972) The Fiscal System of Renaissance France. New Haven, CT: Yale University Press.

RETRENCHMENT AND FLEXIBILITY
IN PUBLIC ORGANIZATIONS

IRENE RUBIN

Institute for Urban Studies
University of Maryland

For an administrator, the necessity of retrenchment poses many difficult problems. One of the most serious of these problems is the lack of flexibility[1] at the time when the organization needs to be most flexible and most adaptive. If changes are to be made, there must be flexibility in the budget to shift funds from one unit or program or budget line to another; if good personnel are to be retained, there must be sufficient flexibility to provide them incentives to stay on; if innovation is to occur, there must be some risk capital. If budget cutters are to maintain their effectiveness, they must have some resources with which to build and maintain coalitions. Otherwise, at the time leaders need the most support to make the most difficult decisions, they will have no support. Growth generates its own political coalitions (see Cyert and March, 1963); retrenchment, with its lack of resources, does not, and creates a crisis of leadership. The level of flexibility in the budget is thus an important factor in the ability of administrators to manage change; yet the level of flexibility in the budget at the time of retrenchment is highly problematic.

The purpose of this essay is to examine the relationship of budgetary flexibility and retrenchment in several actual organizations experiencing

AUTHOR'S NOTE: *This article was originally a paper prepared for a colloquium, "Fiscal Stress and Public Policy," at the University of Maryland, March 1980.*

fiscal stress. The case studies should show what factors or pressures work to reduce flexibility and which ones increase it. Examination of case study materials should also show specific techniques used to increase or decrease flexibility, as well as the organizational consequences (intended and unintended) of applying such techniques. Finally, by comparing the results of the study across organizations, some suggestions may emerge on the impact of the type of organization on the relationship between fiscal retrenchment and budgetary flexibility.

THE CASE STUDIES

The analysis presented here is based on two separate studies: one of five retrenching universities, and the other of a city experiencing severe fiscal stress.[2] Each study took one year. Each relied on a combination of documentary materials, interviews, and participant observation (although the city study made more use of participant observation of decision making than did the university study). Documents used included budgets, audits, newspaper accounts, minutes, memos, internal reports, and the like. There were ten formal interviews in each university, five with department chairmen and five with upper level administrators. There were twenty-four formal interviews in the case study city, including city staff, union representatives, and politicians. Both studies were concerned with retrenchment broadly defined. Flexibility was only one issue which emerged from these studies, but perhaps one of the most important from the point of view of theory and administration.

UNIVERSITIES' FISCAL STRESS AND FLEXIBILITY: THE BACKGROUND

The universities in the study were all state universities located in the same state. They were all subject to the Board of Higher Education. This board was responsible for reviewing university budget requests and cutting them before handing them on to the legislature. In the early 1970s, the state found itself squeezed between higher levels of support for public schools and increased expenditures for a growing post-secondary education sector. When enrollments in the universities began to fluctuate, the board began to cut back the universities' budget requests.

At the time when these cuts occurred, the universities had little autonomy over their revenue. All revenues had to be appropriated by the legislature before the university could use the money. Thus, if the universities strove to increase their revenue from nontax sources, the legislature had to appropriate this new money as well as the tax money. If the legislature so chose, it could reduce *tax* allocations if the universities increased nontax revenues. Moreover, all monies appropriated by the legislature were under the legislature's restrictions on expenditure.

Though there was little formal autonomy over revenues, there was some informal autonomy. During the period of growth, not all monies were in fact appropriated. Money not appropriated was called "local funds." The sources of such funds varied from campus to campus, but generally included auxiliary enterprises such as dormitories, externally raised funds such as contracts, and some types of scholarship aid. In one university, revenue produced by research was placed in a special fund which was not appropriated by the legislature. This fund was spent on seed money for grants and research assistants. Not in the formal budget, these funds were not subject to state budgeting requirements, and were highly flexible.

The universities thus had a little, but not much autonomy over resources. To make up for the rigidities introduced by such complete formal control by the state, the manner in which the budgets were administered left the universities with considerable flexibility. For example, university budgets were appropriated in categories such as personnel, contractual services, commodities, and equipment. During the period of growth, neither the board nor the legislature ever checked to see that actual expenditures below the university or multicampus level conformed to those budget categories. As long as the overall picture conformed to the budget, there could be enormous variation within and between the units. Similarly, salary increments were determined by the legislature, but the allocations of those increments internally was left pretty much to the universities, and there could be considerable variation between and within units. There was no system for checking whether universities spent "new monies," that is, money for new programs, in the manner which had been negotiated. Finally, while there were rules on the manner of exchanging funds between budget categories, it was permissible to do so.

Another source of flexibility in the administration of the budget was the existence of a pool of "lapsing funds." Lapsing funds are monies budgeted but not expended during the year. For example, during the years of growth, many more faculty positions were authorized and budgeted than were actually filled each year. These monies lapsed from the departments to higher levels of administration. If not spent during the year, the funds lapsed back to the state, so administrators tried to reassign the funds before the end of the year. How these funds were to be allocated was at the discretion of the administrator involved. Administrators could use the discretionary money as leverage to gain compliance in other areas: departments which pleased the administrator could get more funds than those who antagonized him or her. Careful use of such funds, even in limited amounts, extended administrative authority and created supportive coalitions.

To summarize, the universities had little control over revenues, and there was not much formal flexibility in the budget, but the administration of the budget and the growth patterns had created considerable flexibility in budgeting before the retrenchment period began.

THE CITY'S FISCAL STRESS AND FLEXIBILITY: THE BACKGROUND

The case study city was a home-rule city, and thus had considerable autonomy over fiscal matters, while under the general direction of the state. Its fiscal stress was not caused by an external decision by the state, in the way that the universities' fiscal crisis was. Rather, the rate of growth of the tax base failed to keep up with increased expenditures, due to inflation and real growth in personnel and purchases. Though the city had little control over its tax base, it had much more autonomy over revenue through taxes than did the universities.

The structure of the budget and the fund accounting system introduced some inflexibility into budgeting. There was a general fund, covering a number of city functions, and a series of other specialized funds, both for revenues and expenditures. Since each fund account is supposed to balance revenue and expenditures, surpluses in one account are not supposed to be applied to deficits in another fund. Some of the rigidity introduced in this manner could be overcome by interfund transfers and interfund borrowing. Such transfers had to be approved by the city council.

The city did not seem to have a functional equivalent of lapsing funds, since unexpended funds could be applied against the following year's expenditures. The most flexible items in the budget were the contingency funds and the capital budget. Strictly speaking, there was no capital budget: capital items were mixed with other items, and the city manager and his staff had considerable discretion over when capital items would be put in the budget and when they would be actually purchased. The flow of such items could be used internally to build support in the same way that lapsing funds were used in the university.

THE UNIVERSITIES: RETRENCHMENT AND REDUCED FLEXIBILITY

At the beginning of the retrenchment period and for the next several years, the state board and the legislature tried to reduce the informal control the universities had gained over their budgets. In addition, the universities depleted their flexible funds to repair the damage done by cuts and to maintain incentives for academics to seek outside funds. The ending of the growth period also reduced the source of flexible funds, lapsing monies.

To elaborate, the first source of reduced flexibility came from the Board of Higher Education. The board took increased control in several areas. First, it took more explicit control of all new programs, freezing the development of universities that had been moving toward research faculties and functions. Particular areas of growth were thus blocked. All new program money was carefully earmarked and proof was required that money had been spent as directed. The board also began to press for internal conformity to the allocation categories in the budget.

The second source of reduced flexibility came from the legislature. The legislature began to press for more control over salary increments, defining which groups within the university should get greater or lesser increments, and what proportion should be used for incentives (unequal distribution) or cost of living (more equal distribution). Particular legislators threatened they would put salary increment restrictions into the appropriations if the universities did not conform to their will in this area. In addition, the legislature made more effort to control and appropriate all local funds, including grant revenue.

The third source of reduced flexibility was the sharp curtailment of lapsing funds, because there were few new positions authorized, and those authorized were quickly filled. There were few budgeted but vacant lines, and very little unspent money. Moreover, the demand for the remaining lapsing funds was so great that one university budgeted it in advance, in essence, planning to spend the same dollars twice, assuming that a proportion of it would not be spent the first time. By budgeting such money in advance, all discretion and flexibility was eliminated.

The fourth source of reduced flexibility was the depletion of reserve funds. In the effort to smooth over the transition from growth to retrenchment and to repair the damage caused by hasty cuts, the universities tended to deplete their reserve funds. One university which had maintained a large fund of money to sponsor research spent it all in three years, creating deficits for itself in the fourth year.

The reduced flexibility that the universities experienced thus had several distinct sources. The first stemmed from their formal dependence on the state and its rigid budget. When the universities lost the minimum levels of political support necessary to maintain their budget levels, they simultaneously lost their ability to maintain the informal systems of flexibility in budget administration. Second, the ending of growth not only eliminated new monies which could be used for new growth, it also eliminated most of the lapsing funds. Third, the constant fear of budget cuts of unknown amounts, combined with the suddenness of cuts when they came, created a situation in which cuts were hastily made in accordance with political or other criteria. To remedy the damage so caused, whatever carryover funds had been accumulated prior on the onset of fiscal stress were used up. The result was an extremely rigid budget.

THE CITY: RETRENCHMENT AND REDUCED FLEXIBILITY

The history of flexibility in the deficit-ridden city differed considerably from that of the universities. Fiscal stress stemmed from lack of growth in the tax base combined with continued expansion of the city's personnel; it did not stem from the action of an outside group cutting off resources. There was no punitive attempt by outsiders to reduce flexibility in an attempt to make the city behave. Consequently, the relationship between fiscal stress and flexibility is somewhat more problematic in the city. The relationship between retrenchment and flexibility can be characterized in terms of three historical phases. In the first phase, the rigidity of the existing budgetary procedures became awkward; in the second phase, flexibility nearly disappeared because budgetary growth stopped; and in the third phase, the city's activities prompted reactions from other groups of actors who limited flexibility still further.

First, the appearance of deficits made budgetary rigidity inconvenient. It was all too apparent to politicians that if only revenue in one fund could be applied against deficits in other funds, much of the city's fiscal problem would disappear.

Second, as the crisis deepened, the revenue increases over the previous year, which had been the primary source of flexible funds, disappeared. There was no new money for capital projects and equipment, yet these resources had held the political system together. Projects were used by politicians to create political backing, and equipment was used by the city manager to maintain authority over the department heads. This latter exchange was particularly necessary because the city manager was structurally weak.

As the city attempted to reduce the rigidity in the budget, it provoked countermoves by other parties that reduced its flexibility again. The state government required the city to pay a greater amount of money into its pension funds, which had the informal effect of turning money the city had been treating as flexible into earmarked money. When the city tried to reduce or question the base acquired by the unions and renegotiate the contracts, it failed, and made labor more adamant about receiving its share.

In short, the city had a fairly rigid budget to begin with, but that didn't matter until deficits occurred. Then the lack of flexibility became painfully obvious. Lack of growth in unearmarked revenues cut off the major source of flexible funds. New money was obligated way into the future. This lack had a negative effect both on the political system and on the politically negotiated autonomy structure within the administration. Finally, many of the city's attempts to increase flexibility caused others to react by reducing the city's flexibility still further.

RE-CREATION OF FLEXIBILITY

The reduction of flexibility had two major impacts on the case study organizations. First, it curtailed the ability of the organizations to take resources from some areas and put them elsewhere where the need was greater or more pressing, or where the rewards were greater; second, it undermined the authority system, making it increasingly difficult for the organization to carry out retrenchment activities.

With respect to the inability to free up funds for new purposes, both the universities and the city were experiencing difficulties. The universities had difficulty encouraging faculty proposals for new programs and for research, and they had difficulty shifting funds away from departments with declining enrollments toward departments with expanding enrollments. Universities also had trouble finding the resources to reward excellent departments of faculty. For the case-study city, it was very difficult to take revenue from some departments to apply to those that were growing more rapidly. And the city lacked the flexibility to innovate in ways that would save money. For example, it was unable to buy software that would make billing cheaper and that would help them maintain inventory controls and regulate equipment purchases.

The problem of budgetary rigidity undermining the authority structure also occurred in both the universities and the city. In the universities, as in many organizations made up of professionals, line authority was not strong. The control of discretionary resources was a part of most administrators' tactics in carrying out policy. Such money, usually consisting of lapsing funds, could be used not just as an incentive to do a particular thing, but could be parlayed into conformity on other unrelated issues. When these funds began to dry up, there was an increasing competition between administrators for control. Administrators who lost control of discretionary funds not only lost their ability to carry out unpopular retrenchment policies, but simultaneously lost support from above (for failing to carry out policy) and from below (for failing to reward compliance). Several such administrators lost their jobs.

In the case-study city, authority patterns were particularly weak and diffuse to start with. Councilmen were dependent on the city's organized employees; hence they were unwilling to take a strong stand in labor negotiations. The city manager was structurally hampered by a police and fire board that curtailed his power over the departments. Effective deployment of discretionary, flexible funds was important in maintaining any semblance of authority. The elimination of these flexible funds meant a curtailing of special projects and new programs that the councilmen wished to provide to gain political support. The weaker they became politically, the less able they were to curtail the unions and the department heads. The city manager too lost authority over his departments when his resources dried up. He was unable to force his department heads to draw up their own reduced budgets.

There were, then, two major consequences of reduced flexibility: the inability to shift between departments or programs, and the weakening of the authority structure at a time when retrenchment policies had to be carried out. For these reasons, as well as a desire to enhance personal authority independent of organizational needs, there was considerable pressure to re-create flexibility.

UNIVERSITIES AND THE RE-CREATION OF FLEXIBILITY

The pursuit of flexibility was a conscious goal in the minds of many university administrators. The techniques used to re-create flexibility and slow down the tendency toward increasing rigidity can be roughly grouped in three categories: (1) building pools of flexible funds; (2) improving techniques of reallocation; and (3) slowing down the increase in fixed costs.

Creating pools of resources. The first of these sets of techniques was building pools of flexible funds. The need to provide buffer funds against future cuts, to shift resources to minimize damage from freezes and cuts, and to maintain coalitions in support of the administration could not be met within the confines of an increasingly rigid budget. The techniques for creating the pools of resources differed according to the intended use. Techniques used to create pools of resources which could be cut if necessary include the following:

(1) Increasing the use of temporary faculty and teaching assistants. All new hiring was in temporary positions. By switching to more temporary

faculty, and/or maintaining a pool of part-timers, temporary faculty, and graduate assistants, administrators created a buffer of faculty members who were outside the confines of AAUP guidelines and tenure requirements, who could be cut when necessary and added when possible.

(2) Increasing the number of faculty on twelve-month rather than nine- or ten-month contracts. If cuts became necessary, these faculty members could be cut back to nine or ten months without losing permanent faculty. Other universities used summer school in a similar but less formal way, contracting or expanding summer school depending on the size of the total budget.

(3) Expending committed funds very slowly. For example, administrators would authorize positions in the departments, but not give final permission to hire. The positions were prioritized and released in batches throughout the year. Thus, there were a few authorized but unfilled lines which could be cut if budget reductions occurred late in the year.

The second goal of administrators in re-creating flexibility was to provide some flexible funds after a major cut to minimize the damage done. This was also done in several different ways:

(1) Underestimating revenues. This tendency was strongest among the budget officers. Individuals (often with the knowledge of only one other person) revised estimates of income downward, making deficits look larger. Since several individuals may do this independently, the actual size of operating deficits became problematic: errors of over a million dollars were found in one university. This technique provides the administrator with a surprise cache of funds when the net balance appears to be zero. One specific use of this technique illustrates how underestimation of revenues can create a windfall during the year. Some universities attempted to underestimate tuition revenue. By estimating low, the universities created a slight but predictable squeeze for themselves. However, the difference between the estimated and actual tuition was put in a special account toward the next fiscal year. Since most revenues could not be carried from one year to another, underestimating tuition revenues provided a cache against a rainy day.

(2) Not spending money for capital items. A series of low-priority projects was approved but never expended, and carried from year to year. With a special request to the legislature, this money could be spent on noncapital costs during severe cutback. (There was always the hope that the legislature would come through with other supplemental requests during the budget year).

Pools of funds were also rebuilt for the purposes of allocating such funds to departments and individual faculty members on a discretionary basis. Such funds served not only as incentive systems, but also to rebuild political support of administrators. Tactics used to re-create discretionary funds included:

(1) Improving the internal accounting systems. Departmental accounts were computerized, and frequent reports on what proportion of the budget had been spent were sent back to the departments. Such reports helped control overspending and also documented where unspent money was. The unspent funds would then be collected several times during the year for reallocation. A supplementary system of line-item trades made the system even more flexible.

(2) Change the source of lapsing funds. The difference in salary between outgoing, more senior personnel and newly hired junior personnel was kept in the university as discretionary funds. Consequently, new hiring was almost exclusively at the most junior levels.

(3) Holding back on the budget. Despite efforts to replace lapsing funds as a source of discretionary funds, the amounts involved remained small. Some universities therefore adopted another tack, withholding money from departmental budgets. Universities which used this technique tended to increase that portion held back as retrenchment eroded other sources of flexibility. The way this technique worked was to budget some kinds of university expenditures that are meant ultimately to be spent on the departments in the office of a higher-level administrator. A good example is salaries for summer school, which, although spent in the department, may be budgeted at the provost's level. There are many other operating items which can be held in this way, such as travel funds and equipment monies. By holding these funds at higher administrative levels, several advantages may be gained: departments may have to compete for funds treated in a somewhat discretionary (and non-public) manner, enhancing the ability of administrators to form support coalitions; the money can be held uncommitted against the possibility of future cuts; and it can be used to handle problems which crop up during the year.

Devising and implementing a reallocation schema. Pools of "flexible" funds created as described were not large enough or permanent enough to fund innovative units or programs, or to help the university adapt to changing demands. To do his, the universities had to reallocate from one program or area to another. There are three ideal types of reallocation systems: attrition, formula, and zero based. The universities tried all three of them with varying success.

Attrition was the most widely used. Whenever a position became vacant, it returned to the dean's or provost's level to be reassigned according to some priority listing. Not all positions would necessarily be returned; fewer might be reallocated than were collected. The method is slow and somewhat haphazard, since positions occur in random locations at random times. The recipients are prioritized but not the donors. The advantage of reallocation through attrition is that it is peaceful; it doesn't stir up too much antipathy between departments or too much resentment against administration.

The second type of reallocation system used was formula budgeting. Several of the universities increased their use of formulas in response to fiscal stress. Because formula budgeting seems to allocate to everyone in the same impersonal way, it reduces conflict, but it may actually take from one department and give to another on a systematic basis. The choice of what criteria will be employed in the formula affects some units negatively, so the choice of what formula to use can turn into a political battle, as it did at one of the universities. While formula allocations are zero based in the sense that they start with no allocations for each unit and build them up according to formulae, there is no real comparison of merit or quality between units or programs.

The universities also tried to use the third type of allocation system, zero-based budgeting, but they had little success with it. They had difficulty in formulating criteria on which to judge units; they also had difficulty getting cooperation from the faculty in setting "negative priorities," that is, priorities for the first things to be cut. When one university tried a modified zero-based budget, cutting back all budgets to 95 percent to create a pool of funds that different units could compete for with innovative ideas, the whole attempt collapsed in a complicated heap.

Since zero-based budgeting appears to be the most rational reallocation system for a retrenching organization, it is worth outlining why this effort to recreate flexibility failed so dramatically. Part of the problem was the time frame: the cuts were to take place over one year. Only the operating budget could be cut in a single year, since it takes several years to phase out a program (the students in a program are normally allowed to finish, while no new students are admitted). The operating budgets for departments do not include personnel, but only items like supplies, printing, contractual services, travel, and equipment. After years of cuts in the operating budget, some departments had little as 5 percent of their budgets in operating lines; these could be cut no further. The second problem was that departments chose not to submit innovative ideas for new programs, because the likelihood of success in competition was seen as too low to be worth the effort of coming up with a proposal. The third reason the zero-based approach failed was that all the units received a 5 percent cut in their budgets, so every unit was hurt and motivated to protest. A more selective approach to cuts would have created a more manageable balance of those hurt and those benefiting.

What is important to note particularly about the reallocation process is that despite its jerky progress, the universities were generally able to cover shifting enrollments by shifting funds. Sometimes the shift was too slow, causing departments with growing enrollment to suffer more stress than departments with shrinking enrollments. But overall, the universities did succeed in maintaining this minimum amount of flexibility.

Controlling aging processes. Two techniques for creating flexibility have been described: the creation of pools of resources and the creation of reallocation techniques. The third set of techniques to recreate flexibility was designed to control "aging processes." Organizational aging results from the combined influence of reduced hiring of new faculty at lower levels and continued progress through the ranks of the current faculty. If unchecked, this byproduct of financial stress will reduce future flexibility by creating an increasingly expensive and tenured faculty. The more faculty members who have tenure, the more difficult reallocation becomes, and the more difficult it becomes to reduce the size of the faculty. Efforts to mitigate the influence of aging can be divided into two groups: one involves holding down the costs of aging, the other involves slowing down the speed of aging.

University administrators controlled the cost of "aging" faculty by controlling rank and salary at entry. Some of the universities issued blanket rules about hiring only junior people at the assistant professor level. Also, in some universities in which salary had been negotiated with each new faculty member, administrators set very narrow ranges of salary for all newcomers. Salary was further controlled by hiring part-timers and temporaries, whose responsibilities were narrower and whose salaries were commensurately smaller. Also, they seldom received raises and so did not become more expensive as time passed.

The second set of techniques for controlling the aging process involved the attempt to slow them down. These techniques included lengthening the probationary period before tenure and promotion, reducing the number of faculty eligible for tenure, and reducing the proportion of eligible faculty who actually obtained tenure. In order to lengthen the amount of time before tenure and promotion, several of the universities stopped awarding "early" tenure and promotion. Recommendations from the departments were not considered unless the full probationary period had been served. In addition, the universities stopped counting unpaid leave toward the probationary period, which drew out the waiting period even longer. To reduce the proportion of faculty eligible for tenure, administrators: (a) raised the proportion of faculty on non-tenure tracks by hiring graduate assistants and temporary faculty; and (b) shifted administrators, librarians, and research staff out of tenure track positions. Finally, to reduce the proportion of eligible faculty actually receiving tenure, the requirements for tenure were tightened, and fewer members of each cohort were granted tenure.

To summarize, university administrators responded to reduced flexibility in a variety of ways: they created pools of funds to use as buffers against future cuts, to repair damage done by cuts, and to maintain political coalitions; they devised and implemented a variety of reallocation schemes to shift resources between units in order to be able to change emphasis and adapt to changing enrollments; and they slowed down the processes of aging.

THE CITY AND THE RE-CREATION OF FLEXIBILITY

The city, like the university, strove to increase flexibility. But the structures of the city and the universities were very different, and led to emphasis on different strategies. The city had more autonomy over revenues than the universities; the universities were less hampered by a fund structure than the city; the universities were more limited to single year as the budgetary time span than the city; and the city was more restricted by labor contracts than the universities. As a result of these differences, the city engaged in less buffering and more borrowing, was less concerned about delaying commitments, and more concerned with delaying expenditures. Also, the city was more involved in a strategy of increasing revenues than the universities were, but was less involved in controlling the aging processes.

Borrowing versus buffering. The city engaged in many different forms of borrowing that were either not required because of the simplicity of the fund structure in universities or were simply forbidden to the universities. The fund structure of the city in a sense exaggerated the deficits because surpluses in one fund could not legally be applied to deficits in other funds. City elected officials began by ignoring the fund structure, paying attention only to the bottom line of total revenues compared with total expenditures. City staffers were opposed to this view, and began to press for formal exchanges between funds. Later, under pressures from deficits and cash-flow problems, formal borrowing between funds was supplemented with informal borrowing. Money that should have been put into pension funds was spent elsewhere. Some of the informal borrowing was not repaid during the year. The fund with the highest cash flow became supplier to the rest of the city's funds, running a net internal loss over a period of several years. Borrowing from the future became more and more acute as expenditures were slid forward into the following year. Finally, bond revenue was used partly to pay off some of the internal borrowing for operating expenses. In addition, there was also short-term borrowing from local banks in anticipation of revenue, to facilitate cash flow, but this last form of borrowing did not appear to be used to cover deficits.

The city borrowed but did little buffering in the manner of the universities. There was little effort to create pools of funds that could be cut or to create pools of personnel which could be cut if necessary. The reason for this difference is that the city did not in fact balance its budget every year as the universities were forced to do, so the city did not anticipate the constant possibility of cuts. Not anticipating it, they never prepared for it. When cuts became necessary, administrators cut into recently hired personnel; slots were not taken from vacant lines or temporary personnel (as in the university).

While the city was supposed to balance its budget every year, there was a procedure for putting items which had been obligated but not yet paid for into the following year's budget. It was a simple matter to put more and more items into that category when the revenues would not cover all the approved budgeted expenditures. Actually, deficits were increasing but not apparent. As a result, cash-flow problems began to be important: if there are routinely more expenditures planned than revenues will cover, some picking and choosing must go on among budgeted items. The consequence of this strategy is that the budget loses some of its power. The budgeting of an expenditure becomes only the first step in getting it. Items which can be (and some which should not be) are delayed, sometimes for several years. Capital projects in particular (including those from local revenue) were carried in the budget for several years before they were actually carried out. When new personnel were added, they were routinely added late in the year, delaying the expenditure as long as possible.

Because the city's strategy was oriented to borrowing rather than buffering, the mechanics of cutbacks were highly problematic. The city manager attempted to employ a modified zero-based budget similar to that used by the universities, but with a difference: the purpose was to allocate cuts, not to redistribute fixed expenditures.

Department heads were asked to generate their budgets from zero up to three specified levels, each representing a cut. Presumably, the city manager would then decide on the levels by comparing department proposals, but this step never occurred. The department heads refused to cooperate, insisting the city manager make his own cuts, which he did. The city had no more success with this form of zero-based budgeting than the universities did. The city manager later tried to deal with the departments through formula budgets, but had difficulty arriving at standards for the formula.

It is interesting to note that even after the cutbacks, when the departments began to anticipate the possibility of future cuts in the same way that the universities did, they did not respond by trying to build in buffer funds or temporary personnel. The only temporary jobs at City Hall (on a year-round basis) were CETA employees, who did not represent a group the city could cut for savings. The departments expressed the feeling that if they had added unnecessary personnel, or personnel not suited to their division of labor and task structure, such people would be cut; the department would be making a target of itself. Actual cuts occurring later suggest that this perception was accurate. The appearance of not having anything to cut was seen as a protection against cuts for city departments, but not for universities.

Revenue generation. The city government was not as rigidly bound by a one-year budget as the universities were. Taxes unspent at the end of the year did not lapse back to the taxpayers, and, due to the fund structure, revenues unspent in a particular fund did not automatically lapse to central administration to be reallocated. Surplus earmarked funds could be used as a cash balance to begin the next year. Since there was so little flexible money in comparison to expenditures, there was no analogue to the universities' lapsing funds. Rather, money had to be taken away from one budgeted item and spent on another budgeted item. Such shifts gave the finance officer a great deal of power in dealing with the departments. His informal authority was enhanced by the cash-flow problems.

By contrast, the city manager, who was responsible more for budget formation than for expenditure disbursements, found his informal power eroded. His formal power was not great, so that his power over discretionary budget allocations was extremely important to his job stability and to his ability to carry out retrenchment. For the departments, he could include or encouragement personnel and equipment requests; for the council members, he could include their requests for special projects. When the budget crisis forced cutbacks, these were the only areas of the budget which could be cut, yet to cut them was to cut off his source of authority. The city manager did attempt to cut them in an effort to balance the budget, but in the process lost the support of the department heads and the council, and was rendered almost helpless in his attempts to manage retrenchment.

For councilmen the picture was equally difficult. With their special projects blocked or delayed, their ability to generate favorable publicity and political support was hampered. They consequently became even more dependent on the city's uniformed employees for support. Because they were so dependent, they were unwilling to curb the unions or even to make firm labor policy. Their political vulnerability made them less and less able to direct retrenchment themselves. The only solution appeared to be an increase in revenues and an end to the fiscal crisis. An increase in tax rates was politically obnoxious, but necessary in the short run; the only long-term solution was regeneration of the tax base. Toward this end much of the council's and city staff's attention was bent from 1973 on, until after the deficits were eliminated.

The city engaged in two large-scale projects between 1973 and 1978. One was the development of a large shopping mall on the edge of town, the second the creation of a downtown shopping mall. Each of these projects was loaded with up-front costs that worsened the city's immediate financial prospects and provoked intense controversy. But, despite these disadvantages, there was a stubborn commitment to the realization of these two projects.

To summarize, the fiscal crisis threatened the only source of flexibility in the political system—increased revenues. In doing so, it weakened the authority of both the city manager and the council in dealing with retrenchment. The focus of the city's response to reduced flexibility was to increase revenue by regenerating the tax base.

Controlling the aging processes. The city was less involved than the universities in controlling aging processes. For one thing, new hiring *was* continued throughout the period of fiscal problems, so the problem of an aging work force was somewhat less obvious. However, the expansion of the labor force was sure to strain the retirement system, especially since "borrowing" from retirement funds (in the sense of underfunding them) was common. The state stepped in at one point and insisted that the case-study city, along with the others in the state, improve its funding of pension funds. Increased pay into the pensions combined with high payments for hospitalization insurance made the issue of organizational aging more salient. Moreover, since the city manager lacked authority over his department heads, renegotiation of union contracts seemed a reasonable approach to holding down cost increases.

Like those in many cities, the labor contracts for police and fire built in successive pay increases to a maximum after a few years on the force. The contracts also determined salary at entry. The cost of "aging" as employees go through the ranks was thus fixed by contract, and not subject to administrative control. The city manager attempted to renegotiate the labor contract, especially where particular wordings had later turned out to be particularly expensive. He had very little success in this effort. Overall, the unions' contracts continued to be an area of inflexibility in budgeting.

Three general issues emerge from the case study data: the first is the apparent necessity for re-creating flexibility; the second is the implications for the organization or city as a whole of the strategies actually adopted; and the third is the possible inferences to be drawn from the comparison between the responses of the universities and the case-study city.

NECESSITY OF RE-CREATING FLEXIBILITY

Despite the differences in structure between the universities and the city, growth had generated in each case a certain amount of flexibility which had helped facilitate change and had bolstered a weak authority system. In each case, the formal rigidities of the budget were not particularly restrictive during growth but became awkward during decline. In the case of the universities, an informal system had grown up during growth that had given the universities considerable flexibility in budget administration, but the same loss of support that ended budget growth also limited budget discretion. There was an attempt to take control of the universities' budgets by outside actors. For the case-study city, the source of revenue decline also had a simultaneous effect of reducing flexibility, since annual budget growth was the major source of flexible (nonearmarked) money. Both the universities and the city strove to recreate flexibility. The question becomes, why did they spend so much effort on recreating flexibility? Is it possible for hard-pressed universities and cities to carry out retrenchment without budgetary flexibility?

The study suggests that in organizations with a weak authority structure, without budget flexibility, retrenchment cannot be carried out. Not only is there not enough flexibility to reallocate resources and reward innovations, there is not enough top-down authority to make cuts or to reallocate. Zero-based budgeting failed both in the universities and in the city. If this suggestion is correct, then the attempt of outside actors to control budgets and limit expenditures by limiting revenues and reducing flexibility will produce strangely ineffective results and paralyze the organizations involved. More discretion within reduced resource levels would be a better combination.

IMPACT OF RE-CREATING FLEXIBILITY

The techniques used for re-creating flexibility had major impacts both on the universities and on the city. For the universities, the major changes involved the shift to more temporary personnel, and the shift upward of control over many personnel and budget decisions. For the city, the pressure to regenerate the tax base led to cycles of over and underdevelopment of capital projects.

The shift to temporary personnel in the universities involved the creation of a group of faculty members with no voting rights and no participation in the running of departments or of the university. Their short stay and the readiness with which they can be let go suggest their utter powerlessness with respect to administration; by increasing the proportion of such temporary faculty, the line authority of administrators over faculty is increased, and the collegial structure of universities is weakened. This is not a minor consequence.

Not only was a new powerless class of faculty created, but many responsibilities which had devolved onto departments during growth were recentralized in an effort to gather up and control "loose" resources. This change too promises to change the nature of the university somewhat.

For the case-study city, the only feasible political solution seemed to be to regenerate the tax base and re-create some flexible money. The periodic thrust toward new shopping centers, even when they may be in direct competition with each other, is liable to create a periodic overproduction of certain types of capital outlay.[3]

While the city tried to regenerate the tax base, it created some flexibility by sliding expenditures forward and creating a constant cash-flow problem. There came to be less and less of a relationship between budgets and actual expenditures. This meant the responsibility for keeping expenditures in line with revenues fell increasingly on the finance officer. Department heads had to argue and persuade him to get items already budgeted to them. These changes are also not inconsequential for the organization. The primary reasons for expending or delaying became the dictates of cash flow and the preferences of the budget officer.

CONCLUSIONS

Within the overall similarity of response between the universities and the city there were not only different tactics, but also different strategies. The universities had less autonomy over resources, and were forced each year to balance their budgets. Since there was no possibility of borrowing or postponing expenditures, a revenue cut meant a budget cut. The universities therefore focused on how to best handle a budget cut, whenever it should come. The relationship of budgets with expenditures remained intact for the university as a whole, but weakened for some individual units when items were budgeted at higher administrative levels to be spent on lower levels. Universities also strove to hold down fixed costs. The city, on the other hand, strove to increase revenues, relied heavily on all kinds of borrowing, and increasingly became dependent on cash-flow management.

The differences in these strategies suggest there is not one kind of response by universities and cities[4] to reduced resources. There seem to be some important structural conditions involved that shape the response. First, if the organization has autonomy over resources, it will drive toward increasing those revenues as a primary objective. Second, if it is possible to slide expenses forward from year to year, to make the budget look more balanced than it is, more and more expenses will be slid forward. Such an organization will borrow money inside the organization (from restricted funds) and outside the organization, accumulating a deficit and aggravating cash flow. The demands of cash flow will come to dominate the organization. This pattern is typical of home-rule cities and private universities in fiscal trouble. If the organization has no autonomy over revenues, it will not seek new revenues and will not borrow. If it is forced to balance its budget each year, it may experience expenditure cutbacks with greater frequency than the more autonomous organization. To the extent that these organizations routinely expect cuts, regardless of what is or is not in the budget, there will be a tendency to buffer. This buffering may take many forms, including underestimating revenue and switching to a less permanent class of personnel. State universities with large private endowments fall between the two models and may show some attributes of each.

If this analysis is correct, then the major attribute of organizations in determining their responses to retrenchment and reduced flexibility is the degree of actual (not only legal) autonomy/dependence. Private universities should behave like home-rule cities; public universities should behave like non-home rule cities. The public/private distinction may not be as relevant in this context as the degree of autonomy.

To summarize the whole argument for organizations like the universities and the city of this study, flexibility not only can be re-created during retrenchment, it must be re-created in order to carry out retrenchment activities. However, the very changes made to re-create flexibility may have some unintended consequences that should be observed and perhaps minimized or offset by other policies. Finally, the particular steps adopted to re-create flexibility may vary with the degree of autonomy of the organization.

NOTES

1. Flexibility is used here to denote budgetary flexibility. Budgets can be more or less flexible, depending upon the number and kinds of restrictions on when and how money may be spent. Common forms of restrictions in public budgeting include: earmarked revenues, fund structures in which revenues must match; budgetary categories with little or no exchange between line items or categories of expense; fixed time periods in which money must be spent.

2. The universities study is taken from Rubin (1977b). The city study is taken from Rubin (n.d.). Also see Rubin (1977a, 1979).

3. The drive to re-create flexibility and political resources may be a better explanation of the city as a growth machine than the self-interest of the landowning class. For a class-oriented approach to urban growth, see Molotch (1976).

4. Naomi Caiden and Aaron Wildavsky, in *Planning and Budgeting in Poor Countries,* suggest that there is a basic similarity between hard-pressed universities, cities, and poor countries in terms of budgetary responses. I am suggesting here that differences may be more interesting than similarities, and that the key variable may be degree of autonomy rather than degree of poverty combined with degree of uncertainty.

REFERENCES

CAIDEN A. and A. WILDAVSKY (1980) Planning and Budgeting in Poor Countries. New Brunswick, NJ: Transaction.

CYERT, R. and J. MARCH (1963) A Behavioral Theory of the Firm. Englewood Cliffs, NJ: Prentice-Hall.

HALE, G. E. and S. DOUGLASS (1977) "The politics of budget execution: financial manipulation in state and local government." Administration & Society 9 (November): 367-378.

LEVINE, C. H. (1978) "Organizational decline and cutback management." Public Administration Review 38: 316-325.

MOLOTCH, H. (1976) "The city as a growth machine." AJS 82, 2: 309-322.

RUBIN, I. (1977a) "Universities in stress: decision making under conditions of reduced resources." Social Science Quarterly 58 (September): 242-254.

——— (1977b) "Financial retrenchment and organizational change: universities under stress." Ph.D. dissertation, University of Chicago.

——— (1979) "Retrenchment, loose structure and adaptability in the university." Sociology of Education 52 (October): 211-222.

——— (n.d.) "Unbalanced accounts: a case study of urban fiscal stress." (unpublished)

SCHICK, A. (1973) "A death in the bureaucracy: the demise of federal PPBS." Public Administration Review 33 (March/April): 146-156.

8

CHANGING FISCAL STRUCTURE AND CREDIT QUALITY: LARGE U.S. CITIES

JOHN E. PETERSEN

Municipal Finance Officers Association

This essay deals with major trends and emerging issues in the financial structure and credit quality of the nation's forty-five largest cities.[1] The period from the late 1960s to the late 1970s has been a turbulent one for city government. And as we enter the 1980s, new uncertainties emerge in the face of high rates of inflation, tax and expenditure limits, and belt-tightening in federal aid.

Commencing during the recession of 1974-75 and spotlighted by the events surrounding the New York City crises of 1975 and 1976, academics, analysts, and the public at large became increasingly aware of the financial plight of many of the nation's cities. Almost all observers acknowledge that many cities are suffering dramatic demographic and economic declines. But the causes, severity, and reversibility of these phenomena are very much in dispute, as are, of course, the appropriate policies which cities, states, and the federal government should take to cure this situation.

The first part of the essay provides a historical overview of the changing revenue and expenditure patterns of the largest cities. Stress is placed on the heavy reliance by the late 1970s of cities on intergovernment payments. Subsequent sections review the bond market difficulties of the mid-1970s and the credit quality of the nation's largest cities as revealed in the ratings given to their general obligation bonds.

PATTERNS IN BIG CITY FINANCE

As a whole, the state and local sector has undergone considerable change in the magnitude and structure of its financing over the last decade. The largest forty-five cities have shared in these changes and have seen their budgets grow under the impact of inflation and an increasingly rich array of services delivered to the public. On average, however, they have had to contend with declining populations and with residents' personal incomes that have been growing more slowly than those of the nation at large. But, as we shall see, the use of averages in describing even the largest cities is a perilous exercise; most jurisdictions have found new sources of revenue to finance most—if not all—of their growing expenditure needs.

Before embarking on our analysis of city finances over the past decade, it is important to define carefully both what is being measured and how it is being measured. This and subsequent sections will concentrate on the general expenditures of the city governments. *General expenditures* are those expenditures carried out by the city government for purposes that are defined as being of a general governmental nature by the U.S. Bureau of the Census. The principal exclusions are expenditures by what the Census defines as local utility functions, namely, water supply, gas, electric, and transit utilities. Also, the cities' general expenditure figures do not reflect expenditures and revenues made by independent entities such as counties, special districts, and school districts that are local government jurisdictions under separate political control. It is always necessary to remember when dealing with city-government revenues and expenditures that only parts of the supply of public services and (consequently) revenues are being counted, since many services are rendered, and taxes and fees collected by jurisdictions other than the city in a given geographic area.[2]

Another fundamental problem in dealing with big city data involves the impact of New York City, which is by far the statistically predominant city in the nation. In fact, in the aggregate, New York City's finances tend to swamp those of the largest 45, since it is the largest. In 1967, New York City expenditures represented 44 percent of the total of the largest 45 city expenditures. In 1977 (despite two years of retrenchment on the part of New York City), the city's total general expenditures still represented 45 percent of the total of the largest 45 cities. To correct for this influence and to permit more meaningful comparisons among cities, the analysis will largely use *unweighted* per capita averages, so that New York City's finances will account for only about 2 percent (one in 45) instead of 45 percent of the experience.

Table 1 documents, on a per capita basis, what has been the trend in outlays and receipts of the largest forty-five cities, using the unweighted

Table 1   Selected Financial Items for Forty-Five Largest Cities, Per
Capita Amounts and Rates of Growth, 1967-1977

	1967	1977	Annual Rate of Growth
General expenditures	$184.06	$550.64	11.6%
Current outlays	$141.99	$449.27	12.2%
Capital outlays	$ 42.07	$101.40	9.2%
General revenues	$179.63	$578.97	12.4%
Own-source revenues	$133.44	$244.89	6.3%
Intergovernmental payments	$ 46.19	$334.89	21.9%
Gross city debt outstanding[1]	$351.57	$655.49	6.4%
General long-term debt outstanding[2]	$226.61	$455.95	7.2%
State and local government price deflator (1970 = 100)	72.5	148.5	7.4%

SOURCES: U. S. Bureau of the Census, *Government Finances,* U. S. Department of Commerce.

[1] Includes general debt, utility debt, and short-term debt before any offsets.

[2] Includes only long-term debt issued by the city government for general government (nonutility) purposes.

city averages and showing annual rates of growth in the individual items. As shown, between 1967 and 1977 (the latest year for which complete comparable information is readily available), city per capita general expenditures and general revenues grew at an average annual rate of approximately 12 percent, from $184 in per capita expenditures in 1967 to $551 by 1977 in the case of general expenditures.

Reviewing the items listed in Table 1, it may be seen that city current outlays grew much more rapidly than capital outlays and, looking at the revenues, those received in the form of intergovernmental payments grew at more than three times the rate of these revenues collected locally from the city's own sources. Also, the largest forty-five cities during the decade under review saw both their gross debt and general government (nonutility) long-term debt rise at fairly modest annual rates of 6.4 and 7.2 percent, respectively.

As noted, several definitional and conceptual caveats need to be borne in mind when reviewing the city averages. But certain generalizations about city behavior are possible. First, growth in expenditures was caused to a large extent by the inflation in prices that cities had to pay for goods and services. As shown in Table 1, between 1967 and 1977, the state and local government price deflator (there is no separate deflator for city governments) rose from 72.5 to 148.5, an annual rate of inflation equal to 7.4 percent. As a result, real per capita expenditures and revenues (adjusted for the rate of price increase) rose at a rate of approximately 4.5 percent.

RELATIONSHIP TO STATE AND LOCAL SECTOR

Despite the fact that the decade saw relatively faster rates of growth in per capita expenditures and revenues in the forty-five largest cities in comparison to the state and local sector as a whole, the cities actually saw their relative importance in the aggregate of state and local finances decline. The total general revenues of the largest cities as a percentage of the total of all state and local government general revenues declined from 10.1 percent in 1967 to 8.4 percent in 1977. The reason for this, of course, was that the population of major cities was declining while that of the nation (and of other state and local governments) was growing.

Table 2 illustrates the major underlying trends in total population and per capita income in the forty-five cities, contrasting their performance and relative stature in relationship to the entire state and local sector. As noted, total population in the largest forty-five cities declined over the decade 1967-1977 at a rate of 0.2 percent a year (of course, some cities lost population much more rapidly, as will be discussed below). Perhaps of

Table 2   Population and Per Capita Personal Income of 45 Largest Cities Compared to National Figures, 1967-1977

	1967	*1977*	*Annual Rate of Growth*
Resident population (millions)			
45 cities total	38.4	37.5	−0.2%
U. S. total	197.5	216.9	0.9%
Cities as a percentage of U. S. average	19.5%	17.2%	—
Per capita personal income			
45 cities average	$2,790	$5,967	7.9%
U. S. average	$3,153	$7,051	8.4%
Cities as a percentage of U. S. average	88.5%	84.6%	—

greatest interest is the slower rate of growth in city personal income (7.9 percent versus 8.4 percent nationally). As a result, the per capita personal income on average in the forty-five largest cities slipped from 88 percent of the national figure in 1967 to an estimated 85 percent by 1977.

The consequences of increasing expenditures, own revenues, and outstanding debt in the face of declining personal income are reflected by the three percentage items shown in Table 3. First, for the forty-five largest cities, general expenditures as a percentage of personal income rose from 6.6 percent to 9.2 percent between 1967 and 1977, an annual rate of growth of 3.4 percent. This was considerably faster than the growth rate in total state and local expenditures as a percentage of personal income in the nation, which grew at an annual rate of only 1.8 percent during the decade. However, because cities were enjoying an appreciably higher rate of increase in intergovernmental aid, per capita revenues raised locally as a percentage of per capita personal income actually diminished during the decade for the largest forty-five cities, while it increased for the state and local sector as a whole (second item in Table 3).

The first item in Table 3 shows the changing burden of gross debt for both the largest forty-five cities and for the entire state and local sector as measured by per capita debt outstanding as a percentage of personal

Table 3   Per Capita General Expenditures, Own Revenues, and Debt
as a Percentage of Personal Income, 45 Largest Cities and
Overall State and Local Sector, 1967-1977

	1967	1977	Annual Rate of Growth
General expenditure as a percentage of personal income:			
45 cities	6.6%	9.2%	3.4%
State and local sector	15.0%	18.0%	1.8%
Own revenue as a percentage of personal income:			
45 cities	4.8%	4.1%	−1.6%
State and local sector	12.2%	14.6%	1.8%
Gross debt outstanding as a percentage of personal income:			
45 cities	12.6%	11.0%	−1.3%
State and local sector	18.3%	16.9%	−0.8%

income. As may be seen, for the largest forty-five cities and for the entire sector, per capita debt to personal income declined; however, the burden of debt outstanding as a percentage of personal income dropped for the cities at a somewhat faster rate than for the state and local sector in the aggregate.

CHANGING REVENUE STRUCTURES

As indicated above, perhaps the most important development in the finances of the largest forty-five cities has not been the rate of growth in expenditures, but rather the revolution in the way in which cities have been financing them. Table 4 focuses on the changing composition of the sources of revenue, giving the percentage breakdown among the various sources.

The largest forty-five cities saw their reliance on general revenues raised from their own local sources drop from 74 percent of total revenues in 1967 to approximately 58 percent by 1977. The largest decline came in the property tax, the proportionate share of which fell from 36 percent to 23 percent of total general revenues during the decade. The slack, of course, was picked up by the growth in intergovernmental payments. And within the intergovernmental category, the most impressive growth was found in federal aid. In 1967, federal aid payments represented 4.7 percent of total general revenues; ten years later, its share was more than 21 percent.

Cities have been financing the growth in their expenditures through sources of funds other than those raised locally. Moreover, reflecting on

Table 4   Percentage Composition of General Revenues: 45 Largest Cities, 1967-1977

	1967	1977
General Revenues	100.0%	100.0%
Own sources	74.3	57.7
Property tax	36.2	22.7
Other taxes	24.9	23.2
Charges and fees	13.2	11.8
Intergovernmental	25.7	42.3
State	18.6	19.3
Federal	4.7	21.1
Local	2.4	1.9

trends of indebtedness, it is clear that cities on average have been using other financing sources, rather than relying more on the capital markets. In fact, own-source revenues and debt have both declined as a percentage of personal income, even in cities that lag considerably behind the national average in personal income. The most interesting conclusion, aside from any speculation on the necessity and desirability of such growth in intergovernmental payments, is that the fiscal fortunes of cities have become intertwined progressively with those of the states and, to a great extent, the federal government.

A source of fiscal uncertainty is the impact of the growing dependency on federal and state assistance payments. These can be of particular importance to city finance because so much of the money flows directly or indirectly (via the state, in the case of some federal grant money) through the city's financial structure. The problem is what this increasing dependency on outside sources will mean in terms of a city's ability to cope with a withdrawal or slowing down of funds from these sources. Current budgeting pressures at both the federal and state level will soon provide evidence on this score.

For example, a highly visible reaction to the cities' fiscal problems has been the three Countercyclical Programs—Anti-Recessionary Fiscal Assistance (ARFA), Local Public Works (LPW), and Title VI of the Comprehensive Employment and Training Act, (CETA). Representing a belated federal response to the 1974-1975 recession, they combined to pump about $15 billion into the state and local sector between late 1976 and 1978. By and large, the Countercyclical Programs were targeted to high employment areas and favored cities that would rank high in terms of both socioeconomic and fiscal distress (Advisory Commission on Inter-governmental Relations, 1978: 15-27).

The sudden influx of federal assistance clearly brought fiscal relief to many governments, although not necessarily stimulating additional state and local spending—its nominal policy objective.[3] Besides substituting against locally financed expenditure, the assistance to some extent was used to restore run-down cash balances, and this constituted a form of saving, adding to the sector's surpluses. The restoration of city fiscal balances may have been inimical to the aims of the aid programs but, of course, it was viewed with relief by credit analysts who were becoming increasingly concerned about cash balances and liquidity. Better city financial conditions in 1977 contributed to an improvement in bond market reception of city securities and the units' ability to finance themselves.

The current reliance on federal (and state) assistance may prove to be a mixed blessing for cities. While it obviously has eased near-term fiscal burdens, it presents a new worry as dependency on external funds has grown. At present, the prospects for further growth in federal aid are bleak, and retrenchment in such assistance—which in many cases accounts for 40 to 50 percent of the city's revenues—may set off new crunches in some cities as they attempt to lower expenditures. The collateral threat of state and locally induced tax and expenditure limitations can also cause problems for local borrowers, depending on the severity and design of the limitation.

COSTS OF CITY BORROWING

In late 1975 and early 1976, several major city borrowers were either excluded from the tax-exempt market or forced to pay very high rates of interest to borrow. New York City and Yonkers got most of the headlines, but Buffalo, Detroit, Boston, Newark, and Philadelphia had worrisome episodes. Even relatively strong borrowers—such as Richmond, Virginia— suffered scrapes in a confused and jumpy market. A division between stronger and weaker borrowers—a two-tiered market for big-city general- obligation bonds—rapidly emerged. Several factors converged to cause these borrowing difficulties. For the greatest part, the difficulties were associated with investor concerns over the credit quality of cities and their ability and willingness to repay loans in the face of deteriorating fiscal and economic circumstances. Doubts about creditworthiness, while bad enough, were compounded by uncertainties regarding legal responsibilities in disclosing fiscal conditions and, in the final analysis, the enforceability of bondholders' rights of repayment against competing claims in the case of a default.

A vivid illustration of the tangible costs of such a decay in confidence is found in the large cost differentials that grew among the various grades of municipal bonds, reversing a decade-long trend of declining risk premia between the highest and lowest grades.

An examination of new-issue, general-obligation bond sales by those cities among the largest one-hundred in the country during the period 1976-1978 gives a summary of what happened to city borrowing costs in relationship to those in the rest of the municipal bond market. Table 5 presents, by Moody's rating category of the bonds sold, the average reoffering yield of twenty-year city general-obligation bonds as measured in basis points deviations from the *Bond Buyer* Twenty Bond Index during the week of the bond sale.[4] The period covered is from the first quarter of 1976, the peak of the crisis in the municipal bond market, through to the 1977 and 1978 market recovery. The final column in the table shows the

Table 5   City New Issue Bond Sales: Spread in Basis Points[1] Between Twenty-Year Reoffering Yield and Bond Buyer 20 Index: by Quarterly Averages 1976 I to 1977 IV and 1978 Semi-Annual Averages

| | Moody Rating | | | | |
Year/Quarter	Aaa	Aa	A	Baa	Baa-Aaa
1976 I	−94	−20	*	270	364
1976 II	−72	−31	22	231	303
1976 III	−82	−51	32	130	212
1976 IV	−89	−42	−25	*	*
1977 I	−52	−34	10	121	173
1977 II	−43	−24	3	128	171
1977 III	−50	−29	−17	*	*
1977 IV	−46	−29	− 7	95	141
1978 (First half)	−56	−32	− 6	27	83
1978 (Second half)	−62	−37	−38	56	118

SOURCE: Based on 148 general obligation bond sales of cities among largest 100 cities in the nation.

* = No observation

[1] Basis point equals one one-hundredth of a percentage point.

spread between the highest grade, "Aaa," and the lowest investment grade "Baa," also in basis points. Table 6 presents the *Bond Buyer* Twenty Bond Index for the same period for purpose of reference.

As may be seen in Table 5, the difference between the yields on new-issue city bonds of the highest (Aaa) and the lowest ratings (Baa) was an astronomical 364 basis points in the first quarter of 1976. By the third quarter of 1976, the spread between Aaa and Baa new-issue city bonds began to shrink but was still over 200 basis points. The shrinkage was evident at both ends of the credit spectrum: the interest advantage of the highest grades diminished, as did the added costs of the lower grades, when compared to the overall market average (See Table 6). By 1977, the market began a relatively smooth glide into smaller but still significant spreads among the grades.

The experiences of 1975 and 1976 dramatized the costs of suspect credit quality and having a low bond rating. As Table 5 shows, units with the highest rating benefited—at least relatively—from the "flight to quality," while the lower grades suffered. Having a low bond rating was highly correlated to paying more money to borrow.[5]

Table 6   Bond Buyer Twenty Bond Index Quarterly Averages,
             1976-1978

Year/Quarter	Bond Buyer 20 Index (percentage)
1976 I	7.37
1976 II	6.96
1976 III	6.76
1976 IV	6.63
1977 I	6.16
1977 II	5.88
1977 III	5.69
1977 IV	5.58
1978 I	5.57
1978 II	5.64
1978 III	6.03
1978 IV	6.16

NOTE: Quarterly averages based on weekly averages falling within respective quarters.

But the interest cost was not the only factor; a low rating and the threat of loss of access to credit has manifold political and economic repercussions. Threats of default or bankruptcy demoralize and frighten and conjure up all sorts of visions of stopping city services and civil unrest. It's not only the bondholders that abhor that kind of uncertainty.

TRENDS IN CITY BOND RATINGS

The turmoil of the municipal bond market in the mid-1970s and the well-advertised misery of certain cities tends to associate the big-city credits generally with the difficulties of certain, mainly northeastern, cities. However, the fact is that there has generally been an upward trend in the ratings of the major cities in the past decade. Unfortunately, the popular perception of the difficulties of the northeastern cities is not misplaced. The upgrading in ratings has shown a heavy regional orientation, with the cities in the West and—to a lesser extent—in the South enjoying the upgradings.

Table 7 presents a description of the distribution of Moody's ratings and changes in ratings of general obligation bonds of the largest forty-five cities for the thirteen-year period 1965 to 1978. Only the major rating categories are shown; the subcategories A1 and Baa 1 are grouped in the respective major category (i.e., A1 is assigned to A, etc.). The distribution of ratings in effect in 1965 for the cities can be read across the bottom of the table; that for 1978 may be read in the righthand stub of the table.

As may be seen in Table 7, the city ratings were evenly clustered in 1965 around the A and Aa categories. However, over the next thirteen years, the number of Aaa and Aa ratings given to city bonds increased, while the number in the lower grades also increased but on a smaller scale.

There was a good deal of movement by the cities among the rating categories. The figures lying above and below the boxed diagonal in Table 7 gives the number of credits rising or falling, respectively, and show from which rating in 1965 to which rating in 1978 the movment took place. For example, of the nineteen borrowers rated Aa in 1965, eleven retained that rating in 1978, five had moved up to Aaa, two dropped to Baa (St. Louis and Buffalo), and one (Cleveland) sank all the way to B.[6]

Looking at the overall totals, only twenty of the forty-five city borrowers (44 percent) retained the same rating during the interval 1965 to 1978. Eighteen borrowers were upgraded (40 percent) and seven were downgraded (16 percent) during this period. Not shown in Table 7, but of some interest, is the fact that fifteen rating changes—ten of the upgradings and five of the downgradings—occurred between 1972 and 1978. Thus, there was a pronounced tendency to upgrade city credits, despite the problems of the mid-1970s.

The changes in ratings had a strong regional flavor to them, as is illustrated in Table 8. The heavy concentration of downgradings occurred in the northeastern quadrant of the nation. Conversely, the South and

Table 7   Ratings and Rating Changes of 45 Largest Cities' General Obligation Debt; 1965-1978 (Moody's Ratings)

	Aaa	Aa	A	Baa	Ba-B	Total	
Aaa	3	5	1			9	
Aa		11	11			22	
A			4	1		5	1978
Baa		2	3	2		7	Ratings
Ba-B		1	1		0	2	
	3	19	20	3	0	45	

1965   Ratings

NOTE: Moody's Investor Service Rating in effect as of December 1965 and December 1978. Ratings are grouped by major categories (i.e, A1 and Baa1 are grouped with A and Baa, respectively).

Table 8   Direction of Changes in General Obligation Bond Ratings
of 45 Largest Cities, 1965-1978

Region	Upgraded	Unchanged	Downgraded	Total Ratings
Northeast	0	1	5	6
Midwest	4	8	2	14
South	6	8	0	14
West	8	3	0	11
	18	20	7	45

West have seen their credit ratings improve. Of the eighteen upgradings,
eight occurred in the West (out of a total of eleven cities), six in the South
(out of fourteen city credits), and four in the Midwest (out of fourteen
cities). At the same time, the Northeast saw five of its six big-city credits
go down; the only one that remained unchanged (Boston) was already
marginal ("Baa") in terms of its credit quality.

Table 9 gives a listing of the individual cities and the direction of their
rating change between December 1965 and December 1978.

CITY ECONOMIC AND FINANCIAL CONDITIONS AND RATINGS

Several studies have identified specific cities that are suffering from a
host of long-term social, economic, and fiscal problems.[7] Numerous
factors have been selected which reflect these difficulties, but the substance of analysis appears to be that older, formerly heavily industrial
areas have suffered reductions in population, loss of jobs, slow growth in
per capita income and property values, and a loss of economic activity,
wealth, and people to the surrounding suburban areas.

Municipal credit ratings, as conferred by the major rating agencies, are
determined by a complex of factors that measure both current and future
fiscal performance, and economic and demographic trends. Thus, ratings
should generally mesh with many of the concerns of the urban expert or
policy maker, who also attempts to establish indices of urban economic
and fiscal conditions, and to assess the prospects of cities in coping with
changing economic, social, and political circumstances. As discussed above,
credit ratings are not merely of academic interest: the premiums charged
those city borrowers with low credit ratings increased drastically in the

Table 9 Changes in Moody's Ratings on City General Obligation Bonds; 1975-1978: A Comparison

Rating Upgraded		Rating Unchanged		Rating Downgraded	
Phoenix, AZ	A → Aa	Long Beach, CA	Aa → Aa	St. Louis, MO	Aa → Baa1
Los Angeles, CA	Aa → Aaa	Oakland, CA	Aa → Aa	Newark, NJ	A → Baa
San Diego, CA	A → Aa	Denver, CO	Aa → Aa	Buffalo, NY	Aa → Baa
San Francisco, CA	Aa → Aaa	Miami, FL	A → A1	New York, NY	A → B
San Jose, CA	A → Aa	Atlanta, GA	Aa → Aa	Cleveland, OH[1]	Aa → B
Jacksonville, FL	Baa → Aa	Louisville, KY	Aa → Aa	Philadelphia, PA	A → Baa
Honolulu, HI	A → Aa	New Orleans, LA	A → A	Pittsburgh, PA	A → Baa1
Chicago, IL[1]	A → Aa	Baltimore, MD	A → A1		
Indianapolis, IN	Aa → Aaaa	Boston, MA	Baa → Baa		
Oklahoma City, OK	A → Aa	Detroit, MI	Baa → Baa		
Tulsa, OK	A → Aa	Minneapolis, MN	Aaa → Aaa		
Portland, OR	Aa → Aaa	Kansas City, MO	Aa → Aa		
Dallas, TX	Aa → Aaa	Omaha, NB	Aaa → Aaa		
Fort Worth, TX	A → Aa	Cincinnati, OH	Aa → Aa		
Houston, TX	A → Aaa	Columbus, OH	Aa → Aa		
San Antonio, TX	A → Aa	Toledo, OH	Aa → Aa		
Norfolk, VA	A → Aa	Memphis, TN	Aa → Aa		
Seattle, WA	A → Aa	Nashville-Davidson, TN	Aa → Aa		
		El Paso, TX	A → A1		
		Milwaukee, WI	Aaa → Aaa		

1. Cleveland was downgraded by Moody's to Caa in 1979. Chicago was lowered to A in 1979.

mid-1970s, and for many large cities, borrowing was difficult and expensive.

Tables 10 and 11 display the largest forty-five cities, grouped by rating category, arrayed against ten economic, demographic, and fiscal indicators that have been widely used to measure city fiscal and economic condition. Shown for each of the characteristics in Table 6 are the group means and the associated standard deviations (shown in parentheses).[8] Table 11 takes the same categories and gives the high and low observed values within each rating category, with the associated cities shown in parentheses.

The first bracket in Table 11 focuses on economic and population factors, containing comparative data on personal income, population changes, city-suburban income disparity, job growth, unemployment rate, and a composite index of urban conditions. The values show a fairly regular association between the mean value of the characteristics of a jurisdiction's economic condition and ratings: the lower the rating category, the weaker the performance of the cities as measured by the indicators.

The relationships among the group averages, however, are not always perfect. The overlapping values of the ranges of the rating groups and the standard deviations shown in Tables 10 and 11 tell us that the rating-group averages are not necessarily tight. There is considerable room for a city that may not do well in one respect to "buck the averages" and be classed in a higher rating category. For example, recent population loss, which has been associated with economic deterioration and fiscal stress, does not show a very strong relationship with rating category.

The second bracket of indicators in Tables 10 and 11 deals more directly with the revenue and debt burdens of the city and city area. As may be seen, the relationships among the group means are fairly consistent: in the case of city government tax (own-revenue effort and debt burden), the Aaa-rated cities show only half the effort and burden exhibited by those cities with ratings of Baa or below.

For example, taking the first item in Table 10, per capita personal income for the Aaa cities averaged $6,563 in 1977, which was greater than the $5,232 average for Baa and lower cities. The group averages for the Aa and A cities fall in the range between the two. In Table 11, the cities in each rating category with the high and low value are given for each characteristic. For example, the range in Aaa cities is from a high value of $7,506 (San Francisco) to a low value of $5,834 (Milwaukee). For Baa and below cities, it is from $6,158 (New York City) to $4,082 (Newark).

Note that the sign and direction of the values as they might be expected to correlate with credit quality depend on the variable in question. For

Table 10   Relation of Selected Factors to Rating Categories: Average
Values for Largest 45 Cities as Classified by Moody's 1978
Rating on City General Obligation Bonds
(standard deviations in parentheses)

Economic and Demographic Items	City G. O. Rating:			Baa or below
	Aaa	Aa	A	
Per capita personal income (1977)[1]	$6,563 (512)	$6,090 (664)	$5,277 (558)	$5,232 (605)
Change in population (1970-75) (annual percentage change)	− .5 (1.5)	− .2 (1.6)	− .1 (2.1)	− 2.0 (.8)
Per capita income disparity (city as % of surburban income)[2]	106.1 (9.5)	103.1 (18.2)	88.4 (10.6)	87.6 (16.5)
Unemployment rate (1977) (percentage rate)	7.3 (2.1)	7.5 (1.7)	9.9 (2.0)	11.3 (3.5)
Employment growth (1970-77) (percentage change)	18.3 (14.2)	22.4 (21.8)	14.9 (15.1)	− 1.3 (6.4)
Urban conditions index[3]	103.7 (55.8)	96.0 (59.0)	137.8 (109.3)	262.3 (56.7)
Fiscal Items				
City tax effort (1977)[4] (own revenue as a % of personal income)	4.4 (2.1)	5.0 (2.2)	5.0 (2.1)	9.2 (4.8)
City debt burden (1977)[5] (general debt as a % of personal income)	5.9 (2.6)	7.4 (4.0)	6.8 (2.7)	10.9 (5.6)
Overall local tax effort (1976)[6] (own revenue as a % of personal income)	10.0 (2.1)	9.5 (2.6)	8.9 (2.0)	13.5 (3.4)
Overall local debt burden (1976)[7] (general debt as a % of personal income)	11.8 (3.9)	13.8 (7.4)	13.9 (2.9)	17.1 (5.8)
(Number of cities)	(9)	(22)	(5)	(9)

[1] Author's estimates based on historical relationship of city per capita personal income to national personal income. (The most recently available official personal income and population estimates for cities are for 1975.)

[2] City per capita personal income as a percentage of per capita personal income in the remainder of the city's metropolitan area estimated as of 1973. Advisory Commission on Intergovernmental Relations, *Trends in Metropolitan America* (1977).

[3] Consists of housing stock age, percentage poverty population, and rate of population change. See Richard Nathan, Paul Dommel, and James Fossett, Testimony before the Joint Economic Committee, U.S. Congress, July 28, 1977.

[4] City government per capita revenues collected from own sources (includes taxes, charges, and fees) divided by city per capita personal income.

continued

notes to Table 10 continued

[5]City government per capita general (nonutility) debt divided by city per capita personal income.

[6]Own-source per capita revenues collected in 1976 by all local general governments (including the city government) that overlap the city's geographic area (includes revenues of counties, school districts, and other local districts, but excludes local utilities) divided by city per capita personal income.

[7]Per capita general (nonutility) debt of all local units overlapping city area (including city government) divided by city per capita personal income.

example, Aaa cities show a higher per capita income in relationship to their suburbs (106 percent) than Baa cities, where city income averages only 88 percent of suburban income. This result supports the thesis that the stronger credits have been able to retain a wealthier citizenry within their boundaries, whereas weaker credits have suffered from a flight to the suburbs. Also, the higher-rated cities show higher growth in jobs and enjoy lower Urban Conditions Index scores (the lower the score, the better the city's conditions as defined by the index).[9]

Trying to gauge effort and burden by looking only at the city government's finances may not be sufficient. As was discussed in the first essay of this series, city governments are typically only one of the local governments providing services, raising taxes, and incurring debt within the city's geographic area. Overlapping units, such as counties and school districts, also add to the revenue and debt burdens of the city's inhabitants. Thus, a broader measure of tax effort and debt burden might take into account the revenues and debts of these overlapping jurisdictions. This can be approximated by the ratios of the per capita own revenues and debt of the city and all other local governments overlapping the city area to the per capita income of city residents.[10]

Adding the revenue and debt burdens of overlapping governments tends to somewhat narrow the differences between the group means. This result implies that cities that have higher ratings tend to be in areas where local taxes and debt burdens are shared with other forms of local government (such as counties, independent school districts, or special districts), whereas lower-rated cities tend to have the burden more concentrated on the city government itself.

More rigorous and quantitative comparisons between rating categories and assorted characteristics are possible. But Tables 10 and 11 illustrate that clusters of stronger and weaker performance tend to be grouped by rating across a broad range of economic, demographic, and fiscal characteristics. Cities that display characteristic values consistently at the lower or upper ranges for a rating category's characteristic would appear to be

Table 11 Relation of Selected Factors to Rating Categories: High (H) and Low (L) Values for Factors and Associated City in Rating Category for Largest 45 Cities Classified by Moody's 1978 Rating of City General Obligation Bonds (Cities Shown in Parentheses)

Economic and Demographic Items	High/Low	City G.O. Rating			
		Aaa	Aa	A	Baa or Below
Per capita personal income (1977)	H	$7560 (San Francisco)	7408 (Seattle)	5915 (Jacksonville)	6158 (New York)
	L	5834 (Milwaukee)	4718 (San Antonio)	4410 (El Paso)	4082 (Newark)
Change in population (1970-1975) (annual percentage change)	H	2.5 (Houston)	3.7 (San Jose)	3.3 (El Paso)	-.6 (Boston)
	L	-2.6 (Minneapolis)	-2.5 (Atlanta)	-1.5 (Baltimore)	-3.0 (Cleveland)
Per capita income disparity (city as % of suburban income)	H	115 (Houston/Dallas)	140 (Honolulu)	100 (Jacksonville)	122 (Buffalo)
	L	85 (Milwaukee)	70 (Cincinnati)	73 (Baltimore)	70 (Cleveland)
Unemployment rate (1977) (percentage rate)	H	10.3 (San Francisco)	12.8 (Oakland)	12.1 (El Paso)	14.8 (Newark)
	L	4.3 (Dallas)	4.9 (Nashville)	6.0 (Jacksonville)	8.5 (Boston)
Employment growth (1970-1977) (percentage rate)	H	49.4 (Houston/Dallas)	107.6 (Honolulu)	34.3 (El Paso)	9.3 (Boston)
	L	6.5 (Los Angeles)	3.7 (Chicago)	1.9 (New Orleans)	-10.7 (St. Louis)

(continued)

Table 11 (continued)

Economic and Demographic Items	High/Low	City G.O. Rating			
		Aaa	Aa	A	Baa or Below
Urban conditions index	H	188 (San Francisco)	226 (Cincinnati)	224 (Baltimore)	351 (St. Louis)
	L	37 (Houston)	10 (San Jose)	60 (Jacksonville)	180 (New York)
City tax effort (own revenue as a % of personal income)	H	9.8 (San Francisco)	12.5 (Cincinnati)	8.6 (Baltimore)	16.7 (New York)
	L	2.9 (Omaha)	2.7 (San Antonio)	3.3 (El Paso)	3.5 (Pittsburgh)
City debt burden (general debt as a % of personal income)	H	9.7 (San Francisco)	20.1 (Atlanta)	9.4 (Baltimore)	23.8 (New York)
	L	1.2 (Portland)	2.4 (San Diego)	2.4 (El Paso)	4.9 (Pittsburgh)
Overall local tax effort (own revenue as a % of personal income)	H	14.7 (San Francisco)	14.9 (Atlanta)	12.0 (Minneapolis)	19.0 (New York)
	L	7.9 (Houston)	6.3 (Oklahoma City)	6.9 (Jacksonville)	8.0 (Pittsburgh)
Overall local debt burden (general debt as a % of personal income)	H	18.2 (Minneapolis)	35.1 (Norfolk)	17.5 (New Orleans)	29.2 (New York)
	L	5.9 (Los Angeles)	4.8 (Honolulu)	10.6 (Jacksonville)	10.1 (Buffalo)

NOTE: For explanation of items, see Table 6.

candidates for climbing up or dropping down in rating. For example, inspection of the underlying data shows that St. Louis, which downgraded from A to Baa in 1978, fell below the A rating group mean in nine of the ten characteristics in Table 10 and below the Baa group mean in seven of the items.[11]

CONCLUSION

This essay has first reviewed the changing fiscal structures of cities during the decade of the 1970s and then turned to an examination of their credit quality, particularly as revealed by the ratings on their general-obligation bonds. The most salient fact is that over the 1970s, cities became much more dependent on intergovernmental payments—especially those emanating from the federal government. Conversely, less reliance was placed on those revenues raised from their own sources and upon borrowing than had previously been the case.

While the shift to outside sources of revenue meant fiscal relief to cities, it also introduced elements of uncertainty: What would happen when the outside aid was withdrawn? That question appeared to be in the process of being answered by the end of the 1970s, with the withdrawal of much federal aid to cities in the offing.

Generalizations about cities are to be made cautiously, however. Clearly, the decade of the 1970s brought greater sensitivity to differences among cities. The lines of demarcation between weak and strong cities are in no way better revealed than by examining the trends in their credit ratings. Over the span 1967 to 1978, city credits became divided into two sets: those that improved their credit standing and those that saw their bond market acceptance slip relative to that accorded to other cities. The importance of bond ratings was vividly demonstrated in the mid-1970s, when those cities with weak credits (and, usually, heavy dependency on borrowing) were forced to pay very high rates of interest to meet the risk premium that investors demanded in making loans to them.

Credit ratings as single-dimensional indicators of city fiscal condition show high degrees of association with other indicators of city condition. Such correlation is of more than academic interest, since credit ratings have large economic and political impacts on governments. It is not surprising that investors are evidently concerned about those conditions that constitute the underlying circumstances of city governments. Loss of population, low incomes, loss of business to the suburbs, and assorted other indicators of troubled cities are also indicative of a worrisome and weak fiscal situation—if not immediately, then at some time in the future.

For these reasons, the student of city conditions is advised to keep a sharp eye on credit ratings, which give an educated estimate of a city's prospects and convey more information than their innocuous letter grades alone would seem to imply.

NOTES

1. For purposes of the analysis, the forty-five largest cities are defined in terms of population as of 1975. The District of Columbia has been excluded because of its unique city-state characteristics. A list of cities is given in the Appendix.

2. For example, citizens of Cleveland, Ohio receive local services from the city, Cuyahoga County, and an independent school district—just to mention the major forms of local governments that overlap the city area. If we take only these three governments into account, the city government accounts for about 53 percent of the total local government expenditures within the city's boundaries, the Cuyahoga County government for 10 percent (assuming County expenditures are equal on a per capita basis for all county residents, including those who live in Cleveland), and the Cleveland school districts for 37 percent, made up by units in the city area.

3. Studies of CETA, ARFA, and LPW all show fairly high levels of substitution of federal funds for local funds. See Robert Reischauer (1978).

4. A basis point is equal to one one-hundredth of a percentage point (0.01%). For a detailed examination of municipal bond credit ratings, see John Petersen (1974).

5. To borrow one million dollars at a 9 percent rate of interest a year instead of 6 percent a year (300 basis points more) with a twenty-year "level debt service" maturity schedule costs a city $101,000 a year instead of $87,000 in debt service. Such a cost-of-capital effect is hardly enough to drive a city into poor financial shape. The nub of the problem is that it signals the possible, perhaps imminent, cutting off of access to the bond market. The latter event can have dire financial ramifications if the city has no other way to raise cash to pay its bills and wages.

6. Subsequently, Cleveland was reduced by Moody's to a Caa rating in early 1979 by virtue of its default.

7. Useful summaries are found in U.S. Treasury (1978) and U.S. House of Representatives (1978).

8. Standard deviation is a statistical measure which means that approximately two-thirds of a large number of observations will fall within a range of values bounded by the mean minus the standard deviation and plus the standard deviation. A large standard deviation relative to a given value of a group mean indicates that the observations in the group are not tightly grouped (or highly dispersed) when classified by the particular characteristic in question.

9. The Urban Conditions Index is a composite index formed from population change, age of housing stock, and percentage of population below the poverty level. See the notes to Table 10.

10. The assumption is that revenues and debts can be prorated on a population basis among the underlying jurisdictions.

11. Below in this sense means had values in the direction expected of a lower-rated credit (i.e., higher unemployment, greater population loss, etc.).

REFERENCES

Advisory Commission on Intergovernmental Relations (1978) Countercyclical Aid and Economic Stabilization. Washington, DC: Government Printing Office.

PETERSEN, J. (1974) The Rating Game. New York: Twentieth Century Fund.

REISCHAUER, R. (1978) "The economy, the federal budget, and the prospects for urban aid, in The Fiscal Outlook for Cities. Syracuse, NY: Syracuse University Press.

U.S. House of Representatives, Subcommittee on the City (1978) City Need and the Responsiveness of Federal Grants Programs. Washington, DC: Government Printing Office.

U.S. Treasury (1978) Report on the Fiscal Impact of the Economic Stimulus Package on 48 Large Urban Governments. Washington, DC: Government Printing Office.

PART III

MANAGING RETRENCHMENT

9

MISPERCEIVING PUBLIC EXPENDITURE:

FEELINGS ABOUT "CUTS"

R I C H A R D   R O S E

Centre for the Study of Public Policy
University of Strathclyde

> *When told that Margaret Fuller had declared, "I accept the universe," Thomas Carlyle responded,*
> *"By God, she'd better."*

Need what goes up come down? This is the chief question about public expenditure today. If public spending were like an elevator (or even like unemployment figures), we would expect it to be coming down as often as it goes up. But a cyclical metaphor is peculiarly inappropriate for public expenditure, since it has been going up and up for decades in absolute terms and as a proportion of the national product in nearly every Western nation. As public expenditure has risen, so too theories have multiplied, purporting to account for the growth of government spending (see Tarschys, 1975).

AUTHOR'S NOTE: *In preparing this article, I was aided by Richard Parry's admirable skill with Treasury statistics, and also appreciated Edward C. Page's comments on an earlier draft of the manuscript. I was assisted by a Ford Foundation Grant for Study of Intergovernmental Relations.*

Today, "cuts" in public expenditure are a prominent concern within every major Western political system. Welfare state proponents often devote as much attention to "fighting cuts" as conservatives opposed to the growth of government spend in advocating "cuts." Confusion has been the result of this controversy, for welfare lobbies speak as if cuts occur frequently, and conservatives as if public spending continues to increase greatly. The confusion can even affect discussions among experienced public officials. For example, President Ford had to correct one of his former assistant directors of the Office of Management and Budget in a public discussion about whether the Ford Administration sought cuts in social security spending (American Enterprise Institute, 1980: 15):

> We did not suggest cuts. We recommended a lower ceiling on the escalation costs under the cost of living. In other words, instead of the 7 per cent increase in social security and others, we recommended a ceiling of 5½ percent. We were accused of cutting social security benefits, but that was inaccurate. We only reduced the rate of increase.

When Presidents and senior budget advisors speak at cross purposes about public expenditure, it is time to ask: what *is* actually happening to public expenditure today?

The purpose of this essay is to examine clearly and systematically the multiple meanings of "cuts." The word "cuts" appears in quotation marks here because changes in political mood need not be matched by a change in public expenditure. So great is the potential for misperceiving public expenditure that two political commentators, given full budget details, may disagree about whether a "cut" has occurred. The first two sections concentrate attention upon the diverse uses of the term "cuts," and particularly distinguish between definitions that derive from contrasting economic criteria and those that are rooted in psychological expectations. The third section reviews the ideological and material sources of anxiety about public expenditure in today's relatively turbulent political economy. The concluding section considers the dynamics of adapting public expenditure expectations, replacing anxiety about "cuts" with a sense of reprieve from possible worse events.

Evidence to illustrate the analysis is drawn from both American and British experience; there are sufficient differences between the two countries so that commonalities will probably reflect generic problems of political economy. In turn, this implies that the resolution of these difficulties is also to be found in measures that are not specific to one country, but common to most Western nations.

Of course, public expenditure is not the only important issue in the management of a political economy. From a broad macroeconomic perspective, budgeting is but a means to other ends, or a byproduct of decisions concerning economic growth, inflation, unemployment, and international terms of trade. But public expenditure can be an important means of influencing these macroeconomic goals. When public expenditure is equivalent to one-third to one-half of the Gross National Product, public officials have the opportunity and challenge to control their own spending as an important element in managing the whole of a nation's economy.

I. TAKING THE MEASURE OF "CUTS"

Whether public spending is said to be rising or falling is a *matter of definition, not fact.* If spending is defined in current-money terms, as is done in the presentation of the United States federal budget, then any cuts will be atypical as long as inflation forces a substantial annual increase in the costs of providing the same (or even a reduced) level of services for a given program. If public expenditure is measured in constant-value units, as is done in the British Treasury's public expenditure documents, then public spending will appear to fall whenever the government buys less in volume terms, even though the total annual outlay in current money terms may be up by as much as 15 or 20 percent.

The cash value of the difference between current-money and constant-money definitions of public expenditure varies with the scale of inflation. If there were no inflation in the price of public-sector goods and services in a given year, then the current-money and constant-value change in public spending would be identical. But the greater the level of inflation, the greater the difference between the two measures. For example, in fiscal year 1979, the United States Federal budget registered a 9.5 percent *increase* of $42.9 billion in current-money terms from the previous year, *and* a 2.2 *decrease* in terms of constant-value dollars (U.S. Department of the Treasury, 1980: 613). Similarly, in Great Britain in fiscal year 1977-78, public expenditure showed an increase of £4.0 billion (7.2 percent) in current-money terms and a decrease of £4.9 billion (7.0 percent) in constant-value terms (H. M. Treasury, 1980: Tables 5.3 and 5.12).

The structural change in the rate of inflation in the 1970s has resulted in a widening gap between these two different methods of assessing public expenditure. When inflation was running at only 1 or 2 percent a year, as was often the case in the 1950s, then a current-value increase in public spending would imply an actual increase in the volume of goods and services provided by government. In the 1960s, public expenditure in current-money terms tended to grow faster for two reasons: an accelerating rate of public spending in constant-money terms, and also an accelerating rate of inflation. By the 1970s, the rate of annual increase in public spending has decelerated slightly—but rates of inflation accelerated. In consequence, the bulk of the increase in public spending now reflects the effects of inflation.

Since the great bulk of public spending is devoted to continuing programs, and popular evaluations of these programs are likely to be made in terms of a "then and now" time span extending over a number of years, it is also important to recognize that the cumulative disparity between current-money and constant-value appreciations of public expenditure is even greater. For example, from 1959 to 1969, U.S. federal public spending rose exactly 100 percent in current-money terms and 45 percent in constant-value terms. In Britain, public spending rose by 119 percent in current-money terms and 42 percent in constant-value terms. In both countries, upward of half of the total increase in public spending during the 1959-69 decade was an actual increase in the volume of spending on public policies (see Figure 1).

By contrast, the great bulk of increased public spending in current money terms in the 1970s has been devoted to meeting the costs of inflation. In Britain, public spending has risen 347 percent in current-money terms, as against an increase of 29 percent in constant-money terms. In other words, only seven pence of each extra pound spent has augmented spending on the volume of public policies. In the United States, federal spending rose by 167 percent in current-money terms, as against an increase of 25 percent in constant-money terms. In short, only 13 cents in every extra dollar spent was actually devoted to increasing the volume of spending on the volume of public policies (see Figure 1).

In a field subject to political controversy, there is no "agreed" (let alone "right") way to evaluate changes in public expenditure. Government publications prepared by civil servants can use both current-money and constant-value figures in calculations. Politicians will select figures for their convenience, and having two different sets of calculations (especially if they appear to show movements in conflicting directions) widens the room for maneuver in partisan debate. Even the same person can take different views at different times. For example, Sir Richard Clarke, a Treasury official responsible for converting British public-expenditure analysis to constant-value pounds, subsequently concluded that it was necessary to return to thinking about "actual" money, "real" money having come to refer to something that no longer existed, namely, a pound of constant

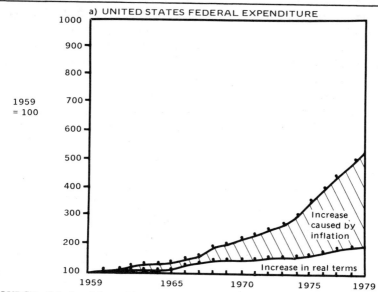

SOURCE: Calculated from *The Budget of the United States* (Washington: Govern ment Printing Office, 1980), Table 22, p. 613.

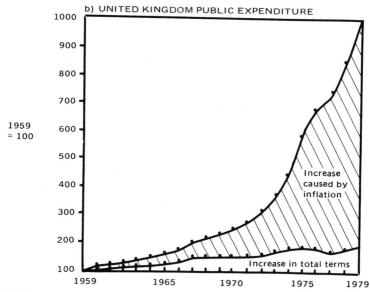

SOURCE: Calculated from *Economic Trends Annual Supplement 1980 edition* (London: HMSO, 1980), p. 12 and p. 143; *Economic Trends* No. 317 (March 1980) p. 8 and p. 56. (Public Expenditures other than general government final consump- tion inflated to 1975. Prices using index of total domestic expenditure.)

Figure 1   Expenditure in Current and Constant Prices, 1959-1979

value (Clarke, 1973: 159). In 1976, the British Labour government switched emphasis from monitoring public expenditure in constant-value pounds to cash limits upon current money spending in order to prevent increased public expenditure from further fueling inflation, then running at a rate of above 20 percent per annum.

Analytically, describing public expenditure in terms of current money values emphasizes *cost inputs,* the actual amount of revenue that must be raised by taxes, borrowing, or other sources in order to finance the total repertoire of government programs. While a macroeconomist may dismiss this as a minor technical difficulty, financial officials concerned with managing the cash flow of government must look to the revenue as well as the spending measures of government. Moreover, the attention given the public-sector borrowing requirement by monetary economists makes revenue shortfalls important influences upon inflation. By contrast, the use of constant-value units to evaluate public expenditure emphasizes the *volume of outputs* of government, that is, the goods and services actually bought by the money that government spends. While a budget official may put money first, a macroeconomist may be concerned with the total resources of society, and in maintaining government activities in volume terms as a stimulus to an economy. It is certain that the staffs of spending agencies are concerned with maintaining (or increasing) the volume of their activities, whatever the nominal cost in current-money terms.

Analytic differences mirror left-right political differences. Constant-value analysis of public expenditure reinforces the bias of American liberals and British socialists in favor of public expenditure. Those who believe that the goods and services produced by government are "good" goods will not want to see a decline in the total volume of government outputs. By contrast, Republicans and Conservatives who think that government controls too much of the economy will not want to see spending rising, for this will require increased taxes and/or borrowing. When public expenditure is under pressure, conservatives can attack rises in current spending, and their opponents attack a fall in the volume of policy outputs. Both can be statistically correct, because each will invoke a different measure of change in public expenditure.

Logically, public expenditure could change in any of four different ways, when measured in terms of both current and constant. Only one of these possibilities would be a "cut without qualification" and only one an unqualified "actual increase" (see Figure 2).

1. *Actual increases* have been the norm for public spending in every major Western country for the past quarter-century. In the affluent 1950s and 1960s, the whole of this increase and then some could easily be paid

Constant-Value Spending

	Up Actual increase	Down Spending squeeze
	Deflationary windfall	Cut without qualification

Current-Value
Spending

Up
Down

Figure 2   Logical Alternatives for Change in Public Expenditure

by the fiscal dividend of economic growth. In the 1970s, economic growth has decelerated, and in some years the economy actually contracted, but public expenditure has still tended to rise in volume terms as well as current cash, not so much from the conscious adoption of new policies as from increased spending for such open-ended entitlements as unemployment benefits or education. The rate of actual increase in spending on the volume of policy outputs has slowed down, but the direction is still upward.

2. *Cuts without qualification* occur as and when public spending decreases in both current- *and* constant-money terms. This is not systematically practicable in an inflationary era unless the volume of spending on public policy is reduced by one-third or more in a few years' time. In turn, this could not occur without repealing statutes mandating "uncontrollable" expenditure on such things as old-age pensions, compulsory education, or health care. In practice, cuts without qualification require a period of stable prices and a government anxious to keep spending down. Even when public expenditure is disaggregated into a variety of policy areas where cuts might be expected in keeping with party changes in government (e.g., defense and social welfare), cuts without qualification are the exception rather than the rule.

3. *A spending squeeze* occurs when public spending increases in current-money terms but decreases in terms of constant-value money. A squeeze reflects a nominal victory by spending departments in a period of fiscal stringency: the budget is increased. But it also represents a victory for budget officials, since the increase is less than the amount required if spending on public policies is to keep pace with inflation. In a period of high inflation and fiscal difficulties such as the 1970s, it would be

expected that government could easily resort to a spending squeeze to reconcile conflicting commitments to expanding public policies, and to a "tough" line on controlling public expenditure.

4. In theory, government could receive a *deflationary windfall* if deflation brought about a general price reduction, yet reduced the actual volume of spending on public programs by less than the overall fall in the price level. But an actual drop in the retail price index is an abnormal event in postwar Britain or America: it has not fallen in Britain since 1959, in the United States since 1955.

Empirically, public spending has in aggregate registered an actual increase for most of the past twenty years in both Britain and the United States. The British experience shows virtually no tendency for public spending to be squeezed; even during the difficulties of the 1970s, it happened only twice. The same is true of federal spending in the United States: it has actually increased in seven of ten years from 1969-1979, the same rate and direction of change as in the 1959-1969 period.

Whichever criterion is used—current or constant money or both—current political and academic discussion of "cuts" in public expenditure is inconsistent with aggregate evidence. In the 1970s as in the 1960s, actual spending increases were the norm in Britain and America, and, for that matter, in other major Western nations as well. Liberal and Socialist attacks upon government for "cutting" public expenditures are wide of the mark. Equally, calls by conservatives to reduce total public expenditure are wildly optimistic, when right-of-center governments in Britain and the United States have normally presided over an increase in total expenditure.

Of course, there are circumstances when particular government programs are squeezed, and occasionally cut without qualification. In Britain

Table 1   Changes in Public Expenditure by Type of Change, 1959-1979

		Britain	*United States*
1.	Actual increase	17	14
2.	Cuts without qualification	0	1
3.	Spending squeeze	3	5
4.	Deflationary windfall	0	0

SOURCES: *The Budget of the United States Government: Fiscal Year 1981* (Washington, D. C.: Government Printing Office, 1980), p. 613, and for the United Kingdom as in Figure 1B.

from 1970 to 1979, a period of successive Conservative and Labour governments, year-by-year cuts without qualification occurred in only 11 of a total of 144 program reviews; 92 percent of the program reviews did not produce unqualified "cuts" (Rose and Peters, 1978: Table 4). Moreover, generalizations that are true of total national expenditure will not be true of all subnational units of government: particular cities or areas may see their spending squeezed, or even cut, because of particular local circumstances.[1] Also, short-term movements can be inconsistent with long-term trends. There have been cases of budget squeeze in both Britain and America in the past decade, and even though this is infrequent, it may be both visible and durable in its impact upon political perceptions.

II. MISPERCEPTIONS AND FRUSTRATIONS

The disparity between the pattern of actual increases in public expenditure and increased discussion of "cuts" in public expenditure is great. It is necessary to recognize that there is today a fundamental disjunction between the practice of political expenditure and the psychology of public expenditure. In other words, the perception of public expenditure by many within as well as outside government is a *misperception*. What people see and what is to be seen by examining the record are two very different things. There is a subjective way of thinking about "cuts," as well as an objective way of viewing evidence of cuts or actual increases in public spending.

Subjectively, much of the discussion about public expenditure in both Britain and the United States today betrays a sense of frustration. There is frustration on the left because of what is perceived as a failure to meet expectations of continued increases in public expenditure. On the right, there is frustration because public expenditure is still increasing in the face of election verdicts interpreted as popular endorsement of government cuts. Frustration about cuts is here defined as a consequence of the relative deprivation arising from a shortfall between expected and actual expenditure. A sense of budget frustration can arise even if public expenditure is actually increasing as the result of feelings about "cuts" rather than thinking about "cuts." If an increase, however clear, is less than is felt to be normal or desirable, then frustration can follow. Frustration is the subjective consequence of a "squeeze" between what is expected and what is received, and can arise in at least three significant ways besides objective deprivation.

1. *Expenditure grows at less than its historic growth in constant-money terms.* The 1950s and 1960s not only witnessed an increase in the scale of

public expenditure, but also a revolution in expectations of government spending, especially within government. Growth in public expenditure came to be taken for granted, along with growth in the Gross National Product. Growth in public spending in Britain and America was relatively low by comparison with other major Western nations, but it was also steady, averaging 4.9 percent in America in the period 1951-1960 and 6.1 percent 1961-1970, and 3.6 percent in Britain in 1951-60 and 4.8 percent 1961-70 (Rose and Peters, 1978: Table 4). Insofar as growth in public expenditure institutionalized expectations, then frustration might result if government "put on the brakes," slowing down the rate at which public expenditure continued to expand. .

A simple way to see whether public spending has lived up to historically institutionalized expectations is to plot the general trend in public expenditure for the period 1955-1970 in constant prices and then see whether, in subsequent years, expenditure has been consistent with the previously established pattern. Figure 3 shows the pattern of annual changes in public expenditure from 1955 to 1979. The evidence shows that public expenditure grows at a relatively stable rate from year to year (see note 1). Growth in constant-value public expenditure in the 1970s has been *above* the long-term mean in five years in Britain, on trend in one and below in three. In the United States, it has been above the trend in six years, on trend in two, and below trend in four. In short, public officials and their clients have no general reason to feel frustrated, for *the growth of public spending in the 1970s has been at or above the standard prevailing previously.*

2. *Expenditure growing less than announced commitments to growth.* When a government makes multiyear budgets or three to five year "plans," budget officials as well as spending agencies agree to significant future increases in public spending. But economic circumstances can change between the date of making plans and delivering spending authorizations. A budget agency finds a long-term spending plan an embarrassment, insofar as prevailing political considerations mean that planned increases cannot be met within current budget constraints. In such circumstances, spending agencies may fairly claim that they are being denied funds notionally "promised," or if spending authority is frozen within a current budget year, denied funds actually appropriated. This source of frustration can hardly be justified in the United States, for multiyear budget plans have no real meaning, given the power of Congress to determine appropriations annually. In Britain, the Public Expenditure Survey has been publishing planned changes in public expenditure for several years ahead since the mid-1960s. Since public expenditure can be "blown off course" by short-

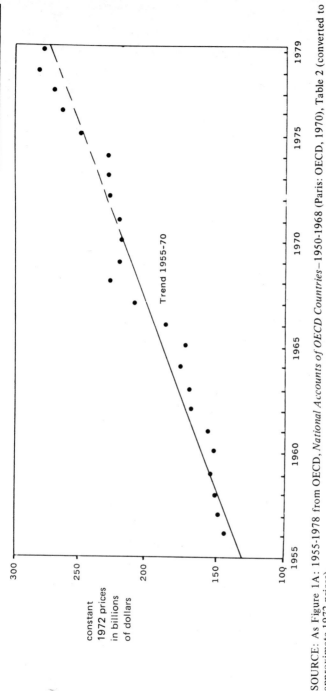

SOURCE: As Figure 1A: 1955-1978 from OECD, *National Accounts of OECD Countries—1950-1968* (Paris: OECD, 1970), Table 2 (converted to approximate 1972 prices).

NOTE: Solid trend line shows actual trend upward in public expenditure, 1955-1970; dotted continuation is a projection of this trend for 1970-1979.

Figure 3 United States Federal Expenditure, 1959-1979, in Constant (1972) Prices

213

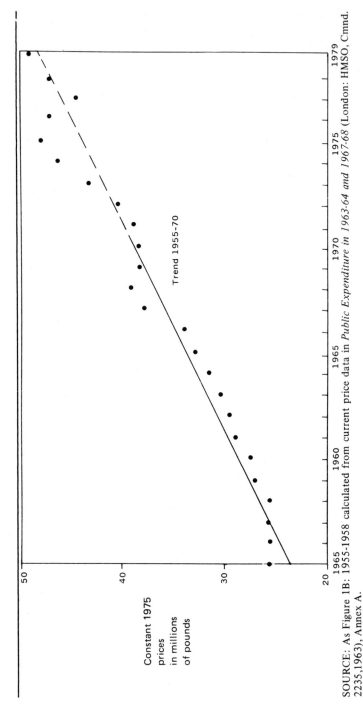

SOURCE: As Figure 1B: 1955-1958 calculated from current price data in *Public Expenditure in 1963-64 and 1967-68* (London: HMSO, Cmnd. 2235,1963), Annex A.

NOTE: Solid trend line shows actual trend upward in public expenditure, 1955-1970; dotted continuation is a projection of this trend for 1970-1979.

Figure 4   United Kingdom Public Expenditure, 1955-1979, in Constant (1975) Prices

term fluctuations in the economy, the extent of under or overshooting of planned expenditure is best assessed for a three- or four-year period. The record shows that the first Wilson government overshot by 9.6 percent its planned increase of 14.8 percent in public expenditure from 1965-66 to 1969-70, and the subsequent Heath government overshot its planned increase of 8.6 percent to the end of 1973-74 by a further 8.8 percent. There could hardly be grounds for frustration when planned expenditure increases were exceeded. Potential for frustration was stimulated by the 1974-79 Labour government, which in January 1975 announced plans for a 5.8 percent increase in public expenditure by 1978-79, but in the event realized only a 0.7 percent increase, the result of one year of a large planned increase and another of an unplanned large increase, and two years of unanticipated cuts in public spending.[2]

Given the alternation in office of Labour and Conservatives in this period, it is also possible to see whether the electorate "frustrates" clients of public policy by returning a party that does not wish to meet planned long-term increases. The 1964 Labour government inherited a Conservative commitment to increase public expenditure by 17.6 percent by 1961-68; in the event it secured a 34.6 percent increase (H. M. Treasury, 1963: 5; Goldman, 1973: 78). The 1970 Conservative government inherited a Labour commitment to increase public expenditure by 10.5 percent by 1973-74; it actually increased public spending by 20.8 percent (H. M. Treasury, 1969: Tables 1.3 and 1.6, 1975: Table 3.2). The 1974 Labour government inherited a Conservative commitment to see public spending rise by 7.4 percent by 1977-78, and it presided over an actual increase of 3.3 percent (H. M. Treasury, 1973: Table 3.2, 1979: Table 5.12). In short, the swing of the electoral pendulum from Labour to Conservative is not itself a cause for frustrating planned increases in public expenditure. Strong secular trends and economic forces outside government can make a party in office responsible for expenditure charges that are the *opposite* of what a party would prefer (see Rose, 1980: Chap. 7).

3. *Underspending.* When the overall economic climate is unfavorable, spending agencies may be subjected to informal advice to watch spending closely or to formal cash limits, notionally restricting the total sum available for spending in the current year. Cash limits represent an attempt to put a ceiling upon current-money increase in public expenditure—whatever the consequences in constant-money terms. With cash limits, spending agencies are given no assurance that the value of their appropriations will be increased to the full extent necessary to keep spending constant in volume terms. Given that budget requests are prepared up to eighteen

months before the end of a given spending year, there is considerable scope for their value to be eroded in times of rapid inflation.

British experience of cash limits, which may not be entirely typical, given the previous strong bias toward non-cash or volume limits, shows that strong political and financial pressures can lead to systematic underspending by public agencies. In 1976-77, there was underspending of 2.6 percent in current money terms, in 1977-78, 1.6 percent, and in 1978-79, 1.6 percent (H. M. Treasury, 1978: Table 4, 1979: Tables 2 and 4). In short, there was a noticeable gap between what the Treasury itself had authorized could be spent and what spending departments actually disbursed.

Whether underspending is regarded as a source of frustration or pride depends upon immediate political factors. When the government of the day is committed to squeezing public spending, then civil servants who so manage departmental funds that they spend less than appropriated may be considered above average in successfully meeting government policy goals, and politician heads of departments may also claim credit for doing so. But if underspending is not consistent with values of political leaders, then it may be regarded as "self-inflicted" frustration.

Formalistically, it might be argued that spending departments should feel frustrated when budget offices do not allocate them all the money that they initially ask for. Budgeting almost invariably involves finance officers reducing the bids of spending departments. But because this is expected to happen, budget requests are normally larger than spending agencies expect to receive. In other words, some "cuts" (that is, disallowance of requested increases) are discounted by spending departments. To be subject to disallowances that are already anticipated is not likely to be a cause of frustration. Most spending agencies would be surprised as well as pleased if given all that they asked for. There is therefore no reason to expect an agency to feel frustrated by getting less than asked for—as long as the final authorization meets expectations of an incremental increase.

While the evidence on frustrated spending agencies is less clear-cut than objective evidence of spending increases, the broad picture remains the same: there is no general and persisting evidence of major shortfalls between expected increases and actual increases in public expenditure. Moreover, even when annual shortfalls do occur, the general trend still favors increased expenditure. Even a small percentage increase can be worth more in constant-value money than a larger increase earlier, when it is applied to a larger base expenditure.

Given the potential ambiguity of public-expenditure data, whether viewed by objective economic criteria or subjective indicators of relative deprivation, we live in an Alice-in-Wonderland world in which "everybody has won and all must have prizes." Inflation virtually guarantees increases in public expenditure desired by those who believe that public spending is a good thing. Concurrently, conservatives who wish the government to "intervene" less in society may hope that, under the guise of fighting inflation, reductions can be imposed upon the volume of goods and services provided by government, even though the total current cost continues to grow.

Since references to spending "cuts" can be ambiguous (as in the case of a spending "squeeze") or confusing (as in the substitution of a subjective sense of frustration for objective reductions), and often plain misleading (when made in the face of actual increases in the volume of outputs), perhaps the term itself should be subject to a moratorium. Yet the concern with "cuts" is now so much voiced in politics (and in academic writing too) that some label is needed to describe this feeling. Perhaps it would be best to speak of a "felicity" rating for government public expenditure. Conventionally, social scientists assume that politicians will be happiest if they preside over acrual increases in public expenditure (e.g., Niskanen, 1971; Brittan, 1975). If this is the case, then the uncertainties surrounding economies of major Western nations today constitute a warning that, potentially at least, there is scope for "unhappy" feelings about public expenditure, whether caused by a spending squeeze or unqualified cuts, or, on the contrary, a conservative's anguish at the failure of government to reduce public expenditure in volume terms.

III. SOURCES OF ANXIETY

The greater the misperception of public expenditure, the greater the level of anxiety that is betrayed about the state of the political economy today.

The disjunction between perceived and actual changes in public expenditure in the past half-dozen years arises in part from frustration that public spending does not always increase as rapidly as before for every program, even though it continues to grow in aggregate. More important, public expenditure is an object of concern because of other changes in the state of the economy. When the national product grows more slowly, it *is* proper that both proponents and opponents of costly government measures should speculate about what is happening to prospects for increased expenditure. Given the difficulties of managing the economy today, it is understandable that many people jump to the conclusion that something has gone wrong with public expenditure, whether this is assumed to be that it is accelerating too rapidly (which inflation makes appear plausible) or that it is not growing rapidly enough (which can appear plausible to public officials who nervously worry that politicians may one day do what they say: impose cuts on public spending).

Public expenditure is a visible symbol of ideas and emotions concerning the contemporary political economy. Because the symbol condenses larger meanings, reactions to public expenditure can be at variance with quantitative data. In the "closed" world of pure ideological reasoning, specific empirical data are irrelevant: an ideology predicts what "must" be true, any evidence to the contrary notwithstanding (Santori, 1969). Reference to public expenditure in political controversy need not be based upon systematic quantitative analysis of what has actually been happening; instead, it may be a symbol condensing a complex ideology that gives meaning to public expenditure from the supraempirical perspective of the analyst.

Theories of structural change in society, whether from the right or the left, give greatest significance to public expenditure. From a Socialist or Marxist perspective, the higher the ratio of public expenditure to the Gross National Product, the more effectively the economy is "socialized," that is, major economic decisions are determined by government. Proponents of "libertarian" political economy share this view, albeit drawing the opposite conclusion, namely, that public expenditure should contract in order to preserve the liberties said to be rooted in the market. Insofar as ideological commitment is primary, then the "correct" course of public expenditure can be predicted. Socialists believe that public expenditure ought to increase, and Marxists proclaim that they have a theory explaining why this must be so. Libertarian political economists start from the assumption that public expenditure has been increasing, but, believing that their philosophy should "change the world," proceed to explain why this trend ought to be reversed. Since theories of structural change concern very general abstract values such as "Socialism" and "Liberty," it is hardly surprising that references to public expenditure in such contexts will often be emotionally charged.

Advocates of collective social programs favor public expenditure on specific grounds. From this perspective, government ought to spend more money for specific programs deemed beneficial to citizens. The selection of programs depends upon changeable, and in some senses, subjective measures of "need," "merit goods," and shadow costs and benefits. On rational grounds, proposals for increased spending on social programs should be rejected by government in the absence of rigorous evidence of need, merit, or a positive cost-benefit ratio. Given the subjective nature of many judgments involved in making such evaluations, it is not surprising that proponents of social programs consistently find ways of justifying increases in public expenditure. Moreover, program advocates usually appear to reason from the a priori assumption that greater spending equals proportionately greater social benefits. Whether current money costs or constant money volume measures are used, there is a mechanical reduction of benefit outputs to spending inputs (Sharkansky, 1970: Chap. 7).

While economists do not think of themselves as ideologues, economic theory does reason from a priori assumptions to deductive consequences that "must be" so, as long as the reasoning is logical, the assumptions accurate, and the results unexamined. Contemporary macroeconomic theories give major theoretical significance to public expenditure. In the Keynesian paradigm, public expenditure is particularly important as a "countercyclical" force, in theory being able to stimulate a deficit-financed increase in aggregate demand during an economic recession and to reduce inflation by a surplus in government revenue. While the theory is internally consistent as far as it goes, it does not go far enough; there are both theoretical and empirical grounds for questioning the simple theory's accuracy as a description of the practice of major Western governments today (e.g., Lindbeck, 1976; Buchanan and Wagner, 1977; Skidelsky, 1977).

Public expenditure, particularly when it causes a large public deficit, as was the case in the 1970s, is regarded as a major cause of inflation by monetarists, who prescribe "cuts" in deficit-financed public spending in order to achieve their macroeconomic goals. In the 1970s, economists of all persuasions have faced the threat of "paradigm shift," as familiar assumptions or propositions—for example, the presumed Phillips curve tradeoff between inflation and unemployment—are demonstrably no longer empirically valid. (cf. Phillips, 1958; Trevithick, 1977: Chap. 4; Buchanan and Wagner: 85-87, 166-168).

Market-oriented efficiency experts are concerned with public expenditure because of its alleged "wastefulness." Reasoning from the assumption that the market is the most efficient allocator of goods, such efficiency theorists conclude that public expenditure "must be" bad because it is normally devoted to producing goods and services that are not marketed, e.g., pensions, health care, education, and military defense.

Resources are assumed to be misallocated by public expenditure, insofar as government produces "too much" of goods and services simply because demand is inflated by making them free at the point of consumption, although they cannot be free at the point of production. Shadow or external "benefits" and the imputed social "costs" of market failures are ignored by efficiency experts. Insofar as efficiency experts are also libertarians, they may oppose public expenditure unconditionally. Otherwise, it is possible for public expenditure to be contingently acceptable—if it is devoted to providing vouchers or a basic income through such a device as the negative income tax, giving citizens a market choice for goods and services.

The relatively turbulent political economy of today is both a threat and an incentive for sustaining "closed" ideological views of public expenditure. It is a threat insofar as such systems of thought are likely to be invalidated by systematic empirical observation, given the recent, relatively rapid and unexpected shifts of major variables of the political economy and also the relationship between them. In a closed system of interdependent variables, the falsification of one major assumption is particularly serious, for it threatens the credibility of the system as a whole. Insofar as the ideology—be it business efficiency, Socialism, or program benefits—is preferred on other grounds, then the risk involved in looking at empirical data is unacceptable to a believer, and he may ignore empirical data in order to maintain a favored belief system intact.

In the opinion of this writer, public expenditure is correctly perceived as a central problem in the political economy of today because the growth in public spending has caused or threatens to cause a cut in the constant value of the take-home pay of most citizens. In the 1950s and 1960s citizens everywhere in the Western world could enjoy the fruits of "double affluence." Growth in the Gross National Product produced a fiscal dividend that could finance both an increase in take-home pay (that is post-tax, pre transfer income) and a growth in public policy benefits (e.g. health, education, and pensions programs). Government could raise tax revenues relatively "painlessly," for net earnings continued to increase in constant-value terms, even after the deduction of increased taxes.[3]

In the 1970s, the national economies of every Western nation have continued to grow in aggregate. Notwithstanding feelings of relative deprivation, the American Gross Domestic Product at factor cost has grown by 32 percent from 1970 to 1979, and the British by 19 percent. While the economy has not expanded in every year of the decade, nonetheless, the average annual American growth rate from 1971 to 1978, 2.9 percent, is higher than that for the decade 1951 to 1960, and the British growth rate, 1.8 percent from 1971 to 1978, is applied to a much larger national product than a similarly low growth rate in the 1950s.

Given that the economy has continued to grow on both sides of the Atlantic, the expression of dissatisfaction about economic growth in the 1970s is a subjective judgment, and, in the case of Britain, based upon refusal to recognize the historical fact that the British economy ought to be expected to grow more slowly.

Concurrently with the slowing down of economic growth, the costs of public policy have continued to grow at more or less their historic rates, 5.1 percent annually in the United States, and 4.4 percent in Britain from 1971 to 1978. Ten or twenty years ago, such an increase would not have jeopardized "double affluence," for it would have claimed only 1.5 to 2.0 percent of a larger fiscal dividend of growth. But in the 1970s, the cumulative increase in public expenditure as a proportion of the national product means that average growth in American public expenditure requires a 1.8 percent growth in the national product for funding entirely from the fiscal dividend of growth, and in Britain a growth in the economy of 2.2 percent, a figure higher than the average British rate of growth in the British economy in this decade.

The result is that continued growth in public expenditure now produces a "negative fiscal dividend" in Britain, and threatens the same in the United States by the 1980s, if historic patterns of growth in the economy and in public expenditure are not altered (see Rose and Peters, 1978: Chap. 7).

When the increased cost of public expenditure cannot be met entirely from the fruits of economic growth, the government's demand for more revenue leads to a cut in take-home pay.

From a macroeconomic perspective, the economy is still growing, and more real resources are available to society in aggregate. But from a microeconomic perspective (namely, that of the ordinary citizen), there is a decrease in constant value earnings. To reverse the old Galbraith slogan, there can be an increase in public affluence, and a decline in private affluence. In Britain, take-home pay has fallen consistently from 1975 through 1979, and by nine percent cumulatively in the four years. In the United States, take-home pay has been up and down, falling in 1975 and 1976, rising in 1977 and 1978, and down again in 1979.

The importance of subjective perceptions of the economy is underlined by the apparent tendency of Americans to protest more about taxes than Britons, even though rising taxes in money terms are consistent with an increase in constant value earnings in the United States, and this is not the case in Britain. The contrast is partly due to differences in fundamental political values; the acceptance of the British welfare state is so strong that, upon occasion, a plurality of Britons say they would prefer to pay higher taxes for more services. It is also due to different expectations in the perceived growth of the economy. Americans have historically been more optimistic about continued growth in personal earnings, whereas many Britons have been ready to adapt to a "revolution of falling expectations" in the face of a decline in constant value take-home pay.

From the perspective of hard-pressed governors, the best terms to describe the control of public expenditure today are probably "unstable" and "uncertain." Instability is demonstrated by the reversals in the national product, contracting in some years as well as growing in others; in the ups *and* downs of inflation rates; and in the occurrence of a "negative" instead of positive fiscal dividend to meet the costs of public expenditure. The British record of about four major public expenditure budgets (or "re-budgets") per year since the mid-1970s shows that the budget reversals of President Carter in the first half of 1980 are not personal, but reflect rapid changes in decision makers' appreciation of national economies.

The more instability has been demonstrated in the 1970s, the greater the cause for uncertainties about the 1980s.[4]

In such circumstances, it is fundamentally wrong to speak of a "standstill" in public expenditure, or to expect a "freeze" to be maintained.[5] While such terms may be revealing of subjective states of mind, they are contradicted by the evidence of actual increases in public expenditure. Equally important, the terms suggest a static equilibrium, when public expenditure today is anything but static or predictable. For example, a budget freeze or standstill could only be produced by the marshaling of substantial countervailing power within government, and by substantial pressures in society sufficient to stop the great inertia forces causing a continuing increase in constant value expenditure.

The "base" as well as the margin of public spending may become open for scrutiny with all that this implies in terms of political disagreements within government.

The dominance of budgets by "uncontrollable" items of expenditure further weakens government efforts to control uncertainties. Uncontrollable elements of expenditure are those that are committed by statute or contract (e.g., transfer payments to the elderly and salaries to tenured public officials). Uncontrollable spending accounts for a majority of public expenditure, and it tends to be rising.

The U.S. federal government estimates that "relatively uncontrollable" spending rose from 66 percent in 1971 to 76 percent in 1980. Another estimate is that only 6 percent of the budget is discretionary in a single year (see LeLoup, 1978: 469). Some of the "uncontrollable" elements in the budget are also fluctuating, and can rise unexpectedly, for example, the cost of interest on the public debt, or the cost of paying unemployment benefits when the number out of work increases. In principle, such "uncontrollables" could be altered, but it would require the government of the day to repeal statutes authorizing open-ended entitlements to benefits.

Insofar as the state of the economy is diagnosed as the principal cause of government's expenditure problems (a reasonable proposition in the abstract), then the governors of a mixed economy find that they share power with financial and industrial groups and trade unions. This realization encourages moves toward tripartite discussions of such economic problems as wages, prices, and investment plans, with the government participating as an equal, rather than as the sovereign authority. While sharing power in the mixed economy, the government of the day finds that it is left with the whole of the responsibility for what goes wrong.

The mass of the electorate does not expect the nation's economy to provide an endlessly expanding cornucopia of benefits (see Rose, 1980b). But it is concerned with protecting what it has, namely, a given level of take-home pay, and a claim to the benefits of public policy. Neither business nor trade union groups need concentrate upon demands for "more" when times are difficult. Instead, their first priority is to hold what they have—that is, to maintain the purchasing power of established wages and to maintain profits against erosion by inflation. But these across-the-board conservative demands are not easy to meet when the inertia of past commitments threatens a "negative fiscal dividend."

Both electors and elected today often find themselves powerless. Whereas elections are about what people want, economics is about what people can have with scarce and uncertain resources. Voters cannot simply set the economy right by turning out one party and installing another, nor can they even be confident of choosing between one horn of a dilemma and another by alternating parties in office. An intensive study of the impact of parties upon the management of the British economy from 1957 to 1979 provides copious evidence of how little difference parties make, whether pursuing consensus goals (e.g., reducing inflation or unemployment) or controversial goals (e.g. altering public expenditure, or the distribution of wealth). The state of the economy today is determined by things stronger than an elected party in government (see Rose, 1980a: Chaps. 7 and 8).

The causes of this sense of "powerlessness" in government are multiple. The most general is the growing interdependence of national economies upon an international economic system. For this reason, governmental leaders who once believed that they could "manage" their own national economies now find them less manageable than expected, because of the increasing importance of exogenous international factors, such as the price of oil. Within a national society, the creation of major welfare state programs has made many programs more or less "uncontrollable" in expenditure terms. Laws concerning health, education, and income maintenance for the elderly confer benefits upon demand to all who are entitled by statute. Demographic changes have increased consumer demand for public expenditure, as more people are entitled to such major benefits. Concurrently, public employees have lobbied for wage increases in keeping with the standards of the capital intensive private sector, even though these are not justified by increased productivity in the labour-intensive public sector. The result of this relative price effect makes it increasingly expensive in constant-price terms to produce the same volume of government goods and services.

Politicians may hope to educate public opinion to moderate claims upon the public purse by demonstrating the costs involved in meeting them. But politicans have a far more anxiety-inducing task insofar as they must also explain to the electorate why they themselves are relatively powerless to achieve what they want to do.

IV. LEARNING TO ADAPT: FROM FRUSTRATION TO REPRIEVE

The costs of governing are finite: the question for budgeters is not whether spending will be limited, but how can this best be done? There is a great practical difference between public expenditure targets decided in advance and more or less successfully met by government, and expenditure totals that can only be derived post hoc, by summing up what departments have actually spent by the end of a fiscal year. In the first instance, the cost of governing reflects political choice (or at least knowledgeable prediction); in the latter, it is an absence of collective choice, with limits finally set by the exhaustion of available resources.

Accepting the universe—that is, setting targets that limit public expenditure—is much easier when the economy is buoyant, when a fiscal dividend can fund the whole of the spending increase and leave something over for an increase in take-home pay. But accepting the universe is very different when the alternative is the frustration of some expectations for public expenditure to increase, *or* imposing a cut in the constant value of take-home pay.

When politicians view the future of public expenditure, the scope for subjective decisions is great, since no one can be certain of what the future will hold. A peculiarity of a budget is that its impact is both immediate and cumulative. It is immediate in that it promptly and publicly concerns this year's level of public expenditure. The annual budget decisions also have a cumulative impact upon public expenditure, as each year's small incremental increase becomes incorporated into next year's base, and thus raises minimum expectations of how much must be spent without imposing a cut in constant-value terms, and how much more must be spent if historic expectations of spending increases are not to be frustrated.

The time horizon of politicians will invariable be short term, by comparison with the permanent accumulation of spending obligations by government. An elected life of five years for a Parliament, four years for a President, and two years for a Congressman sets an outer limit for normal attention, and a limit that is progressively reduced in the life of a government. Moreover, public-opinion polls tell politicans between elections how they stand with public opinion, and the exigencies of life within government departments make their heads face problems with weekly or even daily deadlines.

Given the importance to politicians of today's problems rather than tomorrow's contingent difficulties, a politician is likely to look for measures that will "temporize" or "satisfice" for the moment, whatever the hypothetical consequences in future. The problems of this year's budget may be reckoned to be only "temporary." A temporizing view argues for the adoption of temporary budget expedients that "fudge the books." The repertoire of tricks of the trade is large. The stratagems include: borrowing money from abroad, selling capital assets, postponing capital expenditure, and imposing revenue cuts on other levels of government normally in receipt of transfer funds (e.g., cutting central-government grants to local authorities). Because it has control of the central bank, a central government can also manipulate the money supply in such ways that large increases arising from inflation may camouflage a reduced rate of growth in constant-value spending. By contrast, local authorities may suffer unduly harsh squeezes, insofar as their costs are more buoyant in inflationary times than their sources of revenue.

When the annual increase in government spending *consistently* exceeds the fiscal dividend of growth plus net foreign borrowing, thus forcing a real cut in take-home pay, as is now happening in Britain, then politicians must stop temporizing. The immediate decision becomes whether or not a reduction in take-home pay should be accepted as desirable in itself. Such a conscious choice may be made by persons who hold left-wing values favoring the continued socialization of resource allocation and consumption, or by those who place a very high value upon the presumed benefits of social programs. But it is noteworthy that even Labour and Socialist parties do not fight elections by proclaiming the desirability of reducing take-home pay to finance continued increases in public expenditure. For example, the 1979 Labour manifesto simply promised "high wages" and "fair wages,"[f] a series of specified tax cuts, and additional public expenditure without mentioning where the money might come from.[6]

The challenge to put the brakes on public expenditure by reducing its rate of growth to that consistent with the "fiscal dividend" of the economy as a whole is novel but not unprecedented. It is novel in that it follows the historically unique expansion of public expenditure in the 1960s and 1970s. It is not without precedent, for governments must always impose some limit upon the rate of public spending, and there is a large body of writings suggesting how the growth of public expenditure may be kept within desired limits.[7] Moreover, the agencies responsible for imposing limits upon public expenditure still retain their central place in government, and budget officials are ready to take advantage of changes in the political climate.

The crucial determinant of change is the development of a different perception about public expenditure than that prevailing in the past decade or more. An unemotional evaluation of the subject will emphasize that the size of the problem is relatively small. As long as government can impose a chosen limit on public spending, then it can continue to grow in keeping with the growth of the national economy. The constraints needed are not "amputations," as the word "cut" suggests, but rather "stabilization," that is, the imposition of firm and certain (as well as rising) ceilings upon public expenditure. Misperceptions are unlikely to continue indefinitely, and frustrations can be dispelled by reducing expectations. The lack of success in politicians' efforts to fudge the books will sooner or later reveal the failure of temporizing policies—and failure is itself a good teacher.

The policy process is a continuing activity, and nowhere is this of greater importance than in public expenditure. As Hugh Heclo's (1974) study of the growth of spending on income maintenance policies emphasizes, both public officials and organizations learn from the consequences of the programs that they adopt. The process of learning may be disjointed, as Heclo emphasizes, but it is not "random bumping" (Heclo, 1974: 308). Politicians learn from what goes wrong, as well as from what works. Like military generals, managers of the economy may even be hyperconscious of learning the lessons of battles just past. For example, the rapid progression from using deficit financing to wages policies to dampening inflation by monetary policies when wages policies are eroded represents learning responses to the shortcomings of current policies as they are perceived to emerge. Even though each policy was initially successful, each has been abandoned as it became evident that success was purchased at a progressively more unacceptable price.

Opinion polls provide convincing evidence that ordinary voters can learn from the government's past shortcomings in managing the economy, just as positive expectations can be stimulated by government success. The dominant popular expectations of the economy *are reversible and reverse:* they appear to reflect a reasonable and prompt response to the condition of the economy (Rose, 1980b: 162). For example, the British Gallup Poll shows that in nineteen of the past twenty years a majority or plurality of British people believed that economic conditions would be difficult in the coming year, and the American Gallup Poll found the same dominance of pessimistic views in ten of twelve years since 1965.[8] In the 1960s, Americans usually told the Gallup Poll that they expected the next year to register full employment, but in the 1970s, rising unemployment was the common expectation. British respondents differ only insofar as the expectation of full employment was abandoned in 1966. British people have been consistent in one thing: prices have been expected to rise in each of the 23 years in which the question has been asked by the Gallup Poll. The pessimistic expectations of Britons and Americans are a reasonable reflection of the troubled state of national economies. Insofar as economic conditions vary within a nation or cross-nationally, popular expectations are likely to vary too. The basic point remains true: popular expectations of government's economic performance are changeable, and often negative.

Given that political frustration is caused by a gap between expectations and government achievements, then political satisfaction should follow from expectations being met. If the expectations are of changes for the worse, the result might be better characterized as "no cause for frustration," since the news, however bad, will be anticipated—and may even be welcomed on the grounds that it is *not as bad as expected.*

The longer public-expenditure difficulties continue, the easier it should be to dissipate political frustration, since the general public will learn from experience to expect smaller and smaller increases in public expenditure. The heightened public discussion of budget "cuts" (that is, a reduction in expected increases) itself creates an expectation that spending should be reduced—and ordinary people are likely to interpret this to mean an actual reduction in constant- (or even current-) value money. A second alternative is that continued economic difficulties will lead to the expectation of no increase in public spending in constant-money terms: a "nil norm" can thus replace an expectation of continued public spending growth. In the latter instance, the literal conservatism of bureaucrats—what we have we hold—may be a more accurate forecast than the radical reaction of neoconservatives—what has been rising should now be cut.

Insofar as expectations of public expenditure do change, then we may be entering a period of the politics of reprieve. A *reprieve* promises relief, because the actual fate of public expenditure is not as bad as had been expected or threatened. Insofar as public officials and citizens expect to see public spending reduced in constant terms, and find that government can still manage modest increases in spending as well as increases in take-home pay, this may produce more subjective satisfaction than greater increases under both headings in a period when "accelerating affluence" was a norm for public expenditure.

The politics of reprieve makes explicable why governments successfully survive far worse failures than the relatively minor frustrations resulting from a slowing down in public expenditure increases in the 1970s (cf. Rose and Mackie, 1980). In wartime, citizens come to expect defeats as well as victory. Once the initial shock of the first military setback is accepted, then, by comparison, any lesser setback becomes an improvement ("the enemy is contained"), and a positive or symbolic victory is a cause for positive celebration. In the 1930s, mass publics in both countries accepted depression and high levels of unemployment because this was expected to happen recurringly, as part of a "boom and bust" cycle of economic change beyond the control of government. Today, the gradual rise of unemployment has led to an expectation of more unemployment, and thus a gradual increase in the level of unemployment accepted as tolerable by government and by the electorate.

Politicians, like ordinary voters, are adaptable. The very causes of a country's economic difficulties today are both persisting and well publicized, and many of the sources of difficulties can be blamed upon foreign nations. The very "powerlessness" of politicians in the face of rapidly increasing oil import costs makes it easier for politicians to disclaim responsibility for much of a nation's economic difficulties. The more bad news a government faces, the more politicians become adept at handling bad news—and the more likely the electorate generally will be to accept difficulties without frustration. A governing party can try to encourage the belief that the nation has been reprieved: after all, bad news could be worse still. The sooner that politicians, and political commentators of many different outlooks, learn to understand the facts of contemporary public expenditure, the more quickly misperceptions can be eliminated, and the easier it will be for government decision makers to accept the universe as it is.

NOTES

1. The cross-time trend line results in an r^2 of 0.931 for public expenditure in Britain, 1955-1970, significant at the 0.00000 level, and an r^2 of 0.891 for federal public expenditure in the United States, 1955-1970, significant at the 0.00000 level. See Figures 3 and 4.

2. See H. M. Treasury (1966: 24, 1969: Table 1.1, 1971: Table 1.1, 1975: Table 3.2, 1980: Table 1.6) and Goldman (1973).

3. For the full development of this analysis, see Rose and Peters (1978b), from which the following passage is a condensation.

4. And the more relevant become the types of practices described in Caiden and Wildavsky (1980).

5. Compare Stewart (1980: 9-24), who in fact analyzes interestingly what is clearly a nonstatic situation. The failure to define what *is* there to be perceived is a systematic weakness of the otherwise interesting prose discussions of contributors to Wright's volume.

6. See London Times (1979: 297ff.). For evidence that this oversight was characteristic, not atypical, see the analysis of the 1980 Labour NEC draft "manifesto" by Hugo Young (1980).

7. For the author's own view, see Rose and Peters (1978b: 222-232).

8. See George Gallup and Associates, Inc. (1979: 15ff., 1977: 2) and year-end Gallup Organization reports.

REFERENCES

American Enterprise Institute (1980) A conversation with Gerald R. Ford. Washington, DC: American Enterprise Institute.

BRITTAN, S. (1975) "The economic contradictions of democracy." British Journal of Political Science 2.

BUCHANAN, J. M. and R. E. WAGNER (1977) Democracy in Deficit: The Political Legacy of Lord Keynes. New York: Academic.

CAIDEN, N. and A. WILDAVSKY (1980) Planning and Budgeting in Poor Countries. New Brunswick, NJ: Transaction.

CLARKE, R. (1973) "The long term planning of taxation," in B. Crick and W. A. Robson (eds.) Taxation Policy. Harmondsworth: Penguin.

George Gallup and Associates, Inc. (1977) Gallup Opinion Index. Princeton.

––– (1979) Gallup Political Index 232. London.

GOLDMAN, S. (1973) The Developing System of Public Expenditure Management and Control. London: HMSO.

HECLO, H. (1974) Modern Social Politics in Britain and Sweden. New Haven, CT: Yale University Press.

H. M. Treasury (1963) Public Expenditure in 1963-64 and 1967-68 (Cmnd. 2235). London: HMSO.

––– (1966) Public Expenditure Planning and Control (Cmnd. 2915).

––– (1969) Public Expenditure 1968-69 to 1973-74 (Cmnd. 4234). London: HMSO.

――― (1971) Public Expenditure 1969-70 to 1974-75 (Cmnd. 4578). London: HMSO.

――― (1973) Public Expenditure to 1977-78 (Cmnd. 5519). London: HMSO.

――― (1975) Public Expenditure to 1978-79 (Cmnd. 5879). London: HMSO.

――― (1978) Cash Limits Provisional Outturn, 1977-78 (Cmnd. 7295). London: HMSO.

――― (1979a) The Government's Expenditure Plans 1979-80 to 1982-83 (Cmnd. 7439). London: HMSO.

――― (1979b) Cash Limits Provisional Outturn, 1978-79 (Cmnd. 7681). London: HMSO.

――― (1980) The Government's Expenditure Plans 1980-81 to 1983-84 (Cmnd. 7841). London: HMSO.

LeLOUP, L. T. (1978) "Discretion in national budgeting: controlling the controllables." Policy Analysis (Fall).

LINDBECK, A. (1976) "Stabilization policy in open economies with endogenous politicians." American Economic Review 66, 2: 1-19.

London Times (1979) The Times Guide to the House of Commons 1979. London: Times Books.

NISKANEN, W. A. (1971) Bureaucracy and Representative Government. Chicago: AVC.

PHILLIPS, A. W. (1958) "The relationship between unemployment and the rate of money wage rates in the United Kingdom, 1961-1975." Economica 25 (November): 283-299.

ROSE, R. (1980a) Do Parties Make a Difference? London: Macmillan.

――― (1980b) "Ordinary people in extraordinary economic circumstances," pp. 151-175 in R. Rose (ed.) Challenge to Governance: Studies in Overloaded Politics. Beverly Hills, CA: Sage.

ROSE, R. and T. T. MACKIE (1980) Incumbency in Government: Asset or Liability? Study in Public Policy 54. Glasgow: University of Strathclyde.

ROSE, R. and B. G. PETERS (1978a) The Juggernaut of Incrementalism: A Comparative Perspective on the Growth of Public Policy. Study in Public Policy 24. Glasgow: University of Strathclyde.

――― (1978b) Can Government Go Bankrupt? New York: Basic Books.

SARTORI, G. (1969) "Politics, ideology and belief systems." American Political Science Review 63, 2: 398-411.

SHARKANSKY, I. (1970) "The spending-service cliche," in The Routines of Politics. New York: Van Nostrand.

SKIDELSKY, R. [ed.] (1977) The End of the Keynesian Era. London: Macmillan.

STEWART, J. D. (1980) "From growth to standstill," in M. Wright (ed.) Public Spending Decisions. London: Allen & Unwin.

TARSCHYS, D. (1975) "The growth of public expenditure: nine models of explanation." Scandinavian Political Studies 10: 19-31.

TREVITHICK, J. A. (1977) Inflation. Harmondsworth: Penguin.

U.S. Department of the Treasury (1980) The Budget of the United States Government: Fiscal Year 1981. Washington, DC: Government Printing Office.

YOUNG, H. (1980) "An attempt to be fair to Tony Bern." London Times (July 13).

10

LOCAL GOVERNMENT STRATEGIES
TO COPE WITH FISCAL PRESSURE

HAROLD WOLMAN

The Urban Institute

with the assistance of
BARBARA DAVIS

Local governments are increasingly coming under fiscal pressure to which they must respond. The problems of New York, Cleveland, Detroit, and Washington, D.C. have received national attention as examples of fiscal crisis. Yet there has been little study of how urban administrators and politicians actually respond, or the consequences of their responses both for urban policy outcomes and for the nature and quality of services citizens receive. This essay addresses these questions by examining the response patterns of twenty-three cities and three counties to fiscal pressure.

FISCAL PRESSURE

Fiscal pressure[1] does not necessarily indicate that the government experiencing it is either in a fiscal crisis or fiscally mismanaged. Fiscal pressure may result from any of several situations, all of which, if they persist for any length of time, must call forth a response of increasing revenues, decreasing expenditures, or some combination of the two. These situations include:

(1) A declining base or one growing at less than the rate of inflation.[2]
(2) A reduction in the level of intergovernmental operating assistance.

(3) Unplanned deficits in either the annual operating budget or the general fund. An excess of general-fund expenditures over revenues does not in itself imply the presence of fiscal pressure, since a local government may be quite rationally attempting to reduce a larger surplus accumulated in previous years. However, a budget deficit or successive deficits coexisting with a small or negative fund balance implies the city faces fiscal pressure and must respond by increasing revenues, reducing expenditures or some combination.[3]

(4) A formal fiscal limitation on local expenditures or revenues.[4]

LOCAL GOVERNMENT RESPONSES TO FISCAL PRESSURE

How do local governments respond to fiscal pressure? A review of existing literature plus interviews we have conducted suggests the following possible expenditure and revenue options.

I. Reduce Expenditures (either absolute or in rate increase)
  A. operating expenses
    1. by object of expenditure
      a. reduce personnel cost
        (1) layoffs
        (2) hiring freeze
        (3) cutback on overtime
        (4) wage freeze or reduction in rate of salary increase
      b. reduce nonpersonnel operating costs (utilities, supplies, equipment, travel)
      c. reduce payments to or on behalf of clients
    2. by function
      a. reduce maintenance
      b. reduce service delivery
      c. reduce administration
    3. by program area
      a. reduce spending on social programs
      b. reduce spending on core city housekeeping services (police fire, sanitation)
      c. reduce spending on "optional" city services (parks, recreation, libraries, etc.)
      d. reduce spending on general governmental functions (central administration, courts, etc.)
    4. reduce participation in federal and state grant programs requiring local matching contribution

     5. transfer of functions to other levels of government
     6. administrative and management reforms designed to achieve greater productivity and efficiency (which presumably would be reflected in lower expenditures for the same level of public output)
     7. delay or nonpayment of bills
     8. default
  B. capital expenditures
     1. capital spending freeze for new capital projects
     2. deferral of nonessential capital projects
     3. transfer of cost to private capital
II. Increase Revenues
  A. own source
     1. increase tax revenues through increases in tax rates or change in tax structure
     2. increase tax revenues through increase in tax base (e.g., annexation, new construction, etc.)
     3. increase local fees, licenses, and/or user charges
     4. borrow
     5. liquidate assets
  B. intergovernmental assistance
     1. federal
     2. state

What strategies do local governments in fact pursue when facing fiscal pressure, and which of the above options do they employ? The ensuing discussion and the examples employed derive primarily from an intensive study of responses to fiscal pressure in six local governments (Trenton, Buffalo, and Detroit and surrounding counties—Mercer, Erie, and Wayne) and a broader, less intensive study of twenty cities experiencing fiscal pressure according to one or more of the criteria discussed previously.[5]

There appears to be a strong indication that the overall objective of local-government strategy is to maintain existing employment levels and budget totals, even at the expense of changing the local program mix and priorities. This strategy is likely to dominate the initial response (unless the fiscal pressure occurs very suddenly and is quite severe) and is likely to be an important factor in later stages. The implication of this strategy is that local governments, *ceteris paribus,* will prefer revenue-increasing to expenditure-reducing strategies. However, all other things are seldom equal, and revenue-increasing responses may not be possible, particularly in an era of citizen tax revolt.

Local-government responses appear to follow a rough order reflecting local-government preferences for various options adjusted by their feasibility and political realities. In many cases, however, the pressure of events causes several different options to be pursued simultaneously or in combination.

BUYING-TIME RESPONSES

The first response to fiscal pressure is frequently to draw down existing fund surpluses, engage in interfund transfers, borrow to support operating deficits, and take other action which at a minimum buys time and delays the necessity of choosing between revenue increases and expenditure-reduction strategies. Trenton has drawn down the $3.8 million general-fund surplus present at the end of 1976 to less than $400,000 at the end of 1979. Allentown's surplus of $2.1 million in 1978 (10.6 percent of the general-fund expenditures) will have been reduced to $102,000 (less than 1 percent of general-fund spending) by the end of 1980.

Interfund transfers and fund juggling also occur. In both Baltimore and St. Petersburg, enterprise-fund surpluses have been transferred to the general fund to support current operations. In several cities we examined, expenditures previously made from the general fund have been assigned to special revenue funds, particularly the Community Development Block Grant fund. In others, certain current expenditures, such as street maintenance, had been reclassified as capital spending, in effect, allowing bond issues on long-term repayment schedules to support expenses incurred by the present residents.

Beyond the above "buying-time" techniques, local governments facing pressure must choose either to increase revenues or reduce expenditures. In reality, the choice is a tripartite one: (1) increase intergovernmental revenues, (2) increase own-source revenues, or (3) reduce expenditures.

INCREASING INTERGOVERNMENTAL REVENUES

Our studies suggest that local governments facing fiscal pressure will, not surprisingly, first attempt to increase intergovernmental revenues. If such an effort is successful, the local unit can sustain—or even increase—its existing expenditure and manpower levels without having to resort to a tax increase. However, successful application of this strategy presumes the existence of untapped federal and/or state aid opportunities, a situation which was characteristic of the mid-1970s, but has been much less so, particularly at the federal level, in the latter part of the decade (and substantial increases in federal aid appear even more unlikely in the future). Even so, fourteen of the twenty-three cities experiencing fiscal pressure (see Table 1) did manage to increase intergovernmental revenues in nominal terms (ten had increases in real terms) as a response to the onset of that pressure. (All of these increases occurred in one or more of the years between 1977 and 1980.)

When possible, local governments prefer simply to substitute additional intergovernmental assistance for local funds. In some cases—General Revenue Sharing and Anti-Recession Fiscal Asistance—there is no legal problem involved in this. Trenton, for example, uses its entire General Revenue Sharing payment to support its fire department, thus substituting for what otherwise would have required locally raised revenue. In other cases, federal or state program requirements prohibit or make difficult direct substitution. Nonetheless, it is virtually certain that some such substitution occurs, particularly in programs such as CETA. Trenton, for example, reduced its municipally funded payroll by 247 positions between 1970 and 1979; in 1979, it had 254 CETA employees. Buffalo has reduced its locally funded payroll by 24 percent between 1975 and 1979; CETA in 1979 accounts for approximately 25 percent of Buffalo's work force.

When such substitution is not possible, our studies indicate that local governments faced with the prospect of cutbacks or own-source tax increases will rearrange program priorities, if necessary, to maintain total spending and government employment levels, even if this requires shifting from the locally preferred program mix in order to qualify for the new intergovernmental revenues. In New Jersey's Mercer County, a 34 percent decrease in federal Title XX Social Services revenues (Title XX is essentially a block grant for social services) prompted a search for ways to shift programs to categorical grants. When the opportunities for direct funding replacement were exhausted, county officials created new programs and trimmed old ones in ways that would generate federal funding for the same social services staff. The result was maintenance of the previous total funding level, without new taxes, and maintenance of jobs for existing employees, but a substantially different mix of social services.

OWN-SOURCE REVENUE INCREASES

If local governments facing fiscal pressure are unable to generate sufficient additional intergovernmental revenues, they must then confront the choice of own-source revenue increases or expenditure cutbacks. It is widely believed that in the existing Proposition 13 tax-revolt environment, governments facing fiscal pressure will be forced to cut expenditures rather than increase tax rates or add new taxes, even though they may prefer, as

Table 1 Fiscal Strategies, 1977-1980

City	Increase Revenues — Own-Source				Increase Revenues — Intergovernmental			Decrease Total Spending	
	1977	1978	1979	1980	1978	1979	1980	1978	1979
Allentown		A	A	A				X	
Baltimore		A		D	X	X			X
Boise				D	X	X			X
Buffalo								X	X
Champaign			C		X			X	
Cincinnati				D	X			X	
Detroit	A	A			X			X	
E. Orange			A	A					X
Ft. Wayne			A	A					
Greenville	A		A				X		
Hartford	A		CD		X	X			X
Kettering		C	A			X			X
Macon	B								
New Orleans		A[1]	AD	A	X	X			X
Oakland		A	A	D	X	X			X
Parma									
Pueblo		C		BD	X				
Raleigh			A	A					X
St. Paul		A	A	D	X	X	X		
St. Petersburg		C	D			X	X		
San Francisco		A	A			X			
Trenton	D								X
Tuscaloosa				AB					

SOURCE: City budgets, 1978-1980; annual fiscal reports, 1977-1979.

1. To compensate for reduced assessment equalization.

NOTE: Information not available for all years in each city. Dates refer to fiscal years and represent the years in which the increase or decrease was realized relative to the previous year. Intergovernmental revenue increases are measured in nominal terms, and spending decreases in real (deflated dollars).

A = Increased tax rate.
B = Levied new tax.
C = Increased tax revenues by growth in taxable base (through either addition to tax base, appreciation in value of existing base, or revised assessment equalization).
D = Increase or initiation of fees or user charges.

suggested earlier, to maintain existing budget and employment levels. Conventional wisdom suggests tax increases are now politically unfeasible.

However, despite the political difficulties, fully fourteen of the twenty-three fiscally pressured cities raised local tax rates in at least one of the four fiscal years from 1977 to 1980, and two additional cities imposed new taxes (see Table 1). In addition, three of the twenty-three cities experienced increases in the per capita tax levy through increases in the tax base rather than changes in the rate structure. (If these base increases result from an appreciation in residential property values rather than new additions to the base, they may appear to the average citizen, who is concerned primarily with the total amount of taxes he or she pays, as tax increases imposed by local governments.)

In addition, ten of the governments resorted to new or increased user charges or fees (Kettering, Ohio imposed a recreation charge for use of city recreation facilities, New Orleans imposed a road-use charge—in effect, a tax on motor-vehicle ownership—and several municipalities increased or initiated water and sewer fees). Evidence from California cities suggests that local governments are likely to turn to user fees when other local revenue sources are effectively blocked. California local-government revenue from user fees increased by $200 million in the year following passage of Proposition 13 (California Tax Review Digest, June 1979).

Clearly, the above data suggest that own-source revenue increases remain a viable, if somewhat more difficult, local-government strategy. However, it is also likely that the propensity to increase taxes as opposed to reducing expenditures has shifted more toward the latter than it previously had been. Of the twenty-three fiscally pressured local governments, five actually reduced expenditures in current-dollar terms in either FY 1978 or FY 1979, and a total of fourteen reduced total spending from the previous year's level in real terms for at least one of those years. Eight of the local governments engaged in *both* tax increases and real-expenditure reduction over the 1978-80 period.

EXPENDITURE REDUCTION STRATEGIES

Cutting spending without cutting services. For those cities which do engage in expenditure reduction, it appears that the first line of attack is to attempt to reduce own-source spending through means which do not result in a lower level of service received by citizens.

The rhetoric of expenditure reduction frequently implies that local governments can absorb substantial cuts in spending without any real effect on the level of service provided, simply by cutting waste and achieving greater efficiency. Indeed, public officials faced with the need to reduce spending do seek out areas where greater efficiency can be achieved, and frequently with some success. Many of the governments we examined are making greater use of automatic data-processing systems as a means of increasing productivity. Several cities (Hartford, Greenville, Allentown) have engaged in administrative reorganization which they claim has resulted in savings. Detroit is in the process of switching over to mechanized container garbage collection trucks whose operation requires only one person. Several cities (Buffalo, Greenville, Tuscaloosa, and Macon) have changed from backdoor garbage pickup to curbside pickup, although this may be considered a partial service reduction as well as an efficiency savings.

There also appears to be some increase in contracting out to private-sector firms as an explicit means of achieving efficiency savings. Trenton has contracted out a higher proportion of its engineering work than previously; Allentown has contracted out janitorial work. The "efficiency" advantage of contracting out results from bypassing the high wage rates and work rules of the municipal labor unions; however, the opposition of these unions to this strategy greatly limits its applicability in communities where unions are reasonably strong.

Another means of lowering expenditures without reducing services is to achieve efficiency or productivity gains through reducing the real rate of compensation of local-government employees. Presumably, the same number of employees paid less money will provide the preexisting level of service at a lower cost (with perhaps a small adjustment for lower morale). Since personnel costs account for nearly 80 percent of local-government operating costs, any significant effort to reduce expenditures must affect the level of payment for city manpower. Reductions in payroll costs can be accomplished either by decreasing (in real terms) the average salary per employee or by decreasing the total number of municipal employees. Although we were unable to generate useful data from our twenty-three-city survey on the extent and direction of average salary change, data from other sources indicate that municipal-government public-employee wages have decreased by 5.2 percent in real terms between 1975 and 1978 (U.S. Department of Commerce, Bureau of Census, 1975, 1978), a trend we would expect to characterize fiscally pressured cities as well. Indeed, in two of the three cities we have examined intensively (Buffalo and Trenton), wages have increased at a rate below that of inflation for the past several years. By contrast, in Detroit, a highly unionized city, wage increases have outpaced inflation; indeed, Detroit's employee unions have won, through compulsory arbitration, automatic cost-of-living increases.

Burden shifting and substitution provide additional means of maintaining services to citizens while reducing local-government cost. The burden may be shifted partially or fully to either another level of government or to the private sector. The most common form of burden shifting is to persuade a higher level of government to take over responsibility for administering and funding a specific function. Cincinnati persuaded the state of Ohio to take over the city university system and the county to take over its courts. The state of California is planning to administer the health and possibly the court systems currently operated by counties and the city of San Francisco, and in Boise and Buffalo, various central police functions have been taken over by the county. Erie County has assumed responsibility for many of Buffalo's cultural activities. In addition, the city of Buffalo has given its zoo to the Buffalo zoological society, a private nonprofit organization, and now is responsible for assuming only a portion of the zoo's operating deficit (the county provides the bulk of the required subsidy). Detroit is attempting to transfer its general hospital to a private, nonprofit medical corporation.

Substitution of intergovernmental funds for own-source funds maintains spending and service levels while reducing own-source expenditures. As we have noted, this kind of substitution is particularly prevalent in the CETA program. The Community Development Block Grant program appears to be another source of substitution, particularly as the Anti-Recession Fiscal Assistance and CETA programs phase down. In four of the twenty-three cities, we were able to identify CDBG expenditures which previously had been funded out of general operating revenues.

CUTTING SPENDING AND SERVICES

If expenditure reductions are substantial enough, it is inevitable that government services and programs will suffer. Where are these cuts made?

Uncontrollable costs. This question might best be approached by examining first those areas of the budget that cannot be reduced. Certain items in the budget—debt service and pension-payment contributions—represent essentially fixed costs. These items together may account for a significant portion of the expenditure of some local governments. In Buffalo, for example, debt service and pensions amount to approximately 30 percent of total general-fund expenditures. The problem may be particularly acute for local governments which have not adequately funded their pension systems in the past. Many of these governments are now being forced to make annual payments to the pension fund to amortize the unfunded pension liability as well as to finance the current-year liability for existing employees. Detroit, for example, with an unfunded pension liability of $818 million, made general-fund contributions to its pension fund amounting to more than 18 percent of general-fund expenditures in 1978.

In addition to fixed costs, local governments face mandated costs. These are unavoidable costs imposed on the local government by either federal or state law. State governments, for example, may require local governments to participate in a state general-relief program and contribute a portion of the cost. These costs are essentially out of the local government's control. States may require local governments to operate court systems. The federal government requires local governments to assure that public buildings are accessible to the handicapped. And there are many more.

Research by Catherine Lovell and her associates turned up over 1200 federal mandates (approximately 1000 of which, however, were conditions of receiving federal assistance); on the state level, they found 1479 mandates in California, 534 in New Jersey, 259 in North Carolina, 487 in Washington, and 654 in Wisconsin (Lovell et al., 1979: Ch. 3). Estimates on the portion of local-government budgets mandates constitute varied widely and should be taken as merely indications. In Trenton, Lovell and her associates estimated 10 percent, while in San Bernardino, California, their estimate was 40 percent (Lovell et al., 1979: 160). Several of the cities in our survey complained bitterly of mandates as one of the major factors causing operating-cost increases. Kettering and Parma, both in Ohio, noted that the state has raised employers' contributions to the state-operated pension fund by 45 percent since 1975, primarily to fund increased fire fighters' benefits passed by the state legislature, though similar increases have been levied for the police officers' pension fund as well.

Hartford also claimed hardship due to state requirements that have greatly increased personnel costs, citing mandates for minimum compensation, working conditions, and the bargaining process, as well as minimum requirements for special education and environmental protection.

Controllable costs. What does that leave that can be cut? While most local governments made efforts to economize through reducing the costs of supplies, equipment, travel, and the like, the obvious candidates for expenditure reduction are personnel costs for nonmandated functions and capital outlays.

Most of the cities which had decreases in real expenditures reduced manpower levels. For example, since 1977, Cincinnati's work force has been reduced by 10 percent and Hartford's by 15 percent. The reductions generally occurred in two phases—first, a hiring freeze which, over time, resulted in manpower reduction through attrition, and second, if further reductions were necessary, layoffs. Among cities instituting at least partial hiring freezes were Allentown, Boise, Buffalo, Cincinnati, Detroit, and Hartford, and, in many of these cases, freezes were later followed by layoffs. Reductions in personnel are likely to be translated into reduction both in expenditures and services delivered. Where did these expenditure and—presumably—service reductions occur?

Where are expenditure cuts made? We turn first to the question of whether expenditure reductions occur more frequently in programs funded wholly with local revenues or in intergovernmental programs for which local governments must contribute a percentage matching share. One argument, as commonly formulated, suggests that local governments will cut local spending first from services which are wholly funded locally, even if these are higher priority services, because of the much greater loss in revenues and total spending they would incur by reducing participation in federally funded programs. (A dollar reduction for a 75 percent federal matching grant program would result in the local government losing three additional federal dollars, while a dollar reduction in a locally funded program merely results in the dollar being lost.)

A plausible case has also been made for the opposing proposition, namely, that local governments, when faced with fiscal pressure, will reduce local spending in federal programs because these programs are, from local government's point of view, the lowest-priority services they provide. This proposition implies that federally supported services rank so low in local priorities that, even with federal leveraging, local dollars buy less valuable services than when spent on items of local choice.

Empirically, our intensive case studies indicate that programs wholly locally funded are much more susceptible to expenditure and service reductions. In Trenton, public works and public safety have borne the brunt of expenditure reductions. Trenton's Budget Director commented:

> In general intergovernmental expenditures cannot be cut. . . . Social services have been insulated from the city's budget cuts because they are federally funded. Trenton's cuts have all been in the delivery of essential, but locally funded services.

Buffalo has pursued the same strategy. It has suffered major cuts in public works, streets, and sanitation. In Mercer County, New Jersey, the programmatic areas growing most slowly or declining in real terms have been those nearly completely dependent on local funds (parks, general government), while the areas experiencing the fastest expenditure growth have been those most heavily funded through intergovernmental revenue (human services).

Expenditure reductions by function. In which functional or programmatic areas do expenditure reductions most frequently occur? Perhaps the most common way to respond to relatively severe or sudden fiscal pressure, at least in the short term, is through pro rata, across-the-board reductions.

Trenton, for example, has undergone a series of real-expenditure reductions. The Mayor's professional budget staff has favored targeted and selected cuts, and has presented him with suggested options. However, the Mayor has decided upon more-or-less across-the-board cuts in discretionary items. Buffalo's normal budgetary process involves across-the-board spending cuts from current service-level expenditures for three different priority levels of service: police and fire, which take the smallest percentage reductions; a second group which has suffered severe reductions in previous years, and which will receive a moderate rate in the present year; and a third group which will receive the heaviest reduction. Erie County, New York, when it experienced a major fiscal crisis in 1976-77, cut police and fire by 7.5 percent and all other departments by 15 percent.

A fiscal pressure is prolonged, or in cases of relatively moderate pressure, selective rather than across-the-board cuts are made. The data we gathered from our survey make it difficult to determine the distribution of these reductions, because municipal budgets typically account for federal CETA funds as a single expenditure rather than by distributing them among the various departments in which CETA workers are ultimately employed. Since CETA employees are often moved around to substitute for previously funded municipal employees, we cannot be certain that the distribution and extent of reductions captured by our data represent a true picture.

Data on expenditure change by function was available for thirteen of the cities which reduced total real operating expenditures in one or more years between 1977 and 1979. Public works suffered the largest average expenditure reductions (7.7 percent), followed by general government (4.5 percent) and social services (4.2 percent). However, most of the reduction in social services resulted from involuntary reductions of federal social service assistance. Public safety (2.9 percent reduction) was reasonably well isolated from sharp cuts except in cities facing the most severe fiscal pressure. In Buffalo, for example, police-department employees were reduced by 14 percent and fire-department employees by 5.5 percent between 1976-1979. Surprisingly, our broad sample indicates that parks, recreation, and culture (no reduction) make up the area least adversely affected. However, intensive examination of Trenton, Buffalo, and Detroit strongly suggests that parks, recreation, and culture are likely to be among the functions most severely affected by expenditure reduction.[6] In Buffalo, for example, the parks department suffered the largest percentage of reduction in manpower of any department—24.8 percent between 1976 and 1979.

Within departments or functions, reductions are likely to be made selectively based on one or a combination of several factors. Most cities cut back in areas where reductions would be least noticed or felt and where political conflict was likely to be minimal.

Capital-improvement projects and maintenance, since they are areas where the short-term consequences of cutbacks are relatively invisible, are thus prime targets for cutbacks. Indeed, eleven of the cities in our survey acknowledged in telephone interviews cutbacks in these areas; in some cases, cutbacks of rather mammoth proportions. Raleigh cut capital spending by 60 percent between 1977 and 79, San Francisco 45 percent between 1977 and 78, and St. Petersburg 43 percent. Buffalo has spent only $20 million in capital outlays for water-system projects during the past fifteen years; it now has an estimated $500 million in water-system replacement and repair needs.

The reduction in capital spending is reflected in reduced current outlays for debt services. The thirteen cities in our sample which experienced overall real-expenditure reductions average a 16.7 percent reduction in debt service payments. Maintenance cutbacks also were common, and they undoubtedly explain our finding that the sharpest reduction in current operating expenditures occurred in the area of public works.

Departments also cut back on activities which were considered frills, and were therefore unlikely to be very visible or have strong support. "Frills" are not examples of waste and inefficiency, they are real services which enhance the quality of life, but in ways which are often considered marginal. Thus, one of the victims of Trenton's expenditure reductions was the trimming of shade trees. Allentown reduced leaf pickup activities. Buffalo and Tuscaloosa moved from backdoor garbage to curbside pickup. New Orleans cut back a consumer-assistance program.

This strategy of cutting in the *least* visible areas must be distinguished from the gamesmanship which frequently accompanies the initial debate about how to react to fiscal stress. In an effort to create the climate for an unpopular action such as increasing taxes, or to extract additional resources from other units of government, local officials may first threaten cuts in the *most* visible areas, particularly police and fire protection. The purpose is to demonstrate what terrible consequences might occur if additional revenue is not forthcoming or if the situation is not taken seriously. However, the reductions actually made are seldom in such visible and politically threatening areas.

Indeed, the intensive case studies we have engaged in suggest that, to the maximum extent possible, conflict avoidance is likely to characterize local-official expenditure cutback behavior. One of the most common and successful cutback strategies—because it is relatively invisible and conflict free—is to reduce through inaction. Appropriations for particular programs or activities are simply held steady in nominal terms, thus absorbing cuts through inflation rather than through executive or legislative action.

IMPACT OF CUTS

The foregoing discussion suggests that public officials employ a variety of means to hide and to mitigate the effects of expenditure reductions. It would be wrong to imply, however, that reductions of the magnitude observed in some of the cities in our sample can be absorbed without being perceived by service recipients as adversely affecting them. The effects of cuts, even in relatively invisible areas, cannot be totally hidden. Over time, the citizenry begins to perceive the consequences. When asked whether Trenton's populace had perceived the effects of the cuts (as evidenced by compliants to City Hall), the budget director observed:

> Parks are not being maintained and grass is not being trimmed. People are noticing that. Also streets are not being cleaned as frequently and this is being noticed. In the police area we have had to cut back on walking patrols and people have complained about this.

Detroit's budget director commented that, after several years of expenditure reduction, citizens cannot help but notice the effects:

> They don't see police in scout cars or on the beat as much as they used to, recreation areas are in terrible shape, street lights are out and not replaced, the city is not clean, trees are not trimmed frequently enough, tree stumps are not removed, fire houses have been closed.

DISTRIBUTIONAL CONSEQUENCES
OF EXPENDITURE REDUCTIONS

Who bears the burden of local expenditure reductions? Conventional wisdom assumes that the poor and racial minorities will be most seriously adversely affected, since they are politically disorganized and programs on which they depend enjoy low levels of political support.

We have not systematically traced through changes in the actual quantity and quality of services received by different classes of recipients. Thus, we cannot give a definite answer to the question. However, we can examine the programmatic areas which are most relevant to these groups and attempt to determine whether these receive disproportionate reductions. If conventional wisdom is correct, then the human-services programs would be expected to receive disproportionate reductions. These programs are designed primarily for the poor and have the least political support at the local level.

However, it appears that any propensity to reduce expenditures for these programs is strongly mitigated by two factors. First, the human-service programs are also the most heavily federally funded programs, and thus, as suggested earlier, the ones least likely to suffer reductions. Second, most human-service programs are the responsibility of the county or state rather than municipal government; most cities simply do not have the opportunity to reduce local spending for human-service programs very substantially.

County governments—which do have the opportunity—are generally in better fiscal condition than their central cities and thus not as driven to make massive expenditure reductions. In addition, counties too finance a substantial portion of their human services expenditures from intergovernmental sources. Where local governments—whether cities or counties—do spend own-source funds for human-service purposes (other than as matching funds for intergovernmental assistance), these expenditures do appear to experience substantial reductions.

Local recipients of some human services in fiscally constrained cities may find benefits reduced even though their local government has not reduced human-service spending. The state determines benefit levels for AFDC and other income support programs. In New York State, these benefit levels have not changed since 1974; in New Jersey, these levels have increased by only 7.6 percent for AFDC since 1976, and not at all for general assistance—an indication of a lack of political strength of these groups.

Overall, however, it appears that budget reductions do not occur systematically in programs targeted to poor and minority groups. This does not necessarily imply that the poor do not bear a disproportionate portion of the burden. If they do, however, it is likely to be through a different mechanism than cutting programs aimed at the poor. It is possible, for example, that the reductions in the more traditional locally funded programs are disproportionately focused on poor and minority neighborhoods. However, we have not sought evidence to test this possibility.

APPENDIX

FORTY-FIVE LARGEST U.S. CITIES
(in terms of 1975 population)[1]

Phoenix, AZ	Baltimore, MD	Tulsa, OK
Long Beach, CA	Boston, MA	Portland, OR
Los Angeles, CA	Detroit, MI	Philadelphia, PA
Oakland, CA	Minneapolis, MN	Pittsburgh, PA
San Diego, CA	Kansas City, MO	Memphis, TN
San Francisco, CA	St. Louis, MO	Nashville-Davidson, TN
San Jose, CA	Omaha, NB	Dallas, TX
Denver, CO	Newark, NJ	El Paso, TX
Jacksonville, FL	Buffalo, NY	Fort Worth, TX
Miami, FL	New York, NY	Houston, TX
Atlanta, GA	Cincinnati, OH	San Antonio, TX
Honolulu, HI	Cleveland, OH	Norfolk, VA
Chicago, IL	Columbus, OH	Seattle, WA
Indianapolis, IN	Toledo, OH	Milwaukee, WI
New Orleans, LA	Oklahoma City, OK	Louisville, KY

[1]District of Columbia is not included

NOTES

1. We define fiscal pressure as a situation in which a local government faced with the necessity of achieving a balance between revenues and expenditures must in time choose to (1) increase taxes through changes in the tax-rate structure in order to maintain existing real expenditure and service levels, (2) reduce real expenditures from the level of the previous year, or (3) engage in some combination of these activities. This definition of pressure thus excludes local governments which raise taxes in order to increase the existing level of services, local governments which choose to reduce expenditures in order to reduce taxes from existing levels, and local governments whose tax base permits revenues to expand sufficiently, without changes in the tax rate or structure, to maintain or increase existing expenditure levels.

2. A more precise formulation would specify a tax base growing at a rate less than that required to provide revenues sufficient to pay for the city's fixed costs and maintain the existing level of per capita services. Such a condition might well indicate a higher level of expenditures per capita in a community experiencing population decline.

3. Budget deficits may, in turn, be caused by a slowly growing tax base or a reduction in intergovernmental assistance to which the local government did not make prudent reductions. They can occur even in communities with growing tax bases and increases in intergovernmental assistance. Unplanned deficits may thus result if public officials, whether because of political pressures or mismanagement, increase service levels and thus expenditures at a rate faster than natural revenue growth (or do not anticipate noncontrollable expenditure increases) or if they reduce taxes without equivalent spending cuts.

4. California's Proposition 13 is the most widely known such formal limitation, but it is only one of a growing number (see National Conference of State Legislatures, 1979). New Jersey restricts local government spending increases to a flat 5 percent per year. Michigan prevents local governments from receiving increases in local property-tax revenues which exceed the increase in the consumer price index for the previous year.

5. The author is engaged in both of these studies at The Urban Institute. The first, "State and Local Government Spending Changes in an Era of Fiscal Constraint," is funded by the U.S. Department of Health, Education and Welfare, while the second, "Municipal Responses to Fiscal Pressure," is funded by the Charles F. Kettering Foundation.

6. One reason that the reduction calculated for parks, recreation, and culture is so small on the average, even though the majority of cities studied indicated they were cutting back in this area, has to do with the CETA program. CETA workers are usually concentrated in laborer and maintenance positions, most of them in the

public-works and parks programs. As the number of CETA positions declines, many cities eliminate the parks employees before those in public works, reflecting the common perception that park maintenance is less critical than general city cleaning and maintenance. In many cities, these reductions do not show up in the parks area because CETA is reported separately. In fact, in the cities where some positions formerly funded by CETA are transferred to general fund support, the parks function will even have increased spending, though the service provided is not expanded.

REFERENCES

LOVELL, C., R. MEISEL, M. NEIMAN, A. ROSE, and C. TOBIN (1979) Federal and State Mandating on Local Governments: An Exploration of Issues and Impacts. Final Report to the National Science Foundation. Riverside: University of California.

National Conference of State Legislatures (1979) A Legislator's Guide to State Tax and Spending Limits. Washington, DC: Government Printing Office.

U.S. Department of Commerce, Bureau of Census (1975) Public Employment in 1975. Washington, DC: Government Printing Office.

——— (1978) Public Employment in 1978. Washington, DC: Government Printing Office.

11

CAN PUBLIC POLICY TERMINATION BE INCREASED BY MAKING GOVERNMENT MORE BUSINESSLIKE?

ROBERT D. BEHN

Institute of Policy Sciences and Public Affairs
Duke University

"Government does not terminate its policies often enough." That is a common complaint. But what does "often enough" mean? How do we know that the termination rate is not high enough? What is the standard against which we should compare the termination rate of public programs, agencies, projects, and other policies? How can we tell when the termination rate is satisfactory?

The conclusion that government fails to terminate its activities frequently enough derives, I believe, from an implicit comparison with

AUTHOR'S NOTE: *I would like to thank the National Science Foundation for its assitance in this research. Some of the materials in this work were developed with the financial support of the National Science Foundation Grant on the Termination of Public Policies (SOC-7719116). However, any opinions, findings and conclusions, or recommendations expressed herein are those of the author and do not necessarily reflect the views of the Foundation.*

The original version of this article was a paper titled, "How the Differences Between Private and Public Organizations Affect Their Abilities to Terminate Their Activities," and was presented at the Annual Conference of the American Society for Public Administration in Phoenix, Arizona on April 10, 1978. A number of colleagues provided thoughtful suggestions and criticisms on that paper, and I am grateful for the comments of Graham T. Allison, Jr., James M. Cameron, Philip J. Cook, Willis D. Hawley, Charles H. Levine, Hal G. Rainey, Richard Rose, and Gary L. Wamsley. They should not be held liable, however, for my failure to grasp the wisdom of their ideas.

business. When we say that government does not terminate its policies often enough, we mean that it does not end them as often as business ends its own. The conventional, if unarticulated, wisdom holds that there is a significant difference in the rates at which public and private organizations end their respective activities. The rate of governmental termination is considered inadequate because it does not measure up to the standard set by business.

From this implicit comparison inevitably emerges a common policy proposal: Make government more businesslike. If only government could be changed to be more like business, goes the logic, we could increase government's termination rate. If only corporate executives—people who understand the "bottom line" and other imperatives of business management—ran the government, we could easily and simply increase the termination of obsolete, duplicative, and dysfunctional government policies.

For the purposes of this essay, I accept the assumption that business terminates its activities more frequently than government does. I do so, in part, because I despair at testing the proposition that government and business have different termination rates. In part, I do so because the proposition appears to be quite plausible; the conventional wisdom is not always wrong (although it does provide a convenient strawman upon which to construct academic reputations). But, most importantly, I accept the assumption because I recognize the power of the conventional wisdom and wish to explore the validity of the policy recommendation that, in this case, inevitably flows from it. The difficulty of testing the proposition contributes to its durability; thus it is particularly important to examine carefully the policy changes it implies.

Would making government more like business increase the termination rate in the public sector? What does it mean to make government more businesslike? What are the differences between business and government that contribute to the (assumed) differences in their termination rates? What are the possible actions that would make government more like business *and* increase government's termination rate? My purpose is not to derive, deductively, the existence of a differential in the public/private termination rates from a set of factors that might create such a differential. Rather, assuming that such a differential does exist, I want to examine the policy implications of that assumption: What is it about the well-known differences in the characteristics of public and private organizations that might help explain any difference in their termination rates? And what is the implication of these different characteristics for the prospects of increasing government's ability to terminate its various policies?

My conclusion is simple enough: Business and government are different —and in some very fundamental ways. Some of the most basic organizational characteristics of business and government—the purposes they seek to achieve, the pressures under which their respective managers work, and the environments in which they operate—are inherent to the nature of the two organizations and are major contributors to how they can and do terminate their activities. To the extent that there exists a differential in their termination rates and to the extent that the factors I have identified are the ones that contribute most directly to that differential, it will not be possible to make government more businesslike, at least not in a way that will increase government's termination rate. Those who wish to improve the termination rates of governmental programs had best attempt to cope directly with the characteristics of government that make the termination of its activities so difficult,[1] rather than engage in the futile exercise of reworking the basic nature of government to make it more like business.

SOME EVIDENCE OF A DIFFERENTIAL IN TERMINATION RATES

Testing the proposition that government and business have different termination rates would be quite difficult—perhaps impossible. After all, the nature of their respective activities is quite different, so that the definitions used for "government activities" and "business activities" can predetermine the conclusions. If government activities grew only on vines and business activities only on trees, the results of any test for the size of their respective fruits could depend upon whether you choose to compare pumpkins with cherries, or grapes with coconuts. The definitional problem seems to preclude any reasonable comparison of termination rates.[2]

For example, in his effort to answer the question *Are Government Organizations Immortal?* Kaufman concluded (from data averaged over half a century) that "the annual rate of business failures (56.8 per 10,000) was more than twice the annual death rate (27.9 per 10,000) of the government units" (1976: 54). But there are at least two characteristics of the analysis that bias it toward such a conclusion. First, the governmental death rate was derived calculating how many units alive in 1923 died during the following fifty years. As Kaufman notes: "Since many organizations undoubtedly were born and died in that interval without leaving a record in the specimen population, the mortality figures may be abnormally low" (1976: 54). Second, the government units that Kaufman examined were "departmental headquarters units and . . . the major subdivisions of the departments—essentially, bureaus and groups of bureaus" (1976: 24), while the business data came from Dun and Bradstreet's reports on all business failures. During the first two years of their existence, half of all business firms fail—and the rate is even higher for small businesses—yet Kaufman's sample on the government side specifically excludes small units. Perhaps if intraoffice project teams (the public sector's equivalent of the mom-and-pop grocery store?) were included in the government data, the conclusions would be quite different.

One could, of course, select enterprises that are run by both public and private organizations and test to see if the termination rate of such a common activity is influenced by organizational type. Do private hospitals eliminate useless or outmoded surgical procedures more rapidly than public ones?[3] Yet even the absence of statistically significant differences in the public and private termination rates for such specific activities would not confirm the null hypothesis for the more general proposition. Private organizations supply private goods; public organizations supply public goods. A limited analysis that concentrated on those few situations in which government business provided the same goods would not uncover a differential in termination rates that results from the differences in the basic nature of private and public activities.

And it does seem reasonable that such a differential exists. There exists a wide body of evidence—albeit much of it anecdotal—to support the proposition that government ends its activities much less frequently than business. Such evidence does not provide scientific proof, but it may convince the skeptic that the conventional wisdom is valid.

Think of a business activity that has been terminated and ask: Would government have done the same? If the "Ohio Steel Authority" rather than the Youngstown Sheet and Tube Company had operated the Campbell Works, would it have closed the plant in 1977 and laid off 5000 steel workers (Stevens, 1977)? For those who think it would, consider the behavior of the government-owned British Steel Corporation, which since at least 1972 has wanted to close its antiquated Shotton Works that employ approximately 10,000 Welsh steel workers, (Morgenthaler, 1977); not until the aggressive Tory government of Prime Minister Margaret Thatcher replaced the Labour Party in 1979 did BSC have the political support necessary to announce that it would close the steel-making portion of the plant (while keeping open its steel-processing operations), buying off 6,300 workers with up to £20,000 each in "redundancy pay" (The Economist, 1979). If the U.S. Postal Service had run REA Express (formerly Railway Express) would the 136-year-old firm have been liquidated in 1975 (Jones, 1975)? If the "Federal Cellophane Administration" rather than FMC Corp had been making the wood pulp-based product would it have closed the plant when new, petroleum-based substitutes made cellophane obsolete (Morris, 1978)? Or suppose the Chicago Daily News had been owned not by Field Enterprises but by City Hall; would the government have been as willing to conclude that declining circulation of afternoon newspapers, in part due to the competition from evening television news programs, was inevitable and closed the paper (Kneeland, 1978)? Can you imagine what would have happened if the Edsel, instead of being manufactured by the Ford Motor Company and named for the father of its president, Henry ("the Edsel is here to stay") Ford II, had been built by the U.S. Government and named for the father of Lyndon B. Johnson?

Business may be sentimental about some of its traditional products, but it is quite capable of overcoming that emotion. Textron has gotten out of its original line of business, textiles. DuPont has stopped making dynamite, one of the firm's original and continuously profitable products. Liggett is phasing itself out of cigarettes. Bell & Howell has sold its home-movie camera division. Observed Bell & Howell's chief executive officer, Donald N. Frey (Hayes, 1979):

> Understand that getting out of the photo business for us was an enormously difficult job. Aside from the emotion—and I got past that soon enough—the business was intertwined with so much of what we do. Freeing ourselves of it was a horrendous project.

Commented one employee: "Everyone here feels a certain nostalgia for the home-movie product; it's part of our heritage" (New York Times, 1979). Yet that nostalgia did not prevent Bell & Howell from terminating the product line.

In government, however, the ability to recognize the obsolete, let alone the willingness to terminate it, is not so common. For half a century, the horse cavalry maintained what Katzenbach (1958: 121) called "a capacity for survival that borders on the miraculous" despite a series of challenges from the machine gun, the tank, and the airplane. In part, the cavalry survived (as an institution if not on the battlefield) because of the nostalgia of military commanders—those most hard-headed of all governmental leaders—for the cavalry charge. Katzenbach describes the cavalry charge as "a wave of horsemen, gaily colored (except in the United States), helmets shining, plumes flying, sabers drawn or lances at the ready," and concluded that "basically it was continued because the cavalry liked it" (Katzenbach, 1958: 126). Both Bell & Howell and the U.S. Army possessed a desire to maintain the old and the familiar, but as a basis for decision making, that sentiment seems to be much less important in business than in government.

The case of Chrysler United Kingdom Ltd. illustrates well this difference between the public and private sectors in their tolerance of termination. In the first half of 1975, after a decade of losses, Chrysler's British subsidiary lost another £15.9 million ($36 million), and the company was considering whether or not to close its three British plants and liquidate its subsidiary at a cost, *The Economist* estimated, of £50-100 million (1975a). Chrysler's chairman, John J. Riccardo, reported (New York Times, 1975a):

> We were in the position that we could no longer absorb the losses or provide the cash, so the only alternative was to transfer the company to the [British] government. We were even willing to give them $70 million in addition to giving them the company.

Just the year before, however, the British government had committed £2.8 billion to nationalize and rescue British Leyland Ltd., the only British-owned automobile firm (now called BL Ltd.), and it was in no position to operate two such companies.

So, in December 1975, the British government committed £162.5 million to keep Chrysler: £72.5 million to cover the firm's losses over a four year period, and £90 million in loans and loan guarantees. The government did this despite:

(1) having the previous month established a "new industrial strategy" in which it declared itself willing to assist only promising firms, not "lame ducks" (Kilborn, 1975a);

(2) Prime Minister Harold Wilson's complaint that the company was holding "a pistol to the government's head," and his insistence that "Chrysler will not get one penny" (Will, 1976);

(3) its own study of the British automobile industry concluding that it was plagued by excess capacity and low productivity and recommending that two plants be closed and production reduced by 400,000 cars per year (The Economist, 1975a); and

(4) the inevitability that Chrysler's sales would reduce the sales of cars produced by government-owned Leyland in the limited British market.

Still, the British government agreed to aid the weakest of the four firms producing automobiles in Britain. (In addition to Chrysler and Leyland, there are Ford and General Motors subsidiaries there.)

As Industry Minister Eric Varley explained: "The stark choice is between keeping these 17,000 jobs [that Chrysler agreed to maintain] or losing not only the 25,000 but also many others in firms which depend on Chrysler (Kilborn, 1975b). Moreover, 6,900 of Chrysler's 25,000 workers were employed at the Lindwood plant in Scotland (*The Economist*

[1975b] called it "commercially the most expendable of Chrysler's plants"), and the Labour Government feared that if the plant were closed the Scottish National party would defect from Labour's parliamentary coalition and the government would collapse.

More recently, a similar scenario has played out in the United States, with the federal government providing Chrysler with $1.5 million in loan guarantees. Lee A. Iacocca, chairman of Chrysler Corporation, called the loan "a key step in the preservation of approximately 500,000 jobs" (Miller, 1980). Recent events suggest that if a large business can convince the government that its primary mission is not to produce a product for consumers but to employ workers, the government will feel compelled to save the firm from extinction.

Indeed, government has recently been called upon to rescue a wide variety of private undertakings. Railroad passenger service, transit service, nursing homes, Yankee Stadium, Radio City Music Hall, Chrysler, Lockheed—government is frequently called upon to bail out or take over a variety of what were once business's tasks. If a private organization decides to terminate one of its activities, those who are hurt, wronged, inconvenienced, or offended by the decision look to government to sustain the effort.

Further, people also look to government to establish rules that constrain when and how business is permitted to end one of its enterprises. The Interstate Commerce Commission and the U.S. Railway Association have rules that govern the abandonment of rail service (Railway Age, 1974). The Federal Communications Commission has rules as to how Western Union Corporation can close telegraph offices. In 1980, union officials asked a federal court judge to prevent the United States Steel Corporation from closing its two plants in Youngstown, Ohio. And in Congress and the state Legislatures, a variety of bills have been introduced to prevent or inhibit business firms from closing their plants, with special provisions for advance notification, and severance benefits and transfer rights for employees (Singer, 1979). France, West Germany, and Sweden already have such laws.

On the other hand, can you think of an activity that government wanted to abandon but was rescued by business? I can think of only one: BL Ltd. decided to terminate production of the MG sports car, and a consortium of private firms headed by Aston Martin Lagonda bought the plant and license to produce the car.[5] Of course, the Postal Reorganization Act of 1970 did create the U.S. Postal Service as an independent, businesslike establishment that would operate in a more efficient, businesslike fashion so as to eliminate the annual deficit of the old Post Office

Department. But one reason some members of Congress want to return to more public control over the Postal Service is that the agency has pursued the goal of efficiency by closing a number of rural post offices (U.S. Senate, 1976a).

The records of business and government in terminating their own activities seem to be substantially different. The proposition itself may not be subject to statistical verification. But those who argue the conventional wisdom certainly appear to have a strong case.

PUBLIC, PRIVATE, AND IN-BETWEEN ORGANIZATIONS

Using the terms "public" and "private" does not bisect the universe of organizations into two mutually exclusive categories. Rather, the differences between business and government define an entire spectrum of organizations from the purely private at one end to the purely public at the other. In between, we have a variety of quasi-public, quasi-private organizations.[6] (This creates another barrier to any statistical test of the conventional wisdom: Exactly how do you define "government" and "business"?)

Near the purely public end of this spectrum there are numerous independent agencies and public corporations: the Tennessee Valley Authority; the Urban Development Corporation in New York State; the U.S. Postal Service, Amtrak, the Export-Import Bank (Eximbank); and independent port, turnpike, bridge, tunnel, and airport authorities. Such organizations have been established by government but have been given some specific private characteristics to permit them to function more like businesses than traditional government agencies.

Near the other end of the spectrum are private corporations, such as automobile manufacturers, that must be responsive to government regulation designed to achieve such public purposes as reducing air pollution and increasing passenger safety. There are also businesses, such as defense contractors and some consulting firms, that are dependent almost exclusively on government contracts and thus are not subject to the standard economic discipline of competing in a free market. And further toward the middle of the spectrum are the natural monopolies—private utilities whose most basic economic decisions, production levels and prices, are not made by the firm to maximize profits but are subject to direct government control. Public and private universities are closer to each other on this spectrum than they are to their respective ends.

Along this private-public spectrum, the various characteristics of organizations—including the propensity and ability to terminate their activities—vary continuously. There simply does not exist a neat dichotomy between the public and private sectors, or a few clear characteristics which permit such a distinction to be made. There do, however, exist two hypothetical "ideal types": the purely public government organization, and the purely private business organization. In the following discussion of organizational characteristics,[7] the objective is to distinguish between these two ideal types that define the ends of the private-public organizational spectrum, though obviously the illustrations are taken from real, not ideal, organizations.

GOALS AND MEASURES

The most obvious and frequently mentioned difference between business and government concerns the nature of their goals and of their criteria for measuring performance. Business has a single, simple, clear and well-accepted objective: to make a profit. Furthermore, dollars provide a single, simple, clear and well-accepted measure of business performance. Any business organization will be very well aware of whether or not it is a success.

In contrast, the goals of a government agency are multiple, complex, vague, and subject to much debate. As a result, defining a useful criterion— or even useful criteria—for measuring the performance of any agency, policy, or program is very difficult. Often it is simply not done. Consequently, a public administrator is rarely able to determine unambiguously when an agency or one of its programs, policies, or projects is a success.

Drucker argues that the goals of business are just as intangible as those of government: "To say, as Sears, Roebuck does, 'Our business is to be the informed buyer for the American family' is intangible" (Drucker, 1974: 140). Nevertheless, even if this, rather than profit, is the true goal of Sears, the measure of the firm's success is still the same: are sales greater or less than costs? If costs exceed sales, Sears is clearly doing a poor job at being the American family's informed buyer. For business, the measure of performance is certainly not intangible.

Writing on "The Death and Burial of 'Sick' Products," Alexander suggests that a business's decision to terminate the production of a particular product "should not turn on the sole issue of probability. Profit is the most important objective of a business, but individual firms often seek to achieve both long-run and short-run objectives other than profit (Alexander, 1977: 355), such as market share or growth in sales. At the same time, Alexander observes: "Probably a practical minimum [profit] standard can be worked out, below which a product should be eliminated unless other considerations demand its retention" (1977: 356). Profit—or the lack of it—is clearly the first-order basis upon which a business decides whether to continue or end the production of a product.

Drucker writes that a government agency (or any other service institution) will perform only if it: (1) defines its mission; (2) derives from this clear objectives; (3) thinks through priorities; (4) establishes measures of performance; (5) uses these measurements to feed back from results to efforts; and (6) audits objectives and results to identify obsolete or unattainable objectives, unsatisfactory performance, and obsolete or unproductive activities (Drucker, 174: 158-159). Clearly, such "rational" management would improve performance, though it ought to be equally clear why such "rationality" is rarely achieved.

Why? Bower writes that the objectives of a government agency are set not by its managers but by outsiders—by legislators and constituents (1977). Obviously, an agency's administrators do possess initiative and authority, but they are severely limited in their ability to define their mission, establish objectives, set priorities, create measurements, and rethink objectives. Of course, the ability of business managers to define the objectives of their firm is also constrained—in this case, by the rigors of the marketplace. But, comparing the ideal types at the extreme ends of the public/private spectrum, it should be clear that managers in government have much less influence over the mission of their organizations (and much less flexibility to redefine that mission) than do their counterparts in business.

Furthermore, the outsiders who establish or influence an agency's mission and goals will rarely do so unambiguously. When the legislature creates an agency or program, it seldom defines its own purposes and goals. Not that this is mere oversight. Often, being vague is necessary for the creation of a coalition that will vote for passage. Legislators with conflicting goals can be rallied to support the proposed agency or program only if the purposes and how they are to be achieved are *not* defined in the legislation (see Lowi, 1969).

All this confronts the public administrator with a dilemma. Management requires goals and performance. Yet to attempt to think through, explicitly and publicly, one's mission, objectives, priorities, and measures of performance may well create such controversy and antagonism that the resulting turmoil will divert the agency's energies from those tasks that it is already accomplishing, undermine employee morale, and destroy the administrator's effectiveness. Simon, Smithburg, and Thompson note that agencies "often operate with very inferior statutes in order to avoid opening up legislative debate by asking for needed amendments" (1950: 407).

The difference, then, between the goals and performance measures of an "ideal" business, which are single, simple, clear, and well accepted, and those of an "ideal" government, which are multiple, complex, vague, and debatable, helps explain the difference in their termination rates. The management of a business simply has a much easier time determining which of its activities are contributing to the organization, and how much. Writes Cyert: "The main technique for resolving conflicts arising within contracting organizations is to find objective criteria on which agreement among the contesting participants can be achieved." And, he observes, "the business organization can more easily deal with the conflicts resulting from contraction. Profit is a well-defined criterion of performance and simplifies the measurement of the performance of subunits" (Cyert, 1978: 348).

For example, when, in 1971, RCA was debating the future of its computer division, everyone in top management recognized that the division was not achieving its objectives and knew the exact extent of the problem: a five-year after-tax loss of $90 million. As a result, there was a general acceptance that change was essential, though obviously there was room for disagreement about what that change should be. Still, the existence of clear goals and performance measures narrowed the range of possible options. RCA executives could disagree about whether or not the division could be made profitable, but there existed little opportunity for dissent about its past failures or about how future success should be defined. In the end, RCA dropped out of the computer business, just as General Electric and Xerox have done (Demaree, 1972).

When U.S. District Court Judge Frank J. McGarr was considering the bankruptcy case of the Chicago, Rock Island & Pacific Railroad, he noted that he had received "a veritable flood of mail, telegrams and phone calls" from people asking him to rescue the railroad: "They all implored me to save the Rock Island as if it were within my power to do so." McGarr observed, however, that for the railroad to continue operation, it would have to be able to make a profit. "If I can't make reorganization for the benefit of the creditors work, I have no choice but liquidation" (New York Times, 1975b). Even when a court is making the decision about a business, the goal of profit establishes the criterion for deciding between termination and continuation.

One of the reasons that the Department of Defense is able to close so many military bases may be because its goals are much clearer and more generally accepted than those of other departments. There is disagreement over how to achieve these goals—and over how much to spend doing so—but the defense of the nation is a well-accepted objective. And, although DOD may create much debate by stating that it "needs" a new weapon system, it provokes little dissent when it declares one is obsolete. Consequently, when the Air Force decided that the B-47 was no longer an effective weapon, it was phased out, as were the Air Force bases which supported it (Behn and Lambert, 1979)

With ambiguous goals, however, it is difficult to define failure and thus justify termination, but quite easy to develop a plethora of rationales for continuation. Lindsay Carter Warren, Comptroller General of the U.S. from 1940 to 1954, once observed (Colen, 1977):

> Any bureau can put up a case, at least to suit itself, why it should be retained. Congress can set up a bureau for the edification of the Three Blind Mice or the Rehabilitation of Humpty Dumpty, and within a year those who head them can come in with glowing accounts of their work.

Moreover, when it is impossible to measure success and failure, how can termination even be considered? Termination is such a drastic and final step that it ought to be the overwhelmingly best alternative before this decision is made. Yet, without clear goals and performance measures, how can any alternative be obviously better than the others?

CONSEQUENCES, CONSTITUENCIES, AND CONTROL

The goals of government are not only more numerous and diverse than those of business. The consequences of its actions have greater and broader impact, and, as a result, its constituents are more numerous and diverse. (And this, in turn, feeds back to affect the goals of government: because a government agency has a wider range of constituencies than business, it must also have a wider range of goals.)

The constituents of a business—those individuals and groups most directly and intensely concerned about its actions—are basically those who participate in transactions with it: the owners, the managers, the employees, and the customers. This does not mean that these groups are always in conflict. Owners and employees, for example, may differ over how profits should be divided between them, though neither disagrees with the goal of making profits. The agreement between the United Auto Workers and the major automobile manufacturers on questions of safety and air pollution-control devices further illustrates the point (Serrin, 1973).

When it comes to the termination of a business activity, however, the constituent conflict will be between owners and employees. The reason that termination is even considered is because the customers have abandoned the firm's product or service. There simply are not enough customers to warrant continuation. At this point, the balance of power is clearly on the side of the managers who will favor termination. They have the legal authority to close down a plant or a division (unless Congress passes new legislation), and they have the control of their organization that is necessary to do so. Most labor unions have not been able to negotiate no-cut contracts,[8] so if they want to resist the closing, they must either buy the plant or ask the government to interfere.

The activities of a public organization will have a much broader impact than those of a private one; that is why these activities have been made public responsibilities. Admittedly, the effect of the decisions of Exxon and U.S. Steel are far reaching, though this is, in part, because the policies of these firms are identical to those of Texaco, Mobil, and Gulf or of Bethlehem, Jones & Laughlin, National, and Republic. And, of course, there are the externalities to private transactions that mean the impact of business activities is not limited to the owners, employees, and customers. Still, there ought to be little doubt that, in most cases, the constituents of a government agency are more numerous than those of a business firm of the same size. After all, if nothing else, everyone pays taxes to support the agency, but only those who purchase the firm's products pay to support it.

Furthermore, the diversity of views represented by the constituencies of a public organization is much greater. For every group that believes an agency is pursuing the proper policies, there are others with the opposite opinion. Frequently, all of the constituencies will be dissatisfied—but for different and conflicting reasons.

Still, for a public organization, the views of all constituent groups are to be considered legitimate. Indeed, they are officially sanctioned through the establishment of procedural safeguards and legal constraints (such as the Administrative Procedure Act) to ensure that none of the divergent interests is ignored. Consequently, the managers of a government agency have less control of their organizations than do their business counterparts. They make decisions less than they negotiate compromises—not only with outside constituencies, but also with subordinates who may have cultivated outside supporters. In the public organization, the bias is toward consensus and compromise.

Significantly, the influence that various constituent groups will have on this bargaining process is not only a function of their size but also of their intensity of concern. And, as Bauer, Pool, and Dexter observed, "fear of loss is a more powerful stimulus than prospect of gain" (1963: 142). Consequently, those who fear the losses that will result from termination—

and termination will inevitably inflict losses on someone—will be more intensely motivated than will those who can expect to gain from termination. Furthermore, if the program to be terminated has concentrated benefits and diverse costs, those who gain from the termination will do so only slightly, while those who lose from the termination will lose significantly.[9]

Again, the difference in the impact of business and government is significant. People will lose their jobs both when a government agency eliminates a program and when a business firm closes a plant. But the losses by other constituents due to the termination of a public activity will be greater and more extensive, in part, because of government's monopoly role. If U.S. Steel stops producing high-carbon steel, a number of existing steel firms, and perhaps some new ones, will increase their production of the product (and, in the process, hire some more workers, too). But if the government terminates one of its veterans' programs, who will provide the service? When a public organization terminates one of its activities, there is no one to fill the void.

The consequences of an organization's activities, the constituencies that it attracts, and the control its managers exert are all interrelated. And the differences in these factors between private and public organizations influence the differences in their termination rates. The greater and more extensive consequences of public organizations win them more numerous and diverse constituencies. Constituencies seek to influence decisions, and the more numerous constituencies of government are able to establish rules for political decision making that more severely constrain the control exercised by the public administrator (compared with the relative freedom of the private manager). Thus, although changes in business policy can be made by the organization's managers, changes in public policy must result from bargaining, a process in which those with the most intensive feelings have the greatest influence. And given that the threat of termination—the threat of loss—will arouse intense feelings, the constituencies opposing termination will bargain very hard—and usually be successful. Compromise will result more frequently in the public organization than the private one, and compromise will almost automatically preclude termination.[10]

TIME HORIZONS

Termination is necessarily a long-term solution. In either business or government, it will result in substantial short-run costs, both financial and political, but in few short-run benefits. There are the enemies that will be made by suggesting and implementing the termination—enemies who will be more vocal and dedicated than the few friends earned through the process (Behn, 1977a: 393-394). Moreover, there are the closing costs: the expenses of mothballing facilities and transferring equipment; the severance payments to employees; the size payments to buy off the losers. Only in the long run will the benefits that accrue from termination (increased organizational effectiveness, lower operating expenses, better management, program reform) surpass the costs. Termination can rarely result in short-run savings (see Behn, 1977a: 406-407; 1978b).

In the third quarter of 1977, the Bethlehem Steel Corporation reported the largest net loss in the history of American industry: $477 million.[11] Pretax losses were $894 million, including $750 million resulting from the closing of Bethlehem's plants in Johnstown, Pennsylvania and Lackawanna, New York (a $167 million write-off for facilities not completely depreciated, a $100 million one-time charge to close the plants, and $483 for pension benefits to be paid to the 7300 employees permanently laid off). Offsetting these losses was $417 million in present and future tax deductions that would be taken because of the closings (see Ignatius, 1977). Explained Bethlehem's chairman, Lewis W. Foy:

> Under generally accepted accounting principles, Bethlehem must immediately recognize all estimated costs of the closing of such facilities and employee terminations, even though the major portion of these costs is payable in the future [Salpukas, 1977].

Although both public and private organizations must incur short-run costs to terminate their activities, the time horizons of public and private managers are quite different. Writes Bower: "Public sector managers frequently must ... [a]ccomplish their goals in less time than is allowed corporate managers" (Bower, 1977: 134). It is the rare public official who has the ten years of the Director of the Federal Bureau of Investigation or the fourteen years of a Federal Reserve Board Governor to produce results.

The term of office of top-level public managers is usually fixed at two or four years—either because they must stand for reelection, or because the official who appointed them must do so. And some public agencies, such as the National Park Service, have an established policy of transferring their middle managers between field offices after only two or three years. Moreover, Buchanan reports that public managers possess less organizational commitment than private managers do; they identify less with their organization, are less loyal, and are more likely to leave for another job (1974). Career expectations can certainly shorten a manager's time horizons.

In addition, public officials are pressed by their more numerous and diverse constituencies to achieve success quickly. The short-run costs of starting a new enterprise, or of significantly reforming an existing one, are more recognized and accepted in the business world than they are in government. Consequently, the demand for quick results is much greater in public than private organizations, and further shortens the government administrator's time horizon.

Yet a short time horizon constrains a manager's alternatives. It creates incentives to pursue short-run remedies rather than long-run solutions, or simply to ignore problems that can only be resolved in the long run. For example, J. W. Anderson, an editorial writer for the Washington *Post,* has commented on the attitudes of public and private managers toward employee strikes (1975):

> Municipal unions, in New York and everywhere else, have discovered that city governments can't take long strikes. Sometimes a private company will take a strike that goes on for months, to protect future profits. But city hall is not in the business of protecting profits. It is in the business of delivering peace, order and efficient garbage collection.

Similarly, when short-run considerations dominate a public manager's thinking, termination—which can be only a long-run solution—will be rarely considered.

A series of National Park Service superintendents ignored the problems created by the agency's beach erosion-control program at the Cape Hatteras National Seashore. In part, they may well have been motivated by the (unconscious) recognition that the inevitable turmoil resulting from any termination attempt would reflect badly upon their managerial competence. Yet, since they would be superintendents of the park for only two or three years, the benefits of eliminating the expensive and, many argued, harmful program would appear only during the terms of their successors (Behn and Clark, 1979: 124-125).

When the British government decided to bail out Chrysler U.K., it did so because its short-term desire to save jobs dominated its long-term objective of transforming the British automobile industry. Indeed, the nature of the dilemma was clear to all. Margaret Thatcher, then the opposition leader, declared: "They have gone for the easy option. . . . In the long run, they will not save jobs, they will destroy them" (Kilborn, 1975b). American columnist George F. Will called it "an instance of a government moved by fear of short-term unpleasantness (increased unemployment, possible by-election defeats) abandoning its announced long-term policies" (Will, 1976). *The Economist* (1975a: 76) was equally as critical:

> Each time this sort of short-term decision is made to get round a political problem, it means less money and even less inclination to change the face of British industry and to tackle the main problem: too many people doing the wrong, outdated job . . . one day, now sooner rather than later, it will be more than the car industry that will collapse from obesity.

For Prime Minister Wilson's cabinet, however, the objective of making British industry efficient and competitive could not be achieved if it were out of office.

Business managers, by virtue of their longer time horizons, are in a better position to accept short-run losses to achieve greater, long-run profits than are managers in government. Thus, the differences in time horizons between business and government helps explain the differences between their termination rates.

MODE OF PAYMENT: MARKET VERSUS BUDGET

From the managerial perspective, argues Drucker, the important distinction is between business enterprises and "service institutions" (which include not only government agencies but also the advertising, legal, and research staff departments of business firms). Drucker derives this distinction from the reward systems of the two types of institutions—from their mode of payment. Business is paid by results or performance, by satisfying customers. Service institutions, in contrast, are paid from budget allocations—by promise, not performance. "Their revenues," writes Drucker, "are allocated from a general revenue stream which is not tied to what they are doing but obtained by tax, levy, or tribute" (Drucker, 1974: 141). Wolf makes a similar distinction—between market and nonmarket activities. He defines "non-market activities as those undertaken by governments and other institutions whose sources of revenue come principally from taxes, donations, or other non-price sources, rather than from charging prices in markets" (Wolf, 1979: 115).

The Drucker-Wolf distinction can be illustrated by the differences between public and private schools. Private schools obtain their funds, at least in part, from the tuition payments of the students they educate. Public schools obtain funds not by satisfying their individual customers, but by winning the budget battle with the recreation department, police department, and fire department.

From the mode of payment, Drucker derives other distinctions between business and service institutions. For example, he argues that service institutions possess a unique type of monopoly power: they receive payment even if the service is not used. Parents may elect not to educate their children in the public schools, but they must still pay for this service through their real-estate taxes. Further, Drucker argues, being dependent upon budget rather than customer payments significantly broadens the service institution's constituency and the resultant dilution of the resources reduces its effectiveness (1974: 144, 145):

> Being dependent on a budget allocation militates against setting priorities and concentrating efforts, yet nothing is ever accomplished unless scarce resources are concentrated on a small number of priorities ... the service institution cannot concentrate; it must instead try to placate everyone.

The managers of a private school can concentrate their resources, provide a particular, unique product, and be successful by satisfying a small portion of the educational market. In contrast, the managers of a public school must not just satisfy the students and their parents, but everyone else in the school district who pays the taxes from which the school's budget is allocated. Bower, too, makes this distinction (1977):

> Business strategy has been called the art of imbalance—the application of massive resources to limited objectives. In contrast, a public institution's strategy might be called the art of the imperfect—the application of limited resources to massive objectives.

Drucker also argues that as a consequence of the difference in the mode of payment, the two types of institutions will perform differently, each in response to its own type of reward (1974: 142):

> Being paid out of a budget allocation changes what is meant by performance, or results. Results in the budget-based institutions mean a larger budget. Performance is the ability to maintain or to increase one's budget. Results, as the term is commonly understood, that is, contributions to the market or achievement toward goals and objectives, are in effect, secondary. The first test of a budget-based institution and the first requirement for its survival is to obtain the budget. And the budget is not, by definition, related to contribution but to good intentions.

To the managers of a private school, performance is measured by tuition payments. To the managers of a public school, performance is measured by a "fair" share of the town's budget. "Lacking profit as a measure of performance," writes Wolf, "a non-market agency may view its budget as the proxy goal to be maximized" (1979: 122). (Wolf also suggests that the lack of a clear performance measure may lead to another surrogate: "advanced technology or technical 'quality' as an agency goal" [1979: 124].)

The mode of payment, writes Drucker, also affects an institution's desire and ability to terminate its activities (1974: 145-146):

> being budget-based makes it even more difficult to abandon the wrong things, the old, the obsolete. As a result, service institutions are even more encrusted than business with the barnacles of inherently unproductive efforts.

> No institution likes to abandon anything it does. Business is no exception. In an institution that is being paid for its performance and results and that stands, therefore, under a performance test, the unproductive, the obsolete, will sooner or later be killed off by the customers. In a budget-based institution no such discipline is being enforced. On the contrary; what such an institution does is always virtuous and likely to be considered in the public interest.

> The temptation is great, therefore, to respond to lack of results by redoubling efforts. The temptation is great to double the budget, precisely because there is no performance. The temptation, above all, is to blame the outside world for its stupidity or its reactionary resistance, and to consider lack of results a proof of one's own righteousness and a reason in itself for keeping on with the good work.

> All service institutions are threatened by the tendencies to cling to yesterday rather than to slough it off, and to put their best and ablest people on defending what no longer makes sense or serves a purpose. Government is particularly prone to this disease.

The mode of payment clearly creates different incentives in public and private organizations. The business manager can take the resources saved by terminating an activity and invest them in a more productive enterprise. In contrast, the public administrator, who receives a budget allocation for each activity, does not gain any of the savings that accrue from termination. The monies saved by eliminating an activity are returned to the general pool, and the agency to which they were originally allocated has no more claim to them than any other. The restrictions on the public manager's ability to reallocate resources, when combined with budget size as the dominant measure of organizational success, clearly creates a strong disincentive for termination.

Restrictions on their reallocation of funds clearly distinguishes public from private managers at every level. Notes Hartman: "A President, unlike a business executive, cannot reprogram funds" (1977: 382). Yet this distinction also suggests how government's termination rate can be increased. As Biller has testified, "we must discover how program operators and clients can be rewarded rather than punished for drawing down budgets and ending programs" (1977: 341). He proposes "savings banks" in which program managers could deposit "carry-forward dollars that retained their fungibility—even if very high discount rates were charged." Then, Biller argues, "a declining program . . . would provide an alternative source of venture funding, which if used to create a new effort capable of eliciting budgetary support, could be experienced as a positive incentive" (Biller, 1976: 145).

For the business organization, the market allocation of resources creates the incentive to examine carefully all existing activities to determine if they should be continued or terminated. For the government agency, however, the budget allocation process provides several reasons for resisting termination—and none for considering it seriously.

SUNK COSTS

Anyone familiar with analytical decision making understands the basic rule: Sunk costs don't count.[12] Liabilities already incurred, whether expenses already paid or irrevocable commitments to make future payments, cannot be recovered, no matter what alternative the decision maker chooses. Thus, such "sunk costs" should be ignored when planning future actions. "Sunk costs" are sunk and, although the decision that committed them may now be regrettable, it is too late to do anything about it.

It appears, however, that there exists a significant difference in the attitude of private and public managers toward sunk costs. Business executives ignore sunk costs. Government executives seek to justify them. And the attitude held toward sunk costs may affect the willingness to terminate.

A number of attitudinal differences between public and private managers have been suggested. Banfield writes that although the "incentive system of a business organization is based very largely upon personal, material incentives, especially money," in government at "the top level power and glory are among the principal incentives" (1975: 591, 596).

Rawls, Ullrich, and Nelson found graduate students in management who were planning a career in the nonprofit sector "had a higher capacity for status, and valued economic wealth to a lesser degree than did individuals [i.e., students] preferring the profit sector" (1975: 620). If such differences indeed exist, they might well help explain differences in attitudes toward termination.

In business, where the organization's and individual's criteria of success are measured in dollars, it is easier to discard sunk costs and concentrate on the future implications of present decisions. RCA's decision in 1971 to liquidate its computer division was based on the prediction that computers would not make a profit for RCA for another five years, during which time the firm would have to inject $700 million into the division. Certainly, the $90 million after-tax loss that the division had accumulated during the previous five years affected the reputation of RCA's chairman, Robert W. Sarnoff, who, in an attempt to replicate the success of his father, who built the firm, had committed RCA to becoming number two in the computer business. When the financial implications of continuation versus termination of the computer division became clear, however, Sarnoff was able to disregard the $90 million in sunk costs and make the decision to terminate (Demaree, 1972).

In government, by contrast, sunk costs are not as easily ignored. Often they can dominate the thinking of decision makers. Argued Representative Melvin Price, over the question of terminating the nuclear plane: "It is hard to see why the Defense Department won't move ahead and get a flying aircraft after making such a substantial investment" (Lambright, 1679: 18). Similarly, Representative Nick Galifinakis complained about the failure of the National Park Service to continue its erosion-control program at Cape Hatteras: "It seems to me that we are diluting the investment that we already have there" (Behn and Clark, 1979: 115).

Not that sunk costs do not provide the decision maker with useful information. If large sunk costs are to be subtracted from a *fixed* total expenditure, then the larger the sunk costs, the less it will cost to complete the project and the more sense it will make to do so. If, however, large sunk costs imply a *growing* total expenditure, significantly above the cost estimates originally made, then large sunk costs may imply that the enterprise cannot be completed economically. Sunk costs are significant not because of what they tell about prior expenditures invested in the project, but for what they imply about future expenditures necessary to complete it.

Thus, for example, when evaluating a project, it is necessary to compare *remaining* costs to *remaining* benefits. Before anything is done, all benefits and costs are remaining. But, since most of the benefits will not be realized *until* the project is completed, and since most of the costs will be committed *before* the project is completed, the ratio of remaining benefits to remaining costs will go up as the work progresses. Consequently, because of "sunk costs," it often makes sense to complete half-finished projects even if, using hindsight, it is obvious that the project did not make sense at the beginning. A. Ernest Fitzgerald, Deputy Assistant Secretary of the Air Force for Productivity Management, complained of how this is used to get unwarranted projects authorized and then completed (U.S. Senate, 1976b: 202):

> It is called the "come on theory" you know, just get them accustomed to it a little at a time and then feed it to them a little more each year. And then at the time you come to question it, you are confronted with the "sunk cost" argument. . . . It is either too early, you can't question this program because it is too early, or all of a sudden it is too late. I am sure you have suspected there must be some small window in time at which it is just right to address it, but you never hear about it.

Yet, even when the analysis on a half-completed project is done correctly, and even when the ratio of remaining benefits to remaining costs is less than 1.0, "sunk costs" can still be a justification for not terminating the enterprise. In 1977, the Carter administration undertook to reevaluate thirty-three water-resource projects. At the conclusion of this analysis, it recommended the continuation of nine of these projects "without modification." Of these nine projects, eight had ratios of remaining benefits to remaining costs that were less than 1.0. One continued project, Lyman in Wyoming, was two-thirds complete but still had a ratio of remaining benefits to remaining costs of only 0.5. Under "factors of decision" for Lyman, the Carter administration listed: "The percentage completion of the project (the sunk costs of the project) and the fact that irrigation repayment depends on completion" (White House, 1977). Indeed, one administration official, when asked why eight projects with ratios of remaining benefits to remaining costs of less than 1.0 were recommended for continuation, kept insisting that they were "too far along."

BART, the Bay Area Rapid Transit system, provides another example of how "sunk costs" ensure the continuation of a government enterprise. BART is a highly capital-intensive transit system with correspondingly large sunk costs (to retire $942 million worth of revenue bonds).[13] Still, no matter how large, such sunk costs should be disregarded when deciding between continued operation of the existing system and its termination. The only question is: will the capital plus operating costs of an equivalent (or better) replacement system be greater or less than operating costs of BART? Pozdena has compared BART with equivalent bus systems, operating on either exclusive or priority rights of way, and concluded (1975: 162):

> The fixed costs of these alternatives ... are, in general, not larger than the difference in system [operating] costs between themselves and the rail alternative, suggesting that abandonment in favor of one of those alternative bus systems is economically feasible.

Indeed, Pozdena presents some sample calculations of "the net benefits of abandonment" (1975: 163) to demonstrate the termination is indeed "economically feasible." "Sunk costs" are, however, a political as well as an economic variable, and the large sunk costs of BART make its termination quite politically unfeasible.

In Washington, D.C., one writer (Roth, 1977) suggested that the new Metrorail rapid-transit system be converted into an all-bus system operating along exclusive busways and through the already constructed Metrorail tunnels.

> The basis of future policy, in my view, can be stated quite simply: forget the "sunk" costs—the tunnels built, the railway cars already purchased—and ensure that the avoidable future costs are incurred only if justified by future benefits.

All this struck the editorial staff of the Washington *Post* as absurd:

> There can be no doubt that any such proposal flies in the face of political reality; the public simply isn't psychologically prepared to pay the price—in delays, upheaval and financial support—of a radical departure from the present, long-promised grand design [Washington Post, 1977].

In government, it is not easy to ignore sunk costs.

The most obvious example of government's efforts to justify sunk costs is Vietnam. And a classic column by Art Buchwald suggests that this attitude is not as common in business. Buchwald noted that Robert McNamara had been both Secretary of Defense and President of the Ford

Motor Company and speculated upon what would have happened if Ford had handled the Edsel the way the Department of Defense handled Vietnam. After one Ford executive decided that the "solution is to pour in more men and money," and after Ford sold only 43 cars in one year, Buchwald has another Ford manager comment: "We can't just get out. We've got 50,000 workers committed to making a successful car and we'd be the laughing stock of the world if we quit now." Several years later, after selling only one Edsel—to the Smithsonian Institution—Buchwald has the Ford Motor Company take the ultimate step. As Buchwald has one executive explain it (1967):

> I think we should stop making Fords, Mercurys, Thunderbirds and Continentals and put all our resources into the Edsel. Our engineers say that all they need is 250,000 more workers and another billion dollars, and they'll have General Motors on their knees.

CONCLUSION

It is impossible to compare business and government without quoting Wallace S. Sayre's famous aphorism: "Public and private management are fundamentally alike in all unimportant respects." The fundamentally important differences are numerous, and it has not been my objective to catalogue them all here. Rather, I have sought to take those differences already defined by others and to describe those that seem to be most helpful in explaining why it might be that government and business have different termination rates. I have made no effort to determine exactly how much one characteristic contributes to this (assumed) differential; after all, the characteristics themselves are not distinct but overlapping, and thus so would be their contribution to any differential.[14] Instead, my purpose has been to see if making government more businesslike could help to increase its termination rate.

That approach is not likely to be successful. The differences between business and government that appear to contribute to any differential in their termination rates are derived from the basic nature of the two types of organizations. The differences concerning (1) goals, measures and performance, (2) consequences, constituencies, and control, and (3) the mode of payment are all inherent to the different purposes of government and business. Thus, these characteristics of government are not easily modified to make them more businesslike. For example, the public's desire to achieve goals that are more numerous and diverse than business has proven capable of realizing has led us (in part) to establish governments; it might be possible to increase government's termination rate by collapsing these diverse goals into a single, easily measured one, but then one of the basic purposes of government would be completely negated.[15]

The differences concerning time horizons and sunk costs are characteristics of the managers of business and government rather than of the organizations themselves. Thus, it might be possible to reduce the differential in the public/private termination rates by changing the attitudes of key governmental leaders so that they do have long time horizons and ignore sunk costs. Indeed, policy analysts are constantly telling political leaders that sunk costs don't count[16] and producing analyses that take a long-range perspective. And policy analysts can have some impact—particularly when they take the politically effective step of identifying a constituency that supports the conclusions of their analyses (Behn, 1979: 48). But to alter permanently the attitudes held in government toward time horizons and sunk costs would be rather difficult, since they grow out of more fundamental characteristics of public organizations.

Another approach might be to bring into government business executives who do not share the public manager's attitudes towards time horizons and sunk costs. But that has been tried frequently, with little success. And when private-sector managers prove ineffective in government it is not because they fail to apply their proven business techniques to the task of public management, but because they fail to recognize the very fundamental differences between business and government. Observed George M. Humphrey, Secretary of the Treasury in the Eisenhower Administration (Humphrey and Derieux, 1954: 31):

> When I came to Washington in January [1953], I did not realize so clearly as I do now how different government is from business, and how much more difficult it is to get things done. The job of making changes looked a lot easier from the outside.

Two decades later, Frederic V. Malek, Deputy Director of OMB in the Nixon Administration, reached this conclusion (1972: 67):

> Success in the private sector is not automatically transferable to the public sector. In fact, to succeed in government, the businessman must develop some qualities that are almost the opposite of those he needed to succeed in business.

Still, the myth persists: all that is required to straighten out government is to use a little business common sense. So every new administration brings to Washington, the state capitols, and city halls a fresh crop of corporate executives who must learn the lesson all over again.[17]

The experience of W. Michael Blumenthal, the chairman and chief executive officer of the Bendix Corporation before he came to Washington in 1977 to be Secretary of the Treasury in the Carter Administration, illustrates directly the difference in public and private management when it comes to termination (Blumenthal, 1979: 46):

> Let's say we have at Bendix a certain policy and I think it makes no sense, although its been done that way ever since Mr. Bendix organized the company more than half a century ago. I can get a small group of people together and do all the studies, talk to my bankers, make a decision, and at the right point bring everybody in on it.
>
> Here [in government], the moment I try to do that, everybody wants to get in the act, everybody has an opinion, and I start hearing from Congress before I've even made a decision. And you might as well not fight against it. To move within that process and still come out with the right decision is the essential difference between what you do as a senior executive in government and what you do in business.

Concludes Blumenthal: "Business is simple to succeed in if you follow a few simple rules. Government is harder" (1979: 48).

All this implies that attempting to wipe out the differential in the termination rates between business and government by making government more like business is a futile exercise. Government and business are different—and in ways that cannot be altered (without, at least, discarding some of their respective strengths as well as their weaknesses). If we want government to continue to do those things that it does best (or at least better than business does them), it would be counterproductive to turn it into a business. We might very well increase the termination rate, but we would clearly pay other costs in the process.

Business and government each possess capabilities that the other lacks. For example, in discussing the question of public versus private ownership of industry, Okun argues that it is "vital that private enterprise continue to be the main mechanism for organizing economic activity in those areas where experimentation and innovation are important, and in those where flexibility matters more than accountability" (1975: 61). Okun makes this point because he recognizes that the rules governing the behavior of public officials are different (1975: 61):

> Another commandment proclaims that once something is given, it shall not be taken away. A congressman has to defend to his constituents any loss of government jobs in the district, and will be blamed for such losses far more than if a private firm moves out. As a result, defense bases and veterans' hospitals stay open for decades after they have become inefficient and obsolete. Protections for owners of small farms and businesses and for construction workers that may have made sense in the thirties remain nonsensically on the statute books today. And those irreversibilities can come from good legislators responsive to their constituents, not just evil men tainted by money.

The real challenge is to accept government as it is—with its different goals, rules, pressures, incentives, and constituencies—and to attempt to deal with that reality. We need to identify the forces that sustain governmental activities that have outlived their usefulness and to develop ways to overcome those forces. Wolf writes of "the absence of a reliable termination mechanism for non-market output" (1979: 127), and certainly government does not possess a built-in process similar to the one that helps business terminate its market output. Part of the problem is clearly the lack of incentives for termination in government; thus, to the extent that the incentives for public managers can be altered (without simultaneously creating more perverse incentives), the prospects for termination can be increased.

But part of the problem is created by the search for a single process that can increase termination—a process such as sunset legislation that will simply, quickly, and miraculously eliminate all the forces that sustain governmental policies.[18] Each government program is different; each has different purposes, different consequences, different bureaucratic arrangements, different constituencies. Consequently, terminating each policy requires a different strategy—one carefully designed to overcome the unique forces that sustain it. Such strategies will not always be successful; but if they are developed intelligently with careful attention to the unique features of the termination target, they can be successful (see Behn, 1978a).

Termination in government is—and always will be—a political process. Thus, it takes politically intelligent managers to achieve it.

NOTES

1. For some suggestions as to how this might be done, see Behn (1978a).

2. The problem of definitions complicates any effort to determine a termination rate. For example, if one wishes to determine the rate at which government "programs" are terminated, it is necessary to define "program." And the smaller the activities that are defined as programs, the more termination will be discovered. See Behn (1977a).

3. For a discussion of the problem of terminating useless medical procedures, see Hiatt (1975).

4. Ford is quoted by Brooks (1969: 63).

5. See Hershey (1980). As a former owner of two MGBs (before family expansion forced a switch to more "practical" transportation), I consider Aston Martin's rescue of the MG to be one of truly historical significance.

6. This "'blurring' or convergence of the sectors" is discussed by Rainey et al. (1976: 234). Buchanan (1975: 424) writes of "the conceptually and empirically porous quality of 'public' and 'private' as administrative categories."

7. Most of the following distinguishing characteristics of public and private (and many others) are discussed in more detail in the literature survey of Rainey et al. (1975).

8. In the case of the closing by the U.S. Steel Corporation of the Ohio and McDonald works in Youngstown, Ohio, the United Steelworkers argued in court that this decision violated an oral agreement that the firm had with the union not to close the plant as long as it was profitable. But a federal judge ruled that the union did not have a binding contract. See Salpukas (1979) and New York Times (1980).

9. For a discussion of the distribution of costs and benefits of government programs (and the influence of this distribution on the prospects for change), see Wilson (1973: 331-337). For a discussion of how this affects the prospects for termination, see Behn (1977a: 397-399).

10. For a discussion of how compromise precludes termination, see Behn (1977a: 400-402).

11. Since then, the U.S. Steel Corporation has set a new record: a $561.7 million loss in the fourth quarter of 1979.

12. The costs that count in a decision are the "opportunity costs," i.e., the costs of the opportunities that must be foregone by selecting a particular alternative. Since "sunk costs" have been made or committed by past decisions, they cannot be included in the opportunities that might be foregone by present decisions. For a discussion of the various kinds of costs, see Christenson et al. (1973: 19-45).

13. See Hoachlander (1976: 1).

14. Furthermore, exactly how much one characteristic contributes to the differential will again depend upon the types of private and public activities being compared. Indeed, the research task of determining exactly how much each factor contributes to the differential in termination rates would be even more difficult than testing for the existence of such a differential.

15. Of course, it might be that I have examined the wrong factors. There might be another characteristic—one not identified here—that accounts for the entire difference in the termination rates of business and government. And it might also be

that this characteristic is easily modified in government—without at the same time destroying the basic nature of government—so as to eliminate the differential completely. It is quite possible that I have overlooked this miracle factor; but I am confident that, if I have done so, some reader will quickly point out my error.

16. The attitudes that policy analysts have toward sunk costs is similar to the attitude held in business. See Behn (1979: 12-15).

17. For a further examination of the business executive in government, see Bernstein (1958), particularly pp. 26-37 and 200-208.

18. For an analysis of sunset legislation, see Behn (1977b: 103-118).

REFERENCES

ALEXANDER, R. S. (1977) "The death and burial of 'sick' products," in M. Enis and K. K. Cox (eds.) Marketing Classics. Boston: Allyn & Bacon.

ANDERSON, J. W. (1975) "New York: a moral concept." Washington Post (August 25).

BANFIELD, E. C. (1975) "Corruption as a feature of government organization." Journal of Law and Economics 18 (December).

BAUER, R. A., I de SOLA POOL, and L. A. DESTER (1963) American Business and Public Policy: The Politics of Foreign Trade. Chicago: AVC.

BEHN, R. D. (1977a) "Policy termination: a survey of the current literature and an agenda for future research." Prepared for the Ford Foundation.

——— (1977b) "The false dawn of the sunset laws." The Public Interest 49 (Fall): 103-118.

——— (1978a) "How to terminate a public policy: a dozen hints for the would-be policy terminator." Policy Analysis 4 (Summer): 393-413.

——— (1978b) "Closing a government facility." Public Administration Review 38 (July/August): 332-333.

——— (1979) "Policy analysis and policy politics." Working paper, Institute of Policy Sciences. Durham, NC: Duke University.

BEHN, R. D. and D. P. LAMBERT (1979) "Cut-back management at the Pentagon: the closing of military bases." Presented at the Research Conference on Public Policy and Management, Chicago, October 19.

BEHN, R. D. and M. A. CLARK (1979) "The termination of beach erosion control at Cape Hatteras." Public Policy 27 (Winter).

BERNSTEIN, M. H. (1958) The Job of the Federal Executive. Washington, DC: Brookings.

BILLER, R. P. (1976) "On tolerating policy and organizational termination: some design considerations." Policy Sciences 7 (June).

——— (1977) "Prepared statement," in Sunset Act of 1977. Hearings before the Subcommittee on Intergovernmental Relations of the Committee on Governmental Affairs, U.S. Congress, First Session on S. 2, March 22, 23, 24, 28, 29, and 30. Washington, DC: Government Printing Office.

BLUMENTHAL, W. M. (1979) "Candid reflections of a businessman in Washington." Fortune (January 29).

BOWER, J. L. (1977) "Effective public management." Harvard Business Review 55 (March-April): 131-140.

BROOKS, J. (1969) Business Adventures. New York: Weybright and Talley.

BUCHANAN, B., II (1974) "Government managers, business executives, and organizational commitment." Public Administration Review 34 (July/August): 339-347.

——— (1975) "Red tape and the service ethic: some unexpected differences between public and private managers. Administration & Society 6 (February).

BUCHWALD, A. (1967) "If Vietnam escalator works, why did the Edsel go down?" Washington Post (August 24).

CHRISTENSON, C. J., R. F. VANCIL, and P. W. MARSHALL (1973) Managerial Economics. Homewood, IL: Irwin.

COLEN, B. D. (1977) "Lindsay Warren dies, 'watchdog' of treasury." Washington Post (January 3).

CYERT, R. M. (1978) "The management of universities of constant or decreasing size." Public Administration Review 38 (July/August).

DEMAREE, A. T. (1972) "RCA after the bath." Fortune 76 (September): 122-138.

DRUCKER, P. F. (1974) Management: Tasks, Responsibilities, Practices. New York: Harper & Row.

The Economist (1975a) "Britain after Chrysler: the political economy of cars." December 20: 75-83.

——— (1975b) "The Chrysler retreat." December 13.

——— (1979) "British Steel to buy-out Shotton jobs." July 14.

HARTMAN, R. W. (1977) "Budget prospects and process," in J. A. Pechman (ed.) Setting National Priorities: The 1978 Budget. Washington, DC: Brookings.

HAYES, T. C. (1979) "Talking business with Donald N. Frey." New York Times. (December 13).

HERSHEY, R. D., Jr. (1980) "Aston Martin group buys MG line." New York Times (April 1).

HIATT, H. H. (1975) "Protecting the medical commons: who is responsible?" New England Journal of Medicine 293 (July): 235-241.

HOACHLANDER, E. G. (1976) "Bay area rapid transit: who pays and who benefits?" Working Paper 267, Institute of Urban and Regional Development. Berkeley: University of California.

HUMPHREY, G. M. and J. C. DERIEUX (1954) "It looked easier on the outside." Collier's (April 2).

IGNATIUS, D. (1977) "Bethlehem Steel posts $477 million loss for 3rd quarter: write-off is key factor." Wall Street Journal (October 27).

JONES, W. H. (1975) "REA Express closes doors." Washington Post (November 8).

KATZENBACH, E. L., Jr. (1958) "The horse cavalry in the twentieth century: a study of policy response." Public Policy 8.

KAUFMAN, H. (1976) Are Government Organizations Immortal? Washington, DC: Brookings.

KILBORN, P. T. (1975a) "Britain's Chrysler deal: faith in investment and bending of policy." New York Times (December 26).

——— (1975b) "Britain votes $335 million aid to keep Chrysler open there." New York Times (December 17).

KNEELAND, D. E. (1978) "Chicago Daily News reported to be ready to shut down." New York Times (February 3).

LAMBRIGHT, W. H. (1967) Shooting Down the Nuclear Plane. New York and Indianapolis: Inter-University Case Program and Bobbs-Merrill.

LOWI, T. J. (1969) The End of Liberalism. New York: Norton.

MALEK, F. V. (1972) "Mr. Executive goes to Washington." Harvard Business Review 50 (September-October).

MILLER, J. (1980) "U.S. board approves $1.5 billion backing for Chrysler loans." New York Times (May 11).

MORGENTHALER, E. (1977) "Shotton saga: story of a Welsh mill tells why steelmakers in Europe lag behind." Wall Street Journal (April 25).

MORRIS, W. (1978) "Va. plant is victim of cellophane's decline." Washington Post (February 28).

New York Times (1975a) "Chrysler considered giving away a unit." December 20.

––– (1975b) "Rock Island given extension of life." March 29.

––– (1979) "Another American institution goes by the boards." September 9.

––– (1980) "U.S. Steel allowed to close Ohio plants." March 22.

OKUN, A. M. (1975) Equality and Efficiency: The Big Tradeoff. Washington, DC: Brookings.

POZDENA, R. J. (1975) "A methodology for selecting urban transportation projects." Monograph 22, Institute of Urban and Regional Development. Berkeley: University of California.

Railway Age (1974) "Abandonment rules proposed." December 9.

––– (1977) "Watching Washington: abandonment procedures." November 14.

RAINEY, H. G., R. W. BACKOFF, and C. H. LEVINE (1976) "Comparing public and private organizations." Public Administration Review 36 (March/April).

RAWLS, J. R., R. A. ULLRICH, and O. T. NELSON, Jr. (1975) "A comparison of managers entering or reentering the profit and nonprofit sectors." Academy of Management Journal 18 (September).

ROTH, G. (1977) "Should Metro be derailed?" Washington Post (July 31).

SALPUKAS, A. (1977) "Bethlehem Steel reports a loss, largest ever for a U.S. company." New York Times (October 27).

––– (1979) "Workers bitter in Youngstown." New York Times (December 1).

SERRIN, W. (1973) The Company and the Union: The Civilized Relationship of the General Motors Company and the United Automobile Workers. New York: Knopf.

SIMON, H. A., D. W. SMITHBURG, and V. A. THOMPSON (1950) Public Administration. New York: Knopf.

SINGER, J. W. (1979) "A radical solution to the problem of 'runaway plants,'" National Journal 11 (June): 1040-1043.

STEVENS, W. K. (1977) "Shutdown of steel works stuns Youngstown." New York Times (September 21).

U.S. Senate (1976a) "Cutbacks in postal service." Hearings before the Subcommittee on Postal Service of the Committee on Post Office and Civil Service, U.S. Senate, Ninety-Fourth Congress, May 4 and 5. Washington, DC: Government Printing Office.

––– (1976b) "Government economy and spending reform act of 1976." Hearings before the Subcommittee on Intergovernmental Relations of the Committee on Government Operations, U.S. Senate, Ninety-Fourth Congress, Second Session on S. 2925 and S. 2067. Washington, DC: Government Printing Office.

Washington Post (1977) "Should Metro be derailed?" August 5.

WILL, G. F. (1976) "Britain's Chrysler bailout." Washington Post (January 1).

WILSON, J. Q. (1973) Political Organizations. New York: Basic Books.

White House (1977) "Statement on water projects." Press release, April 18.

WOLF, C. (1979) "A theory of non-market failures." The Public Interest 55 (Spring).

12

LOCAL GOVERNMENT PRODUCTIVITY: POLITICAL AND ADMINISTRATIVE POTENTIAL

R. SCOTT FOSLER

Director of Government Studies
Montgomery County Council

At a conference on government productivity in 1973, one participant dismissed "productivity" as the "latest management-technique fad" and predicted that "it will be dead in six months."

It did not die. In fact, not only did it live on, but the concern about productivity in government, variously defined, exploded five years later into Proposition 13. Meantime, a veritable national preoccupation with the productivity of the economy as a whole has developed within the last year. In 1979, for the first time since World War II, the productivity of the American economy declined while the economy was growing.

The prediction that productivity would disappear as a concern was faulty in its basic premise, i.e., that "productivity" is a "management technique." It is not a technique. It is a concept. And, in fact, it is a concept so fundamental that it will always be present in one guise or another.

The concept of productivity implies a ratio of the quantity and/or quality of results to the resources invested to achieve them. It is what you get for what you give.

In economists' jargon, productivity is the ratio of outputs to inputs, and typically has been measured as output per man hour. That may be a satisfactory definition for some types of industrial economic activity where the definition and measure of output is reasonably precise, and where the principal or most important component of input is labor. For other types of activities, however, the conventional "output per man hour" definition is not so obviously appropriate. In fact, businessmen and economists have questioned its utility in measuring the productivity of industrial activities.

Productivity has two basic dimensions: effectiveness and efficiency. In the conventional definition—output per man hour—effectiveness is more or less assumed to have been achieved when the unit of "output" is produced; the essential question is one of efficiency, or how much labor was required to produce it. In government, however (and the same could be said for many industrial activities), no such assumption can be made. Defining the "output" or result and determining whether or not it has been achieved is a major part of the productivity equation. Determining the efficiency with which the result has been achieved is, of course, all the more difficult when the result is hard to define or measure.

By this definition, government productivity might be improved in one of three general ways. The first is to more precisely identify goals and objectives in order to assure that what government is doing genuinely reflects the needs and desires of citizens as determined through the political process. The second is to select approaches to meeting those goals and objectives which have the highest cost-effectiveness ratio. The third and more traditional productivity concern is to assume the most effective and efficient implementation of the approach selected.

TEN YEARS OF EXPERIENCE

The term "productivity" has been actively applied to government for about ten years. In the early seventies, New York City mounted a formal productivity-improvement program; the federal government undertook to measure and improve the productivity of its civilian work force; the National Commission on Productivity identified as one of its priorities the improvement of state and local government productivity; and numerous public interest groups, such as the International City Management Association, developed productivity programs. Over the past several years, numerous local governments and many state governments have begun efforts to measure and improve productivity.

These efforts, of course, were not the first to demonstrate concern about the effectiveness and efficiency of government. The question of what government accomplishes and what it costs are as old as government itself. In the United States, the application of scientific management and the advance of public administration theory over the past century were part and parcel of efforts to improve effectiveness and efficiency in increasingly bureaucratic, complex, and expensive government operations.

The concept of productivity in government, however, did not gain popularity until the 1970s. And while in most respects it is simply a reiteration of earlier concerns with government effectiveness, efficiency, and economy, it also carries connotations that are new. Thinking about the productivity of government implies that government is bigger and somehow more important, no longer just a housekeeping function or support system for more important private-sector activities, but fundamentally important in its own right. It also implies a greater sense of urgency. If government provides such critical services as education, public safety, housing, provision of water and disposal of wastes, transportation, land-use management, and health, and if it expends an equivalent of one-third of the Gross National Product to do it, then how well it performs those functions and how efficiently it uses those resources is a matter of prime concern.

The first efforts to define and improve government productivity focused heavily on activities that were akin to conventional industrial activities, i.e., those with "outputs" that were relatively easy to measure, and procedures that were relatively routine and hence subject to established industrial-engineering techniques of analysis. Thus, refuse collection was studied ad infinitum, and fire extinguishment was not far behind. These early studies were useful because they demonstrated that conventional private-sector techniques of analysis were in fact applicable to many routine government operations, and because these simpler functions provided an opportunity to compare differences with the private sector. The essential difference, it soon became apparent, was that government operated in a political system, and that the political considerations that set the tone and provided the motivation of government impact fundamentally on questions of productivity.

Analyzing such activities as education and health proved even more difficult because not only were the political factors present, but the goals and objectives were difficult to define and measure.

THE POLITICAL CONTEXT

The purposes of government are, as they should be and inevitably will be, determined politically. And hence the first consideration of productivity—what is the result to be accomplished—is made on the basis of direct political decisions, or at least will be conditioned by political judgments. The second consideration—how is the result to be accomplished—is no less based on a political determination, even if that determination is to leave the selection of approaches to professional judgment. The third consideration—the effective and efficient implementation of the approach selected—is similarly guided by political considerations, including who should be hired to carry out the program, how much they should be paid, and who should be responsible for seeing that the job is done.

The American tradition of government and public administration curiously assumes a certain lack of interest in the making of such decisions. Everyone agrees, for example, that local government should protect life and property, that there should be a police department to provide such protection, and that police officers should be trained and guided in their actions by professional judgment. In practice, of course, the decisions are far more complex and dependent on a host of political judgments. What kind of property should be protected, and at what level of protection? What kind of police operations should be undertaken? What are appropriate standards of pay and qualification for officers? Who should supervise, and with what guidance and restrictions?

Similar questions apply to all government operations. And as government programs and the environments in which they function have become more complex, and as government budgets have grown, such questions have become all the more difficult to answer, both technically and politically.

There are, of course, numerous political constituencies and participants, each of whom has its own set of interests.

Taxpayer. The taxpayer is that part of the personality of each of us which resists higher payments to government and yearns for reductions in government costs that will ease our tax burden. This concern is reflected in an organized fashion through taxpayers' associations and through a preference of candidates for public office who appear to be dedicated to, and capable of achieving, reductions in the cost of government. The advent of Proposition 13 has boosted the taxpayer interest both in organized lobbying and in general consciousness among elected officials. Nonetheless, taxpayers as a class tend to be among the least active political constituencies in terms of persistent and direct political lobbying. The interests of taxpayers, moreover, are more likely to be directed to the simpler matter of cutting costs than to the more complicated task of improving productivity.

Consumer. There is another side of our nature that is pleased to receive or benefit from public services. All of us consume government services of one variety or another, although some groups are more dependent on government than others. As consumers, we may easily argue for more police officers, a new library, newer schools or better educational programs for our children, a new storm water line to curb the flooding of neighborhood streets, and a host of other public services that we either depend upon or would like to have to enrich our lives or alleviate inconveniences. Just as the taxpayer side of us typically underestimates the importance of the services provided by government, the consumer side of us typically ignores the cost of what it is that we demand.

In the private sector, a single individual both purchases and consumes products of his choosing, and hence must evaluate cost compared to value. In government, consumers of public services can press for more without having to bear the full cost, since the cost will be spread among all taxpayers. Because cost is rarely an immediate concern to those arguing for the service, better service is typically equated with more service, rather than more effective use of resources already allocated to that service.

There is, in addition, another type of constituent who is not so much interested in services as in government jobs, contracts, prestige, or political power.

Voter. It is in the voting booth that the taxpayer and consumer sides of our nature must come to grips with each other. Elections also provide a test of political strength between those who see themselves principally as taxpayers and those who see themselves principally as consumers of government services. It is in the voting booth that we either synthesize these concerns or exercise our right to weigh one of these values more heavily than the other in casting our vote for elected officials. And it is, of course, the force of these combined votes and the intricate combination of rational, irrational, self-serving, and community-minded reasoning that determine who is elected.

Elected official. In pondering these conflicting forces, the overriding interest of most candidates for public office, notwithstanding a multitude of nobler motivations, is getting elected. His or her interest in the cost or the effectiveness of government services tends to vary in direct proportion to the degree of interest and intensity to which taxpayers, consumers, and especially voters display similar concerns. Even if general public concern about government cost and performance is great, as it has been in recent years, the aspirant to public office is fully aware of the fact that it is not necessarily the reality of government performance and the actual tax burden that will affect the voting behavior of his constituents; rather, it is the perception of all of these things, and the voter's gut reaction to them. In other words, the *image* of government productivity is generally more important to the candidate and office holder than the reality. In jurisdictions whose voters' perceptions tend to be closely correlated with reality, it may indeed be good politics to achieve real improvements as a way of convincing voters that in fact it has been done. But, of course, it is not contrary to the inclination of many candidates to attempt to convince voters that the reality is something other than it is.

The problem of motivating elected officials to effect real improvements is all the more complicated by the fact that relatively few have competence in the details and drudgery of administration, and most have little interest.

Chief administrative officer. Given the likely outlook of the elected official as suggested above, it typically falls to the city manager or chief administrative officer to bridge the gap between the general public desire for productivity improvement and the more difficult reality of achieving efficient and effective government. The manager is, of course, the employee of his elected boss or, in the case of a council-manager city, his elected bosses. He must, therefore, to a very large extent, pursue their purposes. While most elected officials would like their government to be run as efficiently and effectively as possible, it is an objective that competes with, and often takes a back seat to, other political concerns. And those who do give it high priority are typically at a loss as to how to direct their professional managers to accomplish it, except to command them to do so. Hence, the top manager is more often than not left to his own devices and, perhaps more important, to his own motivation.

In the last seventy years or so, there has been a steady increase in the number of local jurisdictions who employ professional managers. The city-management profession has grown into one of the more serious and respected management professions in the public sector, and boasts among its associates people of real experience and capability who closely identify their own personal roles with doing a genuinely good job of managing government. Part of that professional identification stems from the very practical fact that city managers typically do not stay in one place for more than a few years, and hence must constantly be thinking about future employment opportunities. Whereas a local police or fire chief rarely aspires to a post in another jurisdiction, and hence may depend upon local political support as much as competence to guarantee his job security, the city manager must rely more heavily on his reputation for competence to keep his professional status secure. But to do his job, the top manager must also enjoy the support of those who work for him, i.e., agency heads and other public employees.

Managers and supervisors. The heads of most government agencies have learned over time that there is relatively little reward, aside from personal satisfaction, in doing things exceedingly well or showing imagination or initiative to improve programs. A city manager, a mayor, or a host of council members will always be ready to claim credit for successes, or may simply fail to recognize them. On the other hand, if something goes wrong, or if a new idea does not work out according to plan, there will be innumerable members of the public, an aggressive press, and a variety of elected officials who will be quick to point out the "failure" and to hold the agency head responsible for it. In short, there is little incentive for improvement, but a great price to be paid for failure. It is, of course, one of the legitimate purposes of bureaucracy to screen out and studiously avoid those changes in operation which may threaten the basic efficiency or performance of tried and tested methods of operation. Typically, however, this guardianship role is overdone, and the result more often than not is that good ideas are ignored and obsolete but entrenched practices continue of their own momentum. Innovative managers are bound to make mistakes, suffer failures, and tread on toes, and consequently they are vulnerable to criticism and likely to accumulate political enemies.

Employee. The principal motivation of government employees is refreshingly straightforward. Their first concerns are necessarily with the size of their wages, the generosity of their benefits, the convenience and comfort of their working hours and working conditions, and the security of their jobs. None of these goals is necessarily supportive of the desire to increase either overall agency productivity or personal performance. In recent years, the deficiencies of civil-service systems, once supported as a means of improving the quality and performance of public personnel, have become all too apparent. Merit systems are now regularly accused of being more concerned with protecting mediocrity than encouraging talent. Hiring and promotions typically are awarded on the basis of written examinations which may have little to do with the real capabilities and skills required for the job.

Public employees as a class are no different from employees anywhere. A certain proportion of any working population will always be inclined toward malingering, and an imaginative few will inevitably raise the art to a high level no matter what steps are taken to discourage it. The real problem is that public employees are victims of the system in which they work. Most people would sooner have meaningful tasks to perform and spend their days in productive pursuits, leaving their jobs at the quitting hour with the satisfaction of knowing they had earned their pay and done something useful, than spend their time in the often more tiresome and pressure-ridden enterprise of convincing others that they are engaged in purposeful activities when in fact they know they are not. The extent to which their talents are actually used depends principally upon the skill and motivation of their supervisors in establishing meaningful objectives, organizing work in the manner most likely to achieve those aims, and assigning tasks in such a way that people are performing jobs most suited to their skills and abilities.

Public employees are, of course, also a potent political force. Where they bargain over wages and working conditions, their influence on the cost and operation of government is quite direct. Whether or not they bargain, their political influence is felt in the election of candidates to office.

Higher levels of government. Yet another force is the higher level of government—the county, regional, state, or federal government which has some responsibility for or authority over the jurisdictions within its purview. Until recently, most state governments have been little concerned with the productivity of their local governments, and in fact have permitted or even encouraged unproductive government structures and procedures. However, when New York City's fiscal problems were visited upon New York State in 1975, some state governments began to recognize that they could not ignore the financial and managerial health of the local governments they had created. Likewise, the federal government has discovered that it is not immune to the serious financial problems of the cities and states. Nonetheless, the federal and state governments typically establish objectives, mandate standards, or require procedures that conflict with the goals of local governments or otherwise impede what a city or county may perceive as its own productivity.

WHERE IS THE CONSTITUENCY FOR PRODUCTIVITY?

Few would deny that it is desirable for government to be effective and efficient. But arguments rage over what government should be effective in doing, when effectiveness is achieved, and who should bear the perceived burden of efficiency. In a political system where desires and expectations have proliferated, and where political coalitions aggressively pursue their own interests, there is no organized constituency that persistently and effectively pursues the objective of making the system work in a generally effective and efficient manner. There is, in short, no single political constituency in favor of productivity.

How, then, is productivity to be improved in a system that responds to political demands? Part of the answer lies in focusing such motivation as does exist, and such political pressure as can be mustered, on targets that can yield the greatest return. The following is a suggested list of such targets. They include actions that can be taken in the short run to produce immediate improvements, ways of building organizational capability that in turn can lead to productivity improvement, and strategies and structural changes that aim to improve the overall system of local government that might improve productivity in the long run. Since local governments vary widely in their conditions and capabilities, such a list must of course be general in its applicability.

SHORT-RUN ACTIONS

Actions which have had the most immediate impact in showing results include the following:

(1) *Financial management.* Improved accounting, auditing, revenue collection, disbursement, purchasing, cash management, and insurance policy can produce immediate cash savings. In some cases, the savings or, in the case of cash management, the investment yield can be dramatic. Such improvements are also prerequisites for providing the kind of information and controls essential for making gains in other areas of local government.

Lax accounting and auditing standards and procedures are probably the single greatest source of needless and easily correctable government waste. More stringent revenue-collection procedures for taxes, fines, service charges, and other payments can not only yield additional revenues (and improve equity by assuring that those who are supposed to pay do pay), but produce cash more quickly for investment purposes. Sophisticated disbursement procedures not only avoid illegal or inappropriate payments, but permit rapid payment to take advantage of discounts and bolster creditworthiness and slower payment to maximize the availability of cash. Improved purchasing procedures can cut costs by buying in bulk, and improve agency performance by permitting rapid purchases tailored to specialized needs. Aggressive cash-management and investment policies have proved for some governments to be a substantial source of new revenue. And self-insurance or "risk-management" programs have allowed some governments to substantially cut their insurance costs.

Improved financial management also produces two related benefits that can aid productivity. One is the higher incentive for care in using government funds that stems from knowing that the money is being carefully watched. And the second is the information, financial and otherwise, that results from professional cash management and can be used to identify other targets for productivity improvement.

(2) *Improving output-input ratios in industrial-type activities.* Immediate improvements can typically be made in activities which resemble traditional industrial operations, such as refuse collection, public works, building maintenance, paper processing, and inspections. Such functions generally have precise and quantifiable objectives, and involve largely

repetitive tasks which are susceptible to traditional industrial-engineering analysis and improvement.

Reasonably good quantitative measures normally can be developed for such functions, and the monitoring of such measures over a period of time can indicate whether productivity is improving or declining, and aid in identifying why. One of the earlier productivity studies by the Urban Institute for the National Commission on Productivity discovered that one large eastern city was able to collect three times the number of tons per man hour of refuse as another city of roughly the same size and with generally the same topographical conditions only a few miles away. Closer analysis of the lagging city revealed obvious deficiencies in management practices and basic operations, including an excessive number of men on a truck (in some cases more than five), obsolete equipment requiring frequent repair, crews working as little as four hours a day, and little or no attention to the scheduling of routes in order to minimize the time spent on each pickup.

(3) *Procedures, scheduling, and inventory control.* Immediate improvements can also be realized by the redesign of procedures, more effective scheduling, and greater control of inventory. One of the early discoveries in the New York City productivity program was that the downtime of sanitation trucks was substantially increased by the inability to produce necessary parts for repair at the time when they were needed. Many government activities involve a series of intricate but precise tasks that need to be performed with a reasonably high degree of coordination. Such activities—for example, the processing of applications for licenses—lend themselves to well-established techniques which systematically and in detail identify each task to be performed at the time and in the sequence that it is to be performed. Improvements in scheduling and inventory control not only break production bottlenecks, but also reduce pilfering, which is an outright loss to the government.

(4) *Deployment of resources to match work force to workload.* Few government agencies systematically plot variable workload demands in order to assure that personnel are assigned in equal proportion to the work to be performed. For example, trash collection in most cities is typically higher on Mondays, since there is generally no pickup on Sundays, and residents at home on weekends tend to generate more refuse than on weekdays. Yet most jurisdictions fail to vary their assignment schedules so that a larger number of personnel are on duty during the peak trash-collection days.

Similarly, although the incidence of crime tends to be concentrated during various times of the day, particularly between 6:00 at night and

2:00 in the morning, police departments tend to divide their force into three equal eight-hour shifts, or with a higher proportion of officers on duty during the day hours, when crime tends to be less frequent.

Latent demand or pent-up demand for services in some cases is never even recognized. For example, the hours of many agencies which purport to serve the public are established more for the convenience of the civil servants themselves than for the clients they serve. Departments of motor vehicles typically are open from 9:00 in the morning until 5:00 in the afternoon on weekdays only, precisely the hours when most people are working, and hence unable to get to the department to buy license tags or to get drivers licenses without taking time off from work to do so. Extending the hours of such departments to Saturdays would not necessarily result in any savings, but could significantly increase the convenience to the clientele, itself a productivity improvement.

(5) *Reassignment of tasks to better use individual skills.* Numerous productivity studies repeat the complaint that individual employees are either underutilized or their potential abilities are not being fully tapped. Restrictive classification systems cause one employee to be overburdened with work while another spends part of the day idle. Greater flexibility in position classifications and in the assignment of work can improve the match of work to employee time.

Some jurisdictions have experimented with "job enlargement," where the intricacy or variety of assignments is increased, and "job rotation," where an employee will spend only a part of his day or week (or longer period of time) in one type of job and then switch to a second job to break the monotony. The same concept can be applied to career development; for example, the city of Inglewood, California attempts to utilize as many younger people as possible in such manual work as refuse collection, moving the older collectors into jobs which are not as physically demanding. The advantage here is twofold: the more physically able and aggressive younger workers can accomplish a greater amount of work, while the older workers are not subjected to demanding physical tasks.

(6) *Applying readily available technology.* Finally, immediate steps could be taken to apply technology—both hardware and methods of operation—which is already in use and proving its value in other jurisdictions. Few governments make any systematic attempt to identify the "best practices" available in other jurisdictions and apply them to their own operations, largely because they simply lack the motivation to do so. Nonetheless, the opportunities are virtually limitless. Conferences, manuals, trade journals, and professional exchanges offer endless information about improved methods of operation that are currently in use.

BUILDING CAPACITY FOR CONTINUED IMPROVEMENT

The steps noted above focus on immediate steps that can be taken to improve productivity (most of which are geared to efficiency improvements). However, sustained improvement requires the development of internal capability for being able to regularly identify and implement better ways of operating. The following intermediate steps may not produce immediate improvements, but they are the building blocks upon which regular and more systematic productivity improvement can be pursued.

(1) *Management and supervisory capability.* Most critical are effective managers. While most large local governments have moved toward hiring and developing professional managers, the deficiencies are still severe. Many agency heads are political appointees or functional professionals (e.g., police chiefs who are former police officers, doctors heading health agencies, etc.) who do not necessarily have the training, experience, or personal ability to manage.

Of growing concern is the caliber of supervisory personnel, who have too long been the stepchildren of government manpower development programs. Deficiencies in supervisory personnel become all the more apparent with unionization. In some cases, supervisors are included in unions with their subordinates, a situation that causes confusion for workers, for top management, and for the supervisors themselves. However, the situation is not much better where supervisors are separated out from the unions but remain isolated from top management. They find themselves in a kind of limbo, somewhere between the top management of the organization and strong unions composed of the people they are supposed to supervise and motivate. Middle-level supervisors feel themselves pressed from both sides, and all the more frustrated because they have not been given the kind of training required to perform their jobs.

(2) *Analytic capability to improve decision making and operations.* Many large business organizations typically devote about 1 percent of gross sales to financing personnel whose sole responsibility is the continual improvement of operations. For the most part, these are industrial engineers whose job is to seek out opportunities for cutting costs and improving efficiency or quality. Few governments have anywhere near this level of analytic staff. Many governments have none.

Such personnel can be invaluable to top policy makers in analyzing basic policy options in terms of relative costs and benefits, as well as in the analysis and improvement of operations. Within the line operating agencies, there are endless opportunities for management-engineering and industrial-engineering analyses which can be used to spot opportunities for cost savings, and efficiency and quality improvements.

(3) *Evaluation of programs.* One of the principal deficiencies in government operations is the absence of systematic evaluation of decisions made in the past and of programs underway or that have been completed. In business, sales and profit-and-loss statements provide continual evaluation. In the public sector, for the most part, there is no such systematic and precise evaluation of the quality or the effectiveness of operations. There are, of course, general types of evaluation, including press reports, citizen complaints, and general observation by top managers and elected officials. But these tend to be of limited value, and often reflect the superficial or spotty biases or observations of those who may not be familiar with the details of the operation.

Evaluation is important for two reasons. On the one hand, it can establish accountability, which in turn provides incentive for improvement. On the other hand, it can provide useful information to policy makers and to managers regarding whether programs or specific parts of programs should be continued, and if they are to be continued, how they can be improved. In fact, one of the most useful forms of evaluation is that which is systematically built into the planning and decision-making process, so that future decisions are made on the basis of useful information on how the program has performed in the past.

Legislative bodies, including city and county councils and state legislatures, are taking an increasing interest in evaluation or oversight. A few legislatures have developed the capacity for evaluating executive-branch programs. Others have practically no staff capability for evaluation. The recent interest in "sunset" laws, whereby government programs would be terminated after a specified period of time unless a persuasive case could be made for their continuation, really reflects an implicit understanding of the need for better evaluation of government programs. Serious proponents of sunset legislation have recognized that what they are really attempting to accomplish is more systematic and effective evaluation of government programs.

(4) *Budgeting to improve management.* The budget is potentially the most useful device for forcing policy makers and top managers to focus on productivity. Most budgets, however, do not provide useful or accurate information on objectives and performance. Most legislators feel more comfortable with line-item budgets that deal with the tangibles of staff and equipment. Efforts over the years to implement various forms of performance budgets have typically failed for any number of reasons, including their complexity, the unavailability of staff to undertake the required analyses, the generation of too much paperwork, and the opposition of agencies and various political constituencies who fear the presentation of policy choices in terms of clear options. Nevertheless, performance-

oriented budgeting is found in one form or another in many jurisdictions, and continues to provide potential for improving performance, efficiency, and effective decision making.

Zero-based budgeting has caused confusion and added to the legions of budget skeptics. Zero-based budgeting is typically perceived as an overall and thorough look at an entire program. The more important concept in zero-based budgeting, however, is the importance of assessing the marginal value of various levels of service, or increments of activity that compel some ordering of priorities from essential to desirable. Whatever form of budgeting or other approach to decision making is employed, considering marginal costs and benefits—a fundamental economic and business concept rarely applied except in crude ways in government—is perhaps the single most important potential source of productivity improvement.

(5) *Personnel management and labor-management cooperation.* People are the biggest cost and principal resource of local government. Productivity, therefore, depends largely on the extent to which public employees have the capability, training, motivation, necessary resources, and appropriate organizational environment and leadership to function effectively.

Civil service systems, created to enhance the quality of public employees and protect them from political abuse, have in many ways become impediments to productive government. The fundamental merit principles are still sound—i.e., hiring and promotion on the basis of merit, and protecting employees against arbitrary administrative or political actions—but many of the rules and procedures that were created to enhance those principles now threaten to protect mediocrity, discourage initiative, and frustrate managers in their efforts to make government work. Collective bargaining has added a new dimension to local government which has overwhelmed some administrations that were unprepared for it.

Correcting deficiencies in merit systems—or establishing modern and workable merit systems where they are not currently in place—and building the professional capability to engage in effective collective bargaining are top priorities. Beyond these fundamentals, however, are opportunities for more cooperative and creative personnel management that have only begun to be explored.

While personnel management and labor relations during the past decade have been characterized by confrontation, the opportunities for cooperation, and for releasing and building upon the potential of individuals are great. Personal attitudes and priorities have changed as incomes have risen, old social conventions—such as discrimination against blacks and women—have been challenged, and responsiveness to authority has diminished. The combination of changes presents both problems and opportunities to local-government personnel management, but each of the changes challenges traditional assumptions and requires response.

Skillful redesign of jobs and other basic improvements in the conditions of work will address some of these needs. But longer-term improvements will require more imaginative management approaches that recognize a basic human need to feel a part of a useful and productive undertaking, to believe that one's own contribution is aiding the attainment of broader organization goals, and to sense that one is a genuine participant in the overall operation.

LONG-TERM CHANGES: IMPROVING THE OVERALL SYSTEM

While the short-run actions focus on steps that can be taken for immediate productivity improvement, and the intermediate approach is geared toward building the internal capability for sustained improvement over a longer period of time, long-term changes are required to strengthen the overall system in which local governments function.

(1) *Structure of government.* Prescriptions for modern government structure typically emphasize "rational" organization that integrates program components into functionally oriented departments which in turn are hierarchically responsible to a single strong executive. Such concepts are applicable to many situations; however, preoccupation with supposedly rational and orderly hierarchies occasionally obscures the advantages—or inevitability—of structures that may appear untidy but nonetheless work.

Small units of government conventionally have been alleged to cause fragmentation, duplication, diseconomies, and general confusion. More recently, however, some of their virtues have been rediscovered. Small units—whether municipalities, special taxing districts, or decentralized service units—provide the opportunity for contracting on a competitive basis, tailoring the level and quality of service to more limited requirements, providing greater attention to the operation of services and satisfaction of the consumer, and drawing upon pride and competitiveness to improve performance. These are no insignificant attributes in a world of large governments and complex bureaucracies.

On the other hand, it is equally clear that broader, more comprehensive structures are required for services or functions that transcend municipal or neighborhood boundaries. The effective operations of such functions as water supply, sewage disposal, transportation, emergency communication, and planning, among others, usually benefit from comprehensive geographical coverage.

The question is not whether small or large, decentralized or centralized, disaggregated or comprehensive structures are better. The question is which, in combination with the other, is more appropriate for given functions (or parts of functions) responding to specific needs in individual metropolitan areas. The most likely answer lies in two-tier (or, in larger metropolitan areas, three-tier) structures ranging from metropolitan to community-or neighborhood-level governments, with special-purpose districts for appropriate functions.

(2) *Distribution of functions among levels of government.* Structure will mean little, however, if a jurisdiction is assigned responsibility for a function which it cannot effectively provide, or for which it does not have adequate sources of revenue.

The debate over distribution of functions among levels of government typically breaks down in part because of confusion over what constitutes a "function." In fact, all levels of government are involved in providing some aspect of most "functions," such as education, criminal justice, transportation, and the like. It is more fruitful to look at specific components of various functions. The transportation function, for example, is usefully divided into interstate (a federal concern), intercity (a state concern), principal local arteries (a county concern), road maintenance and traffic control (a county and municipal concern), mass-transit arteries (a regional concern), and mass-transit feeder systems (a county/municipal concern). Appropriate responsibilities vary on a state-by-state and locale-by-locale basis, and they can change over time.

Equally as important as the appropriate distribution of responsibilities is appropriate access to revenue sources. At a time when 80 percent of the nondefense domestic purchases of goods and services in the public sector are made at the state and local levels (including those made with federal grants), it is an anachronism that the basic revenue structure in the United States should so heavily favor the federal government to the extreme detriment of the states and localities. Across the country, school bonds are turned down, taxpayers are rising in Proposition 13-type protests, and elderly residents are pushed to the brink by property taxes that rise faster than their pensions. While the federal government continues to reap a revenue dividend from inflation (since federal income-tax revenues increase by 1.5 percent for every 1 percent increase in the consumer price index), and many state governments continue to show sizable surpluses, local governments struggle to meet costs, and bear the brunt of taxpayer dissatisfaction when they resort to property-tax increases to do so.

It is not surprising, therefore, that the focus of the taxpayers' revolt has been local government and, in particular, the property tax. The irony, of course, is that as local governments become more dependent on the state and federal governments for grants to buttress their sagging revenues, the federal and state governments assume commensurately greater power in determining the nature of local-government operations. The essential linkage between authority for raising revenues and responsibility for delivering services is thus becoming all the more diffuse, with a consequent negative affect on productivity.

(3) *Improving operating relations among governments.* American federalism has variously been compared to a layer cake, marble cake, and fruit cake. Whatever the pattern, the array of laws, programs, regulations, grants, reporting requirements, and administrative and personal relationships that constitute something called the "intergovernmental system" is confusing at best and crippling at worst. Here again, the brunt of the problem is borne by local governments, which have the dual disadvantage of being principally responsible for delivering most programs, and most vulnerable—located as they are at the bottom of the bureaucratic heap—to the legal and administrative whims and miscalculations of other governments.

Some local governments have learned to adjust to the intergovernmental maze by aggressive entrepreneurship that plays the system for all it's worth, and by a street-wise, pragmatic approach that accepts the system for what it is and tries to put things together at the local level as best it can. Other local governments simply limp along.

There are several opportunities for improvement. The first lies with the federal government. Despite early attempts to limit the number and complexity of categorical grant programs, the growth has continued unabated. The block-grant approach has helped. And, of course, general revenue sharing is a favorite with local governments, since there are no strings attached to spending the money. Despite some genuine efforts to improve the categorical grant process, the full potential is far from tapped. Meanwhile, there are questions regarding whether the block-grant and general revenue-sharing programs establish appropriate types of performance standards that assure the federal money is being well spent.

In recent years, the federal government has taken some steps to assist state and local governments in improving management capability. The Intergovernmental Personnel Act was an important step in that direction. Such efforts as the National Center for Productivity and Quality of Working Life, and the capacity-building programs of the Department of Housing and Urban Development have also made a contribution. These efforts, however, have been aimed more at improving state and local government capability than improving the operation of the intergovernmental system.

A second, critical role lies with state governments. Local governments are the creatures of the states; hence, their basic structures, sources of revenue, and legal bases are established by state law. States could take numerous actions to encourage local-government productivity, beginning with the elimination of anachronistic laws, structures, regulations, and administrative procedures. On the positive side, states could establish and enforce minimum standards for budgeting, accounting, and performance and reporting systems in order to provide data on the level, quality, results, and cost of services. They could encourage the use of professional management and analytic staff, and assist those local governments which are too small to provide or to justify professional management expertise on a full-time basis by developing pooling arrangements. State governments could also take action to improve personnel management and manpower development programs in all local governments within the state. And they could, in general, provide the leadership and the technical and financial support for bringing modern and effective management to local governments. Unfortunately, the potential for state action is limited by the quality of some state governments themselves; many are far behind some of their own subdivisions in professionalism and performance.

A third opportunity is improved cooperation among governments at the same level. Many local governments have learned that they can join with neighboring jurisdictions to pool resources, or to develop larger service areas for such functions as solid-waste management or the joint purchase of materials.

The intergovernmental system has probably reached a stage of complexity that will not easily succumb to restructuring or better administrative procedure alone. The various entities that compose the public sector represent important and often relatively autonomous political centers of influence that resist trusting their fate to supposedly neutral administrators or administrative procedures. One possibility for dealing with the complexity and synthesizing or reconciling the political differences lies in providing opportunities and incentives for negotiations among the various governmental units. Such is the aim of the "negotiated investment strategy" currently under experimentation in Chicago, St. Paul, Minnesota, and Gary, Indiana, where federal, state, and local officials are attempting to pull together various programs and needs into formal agreements and informal understandings that can coordinate and focus the resources of the public sector to meet local needs.

(4) *Involvement of the private sector.* Few state and local governments have learned to effectively use the talents and technological capability of the private sector to improve public services. A simple method is to enlist

local businessmen in providing direct assistance in those areas where businesses have special expertise, especially in functions characterized by fairly clear objectives in business-type operations (such as basic management and financial procedures, industrial engineering, purchasing, the operation of food services, transportation, maintenance of facilities, and the like).

There are also opportunities for contracting out public services to private businesses in those instances where a private contractor can do the job more efficiently or, in some cases, more effectively. To assure that there are genuine savings to be had, and that the necessary services will be provided at the same or higher quality level that had been provided by the public operation, contracting out obviously must be undertaken with care. Of special importance is to guard against the potential for graft and corruption in government contracts. However, appropriately structured and monitored, there are untapped opportunities for greater involvement of private contractors.

(5) *Challenging conventional assumptions.* Most of the above measures involve techniques or concepts which are fairly well known but for the most part have been little applied. But there is also a need in the longer run to challenge some of the basic assumptions that have governed the provision of public services in the United States for generations. In the long run, the substantial restructuring or redesign of the way in which public services are provided may offer the greatest potential for improved productivity.

The difficulties involved in challenging old assumptions or testing new ideas are formidable. And the instances in which substantial efforts have been undertaken are rare. One of the most interesting to date is the experiment in Kansas City that tested the assumption that random patrol of police cars is a deterrent to crime. The city was divided into three sectors. In one sector, the level of random patrol was quadrupled; in the second sector, it remained the same; and in the third sector, patrol was eliminated altogether (although police would respond to specific calls or emergencies). At the end of a year, there was no substantial difference in the level of crime or citizens' feelings of security (as determined by survey), and the conclusion was that, at least for a city like Kansas City, it could not be taken on faith that random police patrol had a significant effect on crime levels.

Such conclusions are obviously controversial. And it remains to be seen how they will affect policy or actual police operations. Nonetheless, the experiment is extremely enlightening in demonstrating the possibilities for undertaking systematic experimentation in the public sector as a way of

eliminating, minimizing, or significantly restructuring old modes of operation, and of developing new ways of providing public services more
efficiently and more effectively.

(6) *Research and development.* Finally, there is a need to substantially
increase national as well as state and local government and university
efforts in research and development related to improving the productivity
of government. There are some hopeful signs at the national level. The
creation of Public Technology, Inc., a nonprofit organization established
at the initiative of the major public-interest groups (such as the National
League of Cities and the National Association of Counties) with private
foundation and federal government funding, along with subscriptions from
local governments, has opened the possibility of focusing research and
development resources on problems that plague state, city, and county
government. PTI attempts to pool the resources of local governments that
would not undertake research and development on their own, yet desire to
develop new solutions for problems that they have in common. For
example, PTI, working with its own resources and in combination with
private operations, developed a variety of firefighting apparatus (such as
better breathing equipment and "rapid water," which permits a greater
volume of water to be distributed through a standard-size hose) and street
patching equipment, and has also assisted local governments in developing
the in-house capability required for seeking out opportunities to apply
technology.

The federal government established a science and technology advisory
board of state and local government officials to bring the views of the
states and localities to the federal level, where they can help to assist in
developing a more effective agenda for federal research and development
geared toward problems of public-sector technology.

SUMMARY

Improving productivity means doing a better job with the resources we
have, or doing the same job with fewer resources. It means government
that is more effective and efficient in achieving goals established through
the political process. It means, moreover, setting goals that are appropriate
in the first place—appropriate in the sense that they are reasonable, that
they do in fact reflect genuine and not illusory needs, and that they take
account of the resources available or required to achieve them.

There is no single or simple prescription for improving the productivity
of government. Immediate improvements can be achieved in virtually all
government operations by assuring that the procedures and technology

used are at least up to date. Sustained improvement requires developing the internal capability for continually examining and upgrading operations. In the longer run, productivity improvement requires changes in the overall structure and management of government.

To some extent, such changes are slow in coming because the opportunities for change have not been fully recognized. Because there are no one, two, or three principal changes, but rather a lengthy agenda of changes, there is a tendency to ignore those that are not readily apparent or easily achieved.

The principal reason for failure to take advantage of the opportunities for improving productivity, however, is lack of incentive to do so. While there may be general agreement on the desirability of achieving more effective and efficient government, the incentive to do so is not sufficiently intense, nor sufficiently well organized and focused, to overcome the powerful political and administrative impediments and disincentives that militate against it.

Our system of government is slack. The potential for greater productivity is substantial. But achieving that potential will require overcoming formidable political and administrative obstacles.

NAME INDEX

303

SUBJECT INDEX

ABOUT THE CONTRIBUTORS

DAVID R. BEAM is a Senior Analyst on the staff of the Advisory Commission on Intergovernmental Relations. His recent research has been concerned with the growth of federal domestic programs and administrative problems in federal grants-in-aid.

ROBERT D. BEHN is an Associate Professor at Duke University's Institute of Policy Sciences and Public Affairs. He has written extensively about the problems of policy termination and cut-back management, including: "The False Dawn of the Sunset Law," *The Public Interest* (Fall 1977); "How to Terminate a Public Policy: A Dozen Hints for the Would-Be Policy Terminator," *Policy Analysis* (Summer 1978); and "Leadership for Cut-Back Management: The Use of Corporate Strategy," *Public Administration Review* (November-December 1980).

NAOMI CAIDEN is coauthor of *Planning and Budgeting in Poor Countries* (Transaction Books, 1980), and has published several articles in the area of comparative public administration and public finance. She is currently completing a book on French budgeting history and is collaborating on a study of the financial origins of the welfare state. Dr. Caiden was educated at the London School of Economics, the Australian National University, and the University of Southern California, and has been principally engaged in research and teaching in the social sciences in Australia, Israel, and the United States.

CYNTHIA C. COLELLA is an Analyst on the staff of the Advisory Commission on Intergovernmental Relations. Her recent research has been concerned with the growth of federal domestic programs.

R. SCOTT FOSLER was elected to the Montgomery County Council, Montgomery County, Maryland, in 1978 and is currently serving as its President. He is also Vice President and Director of Government Studies at the Committee for Economic Development, where he has been involved in various projects dealing with productivity, personnel management, labor relations, and urban policy. Mr. Fosler was previously employed at the National Commission on Productivity as Assistant to the Executive Director, and at the Institute of Public Administration as Senior Staff Member. He is the author of numerous books and articles, including *Improving Management of the Public Work Force: The Challenge to State and Local Government* (CED, 1978) and *Improving Productivity in State and Local Government* (CED, 1976). Mr. Fosler received his M.P.A. from the Woodrow Wilson School of Public and International Affairs in 1969 and his B.A. from Dickinson College in 1967.

JAMES GREENFIELD was a Policy Analyst in the Division of Economic Development and Public Finance in the Office of Policy Development and Research at the U.S. Department of Housing and Urban Development. He is now attending law school.

JOHN J. KIRLIN is a Professor of Public Administration at the University of Southern California, stationed at the Sacramento Public Affairs Center. He has written and lectured extensively on the causes and effects of Proposition 13. Dr. Kirlin's other research interests and publications focus upon alternative structures for the governance of metropolitan areas and for municipal service delivery, and upon the intergovernmental system of the United States.

CHARLES H. LEVINE is Director of the Institute for Urban Studies and the Bureau of Governmental Research at the University of Maryland, College Park. A specialist in public management and urban politics, he previously taught at Indiana University, Michigan State University, and Syracuse University, and has held visiting appointments at the University of Southern California, Cornell, and the Federal Executive Institute. He has previously published four books: *Racial Conflict and the American Mayor* (1974), *Managing Human Resources* (1977), *Urban Politics* (1980), and *Managing Fiscal Stress* (1980). In 1979, he received the William E. Mosher Award of the American Society for Public Administration for his article, "Organizational Decline and Cutback Management."

B. GUY PETERS is currently Director of the Center for Public Policy Studies of Tulane University. He is the author of *the Politics of Bureaucracy, Can Government Go Bankrupt?* (with Richard Rose) and a number of scholarly articles.

JOHN E. PETERSEN is the Director of the Government Finance Research Center, Municipal Finance Officers Association. Previously he was Director, Center of Policy Research, National Governors' Conference; Washington Director, M.F.O.A.; Director of Finance, Securities Industries Association; and Economist for the Urban Institute and the Board of Governors—Federal Reserve System. He holds a Ph.D. in Economics from the University of Pennsylvania, an M.B.A. from the Wharton School, and a B.S. degree in Economics from Northwestern University.

RICHARD ROSE is Director of the Centre for the Study of Public Policy at the University of Strathclyde, Glasgow, Scotland. He is Secretary of the Committee on Political Sociology, IPSA/ISA, and has been a visiting fellow at the American Enterprise Institute, the Brookings Institution, and the Woodrow Wilson International Center in Washington, D.C. Among the two dozen books he had authored or edited are: *Presidents and Prime Ministers, Do Parties Make a Difference?, Can Government Go Bankrupt?, Managing Presidential Objectives,* and *Politics in England: An Interpretation for the 1980s.*

JOHN P. ROSS is the Director of the Division of Economic Development and Public Finance in the Office of Policy Development and Research at the U.S. Department of Housing and Urban Development. Dr. Ross received his Ph.D. in Economics from the Maxwell School, Syracuse University. He has written widely in the field of public finance, including coauthoring with Jesse Burkhead *Productivity in the Local Government Section.* His article entitled "The Impact of Urban Aid" recently appeared in *Urban Revitalization.*

IRENE RUBIN has her Ph.D. in Sociology from the University of Chicago. She directed an Urban Studies center at Lewis University in Illinois for three years and is now a faculty member at the Institute for Urban Studies of the University of Maryland. She is an organization theorist who writes about the effects of resource levels on public organizations. Her past work includes a study on universities' responses to fiscal stress and a case study of a city in fiscal stress. Her articles have appeared in *Social Science Quarterly* and *Sociology of Education.*

ALLEN SCHICK is Senior Specialist in American Government and Public Administration at the Congressional Research Service of the Library of

Congress. He has written several books and numerous articles on public budgeting, financial management, and congressional decision making.

HAROLD WOLMAN is a Senior Research Associate in the Public Finance program at the Urban Institute. He holds a Ph.D. in Political Science from the University of Michigan and has been on the political science faculty at both the University of Pennsylvania and the University of Massachusetts, Boston. He has also served as Director of Research for the White House Conference on Balanced National Growth and Economic, and as Staff Director for the House Subcommittee on the City.

6388

THE CATHOLIC UNIVERSITY OF AMERICA
STUDIES IN AMERICAN CHURCH HISTORY

VOL. IV

THE CATHOLIC HIERARCHY OF THE UNITED STATES

1790-1922

BY

REV. JOHN HUGH O'DONNELL, C.S.C.

A DISSERTATION

SUBMITTED TO THE FACULTY OF PHILOSOPHY OF THE CATHOLIC UNI-
VERSITY OF AMERICA IN PARTIAL FULFILMENT OF THE REQUIRE-
MENTS FOR THE DEGREE OF DOCTOR OF PHILOSOPHY

WASHINGTON, D. C.
1922

Library of Congress Cataloging in Publication Data

O'Donnell, John Hugh, 1895-1947.
 The Catholic hierarchy of the United States,
1790-1922.

 Reprint of the author's thesis, Catholic University
of America, 1922, which was issued as v. 4 of the
Catholic University of America. Studies in American
church history.
 Includes bibliographies.
 1. Bishops—United States. I. Title. II. Series:
Catholic University of America. Studies in American
church history, v. 4.
BX4670.O4 1974   262'.02   73-3558
ISBN 0-404-57754-7

Reprinted from the edition of 1922, Washington D.C.
First AMS edition published, 1974
Manufactured in the United States of America

International Standard Book Number
Complete Set: 0-404-57750-4
Volume 4: 0-404-57754-7

AMS PRESS, INC.
New York, N.Y. 10003

TABLE OF CONTENTS

PREFACE

Several attempts have been made to write the history of the Hierarchy in the Church of the United States. John Gilmary Shea, historian of the American Church, was one of the first to undertake this task. In 1886, he published a volume *The Hierarchy of the Catholic Church in the United States*, and while this work deserves the highest praise, it is of little historical value, since the author withheld all references to his sources. In 1888, Richard H. Clarke published a similar work in three volumes entitled *The Lives of the Deceased Bishops of the Catholic Church in the United .States.* Unlike Shea, Clarke has given abundant references in his footnotes with the result that he has approached somewhat more closely to the historical ideal. But, despite this, the work is not reliable.

To Francis X. Reuss must be accorded the honor of being the first to undertake a thoroughly historical treatment of this subject. His *Biographical Cyclopedia of the Catholic Hierarchy of the United States from 1789 to 1898*, published at Milwaukee in 1898, was "nothing more—nor less—than an American supplement to the *Art of Verifying Dates.* It is not a history in the ordinary meaning of the word: it is a manual of fundamental data for the guidance of future historians of the Church in the United States." The work has many source references and in some instances previous historical inaccuracies are corrected.

In the first issues of the *Catholic Historical Review*, the Rt. Rev. Owen B. Corrigan, D.D., Auxiliary-Bishop of Baltimore, published a *Chronology of the Catholic Hierarchy of the United States*, supplementing to a great extent the plan of Reuss. He added the Provinces and the Suffragan Sees in the order of their establishment, following a geographico-chronological division. These articles elicited high commendation and have been exceedingly beneficial to writers in the field of American Church History. But something more is needed, and at the suggestion of Doctor

Peter Guilday, this Manual of the American Hierarchy was
written to fill the lacunae. It combines the work of Reuss
and Corrigan with an added guide to the known sources
of the lives of the Bishops who have ruled the Church
in the United States. Under each diocese is given also a
brief bibliographical guide.

To bring the work up to date, questionnaires were sent
out to the Bishops relative to their biography, as well as
to that of their predecessors, and excellent returns were
received. For their hearty cooperation, as well as that
of the many Diocesan Chancellors, I am duly grateful. To
Doctor Peter Guilday, under whose inspiration and guidance this work was undertaken and completed, my gratitude is due. I also take pleasure in acknowledging my
indebtedness to the Rev. P. W. Browne, S.T.D., to Mr.
Daniel Ryan of the National Catholic Welfare Council, and
to Miss Alice McShane of the Library of the Catholic University of America, as well as to my confrères in the American Church History Seminar at the Catholic University of
America for helpful suggestions and much-needed assistance.

INTRODUCTION

I. SPANISH ECCLESIASTICAL JURISDICTION

The Spanish colonists came from lands where the Catholic Church had been organized for centuries. As a part of their work of colonization they brought with them the Church system of Spain. As a result bishoprics had been erected from the outset and a hierarchical organization had been effected long before Bishop John Carroll was consecrated.

In a work on the Catholic Hierarchy of the United States from 1790 to 1922 it is necessary to sketch briefly the story of this hierarchy, viewed in the light of early Spanish jurisdiction.

The beginnings of episcopàl jurisdiction in the Spanish colonies of America are historically traced to Seville. While in practice the patriarchal honor given to Seville may be cf small import, yet this ancient See of the last of the Western Fathers must ever be regarded as the source of Spanish-American canonical discipline.[1]

The priests who accompanied Columbus on his second expedition received their faculties from Father Buil, who was appointed Vicar-Apostolic of the New World by Alexander VI. It was not, however, until 1511, that a practical acknowledgment of the rights of Seville as the Metropolitan of the dioceses about to be erected was manifested. In that year on the eighth of August, the first actual sees in the New World were created: at San Domingo, Concepcion de la Vega, and San Juan. The first Bishop to arrive was Alonso Manso and with him the American hierarchy may be said to have begun.[2]

In 1518, the Diocese of Baracoa in Cuba was erected, but four years later it was superseded by the creation of

---

[1] RYAN, *Diocesan Organization in the Spanish Colonies*, in the *Catholic Historical Review*. Vol. II. p. 146 seq.

[2] Pope Julius II erected the Province of Hyaguata, with Magua and Bayuana as suffragan sees in 1504, but they never existed except on paper. Their creation on account of the proximity to the mainland, is the foreshadowing of the hierarchy under which we now live.

the See of Santiago de Cuba and it was to this Diocese that our first parish, St. Augustine, organized in 1565, belonged.

The Church in Spanish-America was made independent of the Metropolitan See of Seville in 1545, when the archiepiscopal Sees of Lima, Mexico City, and San Domingo were erected. We are only concerned with the last two, for it is from these Provinces that ecclesiastical jurisdiction and organization in the southeastern and southwestern parts of the United States can be traced.

In the southeastern part of our country, the parish of St. Augustine, was subject ecclesiastically to the Diocese of Santiago de Cuba, which See was at first a Suffragan of the Province of San Domingo. During the next century and a half, subsequent to 1565, Florida received canonical visitations from the Bishops of Santiago and their representatives. As a result, the Holy See instructed the Bishop of Santiago to select an Auxiliary, who was to serve as his representative in Florida. Accordingly, Dionisio Rezino was consecrated in Yucatan in 1709 as titular Bishop of Adramyttium. From 1710 to 1763, Florida received episcopal supervision from the Auxiliary-Bishops of Santiago and in 1762 from the Ordinary of Santiago himself. By the Treaty of Paris in 1763, Spain ceded Florida to England in return for Manila and Havana and the subsequent years until 1783 were disastrous to the Church in that region. In 1783, Florida—then under the jurisdiction of the Diocese of Havana, erected in 1787 —was restored to Spain and remained under her control until 1819, when the territory was purchased by the United States. Thenceforward, Bishop DuBourg of New Orleans, assumed control, notwithstanding the protests of the Bishop of Havana, who maintained that he had not been notified of the change by the Patriarch of the Indies. The question of jurisdiction was finally settled on November 5, 1826, when Bishop Portier became resident Vicar-Apostolic of the Vicariate of Alabama and the Floridas.

In the southwestern part of our country the Church was subject to Mexican Sees and in particular to the Archdiocese of Mexico City, which had been erected in

1545. As a Suffragan of this Province, the See of Guadalajara (erected in 1560) is of prime import, for our southwest enters on the stage of Church history as part of this diocese.'

The jurisdiction of the Bishop of Guadalajara over the future southwest of the United States was transferred to the Bishop of Durango upon the erection of the latter Diocese in 1620. The next ecclesiastical division came in 1777, when the Diocese of Linares was erected, and two years later the See of Sonora was established. These changes, therefore, bring us closer to the origin and development of the present Dioceses in the States of New Mexico, Arizona, Texas, and California. In brief, the Vicariate-Apostolic of New Mexico (which included Arizona), erected in 1850 by Pius IX, with the Rt. Rev. John Lamy as first Vicar, belonged ecclesiastically to the Diocese of Durango. To the Bishop of the See of Linares was given the jurisdiction over the present State of Texas from 1777 until it was created a Prefecture-Apostolic in 1838 under the administration of the Rev. John Timon, C.M.' The Diocese of Monterey (erected in 1850) was formerly part of the Diocese of Both Californias (1840) which in turn was subject to the Bishop of Sonora (1779). In 1851, when Lower California was severed from the jurisdiction of Bishop Alemany of Monterey, the last link with the Spanish-American hierarchy was broken.

II. FRENCH ECCLESIASTICAL JURISDICTION

The Archbishop of Rouen was the first to exercise jurisdiction over the country that was called New France, which at that time included the great central valley of the United States. Consequently in 1647, he appointed Father Jerome Lalemant, as Superior of the Missions in Canada. Notwithstanding the protests of the Archbishop, the Holy See thought it necessary to erect a Vicariate-Apostolic in Canada in order that more personal supervision could be exercised over the growing Church in this continent.

---

³ RYAN. *Ecclesiastical Jurisdiction in the Spanish Colonies*, in the *Catholic Historical Review*. Vol. v. p. 5.
⁴ Erected as a Vicariate-Apostolic in 1841, with the Rt. Rev. John M. Odin, D. D., as first Vicar-Apostolic.

Accordingly, on June 3, 1658, the Vicariate of Canada was established and the Rt. Rev. Francis Montmorency de Laval, was appointed as first Vicar-Apostolic; as a result the immediate jurisdiction of the Archbishop of Rouen ceased.

The territory of the new Vicar-Apostolic was quite extensive. With the exception of the Thirteen Original Colonies and the territory in the southeastern and the southwestern parts of our country, which were under Spanish jurisdiction, Bishop Laval was spiritual administrator over the remaining part of the United States and all of Canada. For our purpose, it suffices to state that he administered this territory by appointing vicars-general with ample powers as his representatives in the Illinois country and in the Mississippi Valley region of Louisiana. In the east and northeast, he exercised personal jurisdiction with the various Jesuit Fathers acting as Superiors.

By way of anticipation, it may be stated that the Far West, the Oregon Territory, remained under the jurisdiction of the Bishops of Quebec until 1822, when the Vicariate-Apostolic of Red River was erected with Bishop Provencher as Vicar Apostolic.[5] It was he who received the first appeal from the settlers in the Oregon Country in 1834 to send priests to that territory to care for their spiritual wants.[6]

In 1722, Louisiana was divided into three great ecclesiastical districts. The first section extending from the mouth of the Mississippi River to that of the Illinois, was assigned to the Capuchins; the second, which was north of the Wabash River (Illinois Country), was given to the Jesuits; while the third, the country east of the Mississippi from the sea (Gulf of Mexico) to the Wabash, was allotted to the Carmelites. The Superior of these respective Religious Orders was to be the Vicar-General of the Bishop of Quebec. During the subsequent years, considerable trouble arose among the Superiors as to the question of

---

[5] The Diocese of Quebec was erected in 1674.

[6] Bishop Provencher had no priests to spare, so the appeal was transmitted to the Bishop of Quebec. In response to this, Fathers Francis Norbert Blanchet and Modeste Demers were sent to this region in 1838, the former being appointed Vicar-General.

jurisdiction. Shortly after the Carmelites retired, and their territory was turned over to the Capuchins.[7]

By the Treaty of Paris in 1763, Louisiana became a province of Spain and ecclesiastical jurisdiction over this territory was withdrawn from the Bishop of Quebec and given to the Ordinary of the Diocese of Santiago de Cuba. In 1789 this diocese was divided; the new bishopric of St. Christopher of Havana was erected, and the Rt. Rev. Cyril de Barcelona, Auxiliary-Bishop of Havana, became resident Ordinary over the Louisiana part of the diocese. The next ecclesiastical change occurred in April, 1793, when Pius VI made Louisiana an independent see with the Rt. Rev. Louis Peñalver y Cardenas as first Bishop. In 1800 Spain retroceded Louisiana to France, and it was later (1803) purchased by the United States. On September 1, 1805, the Congregation of Propaganda issued a decree to the effect that Bishop Carroll was appointed Apostolic-Administrator of Louisiana with power to appoint a resident Vicar-General. The upper part of the Mississippi Valley remained under the control of the Bishop of Quebec, with resident Vicars-General as their representatives until the Very Rev. John Carroll was appointed Prefect-Apostolic of the Church in the New Republic.[8]

III. ENGLISH JURISDICTION OVER THE THIRTEEN COLONIES

The Church in the English Colonies was almost exclusively an English Jesuit Mission and the Superior acted as the representative of the Vicar-Apostolic of London. Whether or not these Vicars had the power to grant the Superiors faculties prior to 1757 is a debated question. But in that year the Sacred Congregation of Propaganda granted to Bishop Petre, Vicar-Apostolic of the London District, full jurisdiction over the islands and colonies. When Bishop Challoner became Vicar-Apostolic he received the same power on March 31, 1759, and he exercised this up to the time of his death in 1781. The Jesuit Superior acted as his Vicar-General in the American Colonies.[9]

---

[7] SHEA, *History of the Catholic Church in the United States.* Vol. i. p. 566 seq.

[8] DILHET, *Etat De L'Eglise Catholique ou Diocese des Etats-Unis De L'Amerique Septentrionale,* translated by Rev. Patrick W. Browne, S. T. D., pp. 158 seq. (notes), Washington, D. C., 1922.

[9] BURTON, *Life and Times of Bishop Challoner.* Vol. ii, p. 123 seq. London, 1909.

Both Bishop Petre and his successor, Bishop Challoner, petitioned the Holy See to erect a Vicariate Apostolic in English America for the government of the Church in the islands and on the mainland, but their efforts were of no avail.

When the Revolutionary War broke out, ecclesiastical relations between Bishop Challoner and the Church in the Colonies came to an end. The Church in the future Republic was not, however, without its head, for the acting Vicar-General, Father John Lewis, continued to be acknowledged by the clergy and laity alike as their Superior. But after the Treaty of Paris in 1783, it was recognized that it would be impossible for the Vicar-Apostolic of London to exercise jurisdiction over the Church in the New Republic, and accordingly, a General Chapter of the American clergy was called at Whitemarsh.

After the first meeting on November 6, 1783, the name of Father John Lewis was sent to Rome as Superior of the whole Mission. He remained as the acknowledged leader until June 9, 1784, when the Holy See appointed John Carroll Prefect-Apostolic of the Church in the New Republic.[10] Thus officially ended the jurisdiction of the Vicar-Apostolic of London over the nascent Church in this country. Father Carroll acted as Prefect-Apostolic during the subsequent five years, and on November 14, 1789, he was appointed first Bishop of the newly created Diocese of Baltimore, thereby becoming the first Bishop of the present Hierarchy of the United States.

[10]GUILDAY, Life and Times of John Carroll. Vol. i, p. 202 seq. New York, 1922.

CHAPTER I

I. THE PROVINCE OF BALTIMORE (1808)

The Metropolitan See of Baltimore was erected by Pius VII on April 8, 1808, with the Right Reverend John Carroll, D.D., as first Archbishop.

When created, the Archdiocese had as suffragan sees the Dioceses of Boston, New York, Philadelphia, and Bardstown, and the jurisdiction of the Archbishop in 1808 extended over Maryand, Virginia, the District of Columbia, the two Carolinas, and over what is now Alabama, Mississippi, Louisiana and Florida. Three years later some islands in the Danish and Dutch West Indies were added to this already extensive jurisdiction. At present the Province of Baltimore has as suffragan sees, the Dioceses of Richmond (1820), Charleston (1820), Savannah (1850), Wilmington, Delaware (1868), Saint Augustine (1870), and the Vicariate-Apostolic of North Carolina (1868).

SHEA, *History of the Catholic Church in Colonial Days*, New York, 1886; ID., *Life and Times of Archbishop Carroll*, New York, 1888; ID., *Hist. of the Cath. Church in the United States*, 1844-68, 2 vols., New York, 1892; Catholic Almanacs and Directories, 1834-1907; O'GORMAN, *The Roman Catholic Church in the United States*, New York, 1895; DAVIS, *Day Star of American Freedom;* SCHARF, *Hist. of Maryland*, Baltimore, 1879; McSHERRY, *History of Maryland*, Baltimore, 1852; SCHARF, *History of Baltimore City and County*, Philadelphia, 1881; TREACY, *Old Catholic Maryland*, Swedesboro, N. J., 1879; KNOTT, *History of Maryland*, Baltimore, s. d.; STANTON, *History of the Church in Western Maryland*, Baltimore, 1900; RIORDAN, ed., *Cathedral Records*, Baltimore, 1906; Archives of Maryland Hist. Society, Baltimore; Diocesan Archives, ibid.; HUGHES, *Hist. of S. J. in N. Am.*, Cleveland, 1907; *Acta et Decreta S. Conc. Recentiorum. Collectio Lacensis. Auctoribus Presbyt. S. J.*, Frieburg, 1875, contains in vol. III, the full text of the decrees of these ten councils; *Concilia Provincialia Baltimori Habita ab Anno, 1829 ad 1849*, Baltimore, 1851, gives the acts of only the first seven provincial councils.

I. Diocese of Baltimore (1789)

The original Diocese of Baltimore, the first to be erected in the United States, was created on November 6, 1789, when Pius VI appointed the Reverend John Carroll to the new See as its first Bishop.

1

The original thirteen colonies were the geographical limits of this diocese in 1789, but throughout the course of the years it has been gradually reduced, so that it now comprises all the counties of Maryland, lying west of Chesapeake Bay, and the District of Columbia with a total area of 6,463 square miles.

1. CARROLL, JOHN.

The first Bishop of the Hierarchy of the United States was born at Upper Marlboro, Maryland, on January 3, 1735. At the age of twelve he went to the Bohemia Manor School, and after a year there he was sent to College of Saint Omer's in France, where he made his classical studies. In 1753, he entered the Society of Jesus, and two years later, at Liège, began his studies in philosophy and theology. Ordained to the priesthood in 1769, he spent the next five years in teaching and in traveling. When the Society of Jesus was suppressed in 1773, he was ordered to return to Maryland, where his mother was living. During the next decade (1779-1789), he served as a missionary to the scattered Catholics of Maryland and Virginia. In 1776 he went to Canada with the three American commissioners, Charles Carroll of Carrollton, his cousin, Benjamin Franklin, and Samuel Chase. He was appointed Prefect-Apostolic of the Church in the United States on June 9, 1784, and five years later, on November 6, 1789, he was appointed first Bishop of Baltimore. He was consecrated in Lulworth Castle, England, on August 15, 1790, by the Rt. Rev. Charles Walmesley, senior Vicar-Apostolic of England. He was elevated to the archiepiscopate on April 8, 1808, and received the pallium on August 18, 1811. Mourned by all classes, he died on December 3, 1815, in Baltimore, Maryland.

ARCHIVAL MATERIAL: There are twenty cases of *Letters and Correspondence Private* and *Administrative,* in the *Baltimore Archives.* Many of these letters are rough sketches and copies of letters sent to Rome and elsewhere, and they have been admirably used by Shea in the second volume of his *History of the Catholic Church in the United States.* Shea procured copies of most of the Carroll correspondence from Rome and elsewhere and these *Shea Transcripts* are now in the *Georgetown Archives,* at the University of Georgetown.

Both the *Baltimore Archives* and the *Georgetown Archives* are card-catalogued. The *Dominican Archives* at the Dominican House of Studies, Catholic University of America, Washington, D. C., contains many photostatic copies of Carroll's letters and reports from foreign archives. *Cf.* C. R. FISH. *Guide to the Materials for American History in Roman and other Italian Archives*, Washington, D. C., 1911. See also, *United States Catholic Historical Magazine*, Vol. ii (1888), pp. 217-220; E. I. DEVITT, S.J., *Propaganda Documents: Appointment of the First Bishop of Baltimore*, in the ACHS *Records*, Vol. xxi, pp. 185-236. (Translation of original documents published in the AHR for July. 1910, pp. 801-839. *Cf.* also *Carroll Correspondence*, edited by E. I. DEVITT, S.J., in ACHS *Records*, Vol. xix (1908), pp. 214, 243, 385, 455, Vol. xx (1909), pp. 49, 193, 250, 432.

BIOGRAPHIES: BRENT. *Biographical Sketch of the Most Rev. John Carroll, First Archbishop of Baltimore, with select portions of his Writings.* Baltimore, 1843; B. U. CAMPBELL, *Memoirs of the Life and Times of the Most Rev. John Carroll*, in the *United States Catholic Magazine*, Vol. iii (1844), pp. 32-41, 98-101, 169-176, 244-248, 363-379, 662-669, 718-724, Vol. v (1846), pp. 595, 676, Vol. vi (1847), pp. 31, 100, 144, 434, 482, 592, Vol. vii (1848), pp. 91-106; SHEA, *Life and Times of the Most Reverend John Carroll*, being Vol. ii of his *History of the Catholic Church in the United States* (1763-1815). New York, 1888; B. U. CAMPBELL, *Desultory Sketches of the Catholic Church in Maryland*, in the *Religious Cabinet* for 1842; GUILDAY, *The Life and Times of John Carroll*, two volumes, New York, 1922.

SECONDARY SOURCES: CLARKE, *The Lives of the Deceased Bishops of the Catholic Church in the United States*, Vol. i, pp. 32-113, New York, 1888; REUSS, *Biographical Cyclopedia of the Catholic Hierarchy of the United States*, p. 21, Milwaukee, 1898; SHEA, *The Hierarchy of the Catholic Church in the United States*, pp. 61-65, New York, 1886; RUSSELL, *Maryland the Land of Sanctuary*, pp. 367, 496-8; (Cf. Appendix U for Carroll genealogy), Baltimore, 1907. McCANN, *History of Mother Seton's Daughters*, Vol. i, pp. 20-69, *passim*, New York, 1917; WEBB, *Centenary of Catholicity in Kentucky*, pp. 36, 161, 187, 201, 213, 215, Louisville, 1884. McSWEENY, *Story of the Mountain* (Mt. St. Mary's College), Vol. i, passim, Emmitsburg, 1911; Cf. Indices of the *Catholic Historical Review*, and the *American Catholic Historical Society Researches*.

2. NEALE, LEONARD.

Archbishop Neale was born at Port Tobacco, Charles County, Maryland, on October 15, 1746. His early instruction was received at home and at the age of twelve he was sent to the College of Saint Omer in France. He entered the Society of Jesus, and after completing his studies was ordained to the priesthood at Liège, Belgium, on June 5, 1773. In 1779, he set sail for British Guiana to engage in missionary work. His attempts meeting with little success, on account of ill-health he returned to Maryland in January, 1783. Bishop Carroll appointed him Vicar-General for the northern district of the Diocese and in 1798, he became

4 STUDIES IN AMERICAN CHURCH HISTORY

President of Georgetown College. The following year he was appointed coadjutor to Archbishop Carroll with the title of titular Bishop of Gortyna. He was consecrated by Bishop Carroll on December 7, 1800, and succeeded to the Archiepiscopal See of Baltimore on December 5, 1815. His death occurred at the Visitation Convent, Georgetown, D. C., on June 18, 1817.[1]

REUSS, *op. cit.*, p. 78, SHEA, *Hierarchy, etc.*, p. 65; CLARKE, *op. cit.*, Vol. i, pp. 116-139; CHR, Vol. i, p. 373. *Notice on the Most Rev. Leonard Neale*, in the USCM, Vol. iii, p. 505; ACHS *Researches*, Vols. iii, p. 65; iv, p. 187; v. p. 151 ʼ(named Coadjutor); vii, p. 30 (Autograph), viii, p. 17 (in Phila., 1793), 52 (mentioned in Carroll's will), pp. 99-104 (in Grassi's *Account of 1818*), 112 (Visitandines), 114 (Sir John James Fund), ix, p. 66 (on election to Balto.), x, p. 62 (elected Bishop), x, p. 67 (consecration), x, p. 182-3 (corresp. with Carroll regarding Egan's successor), xvi, p. 67, p. 198 (regarding John Thayer), xvii, p. 48 (faculties), 68, 78 (and Jesuits), 87 (with Gallagher), 127, 129 (on Washington's death), xix, p. 66 (corresp. with Judge Gaston), xx, p. 20 (shorthand), 152 (and Thomas Lloyd), xxi, p. 64 (appointment as Coadjutor). xii, p. 78 (with Gallagher), 281 (on Church in Georgia), xxiv, p. 73 (consecration), 92 (mother of), xxvi, p. 254 (V. G. of Bishop Carroll), 277 (leaves Phila.), xxviii, pp. 112-113 (on Yellow Fever in Phila.), 193 (church in Delaware), 240 (in Phila.). PINE, *A Glory of Maryland*. Phila., 1917. GUILDAY, *op. cit.*, Vol. ii *passim*.[2]

3. MARECHAL, AMBROSE.

Archbishop Maréchal was born at Ingres, Loiret, France, on August 28, 1764. His parents had destined him for the legal profession, but young Marechal chose an ecclesiastical career. During the turmoil of the French Revolution he entered the Sulpician Seminary at Orleans. After completing his studies, he was ordained to the priesthood at Bordeaux early in 1792. On the same day he embarked for the United States and arrived at Baltimore on June 24, and said his first Mass in that city. He labored as a missionary in Maryland, and in 1799 was appointed professor of Dogmatic Theology at St. Mary's Seminary, Baltimore. He was appointed coadjutor to Archbishop Neale on July 24, 1817, and was consecrated at Baltimore

---

[1] The Rev. Lawrence Graessel was appointed coadjutor to Bishop Carroll in 1793, but he died before being consecrated.
[2] ABBREVIATIONS: ACHS (*American Catholic Historical Society*), ACQR (*American Catholic Quarterly Review*), USCM (*United States Catholic Magazine*), CE (*Catholic Encyclopedia*) CHR (*Catholic Historical Review*), AHR (*American Historical Review*), USCHS, (*United States Catholic Historical Society*), CUB (*Catholic University Bulletin*), ICHR (*Illinois Catholic Historical Review*).

by Bishop Cheverus on December 14, 1817. He received
the pallium December 19, 1819. He died in Baltimore on
June 28, 1828.

REUSS, *op. cit.*, pp. 67-68; SHEA, *Hierarchy, etc.*, p. 67; CLARKE,
op. cit., Vol. i, pp. 239-255; ACHS *Researches*, Vol. viii, p. 75 (declines Presidency of Library Company of Baltimore), Vol. ix, p. 160
("Retributions" for Pastoral Services), Vol. x, pp. 187-188 (corresp.
with Trustees of St. Mary's, Phila.), Vol. xii. p. 113 (Pastoral on
Balto. Cathedral), Vol. xvii, p. 162 (letter from Jefferson regarding
appointments of Bishops in U. S.), also Vols. iv, pp. 7, 158, vi, p. 180
(memories of Church in Maryland), xiii, pp. 149-151, xxv, p. 56, xxvi,
p. 255, xxvii, p. 348; CHR, Vol. i, p. 373 (biog. ref.), *ibid*, Vol. iv,
p. 264-5 (diocesan bibliography). GUILDAY, *op. cit.*, Vol. ii, *passim.*

4. WHITFIELD, JAMES.

The fourth Archbishop of Baltimore was born at
Liverpool, England, on November 3, 1770, of well-to-do
parents. He received a liberal education and made good
use of his opportunities. While touring Europe with
his mother, he met the Rev. Ambrose Maréchal at
Lyons, France, and from this meeting was formed a lasting acquaintance. Due to this influence, Whitfield entered
the theological seminary at Lyons, and on the completion
of his course of studies, was ordained to the priesthood on
July 14, 1809. At the request of Archbishop Maréchal he
came to the United States in September, 1817, and shortly
afterward was appointed one of the assistants at St. Peter's
Church, Baltimore. He was appointed coadjutor to Maréchal on January 8, 1828, but the Bulls did not arrive until
after the archbishop's death. Bishop Flaget consecrated him
on March 25, 1828. He died in Baltimore on October 19, 1834.

REUSS, *op. cit.*, p. 109; CLARKE, *op. cit.*, Vol. i, pp. 456-472; SHEA,
HIERARCHY, p. 69 seq; ACHS *Researches*, Vol. vii, p. 94, Cf. CE
(Biog. Sketch) Vol. ii, p. 232; *Catholic Directory*, 1835; CHR, Vol.
i, p. 373.

5. ECCLESTON, SAMUEL.

Archbishop Eccleston, was born of non-Catholic
parents a few miles from Chestertown, Kent County, Maryland, on June 27, 1801. He received his early education
as an Episcopalian, but when his mother married a Catholic,
after the decease of the Archbishop's father, young Eccles-

ton was sent to Saint Mary's College, Baltimore, where he became a convert to the Faith. He entered the seminary adjoining the college on May 23, 1819, and six years later on April 24, 1825, he was ordained to the priesthood by Archbishop Maréchal. A few months afterward he was sent to France and there entered the Sulpician Seminary near Paris. Upon the completion of his probation, he returned to the United States in July, 1827, and was appointed Vice-President of Saint Mary's College, and two years later became President of that institution. In the summer of 1834, he was appointed coadjutor to Archbishop Whitfield and was consecrated titular Bishop of Thermias on September 14, of that year. He succeeded to the See of Baltimore on October 19, 1834, and died at Georgetown in the Visitation Convent on April 22, 1851.

REUSS, op. cit., p. 38; Catholic Expositor for February, 1843; SHEA, Hierarchy, etc., pp. 72-74; CLARKE, op. cit., Vol. i, pp. 527-546; Researches. Vol. vii, p. 104, Vol. viii, p. 130, Vol. ix, pp. 138-142, Vol. xii, p. 137, Vol. xv, pp. 77, 151, Vol. xix, p. 176, 178; ROTHENSTEINER, Archbishop Eccleston and the Visitandines of Kaskaskia, in the ICHR. Vol. i, pp. 500-509; HERBERMANN, op. cit., pp. 85-86, 276-281; CHR, Vol. i, pp. 37, 373, 374; CE, Vol. v, p. 269; McCANN, op. cit., Vol. ii, pp. 5, 20, 60, 87, 90, 108-115 passim; McSWEENY, Vol. i, pp. 114-123 passim, 171, 339, 348, 380-382, 402-411, 430, 472.

6. KENRICK, FRANCIS PATRICK.

This learned ecclesiastic was born in Dublin, Ireland, on December 3, 1796, and received his early education in that city. He completed his studies in the College of Propaganda, Rome, where he spent seven years. He was ordained to the priesthood in the Eternal City on April 7, 1821. Shortly after his ordination, the Rector of Propaganda College sent him, at the request of Bishop Flaget, to Kentucky to fill the chair of professor in the theological seminary at Bardstown. He attended the First Provincial Council of Baltimore as theologian of Bishop Flaget, and while there was selected for the difficult post of Bishop-Administrator of Philadelphia. He was consecrated Bishop of Arath in the Cathedral of Bardstown June 6, 1830, by Bishop Flaget, and on August 3, 1851, he was promoted to the See of Baltimore. Bishop Timon of Buffalo invested him with the pallium on November 16, 1851; he died in Baltimore on July 6, 1863.

REUSS, *op. cit.*, p. 61; SHEA, *Hierarchy, etc.*, pp. 74-76; CLARKE, *op. cit.* Vol. i, pp. 473-517; see *Index* to ACHS *Researches*, pp. 164-165; CHR, Vol. i, p. 374, Vol. ii, p. 23; O'CONNOR, *Archbishop Kenrick and His Work*. *Philadelphia*, 1867; SWEENY, *op. cit.*, Vol. i, *passim*, esp. pp. 240-248, 274-279; HERBERMANN, *Sulpicians, etc.*, pp. 213, 306-307; O'SHEA. *The Two Kenricks*. Philadelphia, 1904; cf. *Diary and Visitation Record of Bishop Kenrick*. Philadelphia, 1916.

Among his published works are: *The Primacy of the Apostolic See Vindicated* (Baltimore, 1845); *The Pentateuch, Historical Books of the Old Testament, New Testament in 3 Vols.* (Baltimore, 1862); *Theologicae Moralis* in 3 Vols. (Philadelphia, 1842); *Theologicae Dogmaticae* in 4 vols. (Philadelphia, 1840).

7. SPALDING, JOHN.

Archbishop Spalding was born near Bardstown, Kentucky, on May 23, 1810. At the age of eleven he entered Saint Mary's College, Lebanon, Kentucky, and in 1830, he was sent to Propaganda at Rome, and after a brilliant course ordained to the priesthood on August 13, 1834. Upon his return to Bardstown, he became pastor of the cathedral and editor of the *Catholic Advocate*, which was founded in 1835. When the See was transferred from Bardstown to Louisville, he was appointed Vicar-General of the Diocese, and in 1848, was chosen coadjutor *cum jure successionis* to Bishop Flaget. He succeeded to the See of Bardstown-Louisville on February 11, 1850. He was promoted to the archiepiscopal See of Baltimore on May 3, 1864, and died in that city on February 7, 1872.

REUSS, *op. cit.*, p. 101; CLARKE, *op. cit.*, Vol. iii, p. 11 seq.; SHEA, *Hierarchy*, p. 77; SPALDING (J. L.), Life of *Most Reverend M. J. Spalding*, Baltimore, 1873; CE, *Biographical Sketch*, Vol. xiv. pp. 208-209; CHR, Vol. i, p. 374.

Among his published works are: *Sketches of the Life, Times and Character of Benedict Joseph Flaget*, Louisville, 1852; D'AUBIGNYS, *History of the Reformation Reviewed*, Baltimore, 1844; *Sketches of the Early History of Kentucky*, Louisville, 1844.

8. BAYLEY, JAMES ROOSEVELT.

Archbishop Bayley was born at Rye, New York, on August 23, 1814, of distinguished parents, and his early school days were spent at Amherst College. While touring Europe he became a convert and was received into the

Church by Father Esmond, S. J., at Rome on April 28, 1842. He then entered St. Sulpice in Paris for his theological studies and afterwards returned to New York. He was ordained to the priesthood by Bishop Hughes on March 2, 1844. When the Diocese of Newark was established, he was named first Bishop of that See and was consecrated in Saint Patrick's Cathedral, New York City, by Archbishop Bedini on October 30, 1853. At the death of Archbishop Spalding of Baltimore he was promoted to that See on July 30, 1872. He died at Newark, New Jersey, on October 3, 1877, and was buried at Emmitsburg, Maryland, beside the body of his aunt, Mother Elizabeth Seton.

REUSS, op. cit., p. 12; CLARKE, op. cit., Vol. iii, pp. 43-68; valuable letters in McCANN, History of Mother Seton's Daughters, Vol. ii, pp. 185, 186, 190, 192. New York, 1917; references in McSWEENY, Story of the Mountain, Vol. i, pp. 50, 77, 98, 146, 330, 401, 489, 534; documentary material in ACHS, Researches, Vol. vii, p. 104, Vol. viii, p. 5, Vol. ix, pp. 45, 95, 132, Vol. xv, p. 60, Vol. xxv, p. 44, Vol. xxvi, p. 258; SHEA, Hierarchy, etc., p. 81; biog. sketch in CE, Vol. ii, pp. 359-360; FLYNN, Catholic Church in New Jersey. Morristown, 1904, contains numerous references to his work in Newark Diocese; CHR, Vol. i, p. 148 (historical work of), p. 64 (preserved papers of), p. 374 (biog. sketch); CLARKE, op. cit., Vol. ii, p. 67, speaks of his Journal; letters of, in FARLEY, Life of Cardinal McCloskey, pp. 140-142, 207. 316-319, 367; SHEA, History of the Catholic Church, etc., Vol. iv, pp. 120, 463, 497, 502-504; Works of Hughes (Kehoe Edition), Vol. ii, pp. 1—xiv, 211. New York, 1864; MACLEOD, History of the Devotion to the B. V. M. in North America, p. 323. New York, 1866.

Among his published works are: A Brief Sketch of the Early History of the Catholic Church on the Island of New York, New York, 1853; Memoirs of Simon Gabriel Bruté, First Bishop of Vincennes, New York, 1876.

9. GIBBONS, JAMES, CARDINAL.

This distinguished churchman, and at the time of his death one of America's foremost citizens, was born in Baltimore on July 23, 1834. At the age of seven, he went with his parents to Ireland. He returned to the United States in 1847, and in 1855 he entered Saint Charles College to study for the priesthood. After completing his course at this institution, he entered Saint Mary's Seminary, and was ordained to the priesthood by Archbishop Kenrick on June 30, 1861. In October, 1865, Archbishop Spalding made him his secretary. At the age of thirty-two he was appointed Vicar-Apostolic of North Carolina and titular Bishop of Adramyttium and was consecrated by Archbishop Spalding in the Cathedral at Baltimore on August 16, 1868. At the Vatican Council in 1869 he was the youngest of the seven hundred and sixty-seven Bishops present. Three years later on July 30, 1872, he was transferred to the See of Richmond and was installed by Archbishop Bayley of Baltimore on October 20 of that year. When Archbishop Bayley petitioned Rome for a coadjutor, Bishop Gibbons was selected for the office with the title of Bishop of Gionopolis on May 25, 1877. On the death of Archbishop Bayley he succeeded to the See of Baltimore as the ninth incumbent on October 3, 1877. He was notified of his promotion to the Cardinalate on February 10, 1886, and he was invested with the robes of office on June 30, 1886, in the historic Baltimore Cathedral. He died in Baltimore on March 24, 1921.

REUSS, *op. cit.*, p. 48; SHEA, *Hierarchy*, pp. 82-83; O'CONNELL (J. J.), *Catholicity in the Carolinas and Georgia, passim*, New York (n. d.); SMITH and FITZPATRICK, *Cardinal Gibbons, Churchman and Citizen*, Baltimore, 1921; CHR, Vol. i, p. 374; files of *Baltimore Catholic Review*, issue of March 26, 1921.

Among his published works are: *The Faith of Our Fathers*, Baltimore, 1876; *The Ambassador of Christ*, Baltimore, 1896; *A Retrospect of Fifty Years*, Baltimore, 1916.

10. CURLEY, MICHAEL J.

The present incumbent of the See of Baltimore was born in Athlone, Ireland, on October 12, 1879. He began his studies at a school in his native town conducted by the Marist Brothers. At the age of sixteen he entered the Mungret College, where he completed his philosophy in 1900. His theological studies were made at the Propaganda in Rome; he was ordained to the priesthood in the Basilica of Saint John Lateran on March 19, 1904, and afterwards came to the Diocese of Saint Augustine, serving as pastor at DeLand, where he was stationed when notified of his appointment to the See of Saint Augustine (April 3, 1914). When consecrated by Bishop Keiley of Savannah (June 30, 1914) he was the youngest member in the American hierarchy. He was promoted to the See of Baltimore on

July 25, 1921, and was installed on November 30th of that year.[3]

The Rt. Rev. Owen B. Corrigan was born in the city of Baltimore on March 5, 1849, and was appointed Auxiliary Bishop of this See and titular Bishop of Macra on September 29, 1908. He was ordained to the priesthood after the completion of his studies in the American College in Rome on June 7, 1873. He was consecrated by Cardinal Gibbons in Baltimore, Maryland, January 10, 1909.

Bishop Corrigan has written: *The Chronology of the Hierarchy in the United States* in the *Catholic Historical Review* in Vol. i, p. 367 seq.; Vol. ii, p. 127 seq.; p. 283 seq., and Vol. iii, p. 151 seq.

IV. Diocese of Richmond (1820)

The Diocese of Richmond was created on July 11, 1820, and on January 19, 1821, the Rt. Rev. Patrick Kelly was consecrated first Bishop of the See.

When first erected, the Diocese of Richmond included what was then the State of Virginia. At present it comprises the State of Virginia, with the exception of the Counties of Accomac, Northampton (which belong to the Diocese of Wilmington), Lee, Scott, Wise, Dickinson, Buchanan, Washington, Russell, Grayson, Smyth, Tazewell, Carroll, Wythe, Bland, Floyd, Pulaski, Montgomery, Giles and a part of Craig County (which belong to the Diocese of Wheeling), also the counties of Pendleton, Grant, Mineral, Hardy, Hampshire, Morgan, Berkeley and Jefferson, in the State of West Virginia, with a total area of 34,808 square miles.

MAGRI, *The Catholic Church in the City and Diocese of Richmond,* Richmond, Virginia, 1906; PARKE, *Catholic Missions in Virginia,* Richmond, 1850; KEILEY, *Memoranda,* Norfolk, Virginia, 1874; *Proceedings of the Catholic Benevolent Union,* Norfolk, 1875; *The Metropolitan Catholic Almanac,* Baltimore, 1841-61; *Catholic Almanac and Directory,* New York, 1865-95; *Catholic Directory,* Milwaukee, 1895-9; *Official Catholic Directory,* Milwaukee, 1900-11; HUGHES, *The History of the Society of Jesus in North America, Colonial and Federal,* London, 1907; SHEA, *The History of the Catholic Church in the United States,* Akron, Ohio, 1890; foreign references cited by SHEA

---

[3] Data for the biographies of the present Cardinals, Archbishops and Bishops was obtained either from the Prelates themselves or from the diocesan Chanceries. In several instances the diocesan newspapers were consulted.

(1, bk. II, i, 106, 107, 149, 150) ; NAVARETTE, *Real Cedula que contiene el asiento capulado con Lucas Vasquez de Ayllon; Coleccion de Viages y Descubrimientos*, Madrid, 1829, ii, 153, 156; FERNANDEZ, *Historia Eclesiastica de Nuestros Tiempos*, Toledo, 1611; QUIROS, *Letter of 12 Sept., 1570;* ROGEL, *Letter of 9 Dec., 1520;* BARCIA, *Ensayo Cronologico*, 142-6; TANNER, *Societas Militaris*, 447-51; CHR, Vol. i, p. 374.

1. KELLY, PATRICK.

The first Bishop of Richmond was born at Kilkenny, Ireland, on April 16, 1779, and was educated in the Irish College, Lisbon; he was ordained to the priesthood in that city on July 18, 1802. He was acting as President of Saint John's Seminary in Kilkenny when he received news of his appointment as first Bishop of Richmond, on August 24, 1850. Twelve days later he was consecrated by Archbishop Troy of Dublin, and soon sent out for his Diocese in the United States. Upon his own request, he was transferred to the See of Waterford and Lismore in Ireland on January 28, 1822. He died at Waterford on October 8, 1829.

REUSS, *op. cit.*, p. 60 (important data) ; CLARKE, *op. cit.*, Vol. i, pp. 268-270; SHEA, *Hierarchy, etc.*, p. 349; CHR, Vol. i, p. 375; *Catholicity in Virginia* (1850-1872), article by MAGRI, in CHR, Vol. ii, pp. 415-426; ACHS *Researches*, Vol. xix, p. 107, Vol. xx, p. 39, Vol. xxiii, p. 27, Vol. xxvii, p. 347; HERBERMANN, *Sulpicians, etc.*, p. 184; MAGRI, *The Catholic Church in Richmond*, pp. 44-46; cf. bibliography of Richmond Diocese in CHR, Vol. iv, p. 266.

2. WHELAN, RICHARD V.

Bishop Whelan was born in Baltimore on January 28, 1809, and entered Mount St. Mary's, Emmitsburg, where he had as companions and classmates the future Cardinal McCloskey and Archbishop Hughes. Having completed his course at Emmitsburg, he went to St. Sulpice, Paris, and was ordained to the priesthood at Versailles in 1831. Upon his return to the United States Archbishop Eccleston assigned him to the Virginia Missions, where he labored until his appointment as Bishop of Richmond. He was transferred to the See of Wheeling, on July 22, 1850, and he died at St. Agnes Hospital, Baltimore, on July 7, 1874.

REUSS, *op cit.*, p. 108; CLARKE, *op. cit.*, Vol. iii, pp. 108-116; SHEA, *Hierarchy*, p. 350; PARKE (H. F.), *Richard Vincent Whelan;* CHR,

Vol. i, p. 375; CE, Vol. xiii, p. 51; cf., *Freeman's Journal*, issue of June 22, 1850; *Pittsburgh Catholic*, Vol. vii, p. 123; *Glimpses into the History of the Old Dominion Church*, etc., in the *Catholic Mirror*, for year 1888; ACHS *Researches*, Vol. vii, pp. 105-147.

3. McGILL, JOHN.

Bishop McGill was born in Philadelphia, November 4, 1809. His early life was spent in the vicinity of Bardstown, Kentucky, to which locality his parents had moved in the winter of 1818-19. He followed the legal profession for a number of years, but finally decided to study for the church. After completing his theology at St. Mary's Seminary, Baltimore, he was ordained to the priesthood at Bardstown, by Bishop David on June 13, 1835. When Bishop Whelan was transferred to the See of Wheeling, Father McGill was consecrated as his successor in Richmond by Archbishop Kenrick on November 10, 1850. He died in Richmond, on January 14, 1872.

REUSS, *op. cit.*, p. 71; SHEA, *Hierarchy, etc.*, p. 352; CLARKE, *op. cit.*, Vol. iii, pp. 81-93; *Catholic Herald* (Phila.), of January, 1872; MAGRI, *Catholic Church in Richmond*, pp. 74-100. Richmond, 1906; ACHS *Researches*, Vol. xiv, p. 141 (in Phila.), Vol. xv, p. 42 (letter to his father on Catholic life in Phila.), Vol. xxiii, p. 187-8 (Episcopal acts); CHR, Vol. i, p. 375; *ibid.*, Vol. ii, pp. 415-426 (*Catholicity in Virginia during the Episcopate of Bishop McGill*, by Magri); *ibid.*, Vol. iv. pp. 265 (diocesan bibliography).

4. CARDINAL GIBBONS.

The late Cardinal Gibbons was transferred to Richmond from the Vicariate-Apostolic of North Carolina as fourth Bishop of this See on July 30, 1872. Promoted to Coadjutorship of Baltimore, May 15, 1877.

(Cf. Baltimore.)

5. KEANE, JOHN JOSEPH.

Consecrated Bishop of Richmond, and administrator of Vicariate-Apostolic of North Carolina, August 25, 1878. Became Archbishop of Dubuque, on July 24, 1900.

(Cf. Dubuque.)

6. VAN DE VYER, AUGUSTINE.

Bishop Van De Vyer came to Virginia shortly after his ordination in July, 1870, from Belgium, where he was born at Haesdnock, East Flanders, on December 1, 1844. Upon his arrival he was appointed one of the assistants at the Cathedral of Richmond, and later had charge of the mission center at Harpers Ferry. In 1881 he was made Vicar-General of the Diocese, and after Bishop Keane's departure for Washington as first Rector of the Catholic University, acted as Administrator until he was chosen as successor in the See. He was consecrated by Cardinal Gibbons on October 20, 1889 and died on October 16, 1911.

REUSS, op. cit., p. 105; CE, Vol. xiii, p. 51; CHR, Vol. i, p. 375; CURTIS, American Catholic Who's Who, p. 66, St. Louis, 1911.

7. O'CONNELL, DENIS J.

The present Bishop of Richmond is a native of Ireland, where he was born on January 28, 1849. He received his ecclesiastical training at Saint Charles Seminary, Charleston, and at the Propaganda, in Rome, at which place he was ordained to the priesthood on May 26, 1877. He became Rector of the American College in Rome, and later Rector of the Catholic University of America in Washington. While serving in this last capacity he was consecrated titular Bishop of Sebaste by the late Cardinal Gibbons, on May 3, 1908. He was appointed Auxiliary Bishop of San Francisco on December 21, 1908, and was transferred to the See of Richmond on January 19, 1912.

III. Diocese of Charleston (1820)

Pius VII erected the Diocese of Charleston on July 12, 1820, and the Rt. Rev. John England was consecrated as first Bishop on September 20, 1820.

The Diocese of Charleston comprised at first the Carolinas and Georgia. At present, its territorial limits are confined to the State of South Carolina: an area of 30,170 square miles.

SHEA, History of Catholic Church in United States, New York, 1889-92; O'GORMAN, History of the Catholic Church in the United States, New York, 1895; passim; The United States Catholic Mis-

cellany, files, Charleston, 1822-1862; O'CONNELL, *Catholicity in the Carolinas and Georgia,* New York, 1879; CHR, Vol. i, p. 375.

1. ENGLAND, JOHN.

Bishop England was born at Cork, Ireland, on September 23, 1786. He was ordained to the priesthood by Bishop Moylan, of his native city on October 11, 1808, and four years later was designated President of the Diocesan College of St. Mary. When informed of his appointment as first Bishop of Charleston, he was acting as parish priest in Ireland. Bishop Murphy, of Cork, consecrated him on September 21, 1820, and soon afterwards the new bishop started for his See. Twice he visited Haiti as Apostolic Delegate, and several times he crossed the ocean to obtain aid for his needy diocese. In 1826, at its invitation, he addressed Congress. In 1841, he visited Europe for the last time and upon his return he was stricken with a complication of ailments. He died at Charleston on April 11, 1842.

REUSS, *op. cit.,* Vol. i, pp. 271-309; *Researches,* Vols. v-xxix *passim,* chiefly Vol. xiii, pp. 151, Vol. xix, p. 111, Vol. xxviii, p. 245, for which consult *Index; The Works of the Right Rev. John England, First Bishop of Charleston.* Edited with *Introduction, Notes* and *Index,* under the direction of the MOST REV. SEBASTIAN G. MESSMER, Archbishop of Milwaukee. 7 Vols., Cleveland, 1908; CHR, Vol. i, pp. 55, 265, 270, 357, 375-376, 449-450, Vol. iii, p. 40, Vol. v, pp. 239-301 *passim;* CE, Vol. v, pp. 470-471; McCANN, *op. cit.,* Vol. i, pp. 112, 145, 195, 197, 211, 318; vide *The Messenger* for 1890, pp. 769-782, and for 1892, pp. 370-374; READ, *Sketches of Bishop England* in the *Religious Cabinet,* Vol. i (1842), pp. 361-380; O'CONNELL, *Catholicity in the Carolinas and Georgia.*

The Rt. Rev. William Clancy, appointed coadjutor to Bishop England in 1834, was born in Cork, Ireland, in February, 1802. He received his education at Maynooth, and was ordained to the priesthood on May 24, 1823. The Rt. Rev. Edward Nolan, Bishop of Kildare, consecrated him Bishop on December 21, 1834. His stay in Charleston was brief, for he was transferred to British Guiana as Vicar-Apostolic on April 13, 1837, from which place he was removed in 1843. He retired to Ireland and died at Cork on June 19, 1847.

REUSS, *op. cit.*, pp. 23-24 (contains full notes on his erratic career); CLARKE, *op. cit.*, Vol. ii, pp. 44-57; SHEA, *Hierarchy, etc.*, p. 200; ACHS *Researches*, Vol. vi, pp. 121-125, Vol. viii, p. 167, Vol. x, p. 144, Vol. xx, p. 186; CHR, Vol. ii, p. 376.

2 REYNOLDS, IGNATIUS.

Bishop Reynolds was born in Bardstown on August 22, 1798. After commencing his theological studies at the diocesan seminary he entered Saint Mary's, Baltimore, where he completed his course and was ordained to the priesthood by Archbishop Maréchal on October 24, 1823. Upon his return to Kentucky he became President of St. Joseph's College, and later he was called to the Bardstown Seminary to take the chair of theology made vacant by the promotion of Dr. Kenrick. He was acting as Vicar-General of the Diocese when appointed second Bishop of Charleston. Archbishop Purcell consecrated him in the Cathedral in Cincinnati on March 19, 1844. He died in Charleston on March 9, 1855.

REUSS, *op. cit.*, p. 93; CLARKE, *op. cit.*, Vol. ii, p. 292-293; SHEA, *Hierarchy*, p. 201; O'CONNELL, *op. cit.*, p. 105, seq.; CHR, Vol. i, p. 376; WHITE (C. I.), *Substance of a Discourse on Bishop Reynolds*, in the *Metropolitan Magazine*, Vol. iii, 1855; *Freeman's Journal*, issue of August 10, 1850.

Bishop Reynolds edited the works of the Right Reverend John England, D.D., which were published at Baltimore, Maryland, in 1849.

3. LYNCH, PATRICK N.

Bishop Lynch was born at Clones, County Monaghan, Ireland, on March 10, 1817. His parents emigrated to the United States, where the future bishop began his studies in the diocesan school at Charleston. Later he entered the Propaganda, in Rome, and was ordained to the priesthood on April 5, 1840. On the death of Bishop Reynolds he was appointed Administrator *sede vacante* and later was chosen as his successor. His consecration took place on March 14, 1858, by Archbishop Kenrick of Baltimore. He died at Charleston, on February 26, 1882, after a prolonged sickness.

REUSS, *op. cit.*, pp. 65-66; SHEA, *Hierarchy, etc.*, p. 202; O'CON-
NELL, *Catholicity in the Carolinas and Georgia* (1820-1828), pp.
105-137. New York, 1879; CLARKE, *op. cit.*, Vol. iii, pp. 68-80; ACHS
Researches, Vol. xix, p. 7; Vol. xxii, pp. 88, 248-249, 296; Vol. xxiv,
p. 182 (on his mother's name), Vol. xxviii, p. 347 (on his middle
name), Vol. xxii, p. 248 (report on Confederate sympathy abroad),
p. 249 (letter to Secretary of State, 1864); *cf.* ACQR, Vol. i, pp. 100,
475, Vol. vi, p. 85; CHR, Vol. i, p. 376 (bibliographical references),
Vol. iv, p. 265 (diocesan bibliography).

4. NORTHROP, HENRY P.

The fourth Bishop of Charleston was born in that city on May 5, 1842, and studied in Georgetown College and at Mount St. Mary's College at Emmitsburg. His theological studies were completed at the American College in Rome, where he was ordained to the priesthood on June 25, 1865. He was appointed titular Bishop of Rosalia and Vicar-Apostolic of North Carolina on September 16, 1881, and was transferred to the See of Charleston two years later, January 27, 1883. He died on June 7, 1916.

REUSS, *op. cit.*, p. 80; SHEA, *Hierarchy, etc.*, p. 204; *cf.* CARDINAL
GIBBONS, *Reminiscences of North Carolina*, in the USCHS, Vol. 3
(1890), pp. 337-352; ACHS *Researches*, Vol. xxviii, p. 347 (his transfer to Charleston); CHR, Vol. i, p. 376.

5. RUSSELL, WILLIAM T.

The present Bishop of this see was born in Baltimore, on October 20, 1863, and was educated at St. Charles College, Ellicott City; St. Mary's Seminary, Baltimore, and at the American College, Rome. He was ordained to the priesthood on June 21, 1889. He was secretary to Cardinal Gibbons for fourteen years and then became Rector of St. Patrick's Church in Washington. He was appointed Bishop of Charleston on December 4, 1916, and was consecrated by Cardinal Gibbons on March 15, 1917.

IV. Diocese of Wheeling (1850)

On July 23, 1850, Pius IX divided the Diocese of Richmond and erected the See of Wheeling with the Rt. Rev. Richard Whelan as first Bishop.

The western part of the State of Virginia, as it existed at the time the Diocese was created, comprised the terri-

tory of this See.   Now the Diocese of Wheeling comprises
the State of West Virginia except the counties of Pendleton, Grant, Mineral, Hardy, Hampshire, Morgan, Berkeley
and Jefferson; also the counties of Lee, Scott, Wise, Dickinson, Buchanan, Washington, Russell, Grayson, Smythe,
Tazewell, Carroll, Wythe, Bland, Floyd, Pulaski, Montgomery, Giles and a portion of Craig County, in the State of
Virginia.   The total area is 29,172 square miles.

SHEA, *History of the Catholic Church in the United States*, New
York, 1889; DECOURCY-SHEA, *New History of the Catholic Church
in the United States*, New York, 1879; CHR, Vol. i, p. 376; SULLIVAN,
Sacerdotal Jubilee of the Rt. Rev. J. J. Kain, second Bishop of Wheeling, Wheeling, 1891.

1. WHELAN, RICHARD.

Consecrated Bishop of Richmond, March 21, 1849, he
was transferred to Wheeling July 23, 1850.   At his death
in Wheeling, on July 7, 1874, he was the senior member of
the Hierarchy of the United States.

(Cf. Richmond.)

2. KAIN, JOHN J.

Consecrated as second Bishop of Wheeling May 21,
1875.   He was promoted to the archiepiscopal See of St.
Louis May 21, 1893.

(Cf. St. Louis.)

3. DONAHUE, PATRICK.

The present Bishop of Wheeling was born at Mal-
vern, England, April 15, 1849 and came to the United
States after receiving his education at the University of
London.   He engaged in the practice of law in Washington, D. C., until 1882, when he began studying for the
priesthood.   He was ordained to the priesthood in Baltimore on December 23, 1885.   At the time of his appointment to the See of Wheeling on January 22, 1894, he was
acting as Rector of the Cathedral in Baltimore, and was
consecrated as Bishop by the late Cardinal Gibbons on
April 8, 1894.

The Right Reverend J. J. Swint, D.D., was appointed auxiliary to Bishop Donahue, according to a cable dispatch of February 22, 1922. He was born at Pickens, West Virginia, December 15, 1879, and received his seminary training at Saint Mary's, Baltimore. He was ordained to the priesthood on June 23, 1904, and was consecrated on May 11, 1922, by Archbishop Curley of Baltimore.

V. Diocese of Savannah (1850)

Upon the recommendation of the Fathers of the Seventh Provincial Council of Baltimore, Pius IX created the Diocese of Savannah on July 19, 1850. The Right Rev. Francis X. Gartland, was consecrated as its first Bishop on November 10, 1850.

When first erected, the Diocese of Savannah comprised the State of Georgia and the eastern part of Florida. In 1857 Eastern Florida was detached, and the See of Savannah was given its present territorial limits of the State of Georgia; an area of 58,980 square miles.

SHEA, *History, op. cit., passim;* DECOURCY-SHEA, *op. cit.;* O'CONNELL, *op. cit., passim;* CE, Vol. xiii, p. 488; CHR, Vol. i, p. 376-377; *Metropolitan Magazine,* Vol. ii, p. 324; *Freeman's Journal,* issue of August 7, 1858; *Catholic Mirror,* issues of November 11, 1865, September 16, 1861, August 8, 1857, and August 7, 1858; FOLEY, *The Catholic Church in the Diocese of Savannah,* a paper read at the first annual meeting of the American Catholic Historical Association in Washington, D. C., December, 1920.

1. GARTLAND, FRANCIS.

The first Bishop of Savannah was born in Dublin, Ireland, on January 19, 1805. At an early age he came to the United States with his parents, who sent him to Mount Saint Mary's Seminary to be educated. Having decided to study for the priesthood he continued his ecclesiastical course under Bishop Bruté and upon its completion was ordained to the priesthood on August 5, 1831. He was appointed in 1832 assistant pastor in St. John's Church, Philadelphia, and in 1845 became Vicar-General of the Diocese. Upon his promotion to the See of Savannah, he was consecrated by Archbishop Eccleston on November 10, 1850. He died on September 20, 1854.

REUSS, *op. cit.*, pp. 47-48; SHEA, *Hierarchy, etc.*, p. 362; CLARKE, *op. cit.*, Vol. ii, pp. 408-414; CHR, Vol. i, p. 187 (Bishop Gartland to Leopoldine Association, Paris, September 9, 1851), p. 377; ACHS *Researches*, Vol. iv, p. 138, Vol. vii, pp. 33, 103, Vol. xii, p. 36 (letters of 1852), Vol. xiii, p. 80, Vol. xxi, p. 11 (diary of), Vol. xxii, pp. 78, 87; McCANN, *op. cit.*, Vol. i, *passim;* cf. O'CONNELL, *Catholicity in the Carolinas and Georgia.*

2. BARRY, JOHN.

The second Bishop of Savannah was born in County Wexford, Ireland in 1799, and while an ecclesiastical student in Ireland attached himself to the Diocese of Charleston, then governed by Bishop England. He was ordained to the priesthood by Bishop England on September 24, 1825. In 1839 he was appointed Vicar-General for the State of Georgia, and while acting as administrator of the Savannah Diocese he was appointed Bishop of that See. Archbishop Kenrick of Baltimore consecrated him on August 2, 1857, and he died in Paris on November 11, 1859.

REUSS, *op. cit.*, pp. 10-11; CLARKE, *op. cit.*, Vol. ii, 551-554; SHEA, *Hierarchy, etc.*, p. 363; McSWEENY, *Story of the Mountain* (Mt. St. Mary's College), Vol. i, p. 535, Emmitsburg, 1911; CE, Vol. ii, p. 311, Vol. xiii, p. 488; O'CONNELL, *Catholicity in the Carolinas and Georgia* (1820-78); SHEA, *History of the Catholic Church, etc.*, Vol. iv, pp. 99, 373-378, 451-453; *Catholic Directory for 1861*, p. 226; ACHS *Researches*, Vol. x, p. 467; Bishop England's *Works*, Vol. iv, pp. 301, 325, 345 (Cleveland Edition).

3. VEROT, AUGUSTINE.

The third Bishop of Savannah was born in France on May 23, 1805. He was ordained to the priesthood in Paris on September 28, 1828, and shortly afterwards joined the Sulpicians. In 1830 his superiors sent him to Baltimore, and in 1853 he was pastor of the Church at Ellicott Mills, near Baltimore. Archbishop Kenrick consecrated him titular Bishop of Deneba and Vicar-Apostolic of Florida on April 25, 1858. Three years later in the month of July he was translated to the newly erected Diocese of Savannah but still retained jurisdiction over the Vicariate of Florida. When the Diocese of Saint Augustine was erected in 1870, he was appointed as first Bishop of this See. He died at Saint Augustine on June 10, 1876.

REUSS, *op. cit.*, p. 106; SHEA, *Hierarchy*, p. 364; CLARKE, *op. cit.*, Vol. iii, pp. 94 seq.; CHR, Vol. i, p. 577; ACHS *Researches*, Vol. xi, p. 24.

4. PERSICO, IGNATIUS.

Bishop Persico was born in Naples on January 30, 1823, where he was also ordained to the priesthood on January 24, 1846. He was selected as coadjutor to the Vicar-Apostolic of Bombay, India, and was consecrated in that place on June 4, 1854, by the Rt. Rev. Anastasius Hartmann. He was made Vicar-Apostolic of Hindustan in 1856, and resigned the See four years later. On March 20, 1870, he was transferred to Savannah where he resided for two years, again resigning. As ruler of the Diocese of Aquino in Italy, he administered it until forced to resign on account of ill health. He was chosen titular Archbishop of Damiata on March 4, 1887, and was preconized Cardinal-Priest on January 16, 1893. He died in Rome, Italy on December 7, 1895.

REUSS, *op. cit.*, pp. 88-89; SHEA, *Hierarchy*, p. 366; O'CONNELL, *op. cit.*, p. 536, seq.; CHR, Vol. i. p. 377; ACHS *Researches*, Vol. xi, p. 24.

5. GROSS, WILLIAM H.

Consecrated Bishop of Savannah on April 27, 1873. He became Archbishop of Oregon City on February 1, 1885. (Cf. Oregon City.)

6. BECKER, THOMAS H.

Bishop Becker was born in Pittsburgh, Pennsylvania, on December 20, 1832. He was ordained to the priesthood at Rome, Italy, June 18, 1859. Appointed Bishop of Wilmington on March 3, 1868, he was consecrated by Archbishop Spalding in Baltimore, Maryland on August 16, 1868. He was transferred to Savannah on March 26, 1886 and died in Savannah on July 29, 1899.

REUSS, *op. cit.*, p. 13; SHEA, *Hierarchy, etc.*, p. 392; McSWEENY, *op. cit.*, Vol. ii, pp. 80, 173, 180, 196, 318; ACHS *Researches*, Vol. vi, pp. 141, 180, Vol. ix, p. 191, Vol. xi, p. 27, Vol. xix, p. 175; for his connection with the founding of the Catholic University of America, cf. ACQR, Vol. xix (1876), *Plan for the Proposed Catholic University*, pp. 665-670, and *Shall We Have a University? ibid.*, p. 230-236; SHEA, *History of the Catholic Church, etc.*, Vol. iv. p. 432.

7. KEILEY, BENJAMIN K.

Bishop Keiley was born at Petersburgh, Virginia, on October 13, 1847, and received his ecclesiastical education at the American College in Rome, Italy. He was ordained to the priesthood on December 31, 1873. When appointed seventh Bishop of Savannah, April 19, 1900, he was serving as Rector of the Cathedral in that city. Cardinal Gibbons consecrated him in St. Peter's Cathedral, Richmond, on June 3, 1900. He resigned the See on February 23, 1922.

VI. Diocese of Wilmington

The Diocese of Wilmington was created by Pius IX on March 3, 1868, and the Rt. Rev. Thomas A. Becker was consecrated as its first Bishop on August 16, 1868.

The Diocese comprises its original territorial limits of the State of Delaware and the Eastern Shores of Maryland and Virginia. The total area is 6,211 square miles.

Archives of the Diocese of Wilmington; Archives of the Maryland Province, S. J.; JOHNSTONE, *History of Cecil County, Maryland*, Elkton, Md., 1881; CONRAD, *History of Delaware*, Wilmington, 1908. CHR, Vol. i, p. 378.

1. BECKER, THOMAS A.

Consecrated Bishop of Wilmington on August 16, 1868; transferred to the See of Savannah in 1886.
(Cf. Savannah.)

2. CURTIS, ALFRED A.

The second Bishop of Wilmington was born in Somerset County, Maryland on July 4, 1831, the son of Episcopalian parents. In 1872 he visited England, while there he became converted and was received into the Church by Cardinal Newman. Upon his return to this country he entered St. Mary's Seminary, Baltimore, to study for the priesthood and was ordained by Archbishop Bayley, on December 19, 1874. At the time of his appointment to the See of Wilmington, he was acting as chancellor of the Archdiocese of Baltimore. He was consecrated by Cardinal Gibbons on November 16, 1886. He resigned his charge in 1896 and was named titular Bishop of Echinus. The last ten years of his life were spent as Vicar-General of the Archdiocese of Baltimore and he died on July 11, 1908.

REUSS, *op. cit.*, p. 30; MCSWEENY, *op. cit.*, Vol. ii, pp. 301, 329; *cf. Souvenir of Loretto Centenary*, p. 363 (biog. sketch). Cresson, Pa., 1899; portrait in ACHS *Records*, Vol. xx (1909), p. 86; CHR, Vol. i, p. 378; *Life and Characteristics of Rt. Reverend Alfred A. Curtis, D.D., Second Bishop of Wilmington*, compiled by the Sisters of the Visitation, New York, 1913.

3. MONAGHAN, JOHN J.

The present Bishop of Wilmington was born at Sumter, South Carolina, May 23, 1856. He received his education at Saint Charles College, Ellicott City, and Saint Mary's Seminary, Baltimore, and was ordained to the priesthood for the Diocese of Charleston on December 19, 1880. He was appointed Bishop of Wilmington January 26, 1897, and he was consecrated by Cardinal Gibbons on May 9, 1897.

VII. Diocese of Saint Augustine (1870)

Leo XIII raised the Vicariate-Apostolic of Florida to the Diocese of Saint Augustine in 1870, with the Rt. Rev. Augustine Verot as first Bishop.

The Diocese of Saint Augustine comprises the same territory now as at the time of its erection, namely: the entire part of the State of Florida, east of the Appalachicola River; an area of 46,959 square miles.

Diocesan Archives (records go back to sixteenth century); SHEA, *History of the Catholic Church in the United States*, Vols. i and ii *passim;* New York, 1889; DECOURCY-SHEA, *op. cit., A Catholic History of Alabama and the Floridas*, by a Sister of Mercy, in two Vols., New York, 1908; CHR, Vol. i, p. 378, Vol. ii, pp. 146-156; Vol. iv, p. 170; Vol. v, p. 3.

1. VEROT, AUGUSTINE.

He became first Bishop of St. Augustine on March 11, 1870.
(Cf. Savannah.)

2. MOORE, JOHN.

The second Bishop of Saint Augustine was born in County West Meath, Ireland on June 27, 1835, and was ordained to the priesthood in Rome, Italy, on April 9, 1880. He was consecrated bishop at Charleston May 13, 1877, by Bishop Lynch and died there on July 30, 1901.

REUSS, op. cit., p. 76; SHEA, Hierarchy, etc., p. 375; ACHS Researches; Vol. iv. p. 189, Vol. xi, p. 96 church in St. Augustine), Vol. xiii, p. 76 (diocese of Baltimore in 1830); CHR, Vol. i, p. 378.

3. KENNY, JOHN.

Bishop Kenny was born at Delphi, New York, January 12, 1853. He received his education at Saint Bonaventure's College, Albany, New York, and was ordained to the priesthood for the Saint Augustine Diocese on January 15, 1879. Ten years later he served as Vicar-General of the diocese and he acted as administrator of that diocese *sede vacante* (1901-1902). The late Cardinal Gibbons consecrated him bishop at Saint Augustine on May 18, 1902. He died on October 23, 1913.

CURTIS, American Catholic Who's Who, p. 329, St. Louis, 1911; CHR, Vol. i, p. 378.

4 CURLEY, MICHAEL JAMES.

Consecrated Bishop of St. Augustine on June 30, 1914, and was promoted to Baltimore on July 25, 1921.
(Cf. Baltimore.)

5. BARRY, PATRICK.

The present Bishop of St. Augustine was born in Lauraugh, County Clare, Ireland, on November 15, 1868. He received his education at Mungret College, Limerick, Ireland, and at Saint Patrick's College, Carlow

He was ordained to the priesthood on June 9, 1895, and soon after he came to the Diocese of St. Augustine. He was acting as Vicar-General of this Diocese when appointed as successor to Archbishop Curley. He was consecrated by his predecessor on May 3, 1922.

VIII. Vicariate of North Carolina (1868)

On March 3, 1868 the Holy See erected the Vicariate of North Carolina, to comprise the State of that name. The late Cardinal Gibbons was consecrated titular Bishop of Adramyttium and named its first Vicar-Apostolic on August 16, 1868. Pius X, on June 8, 1910, erected eight counties of North Carolina into the Abbacy Nullius of Belmont and decreed that the Abbot of this place should exercise administrative powers over the Vicariate Apos· tolic of North Carolina until it was erected into a Diocese.

Until 1910 the Vicariate comprised the State of North Carolina. At that time the Abbey of Belmont was erected and eight counties were abscinded. At present the Vicariate of North Carolina and Belmont Abbey comprises the entire State, excepting the Counties of Gaston, Lincoln, Cleveland, Polk, Rutherford, McDowell, Burke and Catawba. which by a Bull of His Holiness, Pius X dated June 8, 1910, constitute the diocesan territory of the Abbacy Nullius of Belmont. The total area is 48,580 square miles.

O'CONNELL, op. cit.; WHEELER, History of North Carolina; CE. Vol. xi, p. 14; CHR, Vol. i, p. 379.

1. GIBBONS, JAMES CARDINAL.

Consecrated Vicar-Apostolic of North Carolina on August 16, 1868, he was transferred to Richmond, and finally to the archiepiscopal See of Baltimore.

(Cf. Baltimore.)

2. NORTHROP, HENRY P.

Consecrated titular Bishop of Rosalia and second Vicar.Apostolic, he was transferred to the See of Charleston on January 27, 1883, but still retained jurisdiction over this territory until the appointment of Bishop Haid.

(Cf. Charleston.)

3. HAID, LEO.

The present Vicar-Apostolic was born at Latrobe, Pennsylvania, on July 15, 1849, and joined the Benedictine Order in 1869, and received his training at Saint Vincent's Abbey at Beatty, Pennsylvania. He was ordained to the priesthood on December 21, 1872, and then served as chaplain and professor at his Alma Mater. He received the solemn rite of benediction as Mitred Abbot of Belmont Abbey on November 26, 1885. Appointed Vicar-Apostolic of North Carolina on July 15, 1887, he was consecrated by Cardinal Gibbons titular Bishop of Messene on July 1, 1888. He was made Abbot Ordinary of the Abbacy Nullius of Belmont in 1910.

CHAPTER II

THE PROVINCE OF OREGON CITY (1846)

The Archiepiscopal See of Oregon City was erected on July 24, 1846, with the Right Reverend Francis N. Blanchet as first Archbishop.

When created, the Province of Oregon City included part of Canada and had as suffragan sees, the Dioceses of Nesqually, Walla-Walla, Fort Hall, Calville, Vancouver, Princess, Charlotte's Island and New Caledonia. For some unknown reason, Bishops were only appointed to the Sees of Oregon City, Walla-Walla and Vancouver Island. At present the Province is confined to the States of Oregon, Montana, Washington, Idaho and Alaska, and has as suffragan sees the Dioceses of Helena (1884), Boise City (1903), Baker City (1903), Great Falls (1904), Seattle (1907), and Spokane (1903). Also the Vicariate-Apostolic of Alaska (1916).

BLANCHET, *Historical Sketches* Portland, 1870; O'HARA, *Pioneer Catholic History of Oregon,* Portland, 1911; SHEA, *History of Catholic Church in the United States,* Vol. iii, New York, 1889; DE-COURCY-SHEA, *op. cit.;* DESMET, *Western Missions and Missionaries,* New York, 1859; IDEM, *Oregon Missions and Travels over the Rocky Mountains,* New York, 1847; CHR, Vol. i, pp. 380-381.

I. Diocese of Oregon City (1843)

By a Brief of December, 1843, the Sovereign Pontiff created the Vicariate-Apostolic of Oregon, and the Very Reverend Francis N. Blanchet, was appointed titular Bishop of Philadelphia and Vicar-Apostolic. He was consecrated on July 25, 1845. The Archiepiscopal See was created out of the Vicariate-Apostolic of Oregon.

The Vicariate-Apostolic of Oregon embraced all the territory between the Mexican Province of California at the south, and the Russian Province of Alaska on the north and extended from the Pacific Ocean to the Rocky Mountains. At present, the Diocese of Oregon City comprises the territory in the western part of the State of Oregon with an area of 21,398 square miles.

1. BLANCHET, FRANCIS N.

The first Archbishop of Oregon City, was born near Saint Pierre, Riviére du Sud, Province of Quebec, September 30, 1795. He received his early education in the village school and later entered the Seminary of Quebec, where he was ordained to the priesthood on July 18, 1819. After his ordination he was stationed at the Cathedral in Montreal for a year and was then sent to New Brunswick as a missionary. In 1837 he was chosen Vicar-General of the Oregon Mission by Archbishop Signay. Appointed first Vicar-Apostolic of the Oregon Territory, he went to Montreal for his consecration, which took place on July 25, 1845 with Bishop Bourget as consecrating prelate. When the Vicariate was erected into a Province he became its first Archbishop on July 24, 1846. He signed the See in 1880 and was appointed titular Archbishop of Amida, and died in Portland on June 18, 1883.

REUSS, *op. cit.*, pp. 15-16; CLARKE, *op. cit.*, Vol. iii, pp. 438-509; SHEA, *Hierarchy, etc.*, pp. 150, 320; ACHS, *Researches*, Vol. vi, pp. 48, 188, Vol. ix, p. 183, Vol. xi, p. 158, Vol. xvi, p. 191. Vol. xxviii, p. 348; CLARKE, *op. cit.*, pp. 474-475, refers to a printed *Pastoral* of Archbishop Blanchet of February 27, 1881; SHEA, *Missions and Missionaries*, pp. 470-472; DE SMET, *Letters and Sketches, etc.*, Philadelphia, 1843; ID., *Origin, Progress, and Prospects of the Catholic Missions of the Rocky Mountains.* Philadelphia, 1843; ID., *Western Missions and Missionaries.* New York, 1857; BLANCHET, *Notes on the Oregon Missions;* VAN RANSSELAER, *Sketch of the Catholic Church in Montana,* in the ACQR. Vol. xvii (1887); O'HARA, *Catholic History of Oregon,* Portland, Ore., 1911, refers to *Memoirs of Most Rev. F. X. Blanchet,* by Major Mallet, and also to large collection of letters and documents by both brothers in the Archdiocesan Archives of Portland; MARSHALL, *Acquisition of Oregon,* Vol. ii, pp. 210-211. Seattle, 1911; CE, Vol. ii, pp. 593-594; CHITTENDEN-RICHARDSON, *Life. Letters, and Travels of Fr. Pierre Jean De Smet.* New York, 1905; for the Whitman affair cf. *Catholic World,* Vol. xiv (1872), p. 95; *Historical Records and Studies,* Vol. viii; PALLADINO, *Indian and White in the Northwest.* Baltimore, 1894; CHR, Vol. i, pp. 182, 185-186, 381, 383, 187 (letters, etc.. to the Leopoldine Association), Vol. ii, p. 428, Vol. iii, pp. 187-201 (*Catholic Pioneers of the Oregon Country,* by Edwin V. O'Hara) ; cf. *Dr. John McLoughlin,* by T. J. Campbell, S. J., in the *Historical Records and Studies.* Vol. viii, pp. 83-116; SHEA, *History of the Catholic Church, etc.,* Vol. iv, pp. 310-327; 328, 689-702; ENGELHARDT. *Missions and Missionaries,* Vol. iv, pp. 613-615.

While in the hospital before his death, Archbishop Blanchet, wrote the *Historical Sketches of Catholicity in Oregon,* Portland, 1870.

2. SEGHERS, CHARLES J.

The second archbishop of this see was born at Ghent, Belgium, on December 26, 1839. His early training was received in his native city and his theological preparation at the American College in Louvain. Ordained to the priesthood at Malines on May 30, 1863, he set out for the American Mission, and arrived at Victoria on November 17, 1863. He was appointed to the See of Vancouver Island on March 23, 1873, and was consecrated at Victoria by Archbishop Blanchet on July 6, 1873. He was appointed as coadjutor of Oregon City on December 10, 1878, and two years later he became head of the archdiocese upon the resignation of Archbishop Blanchet on December 20, 1880. He resigned this see to accept the bishopric of Vancouver Island on April 12, 1885. He was murdered by a man named Fuller on November 28, 1886, while on a visitation of Alaska.

REUSS, *op. cit.*, p. 99; CLARKE, *op. cit.*, Vol. iii, p. 508 seq.; SHEA. *Hierarchy.* p. 152; O'HARA, *op. cit., passim;* BLANCHET, *op. cit., passim;* CE, Vol. xi, p. 293; CHR, Vol. i, p. 381-382.

3 GROSS, WILLIAM H.

Archbishop Gross was born in Baltimore, Maryland, on June 12, 1837. After his student days at Saint Charles College, he entered the novitiate of the Redemptorist Congregation in 1857 and upon completing his course of studies was ordained priest at Annapolis, Maryland, on March 21, 1863. He served as Chaplain to the wounded Civil War soldiers at Annapolis the first year after his ordination, and later was appointed a member of the Redemptorist Mission Band. In 1873 he was chosen Bishop of Savannah and was consecrated in Baltimore by Archbishop Bayley on April 27, 1873. He was promoted to the Archiepiscopal See of Oregon City on February 1, 1885, and administered the archdiocese until his death on November 14, 1898.

REUSS, *op. cit.*, p. 51; SHEA, *Hierarchy, etc.*, pp. 153-154; O'HARA, *The Church in Oregon,* pp. 156-165; O'HARA, *Catholic Pioneers of the Oregon Country,* in CHR, Vol. iii, pp. 187-201; HERBERMANN. *Sulpicians, etc.,* p. 263; cf. O'CONNELL, *op. cit.*

4. CHRISTIE, ALEXANDER.

The present Archbishop of this Province was born in Vermont on January 2, 1848, and received his education at Saint John's University in Minnesota and the Grand Seminary in Montreal, where he was ordained to the priesthood on December 22, 1877. He served as pastor of the Church at Waseca, Minnesota, for thirteen years and was stationed in Saint Paul during the following eight years. Appointed Bishop of Vancouver Island on March 26, 1898, he was consecrated on June 29, 1898, by Archbishop Ireland. He was promoted to the See of Oregon City on February 12, 1899.

II. Diocese of Seattle (1907)

This Diocese was created at first as the See of Walla-Walla on July 24, 1846, with the Right Reverend Augustine M. A. Blanchet as first Bishop. The name of the Diocese was changed to Nesqually on May 31, 1850, and on September 11, 1907, the diocesan seat was moved to Seattle.

At first this see comprised the entire State of Washington. When the Diocese of Spokane was created in 1913, it was given the present territorial limits of the western part of the State of Washington comprising the counties of Chelan, Clallam, Clarke, Cowlitz, Grays Harbor, Island, Jefferson, King, Kitsap, Kittitas, Klickitat, Lewis, Mason, Pacific, Pierce, San Juan, Skagit, Skamania, Snohomish, Thurston, Wahkiakum, Whatcom and Yakima; an area of 36,644 square miles.

DE SMET, *Western Missions and Missionaries*, New York, 1859; IDEM, *Oregon, Missions and Travels over the Rocky Mountains*, New York, 1847; PALLADINO, *Indian and White*, Baltimore, 1894; BLANCHET, *Historical Sketches of the Catholic Church in Oregon*, Portland, 1878; SNOWDEN, *History of Washington*, New York, 1909; COSTELLO, *The Siwash*, Seattle, 1895; CHR, Vol. i, p. 383.

1. BLANCHET, A. M. A.

Bishop A. M. A. Blanchet was born at St. Pierre, Rivière du Sud, Province of Quebec, Canada, on August 22, 1797. With his brother, the first Archbishop of Oregon City, he went to Quebec to study for the priesthood and was ordained on June 3, 1821. He held various missionary posts on Cape Breton Island and in the Gulf Provinces, and also in the Vicariate-Apostolic of Montreal. While serving as a Canon in the Cathedral at Montreal he was appointed Bishop of the new Diocese of Walla-Walla and was consecrated in Montreal by Bishop Bourget on September 27, 1846. In February, 1879, after thirty-two years of active service, he resigned his see and was named titular Bishop of Ibora. He died at Fort Vancouver, Washington, on February 25, 1887.

Cf. Bibliography of Archbishop Blanchet of Oregon City.

2. JUNGER, AEGIDUS.

The second Bishop of Nesqually was born on April 6, 1833, at Burtscheid, bei Aix le Chapelle, Germany. He attended the schools of his native city, and in 1853 went to Louvain to study for the priesthood. Ordained priest at Mechlin, Belgium, on June 27, 1862, he left Antwerp for the American mission in September of that year. He served as pastor at Walla Walla City and in 1864 was attached to the Cathedral at Vancouver. Archbishop F. J. Blanchet consecrated him as his brother's successor in the See of Nesqually on October 28, 1879. He died at Vancouver on December 26, 1895.

REUSS, op. cit., pp. 58-59 (important data) ; CHR, Vol. i, 383; see bibliography of Seattle Diocese; SHEA, Hierarchy, etc., pp. 322-323.

3. O'DEA, EDWARD.

The present Bishop of Seattle was born near Boston, Massachusetts, on November 23, 1856, and received his education at Saint Ignatius College in San Francisco and the Grand Seminary in Montreal. He was ordained to the priesthood on December 23, 1882, and served at the Cathedral in Portland under Archbishops Blanchet and Seghers. Later he became secretary to Archbishop W. H. Gross, a position which he held for ten years. He then became pastor of Saint Patrick's Church in Portland. He was consecrated Bishop of Nesqually by Archbishop Gross on September 8, 1896. He was named Bishop of Seattle on September 11, 1907.

III. Diocese of Helena (1884)

Pope Leo XIII erected the Diocese of Helena on March 7, 1884, and appointed the Right Reverend John B. Brondel as first Bishop. When first erected, the See of Helena included the entire State of Montana. At present its territorial limits are confined to the western part of the State with the following counties: Lewis and Clark, Teton, Glacier, Pondera, Flathead, Lincoln, Missoula, Mineral, Sanders, Powell, Granite, Ravalli, Deer Lodge, Silver Bow, Jefferson, Broadwater, Gallatin, Madison, Beaverhead, Meagher, Wheatland, parts of Musselshell and Toole; an area of 51,922 square miles.

PALLADINO (L. B.), *Indian and White in Northwest*, Baltimore, 1894; SANDERS. *History of Montana.* New York, 1913; LAVEILLE, *Life of Father De Smet*, New York, 1915; Cf. Bibliography of Oregon City for *Works of Father De Smet;* CHR. Vol. i, p. 383; Files of the *Catholic News* of New York City.

1. BRONDEL, JOHN BAPTIST.

The first Bishop of Helena was born at Bruges, West Flanders, Belgium, on February 23, 1842, and received his early instruction from the Xaverian Brothers of his native city. He made his philosophical and theological studies at Louvain and was ordained to the priesthood at Mechlin, Belgium, for the Diocese of Nesqually. He set out for his field of labor shortly after his ordination and arrived there by way of Panama. He served as rector of the Church at Heilacoos, Washington Territory, in 1867 where he remained for ten years and was then transferred to Walla-Walla. Archbishop Seghers consecrated him Bishop of Vancouver Island, on December 14, 1879, and he retained this position until appointed administrator of the Vicariate of Montana on April 17, 1883. He was promoted to the See of Helena as first Bishop on March 7, 1884, and he died in that city on November 3, 1903.

REUSS, *op. cit.,* p. 18; CHR, Vol. i, pp. 382-383; PALLADINO, *Indian and White in the Northwest, or a History of Catholicity in Montana,* pp. 361-394. Baltimore, 1894; Palladino made use of Brondel's *Diary,* letters, etc.. for this work; the *Diary* is now in the possession of the present Bishop, John Patrick Carroll; cf. files of

Catholic News (New York), for November, 1903; SHEA, *Hierarchy*, etc., p. 261; VAN RENSSELAER, *Sketch of the Catholic Church in Montana*, in the ACQR, Vol. xix (1887); VAN DER HEYDEN, *History of the American College of Louvain*, p. 259. Louvain. 1909; CE, Vol. ii, p. 798 (biog. sketch); *The Catholic Sentinel* (Portland, 1870-1919), files; *The Intermountain Catholic* (Salt Lake City, 1889-1919), files; *Diocesan Archives; Diocesan Scrap-Book* (Helena Chancery); SANDERS, *History of Montana*, Vol. i, pp. 162, 568; *Records of Historical Society of Montana* (1883-1903); *Life of Father Lacombe; Life of Bishop Brondel* (in preparation).

2. CARROLL, JOHN P.

Bishop Carroll was born in Dubuque, Iowa, on February 22, 1864. His educational training was received at St. Joseph's College, in his native city, and at the Grand Seminary in Montreal. He was ordained to the priesthood on July 7, 1886, and immediately after, was made professor in St. Joseph's College, Dubuque, an institution of which he later became president. Appointed Bishop of Helena on September 12, 1904, he was consecrated by the Most Rev. James John Keane on December 21, 1904.

IV. Diocese of Boise City (1893)

The Diocese of Boise City was erected out of the Vicariate of Idaho on August 25, 1893, with the Right Reverend Alphonsus J. Glorieux as first Bishop.

The Diocese of Boise City has always been coterminus with the State of Idaho; an area of 84,920 square miles.

SHEA, *History, op. cit., passim;* DECOURCY-SHEA, *op. cit.; Works of Father De Smet, cit., supra.* VAN DER DONCKT, *The Founders of the Church in Idaho* in the *American Ecclesiastical Review*, Vol. xxxii, Nos. 1, 2 and 3; CE, Vol. ii, pp. 623-624; CHR, Vol. i, p. 384.

1. LOOTENS, LOUIS.

The first Vicar-Apostolic of Idaho was born at Bruges, Belgium, March 17, 1827, and came to Vancouver as a missionary in 1852, a year after his ordination at Paris, France, on June 14, 1851. Six years later, he served in the Californian missions and was elected Vicar-Apostolic on March 3, 1868. Archbishop Alemany consecrated him titular Bishop of Castabolla at San Francisco, California, August

9, 1868. He resigned his Vicariate on July 16, 1876, and died at Victoria, Vancouver Island, on January 13, 1898.

REUSS, *op. cit.*, p. 64; SHEA, *Hierarchy, etc.*, p. 399; AER, Vol. xxxii, pp. 1, 123, 280; CHR, Vol. i. p. 384.

2. GLORIEUX, JOSEPH.

The first Bishop of Boise City, was born in West Flanders, Belgium, on February 1, 1844. After a college course of six years at Courtrai he entered the American College at Louvain to study for the priesthood. He was ordained at Mechlin on August 17, 1867, and set out for Oregon shortly after as a missionary. He held appointments at Roseburg, Oregon City, and Portland, and in 1884 was chosen second Vicar-Apostolic of Idaho. The late Cardinal Gibbons consecrated him in Baltimore on April 19, 1885. He became first Bishop of Boise City, on August 26, 1893, and he died on August 25, 1917.

REUSS, *op. cit.*, p. 49; CHR, Vol. i, p. 384; ACHS *Researches*, Vol. xxiii; p. 165; VANDERHEYDEN, *The American College of Louvain*, Louvain. 1909. VAN DER DONCKT, *The Founders of the Church in Idaho*, in AER, Vol. xxxii.

3. GORMAN, DANIEL M.

The present Bishop of Boise City was born at Wyoming, Iowa, on April 12, 1861. His early education was received in the high school of his native city, after which he attended Saint Joseph's College, Dubuque, and Saint Francis Seminary, Milwaukee, where he was ordained to the priesthood on June 24, 1893. For one year, he acted as parish priest at State Center, Iowa, and in September, 1894, was appointed professor at Saint Joseph's College, Dubuque. He became president of this institution in 1904, and remained in charge there until his appointment to the vacant See of Boise City. His Excellency the Apostolic Delegate, Most Rev. John Bonzano, consecrated him in Dubuque, Iowa, on May 1, 1918.

V. Diocese of Baker City (1903)

Pius X erected the Diocese of Baker City in 1903, and the Right Reverend Charles J. O'Reilly, was consecrated as first Bishop on August 25, 1903.

The Diocese comprises the original territorial limits of the counties of Wasco, Klamath, Lake, Sherman, Gilliam, Wheeler, Morrow, Grant, Union, Crook, Jefferson, Umatilla, Wallowa, Baker, Harney and Malheur in the State of Oregon; an area of 68,000 square miles.

Cf. Bibliography of *Province of Oregon City*, in CHR, Vol. i, 384; *Catholic Sentinel of Portland*, *Oregon*, Christmas Number, 1921, p. 242.

1. O'REILLY, CHARLES J.

Consecrated first Bishop of Baker City on August 25, 1903; transferred to the See of Lincoln on March 20, 1918.

(Cf. Lincoln.)

2. McGRATH, JOSEPH F.

The present Bishop of Baker City was born at Kilmacaur, County Kilkenny, Ireland, on March 1, 1871. He made his theological studies at the Grand Seminary, Montreal, and was ordained to the priesthood on December 21, 1895. He was acting as Pastor of Saint Patrick's Church in Tacoma, Washington, when he was appointed second Bishop of Baker City on December 21, 1918. He was consecrated by Bishop O'Dea, of Seattle, on March 25, 1919.

VI. Diocese of Great Falls (1904)

Piux X divided the State of Montana into two dioceses on May 18, 1904, making Great Falls the diocesan seat for the eastern part of the State and Helena for the western. The present incumbent, the Right Reverend Mathias Lenihan, was consecrated as first Bishop of the former see on September 21, 1904.

The Diocese comprises the counties of Big Horn, Blaine, Carbon, Cascade, Chouteau, Custer, Dawson, Fallon, Fergus Hill, Musselshell Park, Phillips, Prairie, Rosebud, Sheridan, Stillwater, Sweet Grass, Valley,. Wibaux, and Yellowstone in the State of Montana; an area of 94,158 square miles.

PALLADINO, *op. cit.*, *passim;* SANDERS, *History of Montana. loc. cit.; Works of Father De Smet, cit. supra;* CHR, Vol. i, p. 384; *The Great Falls Catholic Review,* issue of January, 1920, *passim.*

1. LENIHAN, MATHIAS C.

The first and present Bishop of Great Falls was born in Dubuque, Iowa, on October 6, 1854, and received his educational training at Saint John's College, Prairie Du Chien, and the Grand Seminary, Montreal, where he was ordained to the priesthood by Bishop Fabre on December 21, 1879. He was acting as dean and irremovable Rector of the Church at Marshalltown, Iowa, when appointed Bishop of Great Falls by Pius X May 20, 1904. The Most Reverend John Ireland, consecrated him on September 21, 1904.

VII. Diocese of Spokane (1913)

The Diocese of Spokane was erected on December 17, 1913, with the Right Reverend Augustine F. Schinner, D.D.. as first Bishop.

The Diocese comprises the following counties in the State of Washington: Okanogan, Ferry, Stevens, Pend, Oreille, Douglas, Grant, Lincoln, Spokane, Adams, Whitman, Benton, Franklin, Walla-Walla, Columbia, Garfield. and Asotin; an area of 30,192 square miles.

Cf. *Diocese of Seattle;* Cf. Files of the *Catholic Northwest Progress,* Seattle, Washington.

1. SCHINNER, AUGUSTINE F.

The first and present Bishop was born in Milwaukee, on May 1, 1863, and made his studies at Saint Francis Seminary. He was ordained to the priesthood on March 7, 1886, and afterwards was made pastor at Redfield, Wisconsin. Later he was appointed professor at St. Francis Seminary and in 1891 he acted as secretary to Archbishop

Katzer. He was chosen Vicar-General of the Archdiocese of Milwaukee in 1895. Archbishop Messmer consecrated him first Bishop of Superior, Wisconsin, on July 15, 1905, but he resigned that see on January 15, 1913, and on March 18, 1914, was appointed first Bishop of Spokane.

VIII. Vicariate-Apostolic of Alaska (1916)

The territory of Alaska was erected into a Vicariate-Apostolic on December 22, 1916, and the Very Reverend Joseph R. Crimont, S. J., was preconized titular Bishop of Ammaedera and first Vicar-Apostolic on March 22, 1917. The Vicariate comprises the territory of Alaska and the Aleutian Islands, with a total area of 586,400 square miles.

Archives of the Prefecture-Apostolic of Alaska; DEVINE, *Across Widest America,* Montreal, 1905; O'HARA, *op. cit.;* CHR, Vol. i, p. 385.

1. CRIMONT, JOSEPH R.

The first and present Vicar-Apostolic, the Right Reverend Joseph R. Crimont, was born at Ferrierer, France, on February 2, 1858. He was educated at the College of La Providence, Amiens, and in the Jesuit Scholasticates in France and Woodstock, Maryland, having entered the Society of Jesus in 1875. He was ordained to the priesthood in 1888 and acted as missionary and Superior at the Crow Indian Reservation, St. Xaviers, Montana, from 1890 to 1893. The next three years he was stationed at the Holy Cross Mission in the Yucon County where he performed the duties of Superior from 1896 until 1901. He was acting as President of Gonzaga College in Spokane, Washington, when appointed Prefect-Apostolic of Alaska on March 28, 1904. He was chosen first Vicar-Apostolic of that territory and preconized as titular Bishop of Ammaedera on March 22, 1917, and was consecrated on July 25th of that year by Bishop O'Dea of Seattle.

CHAPTER III

THE PROVINCE OF SAINT LOUIS (1847)

The Metropolitan See of Saint Louis was erected on July 20, 1847, and the Rt. Rev. Peter R. Kenrick was appointed first Archbishop. At the time of its erection, the Province of Saint Louis comprised the territory now embraced by the Provinces of Saint Paul and Dubuque, with the Dioceses of Dubuque, Nashville, Chicago, Milwaukee and Saint Paul as suffragan sees. At present the Province is confined to the States of Missouri and Kansas and it has as suffragan sees the Dioceses of Saint Joseph (1868), Leavenworth (1877), Kansas City (1880), Wichita (1887) and Concordia (1887).

ROSATI, *Relazione*, Letters to the Propaganda and Private Letters; IDEM, *Diocesan Archives;* SHEA, *History of the Catholic Church in the United States*, I. Akron. 1888, passim; THORNTON, *Historical Sketch of the Church in St. Louis;* WALSH, *Jubilee Memoirs*, St. Louis, 1891; *Encyclopedia of the History St. Louis*, St. Louis, 1899; *Catholic Directory, Milwaukee;* DECOURCY-SHEA, *op. cit.;* cf. various numbers of the *Saint Louis Historical Review;* SOUVAY, *A Centennial of the Church in St. Louis*, in the CHR, Vol. iv, p. 52 seq.; CHR, Vol. i. p. 52 seq.

I. Diocese of Saint Louis (1826)

The Diocese of Saint Louis was erected on July 2, 1826, and the Rt. Rev. Joseph Rosati was appointed first Bishop on March 20, 1827.

The Diocese covered an immense area when created, including not only the Territory of Arkansas, the State of Missouri and the western part of Illinois, but also all the region of the Louisiana Purchase which extended along the Mississippi River to the northern boundary of the United States and westward to the Pacific Ocean. At present the Diocese of Saint Louis comprises that section of the State of Missouri bounded on the north by the northern lines of the counties Pike, Audrain, Boone and Howard; on the west by the western lines of the counties Howard,

39

Boone, Cole, Maries, Pulaski, Texas and Howell; on the
south by the State of Arkansas; and on the east by the
Mississippi River; an area of 27,092 square miles.

1. ROSATI, JOSEPH.

The first Bishop of Saint Louis was born at Sora,
Naples, Italy, on January 12, 1789, and in his youth he
entered the novitiate of the Congregation of the Mission.
He was probably ordained in 1811 or 1812 and his first
work as a priest was assistant to the Rev. Felix de Andreis
C. M., in Rome. He readily consented to come to the
American mission and when the group of missionaries
departed for the United States Father Rosati was appointed
Director of the seminarians in the party. The zealous
band reached Bardstown, Kentucky, in October, 1817, and
Father Rosati remained at that place as Rector of the
seminary until the following year, when he was transferred to the Barrens, Perry County, Saint Louis, as Superior of the seminary there. Bishop DuBourg consecrated
him titular Bishop of Tenagre and Coadjutor of New Orleans at Donaldsville, Louisiana, on March 25, 1824. Two
years later he was designated Bishop of New Orleans, but
refused the appointment. He was translated to Saint Louis
as first Bishop of this historic see on March 20, 1827, also
serving at the same time as Administrator of New Orleans.
He died in Rome at the House of the Fathers of the Congregation of the Mission on September 25, 1843.

ROSATI, *Relazione*, letters to the *Propaganda* and private letters;
REUSS, *op. cit.*, p. 95; CLARKE, *op. cit.*, Vol. i, p. 23 seq.; SHEA,
Hierarchy, p. 162 seq.; CE, Vol. viii, p. 360 seq.; CHR, Vol. i, p.
386; *St. Louis Catholic Historical Review*. Vol. i, pp. 215 seq., and
pp. 243 seq. (Other volumes contain added information.)
Bishop Rosati wrote the *Life of the Very Rev. Felix DeAndreis*,
which was published at St. Louis in 1900.

2. KENRICK, PETER RICHARD.

The first Archbishop of Saint Louis was born in
Dublin, Ireland, on August 17, 1806. He received his early
education in the schools of his native country and at the
age of twenty-one he entered Maynooth. After five years
of assiduous work at this institution he was ordained to

the priesthood on March 6, 1832, by Archbishop Murray of Dublin. At the invitation of his brother in Philadelphia, he came to the United States and while in Pennsylvania he held the positions of President of the Diocesan Seminary in Philadelphia; Rector of the Cathedral and Vicar-General of the Diocese. His consecration as titular Bishop of Drasa and coadjutor of Saint Louis took place in Philadelphia on November 30, 1841, with Bishop Rosati as consecrating prelate. He succeeded to the See of Saint Louis on September 25, 1843, and was made first archbishop on July 20, 1847. After a most successful administration he retired on May 21, 1859, in favor of his coadjutor and was proclaimed titular Archbishop of Marcianopolis. He died at the archiepiscopal residence in Saint Louis, on March 3, 1896.

REUSS, *op. cit.*, 61, 62; SHEA, *Hierarchy*, p. 164, seq.; SWEENEY, *op. cit.*, Vol. i, p. 303; O'SHEA, *The Two Kenricks*, Philadelphia, 1904, *passim;* CE. Vol. iii, pp. 618-619, AER, Vol. xvi, p. 73; ACQR, Vol. xii, p. 425; CHR, Vol. i, pp. 306-387; late issues of *St. Louis Catholic Historical Review.* Among his important literary works are; *Validity of Anglican Orders Examined,* Philadelphia, 1841, and *The Month of Mary,* Philadelphia, 1843.

3. KAIN, JOHN JOSEPH.

The second Archbishop of Saint Louis was born at Martinsburg, West Virginia, on March 31, 1841, and after attending the Academy in his native city, he entered successively Saint Charles College, Ellicott City, and Saint Mary's, Baltimore. After his ordination to the priesthood on July 2, 1866, he was appointed pastor of Harpers Ferry, West Virginia, and at the age of thirty-four he was chosen Bishop of Wheeling. Archbishop Bayley consecrated him on May 23, 1875, and on May 21, 1893, he was promoted to the Archiepiscopal See of Saint Louis as coadjutor to Archbishop Kenrick. He was officially designated as Administrator of the Archdiocese on December 14, 1893, and he succeeded to the See on May 21, 1895. He died in Baltimore on October 13, 1903.

REUSS, *op. cit.*, p. 59; CHR, Vol. i, pp. 376, 387; CUB, Vol. ii, p. 427; SWEENY, *op. cit.*, Vol. i, p. 369; HERBERMANN, *Sulpicians, etc.*, pp. 263, 308; SHEA, *Hierarchy, etc.*, p. 391.

4. GLENNON, JOHN JOSEPH.

Archbishop Glennon was born in County Meath, Ireland, on July 14, 1862. He was ordained to the priesthood for the Diocese of Kansas City on December 20, 1884, and held the positions of pastor of the Cathedral in Kansas City; Vicar-General of the Diocese and finally Administrator thereof until his appointment as coadjutor Bishop of Kansas City. Archbishop Kain consecrated him titular Bishop of Pinara on June 29, 1896, and he was transferred to Saint Louis as coadjutor to his consecrating prelate on April 27, 1903. He succeeded to the Archiepiscopal See on October 13, 1903.

II. Diocese of Saint Joseph (1868)

On March 3, 1868, the Diocese of Saint Joseph was erected and the Reverend John J. Hogan was consecrated as first Bishop on September 13, 1868.

When erected, the Diocese of Saint Joseph included the territory between the Missouri and the Charleston Rivers in the State of Missouri. The present territorial limits of the diocese comprise that part of the State of Missouri bounded on the north by the State of Iowa, on the east by the Mississippi River, on the west and south by the Missouri River and the northern boundaries of the counties of Howard, Boone, Audrain and Pike; an area of 18,206 square miles.

HOGAN, *On the Mission in Missouri*, Kansas City, 1892; LINNEN-KAMP, *Historical Souvenir of the Immaculate Conception Parish*, St. Joseph, 1907; *Official Catholic Directory*, 1910; CHR, Vol. i, p. 387.

1. HOGAN, JOHN J.

Bishop Hogan was born on March 10, 1828, at Buff, County Limerick, Ireland. His early ecclesiastical studies were made in his native land and completed at the Diocesan Seminary in Saint Louis. Archbishop Peter R. Kenrick, ordained him to the priesthood on April 10, 1852, and afterwards he labored in and around the State of Missouri doing missionary work. When the Diocese of Saint Joseph was erected, he was consecrated first Bishop on September 13, 1868, by Archbishop P. R. Kenrick, and was transferred to the See of Kansas City on September 18, 1880. He died there on February 21, 1893.

REUSS, *op. cit.*, pp. 54-55; CHR, Vol. ii, pp. 387-388; *Catholic Church Annals of Kansas City*, article by KEUENHOF, in CHR, Vol. iii, pp. 326-335; SHEA, *Hierarchy, etc.*, p. 263; HOGAN, *On the Mission in Missouri. Kansas City*, 1892; cf. GARRAGHAN, *Catholic Beginnings in Kansas City, Mo.*, Chicago, 1920.

2. BURKE, MAURICE F.

Bishop Burke was born in County Limerick, Ireland, on May 5, 1845. He received his education at Saint Mary's-of-the-Lake in Chicago, Notre Dame, Indiana, and the American College, Rome. Cardinal Patrizzi ordained him to the priesthood on May 25, 1875, and upon his return to the United States, he labored in the Diocese of Chicago until he was appointed Bishop of Cheyenne on August 9, 1887. His consecration took place in the Cathedral of the Holy Name in Chicago, Illinois, on October 28, 1887, with Archbishop Feehan as consecrating prelate. He was transferred to the Diocese of Saint Joseph on June 19, 1893.

III. Diocese of Leavenworth (1877)

On May 22, 1877, the Vicariate of Kansas was erected into the Diocese of Leavenworth, and the Rt. Rev. Louis M. Fink was appointed as first Bishop.

When first erected the Diocese of Leavenworth included the entire State of Kansas. At present it comprises the following counties of Kansas: Anderson, Atchison, Coffey, Doniphan, Douglas, Franklin, Jackson, Jefferson, Johnson, Leavenworth, Linn, Lyon, Marshall, Miami, Nemaha, Osage, Pottawatomie, Shawnee, Wabaunsee and Wyandotte; an area of 12,524 square miles.

DEFOURI, *Original Diaries and Letters of Jesuit Missionaries;* DECOURCY-SHEA, *op. cit.*, p. 665 seq.; CHR, Vol. i, pp. 387-388; Cf. files of the *Western Watchman* of St Louis, Missouri.

1. MIEGE, JOHN B., S. J.

The first Vicar-Apostolic of Indian Territory was born at La Foret, Upper Savoy, Italy, on September 18,

1815. He studied at the diocesan seminary of Montiers and entered the Society of Jesus at Milan on October 23, 1836. He was ordained to the priesthood on September 7, 1847, and afterwards, he became professor of philosophy at the Roman College. He obtained permission of his superiors to come to the United States to labor among the Indians and was engaged in this work when appointed first Vicar-Apostolic of Indian Territory. Archbishop Peter R. Kenrick consecrated him titular Bishop of Messene on March 25, 1851. Bishop Miege petitioned the Holy See to accept his resignation in 1871, but, instead, a coadjutor was given him in the person of the Rev. Louis M. Fink. He was permitted to resign in December, 1874, and he returned to the Jesuit Order at Woodstock, Maryland, where he died on July 21, 1884.

REUSS, op. cit., p. 75; SHEA, Hierarchy, etc., p. 268; CLARKE, op. cit., Vol. iii, pp. 611-625; CHR, Vol. i, p. 388.

2 FINK, LOUIS M.

The first Bishop of the Diocese of Leavenworth was born at Triftersberg, Bavaria, on July 12, 1834, and when a mere boy emigrated to the United States. He joined the Benedictine Order in 1852 and was ordained to the priesthood at Saint Vincent's Abbey on May 28, 1837. He was consecrated titular Bishop of Eucarpia and Coadjutor to Bishop Miege, by Bishop Foley of Chicago on June 11, 1871. Three years later he assumed complete charge of the Vicariate upon the resignation of Bishop Miege in December, 1875, and was appointed first Bishop of Leavenworth on May 22, 1877. He died on March 17, 1904.

REUSS, op. cit., pp. 41-42; SHEA, Hierarchy, etc., pp. 270-273; CLARKE, op. cit., Vol. iii, p. 623; CHR, Vol. i, p. 388.

3. LILLIS, THOMAS F.

Bishop Thomas F. Lillis was consecrated second Bishop of Leavenworth on December 27, 1904; transferred to the See of Kansas City on March 14, 1910.
(Cf. Kansas City.)

4. WARD, JOHN.

The present Bishop of Leavenworth was born in Ohio on May 23, 1857, and received his ecclesiastical training at Saint Meinrad's Seminary in Indiana. He was ordained priest for the Diocese of Leavenworth on July 17, 1884, after which, he served among the mission stations of that diocese until his appointment and subsequent consecration as Bishop of Leavenworth on February 22, 1911. His Eminence, Cardinal Falconio was consecrating prelate.

IV. Diocese of Kansas City (1880)

The Diocese of Kansas City was erected on September 10, 1880, with the Rt. Rev. John Hogan as first Bishop.

The territorial limits of this Diocese are confined to that part of the State of Missouri south of the Missouri River and west of the eastern boundary of the counties of Moniteau, Miller, Camden, Laclede, Wright, Douglas and Ozark; an area of 23,539 square miles.

GARRAGHAN (G. J.), *Beginnings of Catholicity in Kansas City*, Chicago, 1920; HOGAN, *On the Mission in Missouri*, Kansas City, 1892; CHR, Vol. i, p. 388; *Western Watchman*, St. Louis.

1. HOGAN, JOHN JOSEPH.

Bishop Hogan was consecrated on September 13, 1868, for the Diocese of Saint Joseph; transferred to See of Kansas City on September 10, 1880.

(Cf. St. Joseph.)

2. LILLIS, THOMAS F.

The present Bishop of Kansas City was born at Lexington, Missouri on March 3, 1862, and received his education at Niagara University and Saint Benedict's College, Atchison, Kansas. He was ordained to the priesthood on August 15, 1885, and was consecrated Bishop of Leavenworth, in Kansas City on December 27, 1904. On March 14, 1910, he was transferred to Kansas City as coadjutor to Bishop Hogan and was named titular Bishop of Civira. He became Bishop of Kansas City on February 21, 1913.

V. Diocese of Wichita (1887)

The Diocese of Wichita was erected on August 2, 1887, and the Rt. Rev. James O'Reilley was appointed first Bishop of the new See, but he died before he was consecrated on July 26, 1887. The Rt. Rev. John J. Hennessey was appointed as his successor on August 28, 1888.

New boundaries of the diocese were established by Apostolic Letters dated July 1, 1897. Bounded on the west by Colorado, south by Oklahoma, east by Missouri and north by the north lines of Bourbon, Allen, Woodson, Greenwood, Morris, Marion, McPherson, Rice, Barton, Rush, Ness, Lane, Scott, Wichita, and Greely counties, in Kansas, with an area of 42,915 square miles.

CE, Vol. xv, p. 616; CHR, Vol. i, p. 389; files of the *Catholic Advance*, of Wichita, Kansas.

1. HENNESSEY, JOHN J.

The first occupant of the See of Wichita was born in County Cork, Ireland, on July 19, 1847, and came to the United States at the age of three. He received his collegiate education at the Christian Brothers College in Saint Louis, and made his theological course at Saint Francis, Milwaukee. His ordination to the priesthood took place in Saint Louis on November 28, 1869, and he served as a priest in the Archdiocese of Saint Louis until his appointment as Bishop of Wichita on August 28, 1888; he was consecrated by the Most Reverend P. J. Kenrick on November 30, 1888. He died in Wichita on July 13, 1920.

REUSS, *op. cit.*, p. 53; SHEA, *Hierarchy*, p. 409; CHR, Vol. i, p. 389; files of the *Catholic Advance*, of Wichita, Kansas.

2. SCHWERTNER, AUGUST J.

Bishop Schwertner was born in Canton, Ohio, and received his early training in the schools of that city. Later he attended Saint Canisius College in Buffalo and Saint Mary's Seminary, Baltimore. Bishop Horstmann, of Cleveland ordained him to the priesthood on June 12, 1897. He labored as an assistant at Saint Columba Church in

Youngstown; was pastor at Milan, Ohio, and on June 21, 1907, was sent to Lima in a similar capacity. He was appointed chancellor of the Diocese of Toledo in 1903, and was acting as such when appointed Bishop of Wichita. He was consecrated by Bishop Schrembs in Toledo, Ohio, on June 8, 1921.

VI. Diocese of Concordia (1887)

This Diocese was erected at the same time as the Diocese of Wichita, on August 2, 1887, and the Rt. Rev. Richard Scannell was consecrated first Bishop on November 30, 1887.

The northwestern part of the State of Kansas with an area of 26,685 square miles constitutes the territorial limits of the Diocese of Concordia. It is bounded on the west by Colorado, on the north by Nebraska, on the east by the east lines of Washington, Riley, Geary, Dickinson counties, and on the south by the south lines of Dickinson, Saline, Ellsworth, Russell, Ellis, Trego, Gove, Logan and Wallace counties, in the State of Kansas.

Some Early History of the Pioneer Catholic Settlers and Parishes of Northwestern Kansas, a souvenir booklet published in 1913 by the Capuchin Fathers, of Herndon, Kansas; CHR, Vol. i, p. 389.

1. SCANNELL, RICHARD.

The first Bishop of Concordia was born in Cloyne, County Cork, Ireland on May 12, 1845. His classical studies were made at a private school near Middleton and in 1866 he entered All Hallows College, Dublin, where he was ordained to the priesthood on February 26, 1871. In the year of his ordination he came to the Diocese of Nashville, and was appointed assistant at the Cathedral there, of which he afterwards became rector in 1870. From 1880 to 1883 he acted as administrator of the Diocese *sede vacante* and in 1886 became Vicar-General. Appointed Bishop of Concordia, he was consecrated in Nashville, Tennessee, by Archbishop Feehan, on November 30, 1887, and was transferred to the See of Omaha on January 30, 1891. He died in that city on January 8, 1916.

REUSS, *op. cit.*, pp. 98-99; SHEA, *Hierarchy*, p. 414; CHR, Vol. iii, p. 161; Cf. files of *The True Voice*, Omaha, Nebr., for January, 1916.

2. BUTLER, THADDEUS.

The Rt. Rev. Thaddeus Butler was appointed second Bishop of Concordia, but he died in Rome on July 2, 1897, a short time before his consecration.

3. CUNNINGHAM, JOHN FRANCIS.

The third Bishop of Concordia was born in County Kerry, Ireland, June 20, 1842, and received his preliminary classical education at Listowel in his native country. Coming to the United States he made his theological course at Saint Francis, Wisconsin, and was ordained to the priesthood at Leavenworth, on August 8, 1865. His priestly labors were confined solely to the Diocese of Leavenworth of which he became Vicar-General on January 1, 1881. He was acting as rector of the Cathedral of that city when appointed Bishop of Concordia on May 14, 1808, and was consecrated on September 21st of that year. He died on June 23, 1919.

Cf. CHR, Vol. i, p. 389: Vol. ii, p. 430. Also files of the *Catholic Advance* and the *Catholic Register* for September, 1898, September, 1915, and June, 1919.

4. TIEF, FRANCIS J.

The present Bishop of Concordia was born in New York State on March 6, 1881, and made his studies at Niagara University and Saint Bonaventure's College, Allegheny. He was ordained to the priesthood by Bishop Colton on January 13, 1908. Two years later he became rector of the Cathedral in Kansas City and in 1916 acted as Vicar-General. He was designated Bishop of Concordia on February 22, 1921, and was consecrated by Bishop Lillis of Kansas City on March 30, 1921.

CHAPTER IV

PROVINCE OF NEW ORLEANS (1850)

The Archiepiscopal See of New Orleans was erected cn July 19, 1850, with the Rt. Rev. Anthony Blanc as first Archbishop.

The Province, when erected, had as suffragan sees, the Dioceses of Mobile (1829), Natchez (1837), Little Rock (1843), and Galveston (1847), embracing the States of Louisiana, Alabama, Mississippi, Arkansas and Texas. At present its territorial limits extend to these same States, but the Dioceses of Alexandria (1910), San Antonio (1847), Corpus Christi (1912), Dallas (1890), Oklahoma (1905), and Lafayette (1918), have been added to the original number of suffragan sees.

Archives of the Diocese of New Orleans; Archives of the St. Louis Cathedral; SHEA, *The Catholic Church in Colonial Days,* New York, 1886; IDEM, *Life and Times of Archbishop Carroll,* New York, 1888; IDEM, *History of the Catholic Church in the United States,* 1808-85, 2 Vols., New York, 1892; GAYARRE, *Historie de la Louisiane,* 2 Vols., New Orleans, 1846-7; CHARLEVOIX, *Journal d'un Voyage dans l'Amerique Septentrional,* VI, Paris, 1744; DE LA HARPE, *Journal Historie de l'Etablissement des Francais a la Louisiane,* New Orleans, 1831; KING. *Sieur de Bienville,* New York, 1893; DIMITRY, *History of Louisiana,* New York, 1892; DUMONT, *Memoires Historie sur la Louisiana,* Paris, 1753; LE PAGE DU PRATZ, *Historie de la Louisiane,* 3 Vols., Paris, 1758; FORTIER, *Louisiana Studies,* New Orleans, 1894; IDEM, *History of Louisiana.* 4 Vols., New York, 1894; MARTIN, *History of Louisiana from the Earliest Period,* 1727; KING AND FICKLEN, *History of Louisiana,* New Orleans, 1900; *Archives of the Ursuline Convent,* New Orleans, *Diary of Sister Madeleine Hachard,* New Orleans, 1727-65; *Letters of Sister M. H.* 1727; *Archives of Churches. Diocese of New Orleans,* 1722-1909; *Le Propagateur Catholique,* New Orleans, files; *The Morning Star,* New Orleans, 1868-1909, files; *Le Moniteur de La Louisiane,* New Orleans, 1794-1803, files; French and Spanish manuscripts in archives of Louisiana Historical Society; CHAMBON, *In and Around the Old St. Louis Cathedral,* New Orleans, 1908; *The Picayune,* New Orleans, 1837-1909, files; CAMILLE DE ROCHEMENTEIX, *Les Jesuites et la Nouvelle France au XVIIIe Siecle,* Paris, 1906; CASTELLANOS, *New Orleans as it Was,* New Orleans, 1905; MEMBER OF THE ORDER OF MERCY, *Essays, Educational and Historic,* New York, 1899; LOWENSTEIN, *History of the St. Louis Cathedral of New Orleans,* 1882; MEMBER OF THE ORDER OF MERCY, *Catholic History of Alabama and the Floridas; Centenaire du Pere Antoine,* New Orleans, 1885; HARDEY, *Religious of the Sacred Heart,* New York, 1910.

49

I. Diocese of New Orleans (1826)

On July 18, 1826, Pope Leo XII, divided the Diocese of Louisiana and erected the Dioceses of New Orleans and Saint Louis. Until the consecration of the Rt. Rev. Leo de Neckere, C. M., as first resident Bishop of New Orleans on May 24, 1830, the administration of the Diocese of New Orleans was left to Bishop Rosati of Saint Louis.[1]

As erected in 1826, the Diocese of New Orleans comprised the States of Louisiana and Mississippi. At present the Diocese comprises the territory in the southern part of the State of Louisiana, with an area of 23,208 square miles.

1. PENALVER Y CARDENAS, LOUIS.

The first Bishop of Louisiana was born on April 3, 1749; ordained to the priesthood at Havana on April 14, 1772; appointed Bishop of Louisiana, and the Floridas on April 25, 1793, and was consecrated Bishop in the same year. He was promoted to the Archiepiscopal See of Gautemala on July 20, 1801, and died in Havana on July 17, 1810. A Franciscan, the Rt. Rev. Francis Porro y Penado, was nominated and appointed as successor to Bishop Penalver. It is certain that he never took possession of the see, although it is a disputed matter whether or not he was consecrated as Bishop.

2. DuBOURG, WILLIAM.

The third Bishop of Louisiana was born in San Domingo on February 14, 1766, and made his theological studies in Paris where he was ordained to the priesthood in 1788. After his ordination, he joined the Sulpicians and in 1794 emigrated to the United States. From 1796 to 1799 he was president of Georgetown College and on August 18, 1812, he was chosen Apostolic-Administrator of the Diocese of Louisiana and the Floridas, and was consecrated Bishop of that See in the Eternal City on September 24,

---

[1] On April 25, 1793, the Holy See erected the Diocese of Louisiana the Floridas. and on July 17, 1795, the Rt. Rev. Louis Penalver y Cardenas, appointed first Bishop, arrived in New Orleans. He left in 1801, and then the Diocese was administered by the Vicar-General of Bishop Carroll. Later, on September 24, 1815. Rev. William Du Bourg was consecrated as Bishop of Louisiana, and he administered this Diocese until it was divided and the Dioceses of New Orleans and Saint Louis created.

1815, by Cardinal Joseph Doria Pamfilo, Bishop of Poro.
He resigned his episcopal charge in November, 1826, and
was translated to the Bishopric of Montauban, France, on
August 13, 1826. On February 15, 1833, he was promoted
to the Archiepiscopal See of Bensancon. He died on December 12, 1833.

REUSS, *op. cit.*, p. 34; SHEA, *Hierarchy, etc.*, pp. 120-122; CLARKE,
op. cit., Vol. i, pp. 205-238; *Researches*, Vol. vi, p. 191, Vol. viii. p.
103, Vol. x, pp. 144-152, *Bibliography of Bishop Du Bourg*, Vol. xi,
pp. 157-159, Vol. xii, pp. 10, 94. Vol. xx, p. 22, Vol. xxii, pp. 17, 389,
398, Vol. xxvi, pp. 48, 272, Vol. xxviii, p. 345; HERBERMANN, *Sulpicians, etc.*, pp. 170-180, 199. 222-226, 231; CHR, Vol. i, pp. 64, 277,
630, Vol. ii, pp. 5-21 *passim*, 165-169, 392-416, 448, 470, Vol. iv, pp.
52-75, 448, 452-469. Vol. v, pp. 221, 356; CE, Vol. v, pp. 178-179;
McCANN, *op. cit.*, Vol. i, pp. 39, 49, 118-120, Vol. ii, pp. 70, 114;
McSWEENY, *op. cit.*, Vol. i, pp. 13, 16, 24, 27, 49, 155-156, 390; MIGNE,
Encyclopedie Theologique. pp. 442 seq., Paris, 1863. The Rev. Edward
Hickey, Ph.D., of the Diocese of Detroit, possesses some valuable data
relative to *Bishop DuBourg and the Society of the Propagation of
the Faith.*

3. DeNECKERE, LEO RAYMOND, C. M.

Strictly speaking, the Rt. Rev. Leo DeNeckere was
the first Bishop of New Orleans. He was born at Wevel-
ghem, Belgium, on June 6, 1800, and while a seminarian
in the city of Ghent, he was accepted by Bishop DuBourg
for the Diocese of Louisiana. Coming to this country he
joined the Lazarists and was ordained to the priesthood
in St. Louis on October 30, 1822. While visiting Europe
in 1827 he was summoned to Rome, where he was appointed
Bishop of New Orleans, on August 4, 1829, and upon his
return to that city was consecrated on May 24, 1830, by
Bishop Rosati. He died in New Orleans on September 4,
1833.

REUSS, *op. cit.*, pp. 78-79; SHEA, *Hierarchy, etc.*, pp. 122-123;
CLARKE, *op. cit.*, Vol. ii, pp. 518-527; *Researches*, Vol. ix, p. 88; CHR,
Vol. ii. pp. 128, 428; Vol. iv, p. 69.

4. BLANC, ANTHONY.

The first Archbishop of New Orleans was born on
October 11, 1792, at Sury le Comtal, near Lyons, France.
He was one of the first ecclesiastical students to enter the
seminaries of France after the Restoration and was or-

dained to the priesthood on July 22, 1816, in the Seminary at Lyons. He came to the United States in September, 1817, with several young seminarians and shortly afterwards went south to labor in Mississippi. In 1831 he became Vicar-General of Bishop DeNeckere and after the Bishop's death he acted as Diocesan Administrator until appointed as his successor. Bishop Rosati consecrated him Bishop on November 22, 1835. He was created archbishop on July 19, 1850, and received the pallium on February 16, 1851. He died somewhat suddenly in New Orleans on June 20, 1860.

REUSS, *op. cit.*, p. 14; CLARKE, *op. cit.*, Vol. iii, pp. 438-477; SHEA, *Hierarchy*, etc., p. 123; *Catholic History of Alabama and the Floridas*, by a Member of the Order of Mercy, *passim*, New York, 1908; ACHS *Researches*, Vol. vii. p. 103, Vol. viii, p. 170, Vol. ix, pp. 85-88, Vol. xii, p. 82, Vol. xix, pp. 14-15; DEUTHER, *Life of Bishop Timon*, p. 29, Buffalo, 1897; CHR, Vol. ii, pp. 129, 428; CE. Vol. ii, p. 592 (biog. sketch), Vol. xi, pp. 12, 208; files of the *New Orleans Delta*, for June 23, 1860; ROSATI, *Life of Felix De Andreis*, St. Louis, 1900; SHEA, *History of the Catholic Church*, etc., Vol. iii, pp. 389, 411, 444, 452, 669, 671-680. 700-706, 719; *ibid.*, Vol. iv, pp. 28, 667-671. 695-697; SALZBACHER, *Meine Reise nach Nord-American Jahre*, 1842. p. 310, Vienna, 1845; CAUTHORN, *History of the City of Vincennes*, p. 117. Terre Haute, Ind., 1902.

5. ODIN, J. M., C.M.

Bishop Odin was promoted to the Archiepiscopal See of New Orleans from the Diocese of Galveston on February 15, 1861. He was born at Hauteville, Ambierle, France, on February 25, 1801. While a seminarian in his native country he responded to the call of Bishop DuBourg for missionaries and came to the United States in June, 1822. He was sent to the Lazarist Seminary near St. Louis to complete his theological studies and was ordained to the priesthood on May 4, 1824. His early career as a priest was spent in and around Missouri and Arkansas, and in 1840 he was sent to Texas by his superiors as Vice-Prefect. Archbishop Blanc consecrated him titular Bishop of Claudiopolis and Vicar-Apostolic of Texas on March 6, 1842. He was appointed first Bishop of Galveston on April 23, 1847. While touring Europe, his health failed and he sought relief at his native home in Ambierle, France, where he died on May 25, 1870.

REUSS, *op. cit.*, p. 82; CLARKE, *op. cit.*, Vol. ii, p. 203 seq.; SHEA, *Hierarchy*, p. 125; IDEM, *History of the Catholic Church in the United States*, Vol. iv.. pp. 671-675; CE, Vol. xi, pp. 13-14, p. 208, and Vol. vi, p. 372.

6. PERCHE, NAPOLEON J.

The second Archbishop of New Orleans was born in Angers, France, on January 30, 1805. He completed his studies at the Seminary of Beaupré and was ordained to the priesthood on September 19, 1829. He came to the United States with Bishop Flaget in 1837, and was appointed pastor at Portland, and four years later he went to New Orleans with Archbishop Blanc. Appointed coadjutor to Archbishop Odin, he was consecrated on May 1, 1870, by Bishop Rosecrans, of Columbus. He succeeded to the Archiepiscopal See of New Orleans on May 25, 1870, and a year later he received the pallium from the hands of Pius IX. He died in New Orleans on December 27, 1883.

REUSS, *op. cit.*, pp. 88-89; CLARKE, *op. cit.*, Vol. iii, p. 357; SHEA, *Hierarchy*, p. 127; CE, Vol. xi, p. 14; CHR, Vol. ii, p. 129.

7. LERAY, FRANCIS X.

Archbishop Leray was born at Chateau Giron, Brittany, France, and received his early education in the schools of that town. He made his classical course at the College of Rennes and then came to the United States in 1843. He was ordained to the priesthood at Natchez after the completion of his theology at St. Mary's, Baltimore. During the Civil War he acted as Chaplain for the Confederate Army of Tennessee, and afterwards was appointed Vicar-General by Bishop Elder for the Diocese of Natchez. When the See of Natchitoches became vacant at the death of Bishop Martin, Father Leray was appointed to fill the vacancy and was consecrated bishop at Rennes, France, on April 22, 1877, by Cardinal Mark, Archbishop of that city. Pope Leo XII appointed him coadjutor to Archbishop Perche on October 23, 1879, with the title of titular Archbishop of Jonopolis, but also confided to him the administration of the Diocese of Natchitoches. He became Archbishop of New Orleans on December 27, 1883, and received the pallium from the hands of the late Cardinal Gibbons in January, 1884. In the hope of regaining his lost health, he returned to his native France, where he died on September 23, 1887.

REUSS, *op. cit.*, p. 64; SHEA, *Hierarchy, etc.*, p. 129; CLARKE, *op. cit.*, Vol. iii, pp. 371-376; ACHS *Researches*, Vol. xxiv, p. 191; CHR, Vol. i, pp. 129-130; *ibid.*, Vol. ii, p. 135.

8. JANSSENS, FRANCIS.

The fifth Archbishop of New Orleans was born in Tillburg, Holland, on October 17, 1843. At the age of thirteen he commenced his studies in the Seminary at Bois-le-Duc, and completed them at the American College in Louvain. He was ordained to the priesthood on December 22, 1862, and arrived at Richmond, Virginia, in September, 1868. He held various positions of importance while engaged in work there and when the Diocese of Natchez became vacant he was appointed Bishop thereof and was consecrated in Richmond, Virginia, by Cardinal (then Archbishop) Gibbons, on May 1, 1881. He was promoted to the Archiepiscopal See of New Orleans on August 7, 1888, and he died aboard the steamer Creole, bound for New York City, on June 19, 1897.

REUSS, *op. cit.*, p. 56; SHEA, *Hierarchy*, etc., pp. 313-317; CHR, Vol. ii, pp. 130, 132; AEH. Vol. vi, p. 450, Vol. xvii, p. 70 (necrology); ACHS *Researches*, Vol. v, p. 100.

9. CHAPELLE, PLACIDE LOUIS.

Archbishop Chapelle was born on August 28, 1842, at Runes, Lozere, France, and began his classical studies at Mende in his native country, and completed them in Engheim, Belgium. Upon his arrival in this country, he attended St. Mary's, Baltimore, and was ordained to the priesthood on June 28, 1865. He held various pastorates in and around Washington and Baltimore until his appointment to Santa Fe. He died a victim of yellow fever in New Orleans.

REUSS, *op. cit.*, p. 23; CUB, Vol. xii, p. 137; ACHS *Researches*, Vol. xxiv, p. 357; CHR. Vol. ii, pp. 130, 432, Vol. iii, p. 31; Vol. iv, pp. 331, 362-363; biographical sketch in CE, Vol. iii, p. 579.

The Rt. Rev. G. A. Rouxel was titular Bishop of Curio and Auxiliary to Archbishop Chapelle. Upon his death, he acted as administrator until the selection of Archbishop Blenk on April 20, 1906. He died March 7, 1908.

10. BLENK, JAMES H.

Archbishop Blenk was born at Neustadt, Bavaria, on July 28, 1856. His education was received in the city of New Orleans and at Jefferson College in Louisiana. Having joined the Marist Community, he was sent to France to make his probationary studies and later went to Dublin where he completed his course in theology. He was ordained to the priesthood on August 16, 1885, and that same year returned to Louisiana. Appointed first Bishop of Porto Rico on June 12, 1899, he was consecrated by Archbishop Chapelle on July 2, 1899. He was promoted to the Archiepiscopal See of New Orleans on April 20, 1906. He died on April 20, 1917.

CHR, Vol. ii, p. 130; cf., *Episcopology of Porto Rico*, in the CHR, Vol. iv, pp. 348-364.

11. SHAW, JOHN.

The present Archbishop of New Orleans was born in Mobile, Alabama, on December 12, 1863, and received his educational training at Navan, County Meath, Ireland, and the American College in Rome where he was ordained to the priesthood on May 26, 1888. Upon his return to the United States he labored in the Diocese of Mobile until his appointment as coadjutor to Bishop Forest of San Antonio, on February 7, 1910. Bishop Allen, of Mobile, consecrated him titular Bishop of Castabala on April 14, 1910. On account of the ill health of his immediate superior he was designated Administrator of the Diocese on May 18, 1910. He succeeded to the See of San Antonio on March 11, 1911, and was promoted to the Archiepiscopal See of New Orleans in 1918.

Rt. Rev. John M. Laval, born in New Orleans in 1854, ordained to the priesthood on November 10, 1877; appointed

titular Bishop of Hierocaesarea on September 7, 1911, and
consecrated by Archbishop Blenk on November 20, 1911,
is the present auxiliary Bishop of New Orleans.

II. Diocese of Mobile (1829)

On May 15, 1829, Pius VIII erected the Diocese of Mobile with the Rt. Rev. Michael Portier as first Bishop.
When erected as a Diocese, the See of Mobile comprised
the states of Florida and Alabama. At present the territorial limits are the State of Alabama, comprising an area
of 58,821 square miles.

HAMILTON, *Colonial Mobile*, Boston and New York, 1897; SHEA.
History of Catholic Church in the United States, Akron, O., New
York, Chicago, 1886, 1892; IDEM, *Defenders of Our Faith*, New York,
Chicago, 1886, 1893; MOTHER AUSTIN, *A Catholic History of Alabama
and the Floridas*, I, New York, 1908; *Metropolitan Catholic Almanac
and Laity's Directory*, Baltimore, 1850 seq.; *Official Catholic Direc-
tory*, Milwaukee, New York, 1910; REGER, *Die Benediktiner im Staate
Alabama*, Baltimore, 1898.

1. PORTIER, MICHAEL.

The first Bishop of Mobile was born at Montbrisen,
France, September 7, 1795. He entered the theological
Seminary at Lyons, and when Bishop DuBourg, of Louis-
iana, appealed for missionaries he responded to the call
and arrived at Annapolis on September 4, 1817. After
completing his course of studies at St. Mary's, Baltimore,
he was ordained to the priesthood by Bishop DuBourg at
St. Louis in 1818. Five years later in the same place,
November 5, 1826, he was consecrated titular Bishop of
Oleno by Bishop Rosati. When the See of Mobile was
erected in the year 1829, he became first Bishop of this
Diocese. He died in that city on May 14, 1820.

REUSS, *op. cit.*, pp. 89-90; SHEA, *Hierarchy*, p. 293 seq.; CLARKE,
op. cit., Vol. i, p. 438 seq.; MOTHER AUSTIN, *op. cit.*, Vol. i, p. 366
seq.; CE, Vol. x, p. 411; CHR, Vol. ii, p. 131.

2. QUINLAN, JOHN.

Bishop Quinlan was born in County Clare, Ireland,
on October 19, 1826. He came to the United States at the
age of eighteen; was adopted for the Diocese of Cincinnati

and was ordained to the priesthood on August 30, 1852.
He was consecrated Bishop at New Orleans, Louisiana, by
Archbishop Blanc, on December 4, 1859. He died in New
Orleans on March 9, 1883.

REUSS, *op. cit.*, pp. 91-92; SHEA. *Hierarchy*, p. 296; CLARKE, *op.
cit.*, Vol. iii, p. 378; CHR, Vol. ii, p. 131.

3. MANUCY, DOMINIC.

The third Bishop of Mobile was born in St. Augustine, Florida, on December 20, 1823. He made his theological studies at Spring Hill College, Alabama, and was
ordained to the priesthood at Mobile on August 15, 1850.
After his ordination he held several laborious missionary
charges and was consecrated Bishop of Dulam and Vicar-
Apostolic of Brownsville, Texas, on December 8, 1874, by
Archbishop Perché. On March 9, 1884, he was transferred
to the See of Mobile without being relieved of his duties
as Vicar-Apostolic of Brownsville. Bishop Manucy resigned
the see on October 9, 1884, and was again transferred to
the Vicariate of Brownsville. He died in Mobile on December 4, 1885.

REUSS, *op. cit.*, p. 67; SHEA, *Hierarchy*, etc., p. 298; CLARKE,
op. cit., Vol. iii, pp. 388-396; *A Catholic History of Alabama and the
Floridas*, Vol. i, 360-369, New York, 1908; CHR, Vol. ii, p. 131.

4. O'SULLIVAN, JEREMIAH.

Bishop O'Sullivan was born at Kanturk, County Cork,
Ireland, on February 6, 1842, and came to the United States
in 1863. He made his theological studies in St. Mary's
Seminary, Baltimore, and was ordained to the priesthood
on June 30, 1868, by Archbishop Spalding, of Baltimore.
He held various pastorates in the Metropolitan See of Baltimore and was consecrated Bishop of Mobile by Cardinal
(then Archbishop) Gibbons in St. Peter's Church, Washington, D. C., on September 20, 1885. He died at Mobile
on August 10, 1896.

REUSS. *op. cit.*, p. 85; SHEA, *Hierarchy*, p. 300; CHR, Vol. i,
p. 131.

5. ALLEN, EDWARD P.

The present Bishop of Mobile was born in Boston, Massachusetts, on March 17, 1853, and received his education at St. Mary's College, Emmitsburg, where he was ordained to the priesthood on December 17, 1881. Three years later he was appointed President of Mount Saint Mary's and was designated Bishop of Mobile on April 10, 1897. The late Cardinal Gibbons consecrated him Bishop in the Cathedral at Baltimore on May 16, 1897.

III. Diocese of Natchez (1837)

The Diocese of Natchez was erected on July 28, 1837, by Pope Gregory XVI. The Reverend John J. Chanche was appointed its first Bishop on December 15, 1840.

The territorial limits of the Diocese when erected were and still are confined to the State of Mississippi; an area of 46,840 square miles.

JANSSENS (F.). *Sketch of the Catholic Church in the City of Natchez, Mississippi*, Natchez, 1886; DECOURCY-SHEA, *op. cit.*, p. 601 seq.; SHEA, *History*, Vol. iv, p. 275 seq.; CHR, Vol. ii, p. 131.

1. CHANCHE. JOHN M.

Bishop Chanche was born on October 4, 1795, at Baltimore, Maryland, and at the age of eleven he entered St. Mary's College. Archbishop Marechal ordained him to the priesthood on June 5, 1819. Sometime later Father Chanche joined the Society of St. Sulpice and was made a professor in St. Mary's, of which he became president in September, 1834. Appointed to the See of Natchez on December, 1840, he was consecrated at Baltimore on March 14, 1841, by Archbishop Eccleston. While visiting at Frederick, Maryland, he was attacked with an illness which resulted in his death on July 23, 1852.

REUSS, *op. cit.*, p. 22; CLARKE. *op. cit.*, Vol. ii, pp. 166-190; SHEA, *Hierarchy*, etc., p. 311; McCANN, *op. cit.*, Vol. ii, pp. 5, 56, 107, 114-117, 130; McSWEENY, *op. cit.*, Vol. i, pp. 21, 106, 122; ACHS *Researches*, Vol. iv, p. 146, Vol. xx, p. 48; CHR, Vol. i, p. 175 (his letters to the Leopoldine Association), Vol. ii, p. 132; SHEA, *History Catholic Church*, etc.. Vol. iii, pp. 411, 452-456, 660-665, 706.

2. VAN DE VELDE, JAMES O.

Consecrated Bishop of Chicago on February 11, 1849; transferred to Natchez on July 29, 1853. (Cf. Chicago.)

3. ELDER, WILLIAM HENRY.

Consecrated Bishop of Natchez on May 3, 1857; transferred, as Bishop of Avara and Coadjutor of Cincinnati on January 30, 1880. (Cf. Cincinnati.)

4. JANSSENS, FRANCIS.

Consecrated Bishop of Natchez, May 1, 1881; transferred to New Orleans on August 6, 1888. (Cf. New Orleans.)

5. HESLIN, THOMAS.

Bishop Heslin was born in the parish of Kilboe, County Longford, Ireland, in April, 1847. Upon the completion of his classical studies he came to the United States at the invitation of Archbishop Odin. He completed his theology at the seminary in New Orleans, and was ordained to the priesthood on September 18, 1869, at Mobile, Alabama. He was acting as pastor of St. Michael's Parish, New Orleans, when appointed Bishop of Natchez. Archbishop Janssens consecrated him Bishop in New Orleans on June 18, 1889. He died on February 22, 1911.

REUSS, op. cit., p. 54; CHR, Vol. i, p. 132.

6. GUNN, JOHN T.

The present Bishop of Natchez was born in County Tyrone, Ireland, on March 15, 1863, and received his education at the Catholic University in Dublin and the Gregorian University in Rome, Italy. He taught in the colleges of the Society of Mary in France and England, and later was Professor of Moral Theology in Washington, District of Columbia. He was appointed Bishop of Natchez on June 29, 1911, and was consecrated on August 29, 1911.

IV. Diocese of Little Rock (1843)

Pope Gregory XVI erected the See of Little Rock on November 28, 1843, and the Reverend Andrew Byrne, a priest of New York City, was consecrated as its first Bishop on March 10, 1844.

At the time of its erection, and at the present time, the Diocese of Little Rock comprises the entire State of Arkansas; an area of 53,045 square miles.

GAYARRE, *French Domination*, New Orleans, 1845; IDEM, *Spanish Domination*, New Orleans, 1845; IDEM, *American Domination*. New Orleans, 1845; POPE, *A Tour of the United States*, Richmond, 1792; GREENHOW, *History of Oregon and California*, Boston, 1845); MELISH, *Military and Topographical Atlas*, Philadelphia. 1815; NUTTAL, *Travels in Arkansas*, Philadelphia, 1821; POPE, *Early Days in Arkansas*, Little Rock, 1895; WASHBURN, *Reminiscences of the Indians*, Richmond, 1869; PARKMAN, works; BANCROFT, *History of the United States*, Boston. 1879; REYNOLDS, *Makers of Arkansas History*, New York and Boston, 1905; HEMSTEAD, *School History of Arkansas*, New Orleans, 1889; SHINN, *School History of Arkansas*, Richmond, 1900; ROZIER, *History of the Mississippi Valley*, St. Louis, 1890; JEWELL, *History of the Methodist Church in Arkansas*, Little Rock, 1898; *Publications of the Arkansas Historical Association*, I, II, Little Rock, 1908; HALLIBURTON, *History of Arkansas County, Arkansas*, Dewitt, 1909; SHEA, *History of the Catholic Church*, New York, 1892.

1. BYRNE, ANDREW.

Bishop Byrne was born on December 5, 1802, at Navan, County Meath, Ireland, and at an early age entered the diocesan seminary in his native place. Having arrived at Charleston in 1820, he completed his theological course under the immediate supervision of Bishop England, and was ordained to the priesthood on November 11, 1827. His early career as a priest was spent in the missions of Carolina where he also exercised the powers of Vicar-General. In 1836 he went to New York and assumed charge of various pastorates in that city. He was laboring there when appointed first Bishop of Little Rock in 1843. He was consecrated Bishop in New York City by Archbishop (then Bishop) Hughes, on March 10, 1844. He died at Helena, Arkansas, on June 10, 1862.

REUSS. *op. cit.*, pp. 19-20; SHEA, *Hierarchy*, etc., p. 274; CLARKE, *op. cit.*, Vol. ii, pp. 264-272; cf; COOGAN, *History of Meath; CE,* Vol. iii, p. 93 (biog. sketch); CHR, Vol. ii, p. 133; SHEA, *History of the Catholic Church,* etc., Vol. iii, pp. 328, 508; *ibid..* Vol. iv, pp. 28, 38, 105, 164, 229, 286-287, 678; ACHS *Researches,* Vol. viii, p. 226, Vol. xix. p. 115; *U. S. C. H. Magazine,* Vol. iv, p. 183; McGARR, *Life of Bishop Quarter,* New York, 1850.

2. FITZGERALD, EDWARD.

The second Bishop of Little Rock was born in Limerick, Ireland, on October 28, 1833, and came to the United States with his parents in 1849. He made his theological studies at Mount Saint Mary's at Emmitsburg and at Cincinnati, and was ordained to the priesthood for the Diocese of Cincinnati on August 22, 1857. He was acting pastor of the Church in Columbus, Ohio, when he was notified of his appointment as Bishop of Little Rock on June 22, 1866. Archbishop Purcell consecrated him in Columbus on February 3, 1867. He died on February 21, 1907.

REUSS, *op. cit.*, p. 42; SHEA, *Hierarchy,* etc., pp. 275-276; Mc-SWEENY, *op. cit.*, Vol. ii, pp. 80, 240; CHR, Vol. ii. p. 133; cf. GIBBONS. *Retrospect of Fifty Years,* Baltimore, 1916.

3. MORRIS, JOHN B.

The present Bishop of this Diocese was born at Hendersonville, Tennessee, on June 29, 1866, and received his education at St. Mary's College in Kentucky, and the American College, Rome. He was ordained to the priesthood on June 11, 1892, and upon his return to this country labored in the Diocese of Nashville. Later he held the rectorship of the Cathedral in that Diocese and in 1901 Bishop Byrne appointed him Vicar-General. He was consecrated coadjutor-Bishop of Little Rock, on June 11, 1906, by Bishop Byrne and succeeded to the See as third Bishop, on February 21, 1907.

V. Diocese of Galveston (1847)

The Diocese of Galveston was erected by Pius IX on April 23, 1847, with the Rt. Rev. J. M. Odin as first Bishop.

When erected the Diocese of Galveston comprised the State of Texas, but at present it embraces that part of the State of Texas lying between the Sabine River, on the east, and the Colorado River on the west; with the Gulf of Mexico on the south, and the northern limits of the counties of Lampasas, Coryell, McLellan, Limestone, Freestone, Anderson, Cherokee, Nacogdoches and Shelby on the north; an area of 43,000 square miles.

SHEA, *History of Catholic Church in the United States*, New York, 1894; IDEM, *History Catholic Missions*, New York. 1855; REUSS, *Biographical Cyclopedia Catholic Hierarchy of United States*, Milwaukee, 1898; *Catholic Directory*, 1909; *Freeman's Journal*, New York, *Morning Star*, New Orleans, June, 1870, files; *The History of the Diocese of Galveston*, Galveston, 1922.

1. ODIN, JOHN MARY.

Consecrated titular Bishop of Claudiopolis and first Vicar-Apostolic of Texas on March 12, 1842; in 1847 became first Bishop of Galveston; transferred to the See of New Orleans in 1861.
(Cf. New Orleans.)

2. DUBOIS, C. M.

The second Bishop of Galveston was born at Cautouvre, Loire, France, on March 10, 1817, and was ordained to the priesthood at Lyons on June 1, 1844. He came to the United States at the invitation of Bishop Odin and labored for many years in the missionary fields of Texas. Bishop Odin consecrated him second Bishop of Galveston in Lyons, France, on November 23, 1862. Owing to ill health he resigned his charge on July 12, 1881, but still kept the title of Bishop of Galveston. He returned to France and lived at Vernaison in the Diocese of Lyons, and in 1894 he was promoted to the titular Archiepiscopal See of Arca. He died in his native country at Vernaison, on May 22, 1895.

REUSS, *op. cit.*, pp. 35-36; SHEA, *Hierarchy*, etc., pp. 238-239; *Researches*. Vol. iii, pp. 4-7; CHR, Vol. ii, pp. 135, 149.

Rt. Rev. Peter Dufal, C.S.C., was named coadjutor to Bishop Dubuis on May 14, 1878. He was at that time Vicar-Apostolic of East Bengal and titular Bishop of Delcus, having been consecrated at the Holy Cross Chapel in LeMans by Monsignor Joseph H. Guibert, who later became

Archbishop of Paris. He resigned his charge at Galveston on April 18, 1880, and retired to Neuilly, near Paris, France, where he died in 1898. He never was Bishop of Galveston.

REUSS, *op. cit.*, p. 36; CHR, Vol. ii, p. 135, 429.

3. GALLAGHER, NICHOLAS A.

The Reverend Nicholas A. Gallagher was born at Temperanceville, Belmont County, Ohio, on February 19, 1846, and was ordained to the priesthood at Columbus, Ohio, on December 25, 1868. He labored in the Diocese of Columbus for many years and after the death of Bishop Rosecrans, he acted as Administrator of that Diocese. Afterwards he went to Texas, and while laboring there was appointed to the titular bishopric of Canopus and Coadjutor of Galveston on January 10, 1882. He succeeded to the See of Galveston in 1894, and died on January 21, 1918.

REUSS, *op. cit.*, p. 45; CHR, Vol. i, p. 135; SHEA, *Hierarchy*, etc., p. 239.

4. BYRNE, CHRISTOPHER.

The present Bishop of Galveston was born at Byrnesville, Jefferson County, Missouri, on April 21, 1867. After the completion of his seminary course at St. Mary's in Baltimore he was ordained to the priesthood on September 23, 1891, in St. Louis, Missouri, by Archbishop Peter R. Kenrick. His first appointment was at St. Bridget's Church, St. Louis, and later he held pastorates at other cities in Missouri. He was acting as pastor of Holy Name Church in St. Louis when he was chosen Bishop of Galveston. He was consecrated by Archbishop Glennon on November 10, 1918.

VI. Diocese of Alexandria (1855-1910)

On July 29, 1852, the Diocese of Natchitoches was erected and the Rt. Rev. Augustus Martin was consecrated as first Bishop on November 30, 1853. In 1910, at the request of Bishop Van de Ven, the diocesan seat was changed to Alexandria.

The Diocese comprises its original limits—the northern part of the State of Louisiana, an area of 22,122 square miles.

MARTIN. *History of Louisiana*, New Orleans, 1882; SHEA, *History of the Catholic Church in the United States*, I; CLARKE, *Lives of the Deceased Bishops*, New York, 1888; and the unpublished letters of Bishop Martin; CHR, Vol. ii.

1. MARTIN, AUGUSTUS M.

The first Bishop of this See was born at Breton, St. Malo, Diocese of Rennes, France, on February 2, 1803. He was ordained to the priesthood in 1828, and while Chaplain of the Royal College at Rennes in 1839, he met Bishop de la Hailandière, of Vincennes, who was making a plea for missionaries for his diocese in the United States. Father Martin responded to the call and set out for this country with him. For six years he acted as Vicar-General in the See of Vincennes, Indiana, and when his health failed, he went to Louisiana and labored in this region until appointed Bishop of Natchitoches. Archbishop Blanc consecrated him in New Orleans on November 30, 1853, and he died at Natchitoches on September 29, 1875.

REUSS, *op. cit.*, p. 68; SHEA, *Hierarchy*, etc., p. 318; CLARKE, *op. cit.*, Vol. iii. pp. 397-403; *Year-Book of the Diocese of Indianapolis*, 1919, p. 7; ACHS *Researches*, Vol. xxiii, p. 179, leaves Havre for United States, list of priests with him; CHR, Vol. i, p. 135, *ibid.*, Vol. ii, p. 135.

2. LERAY, FRANCIS X.

Consecrated Bishop of Natchez on April 22, 1877, he was named Coadjutor of New Orleans in 1879, and succeeded to that see in 1883.

(Cf. New Orleans.)

3. DURIER, ANTHONY.

Bishop Durier was born at St. Bonnet, Desquarts, in the Province of Loire, France, on August 8, 1832. In response to an appeal of Archbishop Blanc for missionaries he came to the United States in 1855 and completed his theological studies at Mount Saint Mary's of the West and was ordained to the priesthood by Archbishop Purcell in 1856. He was stationed at Chillicothe, Ohio, and later went to New Orleans, where he began his priestly labors as an assistant at the Cathedral. He was consecrated Bishop of Natchitoches by Archbishop Leray on March 19, 1885, and administered the see until his death on February 28, 1904.

REUSS, op. cit., p. 23; SHEA, Hierarchy, etc., pp. 319-320; CHR, Vol. ii, pp. 135, 429.

4. VAN DE VEN, CORNELIUS.

The present Bishop of this Diocese was born at Oirschot, Holland, on June 16, 1865, and after his training in the primary schools he entered a college at Rumenderg. He made his theological studies in the Diocesan Seminary of Bois-le-Duc and was ordained to the priesthood on May 21, 1890. He came to the United States in the same year and was stationed at New Iberia, Louisiana, as assistant pastor. Before his appointment as bishop he served as Rector of churches at Lake Charles and Baton Rouge. His consecration took place on November 30, 1904, with the Most Rev. James H. Blenk, of New Orleans, as consecrating prelate. He became Bishop of Alexandria in 1910.

VII. Diocese of San Antonio (1874)

Pius IX erected the Diocese of San Antonio on September 3, 1874, with the Rt. Rev. Anthony Pellicier as first Bishop.

The Diocese comprises that portion of the State of Texas which lies between the Colorado and the Rio Grande Rivers except that part south of Arroto de los Hermanos on the Rio Grande, and the counties of Live Oak, Bee Goliad. Refuio and El Paso; an area of 60,810 square miles.

DeCourcy-Shea, *op. cit.*, p. 671; Shea, *History of the Catholic Missions, passim,* New York, 1855; *History of the Catholic Church in the Diocese of San Antonio,* San Antonio, 1897; CHR. Vol. i, p. 136; cf. files of the *Southern Messenger,* San Antonio, for November, 1894, October, 1895; March, 1911.

1. Pellicier, Anthony D.

The first Bishop of San Antonio was born at St. Augustine, Florida, on December 7, 1824, and was ordained to the priesthood by Bishop Portier at Mobile, Alabama, on October 15, 1850. He served as a missionary in the State of Alabama until 1867, when he was called to Mobile and made Vicar-General. He was consecrated Bishop of San Antonio by Archbishop Perchè of New Orleans on December 8, 1874. He died at San Antonio on April 14, 1880.

Reuss, *op. cit.,* p. 86; Shea, *Hierarchy,* p. 359; Clarke, *op. cit.,* p. 404; CHR, Vol. i, p. 136.

2. Neraz, John C.

Bishop Neraz was born on January 12, 1828, at Anse, France. He made his theological studies in the Seminary at Lyons and came to the United States in 1852, and was ordained to the priesthood at Galveston on February 19, 1852. For thirty years he labored in the mission fields of Texas and finally became Vicar-General of Bishop Pellicier. At the death of this prelate he became Administrator of the Diocese, and later was appointed to succeed him. His consecration took place in San Antonio on May 3, 1881, with Bishop Fitzgerald as consecrating prelate. He died in San Antonio on November 15, 1894.

Reuss, *op. cit.,* p. 79; Shea, *Hierarchy,* etc., p. 360; CHR, Vol. ii. p. 136.

3. Forest, John A.

The third Bishop of San Antonio was born at St. Martin, Canton, St. Germain, France, and was ordained to the priesthood in New Orleans on May 3, 1863. His priestly work was confined to the missionary fields of Texas where he labored until his appointment as bishop on August 27,

1895. Archbishop Janssens consecrated him at San Antonio on October 28, 1895. He died in that city on March 11. 1911.

REUSS, *op. cit.*, p. 44; CHR, Vol. ii, p. 136.

4. SHAW, JOHN W.

Consecrated coadjutor Bishop of San Antonio on April 14, 1910, and succeeded to the See on March 11, 1911. He was promoted to the See of New Orleans on January 25, 1918. (Cf. New Orleans.)

5. DROSSAERTS, ARTHUR J.

The present Bishop of San Antonio was born at Freda, Holland, on September 11, 1862, and received his seminary training at Bois-le-Duc in his native land. He was ordained to the priesthood on June 15, 1889, and began his priestly career in the Archdiocese of New Orleans. He was stationed at Baton Rouge, Louisiana, as pastor when appointed to the Bishopric of San Antonio and was consecrated in St. Louis Cathedral, New Orleans, by His Excellency, the Apostolic Delegate, Most Rev. John Bonzano, on December 8, 1918.

VIII. Diocese of Corpus Christi (1912)

On March 23, 1912, the Vicariate of Brownsville was erected into the Diocese of Corpus Christi by Pius X, and on April 4, 1913, the Reverend Paul J. Nussbaum, C. P., was appointed as first Bishop.

The territorial limits of the Diocese of Corpus Christi comprise that part of the State of Texas situated south and east of Las Hermanas and San Roque Creeks—south of the Nueces River as far as the eastern line of McMullen County; south of Alascosa, Karnes, DeWitt, Victoria and Calhoun counties; an area of 22,000 square miles.

CHR, Vol. ii, pp. 136-137; *Catholic Directory,* 1922.

1. MANUCY, DOMINIC.

Consecrated titular Bishop of Dulma and first Vicar-Apostolic of Brownsville on December 8, 1874. He was promoted to the Diocese of Mobile on March 9, 1884, but resigned the same year and was re-appointed to Brownsville with the title of Bishop of Maronia.
(Cf. Mobile.)

2. VERDAGUER, PETER.

The second Vicar-Apostolic was born on September 10, 1835, at San Pedro de Torrello, in the Province of Catalonia, Spain. He was ordained to the priesthood on December 12, 1862, at San Francisco by Bishop Amat of Monterey. His priestly labor was confined to the city of Los Angeles and vicinity and he was acting as pastor of the Church of Our Lady of Angels in that city when appointed titular Bishop of Aulona and second Vicar-Apostolic of Brownsville on July 26, 1890. He returned to Spain for his consecration which took place in Barcelona on November 9, 1890, with Bishop Calala y Albara as consecrating prelate. He died on October 26, 1911.

REUSS, *op. cit.*, p. 106; CHR, Vol. ii, p. 137.

3. NUSSBAUM, PAUL, C. P.

The first Bishop of Corpus Christi was born in Philadelphia, Pennsylvania, on September 7, 1870, and having joined the Passionist Order, he made his studies at Passionist houses in the United States and in Europe. He was ordained to the priesthood on May 20, 1894, and labored in the Middle Atlantic and Eastern States of this country and in South America. He was appointed first Bishop of Corpus Christi on April 4, 1913, and was consecrated by His Excellency the Apostolic Delegate, Archbishop Bonzano, on May 20, 1913, in West Hoboken, New Jersey. He resigned the see in 1921.

4. LEDVINA, EMMANUEL V.

The present Bishop of Corpus Christi was born in Evansville, Indiana, on October 2, 1868. He received his theological training at St. Meinrad's College in Indiana, and was ordained to the priesthood by Bishop Chatard on May 18, 1893. He served as curate at the Holy Trinity Church, Evansville, Indiana, and afterwards was transferred to St. John's pro-cathedral, Indianapolis. Later he was made pastor at Princeton, Indiana, and for fourteen years was Vice-President and General Secretary of the Catholic Church Extension Society. He was acting in this capacity when appointed to the See of Corpus Christi and was consecrated at St. Mary's-of-the-Woods, Indiana, by Bishop Chartrand on June 14, 1921.

IX. Diocese of Dallas (1890)

The Diocese of Dallas was erected by Leo XIII in 1890 and the Rt. Rev. Thomas F. Brennan was consecrated as its first Bishop on April 5, 1891.

The Diocese of Dallas, when erected comprised the northern part of the State of Texas north of Shelby, Nacogdorches, Cherokee, Anderson, Freestone, Limestone, McLellan, Cargelly, Lampasas, Howard, Martin and Gaines Counties and the Colorado River; an area of 98,266 square miles.

CHR. Vol. ii, p. 317; cf. bibliography of *Diocese of Galveston; Catholic Directory*, 1922.

1. BRENNAN, THOMAS F.

Bishop Brennan was born at Tipperary, Ireland, in October, 1853, and was ordained to the priesthood at Brixen-Tyrol on July 4, 1880. He was consecrated Bishop of Dallas at Erie, Pennsylvania, on April 5, 1891, by Bishop Mullin. Two years later, on February 1, 1893, he was transferred to the titular See of Utilla, and was made Auxiliary to Bishop Power of St. John's, Newfoundland. He was called to Rome in December, 1904, and was given the titular See of Cesarea, Morocco, on October 7, 1905. The last years of his life were spent in the Basilian Monastery at Grotta-ferrata, near Rome, where he died on March 21, 1916.

REUSS, *op. cit.*, p. 17; CHR, Vol. ii, pp. 137-138; *Bishop Brennan, in the Texas Catholic*. Vol. ii, August 6, 1892; *Dallas Diocese, ibid.*, for 1891. 1892.

2. DUNN, EDWARD JOSEPH.

Bishop Dunn was born in County Tipperary, Ireland, on April 23, 1848. He was ordained to the priesthood in Baltimore on June 29, 1871, and was laboring in the Archdiocese of Chicago when appointed to the See of Dallas on September 24, 1893. Archbishop Feehan consecrated him in all Saints' Church, Chicago, on November 30, 1893. He died at Dallas on August 5, 1910.

REUSS, *op. cit.*, p. 37; CHR, Vol. ii, pp. 138, 430, Vol. iii, p. 154

3. LYNCH, JOSEPH P.

The present Bishop of Dallas was born at St. Joseph, Michigan, on November 16. 1872. and received his seminary training in St. Mary's, Baltimore, and at Kenrick Seminary, St. Louis. After his ordination he labored in the Diocese of Dallas and later was appointed Vicar-General and Administrator *sede vacante*. His consecration as Bishop took place at the Cathedral in Dallas, Texas, on July 12, 1911, with Archbishop Blenk as consecrating prelate.

X. Diocese of Oklahoma (1905)

On August 25, 1905, Pius X erected Indian Territory into the Diocese of Oklahoma with the Rt. Rev. Theophile Meerschaert, D.D., as first Bishop.

The Diocese comprises the entire State of Oklahoma; an area of 69,414 square miles.

HILL, *History of Oklahoma*, pp. 407-408, Chicago, New York, 1908; ROCH, *History of Oklahoma*, Wichita, 1890; FINDALL, *Makers of Oklahoma*, Guthrie, 1905; DECOURCY-SHEA, *op. cit.*; CHR, Vol. ii, p. 138.

1. MEERSCHAERT, THEOPHILE.

The first, and present, Bishop of this See, was born at Roussigmes, Belgium, on August 24, 1847, and studied at the American College in Louvain and was ordained to the priesthood on December 23, 1871. He came to the United States the following year and labored in the Diocese of Natchez until 1891, when he was appointed first Vicar-

Apostolic of Oklahoma and titular Bishop of Sydima. He was consecrated on September 8, 1891, and became first Bishop of the Diocese of Oklahoma on August 23, 1905.

XI. Diocese of Lafayette (1918)

The formal erection of the See of Lafayette was decreed by Benedict XV on May 23, 1918, and the Rt. Rev. Jules B. Jeanmard was consecrated as first Bishop on December 8, 1918.

The Diocese comprises the civil parishes, or counties, of Acadia, Allen, Beauregard, Calcasieu, Cameron, Evangeline, Iberia, Jefferson, Davis, Lafayette, St. Landry, St. Martin, St. Mary and Vermillion in the southwestern part of the State of Louisiana; an area of 11,090 square miles.

SOUVAY, *An Historical Sketch of the Church of Lafayette, Louisiana*, in the *Saint Louis Catholic Historical Review*, Vol. iii, pp. 242-294; *Catholic Directory* for 1922.

1. JEANMARD, JULES B.

The present Bishop of this Diocese was born at Breaux-Bridge, Louisiana, on August 15, 1879, and received his education at St. Joseph's Seminary, at the Kenrick Seminary, St. Louis, Missouri, and the St. Louis Seminary in New Orleans. He was ordained to the priesthood in St. Joseph's Church, New Orleans, on June 11, 1903. He acted as secretary to Archbishop Blenk from July 6, 1906, to 1914; chancellor of the Archdiocese and later Vicar-General; served as Administrator *sede vacante* from April 20, 1917, to June 2, 1918. He was appointed first Bishop of Lafayette on July 18, 1918, and he was consecrated by His Excellency, the Apostolic Delegate, Most Rev. John Bonzano, on December 8, 1918, at the Cathedral of St. Louis in New Orleans.

CHAPTER V

THE PROVINCE OF NEW YORK

Pope Pius IX erected the Province of New York on July 19, 1850, with the Rt. Rev. John Hughes as first Archbishop.

In 1850, the Archdiocese of New York comprised the State of New York, part of New Jersey, and all the New England States, with the Dioceses of Boston (1808), Albany (1847), Buffalo (1847), and Hartford (1843) as suffragan sees. At present, the Province is confined to the States of New York and New Jersey, and the Bahama Islands, and the suffragan sees are Albany (1847), Buffalo (1847), Brooklyn (1853), Newark (1853), Rochester (1868), Ogdensburg (1872), Trenton (1881), and Syracuse (1886).

SHEA, *History of the Catholic Church in the United States*, New York, 1886; IDEM, *Catholic Churches of New York*. New York, 1878; *Ecclesiastical Records, State of New York, Albany, 1902;* O'CALLA-GHAN, *Documentary History of New York*, Albany, 1849-51; BAYLEY, *Brief Sketch of the Early History of the Catholic Church on the Island of New York*, New York, 1854; FINOTTI. *Bibliographia Catholica Americana*, New York, 1872; FLYNN, *The Catholic Church in New Jersey*, Morristown, 1904; WHITE, *Life of Mrs. Eliza A. Seton*, New York, 1893; SETON, *Memoir, Letters and Journal of Elizabeth Seton*, New York, 1869; FARLEY, *History of St. Patrick's Cathedral*, New York, 1908; SMITH, *History of the Catholic Church in New York*, New York, 1905; *The Catholic Directory;* UNITED STATES CATHOLIC HIS-TORICAL SOCIETY, *Historical Records and Studies*, New York. 1899-1910; *Memorial, Most Rev. M. A. Corrigan*, New York, 1902; HAS-SARD, *Life of the Most Rev. John Hughes*, New York, 1866; BRANN, *Most Rev. John Hughes*, New York, 1892; CAMPBELL, *Pioneer Priests of North America*, New York, 1909-10; *Mary Aloysia Hardey*, New York, 1910; *New York Truth Teller*, files; *Freeman's Journal*, files; *Metropolitan Record*, files; *Tablet*, files; *Catholic News*, files; BROWN-SON, H. F., *Brownson's Early, Middle and Later Life*, Detroit, 1898-1900; BENNETT, *Catholic Footsteps in Old New York*, New York, 1909; ZWIERLEIN, *Religion in New Netherland*, Rochester, 1910.

I. Diocese of New York (1808)

The See of New York was one of the four dioceses created by Pius VII on April 8, 1808. The Rt. Rev. Luke Concanen, O. P., was consecrated first Bishop on April 24,

73

1808, but he never reached the United States. The first resident Bishop of this Diocese was the Rt. Rev. John Connolly, O. P., who was consecrated on November 6, 1814. The original limits of the Diocese of New York were the entire State of that name, and what was known at that time as East Jersey. At present the Diocese comprises the boroughs of Manhattan, Bronx, and Richmond, of the city of New York, and the counties of Dutchess, Orange, Putnam, Rockland, Sullivan, Ulster and Westchester in the State of New York, also the Bahama Islands; the total area is 9,183 square miles.

1. CONCANEN, LUKE, O. P.

Bishop Concanen was born in Ireland (Connaught), in the ecclesiastical Province of Tuam. A letter to Bishop Carroll (December 29, 1803), in which he states that he was then fifty-six years of age proves that he was born there about 1747.

Most probably he entered the Dominican Order in 1765 or 1766. His educational training was received at the Minerva and the College of San Clemente at Rome. He was ordained to the priesthood at Rome some time between the years 1770-1771. He held important offices in the Dominican Order until his appointment as first Bishop of New York on April 8, 1808. He was consecrated at Rome in the Church of St. Catherine of Sienna on April 24, 1808, by Cardinal Michele de Pietro. He died at Naples on June 19, 1810.

REUSS. *op. cit.*, pp. 25-26; CLARKE, *op. cit.*, Vol. i, pp. 140-143; SHEA, *Hierarchy*, etc., pp. 132-133; BENNETT, *op. cit.*, .p. 459; HEWITT, *History of the Diocese of Syracuse*, pp. 21-23, Syracuse, 1909; McSWEENY, *op. cit.*, Vol. i, p. 151; WEBB, *op. cit.*, p. 202; FINOTTI, *op. cit.*, p. 177; FISH, *op. cit.*, p. 174, 175, 192; JOHN TALBOT SMITH, *The Catholic Church in New York*, Vol. i, p. 38-39, New York, 1905; cf. *Index* to ACHS *Researches*, pp. 75-77; the best account of his life is that V. F. O'Daniel, O.P., in the CHR, Vol. i, pp. 400-421, Vol. ii, pp. 19-46, a complete bibliography will be found pp. 400-401 of the CHR, Vol. i (the *Dominican Archives* at Washington, D. C., contain photostatic copies of his correspondence); cf. CHR, Vol. i, p. 311, Vol. ii, p. 140.

2. CONNOLLY, JOHN, O. P.

The first resident Bishop of New York was born at Drogheda, County Meath, Ireland, in 1750. He joined the Dominican Order in his early youth and made his studies at Rome, where he was ordained to the priesthood. Appointed as successor to Bishop Concanen for the See of New York, he was consecrated in Rome on November 6, 1814, by Cardinal Brancadora, and reached New York the following year, on November 24. He died there on February 6, 1825.

REUSS, *op. cit.*, pp. 26-27; CLARKE, *op. cit.*, Vol. i. pp. 192-204; SHEA, *Hierarchy*, etc., p. 133; J. T. SMITH, *op. cit.*, Vol. i, pp. 15-70; HEWITT, *op. cit.*. p. 24; FINOTTI, *op. cit.*, p. 239; MCCANN, *op. cit.*, Vol. i, pp. 88, 125; USCHS *Historical Records and Studies*, Vol. ii (1900), p. 227 (his portrait); *United States Catholic Historical Magazine*, Vol. iv (1891-93), pp. 58-61 and 186-198; (CONNOLLY correspondence), ACHS *Researches*, Vol. xxii, pp. 91. 232, 250, Vol. xxiv, p. 379, Vol. xxxiii, p. 343; see *Rosary Magazine*, for April, 1895; BAYLEY, *Brief Sketch of the History of the Catholic Church on the Island of New York*, New York, 1853; cf. files of the *Catholic Miscellany*, for 1824-1825; biographical sketch in CE, Vol. iv, p. 257.

3. DUBOIS, JOHN.

The founder of Mount Saint Mary's, Emmitsburg, Maryland, and the third Bishop of New York, was born in Paris, on August 24, 1754. He received his early educational training at home until he was prepared to enter the College of Louis le Grand. He was ordained to the priesthood in Paris on September 22, 1787. On account of the French Revolution he was forced to leave his native land, and he came to the United States in 1791. After a few years of missionary activity, he began his career as an educator in 1808. He was consecrated by Archbishop Maréchal on October 29, 1826. He died in New York on December 25, 1842.

REUSS, *op. cit.*, p. 34; SHEA, *Hierarchy*, etc., pp. 34-36; CLARKE, *op. cit.*, Vol. i, pp. 414-437; *Researches*, Vol. vi, pp. 91. 122-124; Vol. viii, pp. 42, 170, Vol. ix, pp. 85-86, Vol. xxix, p. 200; HERBERMANN. *op. cit.*, pp. 187-193, 204; HERBERMANN in the USCHS *Historical Records and Studies*. Vol. x, pp. 124-129 (*Bishop Dubois in New York in 1836*); FARLEY, *Life of Cardinal McCloskey*, pp. 20, 27, 49, 50, 56, 63, 111, 112. 146, 150. 160, 362; FLYNN, *Catholic Church in New Jersey,* pp. 49, 78, 90-98, 101-109. 115, 260, Morristown, N. J., 1904; BAYLEY, *Brief Sketch,* etc., pp. 29-105; CHR, Vol. i, pp. 285-286, Vol. ii. p. 140, Vol. iv, pp. 12, 404, 411, Vol. v, pp. 239, 251, 309; L. W. REILLY, *Bishop John Dubois,* in the CW, Vol. xxxiv, pp. 454-460; CE, Vol. v, p. 178; SMITH, *The Catholic Church in New York,* New York, 1905-1908; FARLEY, *History of St. Patrick's Cathedral,* New York, 1908; McCANN, *op. cit.,* Vol. i, pp. 22-28, 38-49, 81-89, 96-97, 123-134, 170, 198, 224, 244; Vol. ii, pp. 3, 70, 114; McSWEENY, Vol. i, pp. 2-16, 23-76, 81-126, 130-175, 251-285, 301-313, 352-376, 383-397, 401-431, 505-516, 551-555; *Jubilee of Mt. St. Mary's College,* pp. 235-288, New York, 1859; MOREAU, *Les Pretes Francais Emigres aux Etavt-Unis,* Paris, 1856; MULRENAN, *Brief Historical Sketch of the Catholic Church on Long Island,* New York, 1871.

4. HUGHES, JOHN.

This distinguished ecclesiastic was born at Annalogh, County Tyrone, Ireland, on June 24, 1797, and emigrated to the United States with his parents in 1816. He entered Mount Saint Mary's in preparation for the priesthood and was ordained on October 15, 1826. He was appointed coadjutor to Bishop Dubois and titular Bishop of Basileopolis and was consecrated by Bishop Dubois in New York City on January 7, 1738. For a time he had a large share in the administration of diocesan affairs and upon the death of Bishop Dubois succeeded to the see on December 20, 1842. He was made Archbishop on July 19, 1859, and died in New York on January 3, 1864.

REUSS, *op. cit.,* p. 55; SHEA, *Hierarchy.* etc., pp. 136-141; CLARKE, *op. cit.,* Vol. ii, pp. 73-125; CHR, Vol. ii, p. 140 (biographical data); *ibid.,* Vol. iii, pp. 336-339 (documents relative to his mission to France); CW, Vol. iii. pp. 140 *et seq.* (review of Hassard's *Life*); ACHS *Researches,* Vols. vi, vii, viii, xii, xiv, xvii, Vol. xix, p. 171 (necrology), Vol. xxii. p. 93 (Brooks Controversy), Vols. xxiii, xxviii —these volumes best consulted in *Index* of *Researches;* McSWEENY, *op. cit.,* Vols. i and ii *passim,* especially Vol. i, pp. 89, 99, 126, 136, 140-146; HERBERMANN, *Sulpicians.* etc., pp. 191, 228, 306; BAYLEY, *op. cit.,* pp. 133-147; CLARKE, *op. cit.,* Vol. ii, pp. 73-125; HASSARD, *Life of Archbishop Hughes,* New York, 1866; BRANN, *John Hughes,* New York. 1892; KEHOE, *Works of Archbishop Hughes,* 2 Vols., New York, 1864; USCHS *Historical Records,* etc., Vol. i, p. 171, Vol. ii, p. 227, Vol. iii, p. 282; MAURY. *Statesmen in America* in 1846, London, 1847; BAKER, *Works of William H. Seward,* Vol. iii, p. 482 *et seq.,* New York. 1853; the archival material for the episcopate of Hughes is well preserved in the Dunwoodie, New York, archives; LAWRENCE KEHOE edited the *Works of the Most Rev. John Hughes, D.D.,* containing his sermons, letters, lectures and speeches, New York, 1865.

5. McCLOSKEY, JOHN CARDINAL.

The first American Cardinal was born at Brooklyn, New York, on March 20, 1810. He was sent to the leading classical school in New York City for his early training and in 1822 entered Mount Saint Mary's College at Emmitsburg. He was ordained to the priesthood in New York City on January 12, 1834. In February, 1859, he was named professor of philosophy at Nyack-on-the-Hudson and remained there until the college was destroyed by fire. After a sojourn in Europe he returned to his native diocese in 1837 and was appointed pastor of St. Joseph's Church. Four years later he was selected to be the first President of St. John's College, a position he held until his appointment as coadjutor to Bishop Hughes. He was consecrated titular Bishop of Axiere by Bishop Hughes on March 18, 1844, and on May 21, 1847, he was transferred to the See of Albany. He was promoted to the See of New York on May 6, 1864, and was preconized Cardinal on March 15, 1875. He died in New York City on October 10, 1885.

REUSS, *op. cit.*, pp. 69-70; SHEA, *Hierarchy*, etc., pp. 142; CLARKE, *op. cit.*, Vol. iii, pp. 412-437; FARLEY, *Life of John Cardinal McCloskey*, New York, 1918; ACHS *Researches*, Vol. vii, p. 35 (letter from Rome, 1836); Vol. vii, p. 102 (Frenaye corresp.), Vol. ix, p. 152 (Bayley on McCloskey), Vol. xix, pp. 96, 171, 186, Vol. xxiii, p. 339 (First Secular Priest of New York; *The First American Cardinal*, in the *Month*, Vol. xxi, p. 30; HEWITT, *Cardinal McCloskey*, in the CW, Vol. xlii, pp. 367, 570; CHR, Vol. ii, p. 140.

6. CORRIGAN, MICHAEL A.

The third Archbishop of New York was born at Newark, New Jersey, on August 13, 1893. After graduating from Mount Saint Mary's at Emmitsburg, in 1859, he entered the College of Propaganda at Rome. Upon his return to this country he labored in his native Diocese ten years, after which he was appointed Bishop of Newark. He was consecrated in that city on May 4, 1873, by Archbishop McCloskey. He ruled that see for seven years and was then promoted to be coadjutor to Cardinal McCloskey, *cum jure successionis*. He succeeded to the see on October 10, 1885. He died in New York City on May 5, 1902.

REUSS, *op. cit.*, p. 29; SHEA, *Hierarchy*, etc., p. 148; J. T. SMITH, *op. cit.*, Vol. ii, pp. 404-430 (*cf. ibid.*, pp. 542-555 for an account, somewhat partisan of the McGlynn case) ; *The Silver Jubilee of Arch. Corrigan* (with portrait), in the USCHS *History Records and Studies*, Vol. i, (1905), pp. 14-17. See Corrigan's *Register of the Clergy laboring in the Archdiocese of New York from early missionary times* to 1885, begun in the *History Records and Studies*, Vol. i, p. 18; CUB, Vol. viii, p. 382; ACHS *Researches*, Vol. ix, p. 95, Vol. xi, p. 143, Vol. xxii, p. 149, Vol. xxvi, p. 45; MCSWEENY. *op. cit.*, Vol. i, pp. 416, 501, 517, 525, Vol. ii, pp. 1-3, 180-185, 196, 213, 222, 279, 299, 350. See biog. sketch in *Historical Record and Studies*, Vol. iii (1903), pp. 9-13; FARLEY, *op. cit.*, pp. 211, 349-350, 362-363, 369, 376-377; CHR, Vol. ii, pp. 140, 143, 193, 194, 204, 302; *Memorial of Most Rev. Archbishop Corrigan, Third Archbishop of New York*, New York, 1902; FLYNN, *Catholic Church in New Jersey*, Morristown, 1904; FARLEY, *History of St. Patrick's Cathedral*, New York, 1908.

7. FARLEY, JOHN CARDINAL.

Cardinal Farley was born at Newton-Hamilton, County Armagh, Ireland, on April 20, 1842, and came to the United States in 1859. He continued his education begun in Ireland, at St. John's College and at the Seminary in Troy, New York. In 1867 he went to the American College, Rome, and three years later was ordained to the priesthood in that city on June 11, 1879. He returned home in the same year and was appointed assistant at St. Peter's Church, New Brighton, Staten Island. He was made a Domestic Prelate by Leo XIII, and in 1891 was named Vicar-General of the Archdiocese. He was appointed titular Bishop of Zuean and Auxiliary by Archbishop Corrigan on December 21, 1895. He became Archbishop on September 25, 1902, and was created Cardinal Priest with the title, Sancta Maria Super Minervan, on November 27, 1911. He died in New York City on September 17, 1918.

REUSS, *op. cit.*, p. 40; CHR, Vol. ii, p. 140; GUILDAY, *John Cardinal Farley*, in the *Catholic World*, Vol. cvii, pp. 183-193; *Catholic News*, files for September, 1918; USCHS *Records and Studies*, Vol. vi, part ii, p. 5 seq.

He wrote the *Life of Cardinal McCloskey*, New York, 1918, and a *History of Saint Patrick's Cathedral, New York City*, New York, 1908.

8. HAYES, PATRICK J.

The present Archbishop of New York was born in that city on November 20, 1867. He attended St. Joseph's Seminary at Troy, New York, and was ordained to the priesthood on September 8, 1892. He continued his studies at the Catholic University of America for the next two years, after which he was stationed at St. Gabriel's in New York City. In August, 1903, he was made chancellor of the Archdiocese and President of St. John's College. He was elevated to the rank of Domestic Prelate in November, 1907, and on July 3, 1914, he was appointed Auxiliary to the Bishop of New York and titular Bishop of Tagaste. Cardinal Farley consecrated him on October 21, 1914, in New York City. On November 24, 1917, he was chosen Ordinary of the Chaplains of the Army and Navy, and on March 10, 1919, he was promoted to the vacant archiepiscopal See of New York.

The Rt. Rev. John J. Dunn is the present Auxiliary Bishop of New York. He was born in that city on August 31, 1869; was ordained to the priesthood on May 30, 1896, after completing his theological studies at St. Joseph's Seminary of Troy, New York, and was stationed at the Church of Saint John the Evangelist since June 10, 1896. He was consecrated Auxiliary Bishop of New York in St. Patrick's Cathedral on October 28, 1921, by Archbishop Hayes.

II. The Diocese of Albany (1847)

The Diocese of Albany was erected on April 23, 1847, and the Rt. Rev. John McCloskey (later Cardinal) was appointed as first Bishop on May 21, 1847.

When first established the limits of the Diocese of Albany included the future Dioceses of Ogdensburg and Syracuse. At present it comprises the entire counties of Albany, Columbia, Delaware, Fulton, Greene, Montgomery, Otego. Rensselaer, Saratoga, Schenectady, Schoharie, Warren and Washington and that part of Herkimer and Hamilton counties south of the northern line of the townships of Ohio and Russia in the State of New York; an area of 10,419 square miles.

BRODHEAD, *History of the State of New York*, New York, 1853-71; MARTIN, *Life of Father Jogues*, English tr., New York, 1896; *Dongan Reports* in Vol. iii of *Documents relating to the Colonial History of New York*, Albany, 1853; O'CALLAGHAN, *Documentary History of the State of New York*, Albany, 1849-51; FOLEY, *Records of the English Province of the Society of Jesus*, London, 1877-83; OHN GILMARY SHEA, *History of the Catholic Church in the United States*, New York, 1886-92; HOWELL-TENNEY, *History of Albany and Schenectady Counties*, New York, 1886; WEISE, *Troy's One Hundred Years*, Troy, 1891; *Albany Argus*, 26 Jan., 1813; O'CALLAGHAN, *History of New Netherland*, New York, 1846-48; CHR, Vol. ii.

1. MCCLOSKEY, JOHN CARDINAL.

The first Bishop of Albany was appointed on May 21, 1847; transferred to the See of New York, on May 6, 1864. (Cf. New York.)

2. CONROY, JOHN J.

The second Bishop of Albany was born in June, 1819, at Clonaslee, Queen's County, Ireland, and came to this country at the age of twelve. He pursued his classical studies at Montreal, and studied theology at Mount Saint Mary's, Emmitsburg, and St. Joseph's, Fordham. He was ordained to the priesthood on May 21, 1842. After his ordination he held important positions in the Diocese of Albany and in 1857 he was made Vicar-General. He remained in this position until his appointment as Bishop of Albany on July 7, 1865, and was consecrated by Archbishop McCloskey on October 15, 1863. When he resigned his see on October 17, 1877, he was transferred to the titular see of Curium and made his residence in New York City, where he died on November 20, 1895.

REUSS, *op. cit.*, p. 27; SHEA, *Hierarchy*, etc., p. 179; CUB, Vol. vii, p. 128; MCSWEENY, *op. cit.*, Vol. i, pp. 407-411, 545; Vol. ii, p. 180; ACHS *Researches*, Vol. vii, p. 101; FARLEY, *Life of John Cardinal McCloskey*, pp. 223-224, 245, 261, 328; CHR, Vol. ii, p. 141.

3. MCNEIRNY, FRANCIS.

Bishop McNeirny was born on April 25, 1828, in New York City and his early education was begun in the school of Mr. Sparrow, a Catholic teacher. He studied in Montreal and was ordained to the priesthood on August 7, 1854, in New York City; in 1857 was made chancellor of the Diocese. He was appointed Bishop of Rhesina and Coadjutor to Bishop Conroy, on December 22, 1871, and was consecrated in New York City by Archbishop Mc-Closkey on April 21, 1872. Upon the resignation of Bishop Conroy on October 16, 1877, he became third Bishop of Albany and administered the see until his death in that city on January 2, 1894.

REUSS, *op. cit.*, p. 73; SHEA, *Hierarchy*, etc., p. 180; AER, Vol. xxi, p. 278; CHR, Vol. ii, p. 141.

4. BURKE, THOMAS M. A.

Bishop Burke was born in Utica, New York, on January 10, 1840, and was ordained to the priesthood on June 30, 1864, at St. Mary's Seminary, Baltimore, Maryland. He served as Rector of St. Joseph's Church, Albany, until his appointment as Bishop of the Diocese on May 15, 1894. He was consecrated on July 1, 1894, by Archbishop Corrigan, of New York City. He died at Albany on January 10, 1915.

REUSS, *op. cit.*, p. 19; CHR, Vol. ii, p. 141; there was published an official *Souvenir of Consecration* in 1894; HERBERMANN, *op. cit.*, pp. 261, 263, 308; USCHS *Records and Studies*, Vol. viii, p. 258.

5. CUSACK, THOMAS F.

The fifth Bishop of Albany was born in New York City on February 22, 1862. He was educated at St. Francis Xavier College, New York City, and at the Troy Theological Seminary, and was ordained to the priesthood on May 30, 1885. Before his appointment as Auxiliary Bishop of New York, he was Superior of the Diocesan Mission Band from 1897 to 1904. On March 11, 1904, he was made titular Bishop of Theniscyra, and was consecrated by Archbishop Farley on April 25, 1904. He was transferred to the vacant See of Albany on July 5, 1915, and ruled the diocese until his death on July 12, 1918.

CHR, Vol. ii, p. 141; cf. *Catholic News*, New York, for July 20, 1918.

6. GIBBONS, EDMUND F.

The present Bishop of Albany was born at White Plains, New York, on September 16, 1868. He made his ecclesiastical studies at Niagara University, and at the American College, Rome. On May 27, 1893, he was ordained to the priesthood in the Basilica of St. John Lateran by Cardinal Caprocchi. After his ordination, he served as secretary to Bishop Ryan of Buffalo and before his appointment as Bishop, March 10, 1919, he served as pastor in the Diocese of Buffalo from 1902 to the time of his consecration in the new cathedral in Buffalo, March 25, 1919, by the Most Reverend John Bonzano, D.D., Archbishop of Melitene, Apostolic Delegate.

III. Diocese of Buffalo (1847)

The Diocese of Buffalo was erected by Pius IX on April 23, 1847, and the Very Reverend John Timon was consecrated as first Bishop October 17, 1847.

The original limits of the Diocese of Buffalo included sixteen counties in the western part of the State of New York. In 1868 several counties were abscinded, and at present it comprises the counties of Erie, Niagara, Genesee, Orleans, Chautauqua, Wyoming, Cattaragus and Allegany, in the State of New York; an area of 6,357 square miles.

BAYLEY, *History of the Church in New York*, New York, 1870; TIMON, *Missions in Western New York*, Buffalo, 1862; DONOHUE, *History of the Catholic Church in Western New York*, Buffalo, 1904; IDEM. *The Iroquois and the Jesuits*, Buffalo, 1895; *Relations des Jesuites*, Quebec, 1858; MARGRY, *Decouvertes*, Paris, 1893; HENNEPIN, *Nouvelle Decouverte*, Utrecht, 1678; CRONIN, *Life and Times of Bishop Ryan*, Buffalo, 1893; *The Historical Writings of the late Orsamus H. Marshall*, Albany, 1887; *The Sentinel*, files, Buffalo; maps by GENERAL JAMES CLARKE, Auburn; Bishop Timon's diary and unpublished letters.

1. TIMON, JOHN, C. M.

The first Bishop of Buffalo was born in Conewago, Pennsylvania, on February 12, 1797. In April, 1823, he entered the Lazarist Seminary of St. Mary's at the Barrens and later was received into the Lazarist Congregation. He was ordained to the priesthood in 1825. Ten years after,

he was appointed Visitor of his Congregation in the United
States. In April, 1840, he was selected to be Prefect-
Apostolic of Texas, but sent the Reverend Mr. Odin as his
representative. The Bulls appointing him Bishop of Buffalo
were received on October 5, 1847, and he was consecrated
by Bishop Hughes in New York City on October 17, 1874.
He died in Buffalo on April 16, 1867.

REUSS, *op. cit.*, p. 103; CLARKE, *op. cit.*, Vol. ii, p. 337 seq.; SHEA,
Hierarchy, p. 189 seq.; DEUTHER, (C. G.), *Life and Times of the
Right Reverend John Timon*, Buffalo, 1870; CE, Vol. iii, p. 39; CHR,
Vol. ii, p. 142; cf. *Index* to the ACHS *Researches*, p. 298.

2. RYAN, STEPHEN.

The second Bishop of Buffalo was born at Almonte,
Ontario, on January 11, 1825. His family moved to Pennsylvania, where at the age of fifteen the future Bishop
was sent to St. Charles Seminary, at Philadelphia. On
May 5, 1844, he entered the Lazarist Congregation at Cape
Girardeau, Missouri, and on June 24, 1849, he was ordained
to the priesthood by Archbishop Kenrick at St. Louis. In
1857 he was appointed Visitor of the Congregation in the
United States and held this position until his nomination
as Bishop of Buffalo. He was consecrated in the Cathedral
at Buffalo on April 10, by Cardinal McCloskey. He died
at Buffalo on April 10, 1896.

REUSS, *op. cit.*, p. 79; SHEA, *Hierarchy*, p. 193; CRONIN, *Life
and Times of Bishop Ryan*, Buffalo, 1893; CE, Vol. iii, p. 39; CHR,
Vol. iii, p. 142; ACHS *Researches*, Vol. viii, p. 44; Vol. xxi, p. 125.

3. QUIGLEY, JAMES E.

Consecrated Bishop on February 24, 1897; transferred to the see of Chicago on February 19, 1903.
(Cf. Chicago.)

4. COLTON, CHARLES H.

Bishop Colton was born in New York City on October 15, 1848, and graduated from St. Francis Xavier
College in 1872. He completed his studies at the Seminary
in Troy, New York, and was ordained to the priesthood
on June 10, 1876. He served as chancellor of the Arch-

diocese before his appointment to the See of Buffalo on June 10, 1903. He was consecrated on August 24, 1903, and died at Buffalo on May 10, 1915.

CHR, Vol. ii, p. 142; CE, Vol. iii, p. 39; DONOHUE, *History of the Catholic Church in Western New York,* Buffalo, 1904; files of *The Echo,* and of the *Catholic Union and Times* of Buffalo, for May, 1915; TIMON, *Missions in Western New York,* Buffalo, 1862; CRONIN, *Life and Times of Bishop Ryan,* Buffalo, 1893; necrology in the USCHS *Records and Studies,* Vol. viii, p. 258.

Among his works are: *Seedlings,* Buffalo, 1906; *My Trip to Rome and the Holy Land,* Buffalo, 1906; *Buds and Blossoms,* Buffalo, 1910.

5. DOUGHERTY, DENNIS CARDINAL.

Transferred to the See of Buffalo from the Diocese of Jaro, Philippine Islands, on December 6, 1915, and was promoted to the See of Philadelphia on May 1, 1918.

(Cf. Philadelphia.)

6. TURNER, WILLIAM.

The present Bishop of Buffalo was born at Kilmallock, Ireland, on April 13, 1871. He received his education at Mungret College, Limerick, at the Royal University of his native land, and at Propaganda, Rome. He was ordained to the priesthood on August 13, 1893, and the following year he began his career as professor in St. Paul's Seminary. He was professor of philosophy at the Catholic University of America when appointed to the See of Buffalo on February 1, 1919. He was consecrated by Cardinal Gibbons at the Franciscan Monastery, Washington, D. C., on March 30, 1919.

Among his important works are: *History of Philosophy,* Boston, 1903, and *Lessons in Logic,* Washington, D. C., 1911.

IV. Diocese of Brooklyn (1853)

Pius IX erected the Diocese of Brooklyn on July 29, 1853, and the Rt. Rev. John Loughlin was consecrated as its first Bishop on October 30, 1853.

This Diocese comprises the territory assigned to it at the time of its erection, namely, Long Island; an area of 1,007 square miles.

MITCHELL, *Golden Jubilee of Bishop Loughlin*, Brooklyn, 1891; STILES, *History of Brooklyn*, Brooklyn, 1867; (1870); *The Eagle and Brooklyn*, Brooklyn, 1893; *United States Catholic Historical Magazine*, New York, 1890-91; *United States Catholic Historical Society of Historical Records*, New York, 1900; Vol. ii, part I; SHEA, *History of the Catholic Church in the United States*, New York, 1894; MULRENAN, *A Brief Sketch of the Catholic Church in Long Island*, New York, 1871; O'CALLAGHAN, *History of New Netherlands*, New York, 1846-48; *Long Island Star*, files, Brooklyn, 1822, 1823, 1825; CHR, Vol. ii, p. 142.

1. LOUGHLIN, JOHN.

The first Bishop of Brooklyn was born in County Down, Ireland, on February 20, 1817, and at the age of six his parents took him to the United States, settling at Albany, New York. His theological course was made at Mount Saint Mary's, Emmitsburg, after which he was ordained to the priesthood on October 1, 1840. He was appointed Vicar-General of the Archdiocese of New York, and on October 30, 1853, he was consecrated first Bishop of Brooklyn, by Archbishop Cajetan Bedini. He died at Brooklyn, New York, on December 29, 1891.

REUSS, *op. cit.*, p. 65; SHEA, *Hierarchy*, etc., p. 187; cf. *The Diocese of Brooklyn*, by M. VALLETTE, in the USCHS, Vol. 3, 1890, pp. 287-301, pp. 412-421; ACHS *Researches*, Vol. xv, p. 15; Vol. xxiii, p. 93; MITCHELL, *Golden Jubilee of the Rt. Rev. John Loughlin*, Brooklyn, 1891.

2. MCDONNELL, CHARLES.

Bishop McDonnell was born in New York City on February 1, 1854, and received his early education in the parochial schools of that city. He left for Rome in 1872 to study at the American College and was ordained to the priesthood on May 19, 1878. Upon his return to New York, he was engaged in parish work for the next five years, after which he served as secretary to Cardinal McCloskey and chancellor of the Archdiocese under Archbishop Corrigan. He was appointed Bishop of Brooklyn on March 11, 1892, and was consecrated by Archbishop Corrigan in New York City on April 15, 1892. He died at Brooklyn, on August 8, 1921.

REUSS, *op. cit.*, p. 70; CHR, Vol. ii, p. 142; *News Bulletins* of the NCWC for August, 1921.

3. MOLLOY, THOMAS E.

The present Bishop of Brooklyn was born at Nashua, New Hampshire, on September 4, 1885. He completed his ecclesiastical studies at the North American College in Rome and was ordained to the priesthood in that city on September 19, 1908. He was consecrated titular Bishop of Lori by Bishop McDonnell in the Pro-Cathedral of St. James, at Brooklyn, on October 3, 1920, and served as the Auxiliary until the death of the latter on August 8, 1921. He was appointed his successor on November 21, 1921.

V. Diocese of Newark (1853)

In 1853 Pius IX detached the eastern part of New Jersey from the Diocese of New York and the western part of the state from the Diocese of Philadelphia and erected the Diocese of Newark. The Rt. Rev. James Bayley was consecrated as its first Bishop on October 30, 1853.

The original limits of the Diocese of Newark were the State of New Jersey. In 1881, however, the Diocese of Trenton was erected, and Newark now embraces the counties in the northern part of the state; an area of 1,699 square miles.

FLYNN, *The Catholic Church in New Jersey*, Morristown, 1904; SHEA, *History of the Catholic Church in the United States*, New York, 1889-92; BAYLEY, *A Brief Sketch of the Early History of the Catholic Church on the Island of New York*, New York, 1853; GRIFFIN, *Catholics in the American Revolution*, I, Ridley Park, Pa., 1907; TANGUAY, *Documents relating to the Colonial History of New Jersey*, Newark, 1880; *History of the Catholic Church in Paterson, N. J.*, Patterson, 1883; *History of the City of Elizabeth*, Elizabeth, 1899; *Freeman's Journal* and *Truth Teller*, New York, files; *The Catholic Directory*, 1850-1910; CHR, Vol. ii, p. 143.

1. BAYLEY, JAMES R.

The first Bishop of Newark was consecrated October 30, 1853, and was promoted to the See of Baltimore on July 30, 1872.

(Cf. Baltimore.)

2. CORRIGAN, MICHAEL F.

Consecrated second Bishop of Newark on May 4, 1873, and was transferred to the See of New York on October 10, 1885.
(Cf. New York.)

3. WIGGER, W. M.

Bishop Wigger was born in New York City on December 9, 1841, and received his education at Seton Hall College and at Brignole-Sale, Genoa, Italy. He was ordained to the priesthood on June 10, 1865, and was consecrated on October 18, 1881, by Archbishop Corrigan. He died in Newark on January 5, 1901.

REUSS, *op. cit.*, p. 109; SHEA,. *Hierarchy*, p. 324; CHR, Vol. ii, p. 143; HERBERMANN, *Rt. Rev. Winaud M. Wigger, Third Bishop of Newark* in the USCHS *Records*, Vol. ii, p. 292.

4. O'CONNOR, JOHN JOSEPH.

The present Bishop of Newark was born in that city on June 11, 1855. He made his college course at Seton Hall and in 1873 he was sent to the American College at Rome, where he spent the next four years. Afterwards he went to Louvain for a year and was ordained to the priesthood on December 22, 1857. Upon his return to this country he was appointed professor at Seton Hall College and subsequently became Director of the Institution—a position he held for eighteen years. He was Vicar-General of the Diocese of Newark at the time of his appointment as successor to Bishop Wigger. He was consecrated on July 25, 1901, by Archbishop Corrigan of New York.

VI. Diocese of Rochester (1868)

The Diocese of Rochester was erected by Pope Pius IX on March 3, 1868, and the Rt. Rev. Bernard J. McQuaid was consecrated as first Bishop on July 12, 1868.

The area embraced by the Diocese of Rochester extends to the counties of Monroe, Livingston, Wayne, Ontario, Seneca, Yates, Steuben, Cheming, Tioga, Schuyler and

Tompkins in the State of New York, an area of 7,081 square miles.

Conc. Balt. Plen. II acta et decreta; Acta S. Sedis, III; Leonis XIII Acta xvi, xxi; Catholic Directory, 1868-1911; MCQUAID, *Diaries* (fragmentary) ; IDEM, *Pastorals* in *Annual College for Ecclesiastical Students,* 1871-1911; IDEM, *Pastoral,* Jubilee, 1875; IDEM, *Pastoral,* Visitation, 1878; IDEM, *Our American Seminaries in American Ecclesiastical Review,* May, 1897, reprint in SMITH, *The Training of a Priest,* pp. xxi-xxxix; IDEM, *The Training of a Seminary Professor* in SMITH, *op. cit.,* pp. 327-335; IDEM, *Christian Free Schools,* 1892, a reprint of lectures; IDEM, *Religion in Schools in North American Review,* April, 1881; IDEM, *Religious Teaching in Schools* in *Forum,* December, 1889; *Reports of Conferences held by parochial teachers,* 1904-10; ZWIERLEIN, *Catholic Beginnings in the Diocese of Rochester* in the CHR, Vol. v, pp. 42-54, pp. 311-352.

1. MCQUAID, BERNARD J.

The first Bishop of Rochester was born in New York City on December 15, 1823, and received his early education in the schools of that city. His theological training was received at Saint Joseph's Theological Seminary, Fordham, New York, and on January 16, 1848, he was ordained to the priesthood. His first appointment was to the pastorate of the Church of Saint Vincent de Paul at Madison, New Jersey. When Seton Hall College was opened in 1856 he was appointed President of that Institution, and ten years later he became Vicar-General of the Diocese of Newark. His appointment as Bishop of Rochester was received on March 3, 1868, and on July 12, 1868, he was consecrated in New York City by Archbishop McCloskey. His death occurred at Rochester on January 18, 1909.

REUSS, *op. cit.,* p. 74; SHEA, *Hierarchy,* etc., p. 357; AER, Vol. xvi, p. 461, Vol. xvii, p. 101, Vol. xx, p. 72, Vol. xxv, p. 69; CHR, Vol. i, pp. 282-298; *Catholic beginnings in the Diocese of Rochester,* by Zwierlein; *ibid.,* Vol. v, pp. 42-54; pp. 311-352; *Bishop McQuaid of Rochester* by Zwierlein; CE, Vol. ix, pp. 507-508.

2. HICKEY, THOMAS F.

The present Bishop of Rochester was born in 1861, and made his theological studies at the Seminary of Saint John's, Fordham, and at Troy, New York. He was ordained to the priesthood on March 25, 1884, and before his appointment as Coadjutor of Rochester on February 18, 1905, he held various important pastorates. He was consecrated by his predecessor in the See on May 24, 1905, and succeeded to the Diocese of Rochester on January 18, 1909.

VII. The Diocese of Ogdensburg (1872)

Pope Pius IX erected the Diocese of Ogdensburg on February 15, 1872, and the consecration of the first Bishop, the Rt. Rev. Edgar W. Wadhams, took place on May 5, 1872. When erected, as at present, the Diocese comprised that part of Herkimer and Hamilton counties north of the northern line of the townships of Ohio and Russia, with the entire counties of Lewis, Jefferson, St. Lawrence, Franklin, Clinton and Essex in the State of New York, an area of 12,036 square miles.

SHEA, *History of the Catholic Church in the United States*, New York, 1894; WALWORTH, *Reminiscences of Bishop Wadhams*, New York, 1893; SMITH, *History of the Diocese of Ogdensburg*, New York, 1885; *Illustrated History of the Catholic Church in America*, ed. BEGNI, New York. 1910; CURTIS, *St. Lawrence County*, Syracuse, 1894; CHR, Vol. ii, p. 144.

1. WADHAMS, EDGAR P.

He was born on May 17, 1817, at Lewes, Essex County, New York City. He became a convert to the Faith in June, 1846. He began his theological studies anew at Saint Mary's, Baltimore, and was ordained to the priesthood at Albany, New York, on January 15, 1850. He was acting as Rector of the Cathedral and Vicar-General of the Diocese when he was selected to be the first Bishop of Ogdensburg. He was consecrated in Albany by Archbishop McCloskey of New York on May 5, 1872. He died at Ogdenburg on December 5, 1891.

REUSS, *op. cit.*, p. 107; SHEA, *Hierarchy*, pp. 328-329; SMITH, *History of Diocese of Ogdensburg, passim;* CHR, Vol. ii, p. 144.

1. GABRIELS, HENRY.

Bishop Gabriels was born at Wennegem-Lede, Belgium, on October 6, 1838. He graduated from Louvain when a priest (his ordination having taken place in 1861) and, later, he was invited to come to New York and teach in the Seminary at Troy, where he remained for nearly seven years. He was appointed Bishop of Ogdensburg on December 20, 1891, and was consecrated at Albany on May 5, 1892, by Archbishop Corrigan. His death occurred at Ogdensburg on April 23, 1921.

REUSS, *op. cit.*, p. 45; CHR, Vol. ii, p. 144; cf. *Life of Bishop Gabriels* in the USCHS *Monograph Series* for 1905; Bishop Gabriels wrote an *Historical Sketch of Saint Joseph's Provincial Seminary* at Troy, New York, which was published in the *Monograph Series* of the USCHS, New York, 1905.

3. CONROY, JOSEPH H.

The present Bishop of Ogdensburg was born at Watertown, New York, in 1858. He received his theological training at the Grand Seminary, Montreal, and Saint Joseph's Seminary, Troy, New York. He was ordained to the priesthood on June 11, 1881, and was made Vicar-General in March, 1901; a Domestic Prelate in October, 1905, and on March 25, 1912, was appointed titular Bishop of Arindela and Auxiliary Bishop of Ogdensburg. He was consecrated in Saint Mary's Cathedral by Cardinal Farley on May 1, 1912, and upon the death of Bishop Gabriels, after an interim of a few months, he was appointed third Bishop of Ogdensburg on November 21, 1921.

VIII. Diocese of Trenton (1881)

Pope Leo XIII erected the See of Trenton on July 15, 1881, and the Rt. Rev. Michael O'Farrell was consecrated as first Bishop on November 1, 1891. In 1853 it became part of the newly erected Diocese of Newark and remained under the Bishop of that See until January 15, 1881, when it was erected into a separate diocese.

The diocese comprises fourteen counties in the State of New Jersey, namely: Atlantic, Burlington, Camden, Cape May, Cumberland, Gloucester, Hunterdon, Mercer, Middlesex, Monmouth, Ocean, Salem, Somerset and Warren, an area of 5,756 square miles.

FLYNN, *The Catholic Church in New Jersey*, Morristown, 1904; LEAHY, *The Diocese of Trenton*, Princeton, 1907; McFAUL, *Memorial of the Rt. Rev. Michael J. O'Farrell*; FOX, *A Century of Catholicity in Trenton, N. J.*; *The Catholic Directory*, 1852, 1882, 1911; CHR, Vol. ii, p. 144.

1. O'FARRELL, MICHAEL J.

The first Bishop of Trenton was born at Limerick, Ireland, on December 2, 1832. He completed his classics and philosophy at All Hallows College, Dublin, after which he went to Saint Sulpice in Paris for his theology. Later he joined the Sulpicians and was ordained to the priesthood in his native city on August 18, 1855. After his career as professor in the Grand Seminary, Montreal, he left the Society and was incardinated in the Diocese of New York. He was appointed to the new See of Trenton and was consecrated in New York City on November 1, 1881, by Cardinal McCloskey. He died on April 2, 1894, at Trenton, New Jersey.

REUSS, *op. cit.*, p. 82; SHEA, *Hierarchy*, p. 381; CHR, Vol. ii, p. 145.

2. MCFAUL, JAMES A.

The second Bishop of Trenton was born at Larne, in County Antrim, Ireland, on June 6, 1850, and was taken to the United States by his parents when only a few months old. He made his college course at Saint Vincent's College, Beatty, Pennsylvania, and at Saint Francis Xavier's, New York City. He was ordained to the priesthood on May 26, 1877, after completing his theological course at Seton Hall. Under Bishop O'Connor he became chancellor and Vicar-General of the Diocese and at his death was chosen to be administrator during the interim. He was elevated to the episcopate on July 20, 1894, and was consecrated at Trenton by Archbishop Corrigan on October 18, 1894. He died at Trenton on June 16, 1917.

AER, Vol. xxiii, p. 572; Vol. xxxii, p. 302; Vol. xxxviii, p. 444; *Pastoral Letters, Addresses and other Writings of Bishop McFaul*, New York, 1916; CHR, Vol. i, p. 145.

3. WALSH, THOMAS J.

The present Bishop of Trenton was born at Parkers Landing, Pennsylvania, on December 6, 1875. He received his education at Saint Bonaventure's College, Allegheny, and in Rome, Italy. He was ordained to the priesthood on

January 27, 1900. Upon his return to the United States he served as an assistant at the Cathedral at Buffalo, and later became secretary and chancellor under Bishop Colton. He was consecrated Bishop on July 25, 1918.

XI. Diocese of Syracuse (1886)

On November 20, 1886, Pope Leo XIII erected the Diocese of Syracuse, with the Rt. Rev. Patrick A. Ludden as the first Bishop.

The Diocese of Syracuse comprises the seven counties of Broome, Chenango, Cartland, Madison, Oneida, Onondaga and Oswego in Central New York; an area of 5,629 square miles.

MARTIN, *Life of Father Jogues*, New York, 1896; DONGAN, *Reports* in *Documents relating to the Colonial History of New York City*. III, Albany, 1853; ed. THWAITES, *Jesuit Relations*, Cleveland, 1896-1901); O'CALLAGHAN, *Documentary History of the State of New York*, Albany, 1849-51; SHEA, *History of the Catholic Church in the United States*, New York, 1886-92; DONOHUE, *The Iroquois and the Jesuits*, Buffalo, 1895; BRUCE, *Memorial History of the City of Syracuse*, Syracuse, 1891; BANNON, *Pioneer Irish of Onondaga*, Syracuse, 1911; COOKINGHAM, *History of Oneida County*, Utica, 1912; BUGG, *Memoirs of Utica*, Utica, 1884; CAMPBELL, *Pioneer Priests of North America*, New York, 1908; HEWITT, *History of the Diocese of Syracuse*, Syracuse, 1909; LYNCH, *A Page of Church History in New York*, Utica, 1903; *United States Catholic Historical Society, Historical Records and Studies*, New York, April, 1909-February, 1911; FARLEY, *History of St. Patrick's Cathedral*, New York, 1908; ZWIERLEIN, *Religion in New Netherlands*, Rochester, 1910; BAYLEY, *A Brief Sketch of the Early History of the Catholic Church in the Island of New York*, New York, 1870; GRIFFIS, *The Story of New Netherland*, New York, 1909; DIEFENDOFF, *The Historic Mohawk*, New York, 1910; CHR, Vol. ii, p. 145.

1. LUDDEN, PATRICK A.

The first Bishop of Syracuse was born near Castle, County Mayo, Ireland, on February 4, 1836. He was ordained to the priesthood on May 21, 1864, in the Grand Seminary, Montreal. After his ordination he served as rector of the Church of the Immaculate Conception in Albany. Under Bishops Conroy and McNeirny, respectively, he held the position of Vicar-General and was appointed Bishop of Syracuse on December 14, 1886. On May 1, 1887, he was consecrated by Archbishop Corrigan of New York. He died at Syracuse on August 6, 1912.

REUSS, *op. cit.*, p. 65; HEWITT, *History of the Diocese of Syracuse*, p. 25, Syracuse, 1909; ACHS *Researches*, Vol. xxviii, 130, on Knownothings; CHR, Vol. ii, p. 145; USCHS *Records and Studies*, Vol. vii, p. 221.

2. GRIMES, JOHN.
The present Bishop of Syracuse was born at Limerick, Ireland, on December 18, 1852. He made his theological course at Montreal and was ordained to the priesthood on February 19, 1882. Appointed titular Bishop of Imeria and Coadjutor to Bishop Ludden of Syracuse on February 1, 1909, he was consecrated by Archbishop Farley on May 16, 1909. He succeeded to the See of Syracuse on August 6, 1912.

CHAPTER VI

THE PROVINCE OF CINCINNATI (1850)

The Archdiocese of Cincinnati was erected by Pius IX on July 19, 1850, and the Right Reverend John B. Purcell, D. D., was appointed as first Archbishop. The Province, when erected, had as suffragan sees Bardstown-Louisville (1808-1841), Detroit (1833), Vincennes-Indianapolis (1834-1898), and Cleveland (1847). At present the Province includes the States of Ohio, Indiana, Kentucky, Tennessee and lower Michigan, with ten suffragan sees: Louisville (1841), Detroit (1883), Indianapolis (1834-1898), Nashville (1837), Cleveland (1847), Covington (1853), Fort Wayne (1857), Columbus (1868), Grand Rapids (1882), and Toledo (1910).

SHEA, *History of the Catholic Church in the United States*, New York, 1889-1892; KELLY and KIRWIN, *History of Mt. St. Mary's Seminary of the West*, Cincinnati, 1894; HOUCK, *A History of Catholicity in Northern Ohio*, Cleveland, 1902; *The Catholic Telegraph*, Cincinnati, files; LAMOTT, *History of the Archdiocese of Cincinnati, 1821-1921*, New York, 1921, contains a complete bibliography of this Province, and the various suffragan sees; McCANN (*Sister M. Agnes*), *The History of Mother Seton's Daughters, the Sisters of Charity of Cincinnati, Ohio*, 2 Vols., New York, 1917; also *Archbishop Purcell and the Archdiocese of Cincinnati*, Washington, D. C., 1918; O'DANIEL, *Life of the Right Reverend Edward D. Fenwick, O. P.*, Washington, D. C., 1920, exceptionally good bibliography; CHR, Vol. ii, p. 283.

I. Diocese of Cincinnati (1821)

The Diocese of Cincinnati was erected by Pius VIII on June 19, 1821, and the Rt. Rev. Edward Dominic Fenwick, O. P., was consecrated as its first Bishop on January 13, 1822.

The original limits of the Diocese included the State of Ohio and the old northwest Territory. At present it comprises that part of the State of Ohio south of 40' 41", being the counties south of the northern line of Mercer, Anglaize, Hardin, all west of the eastern line of Marion, Union and Madison counties, and all west of the Scioto River to the Ohio River; an area of 12,043 square miles.

1. FENWICK, EDWARD DOMINIC, O. P.

The founder of the Dominican Order in the United States and the first Bishop of Cincinnati was born in Saint Mary's County, Maryland, on August 16, 1768. At the age of sixteen he was sent to the Dominican College at Bornheim in Flanders, and upon the completion of his college course he entered the Dominican Order there on September 4, 1788. He was ordained to the priesthood on February 23, 1793, and spent the early years of his priestly life in Europe as teacher. Appointed Superior of the first band of Dominicans to come to the United States, he arrived at Norfolk in November, 1804. He visited his relatives in Maryland and also Bishop Carroll, who assigned to him and his Order the field of Kentucky as the scene of future labor. The next fourteen years of his life he spent in the missionary fields of what are now the States of Ohio and Kentucky. On January 13, 1822, he was consecrated first Bishop of Cincinnati by the Rt. Rev. Benedict J. Flaget in Saint Rose's Chapel, Washington County, Kentucky. While on an episcopal visit through Ohio he was stricken with cholera and died at Wooster, Ohio, on September 26, 1832.

REUSS, *op. cit.*, p. 41; SHEA, *Hierarchy*, etc., pp. 103-105; CLARKE, *op. cit.*, Vol. i, pp. 328-352; *Researches*, Vol. iii, p. 27, Vol. v, p. 390, Vol. ix, p. 160, Vol. xi, pp. 113, 123; HERBERMANN, *op. cit.*, p. 184; CHR, Vol. ii, pp. 20, 26, 27, 65-68, 312-317; McCANN, *op. cit.*, Vol. i, pp. 146-194 *passim; cf. An Early Pastoral Letter*, 1827, in CHR, Vol. i, pp. 65-68; O'DANIEL, *Right Reverend Edward Dominic Fenwick, passim,* Washington. D. C., 1920; LAMOTT, *History of the Archdiocese of Cincinnati*, 1821-1921, *passim*, New York, 1921.

2. PURCELL, JOHN BAPTIST.

The first Archbishop of Cincinnati was born at Mallow, Ireland, on February 26, 1800, and made his classical studies there. Coming to the United States, he entered Mount Saint Mary's at Emmitsburg on June 20, 1820, to study for the priesthood. He was ordained in Paris on May 20, 1826, and the following year he returned to the United States and was assigned to Mount Saint Mary's as professor and later was selected to be President of this institution. He was serving in that capacity when appointed to the vacant See of Cincinnati, and was consecrated in Baltimore by Archbishop Whitfield on October 13, 1833. He was elevated to the archiepiscopate on July 19, 1850, and he died at the Ursuline Convent in Brown County, Ohio, on July 4, 1883.

REUSS, *op. cit.*, pp. 90-91; CLARKE, Vol. iii, p. 196 seq.; SHEA, *Hierarchy*, p. 105 seq.; MCCANN, *Archbishop Purcell and the Archdiocese of Cincinnati*, Washington, D. C., 1918; MCCANN, *The Most Reverend John Baptist Purcell, D.D., Archbishop of Cincinnati, 1800-1883*, an article in the *Catholic Historical Review*, Vol. vi, p. 172 seq.; LAMOTT, *op. cit., passim;* KELLY and KIRWIN, *op. cit.;* CHR, Vol. ii, pp. 283-284.

3. ELDER, WILLIAM H.

Archbishop Elder was born in Baltimore, Maryland, on March 22, 1819, and desiring to become a priest he entered Mount Saint Mary's at Emmitsburg in 1831. Eleven years later he was sent to Rome to complete his theology at the Urban College, where he received the Doctorate of Divinity. His ordination to the priesthood took place in Rome on March 29, 1846, and upon his return to the United States he was appointed a professor at Mount Saint Mary's, a position he held until his nomination as Bishop of Natchez. Archbishop F. P. Kenvick consecrated him in Baltimore on May 3, 1857. On January 30, 1880, he was transferred to the See of Cincinnati as titular Archbishop of Avara and Coadjutor to Archbishop Purcell. He succeeded to the See on July 4, 1883, and died in Cincinnati on October 31, 1904.

REUSS, *op. cit.*, p. 38; SHEA, *Hierarchy*, etc., pp. 109-111; *Character Glimpses of Archbishop Elder*, Cincinnati, 1911; CE, Vol. v, p. 373; *Archbishop Elder's Jubilee Album*, Cincinnati, 1896; *Catholic Telegraph*, files for October, 1904; MCSWEENY, *op. cit.*, Vol. i, pp. 29, 36, 78, 366-372, 419-438, Vol. ii, pp. 63, 127. 180-182, 197-213, 223-226, 310; LAMOTT, *op. cit., passim.*

4. MOELLER, HENRY.

The present Archbishop of Cincinnati was born in that city on December 11, 1849. He studied philosophy and theology at the American College in Rome and was ordained to the priesthood on June 10, 1876. He served as pastor of St. Patrick's Church, Bellefontaine, Ohio; professor at Mount Saint Mary's of the West and chancellor of the Archdiocese before his appointment to the See of Columbus.

He was consecrated by Archbishop Elder on August 25, 1900. He was transferred to Cincinnati as Coadjutor to Archbishop Elder and titular Archbishop of Aeropolis on April 27, 1903. He succeeded to the see on October 31, 1904.

II. Diocese of Bardstown-Louisville (1808-1841)

The Diocese of Bardstown, one of the four original suffragan sees of the Metropolitan See of Baltimore, was erected by Pius VII on April 8, 1808, and the Rt. Rev. Benedict J. Flaget, D.D., was consecrated as its first Bishop on November 4, 1810. In 1841, the diocesan seat was transferred to Louisville.

Originally, the Diocese included the territory embraced by the States of Kentucky, Ohio, Tennessee and the old Northwest Territory. At present, its territorial limits comprise that part of Kentucky lying west of Carroll, Owen, Franklin, Woodford, Jessamine, Garrard, Rock Castle, Laurel and Whitley counties; an area of 22,714 square miles.

M. J. SPALDING, *Life, Times and Character of Benedict Joseph Flaget*, Louisville, 1852; IDEM, *Sketches of the Early Catholic Missions in Kentucky*, 1787-1827, Louisville, 1846; SHEA, *History of Catholic Church in the United States*, New York, 1886-93; J. L. SPALDING, *Life of Archbishop Spalding*, New York, 1873; WEBB, *Centenary of Catholicity in Kentucky*, Louisville, 1884; DEPPEN, *Louisville Guide*, Louisville, 1887; *Catholic Orphans' Souvenir*, Louisville, 1901; files of *Catholic Advocate, Catholic Guardian* and *Catholic Record;* CHR, Vol. ii, p. 284.

1. FLAGET, BENEDICT J.

Bishop Flaget was born at Coutournat, near Billom, Auvergne, France, on November 7, 1763. His early training was received from his uncle, Canon Flaget, and at seventeen he went to the Sulpician Seminary of Clermont to study philosophy and theology. On November 1, 1783, he entered the Society of Saint Sulpice, and was ordained to the priesthood in 1787 at Issy. He came to the United States on March 29, 1792. Shortly afterward Bishop Carroll sent him to the west, but later he was recalled to become professor at Georgetown College. Appointed Bishop of Bardstown on April 8, 1808, he was consecrated by Arch-

bishop Carroll on November 4, 1810. He died in Louisville
on February 11, 1850.

REUSS, *op. cit.*, pp. 43-44; SHEA, *Hierarchy*, etc., pp. 277-280;
CLARKE, *op. cit.*, Vol. i, pp. 144-163; *Researches*, Vols. v, xxvi *passim*,
for which consult *Index; Spalding, Sketches of the Life of Rt. Rev.
Benedict Joseph Flaget*, etc., Louisville, 1852; SPALDING, *Sketches
of Kentucky*, Louisville, 1844, HOWLETT in ACHS *Records*, Vol. xxix,
pp. 37-60 (*Bishop Flaget's Diary*); MAES, *Life of Nerinckx, passim*,
Cincinnati, 1880; *I* CHR, Vol. i, pp. 315-319; Vol. iii, pp. 5-20,
passim; CE, Vol. vi, pp. 93-94; MCCANN, *op. cit.*, Vol. i, pp. 23-41,
157-158, 215, 216, 277, 290; MCSWÉENY, *op. cit.*, Vol. i, pp. 10, 16,
48, 50, 71, 227, 243, 293, 321-327; *Monseigneur Flaget, Eveque de
Bardstown et Louisville, sa Vie, son Esprit, et ses Vertus, par le
Pretre qui accompagnait le prelat pendant les voyages qu'il fit en
Europe pour l'oeuvre de la Propagation de la Foi*, Paris, 1851;
*Auszuge aus der Geschichte der Dioecese Louisville: Leben des Hoch.
Bischofs Benedict Joseph Flaget*, Louisville, 1884 (translation of
Spalding's *Life*) ; vide *Bishop Flaget's Report on the Diocese of
Bardstown to Pius VII*, April 10, 1815, in the CHR, Vol. i, pp. 305-310.

2. DAVID, JOHN B.

The second Bishop of Bardstown was born at Nantes,
France, on January 4, 1761. His early educational training
was received in and around Nantes, and after joining the
Sulpicians he was ordained to the priesthood on September
24, 1785. He accompanied Bishop Flaget to this country
in 1792, and served as professor at Georgetown and at
Mount Saint Mary's College, Baltimore. In 1810 or the
following year he went to Bardstown to labor as a missionary; he was consecrated coadjutor-Bishop of that see
by Bishop Flaget on August 15, 1819, and upon the resignation of his superior he was appointed as his successor in
November, 1832. He resigned in May, 1833, but he still
continued to labor in the Diocese until his death, on July
12, 1841.

REUSS, *op. cit.*, p. 31; SHEA, *Hierarchy*, etc., pp. 280-282; CLARKE,
op. cit., Vol. i, pp. 256-267; *Researches*, Vol. xiii, pp. 23 ss. (Account
of his appointment as Bishop of Bardstown and of Bishop Flaget's
resignation and assumption of the See) ; *ibid.*, Vol. xiv, pp. 158-
160; Vol. xix, p. 142; Vol. xxiii, p. 277; Vol. xxviii, p. 343; MAES,
Life of Rev. Charles Nerinckx, passim, Cincinnati, 1880; WEBB,
Centenary of Catholicity in Kentucky, pp. 384-353, Louisville, 1884;
SPALDING, *Sketches of the Life, Times, and Character of the Rt.
Rev. Benedict Joseph Flaget, First Bishop of Louisville*, pp. 242-259,
Louisville, 1853; HERBERMANN, *Sulpicians in the United States*, pp.
161-166. New York, 1917; CHR, Vol. i, p. 312, Vol. ii, pp. 77, 227,
229-230. 284; Vol. iv, pp. 32, 71; Vol. v, pp. 240-241; MCCANN, *His-*

tory of Mother Seton's Daughters, Vol. ii, pp. 105, 120. *A Spiritual Retreat of Eight Days*, by Bishop David, edited with additions by M. T. Spalding, Louisville, 1844.

3. FLAGET, BENEDICT J.

Bishop Flaget was reappointed after the resignation of Bishop David in May, 1833, and became third Bishop of Bardstown. When the diocesan seat was changed to Louisville in 1841, he became Bishop under a new title. He died in that city at the advanced age of eighty-seven on February 11, 1850.

As a second coadjutor, Bishop Flaget had the Rt. Rev. Guy I. Chabrat.

He was born at Chambre, France, on December 27, 1787. He came to Kentucky in 1809 and was ordained to the priesthood on December 25, 1811. He was consecrated as coadjutor of Bardstown by Bishop Flaget on July 20, 1834. From 1835-1839, during the latter's absence, he administered the Diocese. He was stricken with a disease of the eyes, resigned his position in 1847 and retired to his native France where he died, at Mauriac, on November 21, 1868.

REUSS, *op. cit.*, p. 22; CLARKE, *op. cit.*, Vol. iii. pp. 282-288; SHEA, *Hierarchy*, etc., p. 282; DECOURCY-SHEA, *op. cit.*, p. 539; MCCANN, *op. cit.*, Vol. i, p. 262, Vol. ii, pp. 15, 21; MCSWEENY, *op. cit.*, Vol. i, pp. 321-323; WEBB, *op. cit.*, pp. 27, 93. 139, 191, 204, 210, 242, 270, 331, 348, 382. Cf. CHR, Vol. ii, p. 285, Vol. iii, p. 8; Bishop Chabrat was the first priest ordained in Kentucky, cf. CHR, Vol. i, p. 312, note 6.

4. SPALDING, MARTIN J.

Consecrated titular Bishop of Lengone and coadjutor to Bishop Flaget on September 10, 1848. He succeeded to the See of Louisville at the death of Bishop Flaget on February 10, 1850. Transferred to the See of Baltimore on June 11, 1864.

(Cf. Baltimore.)

5. LAVIALLE, PETER J.

Bishop Lavialle was born at Mauriac, France, on July 15, 1819, and came to this country with Bishop Chabrat in 1841. He was ordained to the priesthood on February 2, 1844, at Louisville, and assigned to the Cathedral. In 1856 he was made President of Saint Mary's College and was consecrated Bishop of Louisville by Archbishop Purcell on September 24, 1865. Upon his return from the second Plenary Council of Baltimore in 1866 he was stricken with illness and subsequently retired to Nazareth Academy, Kentucky, where he died on May 11, 1867.

REUSS, *op. cit.*, p. 62-63; SHEA, *Hierarchy, etc.*, p. 283; CLARKE, *op. cit.*, Vol. ii. pp. 586-594; SERRES, *Vie de Mgr. Pierre Joseph Lavialle, Eveque de Louisville*, Aurillac, 1891; WEBB, *Centenary of Catholicity in Kentucky*, pp. 492-495, Louisville, 1884; CHR, Vol. iv, p. 271 (diocesan bibliog.).

6. McCLOSKEY, WILLIAM G.

Bishop McCloskey was born in Brooklyn, New York, on November 10, 1823, and went to Mount Saint Mary's at Emmitsburg in 1835. After his ordination to the priesthood in New York City on October 6, 1852, he acted as assistant pastor to his brother (later Cardinal) for a number of years and on December 1, 1859, was chosen to be the first Rector of the American College at Rome. Cardinal August de Reisach, Archbishop of Munich, consecrated him on May 24, 1868. He died in Louisville on September 17, 1909.

REUSS, *op. cit.*, p. 70; SHEA, *Hierarchy, etc.*, p. 285; BRANN, *History of the American College in Rome*, New York, 1910; CHR, Vol. ii, p. 285.

7. O'DONAGHUE, DENIS.

The present Bishop of Louisville was born in Indiana, on November 30, 1848, and received his education at Saint Meinrad's College and Saint Thomas Seminary at Bardstown. After the completion of his theology at the Grand Seminary, Montreal, he was ordained to the priesthood on September 6, 1874. He served as parish priest in Indianapolis and chancellor of that Diocese before he was appointed titular Bishop of Pomario and Auxiliary of Indianapolis on February 10, 1900. He was consecrated by Bishop Chatard on April 25, 1900, and was transferred to the Diocese of Louisville as eighth Bishop on February 7, 1910.

III. Diocese of Detroit (1833)

On March 8, 1833, Pope Gregory XVI created the Diocese of Detroit and the Rt. Rev. Frederick Résé was consecrated as its first Bishop on October 6, 1833. The Diocese of Detroit embraced originally the State of Michigan and the Northwest Territory. At present it comprises the counties of the lower peninsula of the State of Michigan south of the counties of Ottawa, Kent, Montcalm, Gratiot and Saginaw, and east of the counties of Saginaw and Bay; an area of 18,558 square miles.

SHEA. *History of Catholic Missions among the Indian Tribes of the United States*, New York, 1855; IDEM, *Life and Times of Most Reverend John Carroll*, New York, 1881; IDEM, *History of the Catholic Church in the United States*, New York, 1894; CAMPBELL, *Pioneer Priests of North America*, New York, 1908; United States Catholic Historical Society, *Historical Records and Studies*, New York, November, 1907; Vol. v, part i; DILHET, *op. cit.*, *passim* (splendid account of beginnings of Catholicism in Detroit); FARMER, *History of Detroit and Michigan*, 2 Vols., Detroit, 1889; DECOURCY-SHEA, *op. cit.*; HERBERMANN, *op. cit.*, *passim*; O'GORMAN, *op. cit.*, *passim*; SHELDON (E. M.), *History of Michigan from the Earliest Settlements to 1815*, New York and Detroit, 1856; REZEK, *History of the Diocese of Sault Ste Marie and Marquette*, Houghton, Michigan, 1906; WOOD, *Historic Mackinac*, 2 Vols., New York, 1918; MAES, *History of the Catholic Church in Monroe City and County*, Michigan (pamphlet, no date); *Michigan Pioneer and Historical Collections*, especially Vol. ix, p. 128, article on the *Diocese of Detroit* by the late Right Reverend Msgr. F. O'Brien of Kalamazoo; CHR, Vol. ii, pp. 285-280. cf. files of *Michigan Catholic;* (a history of the Diocese of Detroit will be ready for the Centennial in 1933).

1. RESE, FREDERICK.

The first Bishop of Detroit was born at Hanover, Germany, on February 6, 1791, and as a young man he fought under Blücher at Waterloo. He made his theological studies at the College of Propaganda, at Rome, and was ordained to the priesthood on Trinity Sunday in 1832. He was acting as Vicar-General of the Diocese of Cincinnati, when appointed first Bishop of Detroit, and he was consecrated by Bishop Rosati on October 6, 1833. He retired to his native Diocese of Hildesheim on account of ill health, and died there on December 29, 1871.

REUSS, *op. cit.*, p. 95; CLARKE, *op. cit.*, Vol. iii, p. 266; SHEA, *Hierarchy*, p. 221; REZEK, *op. cit.*, Vol. i; CE, Vol. iv, p. 759; CHR, Col. ii, p. 286.

Bishop LeFevre was never actually Bishop of Detroit although he was consecrated Coadjutor Bishop and Administrator-Apostolic by Bishop F. P. Kenvick at Philadelphia on November 21, 1841. He was born at Roulers, near Ghent, Belgium, on April 30, 1804, and emigrated to the United States in 1828. Three years later he was ordained to the priesthood, in Saint Louis, on July 17, 1831. He died on March 4, 1869.

REUSS, *op. cit.*, p. 63; SHEA, *Hierarchy.* etc., p. 222; CLARKE, *op. cit.*, Vol. ii, pp. 191-202; ACHS *Researches*, Vol. xii, pp. 82 (Church in Iowa), 173 (Marquette); Vol. xiii, p. 184 (on Father Cullen), Vol. xiv, pp. 50-61 (on Father Shawe), 155 (on Detroit Church), Vol. xxv, p. 10 (Church in Detroit), p. 83 (Sacred Heart Convent, Detroit), 151 (Church in Detroit), Vol. xix, pp. 163-165. Vol. xxi, p. 130 (on Sobriety), Vol. xxii, p. 209 (on Lincoln's faith) ; (diocesan bibliography).

2. BORGESS, CASPAR.

The second Bishop of Detroit was born at Koppenberg, near Essen, Hanover, Germany, on August 1, 1824, and came to the United States at the age of thirteen. He made his studies in Philadelphia and in Cincinnati, where he entered Saint Francis Xavier College, and finally was enrolled in the Diocesan Seminary. He was ordained to the priesthood on December 8, 1847, and after ten years' service he was named chancellor of the diocese and was acting as such when appointed Coadjutor and Administrator of Detroit by Pius IX on February 8, 1870. Bishop Rosecrans consecrated him titular Bishop of Claydon on April 24, 1870. He became second Bishop of Detroit at the death of Bishop Résé on December 29, 1871. On April 16, 1888, he resigned and received the titular See of Phacuistes. He died at Kalamazoo, Michigan, on May 3, 1890.

REUSS, *op. cit.*, p. 16; CE, Vol. i, p. 685 (biog. sketch); ACHS *Researches*, Vol. xx, 176; CHR, Vol. ii, p. 286; SHEA, *Hierarchy*, etc.. p. 224.

3. FOLEY, JOHN S.

Bishop Foley was born in Baltimore, Maryland, on November 5, 1833. He attended Saint Mary's College and Seminary at Baltimore and completed his theological studies in Rome, where he was ordained to the priesthood on December 20, 1856. He was appointed Bishop of Detroit on September 12, 1888, and was consecrated in Baltimore by Cardinal Gibbons on November 4, 1888. He died in Detroit on January 5, 1918.

REUSS, *op. cit.*, p. 44; HERBERMANN, *op. cit.*, pp. 242, 294; CHR, Vol. ii, p. 286; cf. files of *Baltimore Catholic Review* for November, 1918.

4. GALLAGHER, MICHAEL J.

The present Bishop of Detroit was born at Auburn, Michigan, on November 18, 1866, and received his education at Assumption College, Sandwich, Ontario; Mungret College, Limerick (1885-1889); University of Innsbruck (Austria, 1889-1894). He was ordained to the priesthood on March 19, 1893, and upon his return to the United States he was assigned to parochial work in the Diocese of Grand Rapids. He served as secretary, chancellor and Vicar-General under Bishop Richter, and was consecrated by him Coadjutor *cum jure successionis* and titular Bishop of Tipasa on September 8, 1915. He succeeded to the See of Grand Rapids on December 26, 1916, and was transferred to the Diocese of Detroit on July 18, 1918.

IV. Diocese of Indianapolis (1834-1898)

Pope Gregory XVI erected the Diocese of Vincennes on May 6, 1834, and the Rt. Rev. Simon G. Bruté, was consecrated as its first Bishop on October 28, 1834. The diocesan seat was transferred to Indianapolis on March 28, 1898.

When erected as a Diocese, the territorial limits of this see extended to the State of Indiana and the eastern part of Illinois. Gradually, it was narrowed down to the State of Indiana and, in 1857, upon the erection of the Diocese of Fort Wayne, it received its present extension of the southern half of the State of Indiana; an area of 18,749 square miles.

ALERDING, *History of the Catholic Church in the Diocese of Vincennes*, Indianapolis, 1883; BAYLEY, *Memoirs of the Right Rev. Simon G. Bruté*, New York, 1860-1873; LYONS, *Silver Jubilee of University of Notre Dame*, Chicago, 1869; SHEA, *History of the Catholic Church in the United States*, New York, 1890, III, IV; CLARKE, *Lives of Deceased Bishops of the United States*, New York, 1872; *Catholic Directory*, Milwaukee, 1909; *Catholic Telegraph*, Cincinnati, contemporary files.

1. BRUTE DE REMUR, SIMON G.

Bishop Bruté was born at Remur, France, on March 20, 1779, and received his early education in the schools of that city until the French Revolution broke out. He was ordained to the priesthood on June 10, 1808, and joined the Sulpicians. He taught theology for two years in France and then sailed to the United States in company with Bishop-elect Flaget. In 1834, he was appointed first Bishop of Vincennes, and on October 28, 1834, was consecrated by Bishop Flaget in Saint Louis. While attending the Provincial Council of Baltimore in 1837 he contracted a cold which later developed into consumption from which he died on June 26, 1839, at Vincennes, Indiana.

REUSS. *op. cit.*, p. 18; CE, Vol. iii, p. 24 (biog. sketch); ACHS *Researches.* Vols. vi, ix, x, xii, xv, xviii, xxii, xxiii, xxix *passim;* McSWEENY, *op. cit.*, Vol. i, pp. 8-429 *passim; Berichte* of the Leopoldine Association, Vols. i-xiii *passim;* LADY HERBERT, *Life of Bishop Bruté*, London, 1870; ALERDING, *History of the Diocese of Vincennes, passim*, Indianapolis, 1883; BRUTE DE REMUR, *Vie de Mgr. Bruté de Remur, premier Eveque de Vincennes*, Paris, 1887; BAYLEY, *Memoirs of the Rt. Rev. Simon Bruté*, New York, 1876; CLARKE, *op. cit.*, Vol. ii, pp. 7-44; SHEA, *Hierarchy*, etc., p. 389; WEBB, *Centenary of Catholicity in Kentucky*, pp. 109-207, Louisville, 1884; *A Missionary Bishop's Reminiscences of a Troublous Boyhood*, by E. C. Donnelly in the *Historical Records and Studies*, Vol. 13 (1902), pp. 325-333; for the fate of his valuable papers and *Journals*, cf. CHR, Vol. iii, pp. 492-494, and Vol. iv. pp. 129-130; SHEA, *History of the Catholic Church in the United States*, Vol. ii, p. 398; *ibid.*, Vol. iii, pp. 90, 411, 634, 638, 646, 659, 689, 692; CAUTHORN, *op. cit.*, pp. 114, 194; MACLEOD. *op. cit.*, p. 272; WHITE, *Life of Mother Seton,* pp. 314, 317, 319, New York, 1904; *Memorial Volume of St. Mary's Seminary, Baltimore.* pp. 19-20, Baltimore, 1891; HERBERMANN, *op. cit.*, pp. 267-276; McCAFFREY, *Discourse on Bishop Bruté* (August 19, 1839), Emmitsburg, 1839; SHEA, *History of the Catholic Church.* etc., Vol. iv, p. 101; *Life of Mother Theodore, of the Sisters of Providence,* St. Mary-of-the-Woods, Ind., 1905; *Life and Letters of Sister Francis Xavier,* St. Louis, 1917.

2. DE LA HAILANDIERE, LAURENT CELESTINE RENE.

The second Bishop of this see was born at a small village near Cambourg, France, on May 2, 1798. At the age of twenty-four, he decided to abandon the legal profession and study for the priesthood. Accordingly, he entered the Seminary at Rennes and upon the completion of his course was ordained to the priesthood in Paris on May 28, 1825. Bishop Bruté induced him to come to the United States with him in 1836, where he labored zealously as a missionary in the State of Indiana. While touring Europe in the interests of the diocese in 1838, he was informed of his appointment as coadjutor to Bishop Bruté and titular Bishop of Axierne. His consecration took place in Paris on August 18, 1839, with Bishop Jansen of Nancy as consecrating prelate. Bishop Bruté having died before his consecration, he became Bishop of Vincennes immediately. He resigned the see on July 16, 1847, and retired to his native town of Triandin, France. where he died May 1, 1882.

REUSS, *op. cit.*, p. 51; SHEA, *Hierarchy,* etc., p. 385; CLARKE, *op. cit.*, Vol. iii. pp. 295-312; ALERDING, *History of the Catholic Church in the Diocese of Vincennes,* pp. 162-173, Indianapolis, 1883; CHR, Vol. ii, p. 287; *Discourse on the Occasion of the Entombment of Mgr. Celestin de la Hailandière, Second Bishop of Vincennes,* preached by Bishop Chatard, November 22, 1882, Indianapolis, 1882.

3. BAZIN, JOHN S.

Bishop Bazin was born at Duerne, near Lyons, France, on October 15, 1796. He was ordained July 22, 1822, and left his native country in October, 1830, to labor in the Diocese of Mobile. Soon after he was made Vicar-General by Bishop Portier who sent him to France in 1846 to obtain help for the diocese. Upon recommendation of the Fathers of the Sixth Provincial Council of Baltimore, he was chosen for the See of Vincennes and was consecrated in the Cathedral of that city by Bishop Portier on October 24, 1847. Shortly after he was stricken with a fatal disease and died on April 23, 1848.

REUSS, *op. cit.*, p. 12, where reference is made to a biog. sketch, by Henry S. Cauthorn; ACHS *Researches*, Vol. xi, pp. 27-28; letters in Archives of Mount St. Joseph, Ohio—cf. MCCANN, *op. cit.*, Vol. ii, *ip*. 9; *Annales P. de Fide*, Vol. v, p. 619; CLARKE, *op. cit.*, Vol. ii, pp. 370-372; cf. CE, Vol. ii, p. 361 (biog. sketch), Vol. vii, pp. 741 744, Vol. x, p. 411, Vol. xlii, p. 508; ALERDING. *The Diocese of Vincennes*, Fort Wayne, 1907; cf. CHR, Vol. iii, p. 492 (destruction of Vincennes Archives), p. 287 (biog. sketch); SHEA, *Hierarchy*, etc., p. 386; SHEA, *History of the Catholic Church*, etc., Vol. iii, p. 697; *ibid.*, Vol. iv, pp. 200-203. 281; *Life of Mother Theodore, of the Sisters of Providence*, St. Mary-of-the-Woods, Ind., 1905; *Life and Letters of Sister Francis Xavier*, St. Louis, 1917.

4. DE ST. PALAIS, MAURICE.

The fourth Bishop of Vincennes was born at La Salvatat, in the Diocese of Montpelier, France, on November 15, 1811. After completing his studies he was ordained to the priesthood on May 28, 1836. He arrived in the United States in the same year, having pledged his service to the Bishop of Vincennes. His priestly labors were confined to the northern part of the State of Indiana and during the administration of Bishop Bazin he served as Vicar-General. Appointed as successor to Bishop Bazin, he was consecrated by Bishop Miles on January 14, 1849. He died at Saint Mary's-of-the-Woods, Indiana, on June 28, 1877.

REUSS, *op. cit.*, p. 102; SHEA, *Hierarchy*, etc., p. 387; CLARKE, *op. cit.*, Vol. iii, pp. 313-323; *Researches*, Vol. vii, p. 100. Vol. xxviii, p. 255; ALERDING, *op. cit.*, pp. 190-210; CHR, Vol. ii, p. 287.

5. CHATARD, FRANCIS SILAS.

Bishop Chatard was born in Baltimore, Maryland, on December 13, 1834, and made his studies at Mount Saint Mary's and the University of Maryland. In 1857 he resolved to study for the ministry and was sent to Rome to make his theological studies. He was ordained to the priesthood on June 14, 1862, and the following year he received the degree of Doctor of Divinity. He remained in Rome, where he acted as Vice-Rector and Rector respec-

tively of the American College.   His consecration as Bishop
of Vincennes took place in Rome on May 12, 1878, with
the Prefect of Propaganda, Cardinal Franchi, as consecrating prelate.   He died at Indianapolis on September 7, 1918.

REUSS, *op. cit.*, pp. 22-23; SHEA, *Hierarchy*, etc., p. 388; CHR,
Vol. ii, p. 287; BRANN, *History of the American College of the Roman
Catholic Church of the United States*, Rome, Italy. New York, 1910;
MCSWEENY, *op. cit.*, Vol. i, pp. 47, 475, 485, 490, 520, Vol. ii, pp. 3,
180, 196, 203, 231, 329.

6. CHARTRAND, JOSEPH.

Bishop Chartrand was born in Saint Louis, Missouri,
on May 11, 1870, and received his education at Saint Louis
University, and at Saint Meinrad's, in Indiana.   He was
ordained to the priesthood on September 24, 1892, by
Bishop Chatard and was acting as secretary to Bishop
Chatard and Rector of the Cathedral when appointed
coadjutor and titular Bishop of Flavias on July 27, 1910.
Cardinal Falconio consecrated him on September 15, 1910.

V. Diocese of Nashville (1837)

On July 28, 1837, Pope Gregory XVI erected the Diocese of Nashville as a suffragan of the Archiepiscopal See
of Baltimore with the Rt. Rev. Richard P. Miles as first
Bishop.

The Diocese of Nashville still comprises its original
limits of the State of Tennessee; an area of 41,750 square
miles.

SHEA, *History*, Vols. iii and iv. *passim;* DECOURCY-SHEA, *op. cit.*,
p. 544 seq.; CHR, Vol. ii, p. 288; cf. files of the *Louisville Record*.

1. MILES, RICHARD P., O. P.

The first Bishop of Nashville was born in Prince
George County, Maryland, on May 17, 1791, and at the age
of fifteen he joined the Dominican Order, in Kentucky, to
which he had emigrated with his parents at the age of
five.   He was ordained to the priesthood in September,
1816, and was sent into various parts of Kentucky and
Ohio to labor as a missionary.   He was consecrated Bishop
of Nashville at Saint Rose Convent in Kentucky by Bishop

Rosati on September 16, 1838. He died at Nashville in February, 1860.

REUSS, *op. cit.*, p. 75; SHEA, *Hierarchy*, etc., p. 305; CLARKE, *op. cit.*, Vol. ii, pp. 147-156; ACHS *Researches*, Vol. vi, p. 120 (cornerstone laying, Cathedral, Nashville), Vol. vii, p. 102 (Frenaye corresp.). Vol. xxlii, p. 93 (on way to Europe).

2. WHELAN, JAMES O. P.

Bishop Whelan was born in Kilkenny, Ireland, on December 8, 1823. His early youth was spent in London and New York, after which he journeyed to Ohio. He entered the Dominican Order in Ohio and was ordained to the priesthood on August 2, 1846. In 1854 he was appointed Provincial of the Order for the States of Ohio and Kentucky and his consecration took place on May 8, 1859, with Archbishop Peter R. Kenrick, as consecrating prelate. At the death of Bishop Miles he succeeded to the see on February 21, 1860, and resigned therefrom in 1864. He retired to a convent of his Order, and died at Zanesville, Ohio, on February 18, 1878.

REUSS, *op. cit.*, p. 107; SHEA, *Hierarchy*, pp. 307-308; CLARKE, *op. cit.*, Vol. iii, p. 289; CHR, Vol. ii, p. 288. He published a work entitled *A Golden Chain of Evidences Demonstrating from Analytical Treatment of History, that Papal Infallibility is no Novelty*, 1872.

3. FEEHAN, PATRICK.

Consecrated third Bishop of Nashville on November 1, 1865; transferred to the See of Chicago in 1880.
(Cf. Chicago.)

4. RADEMACHER, JOSEPH.

Bishop Rademacher was born on December 3, 1840, at Westphalia, Michigan, and at an early age he was sent to Saint Vincent's College at Beatty where he completed his classical course. He was ordained to the priesthood on August 2, 1863, at Fort Wayne, and on April 21, 1883, he was appointed Bishop of Nashville and was consecrated in that city on June 24, 1883, by Archbishop Feehan. Owing to ill health he was transferred to Fort Wayne on June 14, 1893, and five years later his health gave way completely and he had to relinquish the administration of diocesan affairs to his Vicar-General. He died in Fort Wayne on June 12, 1900.

REUSS, *op. cit.*, p. 92; SHEA, *Hierarchy*, p. 308; ALERDING, *op. cit.*, p. 46, seq.; CHR. Vol. ii, p. 288.

5. BYRNE, THOMAS S.

The present Bishop of Nashville was born at Hamilton, Ohio, on July 19, 1841, and prepared for the priesthood at Saint Thomas Seminary, Bardstown; Mount Saint Mary's of the West, and the American College in Rome. He was ordained to the priesthood on May 22, 1869, and on his return to the United States he was a member of the faculty of Mount Saint Mary's at Cincinnati, of which institution he later became Rector. Appointed fifth Bishop of Nashville on May 10, 1894, he was consecrated by Archbishop Elder on July 25, 1894.

He translated from the German in collaboration with Dr. Pabisch, *A Manual of Universal Church History, by the Reverend Dr. John Alzog*, Cincinnati, 1874; translated from the Italian, *Jesus Living in the Priest, by the Reverend P. Millet, S. J.*, New York, 1901. He also translated *The Homilies on the Epistles and Gospels for Every Sunday of the Year*, in 4 Vols., by Bishop Bondmailis; also *The Christian Mysteries*, in 4 Vols., by the same author.

VI. Diocese of Cleveland (1847)

The Diocese of Cleveland was erected on April 23, 1847, and the Rt. Rev. Louis A. Rappe was consecrated as its first Bishop on October 10, 1847.

This Diocese embraced about one-third of the northern part of the State of Ohio when erected in 1847. At present it comprises that part of the State of Ohio lying north of the southern limits of Columbiana, Stark, Wayne, Ashland, and Richmond counties, and east of the western limits of Erie, Huron and Richland counties; an area of 8,034 square miles.

SHEA, *Catholic Missions*, New York, 1854; *Catholic Universe, Cleveland*, 13 September, 1881; IDEM, *History of the Catholic Church in the United States*, New York, 1889, 1892) ; *Leben u. Wirken des hochw. Franz Sales Brunner, C.PP.S.*; *The Catholic Miscellany*, Charleston, S. C., 1824-30; *The Catholic Telegraph*, Cincinnati, 1831-47) ; HOUCK, *A History of Catholicity in Northern Ohio and Diocese of Cleveland*, Cleveland, 1902; IDEM, *The Church in Northern Ohio*,

Cleveland, 1889; *Reminiscences of the Right Rev. P. J. Machebeuf* in *The Catholic Universe*, 18 October, 1883, and 31 January, 1889; *Reminiscenses of the Right Rev. Louis de Goesbriand* in *The Catholic Universe*, 27 December, 1888; LAMOTT, *op. cit., passim.*

1. RAPPE, LOUIS A.

The first Bishop of the Diocese of Cleveland was born near Saint Omer, France, on February 2, 1801. He was ordained to the priesthood at Arras, France, on March 14, 1829; labored in his native country for a few years and came to Cincinnati about 1840. His consecration took place at Cincinnati on October 10, 1847, with Bishop Purcell as the consecrating prelate. He resigned the see in August, 1870, and went to Vermont where he labored as a simple missionary priest and died at St. Albans, in that state, on September 7, 1877.

REUSS, *op. cit.*, pp. 92-93; SHEA, *Hierarchy*, p. 205; CLARKE, *op. cit., Vol. iii*, p. 265, seq.; HOUCK, *A History of Catholicity in Northern Ohio and Diocese of Cleveland, passim;* LAMOTT, *op. cit., passim;* CHR, Vol. ii, p. 288.

2. GILMOUR, RICHARD.

The second Bishop of Cleveland was born at Glasgow, Scotland, on September 28, 1824. He became a convert to the Faith at the age of nineteen. He entered Mount Saint Mary's Seminary to study for the priesthood, and was ordained for the Diocese of Cincinnati on August 30, 1852. He labored in the missions of southern Ohio and later acted as professor in Mount Saint Mary's Seminary, at Cincinnati. Chosen for the See of Cleveland on February 15, 1872, he was consecrated by Archbishop Purcell on April 14, 1872. He died at Saint Augustine, Florida, on April 13, 1891.

REUSS, *op. cit.*, p. 48; SHEA, *Hierarchy*, etc., pp. 206-208; HOUCK, *Church in Northern Ohio*, etc., pp. 67-75, New York, 1887; ACHS *Researches*, Vol. xxii, p. 180, Vol. xxiv, p. 66, Vol. xxvi, p. 250; SWEENY, *op. cit.*, Vol. i, pp. 446, 457, 462; Vol. ii, pp. 98, 180, 190, 202, 213; CHR, Vol. ii, p. 228, (Bibliography of Cleveland Diocese); see also two-volume edition of HOUCK, Vol. i, pp. 105-163 (well documented).

3. HORSTMANN, IGNATIUS F.

Bishop Horstmann was born in Philadelphia on December 16, 1840, and received his education at the Cathedral High School in that city, Saint Joseph's College, and the Diocesan Seminary. In 1860 he was sent to the American College, Rome, where he was ordained to the priesthood on June 10, 1865. In the following year he returned to Philadelphia to teach in Saint Charles Seminary, where he remained for eleven years. Later he was appointed Rector of Saint Mary's Church, Philadelphia, and when chosen for the See of Cleveland was acting as chancellor of the Archdiocese. He was consecrated by Archbishop Elder of Cincinnati on February 25, 1892. He was stricken with heart disease and died from its effects on May 13, 1908, at Canton, Ohio.

REUSS, op. cit., p. 35; CHR, Vol. ii, p. 289; CUB, Vol. ii, p. 106; cf. BRANN, History of the American College, Rome, 1898; HOUCK, The Catholic Church in Northern Ohio and in the Diocese of Cleveland, Vol. i, pp. 164-192, Vol. ii, pp. 40-45.

4. FARRELLY, JOHN P.

Bishop Farrelly was born at Memphis, Tennessee, on March 15, 1856. The beginnings of his college course were spent at Georgetown University, Washington, D. C., and later he went to Europe to pursue further study at the college of Notre Dame de la Praix, Namur, Belgium, and at the Propaganda, Rome, where he received a Doctorate in Sacred Theology. Cardinal Lavalette ordained him to the priesthood, in Rome, on March 22, 1888, and upon his return to the United States he was appointed pastor of the Cathedral at Nashville. Having been appointed Secretary to the American Bishops on September 25, 1887, he returned to Rome to fulfil the duties of that office. From 1904 to 1909 he was Spiritual Director at the American College and on March 16, 1909, was appointed to the See of Cleveland and was consecrated by Cardinal Gotti on May 1, 1909. He died at Cleveland on February 12, 1921.

CHR, Vol. ii, p. 289; NCWC News Bulletin for week of his death; CURTIS, American Catholic Who's Who, p. 199, St. Louis, 1911.

5. SCHREMBS, JOSEPH. The present Bishop of Cleveland was born at Wuzelhofen, near Ratisborn, Bavaria, on March 12, 1866. He came to the United States at the age of eleven and after completing a course at Saint Vincent's, Beatty, Pennsylvania, he spent a few years in teaching and then was accepted by Bishop Richter as a student of the Diocese of Grand Rapids and entered the Sulpician Seminary at Montreal in 1884. He was ordained to the priesthood on June 29, 1889. In 1903 he was appointed Vicar-General of the Diocese of Grand Rapids and three years later was made a Monsignor with the rank of Domestic Prelate. Bishop Richter consecrated him titular Bishop of Sophene and Auxiliary on February 22, 1911. He was transferred to the newly created Diocese of Toledo, on August 11, 1911; on the death of Bishop Farrelly was promoted to Cleveland as his successor on June 16, 1921.

VII. Diocese of Covington (1853)

The Diocese of Covington was erected by Pope Pius IX on July 29, 1853, and the Rt. Rev. George H. Carrell, S. J., was consecrated as first Bishop on November 1, 1853.

The diocese still retains its original limits of that part of Kentucky lying east of the Kentucky River and the western limits of Carroll, Owen, Franklin, Woodford, Jessamine, Garrard, Rock Castle, Laurel and Whitley counties; an area of 17,286 square miles.

MAES, Life of Rev. Charles Nerinckx, Cincinnati, 1880; IDEM, Golden Jubilee of the Diocese of Covington, Pastoral Letter, November, 1903; WEBB, The Century of Catholicity in Kentucky, Louisville, 1884; SPALDING, Life of Benedict Joseph Flaget, Louisville, 1852; IDEM, Sketches of Early Catholic Missions in Kentucky, Louisville, 1844; CHR, Vol. ii, p. 289.

1. CARRELL, GEORGE A., S. J.

The first Bishop of Covington was born on June 13, 1803, in Philadelphia, Pennsylvania, and received his education at Mount Saint Mary's and at Georgetown. After entering the Society of Jesus he was sent to the former institution to complete his theological course and was ordained to the priesthood at Philadelphia on December 20, 1827. After a year of priestly labor in the eastern states he was appointed professor at Saint Louis University and afterwards became president of that institution. Chosen for the See of Covington on July 29, 1853, he was consecrated on November 1, 1853, by Archbishop Purcell. He died in Covington on September 25, 1868.

REUSS, *op. cit.*, pp. 20-21; CE, under *Covington;* McCANN, *op. cit.*, Vol. i, pp. 3, 12, 131, Vol. ii, pp. 140, 154, 178; McSWEENY, *op. cit.*, Vol. i, pp. 37-39, 158-178 *passim*, 279, 380, 475, 489, 502-506 *passim*, 515, 545, Vol. ii, pp. 1, 60; WEBB, *Centenary of Catholicity in Kentucky*, p. 350, Louisville, 1884; MAES, *Life of Rev. Charles Nerinckx,* Cincinnati, 1880; MAES, *Golden Jubilee of the Diocese of Covington*, pastoral letter, November, 1903; SPALDING, *Life of Flaget,* Louisville, 1852; SPALDING, *Sketches of Early Catholic Missions in Kentucky*, Louisville, 1844; SHEA, *History of the Catholic Church in the United States*, Vol. iv, pp. 381, 541; cf. M. J. O'BRIEN, *Irish Pioneers in Kentucky*, New York, 1917; WILLCOX, *Historical Sketches of Some of the Pioneer Catholics of Philadelphia and Vicinity*, in ACHS *Records* for December, 1904, pp. 2-4 (see this for the genealogy of the Carrell family); DECOURCY-SHEA, *History of the Catholic Church in the United States*, p. 242, New York, 1879; SHEA, *Hierarchy*, etc., p. 214; CLARKE, *op. cit.*, Vol. ii, pp. 505-513; ACHS *Researches*, Vol. x, p. 19, Vol. xiii, pp. 66, Vol. xiv, p. 90; for his years at St. Louis University, cf. FANNING, *Historical Sketch of St. Louis University*, St. Louis, 1908; ID, *Diamond Jubilee of St. Louis University*, St. Louis, 1904; cf. CHR, Vol. ii, p. 289.

2. TOEBBE, AUGUSTUS M.

Bishop Toebbe was born in Hanover, Germany, on January 15, 1829. He came to the United States in 1852 and entered Mount Saint Mary's, at Cincinnati, and was ordained to the priesthood on September 14, 1854. His priestly labors were confined to Ohio and he was appointed to the See of Covington on September 17, 1869. Bishop Rosecrans consecrated him on January 9, 1870, at Cincinnati, Ohio. He died on May 2, 1884, at Covington, Kentucky.

REUSS, *op. cit.*, p. 104; SHEA, *Hierarchy*, p. 215; CLARKE, *op. cit.*, Vol. iii, p. 216, seq.; LAMOTT, *op. cit., passim;* CE, Vol. ii, p. 463; CHR, Vol. ii, p. 289.

3. MAES, CAMILLUS P.

Bishop Maes was born on May 13, 1846, in West Flanders, Belgium, and made his classical studies in the

college of his native city.   Desirous of devoting himself
to the American missions he entered the American College
at Louvain, where he completed his theological studies and
was ordained to the priesthood in September, 1884.   He
was elected to the See of Covington and was consecrated in
that city by Archbishop Elder on January 25, 1885.   He
died at Covington on May 10, 1915.

REUSS, *op. cit.*, p. 66; SHEA, *Hierarchy*, etc., p. 216; *Character
Sketches of the Right Rev. C. P. Maes, D. D.*, Baltimore. 1917; ACHS
Researches, Vol. xii, p. 94 (on Catholic American Hierarchy), Vol.
xxiii, p. 164; CUB, p. 164; CUB, Vol. ii, p. 105; AER, Vols. xi,
p. 342, xiv, 204, 312, 435, 531, xxix, 33, 113, 570, 579, 1, 394; CHR,
Vol. i, pp. 125-128 (*In Memoriam* by Bishop Shahan), *ibid.*, Vol. iv,
p. 272 (diocesan bibliography).

Among his published works are *The Life of the Rev. Charles Nerinckx*, Cincinnati, 1880; *History of the Catholic Church in Monroe City
and County, Michigan*, n. d.   As General Spiritual Director of the
Priests' Eucharistic League he founded the society's paper, *Emmanuel*.
He also contributed historical papers to many periodicals and maga-
zines.

4. BROSSART, FERDINAND.

The present Bishop of Covington was born in
Buechelberg, Rhenish Bavaria, on October 19, 1849.   He
received his seminary training at Louvain, and was
ordained to the priesthood at Covington, Kentucky, on
September 1, 1872.   After his ordination he performed
priestly duties at Cynthiana, White Sulphur, Paris,
and Lexington.   He was made Vicar-General and Pastor of Saint Mary's Cathedral in 1888.   He was consecrated Bishop on January 25, 1916, with the Most Rev.
Henry Moeller, Archbishop of Cincinnati, Ohio, as the
consecrating prelate.

VIII. Diocese of Fort Wayne (1857)

On January 8, 1857, the Holy See erected the Diocese
of Fort Wayne, and the Rt. Rev. John H. Luers was consecrated as its first Bishop on January 10, 1858.

The Diocese embraces the northern half of the State
of Indiana (its original limits) ; an area of 17,431 square
miles.

SHEA, *History*, Vol. iv, p. 599 seq.; DECOURCY-SHEA, *op. cit.*, p. 565; ALERDING, *History of the Diocese of Fort Wayne*, Fort Wayne, 1907; LAMOTT, *op. cit.*, *passim;* CHR, Vol. ïi, p. 289.

1. LUERS, JOHN HENRY.

Bishop Luers was born near the city of Münster in Westphalia, Germany, on September 29, 1819. He came to the United States with his parents in 1833 and located at Piqua, Ohio. He was sent to the Lazarist Seminary of Saint Francis Xavier by Bishop Purcell, and was ordained to the priesthood on November 11, 1846. When the See of Fort Wayne was erected he was chosen to be its first Bishop and was consecrated by Archbishop Purcell on January 10, 1858. He died at Cleveland, Ohio, on June 29, 1871.

REUSS, *op. cit.*, p. 65; SHEA, *Hierarchy, etc.*. p. 235; CLARKE, *op. cit.*, Vol. ii, pp. 555-585; CHR, Vol. ii, pp. 289-290.

2. DWENGER, JOSEPH, C. P. P.S.

The second Bishop of Fort Wayne was born in Ohio, on September 7, 1837. His primary education was received in the schools of Cincinnati, and while an orphan, a priest, Father Kunkler, fathered him and placed him with the Fathers of the Precious Blood. He completed his studies at Mount Saint Mary's of the West, and was ordained to the priesthood at Cincinnati on September 4, 1859. Before his appointment as successor to Bishop Luers, he held several responsible positions in the Congregation of the Precious Blood. Archbishop Purcell consecrated him on April 14, 1872, and he died at Fort Wayne on January 3, 1893.

REUSS, *op. cit.*, p. 38; SHEA, *Hierarchy*, etc., pp. 236-238; CHR, Vol. ii, p. 290, Vol. v, pp. 311-357, *passim.*

3. RADEMACHER, JOSEPH.

The third Bishop of this Diocese was transferred from the See of Nashville on July 14, 1893, and died at Fort Wayne on January 12, 1900.

(Cf. Nashville.)

4. ALERDING, HERMAN J.
    Bishop Alerding was born in the Province of West-
phalia, Germany, on April 13, 1845. When an infant his
parents emigrated to the United States and settled in Kentucky. His educational training was received at Saint
Thomas', Kentucky, and Saint Meinrad's, in Indiana, and
on September 22, 1868, he was ordained to the priesthood
by Bishop De St. Palais. He was acting pastor of Saint
Joseph's Church in Indianapolis when appointed Bishop of
Fort Wayne on August 30, 1900. He was consecrated
on November 30, 1900.

IX. Diocese of Columbus (1868)

The Diocese of Columbus was erected on March 3, 1868,
and the Rt. Rev. Sylvester H. Rosecrans, then Auxiliary
Bishop of Cincinnati, was appointed as its first Bishop.
    The Diocese comprises its original limits of that part
of the State of Ohio of 40' 41", and between the Ohio
River in the east and the Scioto River on the west, together
with the counties of Franklin, Delaware and Morrow; an
area of 13,685 square miles.

HOWE, *Historical Collection of Ohio,* Cincinnati, Ohio, 1900;
American Catholic Historical Researches, Philadelphia, July, 1896;
files of *Catholic Telegraph,* Cincinnati, and *Catholic Columbian,*
Columbus; *United States Catholic Magazine,* Baltimore, January,
1847, *The Catholic Church in Ohio;* LAMOTT, *op. cit., passim.*

1. ROSECRANS, SYLVESTER.
    The first Bishop of Columbus was born at Homer,
Ohio, on February 15, 1827, and received his collegiate
training at Kenyon College, and Saint John's, Fordham.
After his conversion to the Faith, Bishop Purcell sent him
to Rome to study at the Propaganda, where he received a
Doctorate in Divinity. After ordination on June 5, 1853,
Father Rosecrans returned to the United States and labored
in the Archdiocese of Cincinnati until his appointment in
1862 as Auxiliary to Archbishop Purcell. He was consecrated
as titular Bishop of Pompeipol on March 25, 1862, the
Archbishop of Cincinnati being the consecrating prelate.
For six years Bishop Rosecrans assisted his venerable

Metropolitan until he was transferred to Columbus upon the erection of that see, on March 3, 1868. He died in Columbus on October 21, 1878.

REUSS, *op. cit.*, p. 96; SHEA, *Hierarchy*, p. 209; CLARKE, *op. cit.*, Vol. iii, p. 250 seq.; LAMOTT, *op. cit.*, *passim;* CHR, Vol. i, p. 290.

2. WATTERSON, JOHN A.

The second Bishop of Columbus was born at Bardstown, Westmoreland County, Pennsylvania, on May 27, 1844, and at an early age was sent to Mount Saint Mary's, Emmitsburg, to begin his education. He pursued theological studies at that institution and was ordained to the priesthood on August 9, 1868. In 1877 he was chosen President of Mount Saint Mary's and was acting in this capacity when appointed to succeed Bishop Rosecrans. He was consecrated Bishop of Columbus by Archbishop Elder on August 8, 1880. Bishop Watterson died in Columbus on April 17, 1889.

REUSS, *op. cit.*, p. 107; SHEA, *Hierarchy*, p. 213; LAMOTT, *op. cit.*, *passim;* CHR, Vol. ii, p. 290.

3. MOELLER, HENRY.

Consecrated Bishop of Columbus on August 25, 1900; transferred to the See of Cincinnati on April 27, 1903.

(Cf. Cincinnati.)

4. HARTLEY, JAMES J.

The present Bishop was born on June 6, 1858, in Columbus, Ohio, and received his ecclesiastical training at Mount Saint Mary's College and the Seminary of Our Lady cf Angels, at Niagara, New York. He was ordained to the priesthood on July 10, 1882, and was appointed Bishop of Columbus on December 23, 1903. Archbishop Elder consecrated him on February 25, 1904, at the Holy Name Church, in Steubenville, Ohio.

X. Diocese of Grand Rapids (1882)

The Diocese of Grand Rapids was created on May 12, 1882, and the Rt. Rev. Henry J. Richter was consecrated as its first Bishop on April 22, 1883. The Diocese still comprises its original allotment of the counties of Lower Peninsula of State of Michigan, north of the southern line of the counties of Ottawa, Kent, Montcalm, Gratiot and Saginaw, and west of the eastern line of the counties of Saginaw and Bay and adjacent islands; an area of 22,561 square miles.

REZEK, op. cit., Vol. i, for beginnings of Grand River Mission; BROWN, Historical Sketch of the Diocese of Grand Rapids, in the Michigan Pioneer and Historical Collections, Vol. 38, pp. 509, 522; CHR, Vol. ii, p. 290; cf. files of the Michigan Catholic at Detroit, Michigan.

1. RICHTER, HENRY JOSEPH.

The first Bishop of Grand Rapids was born at Neuenkirchen, Duchy of Oldenburg, Germany, on April 9, 1838, came to the United States in 1854 and settled at Cincinnati. He entered Saint Paul's school in that city, after which he spent five years at Bardstown and Mount Saint Mary's of the West. He was sent to Rome in 1860; five years later received a Doctorate in Divinity, and on June 10, 1865, he was ordained to the priesthood. Upon his return to Cincinnati, he taught in the seminary of that diocese for a time, and was then assigned to parochial work. He was appointed first Bishop of Grand Rapids on January 30, 1883, and was consecrated by Archbishop Elder in the Cathedral of Saint Andrew on April 22, 1883. After a three days' illness he died at Grand Rapids, Michigan, on December 26, 1916.

REUSS, op. cit., pp. 94 and 95; SHEA, Hierarchy, p. 243; BROWN, article cited under the Diocese; cf. files of Michigan Catholic for December, 1916.

2. GALLAGHER, MICHAEL J.

Consecrated second Bishop of Grand Rapids on September 8, 1915. Transferred to Detroit on July 18, 1918. (Cf. Detroit.)

3. KELLY, EDWARD D.

The present Bishop of Grand Rapids was born in Michigan in 1860, and was ordained to the priesthood on June 16, 1886. After his ordination he was stationed at Battle Creek as curate and later was appointed Rector of Bishop Borgess Seminary. His next appointment was the pastorate of the church in Monroe City, followed by pastorates at Dexter and Ann Arbor. He was chosen titular Bishop of Cestro and Auxiliary Bishop of Detroit on December 1, 1910, and was consecrated by Cardinal Gibbons at Ann Arbor on January 26, 1911. He was transferred to the See of Grand Rapids on January 30, 1919.

XI. Diocese of Toledo (1910)

The Diocese of Toledo was erected on April 15, 1910, and the Rt. Rev. Joseph Schrembs was appointed as first Bishop on August 11, 1911.

The Diocese comprises that part of the State of Ohio lying north of the southern limits of Crawford, Wyandot, Hancock, Allen and Van Wert counties and west of the eastern boundaries of Ottawa, Sandusky, Seneca and Crawford counties; an area of 6,969 square miles.

PARKMAN, *La Salle and the Discovery of the Great West*, Boston, 1899, xi, 151; IDEM, *Conspiracy of Pontiac*, I, v, 162; xiii, 281; II, xxxi, 317; SHEA, *The Catholic Church in the United States*, New York, 1886; I, 631; II, (1888), 387, 474 seq.; *Jesuit Relations*, Cleveland, 1900, LXIX, 191; SCRIBNER, *Memoirs*, Western Historical Association, Madison, Wis., 1910; HOUCK, *Catholic Church in Northern Ohio*, I, Cleveland, 1903, 1 seq; *United States Catholic Historical Magazine*, IV, xiii, 22; *United States Catholic Magazine*, March, 1848, 155; *Diocesan Reports*, Cleveland and Toledo, 1911; parish records, St. *Antoine de la Riviére aux Raisins*; St. *Francis de Sales*, Toledo; St. *Mary's*, Tiffin, Ohio; CHR, Vol. ii, p. 291.

1. SCHREMBS, JOSEPH.

Appointed Bishop of Toledo on August 11, 1911; transferred to the See of Cleveland in May, 1921.

(Cf. Cleveland.)

2. STRITCH, SAMUEL.

The present Bishop of Toledo is the youngest member of the Hierarchy in the United States, having been born August 17, 1887, in Nashville, Tennessee. After graduating from the parochial school in his native city he entered Saint Gregory's College, Cincinnati, and remained there as a student for two years. He was then sent to the American College at Rome where he completed his studies and was ordained to the priesthood on May 21, 1909. Upon his return to the United States he was appointed assistant at Saint Patrick's Church in Nashville. He was chancellor of the diocese when appointed Bishop, and was consecrated in Toledo on November 30, 1921, by Archbishop Moeller of Cincinnati.

CHAPTER VII

THE PROVINCE OF SAN FRANCISCO (1853)

The Province of San Francisco was erected on July 29, 1853, with the Rt. Rev. Joseph S. Alemany, O.P., as first Archbishop. When erected, the Province comprised only the State of California, with the Diocese of Monterey as a suffragan see. At present the Province of San Francisco includes the States of California, Nevada and Utah, with the Dioceses of Monterey-Los Angeles (1840-1850), Grass Valley-Sacramento (1868-1886), and Salt Lake City (1890), as suffragans.

MANUSCRIPTS: In the Cathedral Archives, San Francisco— *Diary of Bishop Diego y Morena, continued by Archbishop Alemany; A. S. Taylor MSS.; Records of the Missions of San Francisco de Asis, San Jose, Santa Clara, San Francisco Solano, and San Rafael; Chancery Records.*
In the University of California: *Spanish and Mexican Archives of California* (copies of the originals burnt in the San Francisco fire of 1906) *Bancroft Collection of MSS.; Pioneer MSS.; Seville and Mexican Transcripts.*
Synodus Diocesan Sanct. Francisci Habita, 1862, San Francisco, 1872; *Concilii Prov. S.F.; II, Acta et Decreta,* San Francisco, 1883; GLEASON, *Catholic Church in California,* San Francisco, 1872; BANCROFT, *History of California,* San Francisco, 1885; GREY, *Pioneer Times in California,* San Francisco, 1881; CLINCH, *California and Its Missions,* San Francisco, 1904; HITTEL, *History of San Francisco,* San Francisco, 1878; ROYCE, *California,* Boston, 1886; DWINELLE, *Colonial History of San Francisco,* 3rd ed., San Francisco, 1866); WILLEY, *Transition Period of California,* San Francisco, 1901; SHUCK, *California Scrap Book,* San Francisco, 1868; MOSES, *Establishment of Municipal Government in San Francisco,* Baltimore, 1889; BLACKMAR, *Spanish Institutions of the Southwest,* Baltimore, 1891; RICHMAN, *California under Spain and Mexico,* Boston, 1911; MARRYAT, *Mountains and Molehills,* London, 1855; KELLY, *The Diggings of California,* London, 1852; DE SMET, *Western Missions and Missionaries,* New York, 1863; RIORDAN, *The First Half-Century,* San Francisco, 1905; ENGLEHARDT, *The Franciscans in California,* Harbor Springs, 1897; ROSSI, *Six Ans en Amérique, Californie et Oregon,* Paris, 1863; FRIGNET, *La Californie,* 2nd ed., Paris, 1867; FERRY, *La Nouvelle Californie,* Paris, 1850; LEVY, *Les Francais en Californie,* San Francisco, 1884; MAGUIRE, *The Irish in America,* New York, 1868, xiii; SWASEY, *Early Days and Men of California,* San Francisco, 1894; QUIGLEY, *The Irish Race in California,* San Francisco, 1878; YORKE, *Wendte Controversy,* San Francisco, 1896; SHEA, *Catholic Church in the United States,* New York, 1892; GLEASON,

Golden Jubilee of the Archdiocese of San Francisco, San Francisco, 1903; *Foreign Relations of the United States, Appendix II, Pious Fund of the Californias* (documents), Washington, 1903; O'MEARA, *Broderick and Gwin,* San Francisco, 1881; the Local and County Histories of HALLEY, HALL, FRAZer, BOWEN, MENEFEE, etc.; Silver and Golden Jubilee Memorials of different religious orders of the Archdiocese; *Society of California Pioneers, Annual Reports,* San Francisco; *California Historical Society,* papers, San Francisco; *Academy of Pacific Coast History,* papers, San Francisco; *Metropolitan Directory* and *Catholic Directory,* 1850-1911; *Monitor,* San Francisco, files; *Freeman's Journal,* New York, 1850-60, files; *Alta California,* San Francisco, early files; *Evening Bulletin,* San Francisco, files, especially *A. S. Taylor Papers; Evening Examiner,* San Francisco, files especially.

I. San Francisco (1853)

San Francisco was created an Archdiocese immediately, and included the entire northern part of California. At present it comprises the counties of San Francisco, San Mateo, San Joaquin, Stanislaus, Sonoma, Alameda, Contra Costa, Lake, Marin, Mendocino, Napa Solano, and their portions of Santa Cruz, Santa Clara and Merced, lying north of 37', 5" north latitude, in the State of California; an area of 16,856 square miles.

1. ALEMANY, JOSEPH SADOC, O. P.

The first Archbishop of San Francisco was born on July 13, 1814, at Vich, Province of Catalonia, Spain. After completing his primary studies, he entered the Dominican Order at the age of fifteen and went to Rome to finish his education and was ordained to the priesthood on March 27, 1837, at Viterbo, Italy. In 1841 he chose the American missions for his future work and spent about ten years in missionary activities in Ohio, Kentucky, and Tennessee, during which he held the office of Provincial for a certain period. While at Rome in 1850, attending a general chapter of the Dominican Order, he was chosen Bishop of Monterey (May 31, 1850) and was consecrated in the Eternal City by Cardinal Fransoni on June 30, 1850. He was transferred to the See of San Francisco on July 29, 1853, and resigned on December 28, 1884. He retired to Spain where he died at Valencia on April 14, 1888.

REUSS, *op. cit.*, pp. 7-8; CHR, Vol. i, p. 32, and Vol. ii, p. 293 (biographical sketches) ; CLARKE, *op. cit.*, Vol. i, pp. 196-260; SHEA, *Hierarchy*, etc., p. 170; ENGLEHARDT, *Missions and Missionaries of California*, Vol. iv, pp. 666-816 *passim;* ACHS *Researches*, Vol. xxi, p. 177; articles in *Dominicana* of San Francisco, 1900-1906; GLEESON, *History of the Catholic Church in California*, pp. 205-208, San Francisco, 1872; cf. *The First Ecclesiastical Synod of California* by Engelhardt, in the CHR, Vol. i, pp. 30-37; SHEA, *History of the Catholic Church in the United States*, Vol. iv, pp. 356-357, 369, 703-708; ENGELHARDT, *Franciscans in California*, pp. 199-202, 232, 470; in the Santa Barbara Mission archives are numerous personal letters of Alemany.

2. RIORDAN, PATRICK W.

The second Archbishop of San Francisco was born at Chatham, New Brunswick, on August 27, 1841, and made his early studies at Notre Dame University, whence he went to Rome as one of twelve students who formed the first class in the North American College in the Eternal City. Subsequently, he went to Louvain and received a Doctorate in Sacred Theology, and was ordained to the priesthood at Mechlin, Belgium, on June 10, 1865. Upon his return to the United States he was appointed professor at Saint Mary's-of-the-Lake, Chicago, and also held the rectorship of St. James Church in that city. While in that capacity, he was chosen as coadjutor Bishop of San Francisco and was consecrated on September 16, 1883, at Chicago by Archbishop Feehan. He succeeded to the see upon the resignation of Archbishop Alemany on December 28, 1884. He died in San Francisco on December 27, 1914.

REUSS, *op. cit.*, p. 95; SHEA, *Hierarchy*, p. 172; CHR, Vol. ii, p. 293; ACHS *Researches*, Vol. xxvi, p. 297; *The Monitor*, of San Francisco, issue of April 17, 1915.

Most Reverend George Montgomery, consecrated Bishop of Monterey on May 8, 1894, was chosen as titular Archbishop of Osino and Coadjutor of San Francisco in January, 1903.

(Cf. Los Angeles.)

3. HANNA, EDWARD J.

The present Archbishop of San Francisco was born at Rochester, New York, on July 21, 1860, and made his theological studies at Rome, Munich, and Cambridge. He

was ordained to the priesthood in 1885, taught in the
College of Propaganda for a year, and later in Saint Bernard's Seminary in Rochester. He was appointed Auxiliary
Bishop of San Francisco on October 22, 1912, and consecrated by Bishop Hickey on December 4, 1912. He succeeded to the see on June 1, 1915.

II. Diocese of Monterey and Los Angeles (1840-1850)

The Diocese of the Californias was erected on April
27, 1840, and the Rt. Rev. Francis Garcia Diego y Moreno
was consecrated Bishop. Ten years later the Diocese of
Monterey was created and the Rt. Rev. Joseph S. Alemany
was consecrated as its first Bishop. This change was
necessitated on account of political disturbances with
Mexico.

When erected, the Diocese of Monterey included all
Upper California. At present it comprises the counties of
Fresno, Inyo, Imperial, Kern, Los Angeles, Monterey,
Riverside, San Benito, San Bernardino, Orange, San Diego,
San Luis Obispo, Santa Barbara, Ventura, Tulare, and those
portions of the counties of Santa Cruz, Santa Clara and
Merced, lying south of 37', 5" north latitude, in the State
of California; an area of 80,000 square miles.

Santa Barbara Mission Archives; Bishop's Archives, Los Angeles; ENGLEHARDT, The Franciscans in California, Harbor Springs,
Mich., 1897; REUSS, Biographical Cyclopedia of the Hierarchy of the
United States, Milwaukee, 1898; Catholic Directory; CHR, Vol. ii,
p. 294.

1. GARCIA DIEGO Y MORENO, FRANCIS, O. F. M.

The first Bishop of this see was born on September
17, 1785, in Lagos, Mexico. He commenced his studies for
the priesthood in the Seminary at Guadalajara, where he
remained until 1800. Three years later he joined the
Franciscan Order and was ordained to the priesthood at
Satillo, in the Diocese of Linares, on November 13, 1808.
He was appointed Commissary of the Indian Missions in
Alta California in 1830 with headquarters at Santa Barbara,
a position he held until chosen to be the first Bishop of the
Two Californias on April 27, 1840. He was consecrated by

the Rt. Rev. Abbot Campos on October 4, 1840, and he died at the Franciscan Mission at Santa Barbara on April 30, 1846.

REUSS, *op. cit.*, pp. 46-47 (important data; Reuss claims that the spelling of *Garcia Diego* is incorrect); ENGELHARDT, *Missions and Missionaries of California*, Vol. iv, pp. 194 seq.; CHR, Vol. i, pp. 292, 294; CLARKE, *op. cit.*, Vol. ii, pp. 157-166; SHEA, *Hierarchy*, etc., 169; see important bibliography of San Francisco Diocese supra, cf. *Index* to ENGELHARDT, *Missions*, etc., pp. 31-32.

2. ALEMANY, JOSEPH S.

Consecrated second Bishop of Monterey on June 30, 1850, and was promoted to the Archiepiscopal of San Francisco on July 29, 1853.
(Cf. San Francisco.)

3. AMAT, THADDEUS.

The third Bishop of this diocese was born at Barcelona, Spain, on December 30, 1810, and made his theological studies in the seminary of his native city. At the age of twenty he entered the Congregation of the Mission and was ordained to the priesthood in Paris in 1838. In August of that year he was sent to the American Missions by his Superiors and labored as a missionary in the southwest for many years. On June 29, 1853, Pius IX appointed him to the vacant See of Monterey, and he was consecrated by Cardinal Fransoni at Rome on March 12, 1854. He died at Los Angeles on May 12, 1878.

REUSS, *op. cit.*, p. 9; *Giornale di Roma* of March 13, 1854; CLARKE, *op. cit.*, Vol. i, pp. 637-643; HERBERMANN, *The Sulpicians in the United States*, p. 213, New York, 1916; CHR, Vol. ii, p. 294; SHEA, *Hierarchy*, etc., p. 301; SHEA, *History of the Catholic Church*, etc., Vol. iv, pp. 62, 709-712; ENGELHARDT, *Franciscans in California*, pp. 200-208; id., *Missions and Missionaries*, Vol. iv, pp. 711-712, 717-720, 816. In the episcopal archives are the *Libro de Gobierno*, *Libro Borrador*, and the *Cartas Pastorales* of the bishop.

4. MORA, FRANCIS.

Bishop Mora was born in the Province of Catalonia, Spain, on November 27, 1827, and in 1855 he accompanied Bishop Amat to California to labor in this diocese. He was ordained to the priesthood in Santa Barbara on May 19, 1856, and seven years later he was chosen to be Vicar-General of the diocese. He was appointed Coadjutor to Bishop Amat on May 20, 1873, and was consecrated titular Bishop of Mosynopolis by Bishop Amat on August 3, 1873; succeeded to the see on May 12, 1878. He resigned on February 1, 1896, and retired to his native land and died at Sarria, Catalonia, on August 3, 1905.

REUSS, *op. cit.*, p. 76-77; SHEA, *Hierarchy*, etc., p. 303; CHR, Vol. iv, pp. 389-390 (diocesan bibliography).

5. MONTGOMERY, GEORGE.

Bishop Montgomery was born in Kentucky, on December 30, 1847. He was ordained to the priesthood on December 20, 1879, and was chancellor of the Archdiocese of San Francisco when appointed Coadjutor to Bishop Mora. He was consecrated titular Bishop of Tuni by Archbishop Riordan, on April 8, 1894. He succeeded to the see on May 6, 1896, and was promoted to the Archiepiscopal See of Osino and Coadjutor to Archbishop Riordan of San Francisco in 1913. His activities in rescue work during the aftermath of the famous earthquake of 1904 had a debilitating effect upon his health and he died there on January 10, 1907.

REUSS, *op. cit.*, p. 76; ACHS *Researches*, Vol. xxiii, p. 80 (on *Researches*); Diocesan bibliography; CHR, Vol. ii, p. 294.

6. CONATY, THOMAS J.

The sixth Bishop of this see was born in County Cavan, Ireland, on August 1, 1847, and came to the United States with his parents in 1850. He attended the schools at Taunton, Massachusetts, and made his college course at Holy Cross College, Worcester. He was ordained to the priesthood in Montreal on December 21, 1872, and labored as pastor in Worcester until his appointment as Rector of the Catholic University of America at Washington, D. C., on January 10, 1897. Pope Leo XIII made him a Domestic Prelate on November 1, 1897, and later he was elevated to the episcopate as titular Bishop of Samos and consecrated by Cardinal Gibbons on November 21, 1901. Two years later he was appointed Bishop of

Monterey-Los Angeles (March 27, 1903) and he died at Coronado, California, on September 18, 1915.

REUSS, *op. cit.*, p. 25; CUB, Vol. iv, pp. 487, 493, Vol. viii, p. 124, Vol. ix, p. 439; CHR, Vol. ii, p. 294; cf. files of *The Tidings*, for September, 1915.
Among his published works are *New Testament Studies, The Principal Events of the Life of Our Lord*, New York, 1898; *Celtic Influence in English Literature*, n. p., 1896; *Bible Studies for the Use of Colleges and Schools*, 1898.

7. CANTWELL, JOHN JOSEPH.

The present Bishop of this see was born at Limerick, Ireland, on December 1, 1874. He was educated at the College of the Sacred Heart in Limerick and also at a private Academy in Clonmel. After the completion of his course at Saint Patrick's College, Thurles, he was ordained to the priesthood in the Cathedral of that city on June 18, 1899. In the fall of the same year he was appointed curate of Saint Joseph's Church at Berkeley, and in 1904 Archbishop Riordan chose him to be his secretary. Under the present Archbishop of San Francisco he served as Vicar-General until his appointment to the vacant See of Los Angeles in September, 1917. He was consecrated by Archbishop Hanna on December 5, 1917.

III. Diocese of Grass Valley-Sacramento (1868-1886)

The Vicariate of Marysville was erected into the Diocese of Grass Valley on March 29, 1868, and the Rt. Rev. Eugene O'Connell, D.D., was appointed its first Bishop on March 29, 1868. Pope Leo XIII on May 16, 1886, changed the boundaries of the Diocese and removed the diocesan seat to Sacramento, and the Rt. Rev. Patrick Manogue was appointed as Bishop.

When the Diocese of Grass Valley was erected it comprised the northern part of California and the State of Nevada. At present, the Diocese of Sacramento comprises Alpine, Amador, Butte, Colusa, Calaversa, Del Norte, Eldorado, Humboldt, Lassen, Mariposa, Modoc, Mono, Nevada, Placer, Plumas, Sacramenero, Shasta, Sierra, Siskiyou, Sutter, Tuolumne, Tehama, Trinity, Yola and Yuba counties

in California, and Churchill, Douglas, Esmeralds, Humboldt,
Lyon, Ormsby, Storey and Washoe counties in Nevada; an
area of 92,611 square miles.

SHEA, *The Hierarchy of the Catholic Church in the United
States*, New York, 1886; SHEA, *History of the Catholic Church in
the United States*, IV, New York, 1886-93; *Catholic Directory*, 1911;
Lives of American Prelates in Mem. Vol. 3rd Plenary Council, Baltimore, 1885; *Sacramento Union*, files; *Catholic Herald*, Sacramento,
26 December, 1908; *Monitor*, San Francisco, 16 July, 1910; *Statistics
of Population of California*, compiled for the use of the Legislature,
1911; *Missions Catholicae*, Rome, 1901; CHR, Vol. ii, p. 295.

1. O'CONNELL, EUGENE.

The first Bishop of Grass Valley was born on June
18, 1815, near Navan, County Meath, Ireland. He studied
in the diocesan seminary of his native city and later entered Maynooth, where he was ordained to the priesthood
in June, 1842. After his ordination he was stationed at
the seminary in Navan as professor. He left for California in 1851 and acted as Director of a College at Santa
Iñez. His next appointment was to the Seminary of Saint
Thomas, near San Francisco, where he remained three
years. He left for Ireland in 1854 and accepted a profes-
sorship of theology at All Hallows College. While there
he was selected to be Vicar-Apostolic of Marysville on
September 26, 1860, and he was consecrated titular Bishop
of Flaviopolis on February 3, 1866. When the Diocese of
Grass Valley was created, he became its first Bishop on
March 29, 1868. He resigned the see on March 17, 1884,
and was made titular Bishop of Joppa. He died at Los
Angeles, California, on December 4, 1891.

REUSS, *op. cit.*, p. 80; SHEA, *Hierarchy*, pp. 245-246; CE, Vol. xiii,
p. 294; CHR, Vol. ii, p. 295.

2. MANOGUE, PATRICK.

Bishop Manogue was born in County Kilkenny, Ireland, on March 15, 1821. He came to this country when
a boy and settled in New England. He studied for the
priesthood at the University of Saint Mary's-of-the-Lake,
Chicago, and at Saint Sulpice in Paris, where he was ordained to the priesthood on December 25, 1861. When

appointed coadjutor to Bishop O'Connell he was acting as pastor of the church in Virginia City, Nevada. Archbishop Alemany consecrated him titular Bishop of Ceramos on January 16, 1881, and he succeeded to the See of Grass Valley on the resignation of his predecessor, March 17, 1884. He became first Bishop of Sacramento on May 16, 1886, and died in that city on February 27, 1895.

REUSS, *op. cit.*, p. 66; SHEA, *Hierarchy*, pp. 246; CHR, Vol. ii, p. 295.

3. GRACE, THOMAS.

Bishop Grace was born in County Wexford, Ireland, on August 2, 1841, and made his ecclesiastical studies at All Hallows College, Dubin. He was ordained to the priesthood on June 11, 1867, and shortly after, he left for the missionary field of California. He held several pastorates in the States of Nevada and California and was acting as Administrator of the Diocese when appointed to succeed Bishop Manogue on March 20, 1896. Archbishop Riordan consecrated him on June 16, 1896, and he died at Sacramento on December 30, 1921.

REUSS, *op. cit.*, pp. 49-50; CHR, Vol. ii, p. 295; cf. *The Catholic Herald* of Sacramento, issue of December 31, 1921.

4. KEANE, PATRICK JAMES.

Bishop Keane was born in County Kerry, Ireland, on January 6, 1872. He received his classical training at Saint Michael College and made his theological studies at Saint Mark's College, Carlow, Ireland. While doing postgraduate work at the Catholic University of America, he was ordained to the priesthood on June 20, 1895, in one of the chapels of that institution. He labored in the Archdiocese of San Francisco before he was appointed titular Bishop of Samaria and Auxiliary to Bishop Grace. Archbishop Hanna consecrated him on December 14, 1920, and he was chosen as third Bishop of Sacramento on April 3, 1922.

IV. Diocese of Salt Lake City (1890)

The Diocese of Salt Lake was erected in 1891 and the acting Vicar-Apostolic of Utah, the Rt. Rev. Lawrence

Scanlan, D.D., was appointed as its first Bishop on January 30, 1890.

The Diocese includes the entire State of Utah, the counties of Eureka, Lander, Lincoln, White Pine, Nye, Elk, Clark, in the State of Nevada; an area of 153,768 square miles.

SALPOINTE, *Soldiers of the Cross*, Banning, California, 1898; HOWLETT, *Life of Rt. Rev. Joseph P. Machebeuf*, Pueblo, 1908; DE SMET, letter published in *Precis Historiques*, Brussels, 19 January, 1858; CHITTENDEN, *Father De Smet's Life and Travels among the North American Indians;* HARRIS, *The Catholic Church in Utah*, Salt Lake City, 1909. CHR, Vol. ii, p. 295.

1. SCANLAN, LAWRENCE.

The first Bishop of Salt Lake was born on September 28, 1843, at Ballintarsna, County Tipperary, Ireland. He graduated from All Hallows, Dublin, in 1868, and was ordained to the priesthood in that city on June 24, 1868. Coming to California shortly after, he held various important pastorates in the Archdiocese of San Francisco. He was appointed the first Vicar-Apostolic of Utah on January 25, 1887, and was consecrated titular Bishop of Laranda at San Francisco on June 29, 1887, by Archbishop Riordan. He became first Bishop of Salt Lake City in 1891 and died there on May 10, 1915.

HARRIS, *op. cit., passim;* REUSS, *op. cit.*, p. 98; SHEA, *Hierarchy*, p. 404; CHR, Vol. ii, p. 295.

2. GLASS, JOSEPH S., C. M.

The present Bishop of Salt Lake was born at Bushnell, Illinois, on March 13, 1874. He graduated from Saint Vincent's College at Los Angeles and then joined the Congregation of the Mission. He made his theological course at Saint Mary's Seminary at Perryville, Missouri, and was ordained to the priesthood on August 15, 1897. Two years later he received the degree of Doctor of Divinity at the Minerva in Rome. He was appointed Bishop of Salt Lake on June 1, 1915, and was consecrated by Archbishop Hanna of San Francisco on August 24, 1915.

CHAPTER VIII

THE PROVINCE OF BOSTON (1875).

This Province was one of the four metropolitan sees erected by Pius IX on July 12, 1875, and the Right Reverend John Williams, D.D., was appointed its first Archbishop.

When created, the Archdiocese had as suffragan sees the Dioceses of Hartford (1843), Burlington (1853), Portland (1853), Springfield (1870) and Providence (1872). The Province still embraces the New England States and to the original suffragan sees have been added the Dioceses of Manchester (1884) and Fall River (1904).

SHEA, *History of the Cath. Ch. in U. S.*, New York, 1886; IDEM, *Life and Times of the Most Rev. John Carroll* (Ib., 1888) ; HAMON, *Vie du Cardinal de Cheverus*, Paris, 1838, tr. WALSH, *Philadelphia*, 1839; tr. STEWART, Boston, 1839; FITTON, *Sketches of the Establishment of the Church in New England*, Boston, 1872; CREAGH, *Laity's Directory*, New York, 1822;*Catholic Observer*, Boston, 1847, files; *Mémoires de P. De Sales Laternere* Quebec, 1813; *Gazette de Québec* (22 October, 1789, supplement) ; *American Cath. Hist. Researches*, January, 1889; July, 1902; FINOTTI, *Bibliographia Cath. Americana*, New York, 1872; *U. S. Cath. Magazine* (Baltimore), viii, 102 sqq.; U. S. CATH., HIST. Soc., *Hist. Records and Studies*, New York, October, 1906, IV, parts I and II; SULLIVAN, *Catholic Church of New England, Archdiocese of Boston* (Boston and Portland, 1895) ; LEAHY in *History of Catholic Church in the New England States*, Boston, 1899, I; *Memorial Volume, One Hundredth Anniversary Celebration of the Dedication of the Church of the Holy Cross, Boston* (Boston, 1904) ; H. F. BROWNSON, *Orestes A. Brownson's Early Life;* IDEM, *Middle Life*, Detroit, 1898-99. CHR, Vol. ii, p. 298.

I. Diocese of Boston (1808)

The Diocese of Boston was erected on April 8, 1808, and the Right Reverend John L. De Cheverus was consecrated as its first Bishop on November 1, 1810.

When erected, the Diocese of Boston included all the New England States, but at present it comprises only the Counties of Essex, Middlesex, Suffolk, Norfolk and Plymouth, in the State of Massachusetts, the towns of Mattapoisett, Marion and Wareham excepted; an area of 2,465 square miles.

1. DE CHEVERUS, JOHN LOUIS LEFEBVRE.

The first Bishop of Boston was born at Mayenne, France, on January 28, 1768. His early training was received from his mother who later sent him to the College of Louis le Grand to complete his education. He was ordained to the priesthood in Paris on December 18, 1790, and upon refusing to take the constitutional oath to the Directory, he was cast into prison, from which he made his escape to England. In response to an invitation from his friend Abbé Matignon to come to this country, he arrived in Boston on October 3, 1796, and labored incessantly as a missionary in that city and in various parts of New England. When the See of Boston was erected, he was chosen to be its first Bishop, but he was not consecrated until two years later (on December 1, 1810) by Archbishop Carroll. Owing to ill health he was transferred to the Diocese of Montauban in France on January 15, 1823. He was promoted to the archiepiscopal see of Bordeaux on July, 1826, and preconized Cardinal on February 1, 1836. He died in Bordeaux, France, on July 19, 1836.

REUSS, *op. cit.*, p. 23; CLARKE, *op. cit.*, Vol. i, pp. 164-185; SHEA, *Hierarchy, etc.*, pp. 85-87; SHEA, *Hist. of the Cath. Missions among the Indian Tribes of the United States* (1529-1824), p. 157. New York, 1855; SHEA, *Hist. Cath. Church in the United States*, Vol. iii, pp. 107-131; HAMON, *Vie du Cardinal Cheverus*, Paris, 1837; English translation of Hamon by STEWART, Boston, 1839; DOUBOURG, J. HUEN, *Cardinal De Cheverus*, trans. by Robert M. Walsh. Philadelphia: Hooker and Claxton, 1839; LEAHY, *Archdiocese of Boston in History of the Catholic Church in the New England States*, Boston, 1889; CE, Vol. iii, p. 650; McCANN, *op. cit.*, i, pp. 9, 18, 32, 37-38, 54, 78, 83, 97-99, 103-108, 233—letters of, pp. 19, 30, 103, Vol. ii, pp. 81 (funeral of); McSWEENY, *op. cit.*, Vol. i, pp. 28, 49-50; 124, 156, 172; FINOTTI, *op. cit.*, pp. 40-41, 50, 119-120, 136, 143, 177, 191, 195, 239, 240-242; FISH, *op. cit.*, pp. 176-178; KENNEDY, *Centenary, etc.*, p. 32 (portrait of Cheverus); ACHS *Records*, Vol. xii (1901), pp. 358-361 (*Two letters from Rt. Rev. John Cheverus to Jean Marie Maximilien de Vernous, Marquis de Bonneuil*); *ibid.*, Vol. xv (1904), pp. 35-45 (*Boston's first Catholic Church*, by E. I. DEVITT, S. J., contains also letters of Matignon to Carroll); *ibid.*, Vol. xiv (1903), pp. 229-382 (*An Interesting Correspondence*, by I. M. O'REILLY, contains an excellent historical introduction to Cheverus' life); *ibid.*, Vol. xv (1904), pp. 83-112 (sixty-four letters from the Cheverus papers); *cf.* O'REILLY, *Cheverus in France*, a second series of letters in the ACHS *Records*, Vol. xvii (1906), pp. 97, 211, 348, 486. Cf. also *My Unknown Chum*. New York, 1917 (Devin Adair Co.); *U. S. Cath. Magazine*, Vol. iv (1845), p. 300 (portrait of Cheverus), pp. 261-267 (*Notice of Card. Cheverus*). See *Index* to ACHS *Researches*, p. 70. CHR, Vol. i, pp. 151, 279, 310-11, 369, Vol. ii, pp. 21-29, 40, 77, 228-230, 296, 300, Vol. iv, pp. 38, 42, 48, 403.

Nouvelle Biographic Universelle, Paris, F. Didot Fréres, 1854, Vol. 9, p. 270 *seq.; Boston Monthly Magazine*, June, 1825; *Boston, Memorial History of,* edited by J. Winsor, Boston, Ticknor & Co., 1886, Vol. 3, p. 516 *seq.; Bostonian Society Publications*, Vol. 2, p. 32 *seq.; Metropolitan, The,* Vol. iv, pp. 460, 462; *Figures of the Past,* by Josiah Quincy, Boston, Roberts Bros., 1883, pp. 311, 313; *Recollections of Samuel Breck,* Philadelphia, Porter & Coates, 1877, p. 117; *Cheverus, Vie du Cardinal de,* par M. le Curé de S. Sulpice, Paris, J. Lecoffre & Cie, 1858; *New England, Sketches of Catholic Church in,* by Rev. J. Fitton, Boston, P. Donahue, 1872, pp. 99 *seq.; Boston Herald,* 2, Aug., 1903; *Boston Commercial Gazette,* 20 June, 1827; *Columbian Centinel,* Boston, 20 June, 1827; *Baltimore Archives:* letters Cheverus to Bishop Carroll, 1797-1816, to Arch. Neale, 1816-1817, to Arch. Maréchal, 1817-1823; *Boston Archives:* Memoir for Ecclesiastical History of Boston; letter Fr. Cheverus in reply to article in *Telegraph,* 20 May, 1800, signed *A Catholick,* letter to —— Boston, 17 April, 1801, letter to editor *Boston Anthology,* 4 May, 1807, address of Boston Catholics to Bishop-elect Cheverus, 27 Sept., 1810, letter Bishop Cheverus to god-child, Boston, 2 April, 1816.

2. FENWICK, BENEDICT JOSEPH.

The second Bishop of Boston was born at Leonardtown, Maryland, on September 3, 1782. In 1793 he was sent to Georgetown and in 1805 he entered the Sulpician Seminary at Baltimore to study for the priesthood. Upon the restoration of the Society of Jesus in 1806, he was received as one of its members and was ordained to the priesthood at Georgetown, D. C., on March 12, 1808. As a priest, he labored in New York as pastor, Administrator, and Vicar-General. His appointment as Bishop of Boston was announced on May 10, 1825, and on November 1, 1825, he was consecrated by Archbishop Maréchal. He died at Boston, on August 11, 1846.

REUSS, *op. cit.,* p. 41; SHEA, *Hierarchy, etc.,* pp. 87-89; CLARKE, *op. cit.,* Vol. i, pp. 374-413; *Researches,* Vol. viii, pp. 93, 170, 175, Vol. ix, pp. 95, 159, 191, Vol. x, p. 159, Vol. xx, pp. 3, 173, 176, Vol. xxii, pp. 91, 260, 277, 288, Vol. xxvi, pp. 23, 244, 274, 290; HERBERMANN, *op. cit., pp.* 72, 204; CHR, Vol. ii, p. 296; McCANN, *op. cit.,* Vol. i, pp. 146, 210; McSWEENY, *op. cit.,* Vol. i, pp. 4, 165, 213, 277, 288, 300, 407, 432.

3. FITZPATRICK, JOHN B.

Bishop Fitzpatrick was born in Boston on November 1, 1812, and received his education in the city schools. His studies for the priesthood were made at the Sulpician Seminaries in Montreal and in Paris, and he was ordained to the priesthood on June 13, 1840. Upon his return to Boston, he was made assistant at the Cathedral and later

served as pastor at East Cambridge. He was consecrated
titular Bishop of Callipolis and coadjutor by Bishop Fenwick on March 24, 1844, and succeeded to the see on
August 11, 1846. He died in Boston on February 13, 1866.

REUSS, *op. cit.*, p. 43; SHEA, *Hierarchy, etc.*, pp. 89-91; CLARKE, *op. cit.*,
Vol. ii, pp. 310-336; *Researches*, Vol. ii, p. 93, Vol. viii, p. 5, Vol. ix, p. 185.
Vol. xxvi, p. 234; CHR, Vol. i, pp. 154, 160, Vol. ii, pp. 297.

4. WILLIAMS, JOHN J.

Archbishop Williams was born in Boston on April
27, 1822, and completed his studies at the Sulpician Seminary in Paris, where he was ordained to the priesthood on
May 17, 1845. As Rector of St. James Church in Boston.
he established the first branch of the St. Vincent de Paul
Society in New England. He was consecrated Bishop of
Boston by Archbishop McCloskey on March 11, 1866, and
he became first Archbishop of this See on February 12,
1875. He died at Boston on August 30, 1907.

REUSS, *op. cit.* p. 109; SHEA, *Hierarchy*, pp. 92-93; O'DONNELL, *History
of the Catholic Church in New England*, Boston, 1899; C.H.R. Vol. ii, p.
297.

The Right Reverend John Brady was appointed titular Bishop of Alabanda and Auxiliary to Archbishop Williams and was consecrated by the Archbishop on August 5,
1891. He was born in County Cavan, Ireland, on April 11,
1842. His ordination to the priesthood for the Diocese of
Boston took place on December 4, 1864, and he served as
curate at Newburyport until 1868, when he was made pastor
at Amesbury where he remained until his appointment as
Auxiliary Bishop. He died in Boston on January 6, 1910.

REUSS, *op. cit.*, p. 17; CHR, Vol. ii, p. 297; KENNEY, *Centenary, etc.*,
p. 198; SULLIVAN, *Catholic Church of New England, Archdiocese of Boston*. Boston, 1895; LEAHY, *History of the Catholic Church in the New
England States*, Boston, 1899.

5. O'CONNELL, WILLIAM CARDINAL.

The present Archbishop of Boston was born at
Lowell, Massachusetts, on December 8, 1859. After the
completion of his early studies in the primary schools of

his native city, he attended Saint Charles College at Ellicott City, Maryland.   He graduated from the Jesuit College in Boston (1881) and was sent to the American College in Rome, where he was ordained to the priesthood on June 8, 1884.   The following year he was appointed assistant at Medford and, later, served in Boston in that capacity until 1895, when he was appointed the Rector of the American College in Rome—a position he held during the subsequent five years.   He was then nominated Bishop of Portland, Maine, and was consecrated by His Eminence, Cardinal Satolli, on May 19, 1901.   On account of his success as special envoy to Japan, the Holy Father named Bishop O'Connell coadjutor to Archbishop Williams of Boston and on August 30, 1907, he succeeded to the See.   He was created Cardinal on November 27, 1911.

The present Auxiliary Bishop of Boston is the Rt. Rev. Joseph G. Anderson, who was born in that city on September 30, 1865.   He received his seminary training at Saint John's, Brighton, and was ordained to the priesthood on May 20, 1892, in Boston.   He served as Chaplain at the Massachusetts State Prison; Director of the Charities Bureau and Pastor of St. Paul's before his appointment as Auxiliary Bishop.   He was consecrated on July 25, 1909, by Cardinal O'Connell.

II. Diocese of Hartford (1843)

Pope Gregory XVI created the Diocese of Hartford on November 28, 1843, and the Reverend William Tyler, then Vicar-General of Boston, was consecrated as its first Bishop on March 17, 1844.

Originally, the Diocese of Hartford included the States of Connecticut and Rhode Island.   When the Diocese of Providence was erected in 1872, Rhode Island was abscinded, and Hartford now comprises only the State of Connecticut; an area of 5,004 square miles.

O'DONNELL, *History of the Catholic Church in New England*. Boston, 1899; SHEA, *History of The Catholic Church in the United States*. New York, 1888; FITTON, *Sketches of the Establishment of the Church in New England*. Boston, 1872; LEAHY, *History of the Catholic Church in the*

New England States. Boston, 1899; *The Catholic Transcript,* Hartford, Conn.; *The Connecticut Catholic Year Book,* Hartford, Conn.; DE COURCY-SHEA, *op. cit.,* CHR, Vol. ii, p. 297.

1. TYLER, WILLIAM.

The first Bishop of Hartford, a convert to the Faith, was born on June 5, 1806, at Derby, Vermont. He was ordained to the priesthood at Boston on June 5, 1827, and later distinguished himself in the missions of Maine and Massachusetts. Before his appointment as first Bishop of Hartford, he was Vicar-General of the Archdiocese of Boston. He was consecrated on March 17, 1844, by Bishop Fenwick. At the Seventh Provincial Council of Baltimore, he petitioned the Fathers to accept his resignation as Bishop, but they refused the request. He died at Providence, on June 18, 1849.

REUSS, *op. cit.,* p. 105; SHEA, *Hierarchy,* p. 253; CLARKE, *op. cit.,* Vol. ii, p. 272; CHR, Vol. ii, p. 297.

2. O'REILLY, BERNARD.

The second Bishop of Hartford was born at Columkille, County Longford, Ireland, in 1803 and completed his classical studies in his native land before coming to America. He finished his theology at St. Mary's, Baltimore, and was ordained to the priesthood on October 13, 1831. Bishop Timon, of Buffalo, consecrated him at Rochester on November 10, 1850. Having completed some ecclesiastical business of importance in Europe, he took passage on the ill-fated *Pacific* on January 23, 1856, which was lost at sea.

REUSS, *op. cit.,* p. 84; SHEA, *Hierarchy,* p. 254; CLARKE, *op. cit.,* Vol. ii, p. 391; CHR, Vol. ii, p. 297.

3. McFARLAND, FRANCIS P.

The third Bishop of Hartford was born at Franklin, Pennsylvania, on April 18, 1819. He received his education at Mt. St. Mary's, Emmitsburg, and was ordained to the priesthood on May 18, 1845. He was Administrator of the Diocese of Hartford in 1856, and was consecrated by Archbishop Hughes on March 14, 1858. He died at Hartford on October 12, 1874.

REUSS, *op. cit.*, p. 71; SHEA, *Hierarchy, etc.*, p. 255; CLARKE, *op. cit.*, Vol. iii, pp. 117-127; *History of the Catholic Church in the New England States*, Vol, ii, pp. 149-158. Boston, 1899; CHR, Vol. i, pp. 148-163 (*Early Times in the Diocese of Hartford*, by Rooney); *ibid.*, Vol. iv, p. 391 (diocesan bibliography).

4. GALBERRY, THOMAS, O. S. A.

Bishop Galberry was born at Naas, County Kildare, Ireland, in 1833. He entered the Augustinian Order after his graduation from Villa Nova College in 1851, and was ordained to the priesthood in Philadelphia on December 20, 1856. Archbishop Williams consecrated him on March 19, 1876. While on his way to Villa Nova in October, 1878, he was stricken with hemorrhages at the Grand Hotel in New York City, and died on October 17, 1878.

REUSS, *op. cit.*, p. 45, CHR, Vol. ii, pp. 297-298; SHEA, *Hierarchy, etc.*, pp. 256-257; CLARKE, op. cit., Vol. iii, pp. 128-140; ROONEY, *Early Times in the Diocese of Hartford*, in CHR, Vol, i, pp. 148-163; CUB, Vol. vii, p. 233 *seq.* (History of Hartford Diocese); O'DONNELL, *History of Diocese of Hartford*. Boston, 1900; see bibliography of Hartford Diocese.

5. McMAHON, LAWRENCE S.

The fifth Bishop of Hartford was born at St. John's, Newfoundland, on December 26, 1835. His youth and childhood were spent around Cambridge, Massachusetts, and he entered Holy Cross College at the age of fifteen. His higher studies were made in France and in Italy. He was ordained to the priesthood in Rome, on March 24, 1860. He served as Chaplain during the Civil War and was Vicar-General of the Diocese of Providence when appointed to the See of Hartford. His consecration took place at Hartford, August 10, 1879, with Archbishop Williams as consecrating prelate. He died at Lakeville, Connecticut, on August 21, 1893.

REUSS, *op. cit.*, p. 72; *History of the Catholic Church in New England*, Vol. ii, pp. 166-176. Boston, 1899.

6. TIERNEY, MICHAEL.

Bishop Tierney was born at Ballylooby, County Tipperary, Ireland, on September 29, 1839. He came to the

United States at an early age and spent his youth in the environs of Norwalk, Connecticut. After the completion of his studies in Montreal and at Troy, New York, he was ordained to the priesthood in May, 1866, and immediately after Bishop McFarland made him his chancellor and rector of the Cathedral. He was consecrated on February 22, 1894, by Archbishop Williams, and died at Hartford on October 5, 1908.

REUSS, *op. cit.*, p. 103; CHR, Vol. ii, p. 298.

7. NILAN, JOHN J.

The present Bishop of Hartford was born in Massachusetts on August 5, 1855, and received his educational training at Saint Joseph's Seminary, Troy, New York. He was ordained to the priesthood on December 21, 1878, and commenced his priestly career in the Archdiocese of Boston. He was acting as pastor of Saint Joseph's Church in Amesbury, Massachusetts, when appointed Bishop of Hartford on February 14, 1910, and was consecrated by His Eminence, Cardinal O'Connell, on April 28, 1910, in the Cathedral at Hartford.

Bishop Murray was acting as chancellor of the Diocese of Hartford when appointed titular Bishop of Flavias and Auxiliary to Bishop Nilan. He was born in Waterbury, Connecticut, on February 26, 1877, and he completed his theological training at the American College in Rome, where he was ordained to the priesthood on April 14, 1900. He was consecrated by the Most Rev. John Bonzano, Apostolic Delegate, on April 28, 1920, in Saint Joseph's Cathedral, Hartford, Connecticut.

III. Diocese of Burlington (1853)

The Diocese of Burlington was erected by Pius IX on July 15, 1853, and the Very Reverend Louis de Goesbriand, then Vicar-General of the Diocese of Cleveland, was named as first Bishop and consecrated in New York City on October 30, 1853.

The Diocese comprises its original territory—the State of Vermont; an area of 9,135 square miles.

DE GOESBRIAND, *Catholic Memoirs of Vermont and New Hampshire.*
Burlington, Vt., 1886; MICHAUD in *History of the Catholic Ch. in the New
England States,* Boston 1899, II; SHEA, *Hist. of Cath. Ch. in U. S.,*
New York, 1894; REUSS, *Biog. Cycl. of the Cath. Hierarchy of U. S.*
Milwaukee, 1898; *Catholic Directory,* 1907; CHR, Vol. ii, p. 298.

1. DE GOESBRIAND, LOUIS.

The first Bishop of Burlington was born at Saint
Urbain, France, on August 4, 1816, and received his entire
education in the schools of that country, completing his
theology at St. Sulpice, Paris.   He was ordained to the
priesthood on July 13, 1840, by Bishop Rosati and shortly
after set sail for the United States to labor in the Diocese
of Cincinnati.   When the Diocese of Cleveland was erected,
Bishop Rappe selected him to be his Vicar-General, an appointment he held until his elevation to the episcopate.
He was consecrated in New York City by Archbishop Bedini on October 30, 1853.   He was Dean of the American
Hierarchy at the time of his death on November 3, 1899.

REUSS, *op. cit.,* p. 49; SHEA, *Hierarchy, etc.,* pp. 195-197; CHR, Vol.
ii, pp. 299, 429; *Researches,* Vol. xxviii, p. 160; DE GOESBRIAND, *Catholic
Memoirs of Vermont and New Hampshire,* Burlington, Vt., 1866; DE
GOESBRIAND, *The Young Converts,* New York, 1908.

2. MICHAUD, JOHN S.

Bishop Michaud was born in Burlington, Vermont,
on November 24, 1843, and made his theological studies at
Saint Joseph's Seminary, Troy, N. Y.   His ordination to
the priesthood took place on June 7, 1873.   When Bishop
De Goesbriand asked for a coadjutor in 1892, the choice
fell upon the Reverend John Michaud, then pastor at Ben-
nington, who was consecrated titular Bishop of Modra by
Archbishop Williams on June 29, 1892.   Upon the retirement of his Ordinary, he became Administrator of the
Diocese and succeeded to the See on November 3, 1899.
He died at Burlington on December 22, 1908.

REUSS, *op. cit.,* p. 75; *History of the Catholic Church in New England,*
Vol. ii, p. 470, Boston, 1899; ACHS *Researches,* Vol. xxvi, p. 71 (on
Researches), p. 267 (on cooperation of French Clergy, 1780), Vol. xxiii,
p. 173 (on Fanny Allen's apparition), Vol. xxvi, p. 49 (on French clergy
gift of 1780).

3. RICE, JOHN J.

The present Bishop of Burlington was born at Leicester, Massachusetts, on December 6, 1871, and received his early training at Leicester Academy and at Holy Cross College. After graduating from college, he entered the seminary at Montreal, and on the completion of his course was ordained to the priesthood in Springfield, Massachusetts, on September 29, 1894. After his ordination, he went to Rome for post graduate work at the Propaganda and upon his return, he labored in the Springfield Diocese until 1901, when he accepted the Chair of Philosophy at Saint John's Seminary at Brighton, Massachusetts. Later he returned to his native diocese and served as pastor of St. Peter's Church at Northbridge, Massachusetts. Appointed Bishop of Burlington in 1910, he was consecrated by Bishop Beaven in the Cathedral of the Immaculate Conception at Burlington, on April 14, 1910.

IV. Diocese of Portland (1853)

The Diocese of Portland was erected on July 29, 1853, and the Right Reverend David W. Bacon, D.D., was consecrated as its first Bishop on April 22, 1855.

Formerly, the Diocese of Portland included the States of Maine and New Hampshire, but upon the erection of the Diocese of Manchester, in 1884, this latter State was abscinded from its area. As a result, its territorial extent at present is confined to the State of Maine; an area of 29,895 square miles.

YOUNG, *History of the Diocese of Portland*, Boston, 1899; SHEA, *History of the Catholic Church in the United States*, passim; FITTON, *op. cit.*, p. 209; *Histories of the Catholic Church*, cited under *Province of Boston*; DE COURCY-SHEA, *op. cit.*, p. 519; CHR, Vol. ii, pp. 298-299.

1. BACON, DAVID W.

The first Bishop of Portland was born in New York City, on September 15, 1813, and made his classical studies at the Sulpician College in Montreal and his theological studies at St. Mary's, Baltimore. He was ordained to the priesthood on December 13, 1838, and began his labors in the parishes of New York City. In 1841 he was sent to

Brooklyn to organize the third parish erected in that city and remained there until 1855, when he was appointed Bishop of the newly created Diocese of Portland. His consecration took place in New York City on April 22, 1855, with Archbishop Hughes as the consecrating prelate. Accompanying Archbishop McCloskey on a trip to Europe in 1874, he was stricken with illness while abroad and on the homeward voyage became worse. He survived until the ship reached New York City, where he died on November 5, 1874.

REUSS, *op. cit.,* pp. 9-10; CLARKE, *op. cit.,* Vol. iii, pp. 141-153; KENNEY, *Centenary of the See of Boston,* p. 217. Boston, 1909; CE, Vol. ii, p. 191; *Historical Records and Studies* of the ACHS, Vol. ii, p. 16; MITCHELL, *Golden Jubilee of Bishop Loughlin,* p. 79. Brooklyn, 1891; *Mulrenan,* Brief Historical Sketch of the Catholic Church on Long Island, p. 121: New York, 1871; FARLEY, *Life of John Cardinal McCloskey,* pp. 198, 261, 299, 302, 303. New York, 1918; CHR, Vol. ii, p. 299; SHEA, *Hierarchy, etc.,* p. 344; SHEA, *History of the Catholic Church, etc.,* Vol. iv, pp. 375, 535-539; LYNCH, *A Page of Church History in New York,* pp. 63-65. Utica, N. Y., 1894; *History of the Catholic Church in the New England States,* Vol. ii, pp. 137, 152, 690. Boston, 1899; BAYLEY, *History of the Catholic Church in New York,* p. 227. New York, 1879.

2. HEALY, JAMES A.

The second Bishop of Portland was born near Macon, Georgia, on April 6, 1830. He graduated from Holy Cross College in 1849, and received his theological training in Montreal and in Paris under the Sulpician Fathers. He was ordained to the priesthood in the Cathedral of Notre Dame, in Paris, on June 19, 1854. Upon his return to Boston, he was made secretary to Bishop Fitzpatrick and in March, 1866, became the first chancellor of the Diocese. He was appointed second Bishop of Portland on February 12, 1875, and was consecrated by Archbishop Williams on June 2, 1875. He died in Portland on August 23, 1907.

REUSS, *op. cit.,* p. 52; CHR, Vol. ii, p. 299; *Maine Catholic Historical Magazine, passim,* since 1913; SHEA, *Hierarchy, etc.,* pp. 345-346.

3. O'CONNELL, WILLIAM CARDINAL.

The third Bishop of Portland was consecrated on May 19, 1901; transferred to Boston on January 26, 1906 as titular Archbishop of Tomi and Coadjutor to Archbishop Williams and succeeded to the See on August 30, 1907. (Cf. Boston.)

4. WALSH, LOUIS S.

The present Bishop of Portland was born at Salem, Massachusetts, on January 22, 1858. He received his ecclesiastical training at the Grand Seminary, Montreal, at Saint Sulpice, Paris, and also in Rome where he was ordained to the priesthood on December 23, 1882. He labored in the Archdiocese of Boston as assistant pastor at Saint Joseph's Church and as professor at the Brighton Seminary until September, 1897, when he was appointed Supervisor of Schools in the Archdiocese of Boston. He was appointed Bishop of Portland in August, 1906, and was consecrated in that city by Bishop Harkins on October 18, 1906.

V. Diocese of Springfield (1870)

Pius IX erected the Diocese of Springfield on June 23, 1870 and the Reverend Patrick O'Reilly of Worcester was consecrated as its first Bishop on September 25, 1870.

The Diocese comprises its original territory of five counties in central and western Massachusetts; an area of 4,372 square miles.

McCoy, *History of the Catholic Church in New England*, Boston, 1899; FITTON, *Sketches of the Establishment of the Catholic Church in New England*, Boston, 1872; SHEA, *History of the Catholic Church in the United States*, New York, 1890; MALANEY, *Catholic Pittsfield and Berkshire*, Pittsfield, 1897; *The Official Catholic Directory*, New York, 1911; CHR, Vol. ii, p. 299.

1. O'REILLY, PATRICK T.

The first Bishop of Springfield was born in County Cavan, Ireland, on December 24, 1833, and he came to the United States at an early age and located in Boston. He was ordained to the priesthood in Boston, on August 15, 1857, and labored in that city and at Saint John's, Worcester, until his appointment as bishop, on June 28, 1870. He was consecrated by Archbishop McCloskey on September 25, 1870, at Springfield. He died in Springfield on May 28, 1892.

REUSS, *op. cit.,* p. 85; SHEA, *Hierarchy,* p. 371; FITTON, *op. cit.,* p. 287, *seq.;* CHR, Vol. ii, p. 300.

2. BEAVEN, THOMAS D.

Bishop Beaven was born in Springfield, Massachusetts, in 1851, and studied at Holy Cross College, Worcester, and the Grand Seminary at Montreal before his ordination to the priesthood on December 18, 1875. His priestly labors were exercised in the cities of Spencer and Holyoke, Massachusetts. On August 9, 1892, he was appointed as Bishop O'Reilly's successor in the See of Springfield and Archbishop Williams consecrated him on October 18, 1892. He died at Springfield on October 5, 1920.

REUSS, *op. cit.,* p. 12; CHR, Vol. ii, p. 300.

3. O'LEARY, THOMAS M.

Bishop O'Leary was born at Dover, New Hampshire, on August 16, 1875. His early training was received in the schools of his native city and at Mungret, in Ireland. After the completion of his theological course at the Grand Seminary, Montreal, he was ordained to the priesthood in that city in 1897. In 1904 he was appointed chancellor of the Diocese of Manchester, and on December 8, 1914, was designated Vicar-General. He was acting in that capacity when appointed Bishop of Springfield, in May, 1921. He was consecrated on September 8, 1921, in Springfield, Massachusetts, by Archbishop Sinnott of Winnipeg.

VI. Diocese of Providence (1872)

On February 17, 1872, Pius IX erected the Diocese of Providence and the Right Reverend Thomas F. Hendricken D.D. was consecrated as its first Bishop, on April 28, 1872.

Formerly, the Diocese of Providence included besides the State of Rhode Island, the southeastern portion of Massachusetts (now in the Diocese of Fall River). Its present extent is limited to the State of Rhode Island; an area of 1,085 square miles.

Histories of Church in New England, cited under *Province of Boston;*
DE COURCY-SHEA, *op. cit.;* CHR, Vol. i, p. 150, and Vol. iii, p. 300,
Providence Visitor for May 27, 1921.

1.   HENDRICKEN, THOMAS F.

The first Bishop of Providence was born on May 5,
1827, at Kilkenny, Ireland. All his educational training
was received in his native country and he was ordained to
the priesthood at All Hallows College by Bishop O'Reilly, of
Hartford, in 1853. He came to the United States to labor
in the Diocese of Hartford, where his ability as an Administrator was soon recognized. When the See of Providence
was created he was recommended to Rome by Bishop Mc-
Farland as the most worthy candidate. He was consecrated
by Archbishop McCloskey, of New York, on April 28, 1872.
He died at Providence on July 11, 1886.

REUSS, *op. cit.,* p. 52; SHEA, *Hierarchy, etc.,* pp. 347-384; CLARKE, *op.
cit.,* Vol. iii, pp. 324-338; CHR, Vol. ii, p. 350; *cf.* Bibliography of Boston
Province; *History of the Catholic Church in the New England States,*
Boston, 1889.

2.   HARKINS, MATTHEW.

Bishop Harkins was born in Boston, Massachusetts,
on November 17, 1845, and received his education at the
Boston Latin School, Holy Cross College, and Douai College, in France. He studied theology at St. Sulpice, France,
and was ordained to the priesthood in Paris on May .22,
1869. Upon his return to the United States, he labored in
the Archdiocese of Boston until he was appointed Bishop
of Providence on February 11, 1887. He was consecrated
by Archbishop Williams at Providence, on April 14, 1887.
He died in Providence on May 25, 1921.

REUSS, *op. cit.,* p. 52; CHR, Vol. ii, p. 300. *Cf.* Files of *Providence
Visitor.*

The Right Reverend Thomas F. Doran was appointed titular Bishop of Halicarnassus and Auxiliary
Bishop of Providence on March 11, 1915. He was born
in Barrington, Rhode Island, on October 4, 1856. He received his seminary training at Mount Saint Mary's,
Emmitsburg, Maryland, and he was ordained to the priesthood in Saint Charles Church, Woonsocket, Rhode Island,

on July 4, 1880. He was appointed Vicar-General in January, 1894, and in 1905 became Domestic Prelate. He was consecrated by Bishop Harkins, of Providence, in SS. Peter and Paul's Cathedral, Providence, Rhode Island, on April 28, 1915. He died at St. Joseph's Hospital, in Providence, on January 3, 1916.

The Right Reverend Denis M. Lowney was appointed titular Bishop of Adrianople and Auxiliary Bishop of Providence on July 4, 1917, and was consecrated by Bishop Beaven, of Springfield. He was born on June 1, 1863, in Ireland, and received his seminary training at the Grand Seminary, in Montreal. He was ordained to the priesthood on December 17, 1887; was appointed assistant at the Cathedral in Providence in 1891, and later, chancellor. He became permanent Rector of Saint Joseph's, Pawtucket, on June 3, 1905. In 1918 he returned to the Cathedral at Providence to assist Bishop Harkins as Auxiliary Bishop. He died at the Cathedral Rectory in Providence, on August 13, 1918.

3. HICKEY, WILLIAM A.

The present Bishop of the Diocese was born in Worcester, Massachusetts, on May 13, 1869, and received his primary education in the schools of that city, after which he entered Holy Cross College. His theological studies were made in Paris and he was ordained to the priesthood in Boston on December 22, 1893. He labored successfully as curate and pastor in the Diocese of Springfield until his appointment as Coadjutor *cum jure successionis* to the See of Providence. He was consecrated titular Bishop of Claudiopolis on April 10, 1919, by Bishop Beaven and succeeded to the See on May 25, 1921.

VII. Diocese of Manchester (1884)

Pope Leo XIII erected the Diocese of Manchester, on May 4, 1884, and the Right Reverend Denis Bradley was consecrated as its first Bishop on June 11, 1884.

The Diocese of Manchester still embraces its original territory of the State of New Hampshire; an area of 9,305 square miles.

Diocesan Archives; History of Catholic Church in New England; Guidon, files: *Life of Bishop Bradley,* Manchester, 1905; *Life of Rev. Wm. McDonald,* Manchester, 1909; *Official Catholic Directory* (Milwaukee); CHR, Vol. ii, p. 300.

1. BRADLEY, DENIS.

The first Bishop of Manchester was born in Castle Island, County Kerry, Ireland, on February 25, 1846, and at the age of eight he came to the United States with his mother who decided to make Manchester her residence. He studied theology at Saint Joseph's Seminary, in Troy, New York, and was ordained to the priesthood on June 13, 1871. He was assigned to duty in Portland and later became rector of the Cathedral and chancellor of the diocese, which office he filled until 1880, when he came to Manchester as pastor of Saint Joseph's Church. On May 4, 1884, he was chosen to be the first Bishop of the newly-created Diocese of Manchester and was consecrated by Archbishop Williams on June 11, 1884. He died at Manchester on December 13, 1903.

REUSS, *op. cit.,* p. 17; SHEA, *Hierarchy, etc.,* p. 286; CE, Vol. ii, p. 727 (biog. sketch); GABRIELS, *History of Troy Seminary,* New York, 1906; KENNEY, *Centenary, etc.,* p. 219; ACHS, *Researches,* Vol. xxii, p. 109; CHR, Vol. ii, p. 301; *History of the Catholic Church in the New England States,* Vol. ii, pp. 177-179, 471, 480, 500.

2. DELANY, JOHN B.

The second Bishop of Manchester was born at Lowell, Massachusetts, on August 6, 1864, and made his classical and philosophical studies at Holy Cross and Boston Colleges. He studied at Saint Sulpice, Paris, where he was ordained to the priesthood on May 23, 1891. At the time of his appointment as Bishop he was serving as chancellor of the Diocese and secretary to Bishop Bradley. He was consecrated on July 6, 1904. He died on September 8, 1906.

CHR, Vol. ii, p. 307; [G.C.D.], *Life and Writings of the Rt. Rev. John Bernard Delany, D. D., Second Bishop of Manchester.* Lowell, 1911.

3. GUERTIN, GEORGE A.

Bishop Guertin was born in Nashua, New Hampshire, on February 17, 1869, and was educated in the parochial schools of that city. Later he went to the College of St. Hyacinthe and St. Charles in the Province of Quebec to continue his studies, and afterwards to Saint John's Seminary at Brighton. He was ordained to the priesthood on December 17, 1892, and after his ordination he served as assistant at St. Augustine's Church in Manchester and at Lebanon. He was acting as pastor of St. Augustine's when he was appointed Bishop on January 2, 1907. He was consecrated by Bishop Harkins on March 19, 1907.

VIII. Diocese of Fall River (1904)

The Diocese of Fall River was erected by Pius X on March 12, 1904, and the Right Reverend William Stang D.D. was consecrated as its first Bishop on May 1, 1904.

The Diocese comprises Bristol, Barnstable, Dukes and Nantucket Counties and the towns of Marion, Mattapoisett and Wareham in Plymouth County in the south-eastern part of the State of Massachusetts; an area of 1,194 square miles.

Diocesan Archives; Catholic Directory, Milwaukee, 1908; *Missiones Catholicae,* Rome, 1907; *American College Bulletin,* Louvain, April, 1907; *Catholic Union,* New Bedford, Feb., 1908; *Cf. Histories of New England,* under Province of Boston.

1. STANG, WILLIAM.

The first Bishop of Fall River was born in Langenbrücken, Germany, in 1854. After the completion of his primary work in the schools of his native land, he enrolled in the American College at Louvain in October, 1875. He was ordained to the priesthood in 1878. In September of that year he came to the United States to labor in the Diocese of Providence, where he held the office of Rector of the Cathedral until 1895. Three years later he accepted an appointment as Professor of Moral Theology at Louvain, a position he held until the following year, when he returned to Providence to become Superior of the Diocesan

Mission Band. When appointed first Bishop of Fall River he was acting as pastor of Saint Edward's Church in Providence. He was consecrated on May 1, 1904. He died on February 2, 1907, at Rochester, Minnesota.

CHR, Vol. ii, p. 301.

2. FEEHAN, DANIEL F.

Bishop Feehan was born on September 24, 1855, at Athol, Massachusetts, and received his classical and philosophical training at St. Mary's College, Montreal, graduating in 1876. The next three years were spent at the Seminary of Troy, New York, and he was ordained to the priesthood on December 29, 1879. His priestly activities were exercised in the Diocese of Springfield where he labored until July 2, 1907, when he was appointed second Bishop of Fall River. He was consecrated on September 19, 1907, by Bishop Harkins, of Providence.

CHAPTER IX

THE PROVINCE OF PHILADELPHIA (1875)

The Province of Philadelphia was erected by Pius IX on February 12, 1875, with the Right Reverend James F. Wood, D.D., as its first Archbishop.

The Province is still limited to the State of Pennsylvania, and to the original suffragan sees of Pittsburgh (1843), Erie (1853), Scranton (1868) and Harrisburg (1868), the Diocese of Altoona was added in 1901.

SHEA, *Hist. of the Cath. Church in the U. S.*, New York, 1886-92; MAHONY, *Historical Sketches of the Cath. Churches and Institutions of Philadelphia;* KIRLIN, *Catholicity in Philadelphia*, Philadelphia, 1909; *Catholic Standard and Times*, files; *Am. Cath. Hist. Researches; Official Cath. Directory* (1911); GUILDAY, *Life and Times of John Carroll*, 2 vols., passim., New York, 1922; DILHET-BROWN, *Etat De L'Eglise Catholique ou Diocèse des Etats-Unis de L'Amérique Septentrionale*, passim., Washington, D. C., 1922; DE COURCY-SHEA, *New History of the Catholic Church in the United States*, passim., New York, 1879; CHR, Vol. iii, p. 22.

I. Diocese of Philadelphia (1808)

The Diocese of Philadelphia, one of the four original suffragan sees of Baltimore, was erected by Pius VII on April 8, 1808, and the Rt. Rev. Michael Egan was consecrated as its first Bishop on October 28, 1810.

In the beginning, the Diocese included the States of Pennsylvania, Delaware and West Jersey. At present it comprises all the City and County of Philadelphia, and the Counties of Berks, Bucks, Carbon, Chester, Delaware, Lehigh, Montgomery, Northampton and Schuylkill in the State of Pennsylvania; an area of 5,043 square miles.

1. EGAN, MICHAEL.

The first Bishop of Philadelphia was born in Galway, Ireland, in 1761, and entered the Franciscan Order at an early age. He came to the United States in 1802 and was received into the Diocese of Baltimore, where he served as pastor in various cities. In 1808 he was appointed first Bishop of the newly created See of Philadelphia and was consecrated by Archbishop Carroll in Baltimore on October 28, 1810. He died in Philadelphia on July 22, 1814.

REUSS, *op. cit.*, pp. 38-39 (important letters on his life); SHEA, *Hierarchy, etc.*, pp. 155-156; CLARKE, *op. cit.*, Vol. i, pp. 185-191; *Researches,* Vol. iii, pp. 53, 54, 60, pp. 2, 139, 144, Vol. vi, pp. 43-45, Vol. viii, pp. 65, 154, Vol. iv and x *passim* (*The History of the Schism in Philadelphia*); Vol. xvii, p. 79. Vol. xviii, p. 4, Vol. xxviii, p. 377; consult *Index* to *Researches;* KIRLIN, *Catholicity in Philadelphia,* pp. 195-210; GRIFFIN, *History of the Rt. Rev. Michael Egan, D.D., First Bishop of Philadelphia,* Philadelphia, 1893; CHR, Vol. i, pp. 311, 369, 439, Vol. iii, p. 22; CE, Vol. v, p. 324; see under CONWELL; MCSWEENY, *op. cit.,* Vol. i, pp. 32, 76, 82-85, 95, 100-132 *passim,* 219-25 *passim,* 413-534; MCCANN, *op. cit.,* Vol. i, pp. 94, 112; GUILDAY, *op. cit.,* Vol. i, p. 646 *seq.*

2. CONWELL, HENRY.

The second Bishop of Philadelphia was born at Moneymore, County Derry, Ireland, in 1748. He made his studies for the priesthood at the Irish College in Paris. His ordination to the priesthood occurred, probably in 1776, either at Paris or at Armagh. He was serving as Vicar-General of the Diocese of Armagh when appointed Bishop of Philadelphia on November 26, 1819. He was consecrated by the Vicar-Apostolic of London, Bishop Poynter, on September 24, 1820, and shortly afterward he came to the United States. After years of diocesan strife Bishop Conwell relinquished the affairs of the See to Reverend William Matthews, and the First Provincial Council of Baltimore petitioned the Holy See to appoint a coadjutor with the right of administration for Philadelphia. The request was granted and the Right Reverend Francis P. Kenrick became coadjutor. Bishop Conwell died in Philadelphia on April 22, 1842.

REUSS, *op. cit.,* pp. 27-28; CLARKE, *op. cit.,* Vol. i, pp. 310-327; SHEA, *Hierarchy, etc.,* p. 156; FISH, *op. cit.,* pp. 146-147, 180-182; FINOTTI, *op. cit.,* pp. 139, 141, 143, 149, 151-170 *passim;* MCCANN, *op. cit.,* Vol. i, p. 112; MCSWEENY, *op. cit.,* Vol. i, pp. 60, 150, 164, 277, 241; KIRLIN, *Catholicity in Philadelphia,* pp. 219-266. Philadelphia, 1909. *Cf. Index* to ACHS *Researches,* pp. 78-79. The American Catholic Historical Society began in 1913 (Vol. xxiv, p. 16 of its *Records*) the publication of the *Life of Bishop Conwell* of Philadelphia, written by Martin I. J. Griffith. For the literature on the troubles which burdened Conwell's episcopate, *cf. Index of Historical Pamphlets in the Library of St. Charles Seminary, Overbrook, Pa.,* in the ACHS *Records,* Vol. xxiii (902), pp. 66-119. *Cf.* CHR, Vol. i, p. 357, Vol. ii, pp. 227, 428, Vol. iii, pp. 22, 23, 336. *Cf.* for an account of his funeral by an eye-witness, SALZBACHER, *Meine Reise nach Nord-Amerika in Jahre,* 1842. Vienna, 1895. SHEA, *Hist. C. C. in the U. S.,* Vol. iii, pp. 229-264; GUILDAY, *op. cit.,* Vol. ii, p. 685.

3. KENRICK, FRANCIS PATRICK.

Became Bishop of Philadelphia on April 22, 1843, and was transferred to the See of Baltimore on August 19, 1851. (Cf. Baltimore.)

4. NEUMANN, JOHN.

Bishop Neumann was born at Prachatitz, Bohemia, on March 28, 1811, and began his studies for the priesthood in the Seminary at Budweis in 1831. He completed his course at the University of Prague in August, 1835, and returned to his native city for ordination. While there he decided to come to the United States as a seminarian to labor in the missions of this country, and accordingly set sail for New York, arriving there on June 2, 1836. He was adopted by Bishop Dubois and was ordained to the priesthood a few days later, on June 25, 1836. After laboring as a missionary in western New York, he entered the Redemptorist Congregation in 1840, and the following year was chosen to be Vice-Provincial of the Congregation in America. Under obedience, he was consecrated Bishop of Philadelphia at Baltimore by Archbishop Kenrick on March 28, 1852, Pius IX insisting that he accept the bishopric. He died quite suddenly in Philadelphia on January 5, 1860.

REUSS, *op. cit.*, pp. 79-80; SHEA, *Hierarchy, etc.*, p. 157; CLARKE, *op. cit.*, Vol. ii, pp. 431-467; BERGER, *Life of Bishop Neumann;* KIRLIN, *Catholicity in Philadelphia*, pp. 352-370. Philadelphia, 1909; MANGNIER, *Life of Venerable Bishop Neumann.* St. Louis, 1837; ACHS *Researches*, Vol. v, p. 46, xiv, p. 137 (burial of), xix, p. 186, xxii, p. 11, (fourth Bishop of Philadelphia), 22 (death of), 112 (in Philadelphia), xxiii, p. 263 (consecration), xxvi, p. 289 (consecration), xxviii, p. 212 (schools in Philadelphia), 313 (on Parochial Schools), 341-344 (Forty Hours Devotion), xxix, p. 41 (introduces Forty Hours Devotion in U. S.).

5. WOOD, JAMES F.

The first Archbishop of Philadelphia was born in that city on April 27, 1813. His early education was received there, and in 1827, he went to Cincinnati with his parents and obtained a position as a bank clerk. He was received into the Catholic Church by Bishop Purcell on April 17, 1838, and the next year, having decided to study for the priesthood, he was sent to Rome to pursue his studies at the Propaganda. He was appointed coadjutor-Bishop of the See of Philadelphia and was consecrated by Archbishop Purcell on April 26, 1857. The temporal administration of the diocese devolved on him even during the lifetime of Bishop Neumann and upon the death of the latter, on January 6, 1860, he succeeded to the See. He was made Archbishop on February 12, 1875, and presided over the First Provincial Council of Philadelphia on May 23, 1880. He died in Philadelphia on June 20, 1883.

REUSS, *op. cit.*, p. 110; SHEA, *Hierarchy*, p. 158; CLARKE, *op. cit.*, Vol. iii, p. 533 *seq.*; KIRLIN, *Catholicity in Philadelphia*; CHR, Vol. iii, p. 23; *Cf. Index* of the ACHS, *Researches*, p. 318.

6. RYAN, JOHN.

The second Archbishop of Philadelphia was born in County Tipperary, Ireland, on February 20, 1831. In 1847 he was adopted for the Archdiocese of St. Louis and entered St. Patrick's College, Carlow, to prepare for the priesthood. After the completion of his course in 1852 he came to the United States and by special dispensation was ordained to the priesthood in St. Louis on September 8, 1852. He held various important charges before his appointment as coadjutor to Bishop Kenrick, who consecrated him titular Bishop of Tricomia on February 14, 1872. He was translated to the See (titular) of Salamis as Archbishop on January 6, 1884, and on June 8, 1884, was promoted to the See of Philadelphia. He died there on February 11, 1911.

REUSS, *op. cit.*, p. 97; SHEA, *Hierarchy*, p. 106; CHR, Vol. iii, p. 23; *Cf.* Files of the Catholic Standard and Times; *Cf. Index* of the ACHS, *Researches*, p. 271.

7. PRENDERGAST, EDMOND F.

The seventh Bishop of Philadelphia was born in Clonmel, Ireland, on May 3, 1843, and came to the United States in 1859, and entered the Seminary at Overbrook, where he was ordained to the priesthood on November 17, 1865. He held various charges in Philadelphia until his appointment on November 27, 1865, as titular Bishop of

Scillio and Auxiliary to Archbishop Ryan. He was consecrated by Archbishop Ryan on February 24, 1897, and succeeded to the See on May 27, 1911. His death occurred in
Philadelphia on February 26, 1918.

REUSS, *op. cit.*, p. 90; CHR, Vol. iii, p. 23; Files of the *Catholic
Standard and Times* for May, 1911; ACHS, Researches, Vol. xix, p. 104;
*The Golden Jubilee of the Priesthood of the Most Rev. Edmond F. Pren-
dergast, D.D., and the Dedication of the Cathedral of the Saints Peter
and Paul, Philadelphia*, a brochure published at Philadelphia in 1915.
Archbishop Prendergast directed the translation of the *Diary and Visi-
tation Record of the Rt. Rev. Francis P. Kendrick, Administrator and
Bishop of Philadelphia (1830-1851)*. Philadelphia, 1916, privately printed.

8. DOUGHERTY, DENNIS CARDINAL.

The first Cardinal Archbishop of Philadelphia was
born at Ashland, Pennsylvania, on August 16, 1865. He
received his education at Saint Mary's College, Montreal,
Canada; Saint Charles Seminary at Overbrook, and the
American College in Rome, receiving the degree of Doctor of Divinity from the last school in 1890. On May
31, 1890, he was ordained to the priesthood by Cardinal
Parocchi and, upon his return to the United States, he was
made Professor of Dogmatic Theology at Overbrook. In
1903 he was selected for the bishopric of Neuva Segovia
in the Phillipine Islands and was consecrated in Rome by
Cardinal Satolli on June 14, 1903. His transfer to the See
of Jaro in the same Island group became effective on April
19, 1908, and seven years later he was again transferred
to the vacant See of Buffalo, New York, on December 6,
1915. He was promoted to the See of Philadelphia on
April 30, 1918, and the following year, on May 6, he was
invested with the pallium by the Most Reverend John Bonzano, Apostolic Delegate. He was preconized Cardinal on
March 10, 1921.

The Right Reverend Michael J. Crane, D.D., is the
present Auxiliary Bishop of Philadelphia, having been
consecrated titular Bishop of the See of Curium on August
21, 1921, by Cardinal Dougherty. He was born in Ashland,
Pennsylvania, on September 8, 1863. He was ordained to
the priesthood on June 15, 1889, by Archbishop Ryan and
in the following September he entered the Catholic Univer-

sity at Washington, where he remained a year doing post graduate work. On September 23, 1914, he was made a Papal Chamberlain with the rank of Monsignor, and on March 1, 1920, was appointed Vicar-General.

II. Diocese of Pittsburgh (1843)

On August 8, 1843, Pope Gregory XVI erected the Diocese of Pittsburgh and the Right Reverend Michael O'Connor was consecrated as its first Bishop on August 15, 1843. The Diocese of Pittsburgh embraced the whole of western Pennsylvania until the Diocese of Erie was erected in 1853. It now comprises the Counties of Allegheny, Beaver, Lawrence, Washington, Greene, Fayette, Butler, Armstrong, Indiana and Westmoreland in the State of Pennsylvania; an area of 7,238 square miles.

BARON, *Register of Baptisms and Burials in Fort Duquesne*, 1753-1756; CRAIG, *History of Pittsburgh*, Pittsburgh, 1851—; *The Catholic* Pittsburgh, 18844-1911, files; *St. Vincent's in Pennsylvania*, New York, 1873; O'CONNOR, *Diocesan Register*, Pittsburgh, 1843; LAMBING, *History of the Diocese of Pittsburgh*, New York, 1880; BECK, *The Redemptorists in Pittsburgh*, Pittsburgh, 1889; LAMBING, *Catholic Historical Researches*, Pittsburgh, 1844-86; GRIFFIN, *American Catholic Historical Researches*, Philadelphia, 1886-1911; IDEM, *History of Bishop Egan*, Philadelphia, 1893; *History of Pittsburgh*, Pittsburgh, 1908; *Cathedral Record, Pittsburgh*, Pittsburgh, 1895-1911; SHEA, *History of the Catholic Church in the United States*, New York, 1892; CHR, Vol. iii, pp. 23-24.

1. O'CONNOR, MICHAEL.

The first Bishop of Pittsburgh was born on September 27, 1810, at Queenstown, County Cork, Ireland. His early education was received in the schools of his native city; his ecclesiastical studies were made in France and in Rome. He was ordained to the priesthood in Rome on June 1, 1833, and immediately after he was appointed a professor in the Propaganda. He accepted Bishop Kenrick's offer to come to the United States in 1839 and was appointed professor at Saint Charles Borromeo Seminary. Later he was sent to Western Pennsylvania as Vicar-General, with a pastorate at Saint Paul's, in Pittsburgh. He was consecrated in Rome, Italy, on August 15, 1843, by Cardinal Fransoni, Prefect of Propaganda. He resigned from the See of Pittsburgh on May 23, 1860, and

entered the Jesuit Order at Woodstock, in Maryland, where
he died on October 18, 1872.

REUSS, *op. cit.,* p. 81; SHEA, *Hierarchy,* p. 336; CLARKE, *op. cit.,* Vol.
iii, p. 560; LAMBING, *op. cit.,* p. 59 sq.; CHR, Vol. iii, p. 24; *Cf. Index*
of the ACHS Researches, p. 228.

2. DOMENEC, MICHAEL.

The second Bishop of Pittsburgh was born at Ruez,
near Terragona, in Spain, on December 27, 1816. His
early education was received in Madrid and at the age of
fifteen he went to France for further study. While there
he entered the Lazarist Congregation and came to the
United States in 1838, and a year later was ordained to the
priesthood at the Barrens, St. Louis, Missouri. He served
there as professor for a while and came to Philadelphia in
1845 to take charge of the Diocesan Seminary and also
to act as pastor at Germantown. He was consecrated
Bishop of Pittsburgh by Archbishop Kenrick, of Baltimore,
on December 9, 1860. When the Diocese of Pittsburgh
was divided he was made first Bishop of Allegheny, a post
he held until July 27, 1877, when he resigned from this See
and retired to Spain, where he died at Terragona on January 7, 1878.

REUSS, *op. cit.,* p. 33; SHEA, *Hierarchy, etc.,* pp. 338-339; CLARKE, *op.
cit.,* Vol. iii, pp. 583-591; LAMBING, *History of the Catholic Church in the
Dioceses of Pittsburgh and Alleghany,* pp. 85-116; CHR, Vol. ii, p. 24.

3. TUIGG, JOHN.

Bishop Tuigg was born in Ireland on February 19,
1821, and after his early education had been completed, he
studied for the priesthood at All Hallows College, Dublin,
and at Saint Michael's Seminary in Pittsburgh. He was
ordained on May 14, 1850, by Bishop O'Connor, and later
was assigned to the Cathedral as assistant and secretary to
the Bishop. On January 11th, he was appointed to the See
of Pittsburgh, after serving as Vicar-forane of the eastern
part of the Diocese, since 1869. He was consecrated
on March 19, 1876, by Archbishop Wood, of Philadelphia.
He also acted as Administrator of Allegheny after the
resignation of Bishop Domenec and upon being stricken

with paralysis he solicited the appointment of a coadjutor who aided him in the administration of the Diocese until his death on December 7, 1889.

REUSS, *op. cit.,* p. 105; SHEA, *Hierarchy,* p. 339; LAMBING, *op. cit.,* p. 101 seq.; CHR, Vol. ii, p. 24.

4. PHELAN, RICHARD.

The fourth Bishop of Pittsburgh was born in County Limerick, Ireland, on January 1, 1828. He received his early education in Ireland but came to the United States to complete his theological studies at St. Mary's, Baltimore. He was ordained to the priesthood in Pittsburgh on May 4, 1854. In May, 1855, he was appointed coadjutor to Bishop Tuigg, and upon the latter's death was consecrated Bishop of Pittsburgh, on August 2, 1885, by Archbishop Ryan. He succeeded to the united Dioceses of Pittsburgh and Allegheny on December 7, 1889. He died at Idlewood, Pennsylvania, on December 20, 1904.

REUSS, *op. cit.,* p. 89; SHEA, *Hierarchy,* p. 343, CHR, Vol. iii, p. 24.

5. CANEVIN, J. F. REGIS.

The fifth Bishop of Pittsburgh was born in Westmoreland County, Pennsylvania, on June 5, 1853, and was educated at Saint Vincent's College and Seminary, Beatty, Pennsylvania. He was ordained to the priesthood in Pittsburgh on June 4, 1879. He was Rector of the Cathedral when selected to be Coadjutor of Bishop Phelan and was consecrated titular Bishop of Sabrata on February 24, 1903, by Archbishop Ryan of Philadelphia. He succeeded to the See of Pittsburgh on December 20, 1904, and resigned on November 26, 1920. He was designated titular Archbishop of Pelusium on January 9, 1921.

6. BOYLE, HUGH C.

The present incumbent of the See of Pittsburgh was born in Cambria Borough, now part of Johnstown, Pennsylvania, on October 8, 1873. His early education was received in the parochial schools of that locality and in his fourteenth year he entered Saint Vincent's College at

Beatty, Pennsylvania. He was ordained to the priesthood by Bishop Phelan on July 2, 1898, and was acting Rector of Saint Mary Magdalene's Church in Pittsburgh when chosen to be sixth Bishop of this See. He was consecrated on June 29, 1921, in Pittsburgh, by Archbishop Canevin.

III. Diocese of Erie (1853

The Diocese of Erie was erected on July 29, 1853, and the Right Reverend Josue M. Young was consecrated as first Bishop on April 23, 1854.

The Diocese comprises its original allotment of the following Counties in northwestern Pennsylvania: Erie, Crawford, Mercer, Venango, Forest, Clarion, Jefferson, Clearfield, Cameron, Elk, McKean, Potter and Warren; an area of 9,936 square miles.

LAMBING, *History of the Catholic Church in the Diocese of Pittsburgh,* New York, 1880; BATES, *Hist. of Cranford County;* SMALL, *Legislative Hand-Book;* SHEA, *Hist. of Cath. Ch. in U. S.,* New York, 1894; *Cf. Index* of the ACHS Researches, p. 107; CHR, Vol. iii, p. 25.

1. O'CONNOR, MAURICE.

As first Bishop of Erie he ruled the See for only seven months and then returned to Pittsburgh.
(Cf. Pittsburgh.)

2. YOUNG, JOSUE M.

The second Bishop of Erie, a convert from Episcopalianism, was born at Shapleigh, Maine, on October 29, 1808. He was ordained to the priesthood by Archbishop Purcell on April 1, 1838. He labored as a missionary in Ohio for many years and was selected to replace Bishop O'Connor in the See of Pittsburgh, but declined the appointment. He was consecrated second Bishop of Erie by Archbishop Purcell on April 23, 1854. He died quite suddenly at Erie on September 18, 1866.

REUSS, *op. cit.,* p. 110; SHEA, *Hierarchy,* p. 232, CHR, Vol. iii, p. 25; ACHS, *Researches,* Vol. iv, p. 1881, and Vol. xii, p. 46.

3. MULLEN, TOBIAS.

The third Bishop of Erie was born in County Tyrone, Ireland, on March 4, 1818. He attended Maynooth, and while there met Bishop O'Connor, of Pittsburgh, who prevailed on him to come to the United States to labor in his diocese. He accompanied the Bishop on his return to this country and was ordained to the priesthood on September 1, 1844, and began missionary labors in western Pennsylvania. He was consecrated Bishop of Erie on August 2, 1868, by Bishop Domenec. In May, 1897, he was stricken with paralysis and died on April 22, 1900.

REUSS, *op. cit.*, pp. 77-78; SHEA, *Hierarchy, etc.*, p. 233; LAMBING, *Foundation Stones of a Great Diocese*, p. 221, Williamsburg, 1914; CHR, Vol. iii, p. 25.

4. FITZMAURICE, JOHN E.

The fourth Bishop of Erie was born at Newtown-Sanders, County Kerry, Ireland, on January 9, 1840, and was ordained to the priesthood in Philadelphia on December 21, 1862. He was appointed Rector of the Diocesan Seminary and on February 24, 1898, was consecrated titular Bishop of Amisus and Coadjutor *cum jure successionis* of the Diocese of Erie by Archbishop Ryan of Philadelphia. He became Bishop of Erie on September 18, 1899, and died in that city on June 11, 1920.

REUSS, *op. cit.*, pp. 42, 43; CHR, Vol. iii, p. 25; *Cf.* NCWC, *News Bulletins* for June, 1921.

5. GANNON, JOHN MARK.

The present Bishop of Erie was born in that city on June 12, 1877. He received his collegiate training at Saint Bonaventure's, Allegheny, and in 1899 attended the Catholic University of America at Washington, D. C. He was ordained to the priesthood in Baltimore on December 21, 1901, after which he spent some time in further study at the Appolinaris in Rome, Italy, from which he received a Doctorate of Divinity in 1903. He held several important charges in the Diocese before his consecration as Auxiliary Bishop of Erie on February 6, 1918, by Bishop Hoban, of Scranton. He acted as Administrator of the See from the death of Bishop Fitzmaurice until his installation as the fifth Bishop of the Diocese on December 16, 1920.

IV. The Diocese of Harrisburg (1868)

The Diocese of Harrisburg was erected by Pius IX on March 3, 1868, and the Right Reverend Jeremiah F. Shanahan was consecrated as its first Bishop on July 12, 1868. Originally, the Diocese of Harrisburg comprised fifteen counties in the southern part of Pennsylvania, but two of these counties were abscinded upon the erection of the Diocese of Altoona. At present it comprises the Counties of Dauphin, Lebanon, Lancaster, York, Adams, Franklin, Cumberland, Perry, Juniata, Mifflin, Snyder, Northumberland, Union, Montour and Columbia in the state of Pennsylvania; an area of 8,000 square miles.

HASSETT, *An Historical Sketch of the Diocese of Harrisburg, 1868-1918.* (A brochure printed privately); CHR, Vol. iii, p. 25; *Catholic Directory* for 1922; *Cf.* Files of the *Catholic Standard and Times,* Philadelphia.

1. SHANAHAN, JEREMIAH F.

The first Bishop of Harrisburg was born at Silver Lake, Susquehanna County, Pennsylvania, in July 1834. His educational training was received at Saint Joseph's College, near Binghampton, New York, and at the Seminary of Saint Charles Borromeo in Phiadelphia. He was ordained to the priesthood on July 3, 1859, and a few months later he received the important appointment of Rector of the new Seminary at Glenriddle, Pennsylvania. He was nominated first Bishop of Harrisburg on March 3, 1868, and on July 12, 1868, was consecrated in Philadelphia by Archbishop Wood. He died in Harrisburg on September 24, 1886.

REUSS, *op. cit.,* p. 100; SHEA, *Hierarchy,* p. 25; CLARKE, *op. cit.,* Vol. iii, p. 548, CHR, Vol. iii, p. 25; HASSETT, *An Historical Sketch of the Diocese of Harrisburg,* 1868-1918, p. 2 seq.

2. McGOVERN, THOMAS.

Bishop McGovern was born in County Cavan, Ireland, in 1832. In 1855 he entered Mount Saint Mary's College, Emmitsburg, where he received the degree of Bachelor of Arts. He then enrolled at Mount Saint Mary's Theological Seminary, but completed his studies for the priesthood at Saint Charles Borromeo, Overbrook, where he was ordained to the priesthood on December 27, 1861. He was pastor in Danville when appointed second Bishop of Harrisburg. He was consecrated by Bishop O'Hara, of Scranton, on March 11, 1888. He died at Harrisburg on July 25, 1898.

REUSS, *op. cit.*, pp. 71-72; HASSETT, *An Historical Sketch of the Diocese of Harrisburg*, 1868-1918, pp. 15-18; CHR, Vol. iii, p. 25.

3. SHANAHAN, JOHN W.

The third bishop of this diocese was born at Silver Lake, Pennsylvania, on January 3, 1846. He was ordained to the priesthood at Overbrook Seminary in 1869. He was pastor of a church in Philadelphia when appointed Bishop of Harrisburg and was consecrated by Archbishop Ryan on May 1, 1899. He died in Harrisburg on January 19, 1916.

HASSETT, *op. cit.*, p. 21 seq.; CHR, Vol. iii, p. 25.

4. MCDEVITT, PHILIP R.

The present Bishop of Harrisburg was born in Philadelphia, Pennsylvania, on July 12, 1858. After his graduation from La Salle College in Philadelphia, he entered Saint Charles Borromeo Seminary at Overbrook, and was ordained to the priesthood at Philadelphia on July 14, 1885. He was Superintendent of parish schools in the Archdiocese of Philadelphia when appointed Bishop of Harrisburg on July 10, 1916. He was consecrated by Archbishop Prendergast, of Philadelphia, on December 21, 1916.

V. Diocese of Scranton (1868)

On March 3, 1868, the Diocese of Scranton was erected and the Right Reverend William O'Hara was consecrated as its first Bishop on July 12, 1868.

The Diocese comprises its original territory of eleven counties in northeastern Pennsylvania; an area of 6,710 square miles.

Official Catholic Directory; SHEA, *Life and Times of the Most Rev. John Carroll,* New York, 1888; BRADSBY, *History of Luzerne County,* Chicago, 1893; KIRLIN, *Catholicity in Philadelphia,* Philadelphia, 1909; LA

ROCHEFOUCAULD-LIANCOURT, *Voyage dans les Etats-Unis d'Amérique*, Paris, 1799-1800; MURRAY, *The Story of Some French Refugees and their "Azilum,"* Athens, 1903; CHR, Vol. iii, p. 26. We have been informed that a *History of the Diocese* will be published in the near future.

1. O'HARA, WILLIAM.

The first Bishop of Scranton was born in Dungibben, County Kerry, Ireland, on April 14, 1816. He came to the United States with his parents in 1820, and resided in Philadelphia. He studied philosophy and theology at the Urban College in Rome where he was ordained to the priesthood on December 21, 1842. After his ordination he served as pastor in Philadelphia for some years and was Vicar-General under Bishop Wood in 1860. When the Diocese of Scranton was erected, he was chosen as its first Bishop and was consecrated in Philadelphia by Archbishop Wood on July 12, 1868. He died in Scranton on February 3, 1899.

REUSS, *op. cit.*, p. 83; SHEA, *Hierarchy*, p. 369, CHR, Vol. iii, p. 26 seq.; ACHS, *Researches*, Vol. x, p. 191, and Vol. xxii, p. 337.

2. HOBAN, MICHAEL J.

The present Bishop of Scranton was born at Waterloo, New Jersey, on June 6,, 1853. His early education was received at Hawley, Pennsylvania, where his parents moved after his birth. After his collegiate course at Holy Cross College, Worcester and Saint John's College, Fordham, he spent a year at Saint Charles Seminary, Overbrook, and then went to the American College at Rome. He was ordained to the priesthood in Rome on May 22, 1880. His appointment as coadjutor-Bishop of Scranton was announced on February 1, 1896, and he was consecrated titular Bishop of Atalis by Cardinal Satolli on March 22, 1896. He succeeded to the See, on February 3, 1899, as second Bishop of Scranton.

VI. The Diocese of Altoona (1901)

The Diocese of Altoona was erected by Pope Leo XIII on May 30, 1901, and the Right Reverend Eugene Garvey, D. D., was consecrated as its first Bishop on September 8, 1901.

The Diocese of Altoona comprises the counties of Bedford, Blair, Cambria, Center, Clinton, Fulton, Huntington and Somerset in the State of Pennsylvania; an area of 6,710 square miles.

SHEEDY, *The Quarterly*, Altoona, October, 1901, vii, 263; IDEM, *The Observer*, Pittsburgh, February 25, 1904; LAMBING, *History of the Diocese of Pittsburgh*, New York, 1880; CHR, Vol. iii, p. 26.

1. GARVEY, EUGENE A.

The first Bishop of Altoona was born in Carbondale, Pennsylvania, on October 6, 1845. His educational training was received at Saint Charles College, Ellicott City, Maryland, and at Saint Charles Borromeo Seminary in Philadelphia. He was ordained to the priesthood on September 22, 1869, after which he labored as pastor in the Diocese of Philadelphia and on May 31, 1901, he was appointed first Bishop of Altoona. He was consecrated by Archbishop Prendergast on September 8, 1901. He died in Altoona on October 22, 1920.

CHR, Vol. iii, p. 26.

2. McCORT, JOHN J.

The present Bishop of Altoona was born in Philadelphia on February 16, 1860, and received his Seminary training at Saint Charles Seminary, Overbrook, Pennsylvania. He was ordained to the priesthood on October 14, 1883, and after his ordination was stationed at Saint Charles Seminary as professor. Later he was made rector of a church in Philadelphia and on July 26, 1910, was appointed Vicar-General of the Archdiocese. On June 28, 1912, he was appointed titular Bishop of Azotus and Auxiliary of Philadelphia and was consecrated by Archbishop Prendergast on September 17, 1912. He was named Coadjutor to Bishop Garvey of Altoona with the right of succession on January 27, 1920, and he became Bishop of the See on October 22, 1920.

CHAPTER X.

THE PROVINCE OF MIILWAUKEE (1875)

The Province of Milwaukee was erected by Pius IX on July 12, 1875, and the Right Reverend John M. Henni, D. D., was appointed as first Archbishop.

The Province includes its original limits of the State of Wisconsin and the Upper Peninsula of Michigan. When erected, the suffragan sees were the Dioceses of Sault Sainte Marie-Marquette (1857), Green Bay (1868) and La Crosse (1868). These Dioceses, with the See of Superior, erected in 1905, are the present suffragan sees.

The Metropolitan Catholic Almanac and Laity's Directory, Baltimore; WILTZIUS, *Catholic Directory*, Milwaukee; SULLIVAN, *The Catholic Church in Wisconsin*, Milwaukee, 1895; *Memoirs of Milwaukee County*, Madison, 1909; MARTY, *Johann Martin Henni, erster Bischof und Erzbischof von Milwaukee*, New York, 1888; RAINER, *A Noble Priest, Joseph Salzmann, Founder of the Salesianum*, tr. from the German by BERG, Milwaukee, 1903; ABBELEN, *Die Ehrwuerdige Mutter Caroline Fries*, St. Louis, 1892; SHEA, *History of the Catholic Church, etc.*, New York, 1898; HAUG, *Geschichte der Katolischen Kirche in Wisconsin*, Milwaukee, 1899; CHR, Vol. ii, pp. 26, 27.

I. Diocese of Milwaukee (1843)

In 1843 the Fathers of the Fifth Provincial Council of Baltimore petitioned the Holy See to erect the Diocese of Milwaukee, and on November 24, 1843, Pope Gregory XVI granted the request. The Right Reverend John M. Henni, D. D., was consecrated as first Bishop of the diocese on March 19, 1844.

When erected the Diocese had as territorial limits Wisconsin Territory (the present State of Wisconsin and that part of the present State of Minnesota which lies east of the Mississippi River). At present the Diocese comprises the Counties of Columbia, Dane, Dodge, Fond du Lac, Green, Green Lake, Jefferson, Kenosha, Marquette, Ozaukee, Racine, Rock, Sheboygan, Walworth, Washington, Waukesha, in the State of Wisconsin; an area of 9,321 square miles.

1. HENNI, JOHN M.

The first Archbishop of Milwaukee was born at Misanenga, Switzerland, on June 15, 1805, and studied philosophy and theology in Rome. He pledged his services to the Very Reverend Frederic Résé, then Vicar-General of the Diocese of Cincinnati, to labor in the missionary fields, and together with his fellow-student Kundig arrived in New York in 1828. Bishop Fenwick ordained him to the priesthood in Cincinnati on February 2, 1829, and he labored as a missionary in the State of Ohio, until appointed first Bishop of Milwaukee on November 28, 1843. He was consecrated by Archbishop Purcell on March 19, 1844. On June 3, 1875, he was promoted to the archiepiscopate and he died in Milwaukee on September 7, 1881.

REUSS, *op. cit.*, p. 53; CHR, Vol. iii, p. 27; SHEA, *Hierarchy, etc.*, pp. 111-113; CLARKE, *op. cit.*, Vol. iii, pp. 324-338; HAUG, *op. cit.*, *passim.*

2. HEISS, MICHAEL.

The second Archbishop of Milwaukee was born in Pfahldorf, Bavaria, on April 28, 1818. He entered the Latin School at the age of nine, and completed his theology at the University of Munich. He was ordained to the priesthood on October 18, 1840, after which he spent two years in his home Diocese of Eichstatt and then offered his services to the American Mission. He had charge of a church at Covington until 1844, when he accompanied Archbishop Henni to Milwaukee as secretary. After filling the office of secretary for a number of years he was given the pastorate of Saint Mary's Church in Milwaukee, and later became the first rector of Saint Francis Seminary. He was consecrated Bishop of La Crosse on September 6, 1868, by Archbishop Henni and was transferred to the Archiepiscopal See of Milwaukee as Coadjutor to Archbishop Henni and titular Archbishop of Adrianople on March 14, 1880. He succeeded to the See as Second Archbishop on September 7, 1881. He died at La Crosse on March 26, 1890.

REUSS, *op. cit.*, p. 52; SHEA, *Hierarchy, etc.*, pp. 114-117; CHR, Vol. iii, pp. 27-29; HAUG, *op. cit. passim.* Among his published works are: *The Four Gospels Examined and Vindicated*, Milwaukee, 1863, and *De Matrimonio*, Munich, 1861.

3. KATZER, FREDERICK X.

Archbishop Katzer was born at Ebensee, Upper Austria, on February 7, 1844, and was ordained to the priesthood on December 21, 1866, after completing his theology at the Salesianum in Milwaukee. He was appointed professor at the Seminary after his ordination and in 1875 he went to Green Bay where he acted as secretary, and later as Vicar-General to Bishop Krautbauer. In 1885 he was appointed Administrator of the Diocese. On May 31, 1886, he was chosen Bishop of that See and was consecrated by Archbishop Heiss on September 21, 1886. He was promoted to the See of Milwaukee on January 30, 1891, and died at Fond du Lac, Wisconsin, on August 4, 1903.

REUSS, *op. cit.*, p. 59; CHR, Vol. iii, pp. 27-28; CUB, Vol. ix, p. 574; AER, Vol. vi, pp. 241 *et seq.* (On Forbidden Societies); ACHS *Researches*, Vol. xii, p. 38, Vol. xx, p. 128; *Cf.* STECKEL, *The Catholic Church in Wisconsin* in the ACHS *Records*, Vol. vii, pp. 225-233; HAUG, *op. cit.*, passim.

4. MESSMER, SEBASTIAN G.

Archbishop Messmer was born at Goldach, Switzerland, on August 29, 1847. He completed his theology at Innsbruck and was ordained to the priesthood on July 23, 1871. He came to the United States shortly after and joined the Diocese of Newark. For many years he was Professor at Seton Hall Seminary and in 1889 he was called to the chair of Canon Law, at the Catholic University of America, Washington, D. C. He held this position until his appointment to the See of Green Bay on December 14, 1891. His consecration took place in Newark on March 27, 1892, with the Right Reverend Bishop Zardetti as consecrating prelate. He was transferred to the See of Milwaukee on November 28, 1903.

Bishop Kozlowski was born in Michigan and received his educational training at Saint Francis Seminary, Milwaukee. After his ordination to the priesthood on June 29, 1887, he labored in the Diocese of Grand Rapids before his appointment as Auxiliary Bishop of Milwaukee. He was consecrated by Archbishop Messmer in the Milwaukee Cathedral on January 14, 1914. He died in that city on August 6, 1915.

II. Diocese of Sault Ste. Marie-Marquette (1857)

The Vicariate of Upper Michigan was erected into the Diocese of Sault Sainte Marie on January 9, 1857, and the Right Reverend Frederic Baraga, D.D., was appointed as its first Bishop.

The Diocese comprises its original territorial limits,— the Upper Peninsula of the State of Michigan; an area of 16,281 square miles.

REZEK, *History of the Diocese of Sault Ste. Marie and Marquette,* Houghton, Mich., 1906; THWAITES, *The Jesuit Relations,* Cleveland, 1901; VERWYST, *Life of Bishop Baraga,* Milwaukee, 1900; KELTON, *Annals of Fort Mackinac,* Detroit, 1890; JACKER, *in the American Catholic Quarterly Review,* I, 1876, *History of the Upper Peninsula of Michigan,* Chicago, 1883; *Acta et Decreta, Collectio Lacensis,* III; *Berichte der Leopoldinen Stiftung in Kaiserthume Oesterreich,* Vienna, 1832-65; *Diocesan Archives, Marquette, Mich.; Catholic Directory for 1922;* CHR, Vol. iii, pp. 27–28.

1. BARAGA, FREDERIC.

The first Bishop of Upper Michigan was born in the Austrian Dukedom of Carniola, on June 29, 1797, and in 1816 he entered the University of Vienna to study law. Some time after he went to the Seminary at Laibach where he was ordained to the priesthood on September 21, 1823. For seven years after his ordination he labored in his native land and on October 29, 1830, he came to the United States, arriving in Cincinnati on January 18, 1831. The following Spring he was sent to Arbre Croche where he began his missionary labors among the Indians. For ten years he labored among the natives of this region and for a long time, he was the only priest in that part of the State. He was appointed Vicar-Apostolic of Upper Michigan on July 29, 1853, and was consecrated titular Bishop of Amyzonia at the Cathedral in Cincinnati by Archbishop

Purcell on November 1, 1853. He became first Bishop of
Sault Sainte Marie on January 9, 1857. He died in Marquette on January 19, 1868.

REUSS, *op. cit.*, p. 10; CLARKE, *op. cit.*, Vol. ii, pp. 468-505; SHEA, *History of the Catholic Missions Among the Indian Tribes of the United States*
(1529-1854), pp. 388-401. New York, 1855; list of his writings in CLARKE,
op. cit., Vol. ii, pp. 487-488, and CE., Vol. ii, p. 283; JACKER, *Life and
Services of the Rt. Rev. Frederick Baraga*, in the *Catholic Telegraph* for
Feb. 19 and 26, 1868; ZAPLOTNIK, *A Lecture delivered by Bishop Baraga*,
in *Acta et Dicta*, Vol. v, (1917), pp. 99-110; ELLIOTT, *Baraga Among the
Indians*, in the ACQR, Vol. xxi (1896), p. 106; *Memoirs of Father Mazzu-
chelli, O. P.*, pp. 64-69, Chicago, 1915; REZEK, *History of the Diocese of
Sault Ste. Marie and Marquette*. Houghton, Mich., 1906; VERWYST, *Life
and Labors of the Rt. Rev. Frederick Baraga*. Milwaukee, 1900; biographical sketch in CE, Vol. ii, pp. 282-283; ACHS, *Researches*, Vol. xv, p. 2;
Vol. xiii, p. 180, Vol. xx, p. 69; *Berichte der Leopoldinen-Stiftung, passim*
for the years of his episcopate (1853-1868)—for which see CHR, Vol. i,
pp. 51-62, 175-190, where an analysis is given of his letters to the Leopoldine Society; articles in the Baltimore *Metropolitan* (the first Catholic
magazine) for 1830-34; in 1906, his life appeared in Slovenian—the sale of
which has already reached 100,000 copies; other references in CHR, Vol. i,
pp. 51, 54-55, 182, Vol. iii, p. 28; SHEA, *Hierarchy*, etc., p. 288; SHEA,
History of the Catholic Church in the United States, Vol. iii, pp. 614,
634; *ibid.*, Vol. iv, pp. 576, 589-593; SILAS FARMER, *The History of Detroit
and Michigan*, Detroit, 1884; *The Bi-centenary of the Founding of Detroit*,
issued by the Common Council of the City of Detroit. Detroit, 1902; *Land-
marks of Detroit and History of the City*, by Robert B. Ross and Geo.
Catlin, revised by C. M. Burton. Detroit, 1891; *An Old Indian Mission*,
Translation of the Letters of Father Baroux by Rt. Rev. E. D. Kelly, DD.
Ann Arbor Press, 1913; *A Retrospect*, by A Sister of The I. H. M. New
York, 1916; HEBERMANN, *Sulpicians in the U. S.* New York, 1917; EDWIN
O. WOOD, *Historic Mackinac*, 2 Vols., New York, 1918; ACHS, *Researches*
for July, 1896, April, Oct., 1897, articles by Richard R. Elliott; *The Jesuit
Manuscript*, translated and annotated by R. R. Elliott, Vol. iv, No. 15, in
the *U. S. Catholic Magazine;* CHAS. LANMAN, *The Red Book of Michigan*.
Detroit, 1871; R. R. Elliott's contributions to the *Michigan Catholic; The
Church Farm*, by R. R. Elliott, in the *Detroit Sunday News*, Aug. 23 and
30, 1891; The C. M. Burton *Historical Collections;* Michigan Pioneer and
Historical Collections; *The Diocese of Detroit*, by Rev. F. A. O'Brien, Vol.
ix, 1886; *Italians in Detroit*, by Rev. John Vismara, DD., in the Michigan
Pioneer and Historical Collections, 1918; *Rt. Rev. Edmond Joos, V. G.*, by
Rev. F. A. O'Brien, *ibid.*, Vol. xxx; *The Roman Catholics in Detroit*, by
a Layman, *ibid.*, Vol. i; ENGELHARDT, *Baraga*, in the *Indian Sentinel*, Jan.,
1919. Among his important works are: a *Chippewa Dictionary* (Cincinnati,
1853) ;*Theoretical and Practical Grammar of the Chippewa Language*,
Detroit, 1850; *History, Character and Habits of the North American
Indians*, (Laibach and Paris, 1837).

2. MRAK, IGNATIUS.

The second Bishop of this See was born in Poland,
Diocese of Laibach, Austria, on October 16, 1818, where he
received his ecclesiastical training in the Diocesan Semi-

nary. He was ordained to the priesthood on August 13, 1837, and after spending a few years in parochial work in his own country, he came to the United States in 1845 and proceeded to the Diocese of Detroit. As a missionary among the Indians he labored at Harbor Springs, La Croix, and Eagle Town. On November 20, 1859, he was made Vicar-General of the Diocese of Sault Sainte Marie and was consecrated as the successor of Bishop Baraga in Cincinnati by Archbishop Purcell on February 7, 1869. Owing to ill health he resigned the See in 1878, but remained in the city of Marquette until 1884, when he moved to Eagle Town. He died there on January 2, 1901.

REUSS, *op. cit.*, p. 77; SHEA, *Hierarchy, etc.*, p. 291; CHR, Vol. iv, p. 543 (diocesan bibliography) : REZEK, *op. cit.*, Vol. i, p. 216 seq.

3.   VERTIN, JOHN.

Bishop Vertin was born in Doblin Parice, Province of Carniola, Austria, on July 17, 1844. He made his preparatory and collegiate course in his native country and came to Houghton, Michigan, at the age of eighteen. Bishop Baraga sent him to the Salesianum in Milwaukee in 1864. After completing his theology he was ordained to the priesthood in Marquette on August 31, 1866. He was entrusted with the mission at Houghton and later at Negaunee, where he labored successfully until his appointment to the See of Sault Ste. Marie-Marquette, on May 15, 1875. He was consecrated by Bishop Heiss on September 14, 1879, in Negaunee, Michigan. He died in Marquette on February 26, 1899.

REUSS, *op. cit.*, pp. 106-107; SHEA, *Hierarchy*, p. 292; REZEK, *op. cit.*, Vol. i, p. 260, seq.; CHR, Vol. iii, p. 28.

4.   EIS FREDERICK.

The present Bishop of Marquette was born at Arbach, Diocese of Treves, Germany, on January 20, 1843, and emigrated to the United States in 1855. His studies for the priesthood were made at Saint Francis Seminary, Milwaukee, and at Joliet, Canada. He was ordained to the priesthood on October 30, 1870, and filled many important pastorates until he was named Administrator of the Diocese after the death of Bishop Mrak. He was appointed to the vacant See of Marquette by Leo XIII on June 7, 1899, and was consecrated by Archbishop Katzer on August 24, 1899.

III. Diocese of Green Bay (1868)

The Diocese of Green Bay was erected on March 3, 1868, and the Right Reverend Joseph Melcher was consecrated as its first Bishop on July 12, 1868.

The Diocese comprises its original limits of the Counties of Brown, Calumet, Door, Florence, Forest, Kewaunee, Langlade, Waushara, Winnebago, Manitowoc, Marinette, Oconto, Outagamie, Portage, Shawano, Waupaca, in the State of Winsconsin; an area of 11,583 square miles.

Catholic Directory (Milwaukee, 1909) ; *Catholic Home Almanac* (New York, 1892) ; *Catholic Citizen* (Milwaukee), files ; *Cf. Bibliography* under the Province of Milwaukee for further references ; CHR, Vol. iii, p. 28.

1. MELCHER, JOSEPH.

Bishop Melcher was born in Vienna, Austria, on March 19, 1806, and attended the schools of his native city. He was ordained to the priesthood at Modena on March 27, 1830, and upon his return to Austria he acted as Chaplain to the Court. In response to the plea of Bishop Rosati for missionaries, he set out for the United States in 1843. He labored in Little Rock and in Saint Louis and for a number of years was Vicar-General of the Diocese of St. Louis. He was appointed Bishop of Green Bay, and was consecrated in St. Louis by Archbishop Kenrick on July 12, 1868. He died at Green Bay on December 20, 1873.

REUSS, *op. cit.*, p. 74; SHEA, *Hierarchy, etc.*, p. 248; CLARKE, *op. cit.*, Vol. iii, pp. 339-345. HAUG, *op. cit. passim.*

2. KRAUTBAUER, FRANCIS X.

The second Bishop of Green Bay was born in Bruck, Bavaria, on January 12, 1824. He received his education in his native land and came to the United States after his ordination to the priesthood on July 16, 1850. He began his priestly career in the Diocese of Buffalo, and later proceeded to Milwaukee, where he remained for ten years, until his selection as successor to Bishop Melcher, in February, 1875. Archbishop Henni consecrated him in Milwaukee on June 25, 1875. He died at Green Bay on December 17, 1885.

REUSS, *op. cit.*, p. 62; CHR, Vol. iii, p. 28; ACHS, *Researches*, Vol. iv, pp. 152, 155; SHEA, *Hierarchy, etc.*, pp. 249–250; CLARKE, *op. cit.*, Vol. iii, pp. 346–356.

3. KATZER, FREDERICK X.

The third Bishop of Green Bay was consecrated on September 21, 1886, and was promoted to the See of Milwaukee on January 30, 1891.

(Cf. Milwaukee.)

4. The present Archbishop of Milwaukee served as fourth Bishop of Green Bay until his translation to his present position on November 28, 1903.

(Cf. Milwaukee.)

5. FOX, JOSEPH J.

The fifth Bishop of Green Bay was born in that city on August 2, 1855. His theological studies were made at Louvain and he was ordained to the priesthood on June 7, 1870. He served as secretary to Bishop Krautbauer; Vicar-General of the Diocese of Green Bay, and pastor of Mariette before his appointment as Bishop of this See on May 27, 1904. His consecration took place on July 25, 1904, with Archbishop Messmer as the consecrating prelate. He resigned the See on December 4, 1914, and was made titular Bishop of Ionopolis. He died a few months afterward, on March 14, 1915.

CHR, Vol. iii, p. 29; *Catholic Directory* for 1922.

6. RHODE, PAUL L.

The present Bishop of Green Bay was born in Wegoramo (Neustadt), Prussian Poland, on September 18, 1871. He made his studies at the colleges of Saint Mary's and

Saint Ignatius in Illinois, and was ordained to the priesthood on June 17, 1894. He held various pastorates in the city of Chicago, and on May 22, 1908, was appointed titular Bishop of Barca and Auxiliary Bishop of Chicago. He was consecrated by Archbishop Quigley on July 29, 1908. He was transferred to the Diocese of Green Bay on July 5, 1915.

IV. Diocese of La Crosse (1868)

The Diocese of La Crosse was erected simultaneously with that of Green Bay, on March 3, 1868. The Right Reverend Michael Heiss was consecrated as its first Bishop on September 6, 1868.

When erected, the Diocese included that part of the State of Wisconsin lying north and west of the Wisconsin River. In 1905 it was given its present limits of the Counties of Adams, Buffalo, Chippewa, Clark, Crawford, Dunn, Eau Claire, Grant, Iowa, Jackson, Juneau, La Crosse, Lafayette, Marathan, Monroe, Pepin, Pierce, Richland, Sauk, Trempealeau, Vernon and Wood; an area of 17,299 square miles.

DECOURCY-SHEA, *New History of the Catholic Church in the United States*, New York, 1879; HAUG (compilation) *op. cit. passim;* CHR, Vol. iii, p. 29. *Official Catholic Directory,* 1869–1910; *Catholic Family Almanac,* New York, 1892; *Benziger's Almanac,* New York, 1888, 1893; *The Catholic Citizen* (Milwaukee), files.

1. HEISS, MICHAEL.

The first Bishop of LaCrosse was consecrated on September 6, 1868; transferred to the See of Milwaukee on September 7, 1881.

(Cf. Milwaukee.)

2. FLASCH, KILLIAN C.

The second Bishop of LaCrosse was born at Retzstadt, Bavaria, on July 16, 1837, and came to the United States with his parents at the age of ten years. He made his academic studies at Notre Dame University and completed his theology at Saint Francis Seminary, Milwaukee, where he was ordained to the priesthood on September 16,

1859.   He was a professor at the Salesianum in Milwaukee
when appointed to the See of La Crosse and was consecrated
by Archbishop Heiss in the Chapel of Saint Francis Seminary, Milwaukee, on August 24, 1881.   He died at La
Crosse on August 3, 1891.

REUSS, *op. cit.*, p. 44; CHR, Vol. iii, p. 29.

3. SCHWEBACH, JAMES.

Bishop Schwebach was born at Platten, Luxemburg,
on August 15, 1847.   He made his early studies at the
College of Diekirk, after which he emigrated to the United
States where he completed his theological course at Saint
Francis Seminary, Milwaukee.   He was ordained to the
priesthood on July 17, 1870, and served as rector of Saint
Mary's Church under the administration of Bishops Heiss
and Flasch.   He was Administrator of the Diocese when
chosen as third Bishop of La Crosse and was consecrated
by Archbishop Katzer in the Cathedral at La Crosse on
February 25, 1892.   He died at La Crosse on June 6, 1921.

REUSS, *op. cit.*, p. 99; CHR, Vol. iii, p. 29.

4. MCGAVICK, ALEXANDER J.

The present Bishop of La Crosse was born in Lake
County, Illinois, on August 21, 1863.   At the age of sixteen
he entered Saint Viator's College, where he completed his
classical course, after which he enrolled in the theological
school of that same institution.   Archbishop Feehan ordained him to the priesthood on June 11, 1887, and he
served in Chicago at the churches of All Saints and Saint
John.   He was appointed Auxiliary Bishop to Archbishop
Feehan in December, 1898, and was consecrated by him on
May 1, 1899.   He held the irremovable rectorship of the
Church of the Holy Angels until his appointment to the See
of La Crosse on November 21, 1921.

V. Diocese of Superior (1905)

The Diocese of Superior was erected by Pius X on May
3, 1905, and the Right Reverend Francis Schinner was
consecrated as its first Bishop on July 25, 1905.

The Diocese comprises the Counties of Ashland, Barron, Bayfield, Burnett, Douglas, Iron, Lincoln, Oneida, Polk, Price, Rusk, Sawyer, St. Croix, Taylor, Velas and Washburn in the northern part of the State of Wisconsin; an area of 15,715 square miles.

The Catholic Church in Superior, Wisconsin, Superior, 1905; HAUG, *Geschichte der Katolischen Kirche in Wisconsin, passim,* Milwaukee, 1899; CHR, Vol. iii, p. 26–27.

1. SCHINNER, AUGUSTINE F.

Consecrated Bishop of Superior on July 25, 1905; resigned the See on January 15, 1913, and was appointed Bishop of Spokane on March 18, 1914.

(Cf. Spokane.)

2. KOUDELKA, JOSEPH M.

The second Bishop of Superior was born at Chlistova, Bohemia, Austria, on December 8, 1852. He was educated at the College of Klattan in his native land, and at Saint Francis' Seminary in Milwaukee. He was ordained to the priesthood on October 8, 1875, and served as pastor of several churches in Cleveland until his appointment as titular Bishop of Germanicopolis and Auxiliary of Cleveland on November 29, 1907. Bishop Horstmann consecrated him on February 26, 1908, and he was transferred to Milwaukee as Auxiliary to Archbishop Messmer on September 4, 1911. He was appointed Bishop of Superior on August 6, 1913, and he died in that city on June 24, 1921.

CHR, Vol. iii, p. 29; Cf. NCWC, *news bulletins* for June, 1921; Bishop Koudelka was the author of a series of *Bohemian Readers* for the use of Catholic Schools in Bohemian Congregations.

3. PINTEN, JOSEPH.

The present Bishop of Superior was born in 1867 at Rockland, Michigan, and received his early education in the schools of Calumet. After completing studies in the Seminary at Milwaukee and at the American College, Rome, he was ordained to the priesthood on November 1, 1890. Upon his return to the United States he was stationed at Detour, Michigan, where he remained for a year and then spent four years as pastor of the Italian parish in Iron Mountain. He was sent to Marquette in 1897, and served as pastor there until 1916, when Bishop Eis designated him as Vicar-General of the diocese. He was acting in this capacity when appointed to the See of Superior and was consecrated by Archbishop Messmer on May 3, 1922.

CHAPTER XI

THE PROVINCE OF SANTA FE (1875)

Pope Pius IX erected the Province of Santa Fé on February 12, 1875, and the Right Reverend John B. Lamy, D.D., was appointed its first Archbishop.

When erected the Province had as suffragans the Vicariates-Apostolic of Colorado and Arizona, with the territory embraced by these states and New Mexico. The Dioceses of Denver (1887), Tucson (1897), and El Paso (1914), comprise the suffragan sees at present, with the territory embraced by the original Province and an added part of the State of Texas.

SALPOINTE, *Soldiers of the Cross* (Banning, 1898) ; DEFOURI, *Historical Sketch of the Catholic Church in New Mexico* (San Francisco, 1887) ; ENGELHARDT, *The Franciscans in Arizona*, Harbor Springs, 1899). SHEA, *History, etc.*, Vol. iv ; DE COURCY-SHEA, *op. cit.*, CHR, Vol. iii, p. 30.

I. Diocese of Santa Fe (1853)

On July 29, 1853, the Holy See made a formal division of the Diocese of Durango and erected the Vicariate of New Mexico into the Diocese of Santa Fé, with the Right Reverend John B. Lamy, D.D., as first Bishop.

When erected the Diocese of Santa Fé embraced the territory now covered by the Dioceses of Denver and Tucson. At present, it comprises the State of New Mexico, Dona Ana, Grant and Eddy Counties excepted, with part of Sierra County; an area of 104,168 square miles.

1. LAMY, JOHN B.

The first Archbishop of Santa Fé was born on October 11, 1814, at Lempdes, France, and made his theological studies at the Grand Seminary of Mount Ferrand. He was ordained to the priesthood on December 22, 1838, and for the first months after his ordination acted as assistant priest in a parish of his native diocese. A year later, he received permission from his Ordinary to come to the

Diocese of Cincinnati. He labored as a missionary in Ohio
and Kentucky, until his appointment as Vicar-Apostolic of
New Mexico. Bishop M. J. Spalding of Louisville, consecrated him at Cincinnati on November 24, 1850. When
he was made Metropolitan in 1875, he received the pallium
from the hands of Bishop Salpointe on June 16, 1875. He
resigned the See on July 18, 1885, and was made titular
Bishop of Cyzicus. He died at Santa Fé on February 13,
1888.

REUSS, *op. cit.*, p. 62; SHEA, *Hierarchy, etc.*, p. 174; ACHS, *Researches,*
Vol. x, p. 136 (Visitation of New Mexico), Vol. xviii, p. 28 (MS. *Short
Sketch of the Pueblo Indians,* by Lamy) ; DEFOURI, *Historical Sketch of the
Catholic Church in New Mexico,* San Francisco, 1887; CHR, Vol. iii, p. 30.

2. SALPOINTE, JOHN B.

Archbishop Salpointe was born on February 1, 1825,
at St. Maurice, France, and made his classical studies in
the preparatory Seminary of Agen and his theology at
Clermont, where he was ordained to the priesthood on December 2, 1851. The first five years of his career were
spent in his native land and on August 4, 1859, he set sail
for the United States to labor in the missions of New
Mexico. At Mora and Tucson, respectively, he served as
parish priest and when Arizona was made a vicariate he
was selected to be the first Vicar-Apostolic and went to
France to be consecrated on June 20, 1868, by Monsignor
Feron of Clermont-Ferrand. On April 22, 1884, he was
made Coadjutor to Archbishop Lamy and succeeded to the
See upon the resignation of the latter on July 18, 1885.
He too, resigned on January 7, 1894, and was made titular
Archbishop of Tomi. He died in France on July 15, 1898.

REUSS, *op. cit.*, p. 97 seq.; SHEA, *Hierarchy*, p. 178 seq.; SALPOINTE,
op. cit. passim; CHR, Vol. iii, p. 30. After his resignation, Archbishop
Salpointe spent some time in collecting notes on the ecclesiastical history
of New Mexico, Arizona, and Colorado which he published under the title
of *Soldiers of the Cross,* at Banning, California, in 1898.

3. CHAPELLE, PLACIDUS L.

Was consecrated Bishop on November 1, 1891; succeeded to the See of Santa Fé, on January 7, 1894; transferred to New Orleans on December 1, 1897.

(Cf. New Orleans.)

4. BOURGADE, PETER.

Archbishop Bourgade was born in the parish of
Vollare-Ville, France, on October 17, 1845. While at the
seminary he was struck by the plea of Archbishop Salpointe for missionaries, and went as a deacon to the missions of Arizona. He was ordained to the priesthood in
Santa Fé and labored in the missions of Texas, Colorado
and Arizona. He was appointed Vicar-Apostolic of Arizona, and was consecrated at Santa Fé on May 1, 1885, by
Archbishop Lamy. He was promoted to the See of Tucson
on May 8, 1887, and was transferred to Santa Fé as Archbishop on January 7, 1889. He died on May 17, 1908.

REUSS, op. cit., pp. 16–17; CHR, Vol. iii, pp. 31, 32; CE, Vol. i, p. 720,
Vol. xiii, p. 457, Vol. xiv, p. 78, Vol. xv, p. 84; SALPOINTE, Soldiers of the
Cross. Banning, 1898; DEFOURI, Historical Sketch of the Catholic Church
in New Mexico, San Francisco, 1887; ENGELHARDT, Franciscans in Arizona,
pp. 200, 209.

5. PITAVAL, JOHN BAPTIST.

The fifth Archbishop of Santa Fé was born in
France, on February 10, 1858. He was ordained to the
priesthood on December 24, 1881, and was appointed titular
Bishop of Sora and Auxiliary of Santa Fé on May 15, 1902.
On July 25, 1902, he was consecrated by the Most Reverend
Peter Bourgade, and in January, 1909, he became Archbishop of Santa Fé and administered the diocese until his
resignation in February, 1918, after which he was appointed titular Archbishop of Amida on July 29, 1918.

6. DAEGER, ALBERT T., O.F.M.

The present Archbishop of Santa Fé was born on
March 5, 1872, at Saint Ann's, Jennings County, Indiana.
He entered the Order of the Friars Minor at Oldenburg,
Indiana, on August 15, 1889, and after taking simple vows
a year later, he followed the regular course of studies pre-
scribed by the Franciscan curriculum. On July 25, 1896,
he was ordained to the priesthood by Bishop Silas Chatard.
After his ordination, he acted as assistant pastor in several
States of the southwest and was pastor of Jemes, New
Mexico, when appointed Archbishop of Santa Fé. His

consecration took place on May 7, 1919, at Saint Francis Cathedral in Santa Fé, the Most Reverend John B. Pitaval, D.D., being the consecrating prelate.

II. Diocese of Denver (1887)

The Diocese of Denver was erected on August 16, 1887, and the Right Reverend Joseph P. Machebeuf, Vicar-Apostolic of Colorado, was appointed as its first Bishop. The Diocese includes the original area assigned to it upon its erection in 1887, viz., the State of Colorado; an area of 103,645 square miles.

HOWLETT, *Life of Bishop Machebeuf* (Denver, 1909) ; REUSS, *Biog. Cycl. of the Cath. Hierarchy of the U. S.* (Milwaukee, 1898) ; DE COURCY-SHEA, *op. cit.*; HARRIS (W. R.). *Catholic Church in Utah*, 1776–1909, passim, Salt Lake City, 1909 ; CHR, Vol. iii, p. 31.

1. MACHEBEUF, JOSEPH.

The first Bishop of Denver was born at Puy de Dôme, France, on August 11, 1812, and was ordained to the priesthood at Clermont on December 21, 1836. Three years later he left France for the United States having volunteered his services to Archbishop Purcell of Cincinnati. He labored in this diocese until Father Lamy was appointed head of the newly-created Vicariate of New Mexico, and in 1850 he went West with him. He arrived in Denver on October 29, 1860, and was consecrated Vicar-Apostolic of Colorado and Utah, and titular Bishop of Epiphania at Cincinnati, on August 16, 1868, by Archbishop Purcell. He died in Denver on July 10, 1889.

REUSS, *op. cit.*, p. 66; SHEA, *Hierarchy, etc.*, p. 394; W. J. HOWLETT, *Life of Bishop Machebeuf*, Pueblo, Colo., 1908; ACHS *Researches*, Vol. vi, 95 (reminiscences of missionary labors in Northern Ohio) ; *cf. Catholic Universe*, Cleveland, Oct. 18, 1888; AER, Vol. xl, p. 728; CHR, Vol. iv, p. 543 (diocesan bibliography).

2. MATZ, NICHOLAS D.

The second Bishop of Denver was born at Munster, Lorraine, France, on April 6, 1850, and received his education at the Petit Séminaire at Finstingen. He came to the United States in 1868 and prepared for the priesthood at old Saint Mary's of the West, in Cincinnati. Having been ordained to the priesthood in Denver on May 31, 1874, he held various charges at Georgetown and Denver, until his appointment as coadjutor to Bishop Machebeuf on August 19, 1887. He was consecrated titular Bishop of Thelmessa on October 28, 1887, by Archbishop Salpointe, and became active Bishop of Denver on July 10, 1889. He died in that city on August 9, 1917.

REUSS, *op. cit.*, p. 69; ACHS, *Researches*, Vol. xxiv, p. 383 (on mixed marriages); CHR, Vol. iii, p. 31.

3. TIHEN, J. HENRY.

The present Bishop of Denver was born on July 14, 1861, in Oldenburg, Indiana, and received his education at Saint Benedict's College, Atchinson, Kansas, and at Saint Francis Seminary, Milwaukee. He was ordained to the priesthood on April 26, 1886. He began his priestly career in the Diocese of Wichita, where he became rector of the Cathedral and chancellor of the Diocese until his appointment as Bishop of Lincoln. He was consecrated by Archbishop Pitaval on July 6, 1911, and was transferred to Denver on September 21, 1917.

III. Diocese of Tucson (1897)

The Vicariate of Arizona was erected into the Diocese of Tucson by Leo XIII on May 8, 1897, and the Right Reverend Peter Bourgade was appointed its first Bishop.

The diocesan limits were originally confined to the State of Arizona and part of New Mexico. In 1914, upon the erection of the Diocese of El Paso, the counties in New Mexico were abscinded and the diocese received its present extent in the State of Arizona; an area of 133,058 square miles.

ORTEGA, *Historia del Nayarit, Sonora, Sinaloa, y ambas Californias*, Mexico, 1887; *Rudo Ensayo*, tr. GUITERAS, in *Am. Cath. Hist. Rec.*, V, Philadelphia, June, 1894, No. 2; JOLY, *Histoire de la Compagnie de Jésus*, V, Paris, 1859, ii; ARRICIVITA, *Cronica serafica del apostolico colegio de Querétaro;* SALPOINTE, *Soldiers of the Cross*, Banning, 1898; ENGLEHARDT, *The Franciscans in Arizona*, Harbor Springs, 1899; *Dairy of Francisco Garces*, tr. COUES, New York, 1900, CHR, Vol. iii, pp. 31–32.

1. SALPOINTE, JOHN B.

The first Vicar-Apostolic was consecrated titular Bishop of Dorylaeum on June 20, 1868, and was transferred to the archiepiscopal See of Santa Fé as Coadjutor Bishop on April 22, 1884.
(Cf. Santa Fé.)

2. BOURGADE, PETER.

He was consecrated titular Bishop of Thamacum and second Vicar-Apostolic of Arizona on May 1, 1885. He became first Bishop of Tucson on May 8, 1897, and was promoted to the See of Santa Fé on January 7, 1899.
(Cf. Santa Fé.)

3. GRANJON, HENRY.

The present Bishop of Tucson was born at St. Etienne, Loire, France, on June 15, 1863, and received his seminary training at Saint Sulpice in Paris, and in Rome, where he received a Doctorate in Divinity. He was ordained to the priesthood on December 17, 1887, and joined the Arizona missions in 1890. From 1897 until 1900 he was in charge of the Society of the Propagation of Faith, with residence in Baltimore, and was consecrated Bishop of Tucson in Baltimore, Maryland, by Cardinal Gibbons on June 17, 1900.

IV. Diocese of El Paso (1914)

The Diocese of El Paso was erected by Pius X on March 3, 1914, and the Right Reverend Henry Schuler, S.J., was consecrated as its first Bishop on October 28, 1915.

The diocese comprises the counties of El Paso, Culberson, Presidio, Jeff Davis, Reeves, Brewster, Terrell, Pecos, Crane, Ward, Loving, Winkler, Ector, Andrews and Gaines in the State of Texas, and the counties of Grant, Luna, Dona Ana, Otero, Eddy and part of Sierra in the State of New Mexico; a total area of 68,394 square miles.

The Pro-Cathedral Record of June, 1917, published in El Paso, Texas, contains an historical summary of the Diocese from its beginnings down to the present.

1. SCHULER, HENRY, S. J.

Bishop Schuler was born in Saint Mary's, Elk County, Pennsylvania, on September 20, 1869, and entered the Society of Jesus at Florissant, Missouri, on December 7, 1886. He received his entire educational training at the House of Studies at Florissant, and he was ordained to the priesthood at Woodstock, Maryland, on June 27, 1901. His career as a priest was confined to the States of Texas and Colorado. He was consecrated Bishop of El Paso by Archbishop Pitaval on October 2, 1915, in Denver, Colorado.

CHAPTER XII.

THE PROVINCE OF CHICAGO (1880).

Pope Leo XIII erected the Province of Chicago on September 10, 1880, and at the same time the Right Reverend Patrick A. Feehan, D.D., was transferred from the See of Nashville as its first Archbishop.

When established the Province embraced the entire State of Illinois, with the suffragan sees of Alton (1853), and Peoria (1877). To these have been added the Dioceses of Belleville (1887), and Rockford (1908).

ANDREWS, in *The History of Chicago;* O'GORMAN, *Hist. of the Roman Catholic Church in the United States,* New York, 1895; SHEA, *Hist. of the Cath. Ch. in the U. S.,* New York, 1904; McGOVERN, *The Life of Bishop McMullen,* Chicago; IDEM, *Souvenir of the Silver Jubilee of the Most Rev. P. H. Feehan;* Catholic Directory, Milwaukee, 1908. GARRAGHAN, *The Catholic Church in Chicago* (1673-1871), Chicago, 1921; DE COURCY-SHEA, *op. cit.;* KIRKFLEET, *The Life of Patrick Augustine Feehan, First Archbishop of Chicago,* Chicago, 1922; CHR, Vol. iii, pp. 151-152; *Cf. Illinois Catholic Historical Review,* since commencement of the publication; *Cf.* Files of *New World* (Chicago), especially issue of April 14, 1900 (Historical number).

I. Diocese of Chicago (1843)

The Diocese of Chicago was erected on November 28, 1843, and the Right Reverend William Quarter was consecrated as its first Bishop on March 10, 1844.

The original territory of the Diocese of Chicago was the State of Illinois. At present it comprises the Counties of Cook, Lake, DuPage, Kankakee, Will and Grundy in the State of Illinois; an area of 3,620 square miles.

1. QUARTER, WILLIAM.

The first Bishop of Chicago was born in Killurine, King's County, Ireland, on January 21, 1806. His classical studies were made in private academies and later he attended Maynooth College. Soon after his arrival in America in 1822, he entered Mount Saint Mary's, at Emmitsburg, and on September 19, 1829, he was ordained to the priesthood for the Diocese of New York. He labored at old Saint Peter's and Saint Mary's in New York City until his appointment as first Bishop of Chicago. He was consecrated by Bishop Hughes on March 10, 1844. He died in Chicago on April 10, 1848.

REUSS, *op. cit.*, p. 91; SHEA, *Hierarchy*, p. 95; CLARKE, *op. cit.*, Vol. ii, p. 240; MCGOVERN, *Souvenir of the Silver Jubilee of the Most Reverend P. H. Feehan*, p. 28 seq.; MCGIRR, *Life of Bishop Quarter*, New York, 1850. Numbers of *Illinois Catholic Historical Review;* CHR, Vol. iii, p. 152.

2. VANDEVELDE, JAMES O., S.J.

The second Bishop of Chicago was born at Tirmonde, Belgium, on April 3, 1875. While a student at the seminary in Mechlin, he pledged his services to Father Nerinckx and accompanied him to the United States. He entered the Society of Jesus at Georgetown, D. C., in 1810, and was ordained to the priesthood on September 25, 1827, at Baltimore, Maryland. He was acting as professor when appointed to the See of Chicago and was consecrated by Archbishop Peter R. Kenrick on February 11, 1849. He was transferred to the See of Natchez on July 29, 1853, and died there on November 13, 1855.

REUSS, *op. cit.*, p. 105; SHEA, *Hierarchy*, p. 96; CLARKE, *op. cit.*, Vol. ii, p. 372; JANSSENS, *Sketch of the Catholic Church in the City of Natchez, Mississippi, passim*, Natchez, 1886; CHR, Vol. iii, p. 152.

3. O'REGAN, ANTHONY.

Bishop O'Regan was born in County Mayo, Ireland, in 1809, studied at Maynooth College and was ordained to the priesthood in November, 1834. After his ordination he acted as professor in the episcopal college of Tuam, a position he held for nearly ten years, leaving it in 1849, upon the invitation of Archbishop Kenrick of St. Louis, to come to this country. He was rector of the theological seminary in St. Louis when appointed Bishop of Chicago. Archbishop Kenrick consecrated him on July 25, 1854. He resigned the See of Chicago and was made titular Bishop of Dora on June 25, 1858, after which he retired to London and died there on November 13, 1866.

REUSS, *op. cit.*, pp. 83–84; SHEA, *Hierachy*, p. 97; CLARKE, *op. cit.*, Vol. iii, p. 162; MCGOVERN, *op. cit., passim.;* GARRAGHAN, *op. cit., passim;* CHR, Vol. iii, p. 152; *Cf. New World,* issue of April 14, 1900.

4. DUGGAN, JAMES.

The fourth Bishop of Chicago was born at Maynooth, County Kildare, Ireland, on May 22, 1825, and emigrated to the United States in 1842, taking up his residence in St. Louis. He made his theological studies in that city and was ordained to the priesthood on May 29, 1847. Before his appointment as Coadjutor to St. Louis on January 9, 1857, he was Superior of the St. Louis Theological Seminary; assistant at the Cathedral, and one of the Vicars-General of the Diocese. In March, 1858, he was sent to administer the vacant See of Chicago, and on January 21, 1859, he was appointed to the See. He was removed from active administration on April 14, 1869. He died in St. Louis on March 27, 1899.

REUSS, *op. cit.*, pp. 36–37; CLARKE, *op. cit.*, Vol. iii, pp. 173, 597; CHR, Vol. iii, p. 152; PHILLIPS, *Bishop Duggan and the Chicago Diocese,* in the ICHR, Vol. ii, pp. 365–368; *Catholic Church in Chicago,* pp. 196–201. GARRAGHAN, *op. cit., passim.*

The Right Reverend Thomas Foley was appointed titular Bishop of Pergamus and Coadjutor Bishop of Chicago on November 19, 1869, and although he was appointed administrator of the Diocese he never really enjoyed the title of Bishop of Chicago.

He was born in Baltimore, Maryland, on March 6, 1822, and received his education at Saint Mary's College, and Seminary in his native city. He was ordained to the priesthood on August 16, 1846, and served as pastor at Rockville, Maryland; assistant at Saint Patrick's, Washington; and Rector of the Cathedral at Baltimore, and Vicar-General of the Diocese. He was consecrated in Baltimore, Maryland, by Bishop McCloskey, on February 27, 1870, and died in Chicago on February 19, 1879.

REUSS, *op. cit.*, p. 44; CLARKE, *op. cit.*, Vol. iii, pp. 171–188; SHEA, *Hierarchy, etc.*, pp. 99–100; *Catholic Church in Chicago,* pp. 202–226, Chicago, 1891; CHR, Vol. iii, p. 152. GARRAGHAN, *op. cit., passim.*

5. FEEHAN, PATRICK A.

The first Archbishop of Chicago was born at Springhill, County Tipperary, Ireland, on August 29, 1829, and in 1852 he emigrated to the United States. He was ordained to the priesthood in St. Louis on November 1, 1852. He was consecrated Bishop of Nashville on November 1, 1865, by Archbishop Kenrick and was transferred to the See of Chicago as its first Archbishop on September 10, 1880. He died in that city on July 12, 1902.

REUSS, *op. cit.*, p. 41; SHEA, *Hierarchy, etc.*, pp. 100–103; *Catholic Church in Chicago*, pp. 227–253; CHR, Vol. ii, p. 288, Vol. iii, p. 152. KIRKFLEET, *The Life of Patrick Augustine Feehan, Bishop of Nashville and First Archbishop of Chicago, 1829–1902*, Chicago, 1922; GARRAGHAN, *op. cit., passim.*

6. QUIGLEY, JAMES E.

Archbishop Quigley was born at Oshawa, Ontario, Canada, on October 15, 1855. After his graduation from Saint Joseph's College, Buffalo, he entered the Seminary of Our Lady of Angels, at Niagara Falls, and later was sent to Innsbruck, and finally to the Propaganda in Rome, where he was ordained to the priesthood on April 13, 1879. He was appointed Bishop of Buffalo and was consecrated in that city on February 24, 1897, by Archbishop Corrigan. He was transferred to the See of Chicago on January 8, 1903, and he died in Buffalo, New York, on July 10, 1915.

REUSS, *op. cit.*, p. 91; *Illinois Catholic Historical Review* (Summer, 1915); CHR, Vol. iii, p. 152; *Cf.* Files of *New World* for July, 1915. GARRAGHAN, *op. cit., passim.*

7. MUNDELEIN, GEORGE W.

The present Archbishop of Chicago was born in Brooklyn, New York on July 7, 1872, and received his collegiate training at Manhattan College, New York City. His theological studies were made at the Propaganda in Rome, and he was ordained to the priesthood on June 9, 1895. He served as assistant secretary to Bishop McDonnell of Brooklyn, and later was appointed chancellor of the Diocese. He was appointed titular Bishop of Loryna and Auxiliary of Brooklyn on June 30, 1909. He was consecrated on September 21, 1909, by Bishop McDonnell and was transferred to Chicago on December 9, 1915.

The Right Reverend Edward Hoban is the present Auxiliary Bishop of Chicago. A native of that city, he made his classical studies at Saint Ignatius' College and later went to Saint Mary's Seminary in Baltimore for philosophy and theology. He was ordained to the priesthood by Archbishop Quigley on July 11, 1903, and after some time spent in parish work he was sent to Rome for post-graduate study, receiving there a Doctorate in Divinity at the Gregorian University. He was chancellor of the Archdiocese until his appointment as assistant to Archbishop Mundelein, and was consecrated on December 21, 1921, by his Ordinary.

II. Diocese of Alton (1853-1857)

At the time of its erection on July 29, 1853, the diocesan seat was located at Quincy, and the Very Reverend Joseph Melcher was appointed as its first Bishop. He refused the office, however, and the newly-created See was administered by the Bishop of Chicago. Finally, the diocesan seat was removed to Alton, and the See of that name was erected on January 9, 1857, and on April 26, 1858, the Right Reverend Henry D. Juncker was consecrated its first Bishop.

When erected, the Diocese of Alton included the entire southern part of the State of Illinois. The extreme southern part was abscinded in 1887 to form the Diocese of Belleville. The Diocese of Alton now comprises that part of Illinois lying south of the northern limits of the Counties of Adams, Brown, Cass, Menard, Sangamon, Macon, Moultrie, Douglas and Edgar, and north of the southern limits of the Counties of Madison, Bond, Fayette, Effingham, Jasper and Crawford; an area of 15,139 square miles.

SHEA, *Hist. Cath. Ch. in U. S., passim; Golden Jubilee of St. Boniface's Church* (Quincy); *Silver Jubilee of Highland; New World, Christmas* edition, Chicago, 1900. DE COURCY-SHEA, *op. cit.;* CHR, Vol. iii, p. 153; *New World,* issue of April 14, 1900.

1. JUNCKER, HENRY D.

The first Bishop of Alton was born in Lorraine, France, on August 22, 1809. While a young student in his native country he decided to devote his life to foreign missions, and accordingly emigrated to the United States. Upon completion of his studies he was ordained to the priesthood at Cincinnati by Archbishop Purcell on March 16, 1843. He labored in the State of Ohio until his consecration as first Bishop of Alton on April 26, 1857, by Archbishop Purcell. He died at Alton on October 2, 1868.

REUSS, *op. cit.*, pp. 57–58; CHR, Vol. iii, p. 153; SHEA, *Hierarchy, etc.*, p. 184; CLARKE, *op. cit.*, Vol. ii, pp. 529–535.

2. BALTES, PETER J.

The second Bishop of Alton was born in Ensheim, Bavaria, on April 7, 1827. At the age of six he emigrated with his parents to the United States. His early education was received at Holy Cross College, Worcester, and later he attended Saint Mary's-of-the-Lake in Chicago, and the Grand Seminary in Montreal. He was ordained to the priesthood in Montreal on May 21, 1853, and began his missionary activities in the Diocese of Chicago. His charges were Waterloo and Belleville, Illinois, and in 1866 he was made Vicar-General of the Diocese of Alton. He was consecrated in Belleville on January 23, 1870, by Bishop Leurs of Fort Wayne. He died in Alton on February 15, 1886.

REUSS, *op. cit.*, p. 10; CLARKE, *op. cit.*, Vol. iii, pp. 189–196; CHR, Vol. iii, p. 153; CE, Vol. i, pp. 367–368 (*The Diocese of Alton*), where references are given to the *Golden Jubilee of St. Boniface's Church* (Quincy, Ill.), to the *Silver Jubilee of Highland*, and to the Christmas edition (1900) of the *New World*, Chicago; SHEA, *Hierarchy, etc.*, p. 185; Special historical edition of the *New World* for April 14, 1900.

3. RYAN, JAMES.

The present Bishop of Alton was born in Thurles, County Tipperary, Ireland, on June 17, 1848. His education was received at Saint Thomas' and Joseph's Colleges, Bardstown, and at Preston Park Seminary, Louisville. He was ordained to the priesthood on December 24, 1871, and afterwards spent a few years in Kentucky as a missionary and teacher. When Bishop Spalding was appointed to the See of Peoria, the future Bishop of Alton followed him there. At the time of his own appointment as Bishop, he was rector of Saint Columba's Church in Ottawa, Illinois. Bishop Spalding consecrated him on May 1, 1888.

III. Diocese of Peoria (1877)

Pope Pius IX created the Diocese of Peoria on January 18, 1877, and the Right Reverend John Lancaster Spalding was consecrated as its first Bishop on May 1, 1877.

The Diocese still comprises its original limits of a cross-section of Illinois, bounded on the north by the Counties of Whiteside, Lee, DeKalb, Grundy, and Kankakee, and on the south by Adams, Brown, Cass, Menard, Sangamon, Macon, Moultrie, Douglas and Edgar; comprising the Counties of Bureau, Champaign, Dewitt, Ford, Fulton, Hancock, Henderson, Henry, Iroquoise, Knox, La Salle, Livingston, Logan, Marshall, Mason, McDonough, McClean, Mercer, Peoria, Piatt, Putnam, Rock Island, Schuyler, Stark, Tazewell, Vermilion, Warren and Woodford; an area of 18,554 square miles.

DE-COURCY-SHEA, *op. cit.*, p. 579; CHR, Vol. iii, p. 58; *New World* (April 14, 1900).

1. SPALDING, JOHN L.

Archbishop Spalding was born at Lebanon, Kentucky, on June 2, 1840, and received his education at Bardstown, Mount Saint Mary's, Emmitsburg; American College at Louvain, and in Rome. He was ordained to the priesthood on December 19, 1863. Upon his return from Europe he was appointed an assistant at the Cathedral in Louisville, and in 1870 he became pastor of Saint Augustine's Church in that city. He was also secretary and chancellor of the Diocese until 1872, when he moved to New York and labored in Saint Michael's parish. While there, in conjunction with the Paulist Fathers, he wrote the life of his uncle, the Most Reverend Martin Spalding, of Baltimore. He was appointed Bishop of Peoria on November

27, 1876, and was consecrated in New York City by Cardinal McCloskey on May 1, 1877. He was stricken with paralysis on January 6, 1905, and resigned the See on September 11, 1908, and was made titular Archbishop of Scitopolis. He died in Peoria on August 25, 1916.

REUSS, *op. cit.,* p. 101; SHEA, *Hierarchy,* p. 334–335. CURTIS, *American Catholic Who's Who,* p. 617; CE., Vol. xi, p. 662; CHR, Vol. iii, p. 154. Among his more important works are: *The Life of Most Reverend M. J. Spalding, D. D.,* Baltimore, 1873; *Religion, Agnosticism and Education,* Chicago, 1902; *Socialism and Labor,* Chicago, 1902; *Religion, Art, and other Essays,* Chicago, 1905; *Opportunity, Other Essays and Addresses,* Chicago, 1900.

2. DUNN, EDMUND M.

The present Bishop of Peoria was born in Chicago on February 2, 1864, and received his early education in the parochial schools of that city. His collegiate education and seminary training were received at Saint Ignatius, Chicago, Niagara University, and the American College at Louvain. He was ordained to the priesthood on June 24, 1887. Under Archbishop Quigley he acted as chancellor of the Archdiocese and on June 30, 1909, was appointed Bishop of Peoria. He was consecrated by Archbishop Quigley on September 1, 1909.

Right Reverend Peter O'Reilly was born on April 14, 1850, in County Meath, Ireland, and received his seminary training at All Hallows College, Dublin, where he was ordained to the priesthood on June 24, 1877. Coming to the United States he labored in Champaign, Danville and Peoria, Illinois, before his appointment as Auxiliary Bishop of Peoria. He was consecrated titular Bishop of Lebedos on September 21, 1900, by Cardinal Martinelli.

IV. Diocese of Belleville (1887)

Pope Leo XIII, acting on the recommendation of the Fathers of the Third Plenary Council of Baltimore, created the Diocese of Belleville on January 7, 1887, and the Right Reverend John Janssen, D.D., was consecrated as the first Bishop on April 25, 1888.

The Diocese comprises that part of the State of Illinois

south of the northern limits of the counties of St. Clair, Clinton, Marion, Clay, Richland and Lawrence; an area of 11,678 square miles.

BEUCKMANN, *History of the Diocese of Belleville,* Belleville, 1914; SHEA, *History of the Catholic Church, etc., passim; Missions Catholicae,* Propaganda, Rome, 1907; *Cf. New World* (Chicago) issue of April 14, 1900.

1. JANSSEN, JOHN.

The first Bishop of Belleville was born at Kepplen, in the Diocese of Münster, Rhine, Prussia. He received his entire education in Germany, and, coming to the United States, he was ordained to the priesthood at Alton on November 19, 1858, by Bishop Juncker. After ordination he was pastor of Saint John's Church, Springfield, and the neighboring missions. He was appointed Vicar-General of the Diocese of Alton, and also served as Administrator thereof after the death of Bishop Baltes. He was appointed Bishop of Belleville on February 28, 1888, and was consecrated there by Archbishop Feehan, of Chicago, on April 25, 1888. He died on July 2, 1913, in Belleville, Illinois.

REUSS, *op. cit.,* pp. 56–57; CHR, Vol. iii, p. 154. BEUCKMANN, *op. cit. passim.*

2. ALTHOFF, HENRY.

Bishop Althoff was born in Aviston, Illinois, on August 28, 1873. His collegiate and seminary training were received at Saint Joseph's College, Teutopolis, Illinois; Saint Francis' Solanus College, Quincy, Illinois, and the University of Innsbruck, Austria, where he was ordained to the priesthood in 1902. Upon his return to the United States he became assistant at Damiansville, Illinois, and later became pastor of Okawville and Nashville in the same state. He was consecrated Bishop of Belleville on February 24, 1914, by Archbishop Quigley of Chicago.

V. Diocese of Rockford (1908)

The Diocese of Rockford was erected by Pius X on September 22, 1908, and the Right Reverend Peter J. Muldoon, D.D., was transferred from Chicago, where he was acting as Auxiliary, as its first Bishop, on September 22, 1908.

The Diocese comprises Jo Daviess, Stephenson, Winnebago, Boone, McHenry, Carroll, Ogle, DeKalb, Kane, Whiteside, Lee and Kendall Counties in the State of Illinois; an area of 6,867 square miles.

CHR, Vol. iii, p. 152; *Catholic Directory for 1922; Cf.* Files of the *New World* (Chicago).

1. MULDOON, PETER.

Bishop Muldoon was born at Columbia, California, October 10, 1863, and received his philosophical and theological training at Saint Mary's, Baltimore. Bishop Loughlin of Brooklyn ordained him to the priesthood on December 18, 1886. He was assistant at Saint Pius Parish in Chicago from 1887 to November 18, 1888, and then was appointed chancellor of the Archdiocese of Chicago. He was consecrated Auxiliary Bishop of Chicago on July 25, 1901, by Cardinal Martinelli. He was transferred to Rockford on September 22, 1908.

CHAPTER XIII.

THE PROVINCE OF ST. PAUL (1888).

The Province of Saint Paul was established by Leo XIII on May 4, 1888, and the Right Reverend John Ireland, D. D., was appointed its first Archbishop, on May 15, 1888. When erected, the Province included the States of Minnesota and North and South Dakota, with the Vicariates of Northern Minnesota and Dakota as suffragans. The Province still comprises the territory of the three States with the Dioceses of St. Cloud, Sioux Falls, Jamestown, Fargo and Duluth (all erected in 1889); Lead (1902), Bismarck (1909) and Crookston (1909) as suffragan sees.

HOFFMANN, *St. John's University* (Collegeville, 1907); *Acta et Dicta* (St. Paul, 1907–11); UPHAM, *Minnesota in Three Centuries*, I (St. Paul, 1908); FOLWELL, *Minnesota, the North Star State* (Boston and New York 1908); WILLIAMS, *A History of the City of St. Paul* (St. Paul, 1876); SHEA, *History of the Catholic Church, passim,* New York, 1894;. SCHAEFER, *History of the Diocese of Saint Paul,* in the *Acta and Dicta,* Vol. iv, pp. 32–71, CHR, Vol. iii, p. 154 seq.; *The Catholic Directory* for 1919.

I. Diocese of Saint Paul (1850)

Pope Pius IX erected the Diocese of Saint Paul on July 19, 1850, and the Right Reverend Joseph Crétin was consecrated as its first Bishop on January 26, 1851.

Originally, the Diocese embraced the territory now covered by the Province, but at present it comprises twenty-seven Counties of the State of Minnesota: Ramsey, Hennepin, Washington, Chisago, Anoka, Dakota, Scott, Wright, Rice, Le Sueur, Carver, Nicollet, Sibley, McLeod, Meeker, Redwood, Renville, Kandiyohi, Lyon, Lincoln, Yellow Medicine, Lac qui Parle, Chippewa, Swift, Goodhue, Big Stone and Brown; an area of 15,233 square miles.

1. CRETIN, JOSEPH.

The first Bishop of St. Paul was born at Montluel in the old Diocese of Belley, France, on December 19, 1799, and made his ecclesiastical studies in the seminary of that

195

diocese. He was ordained to the priesthood in Paris, France, on December 20, 1823, and came to the United States with Bishop Loras of Dubuque in October, 1838. For twelve years he was a zealous laborer in the Diocese of Dubuque and during part of the time he served as Vicar-General. He was chosen Bishop of Saint Paul on July 23, 1850 and Bishop Devie of Belley, France, consecrated him on January 26, 1851. He died in St. Paul on February 22, 1857.

REUSS, *op. cit.,* p. 30; CLARKE, *op. cit.,* Vol. ii, pp. 415–430; SHEA, *Hierarchy, etc.,* p. 377; DE COURCY-SHEA, *op. cit.,* p. 639; SHEA, *History of the Catholic Missions, etc.,* p. 400; CHR, Vol. i, p. 63 (letters), Vol. ii, 428 Vol. iii, p. 555–556; ACHS *Researches,* Vol. viii, p. 261, Vol. xii, pp. 82–84 Vol. xv, p. 46. Biog. sketch in CE, Vol. iv, pp. 487–488. Most of the material for Bishop Crétin's life is still in manuscript, but special reference should be given to the *Life of Bishop Crétin,* from the pen of the late Archbishop Ireland, in the *Acta et Dicta* of the St. Paul Catholic Historical Society. The initial chapters are in Col. iv, No. 2, July, 1916. Bishop Crétin's *Diary* is in Vol. i (*ibid.*), No. 1, July, 1907, pp. 39–42. *Cf.* SCHAEFER, *History of the Diocese of St. Paul,* in *Acta et Dicta,* Vol. iv, No. 1, July, 1915, pp. 32–71. *Cf.* THEBAUD, *Forty Years in the United States,* pp. 274–275. New York, 1904. *Cf.* SHEA, *Hist. Cath. Church, etc.,* Vol. iv, pp. 244–246, 258–260, 262, 646–648. *Cf.* also the *Memoirs* of Father Ravoux, who became Administrator of the diocese after Crétin's death (St. Paul, 1892).

2. GRACE, THOMAS L.

The second Bishop of St. Paul was born in Charleston, South Carolina, on November 16, 1814. He received his early education in his native city and at the age of sixteen he entered the Priory of Saint Rose, Kentucky, and on June 12, 1831, was professed as a member of the Dominican Order. Six years later, his superiors sent him to Rome for further studies at the Minerva. He was ordained to the priesthood on December 21, 1839. Upon his return to the United States in 1844, he was assigned to the mission fields of Kentucky and Tennessee where he labored until his appointment as second Bishop of Saint Paul in the early part of 1859. Archbishop Kenrick of St. Louis consecrated him on July 24, 1859. He resigned the See on July 31, 1884, and was made titular Bishop of Menith, and on September 24, 1889, he was appointed titular Archbishop of Siunia. He died in St. Paul on February 22, 1897.

REUSS, *op. cit.*, p. 50; SHEA, *Hierarchy, etc.*, p. 378; CHR, Vol. iii, p. 156; ACHS, *Researches*, Vol. viii, p. 96, Vol. xii, p. 46; CHR, Vol. iv, p. 544 (Bibliography of St. Paul Diocese); SCHAEFER, *History of the Diocese of St. Paul*, in *Acta et Dicta*, Vol. iv, pp. 32–75.

3. IRELAND, JOHN.

Archbishop Ireland was born at Burnchurch, County Kilkenny, Ireland, on September 11, 1838, and came to the United States with his parents in 1852. Bishop Crétin sent the young seminarian to France to complete his collegiate and seminary course; was ordained to the priesthood in Saint Paul by Bishop Grace on December 21, 1861. Soon after he left for the battlefields of the war, where he acted as chaplain of the Fifth Minnesota Regiment. After the war he was stationed in St. Paul as Rector of the Cathedral and on February 21, 1875, he was appointed titular Bishop of Maronea and Coadjutor to Bishop Grace. He was consecrated in that city on December 21, 1875, by Bishop Grace and upon the resignation of the latter on July 31, 1884, automatically succeeded to the See. A year later, on May 15th, he was made first Archbishop of St. Paul and remained as such until his death on September 25, 1918.

REUSS, *op. cit.*, p. 56; CHR, Vol. iii, p. 156; CUB, Vol. iii, p. 89, Vol. xxiv, p. 127 (Necrology); AER, Vol. xxiv, pp. 418 *et seq.* (On the Temporal Power); SWEENY, *op. cit.*, Vol. i, p. 328; SHEA, *Hierarchy, etc.*, p. 379; *Cf.* Files of the *Catholic Bulletin* (St. Paul), for Sept.-Oct., 1918.

4. DOWLING, AUSTIN.

The present Archbishop of St. Paul was born in New York City on April 6, 1868. He received his collegiate education at Manhattan College and made his seminary course at Saint John's, Brighton, Massachusetts. He was at the Catholic University of America from 1890 to 1892, and was ordained to the priesthood on June 24, 1891. He was pastor of Saint Mary's Church, in Warren, Rhode Island, from 1904 to 1905, and at the time of his appointment as first Bishop of Des Moines on January 31, 1912, he was acting as the rector of the Cathedral of Providence. Bishop Harkins consecrated him on April 25, 1912, and he was promoted to the Archiepiscopal See of St. Paul on February 1, 1919.

II. Diocese of Saint Cloud (1889)

The Diocese of Saint Cloud was established on September 22, 1889, and the Right Reverend Otto Zardetti, D.D., was consecrated as its first Bishop on October 20, 1889. When established, the Diocese included the territory in Northwestern Minnesota. In 1909, when the See of Crookston was erected, it received its present limits of the Counties of Stearns, Sherburne, Benton, Morrison, Millelacs, Kanabec, Isanti, Pope, Stevens, Travers, Grant, Douglas, Wilkin, Otter Tail, Todd, Wadena, in the State of Minnesota; an area of 12,251 square miles.

DE COURCY-SHEA, *op. cit.,* p. 664 seq.; O'GORMAN, *op. cit. passim;* CHR, Vol. iii, p. 156.

1. SEIDENBUSCH, RUPERT.

The first Vicar Apostolic of Northern Minnesota (territory out of which the Diocese was erected) was born in Munich, Bavaria, on October 13, 1830, and came to the United States about 1851. He joined the Benedictine Order at Saint Vincent's, Beatty, Pennsylvania, and made his profession there on January 6, 1852. He was ordained to the priesthood there on June 22, 1853, after which he labored successfully as a missionary in Pennsylvania and New Jersey. Bishop Carrell bestowed the abbatial blessing on him in Saint John's Abbey on May 30, 1867. He held this position for eight years, after which he resigned, on May 4, 1875. He was appointed first Vicar-Apostolic of Minnesota, and was consecrated titular Bishop of Halia on May 30, 1875, at St. Cloud by Bishop Heiss of Milwaukee. He died in Richmond, Virginia, on June 3, 1895, after having resigned the vicariate on October 19, 1888.

REUSS, *op. cit.,* pp. 99–100; SHEA, *Hierarchy,* p. 401 seq.; CHR, Vol. iii, p. 156.

2. ZARDETTI, J. F. OTTO.

The first Bishop of St. Cloud, who later became Archbishop of Bucharest, Roumania, was born at Rorsbach, St. Gall, Switzerland, on January 24, 1847. He was ordained to the priesthood in Trent, Switzerland, on August 21, 1870, and in 1881 he was chosen professor of Dogmatic Theology in Saint Francis' Seminary, Milwaukee. Five years later Bishop Marty made him his Vicar-General and when St. Cloud was erected into a Diocese, he was consecrated as its first Bishop in the Benedictine Abbey at Einsiedeln, Switzerland, on October 20, 1889, by Archbishop Gross. He was transferred to the Archiepiscopal See of Bucharest in Roumania in 1894, which See he resigned some years before his death on May 9, 1902.

REUSS, *op. cit.*, p. 111; CHR, Vol. iii, p. 157.

3. MARTY, MARTIN.

Was appointed first Bishop of Sioux Falls on September 22, 1889; transferred to the Diocese of St. Cloud as second Bishop of this See on December 16, 1894. He died on September 19, 1896.
(Cf. Sioux Falls.)

4. TROBEC, JAMES.

Bishop Trobec was born in the province of Carniola, Austria, on July 10, 1838, and came to the United States in 1864. He was ordained to the priesthood in St. Paul on September 18, 1865, and was acting as pastor of a chain of missions in Minnesota when chosen Bishop of St. Cloud in 1897. Archbishop Ireland consecrated him on September 21, 1897. He resigned the See on April 15, 1914, and was named titular Bishop of Licopolis on May 25, 1914. He died at St. Cloud on December 14, 1921.

REUSS, *op. cit.*, pp. 104–105; CHR, Vol. iii, p. 157; *Cf.* Files of *Catholic Bulletin* (St. Paul) for December, 1921.

5. BUSCH, JOSEPH F.

The present Bishop of St. Cloud was born in Red Wing, Minnesota, on April 16, 1866, and made his philosophical and theological studies at Innsbruck, where he was ordained to the priesthood on July 28, 1889. He also spent two years at the Catholic University of America, and upon his return to St. Paul, Archbishop Ireland made him his secretary. In 1902 he founded the Archdiocesan Mission band and on May 19, 1910, was consecrated Bishop of Lead by Archbishop Ireland. He was transferred to the Diocese of St. Cloud on January 19, 1915.

III. Diocese of Sioux Falls (1889)

Pope Leo XIII in August, 1879, created the Vicariate of Dakota which comprised the territory now embraced by the States of North and South Dakota and on February 1, 1880, the Abbot of Saint Meinrad's, the Right Reverend Martin Marty, was consecrated titular Bishop of Tiberias and first Vicar-Apostolic. He became first Bishop of Sioux Falls on September 22, 1889, by virtue of the ecclesiastical division of the territory into the Diocese of Sioux Falls, South Dakota, and Jamestown (Fargo), North Dakota.

Formerly, the Diocese of Sioux Falls comprised the entire State of South Dakota, but upon the erection of the Diocese of Lead in 1902, it received the present limits, viz., that portion of the state which is east of the Missouri River; an area of 35,091 square miles.

LAVEILLE, *The Life of Father De Smet, passim,* New York, 1915 (Early history of this territory) ; CHR, Vol. iii, p. 157; *Cf.* Files of *Dakota Catholic* (Sioux Falls).

1. MARTY, MARTIN.

Bishop Marty was born on January 11, 1834, in Schwyz, Switzerland. At an early age he entered the Benedictine Abbey at Einsiedeln and made his religious profession on May 20, 1855. After his ordination to the priesthood on September 14, 1856, he emigrated to the State of Indiana with a colony of monks who founded the Abbey at St. Meinrads. He was chosen Abbot of this foundation in January, 1871, and received the abbatial blessing from Bishop de Saint Palais on May 21, 1871. His consecration as titular Bishop of Tiberias and Vicar-Apostolic of Dakota took place at Ferdinand, Indiana, on February 1, 1880, with the Right Reverend Silas Chatard as consecrating prelate.   He was appointed first Bishop of Sioux Falls on September 22, 1889, and was transferred to the See of St. Cloud on December 31, 1894.   He died in St. Cloud on September 19, 1896.

REUSS, *op. cit.*, p. 69; SHEA, *Hierarchy*, p. 396; *Year Book of the Diocese of Indianapolis* (1919) ; ACHS *Researches*, Vol. viii, p. 47, Vol xii, p. 31.

2. O'GORMAN, THOMAS.

Bishop O'Gorman was born in Boston on May 1, 1843, and moved to St. Paul with his parents at an early age.   He pursued his theological studies in France, but returned to St. Paul for his ordination to the priesthood, which took place on November 5, 1865.   He served as pastor in Rochester and Faribault, Minnesota, and later was appointed first President of Saint Thomas College, where he also taught Dogmatic Theology.   In 1890 he was appointed to the chair of Church History at the Catholic University of America in Washington, a position he held until chosen Bishop of Sioux Falls on January 24, 1896.   Cardinal Satolli consecrated him in Washington, D. C., on April 19, 1896.   He celebrated the Golden Jubilee of his ordination on November 5, 1896.   He died in Sioux Falls on September 18, 1921.

REUSS, *op. cit.*, p. 83; *Catholic University Bulletin* for April, 1896; *Cf.* Files of *Dakota Catholic* (Sioux Falls, South Dakota).

IV. Diocese of Jamestown-Fargo (1889)

The Diocese of Jamestown was erected on October 3, 1889, and the Right Reverend John Shanley, D.D., was consecrated as its first Bishop on December 27, 1889.   The See was changed to Fargo on April 6, 1897.

Originally, the Diocese embraced the State of North Dakota, but since 1910 it comprises the Counties of Cass, Richland, Sargent, Ransom, Dickey, Lamoure, Barnes, McIntosh, Logan, Kidder, Stutsman, Sheridan, Wells, Foster, Griggs, Steel, Traill, Grand Forks, Nelson, Eddy, Benson, Pierce, Rolette, Towner, Ramsey, McHenry, Bottineau,

Cavalier, Walsh and Pembina in the State of North Dakota; an area of 34,899 square miles.

Diocesan Records; CHR, Vol. iii, p. 157; *Catholic Directory* for 1922.

1. SHANLEY, JOHN.

Bishop Shanley was born at Albion, New York, on January 4, 1851, and received his seminary training in Rome where he was ordained to the priesthood on May 30, 1874. He was consecrated Bishop of Jamestown in St. Paul by Archbishop Ireland on December 27, 1889. He died at Jamestown on July 16, 1909.

REUSS, *op. cit.,* pp. 100–101; CHR, Vol. iii, p. 158.

2. O'REILLY, JAMES.

The present Bishop of Fargo was born in Ireland in 1857, and was educated at All Hallows College, Dublin, where he was ordained to the priesthood in 1882. After his arrival in this country he served as pastor of the parishes of Belle Creek, Lake City and Stillwater in Minnesota, and in 1886 was chosen as pastor of the Church of Saint Anthony of Padua, in Minneapolis. He was consecrated Bishop of Fargo by Archbishop Ireland in the Cathedral at St. Paul on May 19, 1910.

V. Diocese of Winona (1889)

The Diocese of Winona was erected by Pope Leo XIII on October 3, 1889, and the Right Reverend Joseph B. Cotter was consecrated as its first Bishop on December 27, 1889.

The Diocese of Winona comprises twenty-six counties in the extreme southern part of the State of Minnesota; an, area of 12,282 square miles.

UPHAM, *Minnesota in Three Centuries,* I, St. Paul, 1908; *Sadlier's Directory* (1890); *The Official Catholic Directory* (1909); *Acta et Dicta,* published by St. Paul Cath. Hist. Soc.; *History of Winona County* (1883); RAVOUX, *Memoirs,* St. Paul, 1892; VON PAKISCH, *Die St. Peter u. Paul's Gemeinde in Mankato* (1899); *Jubilee Booklet, St. Felix Church,* Wabasha, Minnesota, 1908; CHR, Vol. iii, p. 158.

1. COTTER, JOSEPH B.

Bishop Cotter was born in Liverpool, England, on November 18, 1844. He came to the United States, was adopted by the Bishop of St. Paul and ordained to the priesthood by Bishop Grace on May 23, 1871. Shortly after he was sent to Winona as pastor of the Church of Saint Thomas. He was consecrated first Bishop of Winona on December 27, 1889, by Archbishop Ireland. He died on June 28, 1909.

REUSS, *op. cit.*, p. 29; CHR, Vol. iii, p. 158.

2. HEFFRON, PATRICK R.

The present Bishop of Winona was born in New York City on June 1, 1860, and received his elementary training in the schools of that city. After 1878 he spent six years at the Grand Seminary in Montreal, and was ordained to the priesthood on December 22, 1884. The next two years he spent in study abroad and upon his return he came to St. Paul where he was appointed Rector of the Cathedral. In 1896 he was made vice-rector of the Seminary in St. Paul and the next year was chosen rector. Archbishop Ireland consecrated him second Bishop of Winona on May 19, 1910.

VI. Diocese of Duluth (1889)

The Diocese of Duluth was erected on October 3, 1889, and the Right Reverend James McGolrick was consecrated as its first Bishop on December 27, 1889.

Originally, the Diocese of Duluth comprised the entire northern part of the State of Minnesota, but upon the erection of the Diocese of Crookston in 1910, it was given its present limits of the counties of Aitkin, Carlton, Cass, Cook, Crow Wing, Itasca, Lake, Pine, Koochiching and St. Louis, in the State of Minnesota; an area of 22,354 square miles.

LYDON, *History of the Diocese of Duluth*, Duluth, 1914; RAVOUX, *Memoirs*, St. Paul, 1892; THEBAUD, *Forty Years in the United States*, New York, 1904; Files of the *Directory of the Cathedral Parish*, Duluth, 1905, CHR, Vol. iii, p. 158.

1. McGolrick, James.

Bishop McGolrick was born at Borrisokane, County Tipperary, Ireland, on May 1, 1841, and received his education at All Hallows College. He was ordained to the priesthood on June 11, 1867, and came to the United States shortly after and was made assistant pastor of the Cathedral in St. Paul. He went to Minneapolis where he was pastor for twenty-two years. He was appointed first Bishop of Duluth, on March 15, 1889, and Archbishop Ireland consecrated him at St. Paul on December 27, 1889. He died in Duluth on January 23, 1918.

Reuss, *op. cit.,* p. 71; ACHS *Researches,* Vol. xxiv, p. 263 (On *Researches*).

2. McNicholas, John T., O. P.

Bishop McNicholas was born in Ireland at the town of Kiltimagh, County Mayo. He came to the United States with his parents at an early age, and later entered the Dominican Order at Saint Rose Convent, Kentucky, and was professed on October 10, 1895. He was ordained to the priesthood on October 10, 1901. He acted as Master of Novices of his Order at the Somerset House of Studies; Pastor of Saint Catherine's Church, New York City, and Assistant General of the Order, before his election to the See of Duluth on July 18, 1918. His Eminence, Cardinal Boggiani, O. P., consecrated him in Rome on September 8, 1918.

VII. Diocese of Lead (1902)

Pope Leo XIII erected the Diocese of Lead on August 6, 1902, and the Right Reverend John Stariha, was consecrated as its first Bishop, on October 28, 1902.

The Diocese comprises its original limits of that part of South Dakota which lies west of the Missouri River; an area of 41,759 square miles.

Cf. Bibliography under Diocese of Sioux Falls as the history of this See is intimately connected with that Diocese; CHR, Vol. iii, p. 158.

1. STARIHA, JOHN.

The first Bishop of Lead was born in the Province of Krain (Carniola), Austria, on May 12, 1845, and pursued him classical studies at Rudolph's Werth, Krain, Austria, before coming to this country. He made his theological studies at Saint Francis Seminary, Milwaukee, and was ordained to the priesthood by Bishop Mrak on September 19, 1869. He served as pastor of various missions in Minnesota and as Vicar-General of the Diocese of St. Paul, until his consecration as first Bishop of Lead by Archbishop Ireland on October 28, 1902. Owing to ill health, he resigned the see in 1909 and returned to his old home in Austria. He died at Laibach on November 25, 1915.

CHR, Vol. iii, p. 159; *Cf.* Files of *Dakota Catholic* (Sioux Falls).

2. BUSCH, JOSEPH F.

Was consecrated second Bishop of Lead, on May 9, 1910; transferred to the See of St. Cloud on May 19, 1915. (Cf. St. Cloud.)

3. LAWLER, JOHN J.

Bishop Lawler was born in Rochester, Minnesota, on August 4, 1862, and made his classical studies at Saint Francis Seminary, Milwaukee, after which he went to Europe to complete his theology. He was ordained to the priesthood at Louvain on December 19, 1885, and upon his return to St. Paul he was made pastor of the Cathedral where he remained until he was consecrated titular Bishop of Hermopolis and Auxiliary of Saint Paul by Archbishop Ireland on May 19, 1910. He was transferred to the Diocese of Lead on January 29, 1916.

VIII. Diocese of Bismarck (1909)

Pope Pius X divided the Diocese of Fargo and erected the See of Bismarck on December 31, 1909, and the Right Reverend Vincent Wehrle was consecrated as its first Bishop on May 19, 1910.

The Diocese comprises the Counties of Adams, Billings, Bowman, Burke, Burleigh, Divide, Dunn, Emmons, Golden Valley, Grant, Hettinger, McKenzie, McLean, Mercer, Morton, Montraille, Oliver, Renville, Slope, Stark, Ward and Williams, in the State of North Dakota; an area of 35,998 square miles.

Bishop Wehrle writes that no works have been published relative to the history of this Diocese. The Diocesan Archives, however, contain valuable historical data; CHR, Vol. iii, p. 159.

1.   WEHRLE, VINCENT, O. S. B.

The first and present Bishop of Bismarck was born in Switzerland on December 19, 1855, and received his education at the College connected with the Abbey of Einseldeln. He entered the Benedictine Order in 1876 and was ordained to the priesthood on April 23, 1882. The same year he came to the United States and labored as a missionary in Arkansas and Indiana until 1887 when he went to Yankton, South Dakota, to work among the Indians. He was appointed first Bishop of Bismarck and was consecrated by Archbishop Ireland in St. Paul on May 19, 1910.

IX. Diocese of Crookston (1909)

Pius X erected the Diocese of Crookston on December 31, 1909, and the Right Reverend Timothy Corbett was consecrated as first Bishop on May 19, 1910.

The Diocese comprises thirteen counties in Northwestern Minnesota: Becker, Beltrami, Clay, Clearwater, Hubbard, Kittson, Marshall, Mahnomen, Norman, Pennington, Polk, Red Lake and Roseau; an area of 17,210 square miles.

Bulletin of the Sacred Heart Cathedral, Duluth, Minnesota (Crookston Edition), issue of May, 1910; CHR, Vol. iii, p. 159.

1.   CORBETT, TIMOTHY.

The present Bishop of Crookston was born in Mendota, Minnesota, on July 10, 1858. He was educated privately in his youth by the Right Reverend James McGolrick, who, in 1876, sent him to the old college of Meximieux in France to continue his studies.   Upon his return to the United States in 1880 he entered the Grand Seminary in Montreal and later Saint John's Seminary, Brighton, Massachusetts, to complete his philosophical and theological studies, and was ordained to the priesthood on June 12, 1886.   Three years later he became Rector of the Cathedral in Duluth and was appointed first Bishop of Crookston on April 9, 1910.   He was one of several Bishops consecrated by Archbishop Ireland in St. Paul on May 19, 1910.

CHAPTER XIV

THE PROVINCE OF DUBUQUE (1893)

Pope Leo XIII erected the Province of Dubuque on September 17, 1893, with the Right Reverend John Hennessy as first Archbishop.

The Province still includes the States of Iowa, Nebraska and Wyoming. To the original Suffragan Sees of Omaha (1885), Davenport (1881), Lincoln (1887), Cheyenne (1887), have been added the Diocese of Sioux City (1902), Des Moines (1911) and Kearney-Grand Island (1912-1917).

SHEA, *History of Catholic Church in United States*, New York, 1889–1892; DE CAILLY, *Life of Bishop Loras*, New York, 1897; KEMPKER, *History of Catholics in Iowa*, Iowa City, 1887; *Souvenir Volume of Silver Jubilee of Archbishop Hennessy; Souvenir Volume of Installation of Archbishop Keane;* CHR, Vol. iii, p. 159–160.

I. Diocese of Dubuque (1837)

The Fathers of the Third Provincial Council of Baltimore petitioned the Holy See to erect the Diocese of Dubuque and the request was granted on July 28, 1837. The Right Reverend Mathias Loras was consecrated as its first Bishop on December 10, 1837.

Originally, the Diocese included that part of the Wisconsin Territory which lay between the Mississippi and Missouri Rivers. At present it comprises that part of the State of Iowa north of the counties of Polk, Jasper, Poweshiek, Iowa, Johnson, Cedar and Clinton, and west of the counties of Kossuth, Humboldt, Webster and Boone; an area of 17,404 square miles.

1. LORAS, MATTHIAS.

Bishop Loras was born on August 30, 1792, in Lyons, France, and had as a schoolmate the Curé d'Ars. He was ordained to the priesthood on November 12, 1815, and despite his youth was made Superior of the Seminary

209

at Largentière. When Bishop Portier sought helpers for his diocese in the United States the Reverend Matthias Loras responded to the call and left for Mobile in 1829. When Spring Hill College was opened he was chosen as one of the professors and in 1833 and 1834 acted as President of that institution. Bishop Portier consecrated him first Bishop of Dubuque in Mobile, Alabama, on December 10, 1837. He died in Dubuque on February 20, 1858.

REUSS, *op. cit.*, pp. 64–65; SHEA, *Hierarchy, etc.*, p. 227; CLARKE, *op. cit.*, Vol. ii, pp. 126–146; Biographical sketch in *Freeman's Journal*, of April 17, 1858; DE CAILLY, *Memoirs of Bishop Loras*, New York, 1897; *Acta et Dicta, Letters of Bishop Loras 1829-30*, Vol. i, pp. 14-29; Vol. iv, pp. 275-293, Vol. v, pp. 111-119; ACHS, *Researches*, Vol. viii, p. 167 (1837, setting out for Europe), Vol. xi, p. 160 (account of Church in Mississippi, 1853–54), Vol. xii, p. 82 (church in Iowa), Vol. xxvi, p. 260 (in favor of Prohibition, 1855), Vol. xxviii, p. 346 (death of); CHR, Vol. iv, p. 145 (diocesan bibliography).

2. SMYTH, CLEMENT.

The second Bishop of Dubuque was born in County Clare, Ireland, on January 24, 1810. He joined the Cistercian Order and received the habit on October 7, 1838, after making a collegiate course at Trinity College. He was ordained to the priesthood on May 29, 1841, in Waterford, Ireland, and later came to the United States with some fellow Trappists who finally located in the Diocese of Dubuque, where they founded the New Melleray Monastery. Archbishop Kenrick consecrated him titular Bishop of Thanasis and Coadjutor to Bishop Loras on May 3, 1857. He succeeded to the See of Dubuque on February 20, 1858. He died at Dubuque on September 22, 1865.

REUSS, *op. cit.*, p. 101; SHEA, *Hierarchy*, p. 229, KEMPKER, *op. cit.*, p. 59 seq.; CHR, Vol. iii, p. 160, PERKINS, *History of the Trappist Abbey of New Melleray, passim,,* Iowa City, 1892.

3. HENNESSY, JOHN.

The first Archbishop of Dubuque was born in County Limerick, Ireland, on August 29, 1825. Coming to the United States, he entered the Seminary at Carondelet and was ordained to the priesthood in November, 1850. After a few years he became Rector of the Seminary in St.

Louis and from 1860 to 1866 he was pastor of the church at St. Joseph's, Missouri. He was consecrated Bishop of Dubuque by Archbishop Kenrick on September 30, 1866, and was appointed its first Archbishop on September 17, 1893. He died in Dubuque on March 4, 1900.

REUSS, *op. cit.*, p. 53; SHEA, *Hierarchy, etc.*, pp. 230–231; KEMPKER, *History of Catholic Church in Iowa*, Iowa City, 1887; *Souvenir Volume of the Silver Jubilee of Archbishop Hennessy.*

4. KEANE, JOHN JOSEPH.

The second Archbishop of Dubuque was born in Ballyshannon, County Donegal, Ireland, on September 12, 1839. His early education was received in Baltimore and later at St. Charles College and at Saint Mary's Seminary in that city, where he was ordained to the priesthood on July 2, 1866. He was acting as an assistant at Saint Patrick's Church in Washington when appointed to the See of Richmond, and Cardinal Gibbons consecrated him on August 25, 1878, in the Cathedral at Baltimore. He became the first Rector of the Catholic University of America and was translated to the titular see of Jasso on August 12, 1888. He resigned as Rector in 1897 and went to Rome where he was made titular Archbishop of Damascus, January 9, 1897. On September 24, 1900, he became second Archbishop of Dubuque, a position he held until April 3, 1911, when he resigned the See and was appointed titular Archbishop of Cio. He died in Dubuque on June 23, 1918.

REUSS, *op. cit.*, pp. 59–60; SHEA, *Hierarchy, etc.*, pp. 353–356; CHR, Vol. i, p. 375, Vol. iii, p. 160; CUB, Vol. xxvi, p. 38 (list of his writings on the Cath. Univ. of Amer.) ; HERBERMANN, *Sulpicians, etc.*, pp. 206, 310, 311; CUB, Vol. ii, pp. 97, 103, 214, 305, 367–368, 428, 444, 592; Vol. v, p. 395; Vol. ix, pp. 277, 570; Vol. xii, p. 303; AER, Vol. i, p. 241; Vol. xvi, p. 78 (his resignation of Rectorship) ; ACHS, *Researches*, Vol. ix, p. 191; Vol. xii, p. 97; Vol. xxviii, p. 148; SWEENY, *op. cit.*, Vol. ii, p. 262.

5. KEANE, JAMES JOHN.

Archbishop Keane was born near Chicago, Illinois, on August 26, 1857, and received his education at Saint John's, Collegeville, Minnesota; Saint Francis Xavier's College, New York City, and the Grand Seminary, Montreal.

He was ordained to the priesthood on December 23, 1882. He began his priestly career in Saint Paul, Minnesota, where he acted as curate at Saint Mary's and as pastor at Saint Joseph's. Later he was made President of Saint Thomas' College and was consecrated Bishop of Cheyenne by Archbishop Ireland on October 28, 1902. He was transferred to the See of Dubuque on August 11, 1911.

II. Diocese of Omaha (1885)

Pope Leo XIII erected the Diocese of Omaha out of the Vicariate of Nebraska on October 2, 1885, with the Right Reverend James O'Connor as its first Bishop.

The Diocese originally embraced the States of Nebraska and Wyoming, but at present it comprises the Counties of Boyd, Holt, Merrick, Nance, Boone, Antelope, Knox, Pierce, Madison, Platte, Colfax, Stanton, Wayne, Cedar, Dixon, Dakota, Thurston, Cuming, Dodge, Burt, Washington, Douglas and Sarpy, in the State of Nebraska; an area of 14,051 square miles.

MORTON, History of Nebraska, Lincoln, 1906; SAVAGE AND BELL, History of Omaha, New York and Chicago, 1894; THE WESTERN HISTORICAL Co., History of Nebraska, Chicago, 1882; SHEA, History of the Catholic Church in the United States, New York; PALLADINO, Indian and White in the Northwest, Baltimore, 1894; PERKINS, History of the Trappist Abbey of New Melleray, Iowa City, 1892; DOWLING, Creighton University Reminiscences, Omaha, 1903; CHR, Vol. iii, p. 161.

1. O'GORMAN, JAMES.

The first Vicar-Apostolic of Nebraska was born near Nenagh, County Tipperary, Ireland, in 1804, and received his early education at a boarding school near the city of Limerick. He was invested with the habit of the Trappist Order on November 1, 1839, and was ordained to the priesthood in December, 1843. He remained in his native land for five years and then left for the United States with his confrères and assisted in the establishment of the monastery at New Mellary, in Iowa, of which he was Prior when appointed Vicar-Apostolic of Nebraska. He was consecrated titular Bishop of Raphanea by Archbishop Kenrick in St. Louis on May 8, 1859. He died in Cincinnati on July 4, 1874.

REUSS, *op. cit.*, p. 83; SHEA, *Hierarchy*, p. 331; PERKINS, *op. cit. passim;* MORTON, *op. cit.*, Vol. ii, p. 439 seq.; CHR, Vol. iii, p. 161.

2. O'CONNOR, JAMES.

The first Bishop of Omaha was born at Queenstown, Ireland, on September 10, 1823, came to this country at the age of fifteen and finished his preparatory studies at Saint Charles Borromeo Seminary, Philadelphia. He made his theological course at the Urban College in Rome, and was ordained to the priesthood on March 24, 1848. Upon his return to the United States, he did missionary work for seven years in the Diocese of Pittsburgh and later served in an administrative capacity at the seminaries in Pittsburgh and Philadelphia. In 1876, he was appointed second Vicar-Apostolic of Nebraska and was consecrated titular Bishop of Dibona by coadjutor-Bishop John Ryan of St. Louis. When the Diocese of Omaha was created, he became its first Bishop, on October 2, 1885. He died in Omaha on May 28, 1890.

REUSS, *op. cit.*, p. 81; SHEA, *Hierarchy*, p. 332; MORTON, *op. cit.*, Vol. ii, p. 440, seq., CHR, Vol. iii, p. 101.

3. SCANNELL, RICHARD.

Was consecrated Bishop of Concordia on November 30, 1887; transferred to Omaha on January 30, 1891.

(Cf. Concordia.)

4. HARTY, JEREMIAH J.

Archbishop Harty was born in St. Louis on November 5, 1853, and was educated at St. Louis University, and Saint Vincent's College, Cape Girardeau, and was ordained to the priesthood on April 28, 1878. He labored successfully as pastor in St. Louis until his appointment as Archbishop of Manila, P. I. He was consecrated by Cardinal Satolli on August 15, 1903 and was transferred to the Diocese of Omaha on May 16, 1916.

III. Diocese of Davenport (1881)

Pope Leo XIII erected the Diocese of Davenport on May 8, 1881, and the Right Reverend John McMullen was consecrated as the first Bishop on July 25, 1881.

When first erected, the Diocese included the entire southern part of the State of Iowa. Upon the erection of the Diocese of Des Moines in 1911, it received its present limits in Iowa with the following boundaries: on the east by the Mississippi River, on the west by the Western boundaries of the Counties of Jasper, Marion, Monroe and Appanoose, on the south by the State of Missouri, on the north by the Northern boundaries of the Counties of Jasper, Paweshiek, Iowa, Johnson, Cedar and Clinton; an area of 12,000 square miles.

Church Directory (1840–1908); KEMPKER, *History of the Catholic Church in Iowa,* 1884; DE CAILLY, *Life of Bishop Loras,* New York, 1897; McGOVERN, *Life of Bishop McMullen,* Milwaukee, 1888; CHR, Vol. iii. p. 161.

1. McMULLEN, JOHN.

Bishop McMullen was born at Ballynahinck, County Down, Ireland, on January 8, 1832, and at the age of four he was taken by emmigrants to Chicago by way of Canada. After his graduation from Saint Mary's-of-the-Lake, he was sent to the Urban College at Rome to complete his theology and was ordained to the priesthood on June 20, 1858. Upon his return to the United States he was made pastor of Saint Luke's Church in Chicago and later was chosen President of Saint Mary's-of-the-Lake, a position he held four years, after which he was appointed professor in the Diocesan Seminary. In October, 1870, he was named rector of the Cathedral and seven years later became Vicar-General. After the death of Bishop Foley, he acted as Administrator of the Diocese, and in 1881, he was appointed first Bishop of Davenport. Archbishop Feehan consecrated him on July 25, 1881. He died in Davenport on July 4, 1883.

REUSS, *op. cit.,* p. 73, SHEA, *Hierarchy,* p. 281; CLARKE, *op. cit.,* Vol. iii, pp. 592–610; McGOVERN, *The Life and Writings of the Rt. Rev. John McMullen,* Chicago, 1888; CHR, Vol. iii, p. 162.

2. COSGROVE, HENRY.

Bishop Cosgrove was born at Williamsport, Pennsylvania, on December 19, 1834, and was educated privately by the Very Reverend Mr. Crétin. He was then sent to Saint Mary's, Perry County and the Seminary at Carondelet to complete his theology. He was ordained to the priesthood in August, 1857, and following his ordination he labored successfully in the City of Davenport, and, under Bishop McMullen, he served as Vicar-General. He was Administrator *sede vacante*, and finally appointed Bishop. He was consecrated on September 14, 1884, by Archbishop Feehan. He died in Davenport on December 22, 1906.

REUSS, *op. cit.*, p. 29; SHEA, *Hierarchy, etc.*, p. 219; GIGLINGER, *The Rt. Rev. Henry Cosgrove*, biog. sketch, in *Acta et Dicta*, Vol. ii, July, 1910, pp. 211–218—portrait on page 210; *Cf. The Messenger* (New York), for January, 1907; ACHS *Researches*, Vol. xxii, p. 175; McGOVERN, *Life and Writings of Rt. Rev. John Wm. McMullen, D.D., first bishop of Davenport, Iowa.* Milwaukee, 1888. *Cf.* CHR, Vol. iii, p. 162; KEMPKER, *History of the Catholic Church in Iowa* (1884).

3. DAVIS, JAMES.

The present Bishop of Davenport was born in Ireland, on November 7, 1852, and was ordained to the priesthood on June 17, 1878. He served as Vicar-General under Bishop Cosgrove and was appointed his coadjutor on October 7, 1904. His consecration as titular Bishop of Milopoyamus took place on November 30, 1904, with Bishop Cosgrove as consecrating prelate. He succeeded to the See on December 22, 1906.

IV. Diocese of Lincoln (1887)

Pope Leo XIII erected the Diocese of Lincoln on August 2, 1887, and the Right Reverend Thomas Bonacum was consecrated as its first Bishop on November 30, 1887.

The Diocese retains its original limits in the section of the State of Nebraska lying south of the Platte River; an area of 23,844 square miles.

Catholic Directory, Milwaukee, 1888–1910; *Church Progress*, and *The Western Watchman*, St. Louis, contemporary files; *National Cycl. of Am. Biog.* (New York, 1904). MORTON, *op. cit.*, Vol. ii, p. 456, seq.; *South Platte Catholicism and the Lincoln Diocese*, by Rev. M. A. Shine; *Cf.* Files of *The True Voice;* CHR, Vol. iii, p. 162.

1. BONACUM, THOMAS.

The first Bishop of Lincoln was born near Thurles, County Tipperary, Ireland, on January 29, 1847, and came to the United States with his parents. He received his education at the Salesianum near Milwaukee and the Lazarist Seminary at Cape Girardeau. He was ordained to the priesthood on June 18, 1870, and at the Third Plenary Council of Baltimore he was proposed for the See of Belleville in Illinois; but the Holy See deferred action and he was appointed to the Diocese of Lincoln as its first Bishop. He was consecrated in St. Louis by Archbishop Kenrick on November 30, 1887. He died in Lincoln on February 4, 1911.

REUSS, *op. cit.*, p. 16; CHR, Vol. iii, p. 162; CE, Vol. ix, p. 266, Vol. x, p. 733. HAYES-COX, *History of the City of Lincoln*, pp. 252–257. Lincoln, Neb., 1889; O'GORMAN, *History of the Roman Catholic Church in the United States*, p. 485. New York, 1895; MORTON-WATKINS, *History of Nebraska*, Vol. ii, pp. 462–464, Vol. iii, p. 398. Lincoln, 1906–1913; contemporary files of the *Omaha Bee, Omaha Herald, True Voice, Nebraska State Journal, Church Progress, Western Watchman; Cf. True Voice*, special edition of July 14, 1911, article by Rev. M. A. Shine, *History of the Diocese of Lincoln; Cf.* CE, Vol. ix, p. 266, Vol. x, p. 732.

2. TIHEN, J. HENRY.

Was consecrated Bishop of Lincoln on July 6, 1911; transferred to the See of Denver on September 21, 1917.

(Cf. Denver.)

3. O'REILLY, CHARLES J.

The present Bishop of Lincoln was born at Saint John, New Brunswick, on January 4, 1862, and received his education at Saint Joseph's College, Memramcook, and the Grand Seminary, Montreal. He was ordained to the priesthood at Portland, Oregon, on June 29, 1890, and was appointed first Bishop of Baker City on June 29, 1903. He was consecrated by Archbishop Christie on August 25, 1903, and was transferred to the see of Lincoln on March 20, 1918.

V. Diocese of Cheyenne (1887)

The Diocese of Cheyenne was erected on August 9, 1887, and the Right Reverend Maurice F. Burke was consecrated as its first Bishop on October 28, 1887.

The Diocese comprises the entire State of Wyoming; an area of 97,575 square miles.

Catholic Directory (Milwaukee, 1908) ; CHITTENDEN AND RICHARDSON, *Life, Letters and Travels of Father Pierre-Jean De Smet, S. J.,* New York, 1905, I–II, *passim*. LAVEILLE, *Life of Father De Smet, passim,* New York, 1915; CHR, Vol. iii, p. 5.

1. BURKE, MAURICE F.

Was consecrated first Bishop of Cheyenne on October 28, 1887; transferred to Saint Joseph, Missouri, on June 19, 1893.

(Cf. St. Joseph.)

2. LENIHAN, THOMAS M.

The second Bishop of Cheyenne was born in Ireland on August 12, 1845, and received his early training in Dubuque, Iowa. He was ordained to the priesthood in November, 1866, and after serving as pastor of several parishes he was finally placed in charge of the Church of Corpus Christi in Fort Dodge, Iowa. Archbishop Hennessy, of Dubuque, consecrated him Bishop in Saint Raphael's Cathedral, Dubuque, on February 24, 1897. He died in Cheyenne on December 15, 1901.

REUSS, *op. cit.,* pp. 63–64; CHR, Vol. iv, p. 546 (diocesan bibliography).

3. KEANE, JAMES JOHN.

Was consecrated Bishop of Cheyenne on October 28, 1902; transferred to the See of Dubuque on August 11, 1911.

(Cf. Dubuque.)

4. McGOVERN, PATRICK A.

The present Bishop of Cheyenne was born in Omaha, Nebraska, on October 14, 1872, and received his collegiate education at Creighton University, and his theological training at Mount Saint Mary's, Cincinnati. He was ordained to the priesthood on August 18, 1895, and served as pastor of various churches in Omaha until his appointment by Pius X as fourth Bishop of Cheyenne in January, 1912. Archbishop Keane consecrated him on April 11, 1912.

VI. Diocese of Sioux City (1902)

The Diocese of Sioux City was erected at the same time, (January 15, 1902), that the Bull appointing the Most Reverend John J. Keane to the archiepiscopal See of Dubuque was issued. The Right Reverend Philip J. Garrigan was appointed first Bishop of the See on March 21, 1902.

The Diocese comprises twenty-four counties in the northwest part of Iowa, west of Winnebago, Hancock, Wright, Hamilton and Story Counties, and north of Harrison, Shelby, Audubon, Guthrie and Dallas Counties; an area of 14,518 square miles.

The Church in Sioux City; The Church in the Diocese of Sioux City; these brochures were published in 1918 under the direction of Bishop Garrigan.

1. GARRIGAN, PHILIP J.

Bishop Garrigan was born in the early forties in Ireland and came to the United States with his parents when a mere youth. His educational training was received at Saint Charles College, Maryland, and at the Provincial Seminary in Troy, New York, where he was ordained to the priesthood on June 11, 1870. After his ordination he served as curate at Saint John's Church, Worcester, Massachusetts, and later was appointed rector of the Seminary at Troy, New York. For fourteen years he was pastor at Fitchburg, Massachusetts, and in 1888 he was appointed Vice-Rector of the Catholic University of America at Washington. On March 21, 1902, he was chosen first Bishop of Sioux City and was consecrated at Springfield, Massachusetts, by Bishop Beaven, on May 25, 1902. He died in October, 1919.

CUB, Vol. ii, pp. 214, 575, 585, Vol. x, p. 382, Vol. viii, pp. 385–386 (consecration of), Vol. xxvi, p. 17 (Necrology); HERBERMANN, *Sulpicians, etc.*, p. 214; *Cf. The Church in Sioux City*, and *The Church in the Diocese of Sioux City*.

2. HEELAN, EDMOND,

The present Bishop of Sioux City was born in Ireland on February 5, 1868. He studied philosophy and theology at All Hallows College, Dublin, and was ordained to the priesthood on June 24, 1890. He was acting as pastor at Fort Dodge, Iowa, when he was appointed second Bishop of Sioux City. Archbishop James J. Keane consecrated him on April 8, 1919, in the Cathedral at Sioux City.

VII. Diocese of Des Moines (1911)

Pius X erected the Diocese of Des Moines on August 12, 1911. The first Bishop was the Most Reverend Austin Dowling (present Archbishop of St. Paul), who was consecrated on April 25, 1912.

The Diocese comprises that part of the State of Iowa which is bounded on the east by the eastern boundaries of the Counties of Polk, Warren, Lucas and Wayne; on the south by the State of Missouri; on the west by the Missouri River, and on the north by the northern boundaries of the Counties of Harrison, Shelby, Audubon, Guthrie, Dallas and Polk; an area of 12,446 square miles.

1. DOWLING, AUSTIN.

Was consecrated on April 25, 1912, first Bishop of Des Moines; transferred to the See of St. Paul in January, 1919.

(Cf. St. Paul.)

2. DRUMM, THOMAS W.

The second Bishop of Des Moines was born in Fore, Ireland, on July 12, 1871. He received his theological training at the Grand Seminary, Montreal, and was ordained to the priesthood on December 21, 1901. He labored for twelve years in the diocesan missions of Dubuque, Iowa, and was consecrated on May 21, 1919, in Dubuque, Iowa, by Archbishop Keane.

VIII. Diocese of Grand Island (1912-1917)

Pius X on March 8, 1912, divided the Diocese of Omaha and erected the See of Kearney, with the Right Reverend James A. Duffy as its first Bishop. Pope Benedict XV. at the request of Bishop Duffy, transferred the diocesan seat to Grand Island on April 11, 1917.

The Diocese comprises the Counties of Arthur, Banner, Blaine, Box Butte, Brown, Buffalo, Cherry, Cheyenne, Custer, Dawes, Deuel, Garfield, Grant, Greeley, Hooker, Howard, Keyapaha, Kimball, Logan, Loup, McPherson, Rock, Scotts Bluff, Sheridan, Sherman, Wheeler, Sioux, Thomas, Valley, and those portions of Dawson, Hall, Lincoln and Keith lying north of the South Platte River in the State of Nebraska; an area of 40,000 square miles.

CHR, Vol. iii, p. 163; Catholic Directory for 1922.

1. DUFFY, JAMES A.

Bishop Duffy was born in St. Paul, Minnesota, on September 13, 1873. He made his ecclesiastical studies at the Seminary in St. Paul, where he was ordained to the priesthood on May 27, 1899. After his ordination he served as assistant at the Church of the Immaculate Conception in Minneapolis, Minnesota, and from September, 1902, until 1904, was pastor of Saint Anne's Church, Le Sueur. He was pastor of Saint Mary's Cathedral in Cheyenne, Wyoming, when appointed first Bishop of Grand Island, and was consecrated by Archbishop James J. Keane on April 16. 1913.

CONCLUSION

Twenty priests constituted the assembly of the first Synod of the Church in the New Republic presided over by Bishop Carroll on November 7, 1791. When the Province of Baltimore was erected on April 8, 1808, Archbishop Carroll and the four suffragan bishops-elect comprised the hierarchical organization of the nascent Church in this country.

With the growth and expansion of the Church came a corresponding development of its hierarchy, so that in 1829 at the First Provincial Council of Baltimore the Catholic Hierarchy of the United States consisted of one archbishop and nine bishops. At the First Plenary Council of Baltimore in 1852, six archbishops and twenty-seven bishops comprised the organization, to which number one archbishop and eleven bishops were added before the convocation of the Second Plenary Council of Baltimore. From 1866 to 1895 the hierarchy doubled its number over the period between 1790 to 1866. At present the status of the Catholic Hierarchy of the United States is as follows: Cardinals (2); Archbishops (12); Titular Archbishops (2); Bishops in active administration (82); Bishops resigned (3); Auxiliary-Bishops (9) and Vicars-Apostolic (2). This personnel exercises ecclesiastical jurisdiction over fourteen provinces, eighty-six dioceses and two vicariates-apostolic.

From 1790 to 1922 seven of the members of the Catholic Hierarchy in the United States have been created Cardinals; fifty-nine have been chosen Archbishops; two hundred and fifty-five have held the office of Bishop; eighteen have served as Coadjutors and Auxiliary Bishops and six as Vicars-Apostolic.[1]

[1] Bishops Peñalver y Cardenas, Porro y Penado and García Diego are not included in this tabulation as they served under Spanish ecclesiastical jurisdiction.

A press dispatch of May 23, 1922, chronicles the appointment of the Rt. Rev. Msgr. Bernard Mahoney, D.D., as the successor of Bishop O'Gorman in the See of Sioux Falls, South Dakota.

VITA

Rev. John Hugh O'Donnell, C.S.C., was born in Grand Rapids, Michigan, on June 2, 1895. He received his primary education at St. Andrew's parochial school of that city and was later graduated from the Catholic Central High School of Grand Rapids in June, 1912. The following September he began his studies at the University of Notre Dame, Notre Dame, Indiana, from which institution he received the degree of Bachelor of Letters (Litt. B.) in June, 1916. He then entered the Congregation of Holy Cross, and after the usual period of novitiate began his theological studies at Holy Cross College, Washington, D. C. He was ordained to the priesthood on December 28, 1921, by the Rt. Rev. Edward D. Kelly, D.D., Bishop of Grand Rapids.

In September 1919 he matriculated at the Catholic University of America, Washington, D. C., to pursue graduate work in American Church History. The major course of study was done under the direction of the Rev. Dr. Peter Guilday. The courses in the two subordinate subjects, American Political History and Industrial Ethics, were completed under the supervision of Dr. Charles H. McCarthy and Rev. Dr. John A. Ryan, respectively. The author here wishes to acknowledge his sincere gratitude to these professors as well as to the Rev. Louis Kelly, C.S.C., for their kindness and hearty cooperation during his period of graduate study.